Frommer's®

Iceland

2nd Edition

by Jane Appleton & Lisa Shannen

WILEY

A John Wiley and Sons, Ltd, Publication

Published by:
WILEY PUBLISHING, INC.

Telephone (+44) 1243 779777
Email (for orders and customer service enquiries): cs-books@wiley.co.uk. Visit our Home Page on www.wiley.com

UK Publisher: Sally Smith
Project Manager: Daniel Mersey
Commissioning Editor: Mark Henshall
Development Editor: Nick Dalton & Deborah Stone
Project Editor: Hannah Clement
Cartography: Andrew Murphy
Photo Editor: Jill Emeny
Front Cover Photo: © Hemis / Axiom. Description: Church, Iceland
Back Cover Photo: © Alex Sands / Alamy. Description: Solfar Sun Voyager sculpture in Reykjavik

Wiley also publishes its books in a variety of electronic formats. Some content that appears in print may not be available in electronic books.

For information on our other products and services or to obtain technical support, please contact our Customer Care Department within the U.S. at 877/762-2974, outside the U.S. at 317/572-3993 or fax 317/572-4002.

British Library Cataloguing in Publication Data
A catalogue record for this book is available from the British Library
ISBN 978-0-470-97379-0 (pbk)
ISBN 978-0-470-97932-7 (ebk)
ISBN 978-1-119-99443-5 (ebk)
ISBN 978-1-119-99461-9 (ebk)

Typeset by Wiley Indianapolis Composition Services

Printed and bound in the United States of America

5 4 3 2 1

CONTENTS

4 ACTIVE ICELAND 67

5 SUGGESTED ITINERARIES 84

6 REYKJAVÍK 98

7 NEAR REYKJAVÍK 147

8 WEST ICELAND 180

9 NORTH ICELAND 228

10 SOUTH ICELAND 290

11 EAST ICELAND 332

12 THE INTERIOR 366

13 FAST FACTS 378

14 ICELANDIC PRONUNCIATION & USEFUL VOCABULARY 381

Index 388

LIST OF MAPS

ABOUT THE AUTHORS

Jane Appleton is a writer, translator, proofreader and copy editor who visited Iceland in 2003 and has lived there ever since. She studied literature and politics at the University of Melbourne, and Icelandic and translation at the University of Iceland.

Lisa Shannen is a writer and composer who has been living in Iceland on and off for more than ten years. She studied Sound Technology at LIPA in Liverpool and Literature at the University of Iceland.

ACKNOWLEDGMENTS

The authors would like to thank the following for their generous help: Ásta Tþorleifsdóttir and Tþuríður H. Aradóttir; staff at Útivist, especially Skúli Skúlason; Guðmundur Heiðrekssonfrom from the roads administration of Iceland; staff at tourist information offices from Hellnar to Seyðisfjörður and dozens in between; hotel and restaurant managers, and tour operators all over Iceland, but especially staff at Ferðafélag Íslands and Sterna; Roman Gerasymenko; Fríða Rakel Kaaber; Jean Christophe Salaün; David Anthony Nobel; Pall Guðmundsson for advice on Krafla; Sigga Gróa Tþórarinsdóttir and the Icelandic Tourist Board; Mark Henshall, Jill Emeny, Scott Totman, and especially Nick Dalton for his patience and persistence in the final edit. To Evan Spring and Zoë Preston (authors of the first edition) it has been a wonderful experience for us to update this outstanding travel guide.

Jane thanks Ólöf and Stéphane for office facilities; Cara for keeping me sane on a daily basis; and Villi and Sigmar for being Villi and Sigmar (and the reason I gets to live in this beautiful country). Lisa thanks Stephen, Sindri and Svanur for their daily patience, and especially Roman for his support, good sense and excellent puzzle-solving skills!

HOW TO CONTACT US

In researching this book, we discovered many wonderful places—hotels, restaurants, shops, and more. We're sure you'll find others. Please tell us about them, so we can share the information with your fellow travelers in upcoming editions. If you were disappointed with a recommendation, we'd love to know that, too. Please write to:

Frommer's Iceland, 2nd Edition
Wiley Publishing, Inc. • 111 River St. • Hoboken, NJ 07030-5774

AN ADDITIONAL NOTE

Please be advised that travel information is subject to change at any time—and this is especially true of prices. We therefore suggest that you write or call ahead for confirmation when making your travel plans. The authors, editors, and publisher cannot be held responsible for the experiences of readers while traveling. Your safety is important to us, however, so we encourage you to stay alert and be aware of your surroundings. Keep a close eye on cameras, purses, and wallets, all favorite targets of thieves and pickpockets.

FROMMER'S STAR RATINGS, ICONS & ABBREVIATIONS

Every hotel, restaurant, and attraction listing in this guide has been ranked for quality, value, service, amenities, and special features using a **star-rating system.** In country, state, and regional guides, we also rate towns and regions to help you narrow down your choices and budget your time accordingly. Hotels and restaurants are rated on a scale of zero (recommended) to three stars (exceptional). Attractions, shopping, nightlife, towns, and regions are rated according to the following scale: zero stars (recommended), one star (highly recommended), two stars (very highly recommended), and three stars (must-see).

In addition to the star-rating system, we also use **seven feature icons** that point you to the great deals, in-the-know advice, and unique experiences that separate travelers from tourists. Throughout the book, look for:

special finds—those places only insiders know about

fun facts—details that make travelers more informed and their trips more fun

kids—best bets for kids and advice for the whole family

special moments—those experiences that memories are made of

overrated—places or experiences not worth your time or money

insider tips—great ways to save time and money

great values—where to get the best deals

The following **abbreviations** are used for credit cards:

AE	American Express	DISC	Discover	V	Visa
DC	Diners Club	MC	MasterCard		

TRAVEL RESOURCES AT FROMMERS.COM

Frommer's travel resources don't end with this guide. Frommer's website, **www.frommers.com,** has travel information on more than 4,000 destinations. We update features regularly, giving you access to the most current trip-planning information and the best airfare, lodging, and car-rental bargains. You can also listen to podcasts, connect with other Frommers.com members through our active-reader forums, share your travel photos, read blogs from guidebook editors and fellow travellers, and much more.

THE BEST OF ICELAND

By summer Iceland is moss-covered lava fields, steep rocky mountainsides dotted with freely-roaming sheep, pockets of forest in an otherwise treeless expanse, and bright nights of song and dance in the crisp polar air. By winter, it is bright lights darting across the sky like restless ghosts, people bathing in hot springs with snow melting in the steam just above their heads, fairy lights glowing in all the windows. Iceland's astonishing beauty often has an austere, primitive, or surreal cast that arouses reverence, wonderment, mystery, and awe. Lasting impressions could include a lone tuft of blue wildflowers amid a bleak desert moonscape or a fantastical promenade of icebergs calved into a lake from a magisterial glacier. There are endless variations of magnificent scenery and adventure.

Iceland's people are freedom loving, egalitarian, self-reliant, and worldly. They established a parliamentary democracy over a millennium ago, and today write, publish, and read more books per capita than any other people on earth. The country is still one of the world's best to live in, based on life expectancy, education levels, medical care, income, and other U.N. criteria. Reykjavík has become one of the world's most fashionable urban hot spots.

For somewhere so small, Iceland has made more than its fair share of global news. In 2008, the booming economy overstretched itself wildly and went into meltdown, leading to the collapse of the country's three main banks and leaving the nation with a massive debt. It has since bounced back and effects on the tourist industry have been minimal—one of the main ones being a better exchange rate for most tourists. Then there was the 2010 volcanic eruption in South Iceland, which produced an ash cloud big enough to ground planes across Europe, divert flights from North America, and irrevocably change the landscape of the area. Yet even at the height of the eruption, it was business as usual in most

Iceland

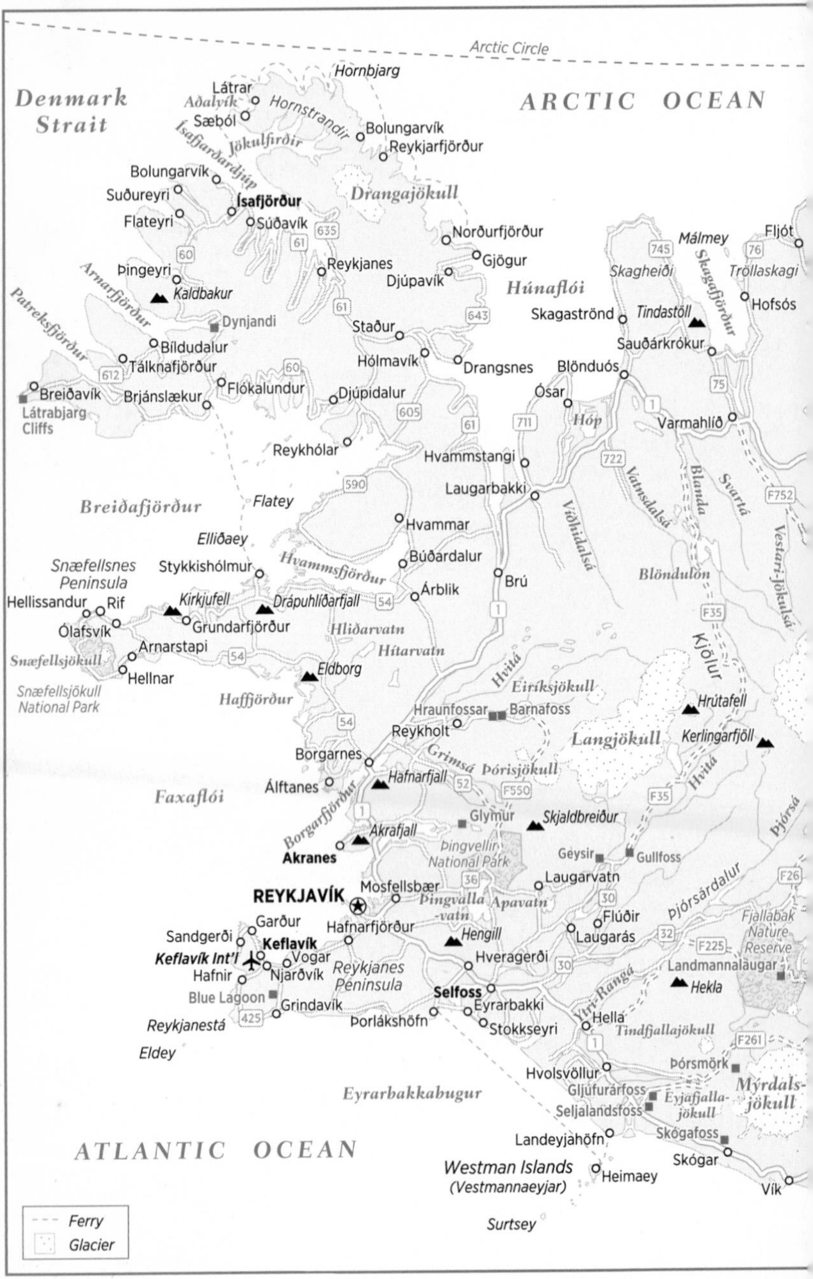
Arctic Circle
ARCTIC OCEAN
Denmark Strait
Hornbjarg
Látrar
Aðalvík
Sæból
Hornstrandir
Ísafjarðardjúp
Jökulfirðir
Bolungarvík
Reykjarfjörður
Bolungarvík
Suðureyri
Ísafjörður
Súðavík
Flateyri
Drangajökull
Norðurfjörður
Gjögur
Reykjanes
Djúpavík
Húnaflói
Þingeyri
Kaldbakur
Arnarfjörður
Patreksfjörður
Dynjandi
Staður
Bíldudalur
Tálknafjörður
Hólmavík
Drangsnes
Breiðavík
Látrabjarg Cliffs
Brjánslækur
Flókalundur
Djúpidalur
Reykhólar
Málmey
Fljót
Skagheiði
Skagafjörður
Tröllaskagi
Hofsós
Skagaströnd
Tindastóll
Sauðárkrókur
Blönduós
Ósar
Hóp
Varmahlíð
Hvammstangi
Laugarbakki
Vatnsdalsá
Blanda
Svartá
Víðidalsá
Vestari-Jökulsá
Breiðafjörður
Flatey
Hvammar
Elliðaey
Búðardalur
Snæfellsnes Peninsula
Stykkishólmur
Hvammsfjörður
Brú
Blöndulón
Árblik
Hellissandur
Rif
Kirkjufell
Drápuhlíðarfjall
Ólafsvík
Grundarfjörður
Hlíðarvatn
Kjölur
Hítarvatn
Arnarstapi
Snæfellsjökull
Hellnar
Eldborg
Hvítá
Eiríksjökull
Snæfellsjökull National Park
Haffjörður
Hraunfossar
Barnafoss
Hrútafell
Reykholt
Langjökull
Kerlingarfjöll
Borgarnes
Grímsá
Þórisjökull
Álftanes
Hafnarfjall
Hvítá
Faxaflói
Borgarfjörður
Glymur
Skjaldbreiður
Þjórsá
Akrafjall
Akranes
Þingvellir National Park
Geysir
Gullfoss
Laugarvatn
Mosfellsbær
REYKJAVÍK
Þingvallavatn
Apavatn
Þjórsárdalur
Garður
Flúðir
Fjallabak Nature Reserve
Sandgerði
Hafnarfjörður
Laugarás
Keflavík
Hengill
Keflavík Int'l
Vogar
Hveragerði
Landmannalaugar
Hafnir
Njarðvík
Reykjanes Peninsula
Ytri-Rangá
Hekla
Blue Lagoon
Selfoss
Grindavík
Eyrarbakki
Reykjanestá
Þorlákshöfn
Stokkseyri
Hella
Tindfjallajökull
Eldey
Hvolsvöllur
Þórsmörk
Gljúfurárfoss
Eyjafjallajökull
Mýrdalsjökull
Eyrarbakkabugur
Seljalandsfoss
Landeyjahöfn
Skógafoss
ATLANTIC OCEAN
Westman Islands (Vestmannaeyjar)
Heimaey
Skógar
Vík
Surtsey
Ferry
Glacier
635
61
60
61
643
612
60
605
61
711
745
76
75
1
722
F752
590
54
1
F35
54
54
52
F550
F35
1
36
30
F26
32
F225
30
425
1
F261

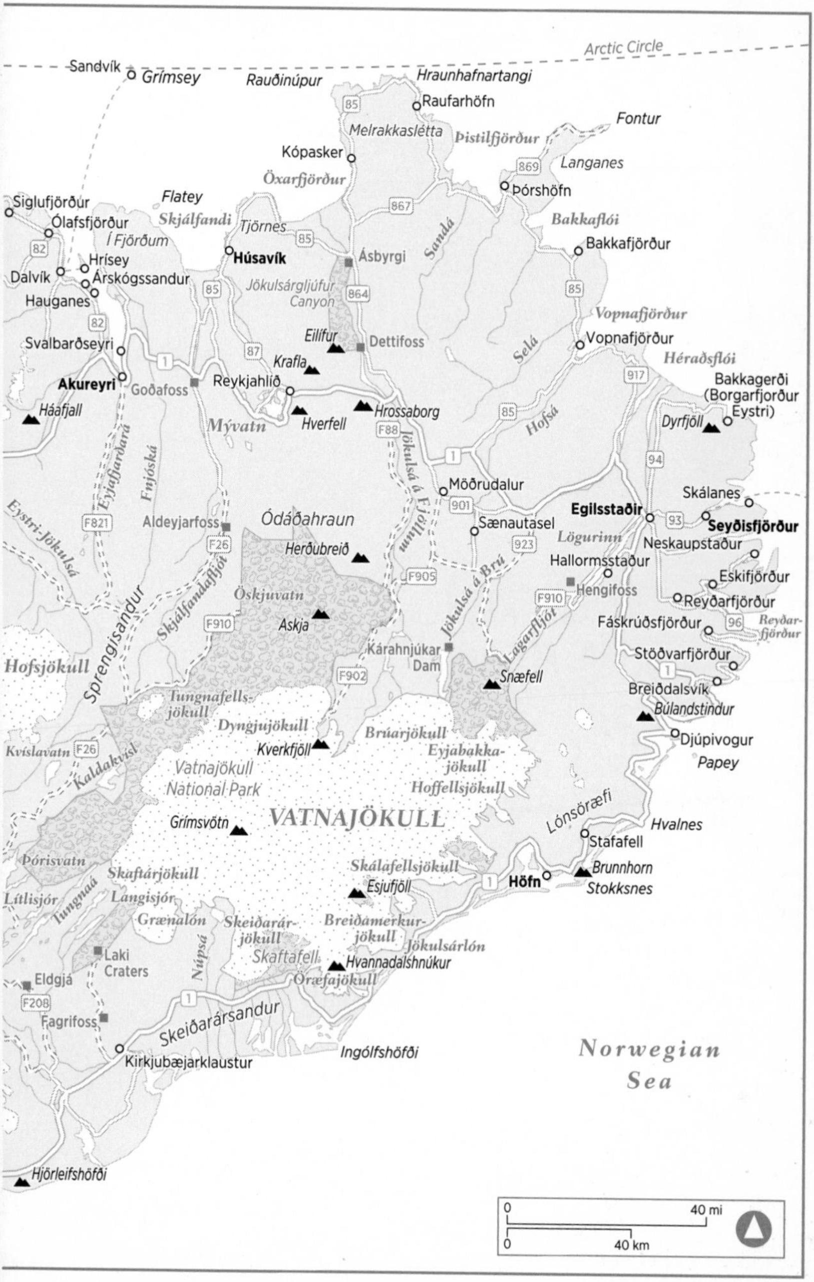
Arctic Circle
Sandvík
Grímsey
Rauðinúpur
Hraunhafnartangi
Raufarhöfn
Fontur
Melrakkaslétta
Þistilfjörður
Kópasker
Langanes
Öxarfjörður
Þórshöfn
Siglufjörður
Flatey
Ólafsfjörður
Skjálfandi
Tjörnes
Bakkaflói
Í Fjörðum
Hrísey
Húsavík
Ásbyrgi
Sandá
Bakkafjörður
Dalvík
Árskógssandur
Hauganes
Jökulsárgljúfur Canyon
Vopnafjörður
Eilífur
Dettifoss
Svalbarðseyri
Krafla
Selá
Vopnafjörður
Héraðsflói
Akureyri
Goðafoss
Reykjahlíð
Bakkagerði (Borgarfjorður Eystri)
Háafjall
Hverfell
Hrossaborg
Mývatn
Hofsá
Dyrfjöll
Jökulsá á Fjöllum
Eyjafjarðará
Fnjóská
Möðrudalur
Skálanes
Egilsstaðir
Seyðisfjörður
Eystri-Jökulsá
Aldeyjarfoss
Ódáðahraun
Sænautasel
Lögurinn
Neskaupstaður
Herðubreið
Hallormsstaður
Jökulsá á Brú
Eskifjörður
Hengifoss
Reyðarfjörður
Öskjuvatn
Sprengisandur
Skjálfandafljót
Askja
Fáskrúðsfjörður
Reyðarfjörður
Lagarfljót
Kárahnjúkar Dam
Stöðvarfjörður
Hofsjökull
Snæfell
Breiðdalsvík
Búlandstindur
Tungnafellsjökull
Dyngjujökull
Brúarjökull
Djúpivogur
Kvíslavatn
Kaldakvísl
Kverkfjöll
Eyjabakkajökull
Papey
Vatnajökull National Park
Hoffellsjökull
Lónsöræfi
Grímsvötn
VATNAJÖKULL
Hvalnes
Stafafell
Þórisvatn
Skaftárjökull
Skálafellsjökull
Brunnhorn
Höfn
Stokksnes
Tungnaá
Langisjór
Esjufjöll
Lítlisjór
Grænalón
Skeiðarárjökull
Breiðamerkurjökull
Jökulsárlón
Núpsá
Laki Craters
Skaftafell
Hvannadalshnúkur
Eldgjá
Öræfajökull
Skeiðarársandur
Fagrifoss
Kirkjubæjarklaustur
Ingólfshöfði
Norwegian Sea
Hjörleifshöfði
0
40 mi
0
40 km
85
867
869
864
82
87
1
917
F88
94
901
93
F821
F26
923
F905
F910
96
F902
F208

places across Iceland. When some areas near the volcano became temporarily inaccessible, tourists were presented with once-in-a-lifetime alternatives, such as lava sightseeing by helicopter.

Throughout this book, we inform you about Iceland's better places to visit, dine, and sleep, and this chapter gives you a taste of the very best. Some are classics, such as the Blue Lagoon, others are less well known. However, we hope you will add your own bests to this list. Perhaps we only gasped in awe at Dynjandi waterfalls because the weather happened to be ideal that day, perhaps the chef was having an exceptionally good day at Tjöruhúsið restaurant. The same applies for this whole book of candid advice: we hope you'll benefit from the inside information, but we can only expect you'll mostly agree with us most of the time. When places change significantly, for better or worse, we let you know on Frommers.com and encourage you to join in the conversation there.

THE most unforgettable TRAVEL EXPERIENCES

- **Boating on the Jökulsárlón Glacial Lagoon:** Hundreds of sediment-streaked, blue-tinted icebergs, seemingly the work of some mad sculptor, waltz in slow motion around this surreal glacial lagoon, the climax of any south-coast trip. Take a boat tour to enter the dance, listen to the music of the cracking, crashing, rotating ice, and watch the seals join in the carnival procession. See p. 329.
- **Being Massaged at the Blue Lagoon:** Floating on your back in womb-like weightlessness, enveloped between a blanket and a floating mat, the masseuse's hands work their magic. Afterward you can resume the central activity at this spa—bathing in an opaque, blue-green lagoon amid a jet-black lava field and smearing white silica mud all over yourself. The massage simply takes the experience of Iceland's top tourist attraction to a new, heavenly level. See p. 166.
- **Gazing at the Northern Lights from a Hot Tub:** You'll have to visit off-peak to be treated to this jaw-droppingly magic display of light dancing across the sky, seen only on clear, cold nights, and best enjoyed from the luxurious warmth and comfort of one of Iceland's countless hot tubs. The *aurora borealis* (Northern Lights) are probably caused by charged solar particles entering the Earth's magnetic field and stimulating molecules in the atmosphere—the fact that scientists aren't certain adds to the mystery. See p. 193.
- **Marvel at a Volcanic Eruption:** Flying by helicopter to watch a volcano erupting while the table is set and dinner is cooked using the heat from the lava flow sounds like a scene from an implausible film. But this was what some visitors were doing between March 21 and April 23 2010 when Eyjafjallajökull filled the sky with flames. If there's another eruption, book your tickets fast to the most spectacular show on Earth. See p. 306.
- **Hiking Laugavegurinn:** A world-renowned 4-day trek between Landmannalaugar and Þórsmörk through a cavalcade of inland scenery. Mossy lava fields, hot spring baths, glacial valleys, and desert expanses combine to make this a hiker's paradise. (Not to be confused with Laugarvegur, Reykjavík's main street and the country's most popular place for shoppers to absorb a more urban scenery.) See p. 304.
- **Seeing History at Glaumbær:** If you visit just one of Iceland's museums housed inside preserved 19th- and early-20th-century turf-roofed farm buildings, make it

Glaumbær in the northwest. Fishskin shoes and other fascinating artifacts are on view, but the most affecting moments are when you imagine the smell of burning peat and the sounds of the family clan pottering about these dark, damp, snug rooms through the long winters. See p. 236.

THE best NATURAL WONDERS

- **Askja:** This staggering whorl of volcanic mountains, circling an 8km-wide (5-mile) bowl formed by collapsed magma chambers, is one of Earth's grandest pockmarks and the most sought-out destination in Iceland's desolate highland interior. Visitors can swim in a warm, opaque blue-green pond at the bottom of a steep crater: a real "if my friends could see me now" moment. See p. 376.
- **Fjaðrárgljúfur:** Iceland has several dramatic gorges, but this one's spiky crags and vertiginous ledges virtually summon the mystics and landscape painters. Fjaðrárgljúfur is close to the Ring Road, near the village of Kirkjubæjarklaustur in south Iceland, and the trail along the rim is a breeze. See p. 322.
- **Hornbjarg:** These sea cliffs in Iceland's far northwest aren't easy to reach, but pilgrims are treated to the most arresting sight on the country's entire coastline. An undulating, razor-backed ridge is etched against the sky: on its inland side, a steep slope scoops down to a meadowed plateau; on its opposite side is a sheer 534m (1,752ft.) drop to the sea. See p. 226.
- **Hverfell:** Of all the monuments to Iceland's volcanism, this tephra explosion crater near Mývatn is the most monolithic: a jet-black bowl of humbling proportions, with a stark, elemental authority. See p. 266.
- **Laki Craters:** This monstrous row of more than a hundred craters, lined up along a 25km (16-mile) fissure, is scar tissue from the most catastrophic volcanic eruption in Iceland's history. Velvety coatings of gray-green moss soften Laki's terrible, bleak beauty. See p. 322.
- **Látrabjarg:** These colossal sea cliffs mark the dizzying, dramatic outer limit of Europe's westernmost reach. 14km (8.7 miles) long and up to 441m (1,447 ft.) high, this is one of the world's most densely populated bird colonies. The sheer volume of birds is unbelievable, and the puffins are particularly willing to have their picture taken. See p. 206.
- **Leirhnjúkur:** In a country with no shortage of primordial, surreal landscapes, this lava field in the Krafla caldera of northeast Iceland out-weirds them all. An easy trail wends its way among steaming clefts, each revealing a prismatic netherworld of mosses and minerals. See p. 268.
- **Raufarhólshellir:** With the right preparations and precautions, anyone can just saunter right into this lava-tube cave and wander more than a kilometer (¾ mile) to its darkest depths, past eerie ice candles and tortured lava formations. See p. 175.

THE best WATERFALLS

- **Dettifoss:** Europe's mightiest waterfall, abruptly marking the southern limit of northeast Iceland's Jökulsárgljúfur Canyon, is a massive curtain of milky-gray glacial water thundering over a 44m (144ft.) precipice. To stand next to it is as hypnotic as it is bone rattling. See p. 283.

- **Dynjandi:** As you approach the six waterfalls of Dynjandi in the Westfjords, it seems a white blanket has been draped across steep giant steps leading up the rocky cliff. The main waterfall, Fjallfoss, tumbles almost 100m (328 ft.) but its majesty also lies in its breadth: 60m (197 ft.) at the bottom, 30m (98 ft.) at the top. It's an easy walk up to the base of the main falls, and worth it for the view of the fjord and the boom of the water. See p. 211.
- **Glymur:** Iceland's tallest waterfall is nimble and graceful: streamlets descend like ribbons of a maypole into a fathomless canyon mantled in bird nests and lush mosses. The hike there is somewhat treacherous, but those who brave it are rewarded with enchanting scenery—and possibly total solitude—all within easy range of Reykjavík. See p. 152.
- **Gullfoss:** Here, the Hvitá river hurtles over a low tier, turns 90 degrees, plunges into a cloud of spray, and shimmies offstage through a picturesque gorge. This astounding waterfall is the climax to the "Golden Circle," Iceland's most popular day tour from the capital. See p. 161.
- **Svartifoss:** In southeast Iceland's Skaftafell area, these falls provide a dramatic white contrast to the surrounding dark columnar basalt gorge. The water begins its descent at a rocky overhang, making it easy to walk behind the falling water below, though raincoats are still recommended. See p. 326.

THE most charming TOWNS & VILLAGES

- **Heimaey (Home Island):** As the only town in the gorgeous Westman Islands, Heimaey—surrounded by magnificent sea cliffs and two ominous volcanic cones—would have made this list for its setting (and cute puffin population) alone. Its distinctive local identity and heroic resilience in the aftermath of a devastating 1973 eruption only add to its luster. See p. 291.
- **Ísafjörður:** The Westfjords region is almost a country unto itself, and its honorary capital has real vibrancy despite its remoteness and small population. Credit the phenomenal setting, thriving dockside, first-rate dining, hip cafes, and festivals ranging from alternative music to "swamp soccer." See p. 213.
- **Seyðisfjörður:** The arrival point for European ferry passengers, and a fashionable summer retreat for Icelandic artists, this dramatically situated Eastfjords village has a cosmopolitan pulse that squares perfectly well with its tiny scale and pristine surroundings. Chalet-style wooden kit homes from the 19th and early-20th centuries provide a rare architectural historicity, and the country's first telegraph station is now a fascinating technology museum. See p. 354.
- **Siglufjörður:** This isolated, untouristy fjord town has a picture-perfect setting and an endearing nostalgia for its herring-boom glory days—case in point, the ambitious Herring Era Museum—and fabulous hiking. See p. 240.
- **Vík:** This southernmost village in Iceland wears its fine setting lightly, but its landscape stays vividly etched in the mind: the lovely beaches of black volcanic sand, the spiky sea stacks offshore, and, on the Reynisfjall cliffs, the most scenic walk on Iceland's south coast. See p. 314.

THE best BIG-NAME HIKING AREAS

- **Hornstrandir Nature Reserve:** This saw-toothed peninsula, the northernmost extremity of the Westfjords, is for those whose eyes always roam to the farthest corners of the map. Protected since 1975, Hornstrandir has no roads, no airstrips, no year-round residents—only the beguiling coastline, flowering meadows, and cavorting birds and Arctic foxes the Vikings first encountered more than a millennium ago. See p. 225.
- **Jökulsárgljúfur Canyon:** This elongated canyon lies within the vast Vatnajökull National Park.. Formed by Iceland's second-longest river, it is bookended by Dettifoss waterfall and Ásbyrgi, a U-shaped ravine reputed to be the hoof print of the Norse godÓðinn's eight-legged steed. Each bend of the river brings a succession of delights on a more human scale: honeycombed basalt, woolly willows, and cascading springs. See p. 280.
- **Landmannalaugar:** This area's undulating, multi-hued rhyolite slopes—with marbled streaks of yellow, red, green, white, and purple scree—make it one of the most photogenic landscapes on the planet and the most celebrated hiking area in Iceland. See p. 301.
- **Skaftafell:** Close to the Ring Road (Route 1) on the southern edge of Vatnajökull, and within the Vatnajökull National Park, Skaftafell is the most accessible of Iceland's major hiking destinations, with startling panoramas of serrated peaks, shimmering icecaps, and barren flood plains stretching toward the sea. At your feet is pleasant scrubland resplendent with wildflowers, berries, and butterflies. See p. 324.
- **Þórsmörk:** This verdant alpine oasis, encircled by monumental glaciers and river-braided valleys of silt, has the aura of an enchanted refuge—a nice counterpoint to the distinctly Martian appeal of most interior regions. See p. 311.

THE best OFF-THE-BEATEN-TRACK HIKING AREAS

- **Borgarfjörður Eystri:** This well-rounded coastal region combines many geological marvels found in the interior—particularly rhyolite mountainsides and their marbled patterns—with an abundance of flowering plants and the romantic melancholy of its formerly inhabited fjords and inlets. Locals have put great effort into designing maps, marking trails, and setting up 4WD tours of the area. See p. 359.
- **Eyjafjallajökull After the 2010 Volcano Eruption:** This area is certainly off the beaten track … there isn't even a beaten track because the track is still evolving. See for yourself brand new lava formations, land freshly sculpted by the flood of melting glacier, and ash (spewed from the volcano at 200 metric tons/441,000 lb per second) which settled across the ground like a giant, grainy shadow. Specific hiking routes are still evolving and are only suitable for experienced hikers. See p. 305.
- **Kerlingarfjöll:** A short detour from the relatively accessible Kjölur Route through the interior, this mountain cluster in the shadow of Hofsjökull has an astonishing

range of scenery: lofty mountains, chiseled ravines, exotic geothermal fields, glimmering icecaps... The clinchers are the hot springs that form enormous natural Jacuzzis and the pleasant lodgings at Ásgarður. See p. 369.

- **Kverkfjöll:** Deep within Iceland's highland desert interior, this geothermally restless mountain spur protrudes from Vatnajökull amid charred expanses of red, brown, and black rock dusted with lichen and moss. Best-known for a wondrous glacial ice cave, Kverkfjöll is anything but a one-hit natural wonder and merits 2 or 3 days to appreciate its austere gravitas. See p. 376.
- **Núpsstaðarskógar:** Accessible only to rugged 4WD vehicles and committed hikers, this magical enclave of scrubby birch, sculpted gorges, and luxuriant waterfalls along the Núpsá river is virtually untouched by tourists. If you can't get there on the ground, consider an exhilarating aerial tour from the Skaftafell airfield. See p. 325 and 327.
- **Sveinstindur-Skælingar:** Landmannalaugar unjustly steals the limelight from many nearby interior regions, most notably this amazing stretch of mountains and sediment-filled river valleys between Landmannalaugar and Vatnajökull. Views from the peak of Sveinstindur over the glacier-gouged Lake Langisjór are among the most otherworldly and sublime in all of Iceland, and in good weather Iceland's vast highland plains can be seen stretching into the distance. See p. 304.
- **Þakgil:** This idyllic campsite is in a perfectly sheltered, stream-fed gully near the southeast edge of Mýrdalsjökull. The surrounding Tuff mountains, formed from compacted volcanic ash, have been elaborately sculpted by wind and water erosion; trails lead right to the moraines of the receding glacier. A modern crop of snug cabins with new amenities added every year means you don't even have to rough it. See p. 318.

THE best MUSEUMS

- **National Museum of Iceland** (Reykjavík; ✆ **530-2200;** www.natmus.is): This museum's permanent but innovative and ever-evolving exhibit, "The Making of a Nation," covers the entire span of Icelandic history and culture. You might anticipate a numbing encyclopedic survey, but the curators' selective restraint manages to say more with less. See p. 128.
- **Einar Jónsson Museum** (Reykjavík; ✆ **551-3797;** www.skulptur.is): The work of Iceland's most revered sculptor draws heavily on classical mythology and traditional folklore, with a virtuoso command of gesture and ingenious meshings of human and beastly forms. His romantic symbolism carries deep emotional and spiritual resonance. Einar spent up to 10 years perfecting each of his works, many of which are displayed exclusively here. See p. 128.
- **Harbor House Museum** (Reykjavík; ✆ **590-1200;** www.artmuseum.is): Erró—the most prominent Icelandic artist of the late 20th-century—has donated most of his life's work to this contemporary art branch of the Reykjavík Art Museum. The exhibit spaces are inside a 1930s-era warehouse, perfectly suited to the vast, cartoon-styled montages for which he is best known. See p. 126.
- **Gljúfrasteinn—The House of Halldór Laxness** (near Reykjavík; ✆ **586-8066;** www.gljufrasteinn.is): This beautiful house in pastureland on the outskirts of Mosfellsbær was home to Icelandic writer Halldór Laxness, winner of the Nobel Prize for Literature in 1955. Walls are adorned with artworks by key Icelandic

artists and the first-rate audio tour provides a touching glimpse into Icelandic life during the 20th century. See p. 150.

- **Settlement Center** (Borgarnes; ✆ **437-1600;** www.landnam.is): With state-of-the-art multimedia exhibits dedicated to *Egils Saga* and the first 60 years of Icelandic settlement, this engaging museum tries almost too hard to turn learning into a kind of amusement-park-fun-house—but we're not complaining. See p. 183.
- **Safnasafnið Folk and Outsider Art Museum** (Near Akureyri; ✆ **461-4066;** www.safnasafnid.is): The curators of this inspiring art museum comb the country for what they call "honesty," ignoring conventional distinctions between contemporary art, folk art, and naïve art. The museum is not anti-elitist so much as immune to all aesthetic dogma. Exhibits spotlight anything from women's needle-working tools, and wooden figurines whittled by a farmer, to fine photography and sculpture. See p. 236.
- **Skógar Folk Museum** (Skógar; ✆ **487-8845;** www.skogasafn.is): This is without a doubt the greatest of Iceland's many folk museums, with an enormous artifact collection ranging from fishing boats to carved headboards and makeshift mousetraps. One of the quirkiest relics is a hollow fishbone used as a straw to feed milk to young boys so that they would not be prone to seasickness. See p. 315.

THE best PLACES TO STAY WITH LOCAL CHARACTER

- **Country Hotel Anna** (west of Skógar; ✆ **487-8950;** www.hotelanna.is): An appealing interlude for road trips along the south coast, this intimate hotel is an ideal blend of a smart B&B and a rural farm stay, though prices reflect the former. See p. 319.
- **Djúpavík Hotel** (Strandir Coast; ✆ **451-4037;** www.djupavik.com): Beautifully situated on the wild and remote Strandir Coast, this former boarding house for seasonal herring workers is so warmly and authentically connected to its past that any luxury deficits are irrelevant. Original driftwood boards creak underfoot, and the decaying herring factory looms wistfully nearby. See p. 223.
- **Faktorshúsið í Hæstikaupstað** (Ísafjörður; **456-3868;** gistias@snerpa.is): In the heart of the Westfjords' happening capital, this painstakingly restored 1788 house—with just one top-floor guest room—is as steeped in Icelandic history as any place you're likely to encounter outside a museum. See p. 217
- **Fljótsdalur Youth Hostel** (Markarfljót valley; ✆ **487-8498;** www.hostel.is): This charmed, turf-roofed hideaway is nestled deep within the Markarfljót valley, on the cusp of Iceland's interior. All beds are in bunkrooms and the amenities are few—but with the real world left safely behind, things couldn't be cozier. See p. 309.
- **Hótel Aldan** (Seyðisfjörður; ✆ **472-1277;** www.hotelaldan.com): Refurbishment of this 19th-century Norwegian kit building struck an exquisite balance of period restoration and sleek modern design. Aldan is easily the Eastfjords' most captivating hotel, in the region's most captivating village. See p. 358.
- **Hótel Borg** (Reykjavík; ✆ **551-1440**; www.hotelborg.is): This luxury hotel opened in 1930 and soon became a city landmark. Since renovations were completed in 2008, Art Deco style dominates and period Icelandic photographs adorn

the walls. Stop to admire the building, overlooking Austurvöllur Square, even if your budget won't allow you to stay the night. See p. 103.

- **Hotel Breiðavík** (Látrabjarg peninsula; ✆ **456-1575;** www.breidavik.is): Around the corner from Iceland's largest sea cliff, this warm and welcoming farm with rooms is in a breathtakingly picturesque bay with Mediterranean-hued waters. Wind down with an evening stroll on the beach, followed by a drink at Europe's westernmost bar. See p. 209.
- **Hótel Búðir** (Snæfellsnes Peninsula; ✆ **435-6700;** www.budir.is): This country-contemporary boutique hotel with an estimable restaurant is surrounded by nothing but ocean, broad sandbanks, sprawling lava, stone ruins of fishermen's huts, and a restored 19th-century church, with Snæfellsjökull glacier loftily presiding over the scene. See p. 196.
- **Hotel Glymur** (Hvalfjörður; ✆ **430-3100;** www.hotelglymur.is): This stylish retreat is just 40 minutes from Reykjavík but feels worlds away, especially when surveying the fjord outside from the vantage point of the hot tub or through the hotel's giant windows. See p. 153.
- **Hótel Tindastóll** (Sauðárkrókur; ✆ **453-5002;** www.hoteltindastoll.com): Each large, handsome room in this lovingly restored 1884 Norwegian kit home is an ideal synthesis of luxury and provincial charm. The natural-stone hot tub is the finishing touch. See p. 243.

THE best DINING EXPERIENCES

- **Fiskifélagið** (Reykjavík; ✆ **552-5300**): Since opening in 2009, "the fish company" has provided stiff competition to other top restaurants in Reykjavík, such as the Sjávarkjallarinn Seafood Cellar. Its exciting menu changes regularly, but think along the lines of smoked and slow-cooked Arctic char with honey purée and apple sauce. See p. 114.
- **Fjalakötturinn** (Reykjavík; ✆ **514-6060**): Traditional yet worldly (for a first course, think smoked lamb carpaccio with chutney and celery root salad), this stellar restaurant has a plain white dining room with a few photos of old Reykjavík on the wall. No glam appeal, but the cooking—and the country's most refined wine list—speak for themselves. See p. 114.
- **Þrír Frakkar** (Reykjavík; ✆ **552-3939**): The hallmarks of a "real Icelandic restaurant" are all here: nautical decor; a wide selection of fresh seafood and seabirds, always complemented by potatoes, familiar vegetables, and rich sauces; and there's nothing dainty about the portions or presentation. See p. 115.
- **Austur-Indía Fjelagið** (Reykjavík; ✆ **552-1630**): Indians know lamb, and Iceland has the world's best lamb meat, so put two and two together. Lobster Kalimirchi followed by Gosht Charminar lamb goes down well, but the vegetarian options are also good. See p. 114.
- **Hamborgarafabrikkan** (Reykjavík; ✆ **575-7575**): Since it opened in 2010 the "hamburger factory" has become the place to go for a gourmet approach to burgers, but the menu offers plenty more including the grilled lamb dish which Reagan and Gorbachev had (at nearby Höfði House) as they celebrated signing the treaty to end the Cold War. See p. 116.

- **Sægreifinn** (Reykjavík; ✆ **553-1500**): Reykjavík's ultimate low-budget dining experience offers a spicy, creamy lobster soup (it's often called simply "the lobster soup place") and other local seafood treats in a tiny seafront warehouse. See p. 118.
- **Strikið** (Akureyri; ✆ **462-7100**): Classy but unpretentious, this restaurant offers Icelandic classics with an international edge (think fried salted cod with a tomato chili sauce and parmesan cheese). Expensive, although not by Reykjavík standards, and with excellent value lunchtime specials. See p. 252.
- **Fjöruborðið** (Stokkseyri; ✆ **483-1550**): Icelanders drive long distances—and sometimes even drop in by helicopter from Reykjavík—to butter their bibs at this famed lobster house on Iceland's southwestern coast. See p. 179.
- **Tjöruhúsið** (Ísafjörður; ✆ **456-4419**): Tucked away in an 18th-century fish warehouse, this no-nonsense Westfjords restaurant serves up generous portions of amazingly fresh and tasty pan-fried fish without the slightest fuss. Ask the cook if the fish is frozen and you'll get a look of utter horror. See p. 218.

THE best OF ICELAND ONLINE

- **www.icelandreview.com: Iceland Review** magazine strikes a fine balance between serious journalism and touristic concerns; the travel articles are great for scouting destinations. Only some articles are featured online but its sister magazine, **Atlantica**, also has excellent travel articles and can be downloaded for free if you didn't get a copy on the plane. Iceland Review Online's daily news update is the best there is in English, and other features include a popular Q&A section about all things Icelandic ("Ask Eygló"). The site links to **What's On Iceland** (**www.whatson.is**), especially good for museum and gallery listings.
- **www.samkoma.com: Samkoma,** which means "meeting place," was set up to foster interchange between Icelanders and Canadians of Icelandic descent, but it also contains the Internet's best collection of Iceland-related links.
- **www.nat.is:** The homepage of **Nordic Adventure Travel** delivers on its cheery promise: "We cover everything you are coming to enjoy! The whole island is air conditioned!" The endless links are particularly helpful for those planning a fishing, hunting, or hiking adventure. Click the trail icons on a national map, and detailed trail maps and descriptions appear.
- **http://kort.bok.hi.is: Antique Maps of Iceland** has high-resolution digital files of vintage, pre-1900 maps of Iceland. Some 16th- and 17th-century maps include sketches of fantastic sea monsters leaping out of the ocean off the coast of Iceland.
- **www.northernlite.ca/19thcenturyiceland/:** Ed Jackson is a connoisseur of rare and long-forgotten Iceland travelogues, and his website **Travels in 19th Century Iceland** presents absorbing extracts with period photographs and illustrations. Entries are cross-indexed by location (Reykjavík, Þingvellir, and so on) and themes, such as dress, customs and manners, and children.
- **www.icelandicmusic.is:** This government-sponsored site, titled **Icelandic Music Export (IMX),** is a great way to sample the country's music scene. Features include news, events, downloadable videos, podcasts, and links to homepages of Icelandic artists. **The Icelandic Music Page** (**www.musik.is**) is another excellent site with links for musical events throughout the country.

- **www.grapevine.is: The Grapevine,** a free left-wing magazine found all over Iceland, is a resource for reviews of art, music, dining, shopping, and trips within Iceland. Issues are archived and searchable online.
- **www.halfdan.is/vestur/vestur.htm: The Emigration from Iceland to North America** is the best site for non-Icelanders of Icelandic descent to trace their ancestry and find living relatives.
- **www.icelandweatherreport.com: The Iceland Weather Report** blog has been offering daily tidbits of news, cultural insights, tips, and whacky facts about Iceland since 2004. It is rarely about the weather (go figure). Icelandophiles will enjoy joining in the conversations and searching the archives.

ICELAND IN DEPTH

2

Tell friends you're going to Iceland, and many will wonder whether they'd be able to place the little country on a map, knowing only that it's somewhere west of Europe, and close enough to clog the continent's skies with ash should a volcano or two decide to awaken, as happened early in 2010.

Iceland, dangling from the Arctic circle between Greenland and Norway like a prickly Christmas decoration, is indeed a land of volcanoes. Eruptions are rare (on a tourist scale if not on a planetary one) but evidence of the country's volcanic history abounds in the landscape—from moss-covered lava fields stretching as far as the eye can see, to geysers and hot springs, to black beaches and basalt-lined bays, to the craters and volcanic mountains themselves (often teasingly hidden away under glaciers).

In some places houses half swallowed by lava have been preserved for show, and the Westman Islands showcase a port extension created during a 1973 eruption (p. 291) when some quick-thinking locals decided to tame the lava stream, hosing it down from boats on one side so that it would flow into the sea to improve the shape of the existing harbor.

Amid Iceland's rocky landscape are grassy meadows, multi-colored mountains, torpid glacial tongues, waterfalls cascading down from impossibly high cliffs into lush valleys, picturesque towns bordering the fjords and one of the trendiest capitals in Europe. The towns boast roofs in rainbow shades and almost every one has its own swimming pool and hot tubs.

The meadows and mountainsides are home to thousands of sheep—legally entitled to roam free during summer—and are crisscrossed with all manner of stream, brook, spring, river, and lake. You see turf-roofed houses and stone-walled sheep-sorting pens, tiny churches and, if you look carefully enough, even tinier elf houses embedded in hillocks, with brightly painted doors.

In this northern, tree-scarce land, the openness of the view is surprising and refreshing, and returning visitors immediately breathe in the crisp, invigorating polar air. It is no illusion—the eye really can see further, the grass really is greener, the summer days are longer, and the spring water coming from your tap is cleaner. In winter, the darkness is celebrated with lights in every window and often in the sky, too, when the magical *aurora borealis*, or Northern Lights, appear like ghosts dancing

Misnomer #1: Iceland Is Much Greener Than Icy Greenland

Iceland is not short of ice, with a couple of dozen glaciers and the whiteness of the winter landscape further enhanced by the lack of trees, but for the rest of the year it is greener than green, literally: the lack of sunshine over the winter months means that the types of grasses and mosses which have survived here need to be super-photosynthesizers and they are consequently more green than you'll find further south of the Arctic. According to the saga of Erik the Red, when Erik set out exploring and came across the southeast tip of Greenland, it looked a fertile enough place to set up shop (and climate scientists today support the theory that it really was much more fertile at that time). So Erik sent a ship back with word of the new settlement, hoping to attract enough people to make the venture worthwhile. But what to call this new land? Greenland had a more promising ring to it than Iceland, so that's what he settled on. Incidentally, the settlement ultimately failed, though experts haven't yet agreed as to what went wrong.

amongst the stars. Small children are pulled to school on toboggans, and people head to the ski areas at the weekend.

In addition to all its natural wonders, Iceland is also a modern nation with a rich culture and sense of history. Consistent with the diverse surroundings, the typical Icelander is a fisherman, a singer, a banker, a sheep farmer, or anything in between—even, quite often, two or three of these at once. You probably saw the 2010 volcanic eruption on TV, and you've probably listened to Björk's music, but we hope you get the chance to see for yourself some of the rest of what this amazing island and its people have to show.

ICELAND TODAY

Iceland's 103,000 square kilometers (39,756 sq. miles), with 4,970km (3,088 miles) of coastline, make it the 16th largest island in the world. Only Madagascar, Britain, and Cuba are larger single independent island states. Hvannadalshnjúkur, Iceland's highest peak, rises 2,110m (6,922 ft.). Roughly 10% of the country is covered in glaciers and the land is a hotbed of geothermal activity. Natural hot water piped into Icelandic homes means most of the population has non-polluting and inexpensive heating.

Only about 2% of Iceland's population (of just under 318,000) lives in rural areas, with roughly three-quarters living in Reykjavík, the capital. If you think the streets are looking more crowded than these figures suggest, keep in mind that the 500,000 tourists each year are out and about too, especially during the summer months. Icelanders boast one of the highest life expectancy rates in the world, and we suspect this has a lot to do with the clean air, clean water, and plentiful fish.

The country's Alþing (parliament) sits in Reykjavík, and its current prime minister is Jóhanna Sigurdardóttir (since 2009). Ólafur Ragnar Grímsson (1996) is serving his third term as president.

Most of the tiny amount of Iceland's arable land is used for grazing and 1 or 2% of Icelanders are engaged in agriculture. Iceland imports a lot of foodstuffs, but also

Gay Leader

Iceland has the world's first openly gay prime minister. In July 2010 when the laws were passed to allow gay couples to marry, she married her long-time partner.

produces vegetables, meat, fish, and dairy. The Icelandic economy has traditionally been driven by fishing and fisheries products, but the other main export today is aluminum.

In 2007, when Iceland was surfing the economic boom, the U.N. named it the world's best country to live in: it had the best life expectancy, best education levels, best medical care, and personal income was at an all time high. When the economy crashed, starting in October 2008, the country suffered great financial loss and many Icelanders were left floundering in an ocean of debt. For months, the people of Iceland protested their outrage on a daily basis outside the houses of parliament, banging on pots and pans and pelting the vehicles of politicians with eggs and *skyr* (an Icelandic milk product). The government was finally driven out of office by what is now known as the "kitchenware revolution."

ELVES IN THE ICELANDIC psyche

Of all the species of Iceland's hidden people, elves are by far the most numerous and prominent. In fact, many 19th-century folk tales use "elves" and "hidden people" interchangeably. Generally elves are said to be good-looking, and dress in rustic styles prevalent in the early-20th century, sometimes with pointy hats. Male elves are skilled craftsmen and often work as farmers and smiths.

Elves are fiercely protective of their homes, which are usually inside rocks, hills, and cliffs, or even in an underground well or spring. Occasionally roads are diverted or building plans altered so as not to disturb them (p. 362). People have been lured into elf homes, never to return from the hidden world. Though elves are quite dangerous, especially if their homes are disturbed, they often help humans and are true to their word. Elf women have suddenly appeared to help women with a difficult childbirth. On the other hand, elves have also been said to steal human babies in the night, replacing them with one of their own. To prevent this, Icelandic mothers would make a sign of the cross both above and below their babies after laying them in the cradle.

The term "**Hidden People**" (*huldufólk*) applies collectively to various humanoid creatures living in Iceland, including elves, dwarves, gnomes, trolls, and so on. When Viking ships first arrived in Iceland, dragon heads were removed from the prows so as not to disturb the guardian spirits of the land. These spirits are ancestral to the hidden people, who have always been strongly identified with features of the landscape. Hidden people are widely mentioned in sagas written during the first centuries of settlement. For the most part they've remained a folkloric phenomenon parallel to Christian belief, but sometimes they were incorporated into Christian frameworks. In one accounting, Eve was washing her children to prepare them to meet God. God arrived sooner than expected, so she kept the unwashed children hidden, and God saw fit to keep them hidden forever.

But while the relatively small size of the country and its economy was one of the reasons it was hit so hard and so early by the global financial crisis, this has also enabled Iceland to bounce back on its feet relatively quickly. Within two years it was already hard to see any outward signs of an economy in trouble, and the government continues to offer tax incentives to people willing to keep constructing buildings or expanding businesses, in order to keep the wheels of commerce turning.

Although some Icelanders went so far as to migrate (mostly to Norway) during the height of the slump, migration to Iceland has steadily continued (almost 7% of the population is foreign) and people on the whole still have an excellent standard of living.

ART & ARCHITECTURE

Art

Art plays a significant role in Icelandic culture, with well over a dozen registered galleries in the Reykjavík area alone. Exhibitions aren't just limited to galleries, many artists exhibit their work in other public places such as in shopping malls, restaurants, and cafes. Sometimes buildings are turned into works of art, such as the illumination of Icelandic lighthouses by artist Arna Valsdóttir in 2004. Some of the more prominent contemporary artists in Iceland include the postmodern artist Erró, Kristján Guðmundsson (the Carnegie Art Award winner of 2010), Ólafur Elíasson (the Danish/Icelandic artist famous for the installation entitled *The Weather Project* at London's Tate Modern) and Ragnar Kjartansson (also of the Icelandic band "Trabant") whose recent exhibition *The End—Venice* won critical acclaim. For more on art in Iceland, **www.sim.is** has good listings for galleries and exhibitions. The Reykjavík Art Museum on Tryggvagata 17, (✆ **590-1201**) also has good online resources at **www.artmuseum.is**.

ICELAND'S THOUSAND YEARS DATELINE

800–1050 The age of the Vikings, when Norsemen brought terror to the coasts of Europe.

871+/-2 The age of settlement. According to the *Íslendingabók* (The Book of Icelanders) the settlement of Iceland began in around 870, with the arrival of Ingólfur Arnarson in Reykjavík. In the 4th century b.c., long before the land was ever settled, it was described by the Greek explorer Pytheas of Marseille who referred to it as "Thule."

930 Alþing. The need for a common law in Iceland led to the creation of the Alþing, an annual political assembly of some 40 local chieftains. A Law Speaker was elected who had to commit the laws to memory and recite them. The first Alþing took place in Lögberg (Law Hill) at Thingvellir and continued for more than

Architecture

Traditional architecture in Iceland was very basic, suffering from the lack of wood. Icelanders built their homes from sod and turf, with supporting constructions often made from driftwood. Some of the later turf houses have been preserved, such as Skógar (p.315), Glaumbær (p. 236), and Keldur (p. 308). During the medieval period, many wooden-framed churches were built, followed by many stone constructions in the 18th century. The church in Hólar (p. 238) is the largest stone-built church from this period.

The first notable influences on Icelandic architecture were Danish and appeared during the expansion of Reykjavík when merchants set up trading posts in Iceland. These houses were typically wooden-framed with pitched roofs.

Another strong influence was the Swiss chalet style bought to Iceland via Norwegian influence. These buildings were modified with corrugated-iron surfacing in place of cladding. Many of these houses can be seen around town, painted in a variety of hues.

MODERN ARCHITECTURE

Some believe one of the greatest tragedies for Icelandic architecture was the arrival of functionalism. The landscape in Reykjavík is dotted with buildings that look like stacks of Lego blocks (though sometimes nicely painted) and concrete apartment blocks. The lack of any decent town planning has resulted in a mish-mash of vastly different styles which continue to clash with every new building project. No lessons have been learnt though, and during the boom period before the economic crash towers were raised next to traditional wooden houses without any consideration for creating an aesthetically pleasing complementary style. The buildings simply look out of place. There are, however, some beautiful buildings, including Alþingi, the current parliament building in the heart of the city, which is hewn out of Icelandic stone, or Háteigskirkja, a beautiful white building crowned with four black turrets

300 years until the Norwegian crown took over.

982 Westward voyages. After being exiled from Iceland, Erikur the Red headed for Greenland and established a settlement of around 300 houses with 3,000 inhabitants. His son, Leifur the Lucky, after hearing about a land west of Greenland, set off and discovered Vinland (North America). They tried to settle there, but were forced to leave after three years by the hostile Indians.

1000 Christianity was brought to Iceland around the year 1000, with missionaries from Norway who converted a southern chieftain (a relative of the King of Norway). For a while Iceland would remain both heathen and Christian, until a compromise was made by the Law Speaker Þórgeir who, after spending a day thinking and reflecting in silence (with a cloak spread over him to discourage people from interrupting), proclaimed that Iceland would become Christian; as long as people were still free to worship heathen gods.

1120 The sagas of Iceland constitute the first extensive body of prose

continues

on Háteigsvegur in the 105 area of Reykjavík. The design of the new Harpa concert hall and conference center on Austurstræti 17, is supposed to be inspired by natural crystallized basalt columns found in Iceland's nature, but the obscure geometric construction fails to bring to mind any natural forms. It's more reminiscent of an alien building from a sci-fi comic book.

FIRE, ICE & THE TALLEST BONSAI FORESTS IN THE WORLD

Chances are that the Icelandic landscape is why you decided to pick up this book in the first place. It's not just that Iceland is a spectacularly beautiful country, which it is, but that there is so much diversity, and that nature at its most stunning is so easily accessible to visitors. There aren't many places on the planet where you can walk behind a waterfall, climb on to a glacier, explore a lava cave, marvel at an erupting volcano (or at the blackened hills still steaming months afterwards), sail among icebergs on a glacial lake, watch water erupting into the air from a geyser, and scuba dive along the rift between two continental plates, all in one weekend. Not just that, but visitors can still spend evenings eating at the finest restaurants, and partying in some of the world's trendiest bars. If it's not summer, you may even be lucky enough to observe some magical Northern Lights as you wander back to your hotel. Perhaps someone added up every tourist's wildest dream and designed a country based on the result: Iceland.

The only thing Icelandic nature does lack is trees. You won't get lost in a forest. (The advice in Iceland if you do manage this unlikely feat is: "Stand up!") It is widely held that Iceland was once much more forested, but that

Impressions

Iceland has "the most magical light of anywhere on earth."
—W. H. Auden.

composed in a European language and largely recount events between 870 and 1350. The fact that most Icelanders would still be able to read and understand them is remarkable. Written in a narrative similar to the modern novel the first manuscripts, the *Íslendingabók* (Book of Icelanders) and *Landnámabók* (Book of Settlements), were written by Ari the Wise. The most famous writer of the sagas is Snorri Sturlasson who wrote *Heimskringla* (Orb of the World), a history of the kings of Norway. The greatest manuscript of the sagas is the *Möðruvallabók* (The Möðruvellir Book) which includes 11 of the Icelandic family sagas.

1262–1380 Norwegian rule. Plans by the Norwegian crown to take over Iceland are first recorded in the year 1220, when Snorri Sturlasson unsuccessfully tried to win Iceland over to the king of Norway. A period of conflict ensued culminating in the Battle of Örlygsstaðir in North Iceland. Conflict continued until 1262 when Gissur (the first earl of Iceland) induced the chieftain of the lands to swear allegiance to the king. Iceland remained in the realm of the Kings of Norway until 1376,

Reykjavík Means 'Smokey Bay' Yet Is Smokeless

When the first settlers sailed toward what we now know as Reykjavík dock, they noticed white plumes dotted around the distant landscape, as though fires were lit in many of the valleys. Hence the name "Smokey Bay." Later, they found these were in fact wisps of steam from the hot springs, but the original name stuck. In modern times this has become even more of a misnomer, given the city's welcome lack of pollution.

the first settlers, being mostly from Norway, didn't understand trees would not grow back as quickly as demand required. Later, when building materials were scarce, driftwood coming from places as far away as Russia became extremely valuable, and laws were devised to govern a person's right to claim driftwood based on where it washed ashore.

Today there are many reforestation efforts in Iceland, but the landscape as a whole is still very bare. All the better to see those lovely undulating hills, many would argue. One might expect the land to seem barren as a result, but that would be forgetting the endless fields of green, green grass and the multifarious moss. It's not just your average garden variety of moss—it's moss in abundance, moss of several dozen species, moss that has grown across lava fields for centuries and centuries, so thick in places that you can't be sure anymore that there are rocks underneath. It reminds you that the soil here is rich, the earth is warm beneath the snow, and the land itself seems vibrant and alive. The landscape takes on a different character and it feels liberating to be able to see for so far without the view being obstructed. If you live in a wooded area, you may even feel a little claustrophobic at first when you return home.

when the crowns of Norway and Denmark were inherited by KingÓlaf. Iceland then became subject to the Danish throne and remained so until 1944.

1300 Fish exports from Iceland to England are recorded in English import records. The industry expanded over the next 100 years as demand increased from Europe, probably because fish was allowed on religious fasts.

1402–1495 The plague swept through Iceland a little later than it did in Europe arriving in the 15th century, with two major epidemics. The first arrived around 1402 and spread rapidly from Hvalfjörður in the west, to the north and south, finally reaching the east by 1403; the plague claimed around 50% of the population before dying out around Easter 1404. The second epidemic occurred in 1494–95 and also claimed a significant proportion of the population, but did not reach the Westfjords.

1536 Religious reformation. The introduction of Lutheranism in Iceland was not as peaceful as the transition to Christianity, bringing violence and murder. The Danish government in Iceland was wiped

continues

ICELAND IN POPULAR CULTURE: MUSIC, BOOKS & FILM

MUSIC

It's quite amazing that a country with only 317,000 people can produce so many talented musicians, with such a diversity of styles and genres. The rise of Iceland as a producer of popular music came with the arrival on the scene of Björk in 1993, and it has since developed into an important international music hub with annual festivals that attract people from all over the world. Artists such as: Mínus, Gus Gus, Emiliana Torrini, Sigur Rós, and Ólafur Arnalds have all made the crossover into international music markets. One of the most notable music festivals in Iceland is "Airwaves" (p. 35), which attracts a lot of media attention from abroad. For 5 days in mid-October Reykjavík is buzzing with talent scouts and journalists from around the globe, there to check out the plethora of local and international bands, showcased on the stages of all available music venues. The festival is affiliated to the national airline, Icelandair, which offers package tours to Iceland during Airwaves. Don't Panic Films, run by up-and-coming film maker Bowen Staines (**www.donticeland.com**), is a good resource with short films profiling new musical talent and documentaries from the festival.

New bands to look out for include: Agent Fresco, Bloodgroup, the Esoteric Gender, Mammút, Sin Fang Bous, Sudden Weather Change, and Worm is Green. Also check out Iceland's best new record label "Kimi", **www.kimirecords.com**, for other great bands. Another good resource for Icelandic music is **www.gogoyoko.com**, an online music market place that operates in a Fairtrade manner. For listings, check *The Reykjavík Grapevine*, a free monthly circular, also available online **www.grapevine.is**.

Apart from pop music, Iceland also has a vibrant classical, opera, and jazz scene, with some dedicated venues in Reykjavík. **Cafe Rosenberg,** Klapparstígur 25–27

	out twice as it tried to convert the Icelanders to protestantism. In 1552 another royal Danish government was established and completed the reformation of Iceland.
1600–1785	The Dark Ages. A particularly pious period for Icelanders as they lived under the repressive thumb of the orthodox Lutheran church. At least 25 people accused of witchcraft were burned at the stake.
1751–1806	Reykjavík. During this period Reykjavík emerged as the capital of Iceland. First with the opening of a wool industry workshop by a team of Icelandic entrepreneurs, then with the abolition of monopoly which led to the establishment of more trading hubs, and finally with the relocation of Iceland's main administration offices.
1830–1904	Fight for autonomy. During this period Iceland struggled with the Danish rule for more power and in 1874 was awarded its own constitution and legislative power, limited to internal affairs. Icelanders had to wait a further 30 years to win complete control.
1873–1914	Emigration. Around 50 million people headed to America from Europe, including 15,000 Icelanders (20% of the population

(✆ **551-2442**) is one of the hosts of the annual Jazz festival in August (p. 35), where many Icelandic jazz musicians can be seen along with international names. Folk and blues are also performed in the venue. The newest opera celebrity in Iceland is Garðar Thór Cortes who can be heard, amongst a wealth of other Icelandic talent, at the Icelandic Opera (p. 145), or check out their website (**www.opera.is/EN/**) for listings in English.

The Iceland Symphony Orchestra (✆ **545-2500**) performs regularly in the Háskólabíó (University Cinema), its home since 1961; in 2011 the orchestra will move to the new 1,800-seat Harpa (Reykjavík Concert and Conference Center).

Books

Iceland's people trace their ancestry back to the Vikings and their language is so close to the Old Norse language of more than a millennium ago that school students have much less trouble reading the old sagas as they were written at the time, than English speakers have trying to decipher Shakespeare who is several centuries more recent. Many consider the sagas Iceland's greatest national treasure and their status is consistent with the Icelandic people's love of literature. With one of the most literate populations in the world, Iceland produces more novels per capita than any other country, so don't be surprised if every second Icelander you meet has published their own book. Icelanders are prolific writers and won't hesitate to self-publish. Its most revered 20th-century writer is Nobel Prize winner Halldór Laxness, whose work is widely available in English and countless other languages. Among other popular modern authors whose books you'll find in English are Einar Már Guðmundsson, Kristín Marja Baldursdóttir, and crime writer Arnaldur Indriðason.

Sagas

Among the great literary works of medieval Europe, the Icelandic sagas retain the most importance and immediacy to the nation that produced them. The Icelandic

at the time). Most left from the north and east of Iceland.

1916 Workers' movement. This year saw the establishment of a national union of trade unions.

1944 Sovereignty. On June 17 1944 independence was established and the Republic of Iceland was formed, with a ceremony in Þingvellir.

1958 Fish fight #1. After World War II, Iceland expanded its fishing boundaries, and in this year set new limits of 12 nautical miles from the coast. British trawlers opposed the boundary under protection of British warships. This first Cod War was eventually resolved through diplomatic settlement.

1955 Halldór Laxness won the Nobel Prize for literature with his book *Independent People*.

1972 Fish fight #2. In 1972, after a low economic period, Iceland extended the fishing boundary to 50 nautical miles. The British answered with a second Cod War.

1975 Fish fight #3. When Iceland further extended their fishing boundary to 200 nautical miles, the Cod War became more destructive. Diplomatic ties

continues

language has changed relatively little in the last thousand years, and today's Icelanders can quite clearly comprehend the original texts. The sagas are still bestsellers in Iceland, and all students must read them.

Most sagas originate from the 12th to 14th centuries, but recount events of the 10th and 11th centuries, when Icelanders were experimenting with self-government and transitioning to Christianity. The sagas do not neatly correspond to any modern literary genre, but might be called historical novels. The storylines follow a general pattern, in which conflicts escalate into multi-generational blood feuds, and personal codes must be reconciled with the maintenance of the social fabric. (Readers expecting stories of handsome knights rescuing fair-haired maidens locked in castles tend to be disappointed.) The narrative style is terse and action-oriented, with infrequent dialogue and not much of the introspective probing expected in modern novels. Yet the sagas seem remarkably contemporary in their depth of character, intimacy of domestic scenes, well-developed sense of irony, and profound grasp of psychological motivation.

About 40 Icelandic sagas have survived, most written anonymously. The two most widely available collections are *The Sagas of Icelanders* (Penguin, 2001) and *Eirik the Red and Other Icelandic Sagas* (Oxford, 1999). As wonderful as these collections are, readers should know that both are highly selective. Of the six most revered sagas—*Egil's Saga, Eyrbyggja Saga, Grettis Saga, Hrafnkel's Saga, Laxdæla Saga,* and *Njál's Saga*—the Penguin collection includes *Egil's Saga, Hrafnkel's Saga,* and *Laxdæla Saga,* while the Oxford collection has only *Hrafnkel's Saga.*

All the major sagas are in print as individual volumes. Which one you choose could depend on which region you plan to visit: *Egil's Saga, Eyrbyggja Saga,* and *Laxdæla Saga* are set in the west; *Njál's Saga* in the south; and *Hrafnkel's Saga* in the east. Grettir the Strong, the hero of *Grettis Saga,* spends his final years on Drangey (p. 237) in the northwest. *Egils Saga* is the subject of a fine exhibit at the new Settlement Center (p. 183) in Borgarnes. *Njál's Saga* is often considered the greatest literary achievement of all the sagas; see "*Njáls Saga* & Its Sites," p. 308.

were severed and the Brits sent in their warships to ram the Icelandic fishing vessels. Iceland fought back with their secret weapon, a sharp hook designed to be dragged under water while crossing the path of British ships. In the end Britain was forced to back down and Iceland regained power of its primary natural resource. A symbolic win for tiny nations around the world.

1970–1980 Girl power and red stockings. In the 1970s a radical women's movement formed called *Rauðsokkahreyfingin* (The Red Stockings) to campaign for the rights of women in Iceland. The movement gathered strength and in 1975 a rally was attended by 20% of the population of Reykjavík with women all over the country taking a mass day off work and domestic duties.

1973 On January 23 of this year a crack appeared in the long inactive volcano Helgafell on Heimaey (Home Island). Fortunately, because of a recent storm, the entire fishing fleet was at hand to assist in the evacuation of the island during a massive eruption.

Modern Fiction

The dominant figure of modern Icelandic literature is Halldór Laxness (p. 25), winner of the 1955 Nobel Prize for Literature. His most renowned work is the 1946 novel *Independent People,* a compassionate and often comic story of a poor sheep farmer determined to live unbeholden to anyone. English translations of several other Laxness novels remain in print. *World Light,* from 1937, is the life tale of a marginal, starry-eyed poet, a kind of foil for Laxness to work out the conflicting imperatives of art and political engagement. *Iceland's Bell,* from 1943, explores Danish colonial oppression of Iceland in the late 17th century, with most characters based on actual historic figures. *The Atom Station,* from 1948, is a more outright political satire dealing with issues stirred up by the American-run NATO base in Iceland. *The Fish Can Sing,* from 1957, is a particularly gentle coming-of-age story about a boy's pursuit of a mysterious male operatic star. *Paradise Reclaimed*, from 1960, concerns a late 19th-century farmer who abandons his family, emigrates to Mormon Utah, and later returns to Iceland as a Mormon missionary.

Currently Iceland's most popular writer—both at home and abroad—is Arnaldur Indriðason, whose crime novels feature inspector Erlendur Sveinsson, a rather gloomy divorcee who spends his evenings reading Icelandic sagas. Seven of Arnaldur's works have been translated into English, and in 2005 his *Silence of the Grave* won Britain's coveted Golden Dagger Award.

Non-Fiction

Iceland was widely venerated in Victorian England, and William Morris's translations of sagas were household reading. Several Victorians wrote Icelandic studies and travelogues, some of which have been reprinted. Letters From High Latitudes (Hard Press, 2006), by the prominent statesman and diplomat Lord Dufferin (1826–1902), is an often wild account of his 1856 travels in Iceland, Norway, and Spitzbergen. (Tim Moore's Frost on My Moustache: the Arctic Exploits of a Lord

The resulting mountain was named Eldfell, and added an extra 233m (764 ft.) to the island's height.

1980 In this year the much admired Vigdís Finnbogadóttir became the world's first democratically-elected female president.

1986 Iceland hosted the famous meeting between Ronald Reagan and Mikhail Gorbachev during the Reykjavík summit, where both leaders took important diplomatic steps towards ending the Cold War.

1993 Björk released her first solo album *Debut* which went on to receive global critical acclaim and propelled her to international stardom, Iceland's biggest star.

2003–2008 Kárahnjúkar hydropower project. A massive dam project created in order to provide power for an aluminum smelter in the east of Iceland caused much controversy and outraged environmentalists. The project went ahead anyway and flooded large areas of Iceland's natural wilderness.

2006 The U.S. pull-out. On September 30 the American forces based in the Keflavík NATO base pulled out of Iceland after a 55-year post-World War II presence in Iceland.

continues

and a Loafer, published in 2000 by Abacus, is a hilarious account of Moore's misadventures while retracing Dufferin's route.) *Iceland: Its Scenes and Sagas* (Signal Books, 2007), by the eclectic scholar, novelist, and folk-song collector Sabine Baring-Gould (1834–1924), is a magnificent account of his 1862 journey across Iceland on horseback, interlaced with learned musings on the sagas. *Ultima Thule; Or, A Summer in Iceland* (Kessinger Publishing, 2007), written in 1875 by explorer and ethnologist Richard Francis Burton (1821–1890), is an equally penetrating and erudite portrait of Icelandic society.

Ring of Seasons: Iceland, Its Culture and History (University of Michigan Press, 2000)—by Terry G. Lacy, an American sociologist who has lived in Iceland since the 1970s—is highly engaging and insightful.

History of Iceland: From the Settlement to the Present Day, by Jón R. Hjálmarsson (Iceland Review Press, 1993), is a tidy, 200-page primer on Icelandic history. Iceland's 1100 Years: History of a Marginal Society, by Gunnar Karlsson (Hurst & Company, 2000; reprinted in the U.S. as The History of Iceland, by University of Minnesota Press), is twice as long and has a bit more intellectual heft. Readers particularly interested in the historical context of the Icelandic sagas should pick up Jesse Byock's authoritative study Viking Age Iceland (Penguin, 2001).

Iceland: Land of the Sagas (Villard, 1990) is a coffee-table paperback, with 150 pages split evenly between Jon Krakauer's evocative photographs and David Roberts' essayistic reflections on Iceland's landscape and literary heritage. *Iceland Saga* (The Bodley Head, 1987) also takes the reader on a kind of literary tour, but from a more informed perspective; author Magnús Magnússon translated many sagas himself.

Film

Iceland is perhaps better know for its fantastic film locations used in big budget films, such as *Lara Croft, Batman Begins,* or *Journey to the Center of the Earth,* than its home-produced creations. Icelanders may not have the money to make similar films, but they do make films and have been doing so for a good 90 years. They even have their own national film awards ceremony, the prestigious (in Iceland) "Edda Award." Though smaller individual films have been made since the 1920s, bigger productions

THE U.S. pull-out

September 30, 2006, marked the end of an era at Keflavík's NATO military base. In an understated ceremony, the U.S. flag was lowered and the Icelandic flag was raised in its place. Iceland now has no armed forces on its territory.

In 1940 the British occupied Iceland to prevent a German takeover. The Americans moved in the following year and have guaranteed Iceland's protection ever since. U.S. forces left after the war, but re-established a large base at Keflavík on behalf of NATO soon after the U.S.–Iceland Defense Agreement of 1951. Iceland was crucial in monitoring Soviet submarines and controlling North Atlantic air space: more Soviet aircraft were intercepted from Keflavík than from any other U.S. base. The base consistently aroused vocal domestic opposition, but commanded governmental support: in 1974, a parliamentary motion to terminate the

HALLDÓR KILJAN LAXNESS (1902–1998)

Halldór Laxness, author of 62 books in a span of 68 years, is the undisputed giant of modern Icelandic literature. (For suggested titles, see p. 23.) Born Halldór Guðjónsson in Reykjavík, he left Iceland after World War I to travel. In France he converted to Catholicism, adopting the last name Laxness and middle name Kiljan, after the Irish saint. In 1927 he published *The Great Weaver from Kashmir*, his first major novel. Three years later, after an ill-fated attempt to break into the Hollywood film industry, he returned to Iceland and became immersed in socialism, which greatly informed his novels: lead characters are typically impoverished and exploited by a corrupt establishment. But his most overriding, lifelong subject was simply the common man; and Catholicism, socialism, absurdism, and Taoism all framed this concern at different stages in his life. After winning the Nobel Prize for Literature in 1955, he was overjoyed that among his many congratulatory notes was one from a local Icelandic society of pipe layers; it was the only card to which he responded.

weren't carried out until 1980, when the Icelandic Film Fund was founded (Kvikmyndamiðstöð). Since then at least 39 Icelandic films have been produced, with some critically acclaimed films like *Englar Alheimsins* (Angels of the Universe) and *Reykjavík 101*. More good films come out every year. Eight films have been released since 2009 including Iceland's first horror flick, *Reykjavík Whale Watching Massacre*, adding to Iceland's growing film making credibility. You can keep up to date with Iceland's film industry at the following website: **http://www.icelandicfilmcentre.is/**.

EATING & DRINKING IN ICELAND

Icelandic cuisine is much improved from 20 years ago, when leaden Scandinavian comfort food was the near-universal standard.Several imaginative and exciting restaurants

1951 agreement was defeated by a petition signed by over half the country.

Before its closing, the Keflavík base hosted 1,200 U.S. servicemen, 100 civilian employees, several fighter jets, and a rescue helicopter squad, at a cost of around $260 million a year to the U.S. government. In March 2006, news of the American pull-out was delivered ham-handedly to the Icelandic government by a State Department underling. Today, the U.S. is still obliged by treaty to defend Iceland, which could one day regain strategic importance due to its proximity to prodigious oil tanker traffic. In the meantime, Iceland has considered starting its own military, but the abandoned base site has been transformed into, amongst other things, cheap housing and an extensive small-business community.

are leading the charge in Reykjavík. The enthusiasm is palpable—sometimes waiters can hardly wait to explain everything happening on your plate. Outside Reykjavík and major towns, however, good food choices can be more restricted. Village restaurants usually conform to a basic model: lamb soup and catch of the day (both of which can be a joy), plus an ever-present array of burgers, pizzas, pasta, and fries. But the reality is, if you like fish you can't really go wrong here. Whether it's cod, salt cod, local lobster or mussels, or various other fish such as herring, there's a sea-loving element which equates with that of the eastern U.S.

Icelanders like their food saucy, salty, and well-seasoned. In good restaurants, this only complements the natural ingredients. Icelandic ingredients are remarkably free of contaminants. Antibiotics, added hormones, and pesticides are rare. The meat could even be described as aromatic, reflecting the healthy outdoor lifestyle of the livestock (and even poultry). The lamb is what you'd expect it to taste like after the lambs have spent the summer roaming the mountains, nibbling on mosses and wild blueberry leaves. The fish is always so fresh that it's difficult to prepare badly, and so abundant that it's still reasonably priced. Restaurant service is almost always friendly and helpful, if not ingratiating. In general, waiters like being asked for advice when ordering. As in much of Europe, you may have to tackle someone to get your bill. Typical dining hours are a little on the late side. On weekends it can be difficult to find anyplace open before 10am, except in hotels. Icelanders usually eat dinner around 8pm or later.

RESTAURANTS

Value-conscious Diners

Food is probably more affordable for tourists now than it was before the economic crash, though it can still be rather expensive.

If you want to save money on food, then the best way is to **cook for yourself.** Icelandic hoteliers are well aware of high food prices, and many places to stay offer

The area, which was home to more than 1,200 service men and women, has since been turned into student housing.

2007 In this year the U.N. named Iceland the world's best country to live in, based on life expectancy, education levels, medical care, income, and other criteria.

2008 Rise and fall. What goes up must come down. After years of thriving, October 2008 saw the global recession take hold, leaving Iceland in an ocean of debt so severe that within three weeks the major banks of Iceland were declared insolvent, the króna plummeted, and suddenly the interest rates for cheap car and house loans—pinned to foreign currency—doubled, leaving many Icelandic families unable to make ends meet. The government came under heavy criticism and was ultimately forced to quit after a massive protest. After a general election in 2009, the Social Democrats were elected to lead the country out of recession.

access to guest kitchens. One way to save money is to focus on lunch as your main meal, since dinner prices are often much higher. If you do want a three-course meal then try the "chef's menu,"; it might look expensive but the price is almost always cheaper than buying the three courses separately. On the other hand, many Icelanders get by on just soup, bread, and salad for lunch. Many convenience stores have relatively inexpensive salad bars. Look out for the daily specials, or the two-person menus, which are often cheaper than other items on the menu. You can also check out the listings in this guide to get an idea of the price of main courses. **Fast food** is often necessary to stay solvent, or when nothing else is available. Thankfully Iceland has the world's best hot-dogs (see "Hot-Dog Utopia," p. 117), available at almost every filling station. Burgers are everywhere, and are often served with a kind of cocktail sauce reminiscent of Russian dressing.

Fish & Lamb

Menu advice can be crudely edited down to two words: *fish* and *lamb.*

Sheep imports are banned, and the lamb stock is exactly what the Vikings brought over. Icelandic lambs roam so freely that they can almost be described as game meat. Many Icelanders claim they can taste the wild berries, moss, and herbs that the lambs feed on. Slaughtering starts in mid-August, peaks in September, and continues into November, so late-season visitors may get the freshest cuts.

Most of Iceland's export income comes from fish. Simply put: Iceland arguably serves up the freshest fish in the world. The most common local species are cod, haddock, catfish, monkfish, halibut, trout, Arctic char, and salmon.

Of course, fish and lamb are hardly the whole story. Icelandic beef is raised in equally healthy circumstances. Delicious wild reindeer from eastern Iceland appears on some menus. Icelanders also have centuries of experience cooking seabirds, especially puffins and guillemots.

2010 On March 20 a vent fissure eruption opened in Fimmvörðuháls, in the south of Iceland, followed shortly by a larger volcanic eruption in Eyjafjallajökull, directly to the west of the first. The ash cloud from the second volcano brought European airspace to a halt for more than a week, creating the biggest-ever shutdown of passenger traffic.

2010 In May 2010 the Best Party (Besti Flokkurinn), led by comedian Jon Gnarr, won control of Reykjavík, with more than a third of the vote, in the city elections. Pledges included "sustainable transparency," free towels at swimming pools, and a new polar bear for the city zoo.

2011 Iceland is special guest at the Frankfurt International Book Fair, the world's leading book marketplace, in recognition of its rich literary heritage.

Crazy Things to Taste in Iceland

Icelanders have faced severe hardship and learned not to let any digestible species or spare parts go to waste—hence the following guide to some of the more peculiar Icelandic specialties on your menu.

- **Hákarl** This is Iceland's most notorious food: Greenlandic shark, uncooked and putrefied. Sharks have no kidneys, so urea collects in their blood and the meat has high concentrates of acid and ammonia. If you eat it raw, you might die. So, it's cut up and placed in an outdoor kiln for 3 months while the toxins drain out. Then it's hung to dry and cure for another 3 months. The shark is served in small cubes that have the look and texture of mozzarella cheese. The taste is indescribable. According to Icelanders, it gives you stamina. Traditionally it's washed down with *brennivín* (wine that burns), an 80-proof clear drink made from angelica root or caraway seeds, and known affectionately as "Black Death."
- **Horse *(hestur)*** The pagan practice of eating horsemeat was banned by Christian authorities in the 11th century, but they relented in the 18th century during a famine. Whatever your personal feelings for these magisterial animals, they're perfectly healthy to eat and don't taste bad either. Traditionally the meat is eaten in stews, but unless you're staying at a farm, you're more likely to find it served very rare, even raw.
- **Cod chins *(gellur)*** These walnut-size delicacies, extracted from Iceland's most bounteous fish species, are surrounded by a thick, fatty membrane that doesn't lift cleanly from the tender, savory meat inside. You'll just have to get it all down. They're best ordered in spring or fall when the cod are leaner, though some say that's missing the point.
- **Dried haddock *(harðfiskur)*** This has been a staple Icelandic food for centuries, and is available in every convenience store. It's best eaten as the locals do, with a little butter, but can also be treated as a healthier alternative to crisps.
- **Whale *(hvalur)*** The only species served up is minke whale, not an endangered species, though Iceland's decision to hunt them again is hardly uncontroversial. Consumption has risen

Produce

Iceland's freshest produce comes from geothermally-heated greenhouses. Locally-grown vegetables are specially marked in supermarkets; top products are tomatoes, cucumbers, and bell peppers. Icelandic salads still have some catching up to do; they're often just iceberg lettuce with a few vegetable shavings.

Dairy

Iceland's dairy products are just as wholesome and exceptional as the fish and lamb, but far less widely known. Icelanders consume lots of whole milk; reduced fat milk is available in markets but is slow to catch on. Iceland also produces great cheese, especially camembert and blue cheese.

But Iceland's greatest food invention is a yogurt-like product called *skyr*, which is gaining popularity abroad too. *Skyr* is a kind of whipped whey that tastes like a cross between plain yogurt, cream cheese, and soft-serve ice cream, yet somehow it's thanks to tourists using the "I'll just try it once and see what its all about" argument. As sashimi it looks more disturbing than it tastes; the raw meat is a deep red, even purplish. Even cooked whale steaks are served very red in the middle. And the taste? A sort of cross between tuna and beef, quite delicious when prepared properly, tough and rank otherwise.

- ***Svið*** This is half of a singed sheep's head, cut down the middle and laid on its side, all the better for eye contact with your meal. If you're sharing, go for the cheeks and lips. Svið is also served cold if you like, and can be found at Kjamminn restaurant in Reykjavík's BSÍ bus terminal—even at the drive-thru window!
- ***Slátur*** Leftover lamb parts, including the liver and blood, are minced, mixed, then sewn up and cooked inside the lamb's stomach lining.
- ***Hrútspungar*** These are ram's testicles pickled in whey, often mixed with garlic and pressed into a kind of cake or spread, which tastes like pâté way past the due date. Some Americans call these "Rocky Mountain oysters."
- **Puffin *(lundi)*** From May to mid-August you'll likely have an opportunity to eat Iceland's unbearably cute unofficial mascot. Puffin can be smoked, pickled, or eaten raw. Traditionally it's overcooked, but in restaurants it's almost always served rare.
- **Cormorant *(skarfur)*** This seabird tastes similar to puffin, only greasier and less fishy.
- **Guillemot *(langvía)*** This coastal bird's meat looks and feels like beef, but tastes like duck, with odd overtones of liver and seaweed.
- **Fulmar eggs *(fillsegg)*** These oily seabird eggs make a good start to a meal.
- **Reindeer *(hreindýr)*** Santa introduced reindeer to eastern Iceland from Norway in the 18th century. All are wild, and only about 300 are culled each year; so prices are high, although reindeer burger patties are often available cheaply from the frozen meats section at markets. Hunting season is late fall, so most tourists eat vacuum-packed meat. If you can tell the difference, your taste buds are superior to ours.

nonfat. Icelanders usually eat it thinned with milk (and sometimes cream) or even as a soup for lunch, served with bread. You'll find all sorts of varieties (blueberry, melon, pear, vanilla…) in markets and convenience stores.

Traditional Foods

For more on Iceland's often terrifying traditional foods, see the box above.

Drink

Coffee in Iceland is simply excellent. Most cafes train their staff as baristas who know exactly how to heat the milk without burning it and apply just the right amount of pressure to the coffee press. An average latte or cappuccino is around 400kr.

Alcoholic drinks in Iceland are very expensive. Beer is served in ½-liter (1 pint) glasses and costs around 650kr. Cocktails are around 1,450kr and an average glass of wine is around 900kr. Icelanders normally buy all their booze from the state-run store Vínbúðinn (© **560 7700**; www.vinbudin.is) with 13 branches in the Reykjavík area. One of the main stores is on Austurstræti 10a in downtown. Nights normally kickoff at home-based parties, with partygoers not venturing out until around 11pm. Unless there's a special promotion (or money is no object for you) don't offer to buy a round!

PLANNING YOUR TRIP

3

This chapter is designed to help you with practical matters in planning your trip to Iceland: when to go, how to get there, how to get around, how to prepare. Advance planning is especially important in high season (mid-June to August), since tourism is booming and services have trouble meeting demand.

For additional help in planning your trip and for more on-the-ground resources in Iceland, please turn to "Fast Facts," on p. 378.

WHEN TO GO

Iceland has a concentrated tourist season, peaking from mid-June until the end of August. Many Icelanders think the summer tourists don't know what they're missing. Iceland offers plenty to do in the other seasons, even winter, and prices are dramatically lower for airfares, car rentals, and places to stay. Icelanders are avid Christmas celebrators, and the *aurora borealis* is remarkably vivid in winter. Most off-season visitors use Reykjavík as a home base, and combine city culture and nightlife with activities such as horseback riding, snowmobiling and visiting spas (see "Iceland in the Off Season," p. 35).

On the other hand, high season is high season for good reason. Most tours and adventure trips to Iceland's most renowned natural attractions end after September. Roads in the hinterlands are generally closed from October to mid-May, and some don't open until early July. Precipitation increases in September, peaking from October to February, and frequent storms and driving rain are enough to dissuade many would-be winter adventurers.

The tourist **high season** corresponds with holiday time for Icelanders, but things don't shut down the way they do in, say, France. Icelanders work longer hours than most Europeans, and students fill seasonal service jobs. Some cultural institutions (theater, symphony, and opera) take the summer off, while most museums outside Reykjavík are *only* open in summer. Arts and cultural festivals are also clustered in summer, except in Reykjavík, where they gravitate to the "shoulder" seasons (April–May and September–October). For annual holidays and events, see the "Calendar of Events," below.

In timing your visit, consider also that the number of daylight hours can have unanticipated physical and emotional effects (see "Staying Healthy," later in this chapter). In early summer there is never complete darkness and the sun stays low to the horizon, creating an ongoing play of light and shadow. Spring and fall daylight hours are roughly the same as in North America or Europe. Days in mid-winter have only 4 or 5 hours of sunlight. These fluctuations are even more extreme in the northern part of the country.

Temperature Celsius / Fahrenheit

	JAN	FEB	MAR	APR	MAY	JUNE	JULY	AUG	SEPT	OCT	NOV	DEC
TEMP. (°C)	-2°-2°	-3°-2°	-2°-2°	0°-7°	3° -9°	6°-11°	8°-13°	7°-13°	5°-12	1°-8°	-1°-4°	-3°-2°
TEMP. (°F)	28°-36°	27°-36°	28°-36°	32°-45°	37°-48°	43°-52°	46°-55°	45°-55°	41°-54°	34°-46°	30°-39°	27°-36°

Calendar of Events

For public holidays, see "Holidays" in "Fast Facts," at the end of this chapter.

JANUARY

New Year's Day. This is really a 2-day holiday, as nothing reopens until January 3. January 1.

Þrettándinn. This day marks the end of the Christmas season. Icelanders celebrate with a kind of New Year's Eve reprise, including bonfires, fireworks, and traditional songs, while children throw snowballs at cars. January 6.

Þorrablót. This ancient Viking mid-winter tradition—named for Þorri, a month in the old Icelandic calendar—was originally a feast of sacrifice involving the blood of oxen and goats. Contemporary celebrations involve dancing, singing, drinking, and eating traditional Norse dishes, including singed sheep's head, pickled rams' testicles, and putrefied shark. Þorrablót dinners can be found in some Reykjavík restaurants; in smaller towns, visitors are often invited to join the locals. From the Friday that falls within January 19 to January 25 through most of February.

FEBRUARY

Food and Fun (www.foodandfun.is). For 4 days Reykjavík's best restaurants create discounted set menus. In a televised competition, top international chefs are challenged to create dishes on the spot from purely Icelandic ingredients. Late February.

Winter Lights Festival (www.visitreykjavik.is). Reykjavík is dramatically lit up for this cornucopia of cultural events: anything from fashion shows to figure skating to outdoor choral performances to belly-dancing troupes. Late February.

Bolludagur. "Bun Day" is celebrated by eating cream puffs *(bollur)* in multiple varieties. In the morning children aim to catch their parents still in bed, and then beat them with decorated "bun wands" *(bolluvondur).* Parents are then obligated to give their children one cream puff for each blow received. Monday before Ash Wednesday.

Sprengidagur. The name of this holiday translates into "bursting day" and is celebrated by eating salted meat and peas to the point of popping. Many restaurants participate. Day before Ash Wednesday.

Ash Wednesday (Öskudagur). Children dress in costume and traipse around town singing for candy. It's much like Halloween, and also a day for pranks. Seventh Wednesday before Easter.

MARCH/APRIL

Beer Day. This unofficial holiday marks the anniversary of the legendary day in 1989 when beer with an alcohol content above 2.2% was made legal. Guess how it's celebrated. March 1.

Easter Sunday. Easter holds special meaning in Iceland, as it marks the end of the long, dark winter. Most workers get a full 5 days off, from Holy Thursday to Easter Monday, and closures cause difficulties for tourists. Families gather and celebrate with

PACKING suggestions FOR ICELAND

The items below are hardly a complete packing list, just a series of suggestions and reminders.

Bathing Suit Yes, even in winter. Icelanders love their geothermal pools and hot tubs year-round, and so should you.

Binoculars These aren't just for bird nerds; you'll be glad to have them when whales, seals, dolphins, and foxes appear in the distance.

Compass/GPS Locational Device The latter is preferred, especially because compasses can be thrown off by Iceland's magnetic minerals.

Driver's License & Passport You wouldn't forget these, now would you?

Earplugs Icelanders can get pretty noisy late Friday and Saturday nights.

Electricity & Phone Adaptors See "Staying Connected," p. 59.

First Aid It's easy to scrape yourself on Iceland's endless lava rocks, so at the very least bring plasters and antibacterial ointment.

Flashlight There's a good chance you'll visit a cave; bring a strong one.

Hair Conditioner The mineral content of Iceland's geothermal water can be pretty rough on hair.

Hiking Shoes Even the most sedate tours often involve walking over rough terrain. Water-resistant shoes with ankle support are advised.

Insect Repellent You'll need this if you plan on visiting the interior or the Mývatn area, especially in spring or early summer. A **head net** is even better.

Motion Sickness Pills Longer ferry rides, as well as whale-watching and sea-angling trips, traverse stretches of open sea. Iceland's winding, bumpy roads can also cause motion sickness.

Multiband Cellphone See "Staying Connected," p. 59.

Raingear Icelanders prefer **raincoats** to umbrellas, since the wind blows rain (and umbrellas) in all directions. It's not *always* windy though, and if you visit any bird cliffs in nesting season an **umbrella** is ideal to protect against attacks by arctic terns. Bring **rainpants** since Iceland is pretty darn rainy.

Sleeping Bag This could save you lots of money; see "Sleeping-Bag Accommodation" in "Tips on Accommodations," p. 61.

Sleeping Mask The midnight sun can make sleeping difficult.

Sunglasses The Icelandic terrain can produce lots of glare, and with the sun so low to the horizon, sunglasses are essential for driving.

Sunscreen The sub-Arctic sun can cause sunburn even when the weather's cool, and the landscape offers few places to hide.

Towel Renting one every time you go to a geothermal pool adds up.

Tupperware Visitors to remote parts of Iceland often have to carry food.

Windbreaker or Windproof Shell Iceland is windy . . . penetratingly windy.

smoked lamb and huge chocolate eggs. Easter weekend is especially lively in Ísafjörður, the cultural heart of the Westfjords, with skiing competitions and the "I Never Went South" rock music festival (p. 216). March or April.

First Day of Summer. Summer starts early in the old Icelandic calendar. The end of long winter nights is celebrated with gift-giving, parades, street entertainment, and sporting events. The Thursday that falls within April 19 to April 25.

MAY

Reykjavík Arts Festival (www.artfest.is). For 2 to 3 weeks Reykjavík is swept up in this government-sponsored event. Many international artists and performers are included. Mid-May.

JUNE/JULY

Seafarer's Day & Festival of the Sea. This holiday salutes those who make their living by the sea, and is celebrated across the country with parades, cultural events, great seafood, and rowdy parties. Fishermen partake in rescue demonstrations, swimming and rowing races, and various strongman competitions. "Festival of the Sea" is the local celebration in Reykjavík, which may take place the following weekend. First weekend of June.

National Day. This public holiday marks Iceland's full independence from Denmark in 1944. The day starts off on a solemn and patriotic note, but by afternoon crowds have flocked to the streets to watch parades, traditional dancing, street performers, and theatrical entertainment. (One of the most meaningful gatherings is at Þingvellir National Park, where the Icelandic parliament first assembled in 930.) Each town celebrates in its own way, so check locally for details. June 17.

Summer Solstice (www.fi.is). On the longest day of the year, many Icelanders gather late at night to watch the sun dip below the horizon and scoop back up again shortly afterward. Formal events are rare, but visitors are usually welcome to join local celebrations. Each year the Ferðafélag Íslands host an all-night climb up to the Snæfellsnes glacier. June 21.

Arctic Open (www.arcticopen.is). This 4-day championship golfing tournament in Akureyri, open to professionals and amateurs, continues into the morning hours under the midnight sun. Late June.

Viking Festival (www.fjorukrain.is). For 10 days, modern-day Viking hordes descend on Hafnarfjörður, a town near Reykjavík, for traditional crafts, merrymaking in period costume, and staged battles with Christian forces. While some participants are Scandinavians, more are Britons and Germans: the Vikings' historic victims. The festival began in 1995 and is run by Hafnarfjörður's Viking Village hotel and restaurant. Between weekends it moves to Sauðárkrókur on the north coast. Mid-June.

Akureyri Summer Arts Festival (www.akureyri.is). For 10 weeks in summer, Iceland's "northern capital" hosts an assortment of concerts and exhibitions in venues across town. Late June to August.

LungA festival (✆ **861-5859;** www.lunga.is), on the third weekend of July is fast becoming one of Iceland's prominent music festivals. It invites young people aged 16 to 25 to join workshops led by artists involved in everything from visual art to circus performance to fashion design. Non-Icelanders are welcome, and the week culminates with live concerts by prominent Icelandic bands.

AUGUST

Verslunarmannahelgi (August Long Weekend or **Bank Holiday Weekend).** On this party weekend, Icelanders often leave town and camp out en masse. The most well-known destination is the Westman Islands, where locals join thousands of visitors at the campgrounds to hear live bands and gather round the bonfire into the morning hours. Plenty of events also take place in towns. First weekend in August.

Gay Pride (www.gaypride.is). The biggest Pride event in Iceland includes a parade, concerts, and all-night parties. Second weekend in August.

Reykjavík Marathon and Culture Night (www.marathon.is). Surely the 3,500 participants in Reykjavík's annual marathon appreciate the purity of the air. Runners can choose between the full marathon, a half-marathon, a 10km (6-mile) run, or 7km (4-mile) and 3km (2-mile) "fun runs." The rest of the day and night are loaded with free concerts and cultural events, and once it's reasonably dark, a fireworks display kicks off. Third weekend in August.

Reykjavík Jazz Festival (www.reykjavikjazz.is). Icelandic and international groups in a variety of styles play clubs and other venues across town. End of August/early September.

Reykjavík Dance Festival (www.dancefestival.is). Contemporary choreographers from around the world are invited to participate in this 4-day event. End of August/early September.

SEPTEMBER

Annual Sheep and Horse Round-up (Réttir). See "The Big Round-Up," below. Early and late September.

Reykjavík International Film Festival (www.filmfest.is). This 10-day event includes film classics, premieres, retrospectives, seminars, and workshops. Late September or early October.

OCTOBER

Iceland Airwaves (www.icelandairwaves.com). This 5-day showcase of Iceland's alternative/indie musical talent (with many international bands thrown in) attracts more visitors to Iceland than any other event. Crowds are thick with journalists and talent scouts; when the bands are through top DJs spin until dawn. Icelandair sponsors Airwaves and arranges special packages from Europe and America. Mid-October.

DECEMBER

Christmas season. In late December, Icelanders only get 4 or 5 hours of daylight, which could explain their enthusiasm for Christmas and its lights. Icelandic children count the 13 days leading up to the holiday with a group of "yuletide lads," all offspring of a grotesque troll named Grýla. (In traditional lore Grýla ate naughty children, but, in the 18th century, threatening them with Grýla was outlawed.) Each day from December 12 to December 24, a different lad descends from the mountains into human homes. Each lad is named for the mischief he gets into: Sausage Snatcher, Door Slammer, Bowl Licker, and so on. At bedtime children leave a shoe in the window, and wake up to find a small present from the nighttime visitor. From Christmas Day through January 6 they come in succession all over again.

New Year's Eve. Private use of fireworks is legal this 1 night only, and the entire citizenry sets the skies ablaze in celebration. (Reykjavík is a particularly chaotic sight.) Oceanside bonfires are another New Year's ritual. For a more refined experience in Reykjavík, try the trumpet and organ recital in Hallgrímskirkja.

For an exhaustive list of events beyond those listed here, check http://events.frommers.com, where you'll find a searchable, up-to-the-minute roster of what's happening in cities all over the world.

ICELAND IN THE OFF SEASON

Tourists arrive en masse in June and disappear just as abruptly in early September, so Icelanders compare them to flocks of migrating birds. However, more and more visitors are coming in the off season, particularly for short vacations in Reykjavík. Nightlife and spas are major draws, and winter adventure travel—particularly backcountry skiing, glacier snowmobiling, and 4WD touring—is also catching on. With fewer tourists around, locals can be especially hospitable and welcoming. Prices are dramatically lower for airfares, hotels, and car rentals, but don't expect price breaks from mid-December to mid-January.

Most museums outside Reykjavík shut down in off season, while some Reykjavík cultural institutions—notably the Icelandic Opera, headquartered at the world's northernmost opera house—are *only* open off season. With fewer tours to choose

THE big ROUND-UP

Visitors in early September—especially experienced horseback riders—can discover beautiful and remote backcountry while participating in an age-old Icelandic farming ritual: the sheep round-up, or *réttir*. Hundreds of thousands of Icelandic sheep spend the summer grazing in highland pastures. Before winter sets in, local groups of farmers spend up to a week herding them home. Historically, this was a man's job, but women have increasingly joined in. Once the flocks are penned and sorted by their earmarks, the farming communities let their hair down for singing, dancing, and drinking into the night. Traditionally many isolated villagers met their spouses during these events.

Most participants are experienced riders, but some accompany in 4WD vehicles or on foot; others just watch and join the party. Visitors are welcome to take part in some local round-ups, though don't expect nonstop excitement: the process could involve holding your position alone for hours in cold rain.

Round-ups for free-roaming horses are in late September or early October, primarily in the north. Figure out which parts of the backcountry you'd like to visit, then contact local tourist offices, travel agencies, and farm accommodations (www.farmholidays.is) for advice. Regional websites posting *réttir* information include www.northwest.is and www.northiceland.is. A lengthy but incomplete list of locations and dates is posted in August on www.bondi.is, website of the Farmers Association of Iceland (e-mail questions to Dr.Ólafur R. Dýrmundsson at ord@bondi.is).

from, visitors usually depend on rental cars to get around. Most major roads are plowed all year, including all of the Ring Road (Route 1). Winter driving conditions can be hazardous, however, and in the dead of winter, some villages can be completely cut off for days at a time. Most mountain roads and interior routes are impassable in the off season, except in specially adapted "Super Jeeps."

Icelandic winters, however, are surprisingly moderate, but they do have just 4 to 6 hours of daylight. Remember that late winter has more sunlight than early winter, with a corresponding increase in arranged tours. From September until March the night is dark enough to see the *aurora borealis*, the startling electromagnetic phenomenon in which shafts and swirls of green (or sometimes orange or blue) light spread across the sky. Of course, depending on the weather, some off-season visitors may see only clouds. (See p. 32 for more on daylight hours and weather.)

The shoulder seasons—April to May and September to October—can be wonderful times to visit, though some destinations are inaccessible. A good general strategy is to shoot for the outlying weeks of the high season for each destination.

For a calendar of festivals and other annual events, see p. 32.

Off-Season Outdoor Activities

See chapter 4 for a thorough outline of outdoor activities, many of which can be enjoyed in the off season. Of particular interest are aerial tours, dog sledding, fishing, glacier tours, hiking, horseback riding, jeep tours, pools and spas, and skiing and ski touring. Icelanders even like to golf on snow-covered courses, using bright orange balls.

Off-Season Destinations

REYKJAVÍK & NEARBY

Reykjavík remains equally vibrant year-round—after all, the weather has little bearing on its appeal. Cultural activities and nightlife show no signs of winter weariness, and Reykjavíkians still throng to their outdoor geothermal pools even if snow gathers in their hair. See the Calendar of Events (p. 32) for Reykjavík's many off-season festivals.

The capital is particularly lively and heartwarming during the Christmas season. Each weekend, starting in late November, the neighboring town of **Hafnarfjörður** hosts an elaborate **Christmas Village** with caroling choirs, trinket stalls, and costumed elves. On New Year's Eve, many visitors shuttle to Reykjavík just to take part in the Bacchanalian celebrations.

Outside of summer, day tours from the capital are less varied but hardly in short supply. The popular **Golden Circle** tour runs year-round, and two of its principal highlights—the **Strokkur geyser** and **Gullfoss waterfall**—are even more captivating in winter. Various companies also lead nightly **Northern Lights tours** in search of the *aurora borealis*. The **Blue Lagoon spa** in Reykjanes Peninsula is strange and magical in wintertime, with far fewer crowds.

OUTSIDE THE CAPITAL AREA

Compelling winter destinations outside Iceland's southwest corner are too numerous to list, but two regions deserve special mention: **West Iceland** and **Lake Mývatn–Krafla Caldera** in the north.

In the west, the wondrously varied scenery of **Snæfellsnes Peninsula** makes for a great road trip year-round, and **Hótel Búðir,** an idyllic getaway on the peninsula's south coast, is always open. **Ísafjörður,** the appealing **Westfjords** capital, is especially buzzing during its Easter Week music and ski festivals. Two marvelous country retreats in the Westfjords remain open all year: the **Heydalur Country Hotel,** along Ísafjarðardjúp Bay, and **Hótel Djúpavík** on the entrancing **Strandir Coast.**

Akureyri, Iceland's northern capital, is alive and kicking in the off season, with the country's best ski slope **Hlíðarfjall** close by. Many winter visitors fly to Akureyri, rent a car, and spend a couple of days surveying the myriad volcanic spectacles of **Mývatn** and **Krafla.** The geothermally heated lagoon of **Mývatn Nature Baths** remains open, and **Sel-Hótel Mývatn** arranges jeep and snowmobile excursions, horseback riding, and go-cart joyrides on the lake. The cross-country skiing is fabulous from February onward, and, in April and May, the lake twitches with birdwatchers ushering in the tourist season.

ENTRY REQUIREMENTS

Passports

All visitors to Iceland must carry a passport, valid at least 3 months beyond the return date. For information on how to get a passport, see "Fast Facts," at the end of this chapter. All U.S. citizens, regardless of age (even newborns), must have a passport to travel abroad. For an up-to-date, country-by-country listing of passport requirements around the world, go to the U.S. State Department website at **http://travel.state.gov** and click the link for "Country Specific Information."

Visas

If your trip to Iceland is under 90 days, no visa is required for passport holders in the U.S., Canada, Great Britain, Ireland, Australia, New Zealand, and many other countries. Iceland is a signatory to the Schengen Agreement, which includes Austria, Belgium, Denmark, Finland, France, Greece, Holland, Italy, Luxembourg, Norway, Portugal, Spain, Sweden, and Germany. Citizens of these countries do not need a visa. If you are from a country not listed here, check with the **Icelandic Directorate of Immigration** (www.utl.is) to see if you need a visa and what the requirements are. In most instances, other Scandinavian embassies will handle visa applications on behalf of Iceland. If you need a visa, it must be secured in advance of your trip.

If you travel to Iceland without a visa and are not from the Schengen Area, the total stay within the Schengen Area must not exceed 3 months in any period of 6 months. If you do need a visa, it will normally apply to the entire Schengen Area.

Work

A visa does not grant the right to work in Iceland. If you are from a European Economic Area (EEA) country, you can apply for Icelandic jobs without first securing a work permit. For more information, check with the **Directorate of Labour** (✆ **515-4800;** www.vinnumalastofnun.is/english).

Medical Requirements

No inoculations are compulsory for travel to Iceland. For more information, see "Health," later in this chapter.

Customs

For complete listings of permitted items, visit the Directorate of Customs website at www.tollur.is, or call ✆ **560-0300** (daily 8am–3:30pm).

WHAT YOU CAN BRING INTO ICELAND

All riding and angling gear must be disinfected, including gloves, boots, and waders. You'll need proof of disinfection from an authorized vet, or the gear will be disinfected upon arrival at your expense. For more information, contact the **Agricultural Authority** (✆ **530-4800;** www.lbs.is).

Alcohol: Visitors at least 20 years of age may bring 1 liter (1 qt.) of wine or 6 liters (6 ½ qt.) of beer, plus 1 liter of spirits (1 qt.). If you're not carrying spirits or beer, you can bring in 2.5 liters (2 1/ 2 qt.) of wine.

Currency: There are no limits on foreign currency.

Food: You may bring up to 3kg of food into Iceland, but no raw eggs, raw meat, or milk.

Pets: All animals require a permit from the Agricultural Authority (above). Permits are hard to get, and the animal must undergo 4 weeks of quarantine, so traveling with pets is usually not an option.

Tobacco: Visitors 18 or older may bring up to 200 cigarettes or 250g (½ lb.)of tobacco, but no "moist snuff."

WHAT YOU CAN TAKE HOME FROM ICELAND

Icelandic law forbids the export of birds, bird eggs, bird nests, eggshells, many rare minerals, all stalactites and stalagmites in caves, and 31 protected plant species. In other words, leave nature where you found it. Objects of historical or archaeological interest may not be taken out of the country without special permission.

U.S. Citizens: For specifics on what you can bring back, download *Know Before You Go* online at **www.cbp.gov** or contact the **U.S. Customs & Border Protection** general inquiries (✆ **1-877-CBP-5511**) or from outside the U.S. **703/526-4200**.

Canadian Citizens: For a clear summary of Canadian rules, pick up the booklet *I Declare,* issued by the **Canada Border Services Agency** (✆ **800/461-9999** in Canada, or **204/983-3500**; www.cbsa-asfc.gc.ca).

U.K. Citizens: For information, contact **HM Customs & Excise** at ✆ **0845/010-9000;** intenquiries@hmrc.gsi.gov.uk (from outside the U.K., **004420/8929-0152**), or consult their website at www.hmce.gov.uk.

Australian Citizens: A helpful brochure available from Australian consulates or Customs offices is *Know Before You Go.* For more information, contact the **Australian Customs Service** (✆ **1300/363-263;** www.customs.gov.au).

New Zealand Citizens: Most questions are answered in a free pamphlet available at New Zealand consulates and Customs offices: *New Zealand Customs Guide for Travellers, Notice no. 4.* For more information, contact **New Zealand Customs** (✆ **0800/428-786**; www.customs.govt.nz).

GETTING THERE & GETTING AROUND

Getting To Iceland

BY PLANE

Virtually all international arrivals come through **Keflavík International Airport** (KEF), about 50km (31 miles) from Reykjavík. Until recently only Icelandair and Iceland Express flew to Iceland, but additional airlines have opened up routes. Typical flight times are 3 hours from London or 5 hours from Boston. Peak season, with correspondingly higher fares, is June to August, plus the 2 weeks before Christmas and the 2 weeks after the New Year.

Icelandair (✆ **800/223-5500** U.S. and Canada; **0870/787-4020** in London; **0207/387-5711** in Glasgow; www.icelandair.com) flies to Keflavík from Boston, New York, Minneapolis, Orlando, Toronto, Halifax (Nova Scotia), London, Manchester, Glasgow, and several other European cities. Flights from North America are usually overnight, though from May to October daytime flights are available from New York and Boston a few times per week.

Icelandair does not have codeshare agreements with North American airlines, so you'll need other means of getting to an Icelandair gateway airport. However, Icelandair does "interline" with major U.S. and Canadian domestic air carriers, allowing passengers to travel from non-Icelandair gateways on "through-fare" tickets. With through-fare tickets, passengers are protected in case of delays or re-routings, and can check luggage to their final destinations.

Icelandair offers a good range of discount packages, combining airfare, hotels, and sometimes tours. Midweek flights are often significantly cheaper. Icelandair fares between the U.S. and Europe can include a free stopover for up to 7 days in Iceland, pending availability. Icelandair's price schemes sometimes make a flight from the

U.S. to London (with a free stopover in Reykjavík for up to 7 days) cheaper than a simple flight to Reykjavík.

If you have any flexibility with your travel dates, sign up for Icelandair's free "Net Club," which alerts you to special online-only fares. All fares, except for some special offers, are discounted for children under 12.

Join Icelandair's **frequent flier scheme,** "Saga Club." Members earn extra miles by flying Air Iceland (Iceland's main domestic airline), upgrading to "Saga" class, or using partner companies. U.S. Diners Club cardholders can exchange their award points for Saga Club miles, and Visa and MasterCard issue credit cards co-branded with Icelandair for earning Saga Club miles.

With average prices that are considerably lower than Icelandair's, **Iceland Express** (© **0118/321-8384** in the U.K.; **01866/512-8364** in U.S. and Canada; **550-0600** in Iceland; www.icelandexpress.com) is a growing force. In summer there are daily flights connecting Reykjavík with London Gatwick and a twice-weekly flight to London Stansted. In summer it flies to 22 other cities, 20 in Europe as well as new 2010 routes to New York (4 times a week) and Winnipeg (twice a week). Winter schedules retain the London and New York flights, with a weekly flight to Winnipeg, plus half a dozen cities across Europe. Children under 12 get 25% off flights and there are e-mail alerts for special offers ... sign up at the website.

SAS Scandinavian Airlines (© **0208/990-7159** from the U.K.; www.flysas.com) flies to Reykjavík from Oslo and Stockholm; prices from Stockholm consistently beat Icelandair.

Atlantic Airways (© **298/341010;** www.atlantic.fo) connects the Faeroe Islands to Europe and Iceland, and is useful to those visiting the Faeroes on their way to or from Iceland.

Arriving at Keflavik International Airport

Keflavík International Airport (airport code KEF; © **425-6000;** www.kefairport.is) is sometimes called "Leifur Eiríksson Air Terminal" or "Reykjavík Airport," even though Reykjavík has a small, domestic airport in the city proper. Extensive renovations to Keflavík International were completed in 2007, and the airport sees over two million passengers each year. Arriving passengers must go through another **security** check before clearing customs. For a list of what you can import to Iceland, see "Customs," p. 38.

For information on **ATMs** and money exchange, see "Money & Costs," p, 46. The airport has a **tourist information** desk with brochures galore, but the staff cannot make hotel or tour reservations. (If you're staying in Reykjavík, see "Visitor Information"

Iceland & Greenland?

If you've ever wanted to explore Greenland, your trip to Iceland could be an ideal opportunity. Iceland is Greenland's closest access point by plane, and you can even visit on a day tour. **Air Iceland** (**570-3030;** www.airiceland.is) flies year-round from Reykjavík to Greenland's east coast, and twice a week in summer to south Greenland. Air Iceland and **Eagle Air** (**562-4200;** www.eagleair.is) both offer Greenland day tours. Two-night packages from Reykjavík are available through **Icelandair.**

in chapter 6 for booking agencies.) The airport has several **car rental** desks; see "Getting Around," below.

Tip: Alcohol prices in the airport may seem high, but they're far lower than elsewhere in Iceland; so consider buying duty-free before you leave the airport. Icelandair prohibits alcohol from being transported in carry-on luggage, so if you're taking this airline and want to buy duty-free, wait until Keflavík. Customs limits you to 1 liter of wine or 6 liters of beer, plus 1 liter of spirits. If you're not carrying spirits or beer, then you can bring in 2.5 liters (2 1/2 pints) of wine.

Note: For tips on getting between the airport and Reykjavík, see "Orientation," in chapter 6.

BY BOAT

The *Norröna,* a Faeroese **car ferry** operated by **Smyril Line** (✆ **570-8600;** www.smyril-line.com), connects Iceland to Denmark and the Faeroe Islands. The ferry sails between April and early September from Hanstholm (Denmark) to Seyðisfjörður in east Iceland. Along the way it stops at Tórshavn (Faeroe Islands).

The *Norröna* arrives in Iceland once a week. The ferry makes a 2- or 3-night stopover in the Faeroe Islands in both directions. Passengers have three sleeping options: their cars, sleeping-bag accommodation in rather primitive rooms for nine people with one bathroom, and cabins. Package deals are advised, especially in summer, though you usually get a windowless room. Some packages also cover tours and accommodation on land in the Faeroes and Iceland. The ferry is best for those who want to bring their own vehicle; otherwise, it does not generally present any savings over flying.

Anyone bringing a vehicle to Iceland must bring registration, proof of insurance, and driving license. A temporary import permit for the car, valid for 1 month, is issued at the port of entry and can be extended. See "Getting Around," later in this chapter, for information on driving in Iceland.

Cruises

Iceland is fast becoming a major cruise ship destination; the number of cruise ship visitors has expanded four-fold in the last 10 years. Iceland is often a featured stopover on transatlantic routes. **Hurtigruten** (from the U.K. ✆ **0844/448-7654;** from the U.S. ✆ **866/552 0371;** www.hurtigruten.com) is one place to check, and **Princess Cruises** (✆ **800/774-6237** in North America; www.princess.com) runs two cruises from London's Southampton port with stops in Iceland. **Voyages of Discovery** (from the U.K. ✆ **0844/822-0802;** www.voyagesofdiscovery.co.uk) includes Iceland in several cruises. **Iceland Experience** (✆ **800/661-3830** in North America; www.greatcanadiantravel.com) lists three North Atlantic cruises that include Iceland. **Roadscholar** (✆ **800/454-5768;** www.roadscholar.org), a nonprofit company setting up trips for visitors age 55 and up, has an excellent Arctic cruise. See "Special Interest & Escorted Trips," p. 56, for an educational cruise within Icelandic waters. The website **www.cruiseiceland.com** has a useful page of links to most cruise companies that make Iceland stops.

Getting Around

Due to the challenges of Icelandic topography, distances are often approximations. Whether by car or by foot, always confirm your exact route before setting out, particularly if you will be visiting more rural regions.

BY CAR

Icelanders love their cars for good reason: Iceland has **no train transport,** and many of Iceland's most beautiful sights are far from populated areas. A private vehicle can be even more necessary in the "shoulder season" (April–May and September–October), when most buses and tours are not operating. Renting a car is costly, but it often stacks up well against air and bus travel, especially if you have three or four passengers. Reykjavík is easy to get around without a car, and parking there can be a nuisance, so many visitors rent a car upon leaving the city.

Route 1, usually referred to as "The Ring Road," is 1,328km (825 miles) long and circles the entire island. Almost all of it is paved, and it's cleared all winter. Only about a third of Iceland's total road network is paved, however.

Bringing Your Own Car

Though many prefer to rent simply because of the beating administered to cars by Iceland's rough roads, Europeans have the option of bringing their vehicles to Iceland on the car ferry (p. 41). This may seem impractical at first glance, but transporting the car costs roughly the same as a regular foot passenger. Visitors bringing their own cars must carry registration, proof of insurance, and a driving license. Permits are issued on the ferry for 1 month, and can be extended. For more information, contact the Directorate of Customs (✆ **560-0300;** www.tollur.is). Make sure to bring a spare wheel, jack, jumper cables, and perhaps other repair tools and supplies.

Rentals

It's generally cheaper to rent a car before you arrive at the airport. If you rent in Reykjavík (as opposed to at the airport, which is over 48km/30 miles away), most agencies will deliver the car to your hotel (or deliver you to the car) and then pick up the car (or deliver you to your hotel) when you're done.

Most agencies offer a choice between limited and unlimited mileage plans. Expect to pay at least 13,000kr per day for a small car with an allowance of 75km or 100km (47 miles or 62 miles) per day, or 16,500kr per day for unlimited mileage. For a 4WD vehicle, prices start around 27,000kr but are usually higher. If you pick up the vehicle in one location and drop it off in another, the drop-off fee is usually at least 8,000kr. Renting a car usually requires a credit card as a form of deposit.

Offices in **Reykjavík** include **Avis,** Knarrarvogur 2 and Reykjavík City Airport (✆ **591-4000;** www.avis.is); **Bílaleiga Akureyrar/National,** Skeifan 9 and Reykjavík City Airport (✆ **461-6000;** www.holdur.is); **Budget,** BSÍ bus terminal (✆ **562-6060**) and Reykjavík City Airport (✆ **551-7570;** www.budget.is); and **Hertz,** Flugvallarvegur, by Reykjavík City Airport (✆ **522-4420;** www.hertz.is).

Local agencies are generally reliable and slightly cheaper, and you're usually getting the same product. Consider taking the Flybus from the airport to Reykjavík, then renting from a local agency once you're ready to leave the city. Agencies in the Keflavík area can also meet you at the airport. Remember that the majors will have more pickup and dropoff locations, and often better resources for dealing with breakdowns and mishaps.

Recommended local agencies that can meet you at Keflavík International Airport include **Geysir,** Blikavöllur 5 (✆ **893-4455;** www.geysir.is) and **SS Bílaleiga,** Iðjustígur 1, Njarðvík (✆ **421-2220;** www.carrentalss.com).

Recommended local agencies that will deliver a car to your hotel in Reykjavík include **ÁTAK Car Rental,** Smiðjuvegur 1, Kópavogur (✆ **554-6040;** www.atak.is), which carries automatics; **Sixt Bílaleiga,** Keflavík (✆ **540-2221;** www.sixt.com).

The travel agency **Touris** (Frostaskjól 105, Reykjavík; ✆ **551-7196;** www.tour.is) has good deals on packages combining 4WD rentals with lodging.

AGE LIMITS & LICENSES Generally you must be 21 to rent a regular car in Iceland and 23 to rent a 4WD vehicle, but company policies vary. No maximum age limit is in effect. All national drivers' licenses are recognized, so you do not need an international one.

INSURANCE Basic third-party liability insurance is included in car-rental rates. Cars usually come with a standard collision damage waiver but a high deductible; in other words, if you get into a scrape you are liable for, say, the first 195,500kr in damages, beyond which the insurance pays. For an extra cost—say, 1,250kr per day—you could bring the deductible down to 25,500kr on a standard car. This is often a good idea as cars face hazardous conditions.

Driving on **prohibited mountain roads** will void your insurance on regular cars. The letter "F" precedes the numbers of mountain roads on maps and road signs. Even with 4WD vehicles, insurance is often voided by attempting to cross rivers. Standard insurance does not cover damage to the car from a collision with an animal, and you may have to compensate its owner. Even for minor accidents, be sure to get a police report so your insurance will cover it.

AUTOMATIC VS. MANUAL TRANSMISSION Even the major Icelandic car-rental companies have very few cars with automatic transmissions. They must be reserved in advance, and usually cost about 10% more.

2WD VS. 4WD Many of Iceland's most beautiful landscapes are accessible only to 4WD vehicles, so if you're in a regular car, be prepared for serious envy as you watch the 4WD vehicles turn off the Ring Road into the great unknown. All the major agencies rent 4WD vehicles and can provide you with ropes, shovels, fuel cans, and GPS navigational systems. On the other hand, the vast majority of roads are accessible to regular cars, and for the more difficult traverses, you can take buses or sign up for 4WD tours. This can save money on fuel, and the environment will thank you.

CAMPERS Icelanders often travel in campers, and the concept of a "portable hotel" holds great appeal in a country with so much open space and so many accessible campgrounds.

Camper Iceland, Grófin 14c, Reykjanesbær (✆ **868-8829;** www.camper.is), near the international airport, has a large selection. Four-person campers start at 215,000kr per week with a 200km (124 miles) per day limit or 246,000kr per week with unlimited mileage.

Other companies near the airport to try are **Geysir,** Blikavöllur 5 Reykjanesbær (✆ **893-4455;** www.geysir.is).

Driving Law

Icelanders drive on the right side of the road. Unless otherwise marked, speed limits are 30kmph (18 1/2 mph) in residential areas, 50kmph (31 mph) in towns, 80kmph (50 mph) on unpaved roads, and 90kmph (56 mph) on paved roads. No right turns are allowed at red lights. In rotaries (aka roundabouts), right-of-way goes to the driver in the inside lane. Headlights must always be on.

Seat belts are mandatory in both front and back seats, and children under 6 must be secured in a car seat designed for their size and weight; these are usually available for rent, but you may want to bring your own. No one less than 140cm (4ft. 7in.)

tall, or weighing less than 40kg (88lb.), or under the age of 12 is allowed to ride in a front seat equipped with an airbag. Talking on phones is prohibited unless you have a hands-free system. Many intersections in the capital have automatic cameras to catch traffic violators.

The blood alcohol limit is extremely strict at .05%, so getting behind the wheel after just one drink could make you guilty of a crime. Drivers stopped under suspicion for drink-driving are usually given a "balloon" or breathalyzer test, which cannot be refused.

To protect the fragile sub-Arctic vegetation, all off-road driving is strictly prohibited, except on some beaches.

Driving Safety

Iceland is not for Sunday drivers. Weather conditions are erratic; roads are winding and narrow, with no guardrails and many blind spots; and most routes are unpaved. We cannot stress enough how important it is not to speed; the majority of fatal car accidents in Iceland involve foreigners unfamiliar with the country's driving hazards.

Before you set out, ask your car rental agency about potentially difficult road and weather conditions, especially in the off season. For road conditions, Icelanders rely heavily on information continually updated by the **Public Roads Administration** at ✆ **354-1777** (May–Oct 8am–4pm; Nov–Apr 8am–5pm) or www.vegag.is. For weather, contact the **Icelandic Meteorological Office** (✆ **902-0600,** press "1" for English; www.vedur.is).

Most roads are steeply sided and do not have shoulders—two seconds of inattention and you could topple off the road into great danger. Many road signs indicate dangers ahead, but few specify how much to reduce your speed, so always be on the safe side. Slow down whenever pavement transitions to gravel; tourists often skid off **gravel roads,** unaware of how poor traction can be on loose dirt and stones. Flying stones launched by oncoming traffic are another hazard on gravel roads, often cracking car windows; slow down and move to the side, especially if a larger vehicle is approaching. For traction, it's often safer to slow down by lowering the gears instead of using the brakes.

Most **bridges** in Iceland are single lane—signposted *Einbreið brú*—and the first car to reach it has right-of-way.

Always bring sunglasses into the car. **Glare** is a common hazard, and the sub-Arctic sun is usually low to the horizon.

Be on the lookout for **sheep** on the road, particularly when a lamb is on one side and its mother is on the other.

MOUNTAIN ROADS & FORDING RIVERS Do *not* attempt highland interior routes in a 2WD car. Roads that require 4WD vehicles are indicated by the letter "F" on road signs and maps. The safest procedure on these roads is to travel with other cars. Always carry repair kits and emergency supplies, and on particularly remote routes, inform someone of your travel plans before setting out. If you don't have a GPS navigation system, at least bring a compass.

Unbridged river crossings for 4WD vehicles are marked on maps with the letter "V." Water flow at these crossings can change dramatically and unpredictably from hour to hour. A sudden increase in flow can be caused not only by rain, but also by the sun melting glacial ice. Water levels are usually lower earlier in the day. Several drivers have drowned in river crossings; always seek advice if you have any doubts.

Many drivers wait and watch other vehicles cross before making their own attempt. Sometimes it's necessary to check the water depth by walking into the current; bring sturdy rubber sandals, a life jacket, and a lifeline for this purpose. Before crossing, make sure the 4WD is engaged. Drive in first gear and use "low" drive if you have it. It sometimes helps to cross diagonally in the direction of the current.

OFF SEASON In winter the weather is particularly volatile and daylight hours are limited. Most roads are open by April or May, but some interior routes are impassable as late as early July. Make sure your vehicle has snow tires or chains, and always pack blankets, food, and water in case you get stranded.

Filling Stations

Iceland has many long gaps between fuel stops, so keep your vehicle filled and know the distance to your next required fill-up. Many pumps are automated and remain open 24 hours. Machines for swiping your credit or debit card usually expect you to know the card's PIN (see "Money & Costs," p. 46). The machines also ask you to input the maximum amount you want to spend, but you are only charged for what is pumped. **N1** and **Olís,** the companies with the most stations in Iceland, both sell prepaid cards. Some small-town places indicated on maps are tiny operations, and you may want to call ahead to make sure they're open.

Road Maps

The **Iceland Road Atlas** (Stöng Publishers), updated every 2 years, is a phenomenal compendium of maps and information, and a must-have for any serious road trip. It's near impossible to find online or abroad, but available at most car-rental agencies and many fuel stops and bookstores. Each map is focused narrowly on short stretches of individual roads, so you may prefer a simpler road atlas that gives you the big picture; these are easy to find.

Carpooling

Samferða (www.samferda.net) effectively connects people looking to carpool on specific routes at specific times. Anyone receiving a ride is expected to share the costs of fuel or car rental. The bulletin board at **Reykjavík City Hostel** (p. 111) is also popular with visitors looking to split car costs.

BY BUS

Iceland's bus system is reliable and punctual. Public buses link all major towns, and even some barren interior routes are covered in summer. (Icelandic buses are impressive machines, chugging right across rocky terrain and raging rivers.) Buses are up to European standards of comfort.

Several bus companies operate in Iceland, but all scheduled routes are coordinated by Iceland's main bus company, **BSÍ** (© **562-1011** daily 4:30am–midnight; www.bsi.is). Bus schedules are available online or at bus stations and tourist information offices across the country. The website **www.nat.is** is also great for bus timetables and bookings; click "Travel Guide," then "Transportation," then "Bus Schedules and Rental." Most long-distance bus routes run only in summer.

Buses on the Ring Road do not require reservations, and you can pay on board with cash or credit card. In small towns the bus stop is usually the main filling station. Coverage of the Ring Road is complete from June through August, but from September through May, it extends only from Reykjavík to Akureyri in the north and to Höfn in the southeast.

Bus travel is not as inexpensive as you might think compared to car and air travel, especially for longer distances. Reykjavík to Egilsstaðir by bus costs around 16,800kr, more than the cost of a flight.

Bus passes can make bus travel more economical. An enjoyable way to see Iceland, if you don't have a car, is on the **Full Circle Pass** sold by **Sterna** (✆ **553-3737;** www.sterna.is) online or at tourist offices. The pass is good for one trip around Iceland on the Ring Road, hopping on and off wherever you like, for 33,000kr. A modified pass includes the Westfjords and costs 50,000kr. **Reykjavík Excursions** (✆ **580-5400;** www.re.is) offers more particular bus passports, available online or at the BSÍ terminal in Reykjavík. For example, the **Highland Circle Passport** includes the interior routes through Landmannalaugar, Sprengisandur, and Kjölur for 34,200kr.

BY PLANE

Air travel in Iceland is common, easy, cost-efficient, and often necessary, especially in winter. Booking online and in advance is likely to save you money. Some routes are very frequent (like Reykjavík to Akureyri, 10 flights per day in summer) and some far less so (Reykjavík to Gjögur, twice per week).

Air Iceland (✆ **570-3030;** www.airiceland.is) handles most domestic air travel, serving seven destinations inside Iceland (Reykjavík, Akureyri, Egilsstaðir, Ísafjörður, Grímsey, Þórshöfn, and Vopnafjörður) as well as the Faeroe Islands and Greenland. The simplest way to buy tickets is online, since they have no direct U.S. or U.K. line, and you can't book directly through Icelandair. Children under 12 get 50% off on Air Iceland.

Eagle Air (✆ **562-4200;** www.ernir.is) connects Reykjavík to Westman Islands, Sauðárkrókur, Hornafjörður (Höfn), Bíldudalur, and Gjögur, and also offers sightseeing tours.

One-way prices from Reykjavík are from 20,000kr to the Westman Islands (25 min.), 9,600kr to Akureyri (45 min.), and 10,500kr to Egilsstaðir (1 hr.).

Note: Because of Iceland's high winds and unpredictable weather, air passengers should always be prepared for delays and cancellations, especially in winter.

BY BOAT

For cruises, see "Cruises" in "Getting There," earlier in this chapter.

Iceland's **ferry system** is often used by tourists; see the map on p. 2 for routes. The only ferries that take cars are the *Baldur,* which connects Stykkishólmur on the Snæfellsnes peninsula to Brjánslækur in the Westfjords, and the *Herjólfur,* which connects Landeyjahöfn to the Westman Islands. For information on particular ferry routes, see the regional chapters of this book.

BY BIKE

For information on biking in Iceland, see p. 68 in chapter 4.

MONEY & COSTS

THE VALUE OF ICELANDIC KRONA VS. OTHER POPULAR CURRENCIES

ISK	US$	Can$	UK£	Euro (€)	Aus$	NZ$
100	$0.86	C$0.88	£0.55	€0.66	A$0.91	NZ$1.17

Frommer's lists exact prices in the local currency, even when the local establishments list prices in a different currency (usually Euro in this case). The currency conversions quoted above were correct at press time. However, rates fluctuate, so before departing consult a currency exchange website such as **www.oanda.com/convert/classic** to check up-to-the-minute rates.

Iceland was a wealthy nation relying heavily on imports, but was hit hard by 2008's financial crisis. Since then, tourism has become a more significant part of the economy. Rather than prices going up, as some might expect, they have dropped dramatically for tourists. Visitors are still entitled to a refund on the value-added tax (VAT, or sales tax) for purchases of eligible goods—see p. 137 for more information. See "Tips on Accommodations," later in this chapter, for more money-saving advice.

Currency

Iceland's monetary unit is the **krona** (sometimes abbreviated as "ISK," but written as "kr" in this book), plural **kronur.** Coins come in 1, 5, 10, 50, and 100 kronur denominations; bank notes are in denominations of 500kr, 1,000kr, 2,000kr, and 5,000kr. Since the collapse of the Icelandic banking sector, the krona and its future have been rather unpredictable. Prices listed in this book reflect **exchange rates** at press time. Visitors to Iceland will find that prices there are often listed only in Euro, or American dollars. Dollars, pounds, and euros are easily exchanged for krona. For more accurate conversion rates, try **www.xe.com/ucc**.

ATMs/Currency Exchange

You could spend a lot of time and effort obtaining Icelandic currency in advance of arrival, but ATMs are the most practical and reliable way to get cash at fair exchange rates. Upon arrival at Keflavík International Airport, you'll easily find ATMs and the currency exchange desk, both run by **Landsbanki Íslands,** which has fair exchange rates. Avoid exchanging money at hotels, which tend to have high transaction fees.

ATMs are found in most villages around Iceland, though not all ATMs are accessible 24 hours. Icelandic ATMs generally accept all major debit, credit, and cash-only cards. **Cirrus** (✆ **800/424-7787;** www.mastercard.com) and **PLUS** (✆ **800/843-7587;** www.visa.com) cards are almost universally accepted in Icelandic ATMs.

Credit & Debit Cards

Credit cards are safe, convenient, and generally offer good exchange rates. Note, however, that many banks now assess a 1% to 3% "foreign transaction fee" on all charges you incur abroad.

In Iceland you'll need a PIN to withdraw cash advances on your credit card. You will *not* need a PIN for most credit card purchases, but occasions may arise (particularly at automated fuel pumps). If you've forgotten your PIN, call the number on the back of your card, or visit your bank website, and ask that it be provided to you.

Icelanders love credit and debit cards, and will commonly whip one out just to buy an ice-cream. Most shops and tourist establishments accept credit cards; you can even charge a taxi ride. Visa and MasterCard are the most widely accepted, though American Express and Diner's Club are useful as well. Electron, Maestro, and EDC debit cards are increasingly accepted at retail stores.

Traveler's Checks

These days, traveler's checks are less necessary because most cities have 24-hour ATMs. However, traveler's checks are still widely accepted in Iceland.

STAYING HEALTHY

Icelanders are blessed with a very healthy environment. The use of geothermal and hydroelectric power has made pollution almost negligible. Some say Iceland has the purest tap water in the world, and even surface water is generally potable. The incidence of insect, water, or food-borne infection is extremely low.

In 2007, smoking was banned in all bars, restaurants, cafes, hotels, and other accommodation. Smokers huddle outside, swathed in blankets under heat lamps.

Iceland's extreme variations in daylight hours may wreak havoc with your body clock, so bring an eye mask to help you sleep in summer. In the short days of winter, Icelanders combat depression through the traditional practice of downing a shot of cod liver oil each morning; the oil is rich in Vitamin D, which is also generated by sunlight on the skin.

The sun can be stronger than many visitors suspect at such a northerly latitude. Bring sunblock and lip balm to protect your skin, and sunglasses to protect your eyes from the glare. In spring and summer you may want to bring insect repellent with DEET to fend off the midges that can be an annoyance in certain interior regions. Iceland has a few bees and wasps, so anyone with an Apoidea allergy should bring a portable remedy. Bring motion sickness pills if you plan on any boating activities, long ferry rides, or bumpy road trips.

Outdoor Safety

Icelanders visiting the U.S. are amused by all the warning signs and guardrails. If Iceland tried to match these precautions, it would be quickly bankrupted. Always use care in Iceland's untamed outdoors. Thoroughly research the potential hazards of any journey, and talk to someone with local knowledge before setting out. Bring a first-aid kit to any remote destination.

Be prepared for Iceland's notoriously abrupt shifts in weather. For forecasts, check with the **Icelandic Meteorological Office** (© **522 6000** and 902-0600; www.vedur.is). Keep in mind that the temperature usually drops about 1° for every 100m (328 ft.) of elevation. Even near the coastline in summer, night temperatures can drop below freezing. Always carry warm and waterproof clothing and footwear, even in summer.

Bring a map and compass for longer walks, or ideally, a GPS unit. A cellphone is also useful for emergencies, though coverage is unlikely in remote areas (see "Staying Connected," below).

ROCKS & FOOTING

Rocks and rock faces in Iceland are often loose and crumbly. Hiking shoes with good ankle support are advised. Be careful not to loosen rocks that could tumble on to someone below you, and be aware of potential rockfalls or avalanches. Take special care to have solid footing on mountaintops and clifftops, where winds are strongest.

GEOTHERMAL AREAS & VOLCANOES

In geothermal hotspots, most tourists know better than to stick their fingers in boiling mud pots, but other dangers are not so obvious. Sometimes unwary visitors step right through a thin crust of earth into boiling mud below. Lighter soil is usually the most dangerous. The main danger of burning comes from the crust collapsing and people getting their feet stuck in the boiling hot mud below it. The crust looks solid and is not particularly hot on the surface, but underneath there may be a pocket of mud boiling its way towards the surface. Stick to paths and boardwalks when provided, and always seek advice before approaching active volcanoes.

Anyone visiting active volcanic areas should be aware of the hazards and the evacuation procedures, clearly set out in the widely available brochure *Eruption Emergency Guidelines.*

GLACIERS

Even road-trippers who seldom stray from their cars are likely to encounter a glacier face-to-face. Do not set off on a glacier without some experience or advice from a local expert. Tours with professional guides are the safest route. Glaciers can collapse without warning, and even a smooth surface can disguise hidden, deadly crevasses. If you walk onto a glacier despite the danger, follow other footprints or snowmobile tracks. Generally, the best time for glacier traverses is from mid-February to mid-July, with optimal conditions between March and May.

Do not venture into ice caves; even experienced guides seldom lead groups there. Also beware of quicksand that can form from meltoff at the glacier's edge.

EMERGENCY SHELTERS

The **Icelandic Association for Search and Rescue** (✆ **570-5900;** www.icesar.com) maintains several bright orange emergency shelters in remote interior and coastline locations, and along some roads, often in high mountain passes. The shelters are identified on most maps and are stocked with food, fuel, and blankets. These are to be used *in emergencies only.* If you are forced to use something, make sure to sign for it so it can be replaced.

SEARCH & RESCUE

Locals constantly encourage visitors to inform someone before venturing into risky areas alone. For most trips you can simply leave your name and itinerary with a local tourist information office or park warden. For more risky ventures, you should register at the Reykjavík office of the **Icelandic Association for Search and Rescue,** Skógarhlíð 14, Reykjavík (✆ **570-5900;** www.icesar.com); local and online registration is in the works.

HEALTH CARE

Iceland has very high-quality medical care and more doctors per capita than any other country on earth. Virtually all doctors speak English reasonably well. Reykjavík and larger towns have hospitals. Most smaller towns have at least one doctor and one pharmacy *(apótek)*; if you need a doctor, ask at any local pharmacy or business. Most pharmacies are open 9am to 6pm, and over-the-counter medicines are accessible, if expensive. Iceland's barren interior is another story entirely: you could be hours from even the most rudimentary form of care.

What to Do If You Get Sick Away From Home

For emergencies in Iceland, dial ✆ **112.**

If you get sick in Iceland, you can usually just call or show up at the nearest hospital or health center. For medical assistance in the Reykjavík area, see "Fast Facts" in chapter 13.

Even insured U.S. citizens may have to pay all medical costs upfront and be reimbursed later. Before leaving home, find out what medical services your health insurance covers. To protect yourself, consider buying medical travel insurance (see "Medical Insurance," under "Travel Insurance," above).

U.K. and E.U. citizens will need a **European Health Insurance Card (EHIC)** available at www.ehic.org.uk to receive free or reduced-cost health benefits during a visit to Iceland. The European Health Insurance Card replaces the E111 form, which is no longer valid. For advice, ask at your local post office or see www.dh.gov.uk/travellers.

We list additional **emergency numbers** in the "Fast Facts" appendix, p. 378.

SPECIAL TRAVEL RESOURCES

In addition to the destination-specific resources listed below, please visit Frommers.com for additional further travel resources.

LGBT Travelers

Iceland was much more homophobic in 1978, when the country's first gay organization was founded in Reykjavík. The small population and close-knit family networks made it difficult for gays and lesbians to escape the disapproval of older generations. Today gay marriages are legal, several prominent cultural figures are openly gay, the Icelandic Prime Minister Jóhanna Sigurðardóttir made history in June 2010 by becoming the first head of State to marry her same-sex partner legally. Outside Reykjavík there isn't any gay scene to speak of, but the worst any gay couple is likely to encounter is a frown.

The main gay and lesbian group in Iceland is **Samtökin '78,** Laugavegur 3, 4th floor, Reykjavík (✆ **552-7878;** www.samtokin78.is), which is open Monday to Friday from 1 to 5pm and holds open-house social gatherings at their **Rainbow Cafe** Mondays and Thursdays 8 to 11:30pm and Saturdays 9pm to 1am. Iceland's main lesbian group is **Konur með Konum** (www.kmk.is), which means "Women with Women." The website posts events and other useful information.

Q-Félag Stúdenta, in the same office as **Samtökin '78,** Laugavegur 3, 4th floor, Reykjavík (✆ **848-5271;** www.queer.is), the gay and lesbian student group at the University of Iceland, welcomes e-mails from young visitors.

www.gayice.is has the best online schedule of gay events. The **Reykjavík Gay Pride Festival** (www.gaypride.is) usually takes place the first week of August. For the gay and lesbian scene in Reykjavík, see "Nightlife," in chapter 5. The following guide is also available: ***GetawayGay Iceland*** (Queer & There Publishing; www.getawaygay.com).

Travelers with Disabilities

Iceland has more options and resources for visitors with disabilities than ever before, but you must call well in advance to secure your plans. Reykjavík and Akureyri are fairly accommodating, and new public buildings have to meet a strict code for wheelchair access. But, in the countryside, accessible facilities are few and far between, and tours often involve traversing long distances over rough ground or unpaved paths. (One bright spot is Iceland's top tourist attraction, **the Blue Lagoon** (p. 164), which has good wheelchair access.)

Always make specific inquiries at hotels before booking. The website www.whenwetravel.com lists wheelchair-accessible hotels around the world; the listings for Iceland are not great at present, but will hopefully improve in the future. All farms in the **Icelandic Farm Holidays** network (p. 62) have been evaluated for accessibility; click the "Facilities for Disabled" link at www.farmholidays.is, or call ✆ **570-2700.**

Most museums and other tourist attractions offer reduced admission prices for travelers with disabilities. Air Iceland do, as does Smyril Line, the ferry connecting Iceland to Europe.

TRANSPORTATION

All **airlines** flying to and from Iceland can accommodate visitors with disabilities, and Air Iceland, the main domestic airline, generally has no trouble with wheelchairs.

Buses in Reykjavík are all wheelchair-accessible, but buses elsewhere usually don't have lifts or ramps. The largest tour operators each have a few wheelchair-accessible buses.

The **car ferries** *Baldur* (which connects Snæfellsnes Peninsula to the Westfjords), *Herjólfur* (which connects the Westman Islands to the mainland) and *Norröna* (which connects Europe to Seyðisfjörður in east Iceland) are all wheelchair accessible.

Hertz Car Rental (✆ **522-4400;** www.hertz.is) offers a specially fitted car for wheelchair users, but does not have cars with hand controls.

TOURS

Tour company **HópferðaÞjónusta Reykjavíkur** (Brunastaðir 3; ✆ **587-8030;** hrtravel@simnet.is) arranges trips for small groups of visitors with disabilities in specially-designed coaches.

Nordic Visitor (Laugavegur 26, Reykjavík; ✆ **511-2442;** www.icelandvisitor.com) is a travel agency with experience in putting together tours for visitors with disabilities. Some travel agencies outside Iceland can put together Iceland tours and itineraries for those with disabilities. Among them are **Flying Wheels Travel** (✆ **507/451-5005;** www.flyingwheelstravel.com) and **Accessible Journeys** (✆ **800/846-4537** or 610/521-0339; www.disabilitytravel.com).

HELPFUL GROUPS

Sjálfsbjörg, Hátun 12, Reykjavík (✆ **550-0300;** www.sjalfsbjorg.is; Mon–Fri 8am–4pm), which literally means "self-help," is Iceland's association for people with disabilities, with 17 chapters throughout the country. This association can answer questions or offer advice on your itinerary. If you call and the recorded message comes on, press "2" to reach an agent. While several hotels have wheelchair-accessible rooms, Sjálfsbjörg also rents out two fully accessible apartments and three guest rooms in their own building.

Groups that offer a vast range of resources and assistance to travelers with disabilities include **MossRehab** (✆ **800/CALL-MOSS;** www.mossresourcenet.org); the **American Foundation for the Blind (AFB)** (✆ **800/232-5463;** www.afb.org); and **SATH (Society for Accessible Travel & Hospitality)** (✆ **212/447-7284;**

www.sath.org). **AirAmbulanceCard.com** is now partnered with SATH and allows you to preselect top-notch hospitals in case of an emergency.

Access-Able Travel Source (© **303/232-2979;** www.access-able.com) offers a worldwide database of travel agents with experience in accessible travel, plus links to resources.

British visitors should contact **Holiday Care** (© **0845-124-9971** in the U.K.; www.holidaycare.org.uk) to access a wide range of travel information and resources for those with disabilities and elderly people.

Family Travel

Iceland is a wondrous and magical place no child will ever forget. Most tour companies welcome children (with the exception of the most rigorous trips, of course) and charge 50% less for children under 12. Discounts are usually available for transportation and tourist attractions, and sometimes for places to stay as well. **Air Iceland,** the main domestic airline, offers 50% off for children aged 2 to 11 when tickets are booked over the phone; even greater discounts may be available online.

A widespread Icelandic custom is for hotels, guesthouses, and farms to offer **"family rooms"** sleeping three to five people, sometimes with cooking facilities. Even youth hostels commonly have family rooms. Often a place has only one or two such rooms; the only way to be sure is to ask. In the **Fosshótel** chain (© **562-4000;** www.fosshotel.is), one child under 12 stays free per room (Fosshótel's prices generally aren't cheap, however). The recommended **Icelandic Farm Holidays** network of farm accommodations (© **570-2700;** www.farmholidays.is) is usually cheaper than hotels and offers children a glimpse of Icelandic country life.

See chapter 4 for a full array of outdoor activities and adventures your children can enjoy. Whale-watching is an obvious choice. Horseback riding is great even for totally inexperienced children, since Icelandic horses are small, even-tempered, and manageable. Horse farms are spread all over the country, so a hired ride is usually within easy reach. Bird-watching may seem like the last thing your child would be interested in, but sidling up to a remote cliff edge and gazing down at the crashing surf, while puffins perch close by and other birds glide upward in the wind currents, is quite a thrill for anyone. Virtually every village in Iceland has a geothermally-heated swimming pool, many with water slides, toys, and games for children. ***Remember:*** Iceland cannot possibly install guard ropes and warning signs at every location that poses danger to children, so mind them at all times.

For activities in or near Reykjavík, see "Reykjavík with Children," p. 127.

Iceland is a safe and personal enough country that parents may feel comfortable leaving their children with local babysitters. You can always ask the staff at your accommodation to recommend someone.

Family Travel Forum (www.familytravelforum.com), a comprehensive site, offers trip planning and has plentiful information on Iceland. The recommended book *Frommer's 500 Places to Take Your Kids Before They Grow Up* includes a few Iceland locales. To locate accommodations, restaurants, and attractions that are particularly child-friendly, look for the **Kids** icon throughout this guide.

Senior Travel

Iceland is often thought of as a travel destination for rugged outdoorsy types. Seniors who fit this description and those who don't will have no trouble finding plenty of adventure in the great outdoors. Age simply shouldn't factor into whether Iceland is the right destination, and senior tourists are anything but a rare sight throughout the country. Chapter 4 lays out a wide range of outdoor activities for all tastes and ability levels.

When deciding whether to rent a car, though, consider that driving in Iceland is hazardous and requires very good reflexes, coordination, and vigilance (see "Getting Around (By Car)," above). Unless you are fully confident in your driving abilities, an arranged tour is the safer bet.

Senior discounts are usually available at museums and other tourist attractions. Note that the retirement age for Icelanders is 67. Visitors aged 65 or 66 are not normally entitled to discounts, though gatekeepers at various attractions may not be inclined to argue.

Many reliable agencies and associations target the 50-plus market. **Elderhostel** (© **800/454-5768;** www.elderhostel.org), a not-for-profit company, arranges worldwide study and adventure for those age 55 and over, with a few "intergenerational" trips. Elderhostel has eight first-rate tours to Iceland, from 9 to 24 days long. **ElderTreks** (© **800/741-7956** or 416/558-5000 outside North America; www.eldertreks.com) offers an 11-day small-group Iceland tour, restricted to visitors aged 50 and older, for around $5,995.

Student Travel

Iceland is tough for students on a tight budget. Youth hostels and "sleeping-bag accommodation" at guesthouses and farms can be lifesavers; see "Tips on Accommodations," later in this chapter. The backpackers' website **travellerspoint.com** offers a number of private rooms in Iceland for as little as $67 per night.

For visitors aged 12 to 26, the **"Youth Restricted Fare" on Air Iceland** offers big savings if you're willing to fly standby and take your chances on availability. Multi-trip **bus passports** from **Sterna** also have student discounts. The **International Student Travel Confederation (ISTC)** website (www.istc.org) offers the **International Student Identity Card (ISIC)** and lists companies, attractions, and places to stay in Iceland that offer student discounts. The card, which also provides students with basic health and life insurance and a 24-hour helpline, is valid for a maximum of 18 months. You can apply for the card online or in person at **STA Travel** (© **800/781-4040** in North America; www.statravel.com); check the web to locate STA Travel offices worldwide. If you're no longer a student but still under 26, STA's **International Youth Travel Card (IYTC)** entitles you to some discounts. **Travel CUTS** (© **800/592-2887;** www.travelcuts.com) offers similar services for both Canadians and U.S. residents. Irish students may prefer to turn to **USIT** (© **01/602-1904;** www.usit.ie), an Ireland-based specialist in student, youth, and independent travel.

Solo Travelers

With so many excellent group adventure tours to choose from, Iceland is a great place to fly solo. Even those normally allergic to tours find the Icelandic experience far more personal and less tame than the usual. (See chapter 4 for a full range of outdoor activities and tours.)

Single holidaymakers can avoid paying a "single supplement" by rooming with other solo visitors or finding a roommate before they go. **Travel Buddies Singles**

FROMMERS.COM: THE complete TRAVEL RESOURCE

It should go without saying, but we highly recommend **Frommers.com,** voted Best Travel Site by *PC Magazine.* We think you'll find our expert advice and tips; independent reviews of hotels, restaurants, attractions, and preferred shopping and nightlife venues; vacation giveaways; and an online booking tool, indispensable before, during, and after your travels. We publish the complete contents of around 130 travel guides in our **Destinations** section, covering nearly 3,600 places worldwide to help you plan your trip. Each weekday, we publish original articles reporting on **Deals and News** via our free **Frommers.com Newsletter** to help you save time and money and travel smarter. We're betting you'll find our new **Events** listings (http://events.frommers.com) an invaluable resource; it's an up-to-the-minute roster of what's happening in cities everywhere—including concerts, festivals, lectures, and more. We've also added weekly **podcasts, interactive maps,** and hundreds of new images across the site. Check out our **Travel Talk** area featuring **Message Boards** where you can join in conversations with thousands of fellow Frommer's travel fans and post your trip report once you return.

Travel Club (✆ **800/998-9099;** www.travelbuddiesworldwide.com), based in Canada, runs small, intimate, single-friendly group trips and will match you with a roommate free of charge; an Iceland trip is usually offered. **TravelChums** (www.travelchums.com) is a respected Internet-only travel-companion matching service.

Rental cars give you unmatched freedom and flexibility as a visitor in Iceland, and solo visitors may want to find car mates to share the costs. One place to start is the bulletin board at the Reykjavík City Hostel (p. 111). **Samferða** (www.samferda.net) is also a useful Icelandic **carpooling website.**

For more information on single travel, go to www.frommers.com/planning.

RESPONSIBLE TOURISM

Each time you take a flight or drive a car, carbon dioxide is released into the atmosphere. You can help neutralize the damage by purchasing "carbon offsets," from **Carbonfund.org** (www.carbonfund.org) and **TerraPass** (www.terrapass.org) in the U.S., and from **Climate Care** (www.climatecare.org) in the U.K. Iceland has its own reputable **Iceland Carbon Fund** (Kolviður; www.kolvidur.is); the website helps you calculate your damages and choose a tree-planting project or other remedy.

Once in Iceland you can base your activities on hiking, biking, horseback riding, or other activities that do not consume fossil fuels. Several Icelandic companies have earned certification from **Blue Flag** (www.blueflag.org), a Danish association that certifies beaches, marinas, whale-watching tours, and other businesses for sustainable oceanside development.

Nordic Swan (✆ **08/5555-2400;** www.svanen.se/en/), certifies places to stay for adhering to strict environmental practices. The only ones in Iceland are the **Reykjavík City Hostel** (p. 111) and **Eldhestar** (p. 178).

Earthcheck (www.earthcheck.org) is another important eco-certification label (formerly known as Green Globe). Icelandic recipients of the Green Globe include **Íshestar,** a horseback riding tour company (p. 76); **Whale Watching Reykjavík** (p. 135); and *every* community on the Snæfellsnes Peninsula (p. 188). Icelandic places to stay (mentioned in this guide) with full Green Globe certifications are **Hótel Hellnar** (p. 197) on the Snæfellsnes Peninsula and the **Country Hotel Anna** (p. 319) in south Iceland.

The village of **Suðureyri** in the Westfjords has set an intriguing precedent by basing their entire economy on environmentally sustainable principles. Visitors can participate in local fishing life; see p. 212 for details.

GENERAL RESOURCES FOR green TRAVEL

In addition to the resources for Iceland listed above, the following websites provide valuable wide-ranging information on sustainable travel. For a list of even more sustainable resources, as well as tips and explanations on how to travel greener, visit www.frommers.com/planning.

- Responsible Travel (www.responsibletravel.com) is a great source of sustainable travel ideas; the site is run by a spokesperson for ethical tourism in the travel industry. Sustainable Travel International (www.sustainabletravelinternational.org) promotes ethical tourism practices, and manages an extensive directory of sustainable properties and tour operators around the world.
- In the U.K., Tourism Concern (www.tourismconcern.org.uk) works to reduce social and environmental problems connected to tourism.
- In Canada, www.greenlivingonline.com offers extensive content on how to travel sustainably.
- In Australia, the national body which sets guidelines and standards for ecotourism is Ecotourism Australia (www.ecotourism.org.au). The Green Directory (www.thegreendirectory.com.au), Green Pages (www.thegreenpages.com.au), and Eco Directory (www.ecodirectory.com.au) offer sustainable travel tips and directories of green businesses.
- Carbonfund (www.carbonfund.org), TerraPass (www.terrapass.org), and Carbon Neutral (www.carbonneutral.org) provide info on "carbon offsetting," or offsetting the greenhouse gas emitted during flights.
- Greenhotels (www.greenhotels.com) recommends green-rated member hotels around the world that fulfill the company's stringent environmental requirements. Environmentally Friendly Hotels (www.environmentallyfriendlyhotels.com) offers more green accommodation ratings.
- For information on animal-friendly issues throughout the world, visit Tread Lightly (www.treadlightly.org). For information about the ethics of swimming with dolphins, visit the Whale and Dolphin Conservation Society (www.wdcs.org).
- Volunteer International (www.volunteerinternational.org) has a list of questions to help you determine the intentions and the nature of a volunteer program. For general info on volunteer travel, visit www.volunteerabroad.org and www.idealist.org.

The **Association of Independent Tour Operators (AITO)** (www.aito.co.uk) is a group of specialist operators leading the field in making holidays sustainable; plenty of Icelandic tour operators are listed.

Environmental issues often come up in conversation with Icelanders, so you may want to read up on the hot topics. Iceland has resumed whaling and the subject often provokes emotional responses (p. 275). For information about the ethics of whaling, visit the **Whale and Dolphin Conservation Society** (www.wdcs.org).

The website **www.savingiceland.org** has a pronounced radical slant but contains links to informative articles on environmental issues facing Iceland.

SPECIAL INTEREST & ESCORTED TRIPS

Special Interest & Educational Tours

Smithsonian Journeys (✆ **877/338-8687;** www.smithsonianjourneys.com), affiliated with the Smithsonian Institution, hosts several educational trips focusing on geology, hydro power, and Icelandic culture.

Travel Quest International (✆ **1-800-830-1998;** www.travelquesttours.com) based in Prescott AZ, lead a 7-day "Fire, Ice and Aurora" tour in October, hosted by a local professional guide and dealing with Iceland's natural wonders. The price is $2,675, air fares not included.

Discover the World (✆ **01737 214 250;** www.discover-the-world.co.uk) lead educational trips to Iceland for schools, with four scheduled itineraries focusing on different topics, such as geography and biology etc. The focus of the itinerary can be negotiated.

Ísafold Travel (✆ **544-8866;** www.isafoldtravel.is) has educational tours in geology and energy technology.

LANGUAGE COURSES

If you want to learn Icelandic, there are a few decent resources on the Internet. A neat, free self-instruction course from the University of Iceland is available here: **www.icelandic.hi.is**

Icelandic Ancestry

The Snorri Program (✆ **551-0165;** www.snorri.is) provides an opportunity for young North Americans of Icelandic descent to explore their heritage. The main 6-week program (mid-June through July) is for ages 18 to 28, but older visitors can join a modified 2-week program in late August.

J.R.J. Super Jeeps (✆ **453-8219;** http://frontpage.simnet.is/jeppaferdir) sets up tours for those tracing their Icelandic ancestry.

Vegetarian Travel

Icelandic diets are meat-heavy, but fresh vegetables have become more widely available in recent years, partly because of local production in geothermally-heated greenhouses. And, of course, there's plenty of fish. Pasta dishes are common on menus. The few vegetarian restaurants and health-food stores in the country are concentrated in Reykjavík and Akureyri.

VegDining.com and **Happy Cow's Vegetarian Guide** (www.happycow.net) are good resources for Iceland's vegetarian dining options.

Volunteer & Working Trips

Seeds Iceland (✆ **845-6178;** www.seedsiceland.org), a nonprofit group founded in 2005, sets up volunteer 2-week "work camps" for projects ranging from environmental clean-ups and trail marking to preparation for local cultural festivals.

Iceland's **Environment and Food Agency** (✆ **591-2000;** http://english.ust.is/of-interest/conservationvolunteers) recruits around 200 volunteers each summer for conservation projects lasting 2 to 11 weeks, and ranging from trail work to wilderness management.

Volunteer Abroad (✆ **720/570-1702;** www.volunteerabroad.com) maintains an excellent database of volunteer vacation opportunities, with several options in Iceland.

Women's Tours

Canyon Calling (✆ **928/282-0916;** www.canyoncalling.com), based in Sedona, Arizona, leads a cost-conscious 8-day multi-activity trip for women in early July. Activities include sightseeing, hiking, rafting, whale-watching, and horseback riding.

Escorted General Interest Tours

Many visitors reflexively dismiss tours and packages, but Iceland is a good place for even the most independent-minded to reconsider. Many of the most fascinating parts of the country are difficult to access on your own, and tour companies can save you lots of time in research and planning. Icelanders themselves often sign up with the same tour companies used by tourists.

For more targeted tours, see the above section, "Special Interest & Escorted Trips." For outdoor activity tours, see chapter 4, "Active Iceland." See also the tours listed in each regional chapter; often the best Icelandic tour companies operate locally.

Major Icelandic Operators

Icelandair (✆ **570-3030;** www.icelandair.com) has all kinds of tours and packages, while its domestic counterpart **Air Iceland** (✆ **570-3030;** www.airiceland.is) offers day tours to Lake Mývatn, the Westman Islands, and several other locations. Icelandair offers not only the usual air/hotel packages but also a good selection of outdoor adventure tours and special-interest tours, including "Ghosts, Elves, and Trolls."

Reykjavík Excursions (✆ **580-5400;** www.re.is), Iceland's largest tour company, has an enormous selection of tours to choose from; most but not all rely primarily on bus travel. **Iceland Excursions** (✆ **540-1313;** www.icelandexcursions.is), Iceland's second largest tour company, is equally prolific and reputable. **Iceland Travel** (✆ **585-4300;** www.icelandtravel.is), one of Iceland's biggest travel agencies, rounds out the big three.

Nordic Adventure Travel (✆ **898-0355;** www.nat.is) is an excellent resource for outdoor adventure tours, often with online booking discounts. **Guðmundur Jónasson Travel** (✆ **511-1515;** www.gjtravel.is), a long-established company, has an interesting range of cross-country adventures, and is especially good for tours that involve light hiking.

Nonni Travel (✆ **461-1841;** www.nonnitravel.is) is the leading tour operator in Akureyri, Iceland's "second city." Offerings include rafting, whale-watching, and other adventures, as well as the usual bus tours.

West Tours (✆ **456-5111;** www.westtours.is), a recommended company with a creative range of tours, is the leading operator in the Westfjords.

North American Operators

Adventures Abroad (✆ **800/227-8747;** www.adventures-abroad.com) has a well-designed 10-day cultural tour of Iceland in August.

Borton Overseas (✆ **800/843-0602;** www.bortonoverseas.com), a Minneapolis-based specialist in Scandinavia, has a good range of Iceland offerings.

Butterfield & Robinson (✆ **866/551-9090;** www.butterfield.com), a prestigious upscale company, has a very well-designed 8-day moderate-activity walking tour, and a trip for families with children 8 and up.

Continental Journeys (✆ **800/601-4343;** www.continentaljourneys.com) is a good clearinghouse for a wide variety of Iceland tours, both escorted and independent, summer and winter. **Five Stars of Scandinavia** (✆ **800/722-4126;** www.5stars-of-scandinavia.com), based in Olympia, WA, is a similar outfit.

The affiliated **Great Canadian Travel Company** in Winnipeg (✆ **800/661-3830**) and **Travel 333 Chicago** (✆ **800/771-4833;** both www.greatcanadiantravel.com) have a good range of tours, including cruises and a 10-day "Iceland on a Budget" self-drive tour for under $1,739, not including air fare.

Iceland Saga Travel (✆ **508/25-9292;** www.icelandsagatravel.com), based in Nantucket, Massachusetts, is particularly good for air/hotel self-drive packages and weekend romps in Reykjavík. **Nordic Saga Tours** (✆ **800-848-6449;** www.nordicsaga.com), based in Edmonds, WA, has a carefully selected list of Iceland tours.

Odysseys Unlimited (✆ **888-370-6765;** www.odysseys-unlimited.com), a well-regarded company based in Newton, Massachusetts, has an excellent 11-day escorted tour crisscrossing the country for $3,195 and up, including airfare.

Scanam World Tours (✆ **800-545-2204;** www.scanamtours.com) is a prominent Scandinavian specialist based in Cranbury, New Jersey, with a good range of Iceland options.

Scantours (✆ **800-223-7226;** www.scantours.com), based in Los Angeles, has an enormous range of Iceland tours impressively laid out by type and departure date. The site is especially useful for scoping out off-season trips, spa trips, and cruise options.

U.K. Operators

Arctic Experience Holidays (✆ **01737/214-250;** www.arctic-experience.co.uk) has basic city break and self-drive tours, plus more singular options, such as horseback riding or diving tours.

Explore Worldwide (✆ **0845/013-1537;** www.explore.co.uk) serves up general small-group tours of Iceland, plus "Super Jeep" and volcano trips.

Scantours (✆ **01206/708-888;** www.scantours.co.uk) has something for every taste, from basic fly/drive packages to multi-day horseback riding tours.

Taber Holidays (✆ **01274/875-199;** www.taberhols.co.uk), a Scandinavian specialist, has a well-rounded list of 8 regional tours, and can also set up your itinerary.

Regent Holidays (✆ **0845/277-3301;** www.regent-iceland.com) focuses on Iceland and Greenland, and offers basic, foolproof, escorted and self-drive tours to popular sites. **Yes Travel** (✆ **01778/424-499;** www.yes-travel.com), an Iceland specialist, has an excellent website with a wealth of independent and escorted tour options.

STAYING CONNECTED

Telephones

Calls to Iceland from overseas require the **country code prefix,** which is **354.** All phone numbers within Iceland are seven digits. Numbers beginning with 6, 7, and 8 are reserved for cellphones. No calls are "long distance" within Iceland, and you don't need to dial the prefix.

To call Iceland: Dial the international access code (011 from the U.S.; 00 from the U.K., Ireland, or New Zealand; or 0011 from Australia), then **354** and the seven-digit number.

To make international calls from Iceland: Dial 00, then the country code (U.S. or Canada 1, U.K. 44, Ireland 353, Australia 61, New Zealand 64), then the area code and number. Rates do not vary by time of day.

For directory assistance from within Iceland: For numbers inside Iceland, dial ✆ **118; Icelandic phone books** are found beside public phones and list residents by their first name and profession.

An **online Icelandic telephone directory** can be found at **www.ja.is**. The site is only in Icelandic, but is still easy to use. Simply enter the name of the person or business in the search box and hit *leita* (find). If your keyboard isn't equipped for Icelandic letters, click *"Íslenskir stafir"* to access a row of special characters.

Toll-free numbers: Icelandic numbers beginning with 800 are toll free, but calling a U.S. 1-800 number from Iceland counts as an overseas call.

Public phones: Coin- and card-operated public phones can be hard to find, but post offices are a good bet. Using a public phone for local calls is usually cheaper than calling from a hotel. Charges for calls within Iceland vary according to time of day. Phone cards are easily found at post offices, gas stations, and markets. The smallest denomination is 500kr. Increasingly, public phones also accept credit cards.

International calling cards are widely available at fuel stations and convenience stores across Iceland. These cards usually provide better rates than calls made from hotels or directly from public phones.

Rechargeable online phone cards: Ekit (**www.ekit.com**) offers rechargeable phone cards with good rates and a toll-free access number in Iceland (✆ **800-8700**). Rates to the U.S. and Canada are currently 27¢ per minute, plus a 59¢ service charge per successful call. Rates to the U.K. are 17p to 67p per minute depending where you call, or £1.14 to a cellphone, plus a 39p service fee per successful call.

Cellphones (Mobile Phones)

Iceland has the world's highest per capita number of cellphones, and coverage is reliable in most populated areas. The "Ring Road" circling Iceland is entirely covered.

The three letters that define much of the world's wireless capabilities are **GSM.** GSM phones function with a removable plastic **SIM card.**

All Europeans and most Australians use GSM.

In the U.S., T-Mobile, AT&T Wireless, and Cingular use this quasi-universal system; in Canada, Microcell and some Rogers customers are GSM. Many phones, especially in the U.S., are not "multiband" (synonymous with "tri-band" or "quad-band") and will not work in Iceland. For U.S./Canadian visitors, even if your phone uses GSM, and you have a multiband phone (such as many Sony Ericsson, Motorola, or Samsung models), the company you're contracted to has probably "locked" your phone. In this case, you cannot simply buy an Icelandic SIM card, insert it into your phone, and start making calls.

Those with **multiband phones** can call their wireless operator and ask for "**international roaming**" to be activated on their existing account. This option is usually expensive. If you plan on using a cellphone in Iceland, you may well want to buy a **prepaid GSM** plan after you arrive, and either buy a phone—new phones in Iceland start around 10,000kr —or bring a rented one from home.

North Americans can **rent a phone** before leaving home from **InTouch USA** (✆ **800/872-7626;** www.intouchglobal.com) or **RoadPost** (✆ **888/290-1606** or 905/272-5665; www.roadpost.com). InTouch will also, for free, advise you on whether your existing phone will work in Iceland; simply call ✆ **703/222-7161** between 9am and 4pm EST, or go to http://intouchglobal.com/travel.htm.

Pre-paid GSM phone cards are available from 2,000kr with four main Icelandic phone companies, **Síminn** (✆ **800-7000;** www.siminn.is), **Vodafone** (✆ **1414** or **1800**; outside Iceland ✆ **599-9000;** www.vodafone.is), Nova (✆ **519-1919;** www.nova.is), and **Tal** (✆ **1871** or **445-1600;** www.tal.is). All companies also offer GPRS and 3G services for Internet access through your phone; almost all areas in Iceland with GSM also have GPRS (a notable exception is the Westman Islands).

Branches of Síminn in Reykjavík include Armulí 25, east of the city center, near the Nordica Hotel (✆ **550-6000** or 800-7000); Kringlan Mall (✆ **550-6690**); and Smáralind Mall (✆ **550-6500**). **Vodafone branches** (all locations, ✆ **599-9000**) in Reykjavík are at Kringlan Mall, Smáralind Mall, and Skútuvogur 2, which is a little closer to downtown but harder to get to by bus. **Nova** and **Tal,** the two main new companies, have branches in the major shopping malls, Kringlan and Smáralind. Síminn (✆ **460-6709**), Nova(✆ **460-6709**), and Vodafone (✆ **460-6709**) also have branches in **Akureyri** on Glerártorg.

When you sign up for a pre-paid GSM plan in Iceland, the SIM card is typically free, and the lowest starting credit is 2,000kr. Typical rates within Iceland are 21kr per minute for the first minute then 25% less after that, and 11kr for a text message, no matter what time of the day or week. For the other companies, the price of a call drops as much as 50% within Iceland if you are calling another cellphone operated by the same company. They also have a "friends" option where you can choose a few numbers to call for free. Calls are all free between users of Nova SIM cards. GPRS costs are typically 20kr per 5 megabyte from Nova and slightly higher with other companies.

Tip: Be sure to ask for your voicemail and other prompts to be in English.

In Iceland only the caller pays for the call, even for calls from overseas. This makes cellphones a great way for people from home to keep in touch with you. Currently the Nova rate for international calls from Iceland per minute to the U.S. is 50kr.

Your phone account can be continually restocked by buying pre-paid cards called *Frelsi* (Freedom) at fuel stations and convenience stores around the country. To make sure you buy the right card, specify whether your cellphone uses Síminn or Vodafone, Nova etc.

Satellite Phones

"Satphones" can be helpful in more remote parts of Iceland. Two providers serve the country: Iridium satellite phones get the best coverage, whereas GlobalStar phones get only marginal coverage with a weaker signal. Iceland has no satellite phone agency, but products can be rented or purchased from two companies.

You can rent satphones from **RoadPost** (✆ **888/290-1606;** www.roadpost.com). Phone rental costs $8.99 per day, and the rate is $1.79 per minute. **InTouch USA** (✆ **800/872-7626;** www.intouchglobal.com) offers a wider range of phones, but phone rental costs $1.49 per week with a per-minute rate of $2.49.

Voice-Over Internet Protocol (VoIP)

If you have Web access while on your travels, you might consider a broadband-based telephone service (in technical terms, **Voice-over Internet Protocol,** or **VoIP**) such as Skype (www.skype.com) or Vonage (www.vonage.com), which allows you to make free international calls from your laptop or in an Internet cafe. The people you're calling may also need to be signed up. Check the sites for details.

Internet & E-Mail

Several factors make Iceland a good place to bring your own computer: the widespread availability of free Wi-Fi; the difficulty of finding public Internet access terminals; the high cost of those public terminals; and the low crime rate. In Reykjavík and Akureyri you won't have trouble finding a cafe with free Wi-Fi, but in the rest of the country you'll have to ask around. Creative solutions can usually be found, from sitting in hotel lobbies (you're unlikely to be thrown out) to loitering outside library doors after closing hours. Reykjavík's international airport has a free hotspot at the **Kaffitár** cafe in the departure lounge.

Remember to bring a power adapter, and perhaps an Ethernet cable and phone cord as well. As in other European countries, Icelandic electricity runs at 220 volts, 50 Hz AC, and electric sockets have two round plugs; you may need an "international" power adapter that properly regulates the current to prevent computer damage. Icelandic phone jacks are the same as in North America, so Europeans will need an adapter.

Without Your Own Computer

Most places to stay do not provide Internet terminals for guests, so your best and least expensive resource is often the public library, which usually charges around 200kr per hour. Most cafes have free Wi-Fi access.

TIPS ON ACCOMMODATIONS

Iceland's tourist season is concentrated from mid-June through August, and tourism is growing by about 10% each year; so booking ahead is often essential. Prices fall as much as 40% in the off season, but many places close in winter, especially guesthouses.

Iceland is not the poor and provincial country it once was, and virtually all places meet good basic standards of comfort and cleanliness. Mattress standards are particularly high.

Anti-smoking legislation that took effect in 2007 forbids smoking *anywhere* inside Icelandic hotels and other places you might stay.

Options

HOTELS

The word "hotel" generally signifies the most luxurious choice in town, but not all hotels are superior to or more expensive than guesthouses (see below), and not all "hotel" rooms even have private bathrooms. Expect to pay at least 16,000kr for the most basic hotel double with a private bathroom, 10,000kr for one without a private bathroom, or 23,000kr for an average business-style room.

ICELANDIC HOTEL CHAINS International chains have few footholds in Iceland. Icelandic chains are more common. **Icelandair Hotels** (**✆ 444-4000;** www.icelandairhotels.com) has seven three- and four-star hotels around the country. **Edda Hotels ✆ 444-4000;** www.hoteledda.is), in partnership with Icelandair, has 13 summer-only hotels, most of which use student housing; **Fosshótel** (**✆ 562-4000;** www.fosshotel.is) has 10 hotels and one guesthouse ranging from one to three stars; and **Kea Hotels** (**✆ 460-2000;** www.keahotels.is) has six two- to four-star hotels. **Reykjavík Hotels** (**✆ 514-8000**; www.reykjavikhotels.is) has three quality hotels in the Reykjavík area.

GUESTHOUSES

Gistiheimilið (guesthouses) are a time-honored Scandinavian institution that is closely related to the "bed-and-breakfast." Rooms, which are usually in private houses, are most often cheaper than hotels and range in quality from the equivalent of a two-star hotel to a hostel. While private bathrooms are rare, most guesthouses are likely to have cooking facilities, sleeping-bag accommodation (see below), or a family-size apartment fitting four to six people. Because Icelanders have a highly developed sense of personal privacy, the proprietors often live in a separate house. Standards of cleanliness are usually very high.

Guesthouse prices vary greatly, but a double with a shared bathroom ranges from 9,000kr to 23,000kr. About half of Icelandic guesthouses include breakfast in the room price, and the rest usually offer breakfast for an extra 1,200kr or so per person.

CABINS

Small timber cabins for visitors are sprouting up all over Iceland, usually in conjunction with an existing hotel or guesthouse. Some visitors seek them out for their comparative privacy, quiet, and convenience. The cabins are often designed for family groups of around four, with private bathrooms and cooking facilities. Prices are comparable to regular doubles.

FARM HOLIDAYS

Staying at farmhouses is the classic Icelandic way to travel, and helps visitors feel more in tune with Iceland's cultural traditions. Every farm in Iceland has its own road sign, and farm names are often unchanged from the Age of Settlement. Towns and villages did not exist for most of Icelandic history, so farmsteads have traditionally been the organizational basis of Icelandic society.

A farm stay is simply a guesthouse in farm surroundings; expect comforts to be on par with those of a European bed-and-breakfast. **Icelandic Farm Holidays (IFH)** (**✆ 570-2700;** www.farmholidays.is) classifies its 150 places as "farmhouses" (where you stay in the family's home); "farmer's guesthouses" (where you stay in a separate building); "country hotels" (with hotel-like facilities, though not always private bathrooms); and "cottages" (see "Cabins," above). All are rated from the most basic, Category I, through Category IV, which guarantees well-equipped rooms with private bathrooms. Many farms offer sleeping-bag accommodation (see below) or camping. Most provide meals on request and allow use of a guest kitchen. Many have hot tubs.

Many farms offer horseback riding or other activities. Most do not offer visitors a chance to participate in the rituals of farm life, but you can always ask—they might be pleasantly surprised.

SLEEPING-BAG ACCOMMODATION

For hardy visitors on a budget, the Icelandic custom of *svefnpoka gisting,* or "sleeping-bag accommodation," can feel like a gift from the travel gods. In many guesthouses, farm stays, and even some hotels, visitors with their own sleeping-bags can get around 35% to 50% off on room rates. (You *can* bring other linens, but sleeping bags are preferred for their warmth and portability.) For the most part the beds, rooms, and amenities are the same; you're simply sparing the management the trouble of washing sheets. You won't find sleeping-bag rooms with private bathrooms, however, except in rare instances. We list sleeping-bag accommodation availability and pricing in our accommodation listings, but you should always ask, nonetheless. Some places offer sleeping-bag accommodation only in the off season. In Reykjavík sleeping-bag accommodation has been almost entirely phased out.

CAMPING

Iceland's many campsites make the country far more accessible to visitors of limited means. Camping typically costs only 700kr to 1,400kr per person per night, and a few municipal campsites are free.

Icelandic campsites are safe, conveniently located, and plentiful: virtually every village has one. (Even in Reykjavík the campground is right next to the city's biggest

THE case FOR HOSTELS

Iceland's 36 youth hostels are hardly the exclusive domain of young backpackers. All hostels have good basic standards of service and cleanliness. Some are almost indistinguishable from guesthouses or farm stays. Most offer doubles, though the majority of rooms sleep three to six; and private bathrooms are an extreme rarity. All hostels give you the option of sleeping-bag accommodation or sheet rental. All have guest kitchens, and some offer meals and self-service laundry. In some remote destinations in Iceland, hostels may be your only option for lodging and dining, as well as an excellent source of tourist information.

All youth hostels in Iceland can be booked through one convenient **central office** (✆ **575-6700;** www.hostel.is). The website includes good deals on adventure tours and a popular car rental package with hostel vouchers. Hostels tend to fill up even faster than hotels and guesthouses in high season, so plan ahead. Many hostels close in winter. Children aged 5 to 12 usually stay for half price.

A **Youth Hostelling International membership** (**www.hihostels.com**), which gives you a 20% discount on rates, can be purchased before you leave home.

geothermal pool, and near buses to the airport and city.) Many campsites are adjoined to farm accommodations, even to guesthouses or hotels, not to mention all the hiking trails. Because Icelanders themselves love to camp, campsites can also be great places to meet natives.

Camping and car rental are a perfect duo in Iceland. The money you save on accommodations can go toward the car, and the car grants you the flexibility, mobility, and secure luggage storage camping doesn't normally afford. Many visitors on a budget try to do without a rental car, only to wish they had brought a tent and sleeping bag instead.

The **Camping Card** (www.campingcard.is), instituted in 2006, is an unbeatable deal. It grants you (plus your spouse and up to four children under the age of 16) unlimited access to 39 campsites across the country for the entire summer at a cost of only 13,900kr. See their website for a list and map of participating sites; many desirable campgrounds, such as those in Þingvellir National Park, are not included. The card can be purchased online or in Iceland at Olis stations and post offices.

Facilities at campsites vary greatly. Some have washing machines, electricity, hot showers, and kitchens; others have only a cold-water tap and toilets. In parks and nature reserves, camping is permitted only in designated areas.

Most campsites are open June through mid-September. Camping is usually not feasible in winter, though some campsites remain open, and you can always shower at the local pool.

Iceland's heavy winds and rains present a serious challenge for campers. You'll need a very strong, waterproof tent, with the maximum number of pegs, a good sleeping mat, and a waterproof sheet for under the tent. Wood can rarely be found for campfires even when they're allowed, so bring a good stove, too. Canisters for common stove fuels are easily found in filling stations.

Campsites are not listed in this book, but as you can see, we hardly mean to discourage their use. A comprehensive list of campsites can be found at **www.camping.is**. **Nordic Adventure Travel** (**www.nat.is**) also has a helpful map of the sites. The free **camping directory** *Tjaldsvæði Íslands* is available at any tourist information center.

MOUNTAIN HUTS

Hiking groups maintain about 70 "mountain huts" in remote interior and coastal locations, many accessible only to hikers (see "Hiking," in chapter 4). Mountain huts can be anything from multi-story structures with kitchens and wardens to bare-bones shacks. Be prepared for a lack of privacy in these accommodations: as many as 30 people can be sleeping in sardine formation on narrow foam mattresses on the floor. Sleeping space can be reserved in most huts, and many are fully booked weeks or months in advance in high season. Costs in the most popular huts are typically around 4,500kr per person per night. For specific mountain huts, see the regional chapters of this book.

RENTALS

Renting a house or apartment can be a wonderful and economical option. **RENT** (www.rent.is; rent@rent.is) is Iceland's best resource for rentals, from individual rooms to fully furnished apartments to a cabin near Þórsmörk, short-term or long-term.

Also see the box, "House- & Couch-Swapping," below.

The Star-Rating System

Icelandic hotels are rated on a voluntary basis by the government on a one- to five-star scale. One star means breakfast is available and your room has a sink, among other minimum standards. Two stars means more options for meals and refreshments. Three stars means all rooms have private bathrooms, phones, TVs, radios, and desks. Four stars means easy chairs, satellite channels, room service, and laundry service. Five stars means room safes, secretarial services, exercise facilities, and shops—but not a single Icelandic hotel has earned this designation.

Many fine hotels and guesthouses opt out of the rating system, however, because the standard criteria do not serve them well. A hotel in an old house, for instance, could be demoted a star if just one of its rooms lacks the requisite square footage. Places with individualistic room designs are particularly ill-served by the system.

Searching For Rooms

This guidebook lists and describes the best places to stay Iceland has to offer. The options listed here could all be full, however, or you may need to find something better suited to your itinerary.

The free 232-page booklet ***Around Iceland*** lists every option in the entire country, along with all restaurants; museums; filling stations; notable sites, hikes and events; as well as services. It's available wherever tourists roam in Iceland, or you can download each chapter free at www.heimur.is/world. ***Áning,*** another useful publication from the same source, focuses exclusively on places to stay—and features photographs and more service details—but is less complete.

USEFUL WEBSITES

Icelanders' embrace of the Internet has made finding rooms radically easier. The websites of regional tourist offices, listed in the respective chapters of this book, have good listings. Most Icelandic villages also have their own websites detailing lodging and other services; the website is usually the name of the village (disregard the accents, and substitute "d" for "ð" and "th" for "Þ") with "www." before and ".is" after. Note, however, that many Icelandic villages have the same name.

The site **www.accommodation.is** has a user-friendly search engine that lists information by location. Hotels in Iceland (**www.hotels.is**) and Reykjavík Center (**www.reykjavikcenter.is**) take it up a notch by indicating availability of rooms or sleeping spaces within a specified time frame. The latter site, despite its name, covers the whole country.

MORE MONEY-SAVING TIPS

- **Book rooms with access to a kitchen.** Restaurants are particularly expensive in Iceland, and you can save money by cooking for yourself.
- **Ask about apartments and "family rooms" if you are in a group of three or more.** These types of rooms are very common in Iceland, but are not always well-advertised.
- **Act noncommittal.** Many Icelandic guesthouses quote different prices to different people. Always ask for a price before committing, even if the guesthouse has a published rate. They could quote something lower to snag your business.
- **Be wary of packages and group tour rates.** Icelandic guesthouses often quote a *higher* rate to a travel agent than to an individual calling directly, especially outside of Reykjavík.

- **Ask about special rates or other discounts.** You may qualify for corporate, student, military, senior, frequent flier, trade union, or other discounts. Children's discounts are very common in Iceland.
- **Book online.** Internet-only discounts are very common in Iceland; many places have a standard discount *every* time you book online. Some supply rooms to Priceline, Hotwire, or Expedia at rates lower than the ones you can get through the hotel itself.
- **Remember the law of supply and demand.** You can save big on hotel rooms by touring in Iceland's off season or shoulder seasons, when rates typically drop, even at luxury properties.

Landing the Best Room

Visitors often assume they want a room with lots of natural light. In the nonstop daylight of Iceland's early summer, however, you might want to request a room with less sun exposure and/or good blackout curtains.

If you're a light sleeper, ask for a quieter room away from vending or ice machines, elevators, restaurants, bars, and nightclubs. Icelanders have a well-earned reputation for late-night partying on Friday and Saturday nights.

Note: Top sheets are generally not even an option in Iceland. Also, filter coffeemakers are rare: coffee/tea-making facilities usually consist of an electric hot water kettle, instant coffee, and teabags.

House- & Couch-Swapping

House-swapping (along with its humble cousin, couch-swapping) is becoming a more popular and viable means of travel; you stay in their place, they stay in yours, and you both get a more authentic and personal view of a destination. **HomeLink International** (homelink.org; $150 yearly membership) is the largest and oldest home-swapping association, founded in 1952, with more than 13,000 listings worldwide. **InterVac.com** ($99 yearly membership) with over 10,000 listings is also reliable. Both sites have plenty of Icelandic offerings. **www.couchsurfing.com** is a free online forum for finding (and offering) a free bed, and hundreds of Reykjavíkians are signed up.

ACTIVE ICELAND

4

Just being in Iceland is enough for many people; the land itself with all its dynamic charm is a magnet for visitors who are happy to observe at a safe distance; but for people who would like to get a closer look at the wonders Iceland can offer, this chapter is full of activities to engage you in an unforgettable experience. It's not just for athletes and adrenaline addicts, but also for anyone seeking recreation and adventure in Iceland's great outdoors.

Some Reykjavík companies, all of which blur the line between tour operator and travel agency, offer a wide range of tours across Iceland. **The Activity Group,** Skútuvogur 12e (© **580-9900;** www.activity.is), and **Mountaineers of Iceland,** Skútuvogur 12e (© **580-9900;** www.mountaineers.is), lean toward private tours and tend to be pricier. **Arctic Adventures,** Laugavegur 11 (© **562-7000;** www.adventures.is), goes for more robust sporting activities and has very reasonable prices. **Nordic Adventure Travel,** Svarthamrar 17 (© **898-0355;** www.nat.is), and **Touris,** Fiskislóð 77 (© **517-8290;** www.tour.is), serve mostly as travel agencies but are also licensed to lead tours. The two regional companies with the most creative roster of outdoor adventures are **Nonni Travel,** Brekkugata 5, Akureyri (© **461-1841;** www.nonnitravel.is), in north Iceland, and **West Tours,** Aðalstræti 7, Ísafjörður (© **456-5111;** www.westtours.is), in the Westfjords.

Iceland's two preeminent hiking groups, **Ferðafélag Íslands,** Mörkin 6, Reykjavík (© **568-2533;** www.fi.is), and **Útivist,** Laugavegur 178, Reykjavík (© **562-1000;** www.utivist.is), lead small groups in down-to-earth expeditions that usually include Icelanders and revolve around hiking; others delve into anything from skiing to yoga under the midnight sun. A good general web resource for activities in Iceland is http://www.randburg.com/is/tourism/plans.html.

Keep in mind that the regional sections of this book may include local tour operators not mentioned in this chapter. Agencies offering outdoor activity tours are also listed in chapter 3, under the heading of "Special Interest & Escorted Trips" (p. 56).

Unless otherwise indicated, tour prices quoted below include transportation (within Iceland only), meals (except for day tours), accommodation, and a guide.

AERIAL TOURS

Aerial sightseeing is mushrooming these days, and it's easy to see why. Pilots can fly almost anywhere, and many remote areas are difficult to reach by other means.

Prices may be less prohibitive than you think. Airplane tours run anywhere from 10,000kr for 20 minutes aloft to 30,000kr for 1½ to 2 hours. Helicopter tours are far more expensive, but maneuvers are more thrilling.

Aerial tours are scheduled by arrangement, and flight paths are usually negotiable. The minimum number of passengers ranges from two to six. If your head count is fewer, ask to team up with another group. Flights are frequently cancelled because of weather and wind conditions, so leave wiggle room in your itinerary. And prepare yourself for buffeting in the wind—all the planes are 4- to 10-seaters.

Tour Operators

Reykjavík has three similarly priced tour operators, all based at the city's domestic airport. **Eagle Air** (✆ **562-4200;** www.eagleair.is) has a 30-minute tour of the area (19,000kr per person) and package tours combining aerial sightseeing with boat trips, white-water rafting, and snowmobiling on Vatnajökull. **Odin Air** (✆ **551-0880;** www.odinair.is) also has tempting flight menus.

Mountaineers of Iceland, Skútuvogur 12E, Reykjavík (✆ **580-9900;** www.mountaineers.is), and **Mountain Taxi,** Trönuhrauni 7, Hafnarfjörður (✆ **544-5252;** www.mountaintaxi.is), tie helicopter rides into Super Jeep romps on glaciers for groups. You could also contact the **Helicopter Service of Iceland** (✆ **561-6100;** www.helicoptericeland.com) directly which now offers aerial film and photography tours with the option of creating your own tour. **Norðurflug** (✆ **562-5200;** www.heli.is) offers a range of helicopter tours including the Journey to the Center of the Earth tour of Snæfellsjökull glacier (p. 192); it was also the main company operating tours of the eruption in Fimmvörðuháls (p. 314) in March 2010.

Outside **Reykjavík, Mýflug Air** (✆ **464-4400;** www.myflug.is), based at **Mývatn's** Reykjahlíð airfield, is conveniently close to Krafla, Jökulsárgljúfur, Askja, Kverkfjöll, and other striking landmarks (p. 269). Eagle Air and Mýflug Air all arrange tours from **Akureyri** (p. 245). **Atlantsflug** (✆ **478-2406;** www.atf.is) is based at **Skaftafell,** close to Núpsstaðarskógar, the Laki craters, and Landmannalaugar (p. 324).

BIKING

Iceland is a rewarding but also demanding locale for a long-distance bike trip. The major hazards are volatile weather, harsh winds, sandstorms, rough roads, and stones flung by passing vehicles. Any bike brought to Iceland should be very high quality. Bring along a repair kit and be prepared for several flats since supplies are difficult to find outside Reykjavík. Make sure you are easily visible to motorists, and always wear a helmet (it's a legal requirement for all children under 15). To protect Iceland's vegetation, all off-road riding is forbidden.

Cyclists along the Ring Road can use the bus as a backup in bad weather. Bikes are stored in the luggage compartment, so you might want to bring padding to prevent damage.

The **Icelandic Mountainbike Club,** Brekkustígur 2, Reykjavík (✆ **562-0099;** www.fjallahjolaklubburinn.is), has some guided bike tours and rentals for tourists but mainly offers advice, including suggested itineraries, a packing checklist, a message board, and tips on where to store your bike box.

See regional chapters for more information on biking by destination.

Tour Operators

From April until August, **Arctic Adventures,** Laugavegur 11 (✆ **562-7000;** www.adventures.is), leads 4-hour bike tours of Reykjavík for 9,990kr with only a six-person minimum (book in advance). The **Icelandic Mountainbike Club** (see above) runs informal weekend trips for its members, and visitors are often welcome to tag along.

West Tours, Aðalstræti 7, Ísafjörður (✆ **456-5111;** http://www.vesturferdir.is), rents mountain bikes for 3,500kr per day and can help with basic logistical support, such as plotting out wonderful routes in that region; though it does not lead guided tours.

Freewheeling Adventures (from North America ✆ **800/672-0775;** outside North America ✆ **902/857-3600;** www.freewheeling.ca/iceland), based in Nova Scotia, Canada, schedules two guided 8-day trips each year, both with fantastic itineraries. The price is $3,895 (including luggage transport), with a self-guided version for $3,595 and leave anytime. Both include domestic transport, but not international.

BIRDWATCHING

In Iceland, even non-birders are at some point drawn to birdwatching. Iceland lies at a major junction of migratory routes, and hosts at least 278 species. Puffins (p. 296), universally beloved for their clownish looks and slapstick antics, are pictured on every other tourist brochure. Other common types are guillemots, arctic terns, gannets, fulmars, cormorants, kittiwakes, and razorbills. Especially coveted sightings include the barrow's goldeneye, found all summer at Mývatn; harlequin ducks, seen on several Icelandic rivers; the white-tailed eagle, occasionally spotted in Breiðafjörður bay; and the gyrfalcon, Iceland's national bird.

Hard-core birders initiate the tourist season in April and May, when nesting season reaches full swing. May and June have the optimal convergence of species variety, fine plumage, and decent weather, though a few nature reserves—notably Dyrhólaey in the south, and the northern end of Hrísey Island in the north—are closed to visitors at precisely this time to protect the birds and their young. By August, bird numbers are down dramatically, but enthusiasts can find ways to keep busy all year.

Prime coastal sites include **Hafnaberg** (p. 172) and **Valahnúkur** (p. 172) on Reykjanes peninsula; **Arnarstapi** (p. 191) on Snæfellsnes Peninsula; **Breiðafjörður** (p. 199), the bay between Snæfellsnes and the Westfjords; **Látrabjarg** (p. 206) and **Hornbjarg** (p. 226) in the Westfjords; **Hrísey Island** (p. 259) near Akureyri; **Langanes peninsula** (p. 287) in the northeast; the **Westman Islands** (p. 291), **Dyrhólaey** (p. 316), and **Ingólfshöfði** (p. 328) in the south; and **Papey Island** (p. 341) in the east. Inland, the foremost locale is **Mývatn** (p. 263), Europe's most diverse waterfowl habitat. The birding map *Fuglakort Íslands,* with English text and handy illustrations, is commonly available in Iceland, or order at **www.nordicstore.net** before you go.

The best online resource, **www.birdingiceland.com** has fantastic photography, extensive diaries, and a gripping "Rare Bird News" feature.

Tour Operators

Gavia Travel, Álfaheidi 44, Kópavogur (✆ **511-3939**; www.gaviatravel.com), is the only Icelandic company devoted exclusively to birding tours. Gavia Travel offers scheduled day tours around the Reykjanes Peninsula (22,600kr) and Snaefellsnes Peninsula (28,600kr) from April until July, and other longer tours from 4- to 12-day regional trips.

Icelander Tours/Highlander Adventures, Seljavegur 19, Reykjavík (✆ **561-2555 or 892-5509;** www.icelandertours.com), schedules 10-day bird-watching tours in May and June for around 330,000kr. The itinerary, which circles the country, includes half-board, a dip at Mývatn Nature Baths, a boat trip through the glacial lagoon Jökulsárlón, and other fun extras.

Valtours (✆ **445-6390;** www.valtours.is), a small and cost-effective eco-tour operator offering scheduled and custom birding tours from May to September 7. One-week trips with half-board at guesthouses typically cost 316,500kr.

CAVING

Iceland has some of the world's longest **lava-tube caves,** formed after volcanic eruptions when conduits of molten rock drain downhill. Lava pillars, mineral stalactites, ice candles, and snaking side passageways are among the intriguing formations within. Walking through these caves generally requires agility and sure-footedness but no particular training or equipment, so experts tend to devote their energies elsewhere. **Ice caves** are also common in Iceland, but they're too dangerous to enter.

Among the many lava-tube caves worth seeking out are **Raufarhólshellir** (p. 175), near Hveragerði in southwest Iceland; **Surtshellir** and **Víðgelmir** (p.184) in west Iceland; and **Lofthellir** (p. 269) near Lake Mývatn.

If you plan to explore any caves on your own, bring a strong flashlight, warm clothing, and sturdy shoes. Helmets, kneepads, gloves, and headlamps are also advised, and caves with icy floors may require studded boots. The smartest procedure is always to seek out expert local advice beforehand.

Tour Operators

Several Reykjavík companies offer caving tours, with all equipment provided. **Arctic Adventures,** Laugavegur 11 (✆ **562-7000;** www.adventures.is), and **Iceland Excursions,** Hafnarstræti 20 (✆ **540-1313;** www.icelandexcursions.is), offer 3-hour tours of Leiðarendi for 9,200kr. Arctic Adventures has a 3–4 hour trip to Gjábakkahellir between Þingvellir and Laugarvatn for 12.990kr, including pickup from Reykjavík. **Iceland Rovers** (✆ **567-1720;** www.icelandrovers.is) has a 6-hour tour that begins with caving and ends with a hike to the swimmable hot springs in Reykjadalur (p. 176). The cost is rather high at 19,990kr. Set departures are on Sundays, and private trips are on request with a two-person minimum.

DOGSLEDDING

Dogsledding on glaciers is not an authentic Icelandic tradition, but it's a quiet and graceful alternative to roaring around on snowmobiles, ATVs, or Super Jeeps, and the sled dogs—all Greenlandic huskies—are very cute. Tours are possible all year, but conditions may be too poor in fall and early winter. Forget about epic dogsledding treks; all that's usually offered are short jaunts of 45 minutes to 2 hours on Langjökull. Snowsuits and gloves are included in tour prices, but make sure to bring sunglasses for snow glare. From Reykjavík, **Eskimos** Skutuvogur 1b, (✆ **414-1500;** www.eskimos.is), runs scheduled day trips to Langjökull in summer and winter, starting at a whopping 33,900kr per person.

If you have your own transport, the best option is to drive to the base camp of **Dog Steam Tours** (✆ **487-7747;** www.dogsledding.is), where there are 1-hour tours of Langjökull 3 times a day for 14,900kr.

FISHING

Freshwater Fishing

Many Iceland visitors are needlessly put off from the idea of freshwater fishing once they learn Eric Clapton and Prince Charles pay upward of 200,000kr per day to cast for salmon. However, cheaper salmon permits are as low as 16,000kr per rod per day, and lake fishing for trout and Arctic char is inexpensive and sometimes free. Virtually every village has reasonably priced fishing locales nearby, and permits, when necessary, can be bought at the local filling station. The ***Veiðikortið*** **fishing card** (✆ **517-4515;** www.veidikortid.is), available at all N1 filling stations, gives you unlimited access to 32 lakes around the country for 6,000kr.

Iceland has more than a hundred self-sustaining **salmon rivers,** of which 20 fall into the elite class. Most elite rivers are leased to private clubs, and fishing these rivers usually means booking through the club, staying at the club lodge, and using club equipment and guides. Less expensive permits tend to be a simpler and more straightforward matter. Most rivers have a strict fly-fishing-only policy.

Fishing season for many lakes, including most lakes in the *Veiðikortið* network, is restricted to April until September. Some lakes remain open all year, even for ice fishing. Salmon season cannot exceed 90 days per river, and the dates are usually set from the first half of June to the first half of September.

The best all-around information source for freshwater fishing in Iceland—including lake fishing—is the **Federation of Icelandic River Owners,** Hagatorg Square, Reykjavík (✆ **553-1510;** www.angling.is). The website lists all the best fishing waters and how to get there, contacts for tours and permits, regulations on fishing tackle, and the ins and outs of ice fishing. For equipment, the best store in Iceland is **Veiðihornið,** with two Reykjavík locations: Krókháls 5g (✆ **517-8050**) and Síðumúli 8 (✆ **568-8410;** both locations Jun–Aug Mon–Fri 9am–6pm, Sat 10am–4pm, Sun noon–4pm; Sept–May Mon–Fri 10am–6pm, Sat 10am–4pm). The Veiðihornið website, **www.rifflehitch.com**, posts ongoing "catch reports" for all of Iceland's salmon rivers. The shop has an out-of-hours service number (✆ **696-4700**).

Note: All fishing equipment—including rods, reels, waders, and tackle boxes, except for brand-new items—must be disinfected before entering Iceland. Customs officials will need to see a veterinarian's certificate for proof; if you do not have one then Icepack (✆ **425-0444;** www.icepack.is) runs a disinfecting service from Keflavík airport and can process fishing gear within 30 minutes. The minimum cost is 4,900kr. Importing any organic bait is out of the question, unless it's thoroughly cooked.

TOUR OPERATORS For many elite rivers and some lakes, the tour operators are the fishing clubs that control the leases. The two most prestigious clubs are

Angling Club Lax-á, Akurhvarf 16, Kópavogur (✆ **557-6100;** www.lax-a.is), and **Reykjavik Angling Club,** Háaleitisbraut 68, Reykjavík (✆ **568-6050;** www.svfr.is), with 29 rivers and several lakes between them. Packages range from full-service pampering in luxury lodges to basic accommodation in self-catering cabins. Rivers tend to book up in advance, but it's always worth checking for cancellations. Other clubs worth scouring for package deals are **Angling Service Strengir,** Smárarima 30, Reykjavík (✆ **567-5204;** www.strengir.is), **G & P,** Hallveigarstíg 10a, Reykjavík (✆ **551-2112;** www.vatnsdalsa.is), and **Sporður,** Suðurlandsbraut 52, Reykjavík (✆ **587-0860;** www.spordur.is).

The tour company **Fly Fishing In Iceland,** Freyjugata 38, Reykjavík (✆ **551-2016;** www.gofishing.is), does not control any leases on rivers or lakes, but can arrange all sorts of fishing itineraries in Iceland, with or without a guide, while taking care of the permit headaches. Day trips from Reykjavík are also offered.

Outside Iceland, **Angler Adventures** (from North America ✆ **800/628-1447,** outside North America **860/434-9624;** www.angleradventures.com), based in Old Lyme, CT, is affiliated with Angling Club Lax-á and designs custom packages. **Frontiers International** (from North America ✆ **800/245-1950;** from the U.K. ✆ **0128/574-1340;** www.frontierstravel.com) offers two week-long fishing packages, each focusing on a specific salmon river. **Sportfishing Worldwide** (from North America ✆ **800/638-7405;** outside North America ✆ **513/984-8611;** www.sfww.com) based in Cincinnati, OH, arranges 4- to 12-day guided trips and works directly with property owners, bypassing the fishing clubs.

Sea Fishing

Sea fishing is so integral to Icelandic life that someone can take you out in virtually every coastal village; if no tours are advertised, just ask around. Success is near guaranteed, at least for cod, and most tours arrange for you to eat your catch for dinner. Unlike freshwater fishing, permits aren't required, as long as you don't return to port knee-deep in fish. A 2- to 3-hour jaunt is around 4,900kr to 7,000kr per person. The regional sections of this book list specific sea-angling **tour operators** based in Reykjavík (chapter 6); Stykkishólmur, Önundarfjörður (Flateyri), and Djúpavík in the west (chapter 8); Akureyri, Dalvík, Grímsey Island, and Húsavík in the north (chapter 9); the Westman Islands in the south (chapter 10); and Djúpivogur, Fáskrúðsfjörður, and Stöðvarfjörður, in the east (chapter 11).

As with freshwater fishing, all equipment must be disinfected before entering Iceland, and a veterinarian's certificate must be supplied for proof.

GLACIER TOURS

Glaciers, which cover around 10% of Iceland's surface, are enduring objects of fascination to Icelanders (see "The Glacier Mystique" box, p. 325). Traversing glaciers is generally done on snowmobiles, Super Jeeps (see also "Jeep Tours," below), skis (see "Skiing & Ski Touring," later in this chapter), dog sleds (see "Dogsledding," above), or by foot. On hiking tours, participants often wear crampons and walk a set distance apart in single file, fastened to each other with ropes and safety harnesses; some tours also involve wielding ice axes or rappelling (abseiling) into crevasses. Snowmobile tours can be tamer than expected, proceeding single-file with the slowest driver setting the pace. Expect to pay 15,000kr to 22,000kr for an hour in a snowmobile seat. Advertised prices assume two people per snowmobile, and riding solo costs an extra 3,000 to 6,000kr.

Glaciers can be mortally dangerous; for more on glacier safety, see p. 49.

Tour Operators

Several companies offer glacier tours that start in Reykjavík and often tie in sightseeing and other outdoor activities. A popular new tour is the Eyjafjallajökull Volcano Tour.

Arctic Adventures, Laugavegur 11, Reykjavík (✆ **562-7000;** www.adventures.is) has a 9-hour tour which gives you a great view of the area surrounding the volcano (the one that brought European air travel to a standstill in 2010). The cost including lunch and a visit to Skógafoss (p. 315) is 34,000kr with a 2-person minimum. Another great location is Langjökull, Iceland's second-largest glacier—and the glacier closest to Reykjavík—is a popular and convenient destination. **The Activity Group,** Skútuvogur 12e, Reykjavík (✆ **580-9900;** www.activity.is), slips snowmobile rides on Langjökull into some day-long Super Jeep sightseeing tours for 34,200kr. The year-round Express Activity Tour is for unadulterated snowmobiling; the 24,500kr price tag includes transportation from Reykjavík, with only a 4-person minimum. **Glacier Guides** (✆ **571-2100;** www.glacierguides.is) do hiking and ice-climbing trips to Sólheimajökull, Iceland's most southerly glacier, all year round for 32,000kr. **Iceland Rovers,** Vagnhöfða 7 (✆ **567-1720;** www.icelandrovers.is) offers 11-hour Super Jeep trips, with a 4-person minimum, from Reykjavík to the magical Þórsmörk, just behind the now famous Eyjafjallajökull volcano, for 30,900kr. The tour includes a visit to Seljalandfoss (p. 313) on the way back. **Mountain Taxi,** Trönuhrauni 7, Hafnarfjörður (✆ **544-5252;** www.mountaintaxi.is), has many options. The Midnight Sun tour takes 11 hours and costs 42,600kr, with stops at Þingvellir, Strokkur, and Gullfoss, plus a snowmobile break on Langjökull. The Northern Lights tour is a winter version of the same itinerary.

If you would like to get married on a glacier, **Nordic Experience** (✆ **0120/670-8888;** www.scantours.co.uk), based in Colchester, England, can create an itinerary and make all the legal and logistical arrangements. Just don't get cold feet.

Several tour operators are listed in this book's regional chapters. For snowmobile and snow cat tours of Snæfellsjökull—the glacier visible from Reykjavík on a clear day—see p. 193. Vatnajökull, the largest glacier between the Arctic and Antarctic Circles, can be approached from several directions. For hiking, mountaineering and ice-climbing tours from Skaftafell, see p. 327. For snowmobile and Super Jeep tours from Jöklasel, near Höfn, see p. 330. For an unforgettable day hike from Kverkfjöll, deep in the interior, see p. 377.

GOLF

Despite its high winds and changeable weather, Iceland is a golf-loving nation with more than 50 courses. Most are open from May until September, and a few try to stay open all year. Course fees range from 1,500kr to 6,500kr. Settings are spectacular, of course, and teeing off under the midnight sun is especially memorable.

For golfing in the Reykjavík vicinity, see p. 136. Other golf courses singled out in regional chapters include **Hamarsvöllur** in Borgarnes (p. 185), **Vestmannaeyjavöllur** in the Westman Islands (p. 297), and Akureyri's **Jaðarsvöllur,** the site of Iceland's best-known tournament, the **Arctic Open** (p. 34).

The best online resource, with basic descriptions and contact information for every Icelandic course, is **www.nat.is**; click the "Golf Guide" link.

Britannia Golf (from North America ✆ **877/249-7354;** outside North America ✆ **1804/346-8716;** www.britanniagolf.com), a golf tour company based in Glen Allen, VA, arranges Iceland golfing itineraries lasting 2 days to a week.

HIKING

Of all the outdoor activities outlined here, hiking is the most fundamental to an Iceland visit. With its stunning landscapes, fresh air, and wide open spaces, Iceland is a hiking utopia. More than 70 mountain huts across the country (p. 64) provide the infrastructure for an extensive network of backcountry routes; though hiking in Iceland hardly has to mean donning a heavy backpack and eating freeze-dried food. The country is equally blessed with short, easy hikes, not to mention tour operators who will transport luggage from hut to hut.

Independent-minded hikers who shy away from arranged tours should at least reconsider the issue. Icelandic hiking tours are often just a practical means to have luggage transported and logistical hassles eased. Hiking groups tend to be small, laid-back and fun, and you can keep to yourself when you want to. Moreover, Icelanders often travel with the groups—especially with the "Big Two," below.

Prime hiking season lasts from early June until mid-September, though some routes at higher altitudes are inaccessible until July. (Occasionally visitors plan their entire trip around a specific trek, and arrive in mid-June only to find snow obstructing the trail and the mountain huts still closed.) For hiking preparations and precautions, see "Staying Healthy"—particularly the "Outdoor Safety" subheading (p. 48)—in chapter 3.

For a summary of top hikes, flip to "The Best Big-Name Hiking Areas" (p. 7) and "The Best Off-the-Beaten-Track Hikes" (p. 7) in chapter 1.

Tour Operators

Several additional tour operators are recommended for specific destinations in the regional chapters of this book.

THE "BIG TWO" HIKING GROUPS

When Icelanders sign up for hiking tours, they usually go with **Ferðafélag Íslands,** Mörkin 6, Reykjavík (✆ **568-2533;** www.fi.is) or **Útivist,** Laugavegur 178, Reykjavík (✆ **562-1000;** www.utivist.is). Neither hankers too much for your business. Trips range from a few hours to several days, with set departure dates. No frills are added, so prices remain relatively low. Generally all that's provided is transportation from Reykjavík and a guide, plus sleeping-bag accommodation in mountain huts for overnight trips, and, occasionally, luggage transport. Participants are expected to bring and cook their own food.

As far as visitors are concerned, not much distinguishes the two. Útivist has slightly lower prices and schedules more trips per year: about 145, as opposed to 70 for Ferðafélag Íslands. However, Ferðafélag Íslands has a few local affiliates, some of which lead trips of their own. The key affiliates are **Ferðafélag Akureyrar**

(✆ **462-2720;** www.ffa.is; ffa@ffa.is) in Akureyri and **Ferðafélag Fljótsdalshéraðs** (✆ **863-5813;** www.fljotsdalsherad.is/ferdafelag; ferdafelag@egilsstadir.is) in Egilsstaðir. Their trips focus on north and east Iceland respectively, but range all over the country. Both affiliates now have translated websites and some brochures in English.

OTHER ICELANDIC COMPANIES

Arinbjörn Jóhannsson, Brekkulækur Farm, Hvammstangi (✆ **451-2938;** www.geysir.com/brekkulaekur), leads a fabulous 12-day hiking excursion across the country from June until early September, with set departure dates and a maximum group size of 14. Accommodation is in simple guesthouses, hostels, and mountain huts keeping the price down to a reasonable 206,500kr. Priorities include birdwatching at sea cliffs, finding rare ferns, and making friends.

Fjallabak (✆ **511-3070;** www.fjallabak.is) offers an impressive variety of well-designed hiking tours for day-trippers and serious backpackers alike, with set departure dates as early as April. Trips last 6 to 11 days and cost 105,000kr to 201,250kr—a decent price, considering the maximum group size is only 9 to 12.

Icelandic Mountain Guides, Vagnhöfði 7b, Reykjavík (✆ **587-9999;** www.mountainguide.is), has staked out some extremely interesting and remote backpacking routes well off the tourist radar. Tours last 4 to 30 days, with set departure dates, small group sizes (6–12), and good prices—a 9-day trek from Laki Craters to Skaftafell, for instance, is 99,900kr.

INTERNATIONAL COMPANIES

Dick Phillips Icelandic Travel Service (from the U.K. **0143/438-1440;** outside the U.K. ✆ **44143/438-1440;** www.icelandic-travel.com) leads a series of 1- to 2-week backpacking adventures well off the beaten track from mid-May to early September, with group sizes of 4 to 16. Dick Phillips has toured extensively in Iceland since 1960, and can serve as a consultant for self-guided wilderness treks.

REI Adventures (from North America ✆ **800/622-2236;** outside North America ✆ **1253-437-1100;** www.rei.com/adventures http://www.rei.com/adventures/ trips/europe/iceland.html) offers an exciting 9-day Fire & Ice Adventure tour of south Iceland, with four departure dates in summer. Most days are spent hiking 3 to 6 hours, and most nights are spent in small hotels. The $4,425 price is higher than average, though part of your fee goes toward keeping the tour carbon neutral.

Southern Treks (✆ **706/291-2471;** www.southerntreks.com), based in the U.S. state of Georgia, has a wonderful 11-day trip for **$4,606,** led by a PhD of Old Icelandic Law, with easy to moderate day hikes all across the country. The trip may not run every year, unfortunately.

Wilderness Travel (from North America ✆ **800/368-2794;** outside North America ✆ **1510-558-2488;** www.wildernesstravel.com) is a respected high-end tour company, whose 8-day hiking circuit of south Iceland—with four summer departures—costs around $5,895. Hikes are moderate, taking 4 to 6 hours per day, and accommodation is in Iceland's nicer hotels.

World Expeditions (from the U.S. ✆ **613/241-2700;** from Canada ✆ **613/241-2700;** from the U.K. ✆ **020/8545-9030;** from Australia **6128/270-8400;** from New Zealand **6409/368-4161;** www.worldexpeditions.com), based in Australia, leads an exciting and well-conceived 5-day trip through south Iceland, with moderate hikes each day and most nights spent in comfortable hotels. The cost is $1,790 (twin share), with two departures each summer.

HORSEBACK RIDING

Beginners and seasoned riders alike are enraptured by the Icelandic horse, a small breed with a gentle temperament and remarkable stamina, agility, and intelligence. One of their best-known talents is *tölting,* a kind of running trot with one foot always touching the ground. (In a popular stunt during Icelandic horse demonstrations, the rider breaks into a tölt while holding a tray of drinks in one hand.)

In summer, many young horses are released into the wilds to adapt them to Iceland's rugged terrain. In September and October, free-roaming horses and sheep are rounded up and brought home for the winter. Visitors are often welcome to participate in these important cultural rituals; see "The Big Round-Up," p. 36.

Riding tack (bridles, saddles, and such) may not be brought into Iceland. Other riding equipment (such as boots, clothing, helmets, and saddlebags) must be sterilized prior to arrival, and a veterinarian's certificate of disinfection must be presented at customs. Alternatively you can get your gear sterilized with Icepack (✆ **425-0444;** www.icepack.is) who run a disinfecting service from Keflavík airport.

Tour Operators

The best tour operators are listed below, but virtually any populated area in Iceland will have riding opportunities nearby—just ask around. Several additional tour operators are recommended throughout the regional chapters of this book, specifically for Snæfellsnes Peninsula and Hornstrandir Nature Reserve in the west (chapter 8); Húnaflói, Skagafjörður, Dalvík, and Mývatn in the north (chapter 9); Landmannalaugar, Hella, Hvolsvöllur, and the Markarfljót valley in the south (chapter 9); and Borgarfjörður Eystri in the east (chapter 11).

Booking horse trips directly through Icelandic tour companies brings the price down in almost every case. Plus, no international companies lead tours themselves; the best they can do is recommend specific routes and arrange packages that save you the trouble of finding flights and lodging in Reykjavík.

Arinbjörn Jóhannsson Touring Service, Brekkulækur Farm, Hvammstangi (✆ **451-2938;** www.geysir.com/brekkulaekur) at a horse farm in the northwest, has been leading wonderful 1- to 2-week pack trips (217,500kr–444,000kr) since the 1970s. Some tours join the September round-ups for horse and sheep.

Eldhestar, Vellir Farm, Hveragerði (✆ **480-4800;** www.eldhestar.is), has a fabulous tour menu with tons of trips and departure dates: 5 days around Þórsmörk is 166,000kr while 9 days around Landmannalaugar goes for 285,000kr. Day tours explore neighboring lava fields and the Mt. Hengill hiking area. The farm and its eco-hotel (p. 178) are just 40 minutes from Reykjavík.

Hestasport, Vegamót, Varmahlíð (✆ **453-8383;** www.riding.is), based in the Skagafjörður area, offers single-day trips ranging from 1 hour to a full day excursion (4,500kr–14,000kr) as well as multi-day riding trips up to 9 days in length through the interior (270,000kr–380,000kr). Group sizes remain small, with 4 to 12 participants.

Íshestar, Sörlaskeið 26, Hafnarfjörður (✆ **555-7000;** www.ishestar.is), is based in the Reykjavík metropolitan area but offers a staggering range of trips in all corners of Iceland. The 6-day trip along the historic Kjölur trail, in Iceland's desert interior highlands, is 265,500kr.

Laxnes Horse Farm, Laxnes Farm, Mosfellsbær (✆ **566-6179;** www.laxnes.is), located 15 minutes outside Reykjavík in Mosfellsdalur Valley, is an excellent choice for day tours from Reykjavík. (It's also something of a rock star haunt, judging by recent visitors Lou Reed, Nick Cave, and Metallica.) A 3-hour tour goes for a reasonable 7,000kr including pickup and dropoff in Reykjavík.

Polar Hestar, Grýtubakki II Farm, Akureyri (✆ **463-3179;** www.polarhestar.is), based in Eyjafjörður Valley near Akureyri, has created two memorable 8-day itineraries through Iceland's northeastern regions; prices are 187,500kr to 242,500kr with 12 departure dates.

HUNTING

Game animals in Iceland are reindeer, seals, foxes, geese, ducks, ptarmigan, and a variety of seabirds, particularly shags, guillemots, cormorants, and razorbills. Reindeer season is from August 1 to September 15, but only around 1,300 licenses are auctioned each year, with a cap on the number of foreign buyers. Ptarmigan—by far the most popular target for wing shooting—can be hunted from October 15 until December 20. Most seabirds are fair game from September until early May.

Most visiting hunters bring their own guns and ammunition. To do this, you must be sponsored by one of the operators below; customs will require a police permit, which only a sponsor can secure for you. Guns can also be rented from the tour operators. ***Note:*** Bringing dogs of any kind to Iceland is prohibited.

Arranged tours are especially convenient because the tour company takes care of the paperwork for securing licenses and exporting trophies. Group sizes are small, usually two to five hunters. **Angling Club Lax-á,** Akurhvarf 16, Kópavogur (✆ **557-6100;** www.lax-a.is), offers hunting expeditions lasting 4 to 8 days, with everything arranged from the moment you step off the plane. **Angling Service Strengir,** Smárarima 30, Reykjavík (✆ **567-5204;** www.strengir.is), puts together hunting trips for ptarmigan, geese, and ducks. The **Icelandic Hunting Club** (✆ **894-3905;** www.huntingiceland.com) can arrange just about any private or group tour.

4WD TOURS

Most tours are in "Super Jeeps," which are not your average 4WD vehicles. These swaggering behemoths, with meter-high tires, souped-up engines, and state-of-the-art GPS navigational systems, could guide drivers through a complete whiteout. Super Jeeps are especially gifted at fording rivers and driving on snow. Super Jeep tours offer unmatched privacy, comfort, flexibility, and back-road access, but you'll pay handsomely for the privilege. (If you're on a budget, be consoled that Iceland's buses are pretty tricked-out themselves.)

Note: Super Jeep tour brochures all brag about driving "off-road," but this only means the tours venture to remote locations on difficult roads. Off-road driving is forbidden in Iceland (except on some beaches).

Tour Operators

Most Super Jeep tours are day-long excursions from Reykjavík. Popular destinations include the Golden Circle, Þjórsárdalur, Mt. Hekla, Þórsmörk, Landmannalaugar, and Langjökull. Hiking, snowmobiling, sightseeing, and other activities are usually worked into itineraries. Since the tour group is often just you and the driver, routes can be highly flexible. Prices are typically 34,000kr to 39,500kr per person for a 9- to

12-hour tour, including Reykjavík pickup and dropoff, but not lunch. Extended tours can be arranged with the operators, but the price will depend on the destinations and accommodation bracket.

The top tour operators near Reykjavík are **Iceland On Track,** Grófarsmári 18, Kópavogur (✆ **899-5438;** www.icelandontrack.com), **Iceland Rovers** (✆ **567-1720;** www.icelandrovers.is), **Mountain Taxi,** Trönuhrauni 7c, Hafnarfjörður (✆ **544-5252;** www.mountaintaxi.is), **Mountaineers of Iceland,** Skútuvogur 12e, Reykjavík (✆ **580-9900;** www.mountaineers.is), **Safaris,** Vallarás 2, Reykjavík (✆ **822-0022;** www.safaris.is), and **Touris,** Fiskislóð 77, Reykjavík (✆ **517-8290;** www.tour.is). **JRJ Super Jeep Tours,** Mánaþúfa, Varmahlíð (✆ **453-8219;** www.simnet.is/jeppaferdir) is based near Skagafjörður in northwest Iceland, but can also launch tours from the capital. Safaris are ideal for visitors who want to drive Super Jeeps themselves in guided convoys. Otherwise, very little distinguishes the offerings of these companies.

KAYAKING

Iceland's fjords, inlets, and sheltered coastlines are ideal for sea kayaking, which can bring you up-close to seal colonies, bird cliffs, and sea caves that are inaccessible from land. All tours recommended below are guided, and none require prior experience.

The best tour operator is **Seakayak Iceland** (✆ **690-3877;** www.seakayakiceland.com), which leads excursions all over the country, anything from 2- to3-day trips to 2-week long tours. The company is based in Egilsstaðir in the east of Iceland. All tours must be planned in advance, where prices are negotiated depending on the destinations and length of trips. **West Tours** (✆ **456-5111;** www.westtours.is), the leading Westfjords tour operator, offers 2- to 6-hour tours (5,000kr–12,900kr) around Ísafjörður and Ísafjarðardjúp, with a two-person minimum; the tour in Mjóifjörður is particularly idyllic, with friendly seals en route. The best tour operator in the Eastfjords is **Kayakklúbburinn Kaj** (✆ **863-9939;** www.123.is/kaj), offering splendid 2-hour tours for 5,000kr from their base in Neskaupstaður.

PHOTOGRAPHY

Iceland's phenomenal scenery and magical light have long enticed professional nature photographers—and even amateur snapshooters are almost guaranteed impressive results. From experience, we offer two small bits of advice. First, don't neglect the close-ups. Iceland's broad vistas always command attention, but the landscape's finer textures and patterns create fascinating worlds unto themselves. Second, have prints made by a quality developer. Iceland's subtleties of light and detail—always so enthralling in person—often don't come across in inferior prints.

In late July or early August, **Borea Adventures** (✆ **899-3817;** www.borea adventures.com) can organize a 5-day excursion around Hornstrandir Nature Reserve. The cost is 232,000kr, and participants are whisked from fjord to fjord on an 18m (60ft.) racing yacht. Nature photographer **Daniel Bergmann** (✆ **697-9515;** www.danielbergmann.com), who lives in Stykkishólmur, conducts 10-day workshop tours around the country from mid-June through August. **Strabo Tours** (from North America ✆ **866/218-9215;** outside North America **1607/756-8676;**

www.phototc.com), a U.S.-based photography tour company, puts together an annual 10-day Iceland trip led by a professional photographer for $5,195. A new itinerary for Iceland is in development.

POOLS & SPAS

Three things are reliably found in every Icelandic village: a Lutheran church, a filling station selling hot-dogs, and a public pool heated by the country's plentiful hot springs. (To put this in perspective, consider that New York City has 25 times the population of Iceland, but half as many public pools.) Geothermal pools are so important to Icelanders that the Icelandic word for "Saturday" (*laugardagur*) means "pool day" or "hot springs day." During work hours, it's not unusual to see business meetings conducted in the hot tubs. Icelanders visit the pools year-round, even in rain and freezing weather, and credit them for their long lifespans (81 years on average for men and 86 for women) and low stress levels.

The regional chapters of this book do not mention all the village pools, only because they're so ubiquitous and easy to locate: just look for street signs depicting a bather. Obscure villages may only have a small pool, hot tub, shower, and changing room, while larger towns could also have lockers, lifeguards, fitness equipment, water slides, kiddie pools, an indoor pool, saunas, and a row of hot tubs, each set at a different temperature. Some farms also have pools that are open to the public, and nature has fashioned a few nice baths as well. For pools in Reykjavík, see p. 133.

Health spas take things to the next level, with massages, beauty treatments, fitness classes, and so on. For spas in **Reykjavík,** see p. 133. The best spas outside Reykjavík are the **Blue Lagoon** (p. 164) in Reykjanes Peninsula, the **NLFÍ Rehabilitation and Health Clinic** (p. 175) in Hveragerði, and **Mývatn Nature Baths** (p. 268).

Pool Etiquette

Icelanders are especially strict about pool rules, especially when they pertain to hygiene. (Remember that Icelandic pools are far less chlorinated than pools abroad, so the concern over spreading germs is not paranoia.) To avoid stern looks of disapproval—or even lectures by pool monitors—follow the simple procedures below:

- **Leave shoes outside the locker room, unless a sign specifically permits you to take them in.**
- **Undress completely at your locker and then walk to the showers carrying your towel and swimsuit. Stash your towel by the showers.**
- **Shower first, and then put your suit on. Rarely will you find a shower curtain or stall to hide behind; if you feel shy, be assured that Icelanders are both respectful of privacy and very nonchalant about this everyday routine. (Also, be prepared for voluntary nudity in steam rooms, which are sex-segregated.)**
- **When showering, use soap, which is usually provided. Most shower rooms post a notorious sign—often photographed by visitors—depicting a human body, with red blotches over the "trouble areas" requiring particular attention.**
- **Don't go down water slides headfirst.**
- **After your swim, shower again and dry off before entering the locker room. Dripping on the locker room floor is frowned upon.**

RAFTING

Iceland has four glacier-fed rivers that are ideal for white-water rafting amid glorious scenery. For trips on the **Hvitá**—in the Golden Circle area, about an hour from Reykjavík—see p. 162. For trips on the **Eystri-Jökulsá** and **Vestari-Jökulsá**—both near Skagafjörður in northwest Iceland—see p. 242. Tours on these three rivers cater to most temperaments and ability levels, but the most experienced (and adrenaline-addicted) rafters head to the **Hólmsá** in south Iceland, 230km (143 miles) from Reykjavík. Hólmsá tours are run by **Arctic Adventures** Laugavegur 11, Reykjavík (✆ **562-7000;** www.adventures.is; only for experienced groups, with a minimum age of 18, and by advance booking only). The most popular trip is the 8-hour day tour from Reykjavík, with 5 hours on **Hvítá,** which goes for 10,990kr (May 20 until August).

ROCK CLIMBING

Iceland is not a major rock-climbing destination because its rock faces tend to be crumbly and insecure. You'll still find plenty of established routes, all detailed at **www.outdoors.is/rock-climbing-areas**. Further inquiries or requests for private guides should be directed by e-mail to the **Icelandic Alpine Club** (info@isalp.is); their website, **www.isalp.is**, is scheduled to have extensive information posted in English. The Alpine Club plans some expeditions for members, and visitors who are serious climbers can often schmooze their way into being invited. **Klifurhúsið,** Skútuvogur 1g, at Holtavegur (✆ **553-9455;** www.klifurhusid.is; May 20–Aug Mon–Thurs 5–10pm, Fri 4–8pm, Sat noon–6pm. Sept–May 19 Mon and Wed 5–10pm, Tues and Thurs 3–10pm, Fri 4–9pm) is Reykjavík's only place for indoor climbing. Climbs cost 700kr plus 200kr for shoe rental.

Arctic Adventures, Laugavegur 11, Reykjavík (✆ **562-7000;** www.adventures.is), leads a 4-hour climbing tour to a vertical rock face in Hvalfjörður, an hour north of Reykjavík. Tours cost 12,990kr and run from April to November—when the weather cooperates—with a four-person minimum—if you're less than four, see if you can combine groups with others who are signed up. No experience is necessary, and the minimum age is 12. More challenging trips can be arranged on request.

SCUBA DIVING & SNORKELING

Iceland's top two diving sites feature some fish sightings, but the main attractions are geological formations quite unlike the scenery typically found in warmer waters. The most popular site is **Silfra,** a deep, dramatic fissure at the bottom of Lake Þingvallavatn, next to Þingvellir National Park. Þingvallavatn's waters are so clear that divers experience a heady flying sensation as they plunge through the waters. The other main site, in the ocean near Akureyri, is **Strýtan,** a 55m-high (180 ft.) limestone pillar formed by a geothermal spring 70m (246 ft.) beneath the surface. Another diving highlight is *El Grillo,* an English oil tanker sunk by a German air raid on Seyðisfjörður during World War II.

The only diving-tour operator in Iceland is **DIVE.S,** Skipasund 85, Reykjavík (✆ **663-2858;** www.dive.is). All participants must be certified for diving in a dry suit; if you want to learn in Iceland, DIVE.IS offers a 4-day certification course for 74,990kr. Day tours from Reykjavík—either to Silfra or the ocean off Reykjanes

Peninsula—are 29,900kr. Multi-day tours of Iceland's best diving sites, with some sightseeing thrown in, range from 123,500kr to 312,500kr, not including lunches and dinners.

For non-divers, DIVE.IS offers a 5-hour **snorkeling** tour of Silfra from Reykjavík for 14,900kr.

SNOW SPORTS

Icelanders are just as passionate about their snow activities as any other Scandinavian country, especially in the north and Westfjords where the main ski areas are located.

Apart from the more traditional cross-country and downhill skiing, snowboarding is an increasingly popular activity, with many of the resorts building ramps and big jumps and holding competitions. Other options include: Telemark skiing, backcountry skiing, and ski mountaineering.

Downhill skiers can find some perfectly nice diversions, and the scenery, sometimes with views across fjords, often compensates for deficiencies in slope lengths and vertical drops. (Skiers that are more cautious may even appreciate Icelandic slopes' lack of trees.) The season runs from November until April, though conditions are most reliable from February to early April. Because of limited winter daylight, the major slopes are floodlit and have extended evening hours.

Some smaller towns, such as Dalvík and Siglufjörður, have ski lifts on local mountains.They might not satisfy experts, but are great for beginners; ask at local tourist information offices for more details. The largest ski area in Iceland is **Bláfjöll** (✆ **530-3000;** www.skidasvaedi.is; day pass 2,200kr adults, 650kr children; call ahead for opening hours and conditions), 33km (21 miles) southeast of Reykjavík, off Route 417. Bláfjöll has 15 lifts, a snowboard course, cross-country tracks, equipment rental, a snack bar, and a ski school on weekends. When Bláfjöll is open, one daily bus leaves for the slopes from the Mjódd bus terminal at Þönglabakka 1 in southeast Reykjavík (Mon–Fri 5:20pm, returning from Bláfjöll at 9:05pm; Sat–Sun 12:40pm, returning from Bláfjöll at 6pm), and several buses connect Mjódd to downtown.

The two other notable ski areas—both with equipment rental and cafes—are **Tungudalur/Seljalandsdalur** (✆ **456-3793;** www.isafjordur.is/ski), near Ísafjörður in the Westfjords, and **Hlíðarfjall** (✆ **462-2280;** www.hlidarfjall.is), near Akureyri in the north (for more on Hlíðarfjall, see p. 256). Tungudalur/Seljalandsdalur is actually two areas, the latter is a cross-country park. The former has two main lifts and a children's lift on treeless slopes and hosts Iceland's biggest skiing event, **Ski Week (Skíðavikan);** see p. 216. It also has rentals and a cafe.

The ski touring season generally runs from January through June, with glacier traverses more prevalent later in the season. Touring skis now come in a bewildering variety of forms, from traditional cross-country (aka Nordic) skis to heavier, wider Telemark skis and stubby mountaineering skis that convert into a kind of snowshoe.

The **Icelandic Alpine Club,** Skútuvogur 1g, Reykjavík (no phone; www.isalp.is; info@isalp.is), posts ski touring information on its website, and can answer questions if you're planning an expedition on your own.

Tour Operators

Borea Adventures, Hlíðarvegur 38, Ísafjörður (✆ **899-3817;** www.boreaadventures.com), offers two backcountry winter tours in the Westfjords. The first is a 6-day training course in winter mountaineering, starting in early March, for 196,000kr; some nights are spent in guesthouses, and others are spent in snow caves or igloos that you construct yourself. The second, with 10 departures from March to May, is a 6-day trip into Hornstrandir Nature Reserve aboard a 18m (60-ft.) yacht, with daily excursions on skis, snowshoes, snowboards—whatever you like—and the yacht stashes for exploring the fjords, inlets and sea cliffs. The cost is 239,000kr.

All year round, **From Coast to Mountains,** Hofsnes Farm, Öræfi (✆ **894-0894;** www.oraefaferdir.is), offer extra-challenging 15-hour ascents of Hvannadalshnúkur, Iceland's highest peak, on Vatnajökull east of Skaftafell. If conditions are right, participants can ski all the way down from the summit almost to sea level—a distance of 11km (7 miles). Departures are by arrangement, and the cost is 35,000kr per person for three to six people, 50,000kr per person for two, and 75,000kr for one.

Icelandic Mountain Guides, Vagnhöfði 7b, Reykjavík (✆ **587-9996;** www.mountainguide.is), escorts the most epic cross-country skiing tours, with set departures in March and April. Possibilities include a 10-day expedition through Sprengisandur (199,000kr), and a 9-day traverse of Vatnajökull (192,000kr).

Útivist, Laugavegur 178, Reykjavík (✆ **562-1000;** www.utivist.is), offers the best selection of well-priced cross-country ski tours. Day trips from Reykjavík leave every Sunday from mid-January to mid-March, for only 5,200kr. Longer excursions—available from January to July—head to Þórsmörk, Strútur, Mýrdalsjökull, Drangajökull, Vatnajökull, and other popular destinations. The website does not list trips in English, but you can skim the Icelandic listings by clicking on "*Ferðaáætlun*" (itineraries), "*Dagsferðir*" (daytrips) or "*Lengri Ferðir*" (longer trips).

VOLCANOES

With the eruption of **Eyjafjallajökull,** the volcano whose ash cloud closed the skies across Europe in spring 2010, volcano tourism has hit the big time. If you're reading this as smoke plumes from any one of a number of possible volcanos fill the sky outside your hotel window, you might tomorrow find a tour being arranged that could get you up close. There are various volcano-friendly operators across the country, while others can be found in specific chapters.

Tour Operators

Glacier Guides (✆ **571-2100;** www.glacierguides.is), is one of the biggest, with super truck rides to the best possible viewpoints. **Extreme Iceland** (✆ **565 9320;** www.extremeiceland.is) is similar, with Super Jeep rides to the volcanic areas. Norðurflug (✆ **562-2500;** www.nordurflug.is) operates stunning helicopter tours over active volcanoes.

WHALE-WATCHING

Whale-watching tours have taken off in recent years, partly in response to all the publicity raised by Iceland's return to whale hunting (see "The Saga of Icelandic Whaling" box, p. 275). The season runs from late April to early October; expect to pay up to 7,700kr for 3-hour tours. The most common sightings are minke whales—which are not particularly huge or entertaining—but lucky tour-goers also spot humpback whales, blue whales, orcas, sei whales, fin whales, white-beaked dolphins, and harbor porpoises.

The regional chapters of this book provide tour information for all the major whale-watching launch points: Reykjavík (p. 135); Keflavík, on Reykjanes Peninsula (p. 166); Ólafsvík, on Snæfellsnes Peninsula (p. 188); Dalvík near Akureyri (p. 258), and Húsavík (p. 272). Húsavík is the most popular launch point, with a slight edge in dramatic sightings.

SUGGESTED ITINERARIES

5

Advance planning can save you a lot of grief in Iceland. From mid-June until the end of August, places to stay and tours often fill up, and knowing some things in advance, such as if and when you'll have a rental car—and whether it will have 4WD—will affect your itinerary.

We also suggest allowing for some free time in your itinerary. In Iceland, the factors most likely to derail an overbooked itinerary are the weather and weather-based cancellations of domestic flights. Free time is also useful for when you find a place you'd like to explore more thoroughly or for when a local fisherman suddenly offers you a free boat trip around a nearby island, as has happened in our experience.

To jumpstart your planning, a few Iceland itineraries are suggested below. Others are found throughout the book, just waiting for you to string them together—we've even known people to flag all the swimming pools and hot springs for an itinerary, treating this pool-crazed country as a giant (albeit non-tropical) resort.

THE BEST OF ICELAND IN 4 DAYS

Word is getting around that Iceland is great for casual 3- or 4-day escapes. The basic components of an Iceland long weekend are Reykjavík and excursions from Reykjavík, often including the Blue Lagoon spa. Every night of this itinerary is spent in Reykjavík. In high season, make sure to call a few days ahead for dinner reservations (and for in-water massages at the Blue Lagoon).

Day 1: Reykjavík

If you're out and about before 9am, head to **Grái Kötturinn** (p. 119) for pancakes, bacon, and strong Icelandic coffee. Begin the sightseeing stage at the **Tourist Information Office** (p. 99), where you can pick up maps and brochures, and arrange tours and car rental if necessary. Nearby are three compelling sites—the 871±2 Settlement Museum (p. 125), the **City Cathedral (Dómkirkjan)** (p. 121) in **Austurvöllur Square,** and the **Harbor**

Iceland in 4 Days

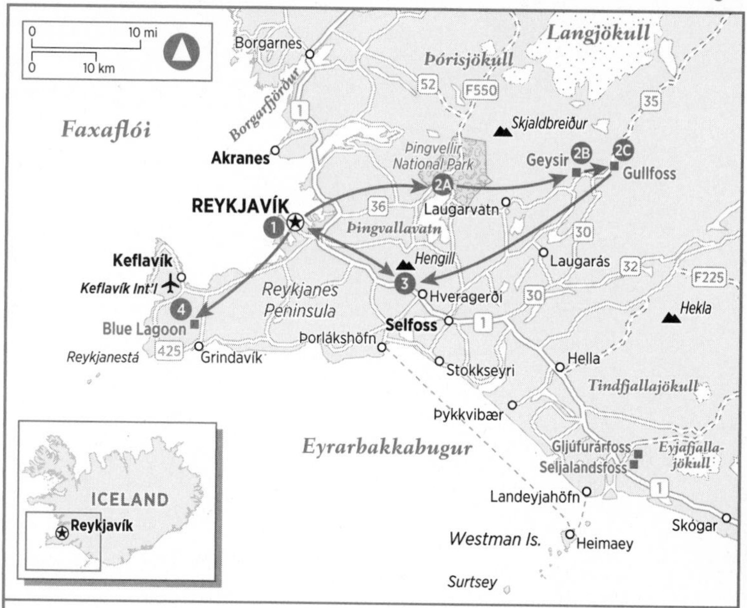

1 Reykjavík
2A Þingvellir
2B Geysir
2C Gullfoss
3 Mt. Hengill/ Reykadalur Valley
4 Blue Lagoon

House Museum (Hafnarhús) (p. 126), dedicated to contemporary art. All three open at 10am; if you need to kill time until then, stroll over to **Tjörnin Pond** (p. 126) and gaze at the enormous 3-D map of Iceland inside the **Town Hall (Ráðhús)** (p. 127).

For a casual lunch, visit **Sægreifinn** (p. 118) for lobster soup and a seafood kebab. After lunch, head to the eastern half of the city and survey Reykjavík's two main shopping streets, **Laugavegur** and **Skólavörðustígur.** Nearby is the **Culture House** (p. 125), with a wonderful exhibit of medieval manuscripts. To recharge, drop into the city's oldest cafe, **Mokka Kaffi** (p. 119) and try its famous waffles.

Skólavörðustígur leads uphill to Reykjavík's most iconic landmark, **Hallgrímskirkja** (p. 128), where you can ascend the elevator for a panoramic view. Don't miss the **Einar Jónsson Museum** (p. 128) next door, dedicated to Iceland's most renowned sculptor; weekend hours are 2 to 5pm. From here it's a half-hour stroll down Njarðargata and across the park to the **National Museum** (p. 128) south of Tjörnin Pond. Alternatively, skip the museum and catch bus 14 to **Laugardalslaug** (p. 134) for a rejuvenating taste of Iceland's geothermal bathing culture, and ply your hot tub companions for travel advice. (Be prepared for the ubiquitous question, "How do you like Iceland?".)

Enjoy an unforgettable dinner at **Fiskifélagið** (p. 114), followed by nightclub-hopping into the wee hours—but keep in mind that Reykjavík's night scene hardly *begins* until the wee hours—and a 2am hot-dog with "the lot" at **Bæjarins Bestu** (p. 117).

Day 2: The Golden Circle

An enormous wealth of day excursions depart from Reykjavík, but the most popular is the **"Golden Circle" tour** (p. 154) to **Þingvellir** (p. 155), the historic rift valley where the Icelandic parliament first convened in 930; **Geysir** (p. 160), the geothermal hotspot that lent its name to all geysers; and the majestic **Gullfoss waterfall** (p. 161). Sign up for an 8-hour bus tour (p. 155) or, for more flexibility, rent a car.

Day 3: Hot Springs Tour

The geothermal hot springs of **Reykjadalur Valley** (p. 176), tucked inside the scenic **Mt. Hengill hiking area,** near Hveragerði, are a bather's delight. The most memorable way to reach Reykjadalur is on horseback; **Eldhestar** (p. 175) offers a 9-hour tour from Reykjavík, with 5 or 6 hours in the saddle. (The small, manageable, good-natured Icelandic horse is great for beginners.) Alternatively, rent a car for the day and hike the route, or sign up for a group hike. The drive is less than an hour one-way, and the hike can be accomplished in as little as 2½ hours round-trip. Don't forget your swimsuit.

Day 4: The Blue Lagoon

The **Blue Lagoon spa** (p. 164)—built around a blue-green geothermal lake within a jet-black expanse of lava—is Iceland's most popular visitor destination. Sign up with tour company Netbus (p. 165) for transportation to the lagoon on the way to the airport, then bathe and exfoliate to your heart's content until it's time to catch your flight home. Allow 2 hours at the lagoon, more if you plan on spa treatments or eating at the restaurant.

THE BEST OF ICELAND IN ONE WEEK

A driving tour through south Iceland's natural wonders—capped off by a journey to the magnificent Westman Islands—is hard to beat. This itinerary is designed for summer; for off-season travel, see "Iceland in the Off Season," in chapter 2.

Day 1: Reykjavík

See p. 84 for our recommended Reykjavík itinerary, which includes a full day's worth of activity and an overnight stay.

Day 2: Höfn & Vatnajökull

Take the morning flight (weekdays only) to Iceland's southeast hub, **Höfn** (p. 332). Rent a car and drive to the intersection of Route F985 and the Ring Road to catch the 2pm **snowmobiling** tour (p. 330) on Europe's largest glacier,

Iceland in 1 Week

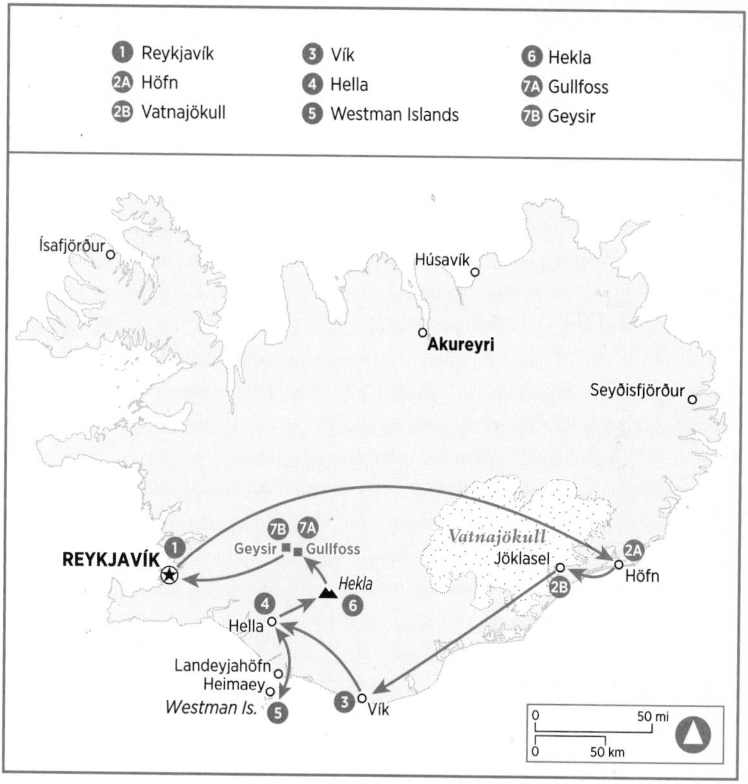

Vatnajökull (p. 330). (Alternatively, try cross-country skiing on Vatnajökull with outfitter **From Coast to Mountains;** p. 327.) Spend the night in Höfn or any farmstay close by.

Day 3: Höfn to Vík

Drive west along the southern coast from Höfn to **Vík** (p. 314), along what is probably the most mind-boggling stretch of the Ring Road. The first stop is the bizarre yet majestic **Jökulsárlón glacial lagoon,** full of parading icebergs. The next stop is **Skaftafell**, within the **Vatnajökull National Park,** for a 2-hour hike to the striking basalt formations of **Svartifoss** (p. 326). After a coffee break at **Systrakaffi** in the hamlet of **Kirkjubæjarklaustur** (p. 321), take an hour to peruse the rim of the **Fjaðrárgljúfur gorge** (p. 322). Spend the night in Iceland's southernmost village, Vík.

Day 4: Vík to Hella-Hvolsvöllur

The day starts with the best walk on Iceland's south coastline: a 3-hour jaunt along the **Reynisfjall sea cliffs** (p. 317). (If this is too much hiking, take a casual stroll on the black-sand beach next to Vík.) After resuming your trip westward on the Ring Road, detour on Route 215 south to the Reynisfjara **beach** (p. 317), just west of Reynisfjall, and witness the awe-inspiring sea cave **Hálsanefshellir.** The next stop is **Dyrhólaey** (p. 316), a promontory and nature reserve with bustling bird cliffs and an iconic rock archway over the sea. In the village of **Skógar,** investigate the towering **Skógafoss waterfall** (p. 315) and the prolific collection at Iceland's best **folk museum.** You are now very close to the site of the 2010 **Eyjafjallajökull** eruption. If you decide to take a glacial tour to see the eruption site up close (p. 306) take the later ferry to the Westman Islands (below), or wait until you return on Day 6. But even without booking a tour, you can see new features in the landscape caused by the eruption, such as lava formations and fissures. Head south at Hvolsvöllur (p. 305) to reach the port of **Landeyjahöfn** (p. 293) for the 6:30pm or 9:30pm ferry (7:30pm or 10:30pm weekends) to the spectacular **Westman Islands** (p. 291), where you'll spend 2 nights in the village of **Heimaey** (p. 293).

Day 5: Westman Islands

Take a boat trip into the sea caves, play a round of golf inside a volcano crater, stroll the coastlines spotting puffins, and investigate the after-effects of a devastating 1973 volcanic eruption. Street signs have been erected in the lava above where the corresponding streets once were, and a few houses, hauntingly half-swallowed by lava, are preserved.

Day 6: Westman Islands to Hekla

After another walk along the Westmans' dramatic coastline, take a morning or early afternoon ferry back to Landeyjahöfn and continue west. From the Ring Road west of Hella, take Route 26 northeast into **Þjórsárdalur valley** (p. 298) for views of Iceland's other notorious volcano, **Hekla** (p. 300). Head for the **Hekla Center** and check on the volcano's seismometer readings, then stay the night at **Leirubakki** hotel on the same property.

Day 7: Gullfoss & Geysir to Reykjavík

Turn on to Route 32, then walk or drive to the lithe and beautiful **Háifoss** (p. 300), Iceland's second tallest waterfall. After visiting **Þjóðveldisbærinn** (p. 299), a reconstruction of a Viking longhouse from the settlement era, drive to **Stöng** (p. 299) to see the ruins that Þjóðveldisbærinn was based on. From Stöng, a short walk extends to **Gjáin gorge** (p. 299), a lush and bewitching enclave. Turn right on Route 30 and proceed north to the majestic **Gullfoss** (p. 161). Ten minutes away is **Geysir** (p. 160), where you can witness eruptions of the **Strokkur** geyser. Return to Reykjavík for a final evening in the capital.

THE BEST OF ICELAND IN 2 WEEKS

With 2 weeks at your disposal, consider this epic driving tour around the whole country, with plenty of opportunities to leave the car behind and experience Iceland's great outdoors directly underfoot. This whirlwind itinerary circles the country clockwise, with Reykjavík as the start and finish point. Technically Iceland's Ring Road can be "done" in 3 days, but a week is a sensible minimum, and two weeks if you're adding the Westfjords as we are here. As with most driving tours of Iceland, this itinerary is

Iceland in 2 Weeks

possible in spring or fall, but is best experienced from early June until mid-September. A conventional rental car can easily handle the route, though a 4WD vehicle expands your options considerably, particularly for excursions into the interior. ***Note:*** Some museums and other sightseeing stops may be closed outside of summer.

Day 1: Reykjavík

The first day and night is spent in the Iceland's thriving first city; see p. 84 for our recommended full-day itinerary.

Day 2: Reykjavík to Stykkishólmur

Set off from Reykjavík around 9am and drive 74km (46 miles) north of Reykjavík to the **Settlement Center** (p. 183) in Borgarnes, for an entertaining multimedia primer on early Icelandic history. Then it's time to explore the beautiful **Snæfellsnes Peninsula.** From the village of **Arnarstapi** (p. 191), on the peninsula's south coast, sign up for a snowmobile tour of **Snæfellsjökull glacier** (p. 192), then take a 2-hour walk along the sculpted lava coastline between Arnarstapi and

Hellnar, where you can stop for afternoon tea at the little shoreside cafe **Fjöruhúsið** (p. 198) overlooking a cavernous lava archway. Stroll through **Djúpalónssandur,** a picturesque beach tucked inside a rocky cove, and drive through the gnarled lava field **Berserkjahraun** (p. 196). Spend the night in Stykkishólmur.

Day 3: Stykkishólmur to Breiðavík

Witness the uncountable islands and shallow marine habitat of **Breiðafjörður**—whilst eating shellfish straight from the shell—on the 11am **Unique Adventure boat tour** (p. 201) from Stykkishólmur. Then board the 3:30pm car ferry to **Brjánslækur** on the Westfjords' south coast. Forming the convoluted claw-shape in Iceland's northwest corner, the **Westfjords** (p. 203) have been criminally overlooked by the tourist industry. Drive to **Látrabjarg Peninsula** and stay overnight at **Breiðavík** (p. 209), winding down with a stroll on the white sands of the idyllic bay.

Day 4: Látrabjarg to Ísafjörður

Today's main event is a 2- to 3-hour hike along the rim of **Látrabjarg** (p. 206), Europe's largest sea cliff; sidle up to the ledges for wonderful views of the crashing surf and multitudes of puffins and other nesting birds. Stop at **Dynjandi** (p. 211)—an entrancing waterfall shaped like a wedding cake—en route to **Ísafjörður** (p. 213), the Westfjords' appealing capital, where you'll spend the next 2 nights.

Day 5: Ísafjörður & Environs

Having spent the last 3 days driving quite intensely, change pace with a day excursion to **Hornstrandir** (p. 225), Iceland's most wild and pristine coastal nature reserve. Walk through diversely vegetated meadows and tundra, observe native Arctic foxes, and inspect the eerie remnants of abandoned settlements. (For the most part, day tours of Hornstrandir are practical only in July and Aug, but there are plenty of alternatives such as a boat trip out to the nearby **Vigur** Island, p. 220.) For dinner, enjoy a generous dish of pan-fried fish at **Tjöruhúsið** restaurant (p. 218) next to the Heritage Museum.

Day 6: Ísafjörður to Hólmavík

Drive along the winding coastline of **Ísafjarðardjúp Bay** to the **Heydalur Country Hotel** (p. 220), and chat up the resident parrot over lunch in a converted barn. Choose among Heydalur's recreational activities—sea kayaking, horseback riding, fishing, and hiking—relaxing afterward in the natural geothermal pool. Cross the "neck" of the Westfjords to Hólmavík, where you can grab a bite to eat before driving a short 12km (7 miles) south and turning in for the night at **Kirkjuból** guesthouse (p. 212).

Day 7: Hólmavík to Akureyri

Prepare for the lengthy drive (330km/205 miles) to Akureyri—Iceland's northern capital—by taking a refreshing morning stroll across the road from Kirkjuból. Those rocks sticking out of the water will probably turn out to be seals, so keep your camera ready. Back on the road, once at **Varmahlíð** (p. 234), in the **Skagafjörður region,** turn left on Route 75 toward Sauðárkrókur. Not far ahead is **Glaumbær folk museum** (p. 236), the best of Iceland's many museums dedicated to preserving 19th-century turf-roofed farmhouses, which are vital repositories of Icelandic cultural memory (closing time is 6pm). Leaving the Skagafjörður region, the Ring Road ascends through a gorgeous mountain pass surrounded by spiky, serrated ridges. Reach **Akureyri** (p. 245) by dinnertime.

Day 8: Akureyri

Begin with a late breakfast at the **Bláa Kannan** cafe (opens 9am) on the main shopping street Hafnarstræti. Visit the **Akureyri Art Museum,** the **Akureyri Church,** with its distinctive and appealingly grandiose Art Deco twin spires, and Einar Jónsson's poignant 1901 sculpture **The** Outlaw **(Útlaginn).** Head 10km (6¼ miles) south of Akureyri on Route 821 to visit the **Christmas House** (p. 262) for some summer Christmas cheer and cinnamon-coated almonds. Visit the outdoor restroom here, it's hilarious. Back in Akureryi, wind down with the massaging water jets at the **Akureyri Swimming Pool**. Dine at **Strikið**, where you can enjoy views of the city and the mountains across the fjord.

Day 9: Akureyri to Mývatn

On your way out of Akureyri, stop at **Safnasafnið,** an innovative art museum seeking to transcend the divide between contemporary and folk art (opens at 10am). The next road stop, 50km (31 miles) from Akureyri, is the elegant **Goðafoss waterfall** (p. 263). Backtrack 4km (2¼ miles), and turn right on Route 85 north to **Húsavík** (p. 272), Iceland's **whale-watching** mecca. (Call ahead if the weather is iffy.) Buy your boat tickets, then bone up before the tour at the **Whale Museum.**

After the 3-hour excursion, head for the **Húsavík** Museum or the **Phallological Museum**. Stock up on groceries before dining at one of Húsavík's two best restaurants, **Gamli Baukur** and **Salka.** Head back south on Route 85, then take Route 87 to **Reykjahlíð village** (p. 265) on **Lake Mývatn,** where you'll spend the next 2 nights.

Day 10: Mývatn–Krafla

Today is devoted to sampling the geological marvels of **Mývatn** (p. 263) and **Krafla** (p. 263). Drive first to **Grjótagjá,** an eerie fissure and geothermal vent, then take an hour to climb to the rim of **Hverfell,** a tephra explosion crater. Drive on to **Dimmuborgir lava field**—or, if you feel like a more challenging hike, descend the south side of Hverfell down to Dimmuborgir. Don't miss **Kirkjan** ("The Church") lava archway—the clearly marked Kirkjuvegur trail will take you right through it. Continue circling Mývatn, until you reach the **Skútustaðagígar** pseudocraters for another 30-minute ramble. Tireless visitors can add the 2-hour round-trip hike up **Vindbelgjarfjall** to survey the day's triumphs thus far.

Drive east of Mývatn to **Hverir** (p. 267), pinch yourself to make sure this hellish geothermal hotspot is not a bizarre Martian dream, then head into Krafla and spend an hour exploring the strange and beautiful **Leirhnjúkur lava field** (p. 268). On your way back to Mývatn, enjoy a rejuvenating swim in the mineral-rich waters of **Mývatn Nature Baths** (p. 268). At 6pm, drop into **Vogafjós Cowshed Cafe** (p. 272) and enjoy a homemade smoked trout treat, while cows are milked on the other side of a plate glass window. For dinner, reserve at **Hótel Reykjahlíð** or the more casual **Gamli Bærinn** (p. 272).

Day 11: Mývatn to Seyðisfjörður

The next fuel stop is a long way off, so fill the tank before setting out and confirm with staff that road conditions to Dettifoss are suitable. About 36km (22 miles) east of Reykjahlíð, exit the Ring Road on to Route 864 and proceed 32km (20 miles) to **Dettifoss** (p. 283), Europe's mightiest waterfall. From Dettifoss, hike 1.5km (1 mile) to the more understated **Selfoss falls** (p. 283).

Return to the Ring Road and continue east. In clear weather you should have fantastic views south to **Herðubreið,** voted Iceland's most-loved mountain in a national poll. Sixteen kilometers (10 miles) east of the Route 864 junction, turn right on Route 901 and proceed 8km (5 miles) to **Möðrudalur** for lunch at the **Fjalladýrð cafe** (p. 365). Ask about road conditions further ahead on Route 901, to help choose the best route to **Sænautasel** (p. 365), a reconstructed turf farm serving coffee and pancakes in the middle of Nowheresville. Keep this place in mind on the final day of the trip as you pass through the farmland that endured the most ashfall during the 2010 Eyjafjallajökull eruption—Sænautasel fared much worse and was abandoned in 1875 after the Askja eruption fouled the area with ash.

From Sænautasel, return to the Ring Road and continue to **Egilsstaðir** (p. 346), the commercial hub of east Iceland. From here it's a 28km (17-mile) detour to the lovely coastal village of **Seyðisfjörður** (p. 354), with a breathtaking descent into the fjord. Dinner is at **Skaftfell** cafe/gallery, followed by a stroll along the waterfront.

Day 12: Seyðisfjörður to Höfn

Linger in Seyðisfjörður, walking among the 19th- and early 20th-century chalet-style kit homes. Devotees of outmoded technology should visit the old telegraph station at the **Technical Museum of East Iceland** (p. 356). After returning to Egilsstaðir, decide on a route to **Höfn** (p. 333), the regional hub of southeast Iceland. The Ring Road is the most direct. The longer route—which affords more Eastfjords coastal scenery—follows Route 92 to Reyðarfjörður, then Route 96 through a tunnel to Fáskrúðsfjörður and along the coast before it rejoins the Ring Road. Stops along Route 96 include **Steinasafn Petru** (p. 342), a magnificent rock collection in **Stöðvarfjörður** (p. 341) begun by a local woman in 1946. Both routes pass **Djúpivogur** (p. 340), a charming fishing village and the launch point for 4-hour boat trips to **Papey Island** (p. 341). Before dinner at Höfn's inviting **Kaffi Hornið** (p. 336), visit the supermarket on Vesturbraut to pick up lunch for tomorrow.

Day 13: Höfn to Vík

The 272km (169-mile) stretch of Ring Road from Höfn to Vík is a nonstop procession of stunning scenery. The first requisite stop is **Jökulsárlón** (p. 329), an otherworldly lake full of icebergs calved from **Vatnajökull,** Europe's largest glacier. After another 55km (34 miles), turn into **Vatnajökull National Park** at **Skaftafell** (p. 280) and bring your lunch along for a 2- to 3-hour hike to **Svartifoss waterfall,** the turf-roofed **Sel farmhouse,** and **Sjónarsker viewpoint,** overlooking an incredible panorama of majestic peaks, looming glaciers, and barren flood plains. In the tiny, isolated village of **Kirkjubæjarklaustur** (p. 321), recharge with afternoon tea or a taste of Iceland's infamous fermented shark (p. 324) at **Systrakaffi.** Shortly west of Kirkjubæjarklaustur, exit on Route 206 and proceed 3km (2 miles) to the lovely, contemplative **Fjaðrárgljúfur gorge** (p. 322) for an hour-long walk along the rim. For dinner in Vík, set out for the casual **Halldórs Café** (p. 321).

Day 14: Vík to Reykjavík

The morning is devoted to Vík's magnificent coastal environs. Allow 3 hours for the round-trip walk along the **Reynisfjall sea cliffs** (p. 317) to the viewpoint looking west toward **Mýrdalsjökull** and the **Dyrhólaey promontory** (p. 316), identified by its enormous, natural arch of rock. (If this is too much hiking, just stroll on Vík's black sand beach and gaze at the iconic **Reynisdrangar** sea stacks.) Back behind the wheel, take Route 215 from the Ring Road to the pebbly **Reynisfjara beach** (p. 317) on the western side of Reynisfjall, and peer into the spellbinding sea cave **Hálsanefshellir.** If you have time, Dyrhólaey is another enticing side trip, especially for birders. West of Vík, you're in the area most affected by the 2010 **Eyjafjallajökull** eruption, though it's easy to pass by without noticing the new features in the landscape if you're not familiar with the way it was before (see p. 306). Thirty-three kilometers (21 miles) from Vík is the **Skógar Folk Museum** (p. 315), Iceland's most glorious and affecting collection of folk artifacts. One kilometer (¾ mile) away is the hypnotic **Skógafoss waterfall** (p. 315). Now you can hightail it back to Reykjavík, with a detour to the **Fjöruborðið** (p. 179) lobster house in **Stokkseyri** for a valedictory feast.

HOME BASE REYKJAVÍK: 5 DAYS WITH THE FAMILY

Depending on the age of the children, the itineraries above are easily modified for families, especially going around the Ring Road, which could make an unforgettable family road trip. But sometimes basing the family in one place and taking day trips makes for a much more relaxed holiday. The order of days can be switched around based on everyone's mood and the latest weather report. This itinerary is designed for a family staying in Reykjavík for 5 days, exploring the city and going on a few adventures further afield. Keep in mind less central—hence less expensive—accommodation for this sort of trip, especially if you're hiring a car for the whole period.

Day 1: Árbær Museum & Reykjavík Zoo

Get your bearings in the city with a morning stroll along Reykjavík's two main shopping streets, **Laugavegur** and **Skólavörðustígur.** At the top of Skólavörðustígur, ascend the Hallgrímskirkja (p. 128) elevator for a panoramic view. From here you could walk down Njarðargata and across the park to the **National Museum** (p. 128)—which has multimedia exhibits and a dress-up room for children—but we recommend catching a bus to the **Árbær Museum** (p. 132) instead. People in period costume explain how to weave

5 Days with the Family

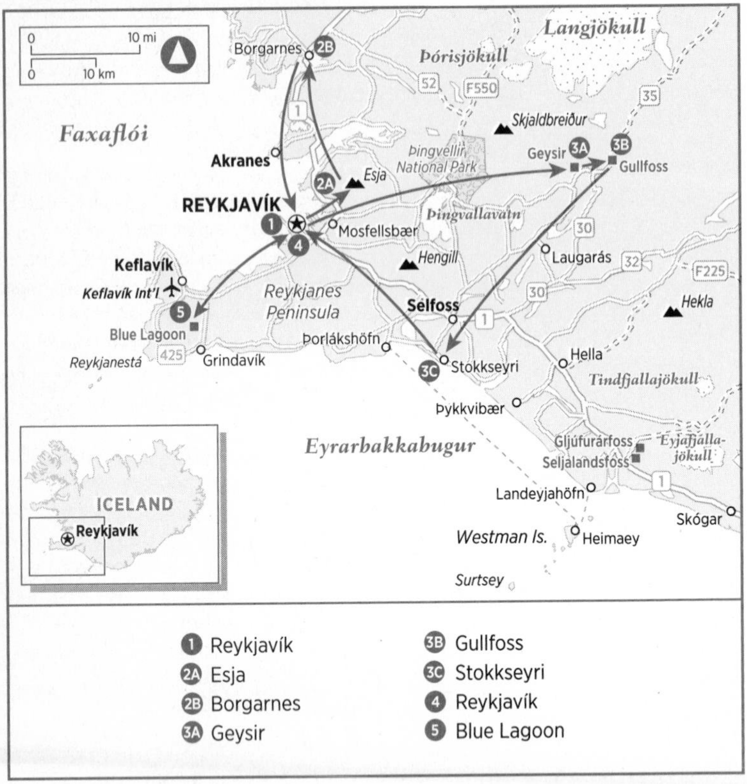

wool or smoke meat, and as the children explore the turf-roofed houses, Icelandic history is put in context without the yawn factor. (If you're reading this as you head down Njarðargata to the more convenient National Museum, note the modern residential rendition of a turf roof at the corner with Fjólugata so that you won't miss out entirely!)

Bus 19 will take you from Árbær Museum to the **Reykjavík Zoo** (p. 130)—ask the driver to let you know when to get off. Have lunch at the nearby botanical garden's greenhouse cafe, then meet the animals of Iceland; from domestic chickens and sheep, to wild reindeer and Arctic foxes. Check the animal petting schedule, posted each day, There's also a Family Park and "science world" for any tireless children, before calling it a day.

Day 2: Laxnes, Esja & Borgarnes

Rent a car for two days. Set off from Reykjavík on the Ring Road heading north to drive 74km (46 miles) to Borgarnes, but take a short detour at Route 36 to sign up for a 9:30am horse ride at **Laxnes Horse Farm** (p. 151). Next stop is **Esja,** Reykjavík's "home mountain" (p. 152) where you can stretch your legs while exploring the small wooded areas at the mountain's base. Head up the mountain until you're happy with the view or overcome by thoughts of lunch. Continue on to Borgarnes, heading for the **Center for Puppet Arts** (p. 183) which boasts an excellent cafe. Explore this unusual museum, then sit back and watch the kids put on their own puppet show while you have a coffee. Back in Reykjavík, enjoy a quick dip in the closest pool before dinner.

Day 3: Geysir & Stokkseyri

Gullfoss is a mighty and beautiful waterfall, but if that's not enough to impress children, **Geysir** is sure to get their attention. To follow the typical **"Golden Circle"** route (p. 154), take Route 1 north of Mosfellsbær, then turn right on Route 36. From Þingvellir, continue east on Route 36, turn left on Route 365, and turn left again on Route 37 in Laugarvatn; when Route 37 ends, turn left on Route 35. From there it's a short way to Geysir, where you can all marvel at the enormous jets of water suddenly shooting into the air, and another 10 minutes to Gullfoss. Watch your footing at both places and keep children close—the unimposing rope barriers belie the dangers of Geysir's multiple hot springs and the steep, deep gorge at Gullfoss.

Head south on Route 35 back to the Ring Road and then via Selfoss on to Route 34, turning left at Route 33 to the coastal town of **Stokkseyri** (p. 177). The artificial ice cave at the **Icelandic** Wonders museum (p. 177) will give you a glimpse of northern lights usually not afforded to summer visitors, as well as show you elves and trolls in their typical dwellings. You might be tempted by the **Ghost Center** next door, but beware that this is a truly scary place and not recommended for the under 12s. The **Töfragarðurinn** ("Magic Garden") theme park and zoo (p. 177) makes an excellent stop to let the children run around, play mini golf, climb a miniature castle, and get up close to the animals before jumping back in the car and heading back to Reykjavík.

Day 4: Sagas, Seaside, and Shopping

Pack swimming gear and towels but begin with a trip to the **Saga Museum** at **The Pearl** (p. 131). These lifelike models bring history to life with the aid of well-narrated audio guides. Have lunch at the cafe upstairs and go outside to admire a 360-degree view of the capital. From here, walk down through the wooded Öskjuhlíð hill, and across to **Nauthólsvík** beach (p. 130). Watch the children play on the white sand (imported!) from the comfort of the long hot tub. Who said Iceland wasn't a beach holiday destination? For a spot of shopping, catch a bus to **Kringlan** shopping mall (p. 140) where you can choose to leave your children (ages 3–9) at the **Adventure Land** child-minding area for an hour or two. From Kringlan you can take a longish but leisurely walk back to the heart of town via Miklatún Park, popping into **Kjarvalsstaðir** Art Museum (p. 129) for a peek at the works of Jóhannes Kjarval, one of Iceland's most admired artists (free for children under 18).

Day 5: The Pond to the Blue Lagoon

On your final day, begin by strolling over to **Tjörnin Pond** (p. 126) where you can feed the ducks and gaze at the enormous 3-D map of Iceland inside the **Town Hall (Ráðhús)** (p. 127). See if the children can work out where they've been, and show them (if you can find it!) where the big Eyjafjallajökull eruption happened in 2010. Sign up with tour company **Netbus** (p. 165) for transportation to the **Blue Lagoon spa** (p. 164) on the way to the airport, then bathe and exfoliate to your heart's content until it's time to catch your flight home. The children will especially enjoy covering each other in the white silica mud without knowing they're getting a health treatment. It's hard to omit this unique send-off from any itinerary in Iceland.

HIKING ICELAND

Iceland's most world-renowned trek—a 4-day route blessed with astonishing scenery—is the 4-day trek known as **Laugavegurinn** (p. 304), connecting the interior wonderland of **Landmannalaugar** (p. 301) to the alpine oasis of **Þórsmörk** (p. 311). Facilities along the route are hardly luxurious, but you can hire a tour company to transport your bags from mountain hut to mountain hut. The Laugavegurinn is passable from roughly the beginning of July to early September. Book the mountain huts well in advance.

Day 1: Reykjavík

See p. 84 for our full-day Reykjavík itinerary. You'll also need this day to stock up on **groceries** (and perhaps some last-minute supplies) since provisions are generally unavailable on the trail—if you are going with a tour group, check with the operator to see if food is provided.

Days 2 & 3: Landmannalaugar

Board the morning bus from Reykjavík to **Landmannalaugar,** whose rhyolite landscape is a photographer's dream. This wondrous hiking zone within **Fjallabak Nature Reserve** (p. 301) is one of the best in the country. Plan to spend 2 nights at the mountain hut run by Ferðafélag Íslands to allow yourself a leisurely day-and-a-half for exploring the region. Bathing in the natural hot springs near where you're staying is a perfect nightcap.

Days 4 to 7: The Laugavegurinn

Four days is the ideal amount of time to hike through this fabulous procession of interior scenery. The entire route is 55km (34 miles), with **mountain huts** spaced at roughly 14km (9-mile) intervals. You may be hankering for privacy by the time you reach Þórsmörk, so consider booking a private room at the **Húsadalur mountain hut** (p. 312) for your last night in the region.

Day 8: Back to Reykjavík

Enjoy another day hike (p. 313) in Þórsmörk before catching the 3pm bus back to Reykjavík for your final evening in the capital. Round out the evening with a meal at **Þrír Frakkar** (p. 115)—welcome back to the real world indeed—and prepare for your next-day departure back home.

Hiking Iceland

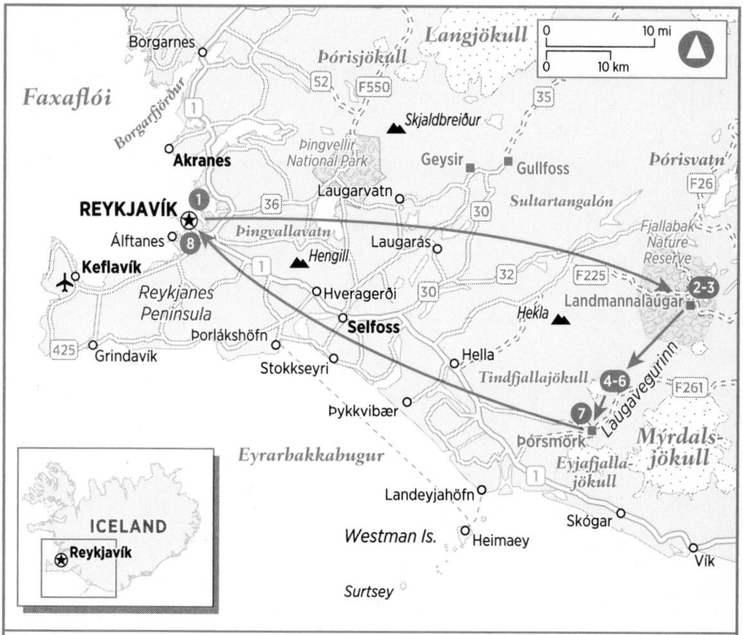

1 Reykjavík
2-3 Landmannalaugar
4-6 The Laugavegurinn
7 Þórsmörk
8 Reykjavík

6 REYKJAVÍK

Reykjavík, the world's northernmost capital, is more cosmopolitan than you can shake a martini at, yet the city also clings affectionately to its parochialism. Greater Reykjavík is home to more than half the country's population and almost all visitors to Iceland pass through the city, many venturing no further than the city limits before heading back to the airport. Reykjavík has become a destination in itself. Whether or not you're packing hiking boots, fishing rods, or zoom lenses, it's easy to fill a long weekend or a whole fortnight in Reykjavík.

For most of its history, Reykjavík suffered a backward reputation among European cities, but this has only intensified its heady sensation of newfound wealth and authority. Thirty years ago, no one even dreamed Reykjavík would become an international arbiter of hipness, especially in music and nightlife.

Despite its reputation for wild nights, Reykjavík by day is the most subdued of European capitals. Its cosmopolitan edge seems at odds with its squat, boxy architecture. It almost feels wrong to leave the world's problems so far behind: Iceland's urban life is virtually free of crime, homelessness, and pollution. Reykjavík is committed to sustainable development, with aggressive tree planting, home heating and electrical systems powered by underground hot springs—that faint egg smell in bathrooms is a natural by-product—and a few buses running on hydrogen fuel (look for steam emissions from the roof). One night a year, since 2006, the entire city turns off all lights for 30 minutes simultaneously. Sleepy children stand outside gazing up at the sky alongside their parents: Reykjavíkians paying tribute to the romance of their town's original, natural state.

Reykjavík hosts a multitude of festivals. Most events take place outside of summer, belying the widespread perception of Iceland as a one-season destination. See "When to Go," on page 31, for a schedule of annual events.

ORIENTATION

Arriving

BY PLANE International flights arrive at Keflavík International Airport, about 50km (31 miles) from town. (For Keflavík arrival information, see "Getting There," in chapter 3.) Taxis to Reykjavík cost around 12,000kr for up to 4 people, so most visitors come to town on the **Flybus** (✆ **580-5400;** www.re.is). Tickets are 1,950kr for adults, 950kr for children 12 to 15, and free for children 11 and under. Taxis and the Flybus are clearly positioned outside the arrival hall; both accept credit cards, but Flybus tickets must be purchased before exiting the terminal. The Flybus stops at the BSÍ bus terminal, almost all hotels and guesthouses, and the City Hostel. Call or check the Flybus website for a complete list of stops. Check with your accommodation if it doesn't appear on the list; but they usually offer a free transfer from the BSÍ terminal, or there might be a stop within easy walking distance. If that fails, you could still save money by taking the Flybus to the BSÍ terminal and catching a taxi from there. Flybus departures from Reykjavík to the airport are timed to coincide with departing international flights.

Domestic flights (and flights from Greenland and the Faeroe Islands) arrive at Reykjavík Airport, just south of the city. For more information on domestic air travel, see "Getting Around," in chapter 3.

BY FERRY No scheduled international ferries arrive in Reykjavík; ferries from Europe arrive at **Seyðisfjörður** on the east coast. For information on cruise ships, see "Getting There," in chapter 3.

Visitor Information

INFORMATION OFFICES

The main **Tourist Information Office** (Aðalstræti 2; ✆ **590-1510;** www.visit reykjavik.is; June–Sept 15 daily 8:30am–7pm; Sept 16–May Mon–Fri 9am–6pm; Sat–Sun 10am–2pm) is in the northwestern sector of the city, near the old port. On the premises is the fee-free **City Center Booking Service,** which can book places to stay, car rentals, and tours.

A smaller branch of the tourist information office is inside **City Hall (Ráðhús)** at Tjarnargata 11 (✆ **411-1000;** year-round Mon–Fri 8:30am–4:30pm, Sat noon–4pm; May 10–Sept 15, also Sun, noon–4pm).

The **Iceland Visitor Center,** Laugavegur 26 (✆ **511-2442;** fax 511-2443; www.icelandvisitor.com; June–Aug daily 9am–10pm, Sept–May daily 10am–6pm), is a privately run, brochure-packed travel agency that's very helpful with tours, car rentals, and other services, but they can't help with hotels.

ONLINE

Run by the city's tourist office, **www.visitreykjavik.is** has thorough, well-mapped listings of hotels, restaurants, museums, and sights, as well as a schedule of events. *What's On in Iceland* (**www.whatson.is**) covers dining, places to stay and city activities and events. *The Reykjavík Grapevine* (**www.grapevine.is**), a free English-language circular, is a useful guide to current happenings.

GETTING AROUND

BY BICYCLE Reykjavík is easily explored by bicycle and has a good network of bike paths. Riding on sidewalks and footpaths is widely tolerated, and most trails are illuminated in fall and winter. A free biking map is available at the Tourist Information Office (above). We recommend the popular route that takes you around the coastline and into the peaceful Elliðaár Valley.

The only major **bike rental** business in town is **Borgarhjól,** Hverfisgata 50 (✆ **551-5653;** www.borgarhjol.net; Mon–Fri 8am–6pm, Sat 10am–2pm). It carries high-quality Trek bicycles and provides studded tires in winter. Rates are 4,200kr per day with discounts for half days or longer rentals. There's an outpost at the City Hostel at Laugardalur (p. 111), and some other hotels also arrange bike rentals.

BY BUS Reykjavík's bus service **Stræto** (✆ **540-2700;** www.bus.is) is very reliable. The major bus hubs are Lækjartorg (in the city, at the north end of Lækjargata), Hlemmur (on the eastern end of Laugavegur), and the **BSÍ bus terminal** (Vatnsmýrarvegur 10; www.bsi.is) south of downtown. Free bus maps are available at www.bus.is (check out the impressive "Journey Planner" feature), the Tourist Information Office, and bus hubs. Most travelers use buses only to reach outlying hotels or sights such as the Pearl, Laugardalur Park, and the Árbær Museum. Local routes venture as far as the suburbs of Hafnarfjörður, Mosfellsbær, and Akranes (see chapter 7). Most long-distance routes leave from the BSÍ terminal.

Buses operate Monday to Saturday from 7am to midnight, and Sunday from 10am to midnight, with set departure times usually every 20 minutes, or every 30 minutes evenings, weekends, and on some routes during summer. The flat fare of 280kr for adults or 100kr for children 6 to 18 is collected on the bus. No change is given, so make sure you have the exact amount. Discounted books of 11 tickets for 2,500kr and 2-week passes *(gula kortið)* for 3,500kr are available at the bus hubs, shopping malls, and the Tourist Information Office (11-ticket books are also available on buses if you have the exact cash). Transfers *(skiptimiði)* are free within a certain timeframe (normally 45 min.) and must be requested from your first driver. The **Reykjavík Welcome Card** (p. 121) includes free unlimited bus travel for 1, 2, or 3 days.

BY CAR Reykjavík's narrow one-way streets and parking regulations discourage many drivers, but by international standards the city is quite negotiable. Public parking—marked on most tourist maps—usually requires buying a ticket at a kiosk and placing it on the dashboard. Meters vary in cost but are usually around 100kr per hour; fees must be paid from 10am to 6pm weekdays and from 10am to 2pm Saturday. Parking is free Sundays and evenings. One parking strategy is to simply park just outside the city's heart where there are no meters. For information on car rentals and driving in Iceland, see "Getting Around," in chapter 3.

BY FOOT Reykjavík is a good walking town, easily navigable on foot, with most of the tourist sites, restaurants, and shops concentrated along the central streets.

BY TAXI Taxis are expensive: meters start at 520kr, and a short ride across town is routinely 1,000kr. Sharing helps, as taxis charge per ride, not per passenger. The best taxi companies are **BSR Taxis** (✆ **561-0000**) and **Hreyfill** (✆ **588-5522**). Both accept credit cards inside the taxi. There is no need to tip (see chapter 13, p. 379, for more on tipping).

TOURS

Reykjavík Excursions A 2½-hour **"Reykjavík Grand Excursion"** bus tour daily at 1pm lets you "do" the waterfront, Hallgrímskirkja, the Pearl, and the National Museum all before afternoon tea. The price is 4,900kr for adults, half-price for children 12 to 15, and free for children under 12, including museum admission and pickup/dropoff service. To go at your own pace, choose the **"Hop On–Hop**

Off" tour, which runs 3 or 4 times a week (check website) June to August on open-topped double-deckers for 3,000kr adults, half-price for children 12 to 15, and free for children under 12. Sights include Hallgrímskirkja, the Pearl, the National Museum, the old port, Kringlan Mall, and Laugardalur Park. The bus completes the loop once each hour, so you can stop wherever you like and catch another bus an hour or two later. Your ticket is valid for 24 hours from the first use, so you can continue hopping the next morning. No advance purchase is necessary, though only cash is accepted onboard. Note that if you have no trouble navigating your way around on the regular city buses, buying a multi-pass (11 tickets stuck together, see p. 100) will probably end up cheaper and will allow more flexibility—for starters you don't have to use them all in one day.

BSÍ bus terminal and Hilton Reykjavík Nordica. ✆ **580-5400**. www.re.is.

Iceland Excursions The 2½-hour **"Greater Area Reykjavík Sightseeing"** bus tour, which leaves daily at 9am in summer, runs at a near-manic pace through sights outside the heart of the city, such as Hafnarfjörður (see chapter 7), Laugardalur Park, and the Ásmundur Sveinsson museum. The price, including hotel pickup and dropoff, is 420kr, half-price for children 12 to 18, and free for kids under 12.

Höfðatún 12, just east of Hlemmur bus station. ✆ **540-1313**. www.icelandexcursions.is.

Literary Walking Tours 🎁 On Thursdays at 5pm in July and August, the City Library sponsors free, little-known tours of Reykjavík, led by a literary critic or an actor. Tours, which last around 1½ hours, leave from the main branch and could include anything from the Settlement Museum (for a saga reading) to the cafe/nightclub Kaffibarinn (site of debauched scenes from the cult novel *Reykjavík 101*). Call ahead to make sure the time hasn't changed.

Tryggvagata 15. ✆ **563-1750**.

Goecco This upstart offers two walking tours daily from May to mid-September. Guides for the 1pm **"Reykjavík Free Walking Tour"** present a personal, opinionated outlook on city history and culture. The popular **"Haunted Walk of Iceland,"** kicking off at 8pm, focuses on ghost stories and lingers over the macabre, such as the grave of a 6-year-old accused of being the devil's child. What steers these tours clear of potential corniness is the guides' healthy infusion of modern skepticism. Each tour lasts 1½ to 2 hours, covers about 2km (1¼ mile) on foot, and leaves from the Tourist Information Center at Aðalstræti 2. Reservations are recommended, but you can just show up and pay in cash.

✆ **696-7474.** www.goecco.com. "Haunted Reykjavík" 2,500kr adults; 2,000kr seniors/students; children 11 and under free.

[FastFACTS] REYKJAVÍK

Airport See "Arriving," earlier in this chapter.

American Express American Express has no branch offices in Iceland.

Banks/Currency Exchange Banks are usually open Monday to Friday 9:15am to 4pm, or until 6:30pm in Kringlan Mall (p. 140). All banks change foreign currency and many have 24-hour ATMs.

Bike Rentals See "Getting Around," earlier in this chapter.

Car Rentals See "Getting Around," earlier in this chapter and "Getting Around Iceland," in chapter 3.

Cellphones See "Staying Connected," in chapter 3.

Doctors & Dentists See "Medical Help," below.

Drugstores Drugstores *(Apótek)* are usually open Monday through Friday 9am to 6 or 7pm, and Saturday to 4pm. Drugstores that stay open late include **Lyfog heilsa** (Háaleitisbraut 68 at Austurver, close to Kringlan Mall; ✆ **581-2101;** daily 8am–10pm) and **Lyfja Apótek** (Lágmúli 5, near Laugardalur Park; ✆ **533-2300;** daily 7am–1am).

Embassies See "Embassies & Consulates," p. 378.

Emergencies Dial ✆ **112** for ambulance, fire, or police. See also "Medical Help," below.

Grocery Stores/Supermarkets **Bónus** (Laugavegur 59 ✆ **562-8200** and Hallveigarstígur 1 ✆ **517-0425;** Mon–Thurs midday–6:30pm; Fri 10am–7:30pm; Sat 10am–6pm; Sun midday-6pm) is the best market in the city center. **10–11** markets are open 24 hours; a small branch is on Austurstræti 17 (✆ **552-1011**) and a larger one is at Barónsstígur 4 (corner of Hverfisgata; ✆ **511-5311**). At Kringlan Mall is **Hagkaup** (✆ **563-5200;** Mon–Wed 10am–8pm; Thurs 10am–9pm; Fri, Sat 10am–8pm; Sun midday–8pm).

Hospitals See "Medical Help," below.

Internet Access Many hotels offer Wi-Fi or guest terminals, and most cafes have free Wi-Fi. Otherwise, the cheapest Internet outlets are libraries (see below), usually 300kr per hour. The Tourist Information Office (p. 99) has Internet terminals; 30 minutes cost 350kr and 1 hour is 500kr.

Laundromat Reykjavík has no self-service laundromats. If you're near Laugardalur Park, you can use the machines in the City Hostel (p. 111). One centrally located laundry service is **Úðafoss** (Vitastígur 13, north of Laugavegur; ✆ **551-2301;** Mon–Thurs 8am–6pm; Fri 8am–6:30pm). The minimum charge is 2,150kr for up to 2kg (4.4 lb.) and goes up to 2,950kr for 5kg (11 lb.); they also do dry cleaning.

Libraries **The City Library** (Tryggvagata 15; ✆ **411-6100;** www.borgarbokasafn.is; Mon 10am–9pm; Tues–Thurs 10am–7pm; Fri 11am–7pm; Sat–Sun 1–5pm) has a large selection of books in English, but non-Icelanders can't sign them out. Internet access is also available.

Lost & Found This service is located in the **police station** at Borgartún 7b (✆ **444-1400;** Mon–Fri 10am–noon and 2–4pm). Bus: 12, 14, or 16.

Luggage Storage Hotels can usually store luggage; otherwise, use the **BSÍ bus terminal** (Vatnsmýrarvegur 10; ✆ **580-5400;** daily 4:30am–midnight). The charge is 500kr per item for the first 24 hours, 300kr each additional 24 hours.

Mail See "Post Offices," below.

Markets See "Grocery stores," above.

Medical Help For emergencies, dial ✆ **112.** The main 24-hour emergency room is at **National University Hospital,** Fossvogur (✆ **543-2000;** Bus: 11, 13, or 18). For non-emergencies, **standard hours** are 9am to 5pm Monday to Friday; doctors are on duty 24 hours at the National University Hospital (✆ **525-1000**) and during non-working hours at the **Kópavogur Medical Center,** Smáratorg 1 (✆ **1770;** Mon–Fri 5–11:30pm, Sat–Sun 9am–11:30pm; Bus: 2, 24, or 28). After 11:30pm, or on weekends and holidays, you can call for a telephone consultation, or possibly a "home visit." Standard appointment fees are around 4,000kr, but phone consultations are free. For **dental emergencies,** call ✆ **575-0505.**

Pharmacies See "Drugstores," above.

Police For emergencies call ✆ **112.** The main

station (✆ **444-1000**) is at Hverfisgata 113–115, opposite the Hlemmur bus station.

Post Offices Post offices are open 9am to 6pm weekdays. The central branch is at Pósthússtræti 5, at the corner of Austursræti (✆ **580-1200**). You can also buy stamps at some bookstores and tourist shops.

Restrooms Public coin-operated restrooms (50kr) are in a few downtown locations, indicated by "WC" icons on tourist maps. City Hall (p. 99) has free restrooms, and most cafes are tolerant of walk-ins.

Taxis See "Getting Around," above.

Telephone Public phones are sparse in Reykjavík, but you can find them at post offices, on the southwest corner of Austurvöllur Square, and on Lækjargata. They accept coins or phone cards, which are available at post offices, filling stations, kiosks, and convenience stores.

Tipping Tipping is not expected. See p. 379, chapter 13.

WHERE TO STAY

With seemingly every Reykjavík hotel constantly in a state of renovation or expansion, it's no surprise that nightly rates have been on the rise too. The upside is that you can expect high standards, and big discounts in the off season. High season is longer in Reykjavík than in the rest of Iceland, so you are likely to encounter peak prices and limited availability in May, June, and September as well as during the country's peak months of July and August. Sadly, the budget-friendly practice of "sleeping-bag accommodation"—bringing your own bedding and paying half-price—is almost gone in the city.

Places are generally classed as either a hotel or a "guesthouse," which is an Icelandic rendition of the B&B. (For more on accommodation types, see "Tips on Accommodations," in chapter 3.) As offerings are similar at both, price and location are more likely to influence your choice. Be aware that many tour packages automatically place unsuspecting visitors outside the heart of the city. Conversely, light sleepers in downtown hotels may wonder why they paid more for the privilege of being amidst the late-night revelry.

In the Amenities section following each review below, "Flybus" (see "Arriving," earlier) indicates airport pickup and dropoff; but note that Flybus will often arrange a free transfer anyway, so have the name and address handy when you're getting your Flybus ticket.

Central Reykjavík

VERY EXPENSIVE

Hótel Borg ★★★ Designed by Guðjón Samúelsson, the same architect responsible for Hallgrímskirkja, the Borg opened in 1930 as Iceland's first luxury hotel. Major 2007 renovations affirm the hotel's Art Deco roots—call it a streamlined, modern Scandinavian update on the style's bold outlines and geometric shapes. Renovated fifth-floor standard rooms have snazzy new mattresses and TVs without the extra cost. If these aren't available, ask for a room in the back; Austurvöllur Square can be a zoo on weekend nights. The stupendously luxurious "tower suite" in the spire, complete with living room and a 360-degree view of the city, is usually booked a year in advance.

Where to Stay & Dine in Reykjavík

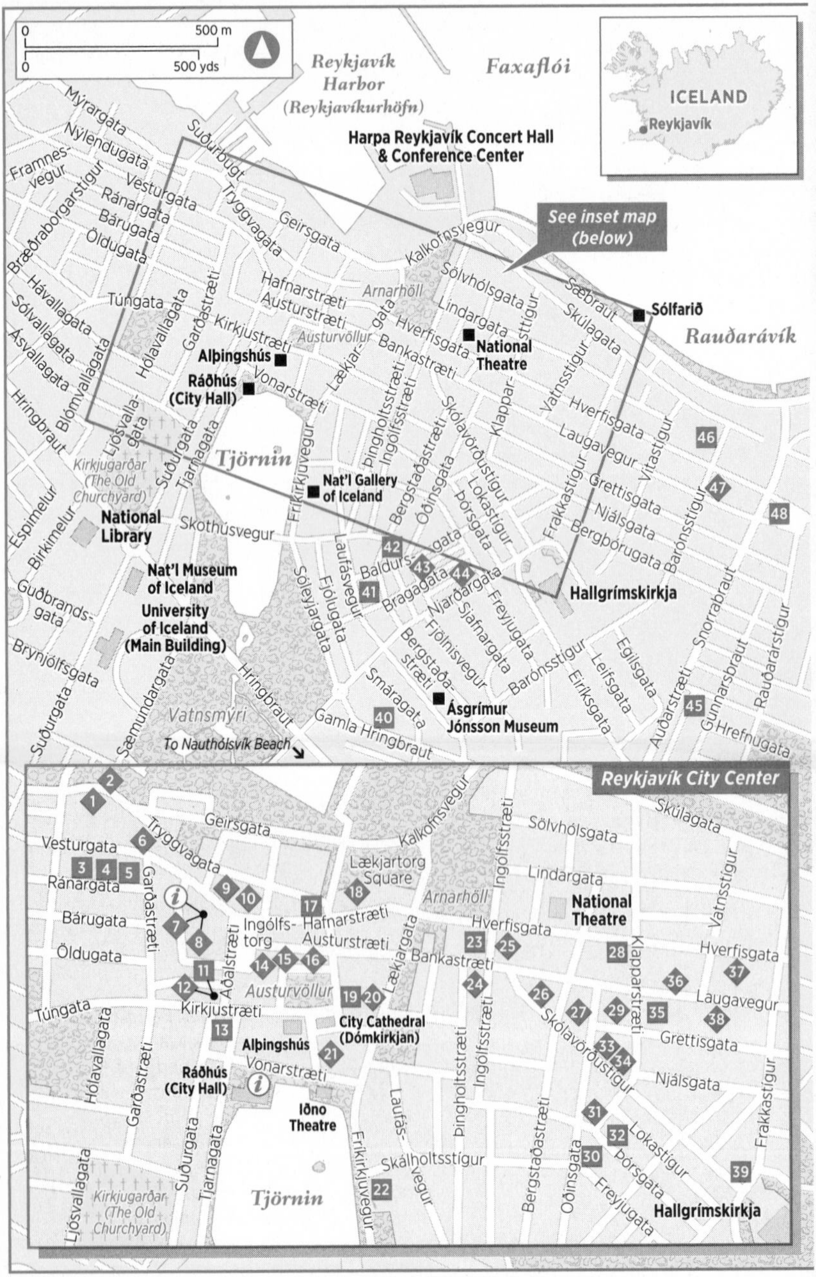

ACCOMMODATIONS ■

Álfhóll Guesthouse **4**
Anna's Guesthouse **40**
Baldursbrá Guesthouse **41**
Butterfly Guesthouse **3**
Castle House & Embassy Luxury Apartments (Kastallin Hotel) **22**
CenterHotel Klöpp **28**
Fosshótel Baron **46**
Grand Hotel Reykjavík **53**
Guesthouse Óðinn **30**
Guesthouse 101 **48**
Hilton Reykjavík Nordica **54**
Hotel Björk **51**
Hótel Borg **19**
Hótel Frón **35**
Hotel Holt **42**
Hotel Leifur Eiríksson **39**
Hotel Óðinsvé **32**
Hótel Phoenix **49**
Hótel Reykjavík Centrum **11**
Hótel Vík **56**
Kríunes Guesthouse **52**
Metropolitan Hotel **5**
101 Hotel **23**
Radisson Blu 1919 Hotel **17**
Reykjavík City Hostel **55**
Salvation Army Guesthouse **13**
Snorri's Guesthouse **45**

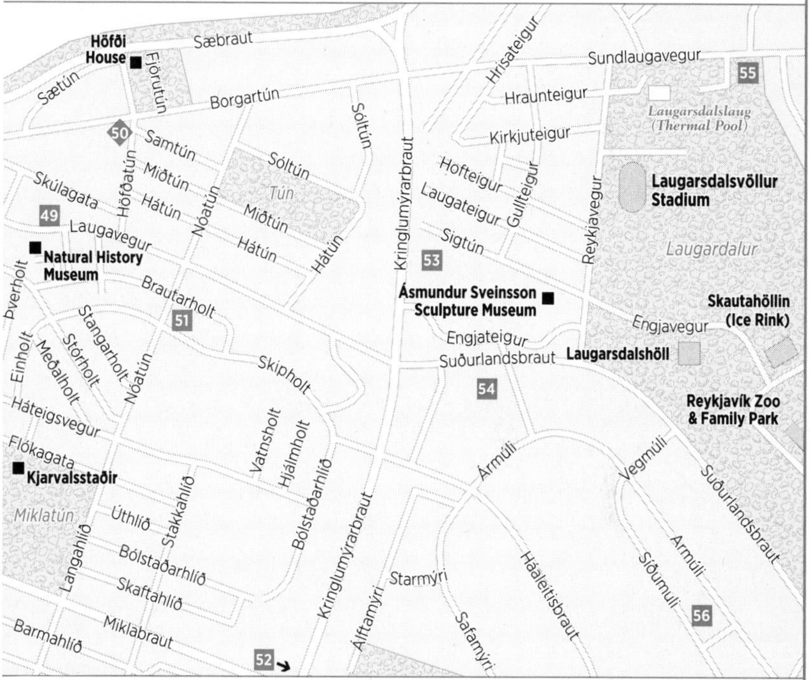

DINING ◆

Á Næstu Grösum **29**
Argentina **47**
Austur Indía Fjélagið **37**
Bæjarins Bestu **18**
C is for Cookie **31**
Cafe Paris **16**
Einar Ben **14**
Eldsmiðjan **44**
Fiskifélagið **9**
Fjalakötturinn **12**
Geysir Bistro & Bar **8**
Grái Kötturinn **25**
Hamborgarafabrikkan **50**
Icelandic Fish & Chips **1**
Jómfrúin **20**
Kaffitár **24**
Krúa Thai **6**
Mokka Kaffi **26**
Restaurant Reykjavík **10**
Sægreifinn **2**
Sandholt Bakarí **38**
Sjávarkjallarinn (Seafood Cellar) **7**
Skólavörðustígur **34**
Té og Kaffi **33**
Thorvaldsen **15**
Tíu Dropar **36**
Vegamót **27**
Við Tjörnina **21**
Þrír Frakkar **43**

Pósthússtræti 11, on Austurvöllur Square. ✆ **551-1440.** Fax 551-1420. www.hotelborg.is. 56 units. May–Sept and Dec 28–Jan 2, 46,000kr–55,000kr double; 71,000kr–110,000kr tower suite. Rates 25% lower Oct 1–Dec 27 and Jan 3–Apr 30 except suites. Children under 12 stay free in parent's room. AE, DC, MC, V. Limited street parking. **Amenities:** 4-star restaurant; bar; concierge. *In room:* TV/DVD, CD player, DVD/CD library at reception, minibar, hair dryer, free Wi-Fi.

Hotel Holt ★★ The reputation of this intimate four-star hotel, situated on a central but quiet residential street, rests on its Icelandic art collection and first-rate French restaurant. The original owner Þorvaldur Guðmundsson died in 1998, but rooms and common spaces are adorned with his prodigious stockpile of paintings and drawings, including several by Jóhannes S. Kjarval. Rooms are a bit small and not all that luxurious but are all tastefully decorated with dark wood furniture. The library, sitting room, and lounge are especially appealing. The restaurant, appropriately called "The Gallery," has the most impressive art display of all, and a dress code is enforced (main courses 3,900kr–5,490kr). Hotel staff is accommodating, and downtown is just a 5-minute walk.

Bergstaðastræti 37. ✆ **552-5700.** Fax 562-3025. www.holt.is. 40 units. Jun–Aug 30,200kr double; 37,000kr–43,400kr and up junior suite and suite. Rates 11%–12% lower Sept–May. AE, DC, MC, V. Free parking. **Amenities:** Restaurant; bar; small health club/massage room; free access to nearby fitness studio; concierge; room service. *In room:* TV, hair dryer, minibar, free Wi-Fi.

Hotel Óðinsvé ★★★ Like the Hotel Holt nearby, the Óðinsvé is an ideally situated mid-size luxury hotel—close to the city's heart, but mercifully quiet on weekends. The Óðinsvé, however, has undergone extensive renovations for a sleeker, more contemporary look. (Indoor plants have replaced all the stuffed seabirds.) Rooms vary considerably in size, though almost all are full of light. Standard rooms on the first three floors have common balconies and a patio. Double deluxe rooms on the third and fourth floors have private balconies, and the fourth floor, added in 2004, has especially good views of Mount Esja and Hallgrímskirkja. All double deluxe rooms have bathtubs, though not all junior suites do. The restaurant, **Brauðbær,** is good when it's open, but is only open for dinner three nights a week and has been known to "take a holiday" for extended periods even during summer (main courses 3,900kr–5,900kr).

Ódinstorg Square (at the intersection of Þórsgata and Týsgi). ✆ **511-6200.** Fax 511-6201. www.hotelodinsve.is. 43 units. May–Aug 27,500kr double; 35,500kr deluxe double. Rates around 15% lower Sept; 30% lower Oct–Apr. Rates include breakfast. Children under 12 stay free in parent's room. AE, DC, MC, V. Limited street parking. **Amenities:** Restaurant; concierge. *In room:* TV, hair dryer, minibar, free Wi-Fi.

Hótel Reykjavík Centrum ★★ This unaffected and relaxed hotel, focused on service and devoid of snob appeal, is a relief from the über-slick luxury places that dominate the city. Rooms are well equipped and rather old fashioned, complete with rubber mat in the shower. Triple-paned windows eliminate most street noise, and the blackout curtains are a real sleep-saver in early summer. The hotel spans three buildings: a 1764 house and two new structures that wrap around it, with coordinated design. Rooms in the old house have a bit more character, but no exceptional antiques or original fixtures or floorboards. Guests in standard rooms are charged for Wi-Fi and extra TV channels. "Triples" are deluxe doubles with a pull-out bed. The most coveted dwelling is the "Hunchback of Notre Dame" suite in the tower.

Aðalstræti 16. ✆ **514-6025.** Fax 514-6030. www.hotelcentrum.is. 89 units. 43,200kr–48,300kr double; 66,500kr junior suite. Rates 36%–45% lower Oct–Apr. In deluxe rooms, children under 12 stay free in parent's room. MC, V. Limited street parking. **Amenities:** Fjalakötturinn Restaurant (p. 114); bar; cafe; concierge; room service. *In room:* TV, minibar, hair dryer, Wi-Fi.

101 Hotel ★★ Opened in 2003, this dauntingly trendy "design hotel" is for the fashionable jetsetter. The exterior is nondescript, the entrance hardly noticeable, as if to show it's for folks in the know. Room decor is undeniably chic, but a bit overdone; the glossy black and white surfaces alone are enough to cause eye strain, and the sink, set at an oblique angle to the rest of the room, looks like a mistake. All beds are queens or kings; bathrooms have no doors; and showers are walled with clear glass and mirrored on the inside. All rooms are spacious, so the main advantage of the double deluxes are the tubs and the quiet, as they face a (designer) inside wall. As with most expensive or very expensive hotels listed here, rates are usually discounted 10–20% when booking online.

Hverfisgata 10. ✆ **580-0101.** Fax 580-0100. www.101hotel.is. 38 units, 1 apt. Standard double and double balcony rooms have walk-in shower only; all others have walk-in shower and bathtub. 54,900kr-62,900kr double; from 75,900kr for deluxe and balcony room, up to 144,900kr for the apt suite. Limited street parking. **Amenities:** Restaurant; bar; small exercise room; small spa with steam room; room service. *In room:* TV/DVD, CD player, minibar, hair dryer, free Wi-Fi.

Radisson Blu 1919 Hotel ★★★ Of all the top hotels here, this SAS takes top place for stylishness, value, and service. The historic 1919 building is the former headquarters of Eimskip, the first major shipping line in Iceland, and almost matches the Borg in grandeur. Much has been made of the avant-garde sculptures of silver-coated human bodies embedded in the walls of the lobby, and the original grand marble staircase. Modern Scandinavian design—with wood lending the only warmth to the cold minimalism—rarely feels so sumptuous. Bathrooms are large. The added value of a deluxe room is simply more space, but rooms with waterfront views book fast. Downstairs is the surprisingly well-priced **1919 Restaurant** (main courses 2,500kr–3,400kr), and a wonderful lounge with a sophisticated and subdued vibe.

Pósthússtræti 2. ✆ **599-1000.** 1800/333-3333 from U.S.; 800/3333-3333 from U.K. Fax 599-1001. www.radissonblu.com/1919hotel-reykjavik. 88 units. Jun-Aug and Dec 28-Jan 2 28,000kr—38,000kr double; from 43,500kr for suite. Rates 18% lower Feb-Mar and Sept-Oct; 30% lower Nov-Jan, except Dec 28-Jan 2. AE, DC, MC, V. Limited street parking. **Amenities:** Restaurant; bar and lounge; small exercise room; concierge; room service. *In room:* TV, hair dryer, minibar, free Wi-Fi.

EXPENSIVE

Center Hotel Klöpp ★★ One block from Laugavegur and right smack in the action, Klöpp belongs to a small Icelandic chain but has the feel of a boutique hotel. Rooms are modern, sleek, and understated, distinguished by medium-dark wood floors, granite-dominated bathrooms, and majestic red walls set off against otherwise neutral colors. Mattresses are softer than the extra-firm Scandinavian standard. The fourth floor has partial views of Mount Esja, and the fifth floor has full views. Rooms 507 and 508, the "superior" doubles, are definitely worth the expense but are often booked far in advance. The corner singles, with their rounded walls, are very appealing. Interior rooms are quieter, but you can't really escape the late-night revelry outside.

Klapparstígur 26. ✆ **595-8520.** Fax 595-8521. www.centerhotels.com. 46 units. Jul-Aug 26,000kr-29,500kr double. Rates around 20% lower May-Jun and Sept; 50% lower Oct-Apr. Closed Dec 17-Dec 26. 50% off for children 7-12; free for those 6 and under. Rates include breakfast. AE, DC, MC, V. Free parking nearby. **Amenities:** *In room:* TV, minibar, hair dryer, free Wi-Fi.

Hotel Leifur Eiríksson The rooms of this family-run hotel are small and uninspired, with narrow beds, small bathrooms, and generic furniture—but the location and friendly, relaxed atmosphere are key. The building itself is quite respectable, at the head of Skólavörðustígur, the most appealing commercial street in Reykjavík. All the action is close by, but not too close. Hallgrímskirkja and its statue of Leifur are virtually next door. Half the rooms have church views, and a few have balconies. Free coffee and juice in the lobby. And if you're out late and can't remember the route home, just look for the church steeple.

Skólavörðustígur 45. ✆ **562-0800.** Fax 562-0804. www.hotelleifur.is. 47 units. May–Sept 21,200kr double; 25,000kr triple. Rates around 30% lower Oct–Apr. Rates include breakfast. Free for 1 child under 12 in parent's room. Special offers available online. AE, MC, V. Free parking. **Amenities:** Room service, free Wi-Fi (in lobby). *In room:* TV.

Metropolitan Hotel Simple three-star comfort, convenience, and friendly service. The location is ideal: in the heart, on a pretty residential street. Rooms are small and rather spartan. Views are nothing to speak of, and curtains should be thicker to defend against the late-night sun. A practical if unexciting choice, with excellent discounts in the off season.

Ránargata 4a. ✆ **511-1155.** Fax 552-9040. www.metropolitan.is. 31 units w/bathroom and shower. May–Sept 20,500kr double; 23,900kr triple. Rates up to 50% lower Oct–Apr. Rates include breakfast. Discount for children ages 7–12 in parent's room; free for children 6 and under. AE, DC, MC, V. Limited street parking. **Amenities:** Concierge. *In room:* TV, fridge, Wi-Fi.

MODERATE

Anna's Guesthouse ★ Housed in the former Czechoslovakian embassy, this cheerful and nicely decorated haven feels more "B&B" than most Reykjavík guesthouses. Rooms are large and individual, and guests share breakfast space around a single table in a living room with a piano. The guesthouse is close to the BSÍ bus terminal and a 15-minute walk from the heart of things.

Smáragata 16. ✆ **562-1618.** Fax 562-1656. www.guesthouseanna.is. 11 units, 7 w/bathroom. May–Sept 12,900kr double without bathroom; 16,200kr double w/bathroom; 16,400kr triple without bathroom; 19,700kr triple w/bathroom. Rates 30%–45% lower off season. Children ages 7–12 pay 1,500kr when sharing bed with parent, or 3,200kr for extra bed; free for children 6 and under. Rates include breakfast. MC, V. Easy street parking. **Amenities:** Flybus. *In room:* Free Wi-Fi.

Baldursbrá Guesthouse ★ Close to Tjörnin pond and a short walk north of the BSÍ bus terminal, this guesthouse is surrounded by foreign embassies. Rooms are large, comfortable, and clean; the street is quiet and reasonably close to town; and the sitting room and TV lounge are appealing—but the clinchers here are the hot tub, sauna, and grill in the back yard. The manager is very friendly and actively interested in making your stay pleasant.

Laufásvegur 41. ✆ **552-6646.** Fax 562-6647. http://notendur.centrum.is/~heijfis. 8 units without bathroom. July–Aug 16,000kr double; June 15,500kr double. Rates around 15% lower in May and over Christmas/New Year; 25% lower Oct and Mar–Apr; and 40% lower Nov–Christmas period and New Year period–Feb. Rates include breakfast. Discounts on payments with cash/traveler's checks. MC, V. Free parking. **Amenities:** Outdoor Jacuzzi; sauna; free Wi-Fi (in lobby). *In room:* No phone.

Butterfly Guesthouse ★ Originally designed as therapists' offices, the rooms at this good-value, central guesthouse are furnished simply and painted in soothing shades with good soundproofing. Rooms are small but spotless, and no more than two or three share each bathroom. Families and groups of three or four should look into the two sky-lighted apartments on the top floor; one apartment is smaller but has a balcony. Breakfast is free but minimal—cereal, biscuits, and coffee—but you can cook in the shared kitchen, an increasingly rare amenity. This guesthouse is one of the few to still observe the Icelandic custom of removing one's shoes upon entering. Even rarer is the accessible washer and dryer. Apartments available for a minimum of 2 nights.

Ránargata 8a. ✆ **894-1864.** www.kvasir.is/butterfly. 8 units, 4 without bathroom. Late May through early Sept 12,000kr–13,600kr double without bathroom; 14,500kr double w/bathroom; 16,000kr family room w/ bathroom; up to 24,000kr apt. Closed early Sept to mid-May. AE, DC, MC, V. Limited street parking. *In room:* Free Wi-Fi. Apts have TV and kitchen.

Castle House & Embassy Luxury Apartments (Kastallin Hotel) ★ Don't shy away from these condo-like places, which are increasingly common throughout Iceland. Apartments offer kitchens and more space for the money, and rooms are cleaned daily; they even wash your dishes. No desk staff is available, but a buzzer can summon the manager. Walls may be thin and bathrooms small, but beds are comfortable and service reliable. The units are in two separate properties, both equally central. Castle House is right on Tjörnin Pond and has the edge in scenery, while Embassy is west of the pond and offers more seclusion. If the apartment is ready, you can check in early without paying extra.

Skálholtsstígur 2a. ✆ **511-2166.** Fax 562-9165. www.mmedia.is/apartment. 12 units. Summer 14,000kr–50,000kr for 1–6 people. Rates vary with size of apt, number of occupants, and length of stay. Online discounts available. Rates 40% lower in winter. AE, MC, V. Easy street parking. *In room:* TV, kitchen, free high-speed Internet.

Fosshótel Baron ★ ☺ The Fosshótel chain isn't known for style, sophistication, or classy furnishings, but this solid choice is in the middle of town and has a range of family-friendly rooming options. Rooms and bathrooms are bright, modern, clean, and large. Studio apartments have fully equipped kitchens and comfortably sleep two adults and two children, all for the same price as the doubles. The two-bedroom apartments sleep four adults and two children, which means even bigger savings. Fosshótel's family policy is especially beneficial to parents with two young children: two doubles for the price of two singles saves you 2,800kr. Children like the kiddie-themed duvets, games, and coloring books. ***Tip:*** Light sleepers should bring ear-plugs to contend with late-night street noise from nearby Laugavegur.

Barónsstígur 2–4. ✆ **562-4000.** Fax 552-4425. www.fosshotel.is. 121 units. May–Sept 26,000kr–32,000kr double and studio apt; 33,000kr–36,000kr apt. Rates 30%–40% lower Mar–Apr and Oct–Dec. Children aged 11 and under stay free in parent's room. Rates include breakfast. AE, DC, MC, V. Free parking. **Amenities:** Bar. *In room:* TV, hair dryer, free Wi-Fi. All apts have kitchen, fridge, coffee/tea.

Guesthouse 101 Not to be confused with 101 Hotel (above)—Jude Law and Leonardo DiCaprio will not be seen in the lobby—this well-run, friendly place is about functionality, value, and basic comforts. The spare, decent-size rooms (all with twin beds) in this converted office building have a generic modern look, but the free breakfast sees you to your next meal without complaint. At the far eastern end of Laugavegur, bordering on a business district, the 101 is a short walk from the action, and Hlemmur bus station is right around the corner.

Laugavegur 101. ✆ **562-6101.** Fax 562-6105. www.iceland101.com. 18 units, 4 w/bathroom. May–Sept 12,600kr double; 14,000kr triple; 16,000kr family room with 4 beds. Rates up to 50% lower Oct–Apr. Rates include breakfast (May–Sept only). MC, V. Free parking. *In room:* Sink, no phone.

Guesthouse Óðinn ★ With two adjoining houses in an ideal residential location close to downtown, this summer-only guesthouse immediately registers adept and conscientious management, value, and comfort. Bright, simple rooms have no unnecessary trimmings. The small house at the back has five double rooms, whose guests share one small bathroom and a huge kitchen—larger groups can rent the whole thing. The main house has apartments and family rooms on the lower floors and renovated doubles on the top; the best double has a balcony.

Óðinsgata 9. ✆ **561-3400.** www.odinnreykjavik.com. 10 units, 1 w/bathroom. June–Aug 13,500kr double without bathroom; 15,600kr triple/double w/bathroom; 26,500kr apt for up to 6 people (2 night minimum). Rates include breakfast. Closed Sept–May. No credit cards. Limited street parking. **Amenities:** Car rental; apts come with either private or shared kitchen. *In room:* Wi-Fi.

Hótel Frón ★ This government-rated three-star hotel spanning three buildings is at the epicenter of Reykjavík shopping and nightlife. What the rooms lack in character they make up in spaciousness, price, and location. The 15 rooms facing Laugavegur—especially those with balconies—are for those who want to breathe in the chaos on weekends. "Zip-and-link" beds easily transform twins to doubles. The 20 "studio" apartments with kitchenettes are big enough to pass for suites. Most rooms on the fourth and fifth floors have good views. The Frón makes a sincere effort to accommodate early arrivals on the red-eye from North America, with free entry to your room as early as 8am.

Laugavegur 22a. ✆ **511-4666.** Fax 511-4665. www.hotelfron.is. 89 units. May–Sept 19,900kr double; 20,900kr–23,900kr studio apt; 24,900kr–31,900kr apt, both with Jacuzzis and 1 with a sauna. Rates around 30% lower Mar–Apr and Oct, and 40% lower Nov–Feb. Rates include breakfast. AE, DC, MC, V. Free parking. **Amenities:** Restaurant; bar. *In room:* TV, minibar, Wi-Fi. All apts have kitchenette, fridge, microwave, and coffeemaker.

Hótel Phoenix ★ This hotel is in a quiet part of the main street, a block away from the main city bus terminal Hlemmur. Rooms are comfortably mid-sized if eclectically decorated. Phoenix is one of half a dozen hotels and guesthouses officially gay-owned and -operated and/or gay-friendly (see www.gayice.is for the full list). The staff can assist with travel arrangements, provide travel tips and advice, and make bookings on your behalf.

Laugarvegur 140. ✆ **511-5002**. www.pheonix.is. 9 units. June–mid-Sept 22,000kr double; May, late Sept and around Christmas 16,800kr; otherwise 12,600kr. Rates include breakfast. AE, DC, MC, V. **Amenities:** Wi-Fi.

INEXPENSIVE

Álfhóll Guesthouse ★ Rooms in this summer-only 1928 guesthouse are tasteful, airy, and uncluttered. The location, residential but close to the old port, is ideal. The place is furnished with antiques. Rooms facing the street are larger but potentially louder on weekend nights. The top-floor studio apartments, which have kitchens and sleep up to four, have wonderfully odd multi-gabled roof contours.

Ránargata 8. ✆ **898-1838.** www.islandia.is/alf. 11 units. May 15–Sept 14,500kr double without bathroom; 18,500kr double w/bathroom/triple; 22,000kr–27,000kr studio apt for 2–4 persons. Rates include breakfast, except studios. No credit cards. Closed Sept 2–May 14. *In room:* Free Wi-Fi. Apts have kitchen.

Salvation Army Guesthouse In case you're wondering, no one will try to save your soul, and the location and value are unbeatable. Sure, the furniture is aging and threadbare, the rooms are charmless and cell-like, and you'll find only one bathroom per gender on each floor. But the place is perfectly clean, and cooking for yourself in the communal kitchens makes it even more of a deal. Drinking is forbidden on the premises, but unlike the old days, the management doesn't prohibit card games.

Kirkjustraeti 2. © **561-3203.** Fax 561-3315. www.guesthouse.is. 50 units. 11,400kr double; 16,100kr triple; 20,100kr room with 4 beds; 3,300kr sleeping-bag accommodation and 800kr to rent quilt. Breakfast available for 800kr. Limited street parking. AE, DC, MC, V. *In room:* No phone.

Snorri's Guesthouse ★ If you're on a budget, would like to do your own cooking, and don't mind walking 10 minutes to the action, it's hard to find a more pleasant lodging than Gistiheimili Snorra. The simple, modern rooms are decent-size; those in the original house have sinks and shared TV, while rooms in the adjoining house have TVs but no sink. Each house has a large, well-equipped kitchen, and both share a leafy patio and very agreeable breakfast area. The guesthouse is on a wide avenue with some traffic noise, so you might request a room off the street. The friendly staff is especially helpful with tours and other travel arrangements, though they take afternoons off in the low season.

Snorrabraut 61. © **552-0598.** Fax 551-8945. www.guesthousereykjavik.com. 23 units. May–Sept 12,400kr double without bathroom; 17,100kr double w/bathroom; 23,500kr family room w/bathroom; 2,500kr sleeping-bag accommodation (Oct–Apr only) in doubles. Made-up bed rates 22%–27% lower Oct–Apr. Made-up bed rates include breakfast. DC, MC, V. Free parking. **Amenities:** Car rental; Flybus (ask driver for Flóki Inn across the street); free Wi-Fi in lobby. *In room:* Family rooms have TV/DVD, fridge.

Outside The City's Heart

Perhaps you think of hostels as the exclusive domain of scruffy young backpackers, but Iceland's hotel prices have driven you to despair. The **Reykjavík City Hostel ★**, Sundlaugavegur 34 (© **553-8110;** fax 588-9201; www.hostel.is; 40 units without bathroom; May–Sept 12,000kr double; bed linens 1,900kr for entire stay; discounts Oct–Apr), is really not all that different from other accommodations. You can get your own room and rent sheets. You don't need a membership card (members get discounts though). You'll see plenty of families and seniors and people from all walks of life. The hostel even has more amenities than most hotels: guest kitchens, sauna, free parking, cafe/bar, game room, playground, free Wi-Fi (in common area), and laundry rooms, plus fun events like film showings and "pub crawls." Many tour operators offer their lowest prices through the helpful front desk. Admittedly, the ambience is sterile and the location is not central; but Flybus and airport connections are easy, and you're right next door to the Laugardalslaug pool (p. 134). Book way in advance, particularly for doubles; summer rooms sell out as early as January.

VERY EXPENSIVE

Grand Hotel Reykjavík ★★ The Grand was the talk of the hotel trade in 2007, when it added two new 13-story towers connected via a glass-enclosed atrium, making it the largest hotel in the country. Later the same year it unveiled Grand Spa, a small luxury spa and fitness facility. Of all Reykjavík's luxury hotels, this is the most business-oriented, with top facilities and amenities, but considerably less aesthetic appeal than rivals like the Nordica or Borg. The old wing is dowdier, but until it's renovated you can save money by staying there. The new rooms are snazzy, though they won't be featured in design magazine spreads. Bathrooms all have heated tile floors and separate bathtubs and showers. Although the new towers were designed to be free of electromagnetic pollution, beware of rooms on the fifth floor or below facing the atrium, as lobby noise filters in. The fitness room and Wi-Fi aren't included in the room price, which seems stingy.

Sigtún 38, 105 Reykjavík. ✆ **514-8000.** Fax 514-8030. www.grand.is. 314 units. May–Sept 38,000kr double; 43,400kr triple; 41,300kr and up for deluxe room and up to 155,000kr for suite. Rates up to 45% lower Oct–Apr (exclude apt suites). Rates include breakfast. Children under 12 stay free in parent's room. MC, V. Free parking. **Amenities:** Restaurant; bar; Grand Spa (3,900kr) with exercise room, spa; sauna, Jacuzzi, salt-water hot tub, massage; room service; executive rooms; shuttle to city center (10am, 1pm, and 5pm); bike rental. *In room:* TV, minibar, hair dryer, Wi-Fi.

Hilton Reykjavík Nordica ★★★ The Nordica represents the pinnacle of sleek Scandinavian chrome-glass and natural-wood interior design. (Yoko Ono told the management she was reminded of Japan.) All rooms are "deluxe" with bathtubs, ample light, and a fine sensibility for texture, harmony, and luxury; some have mountain views. Business and executive rooms are on the eighth and ninth floors and include free access to the exceptional **NordicaSpa** (p. 133) and the panorama lounge, which has a fireplace and free wine, beer, and soda. You can upgrade for 12,000kr a night pending availability: a good deal if you make use of the spa (normally 4,500kr) and free drinks. The well-known restaurant **Vox** has a fantastic lunch buffet for a very reasonable 2,950kr.

Suðurlandsbraut 2. ✆ **444-5000.** Fax 444-5001. www.reykjavik.nordica.hilton.com. 252 units. June–Oct 34,000kr double; from 42,400kr up to 139,700kr for business/executive/deluxe room and suite. Rates 25%–40% lower off season. Free valet/self parking. **Amenities:** Restaurant; bar; NordicaSpa; room service; shuttle bus to city center. *In room:* TV, minibar, hair dryer, Wi-Fi.

EXPENSIVE

Hotel Björk No, this modest three-star hotel has nothing to do with Iceland's foremost international star; *björk* simply means "birch." The staff is friendly and competent, rooms are spacious, beds are comfy and new, the breakfast buffet is ample, and customer satisfaction is consistently high. Beyond that, not much distinguishes the Björk from any chain hotel. (The elegant and historic Hotel Borg is also owned by Keahotels but you'd never know.) In a quiet and rather anonymous business district, the Björk is a 15-minute walk from the main streets, close to Laugardalur Park and its delightful pool. Be sure to ask if you want a queen-size bed or view of Mount Esja.

Brautarholt 22–24. ✆ **460-2000** or 511-3777. www.bjorkhotelreykjavik.com. 55 units. May–Sept 28,700kr double; 29,000kr triple. Online discounts available; as much as 55% lower Oct–Apr. Free parking. **Amenities:** Restaurant; concierge. *In room:* TV, hair dryer, free Wi-Fi.

MODERATE

Hótel Vík Since its expansion and renovations in 2007 and 2008, the Vík has taken on a crisp Scandinavian feel without losing its charm. The prices, lower than the level of comfort deserves, are kept down by the dull surroundings and location, a 20-minute walk from the main action. But this means you'll find peace and quiet at the Vík, and easy parking. Families will appreciate proximity to the Laugardalur pool, zoo, and family park, and can get big savings in the studio apartments with kitchenettes. Second-floor rooms have mountain views. The new wing gets the nod for its nice breakfast room.

Síðumúla 19. ✆ **588-5588.** Fax 588-5582. www.hotelvik.is. 33 units. May 1–Sept 16 18,700kr–21,200kr double; 22,600kr triple; 20,000kr studio apt; 23,800kr suite. Rates 35%–40% lower Sept 17–Apr 30. Rates include continental breakfast. Online discounts available. Free parking. **Amenities:** Bar. *In room:* TV, fridge, free Wi-Fi.

Kríunes Guesthouse ★ If you want to stay in an idyllic country setting, but without forsaking the capital, this lakeshore retreat is a great option. The guesthouse operates a shuttle to the city and airport, but it's really best reached by car (15 min.). The closest bus stop (bus 28) is 530m (1739 ft.) away. The ranch-style building is Mexican-themed, but all this amounts to is a few ornate headboards. The restaurant features local trout, which you can cast for in the lake. Canoes and foot-pedal boats are available for a fee, and horse rentals are nearby. Rooms are spacious and inviting, and the "bridal suites" (more space, a bathtub for two, and, in the larger suite, an open fireplace) won't make non-honeymooners feel out of place.

Við Vatnsenda. ✆ **567-2245.** www.kriunes.is. 12 units. Early May–late Sept 18,000kr double; 24,000kr-30,000kr suite year-round (some weekends more expensive). Rates include breakfast. MC, V. Free parking. **Amenities:** Restaurant. *In-room:* TV.

WHERE TO DINE

Over the past three decades, Reykjavík has transformed from a culinary wasteland into a culinary destination, though the Icelandic landscape still upstages all other attractions. Iceland now has more wine stewards per capita than any other country in the world. With relatively few venerated food traditions to uphold, innovative young chefs have been free to create Icelandic food in their own image, drawing inspiration wherever they find it. The quality and diversity of ingredients is astounding for such a remote outpost of the world, and little by little, one kitchen at a time, the rest of Iceland is catching on.

A few years ago, restaurant prices in Reykjavík seemed outlandish. Now, largely thanks to an exchange rate which helps tourists from just about anywhere, high quality food is more affordable. But there's still a peculiar dynamic to be aware of: ingredients and staff are so costly that all meals have a high base cost, but you're still getting good value at the margin: spend 5,000kr per person and you'll likely have a good meal, spend 6,000kr and you'll likely have a fantastic one. For the best budgeted balance, we recommend visiting the grocery store (and the hot-dog stand) a few times, filling up on that breakfast buffet, and then splurging on a few top quality meals to remember.

VERY EXPENSIVE

Argentina ★★ STEAKHOUSE It's easy to picture a gaucho smoking a cigar in this windowless cavern of meat consumption, and hard to find a better steak in Iceland. The meat is sold by weight, not carved from a spit at your table, as you might find in Buenos Aires—but an Argentinian chef does visit occasionally to check up on things. Whenever possible they use the Icelandic cattle breed, which grazes widely, eats healthily, and develops slowly and naturally. The menu includes seafood, but you can't go wrong with the beef or lamb tenderloin and the good house red wine. Portions are large, and the menu doesn't even mention the accompanying baked potato and grilled vegetables. The four-course menu is well below a la carte prices, and the two-for-one "pre-theater" deal (Fri and Sat only) offers dramatic savings before 8pm.

Barónsstígur 11a. ✆ **551-9555.** Reservations recommended. Main courses 3,670kr-6,220kr; 4-course menu 7,900kr. AE, DC, MC, V. Sun-Thurs 6pm-midnight; Fri-Sat 5:30pm-1am; kitchen closes 90 min. before restaurant.

Einar Ben ★★ CONTINENTAL If you want nouveau or fusion cuisine, look elsewhere. This old-guard restaurant is on the second floor of a century-old gentry townhouse, and the velvety curtains and brass chandeliers are a welcome relief from all the hip, minimalist interiors elsewhere in the fine-dining register. The menu's subtitle of "pure Icelandic" refers to native ingredients, not the dishes, which are honest French peasant fare with decent portions and hearty sauces. Lamb is always a safe choice in Iceland: locals tend to order the filet of lamb Dijon with mountain thyme crust, lamb shank confit, and dill glaze; while foreigners tend to order the fall-off-the-bone tender lamb shank with creamed vegetables and red wine jus. The wine list is exceptional, and the spacious bar on the third floor is a wonderful spot for an after-dinner Cognac.

Veltusundi 1, on Ingolfstorg Square. ✆ **511-5090.** Reservations recommended. Main courses 5,400kr–12,900kr; AE, DC, MC, V. Mon–Fri 6–10pm; Sat–Sun 6–11pm; bar open 3am.

Fiskifélagið ★★★ Since opening in 2009, this restaurant has become known for its exciting menu (which they make a point of completely changing several times a year) and beautiful, modern, medieval interior, complete with knitted curtains and a candle-lit graffiti wall. Check out the (cow photo) restrooms and the fur wall.

Versturgata 2a ✆ **552-5300.** Reservations recommended. Main courses 4,300kr–6,500kr; AE, DC, MC, V. Mon–Fri 6pm–11:30pm.

Sjávarkjallarinn (Seafood Cellar) ★★ SEAFOOD FUSION Even if you distrust "concept food," give this wildly popular restaurant a chance. The decor may be silly (you expect mermaids to appear in the fish tanks), the menu may be alienating (filet of salted cod "yellow brick": limequat, shiitake, beetroot), and the presentation may be melodramatic (even the sorbet arrives in bamboo and a plume of dry steam). Nevertheless, no one is trying to distract you from the food, which will likely be the best you'll eat in Iceland. The menu changes every 3 months, though one consistent item is the lobster pick-me-up: the most delicate steamed langoustine in a foie-gras sauce with cauliflower, truffles, and black pepper. Plenty of non-seafood choices are also on-hand. If you have the money and 2 hours to spare, by all means get the chef's exotic menu and sample several dishes, with a few surprises thrown in.

Aðalstræti 2. ✆ **511-1212.** Reservations recommended. Main courses 4,900kr–5,400kr; exotic menu 8,900kr. AE, DC, MC, V. Mon–Thurs 6–10:30pm; Sat–Sun 6–11:30pm.

EXPENSIVE

Austur India Fjélagið ★★★ INDIAN Run by an Indian woman married to an Icelander, this is hands-down the best non-European restaurant in Iceland. The chefs hail from all over India, as reflected in the menu, which describes each regional special in detail. Freshness is not compromised at this latitude: meat and fish are all locally produced, and imported herbs and spices are ground and mixed on-site. Half the dishes are made in the tandoor oven, and the mixed grill is stupendous. Ambience is casual but classy, with Indian antiques on display.

Hverfisgata 56. ✆ **552-1630.** Reservations recommended. Main courses 2,795kr–4,995kr. AE, MC, V, MC. Sun–Thurs 6–10pm; Fri–Sat 6–11pm.

Fjalakötturinn ★★★ INTERNATIONAL This unpretentious restaurant in the Hotel Centrum doesn't seem to consider itself upmarket, yet the food quality matches almost anything in Iceland's highest price range. It's also the *only* restaurant in Iceland with a Wine Spectator award of excellence (2 years running), yet wine prices are marked up much less than elsewhere. Asian touches are superbly integrated with European preparations. The menu changes with the season, but is always based around the new Nordic cuisine style, using local products.

Aðalstræti 16, in Hótel Centrum. ✆ **514-6000.** Reservations recommended. Main courses 3,500kr–5,900kr. MC, V. Mon–Thurs 7–10am and 6–10pm. Fri–Sat 7–10am and 6–11pm, Sun 7–11am and 6–10pm.

Við Tjörnina ★★★ ICELANDIC None of the experienced chefs at this long-running Reykjavík institution went to cooking school. If they had, they would have been told never to mix fish, fruit, and cheese, and the world would never have known their delicious plaice with banana and blue cheese. The menu has scarcely changed over the years, as they merely refine their unique trial-and-error creations. As outsiders, perhaps they feel a certain sympathy for unpopular fish and meat—this is a great place to try something new, whether it be shark; trout sushi; cod chins; or perhaps guillemot in an expertly balanced sauce of berries, honey, and lamb stock. If this sounds like a horror show to you, you'll delight in the more conventional offerings. The ambience matches the food's blend of tradition and eccentricity: the two intimate rooms have a great folksy-kooky aesthetic, with floral wallpaper, embroidered tablecloths, display cabinets full of old china, and an enormous, wall-mounted wax halibut.

Templarasund 3. ✆ **551-8666.** Reservations recommended. Main courses 3,800kr–4,900kr. AE, MC, V. Daily 6–11pm.

Þrír Frakkar ★★★ ICELANDIC You've come all this way and want to try "real Icelandic food"—a rather fleeting concept, but odds are this is your place. Tables are packed together and nautical miscellany clutters the walls. The menu closely follows the seasons, so the selections of fish and seabirds are there for good reason. This may be the time to sample puffin, cormorant, or whale (sushi or steak), if your conscience allows. The hashed fish with traditional, cakey Icelandic brown bread is a popular favorite, though we preferred the fantastic butter-fried halibut with lobster and lobster sauce. Presentation and the wine list are afterthoughts, but service is fast.

Baldursgata 14, at Nönnugata. ✆ **552-3939.** Reservations recommended. Main courses 2,890kr–3,990kr. AE, DC, MC, V. Mon–Fri 11:30am–2:30pm and 6–10pm; Sat–Sun 6–11pm.

MODERATE

Á Næstu Grösum VEGETARIAN Pleasantly perched above Laugavegur, this casual, cafeteria-style eatery is a long-running vegetarian standby. Ordering is simple: you point, they scoop, and all dishes and combo plates come with unlimited hummus, date chutney, and yeast- and sugar-free bread. Most ingredients are organic, and about half the dishes are vegan. The most consistent offerings are vegetable gratin with soy cheese; lasagna with spinach, basil, and cottage cheese; and whole wheat bread with lashings of lovely hummus. On Fridays you can enjoy an Indian-inspired menu. The dishes can be a bit gloppy and oddly indistinct, but it's hearty comfort food all the same. Try an organic beer or the impressive sugar-free banana cake.

Laugavegur 20b. ✆ **552-8410.** Reservations recommended weekends. Main courses 1,490kr–1,990kr. MC, V. Mon–Sat 11:30am–10pm; Sun 5–10pm.

Geysir Bistro & Bar ★★ ICELANDIC/INTERNATIONAL One of our top tips, this bistro has great food and friendly service in a warmly lit room decorated in hues of strawberries and cream. We recommend the steak sandwich or the catch of day, along with the best crème brulée to be found in Reykajvík.

Aðalstræti 2. ✆ **517-4300.** Reservations recommended weekends. Main courses 1,695kr-4,395kr. MC, V. Sun-Thurs 11:30am-10:30pm; Sun 11:30am-10pm.

Hamborgarafabrikkan ★ BURGERS/ICELANDIC "The hamburger factory" opened in 2010 and quickly established itself as the place to go for a gourmet approach to burgers, but the menu offers plenty more including the lamb dish Reagan and Gorbachev had (at Höfði House opposite the restaurant) as they celebrated signing the treaty to end the Cold War. The place has its own beer label and a car service will take you back down into town.

Höfðatúni 2, ✆ **575-7575** Main courses 1,295kr-3,595kr. MC, V. Sun-Wed 11am-10pm. Thurs-Sat 11am-midnight (kitchen closes at 11pm).

Icelandic Fish & Chips ★ FISH This new, waterfront organic bistro is a wonderful take on an English tradition. The fish—cod, spotted catfish, monkfish, and the catch of the day—is tossed in barley batter (free of white flour and refined sugar) and fried in all-natural canola oil for a remarkably light, crispy finish that doesn't obstruct the fish's delicate taste. Pair your fish with malt vinegar or "skyronnaise," the *skyr*-based house sauce in eight varieties, including coriander-lime and mango chutney. For "chips," choose between green salad, mango salad, orange salad, and oven-baked crispy potatoes, yum!

Tryggvagata 8, at Geirsgata. ✆ **511-1118.** Main courses 1,850kr-3,790kr. MC, V. Mon-Fri 11:30am-9pm. Sat noon-9pm, Sun 5-9pm.

Jómfrúin DANISH "Open-faced sandwich" doesn't really make sense, but connoisseurs of Danish *smørrebrød* love them anyway. Copenhagen even has a *smørrebrød* school, and in 1995 Jómfrúin's head chef was the first male ever to graduate. You can't go wrong with anything based on smoked salmon, and the rye bread (heavy and dense, with whole grains and nuts) is delectable. The most famous sandwich is the H. C. Andersen: rye bread with butter, crisp bacon, liver pâté, port aspic, horseradish and parsley. The most frequently ordered item, for good reason, is the fried plaice on rye with butter, tartar sauce, shrimp, asparagus, and lemon. Service is quick, though mind the odd closing time.

Lækjargata 4. ✆ **551-0100.** Sandwiches 920kr-2,250kr. MC, V. Daily 11am-6pm.

Restaurant Reykjavík ICELANDIC/INTERNATIONAL This cafe-restaurant, is best known for its **Ice Bar** (p. 143) but the restaurant itself serves a good range of reliable fish and meat dishes.

Vesturgata 2. ✆ **552-3030.** Main courses 3,400kr-5,900kr; regular group, seasonal and buffet specials. 11am-midnight. Kitchen closes at 10pm.

Thorvaldsen ★ FUSION One team runs both Sjávarkjallarinn (the Seafood Cellar) and this restaurant-bar. The food is similarly playful and inventive with options such as the jungle curry with chicken, coconut milk, boc choy, asparagus, mushrooms, chili, bacon, and cashew nuts. For something simpler, the fish of the day is always a good choice. After 10pm Thorvaldsen becomes a suave nightspot for snappy dressers and there are free salsa lessons every other Thursday evening.

Austurstræti 8-10. ✆ **511-1413.** Reservations recommended on weekends. Main courses 1,790kr-3,900kr; tasting/party menu 8,790kr per person. Sun-Thurs 11am-1am; Fri 11am-5:30am; Sat 11am-5:30am. Kitchen closes at 10pm.

Hot-Dog Utopia

Icelanders are well aware that their *pylsur* (hot-dogs) are among the best on the planet, and they consume them in enormous quantities—usually *ein með öllu,* or "one with everything." This expression is so ingrained in the national psyche that Akureyri began calling its Bank Holiday Weekend celebrations (p. 34) "Ein með öllu" a few years ago. A familiar and welcoming sight inside every filling station is the undulating metal rack that holds your hot-dog as you dispense mayo, ketchup, and a tangy rémoulade (with finely chopped pickle) from enormous squeezy tubes. Toppings also include raw and crispy onions. However, the key ingredient is the hot-dog itself: the addition of lamb to the usual pork and beef mellows and deepens the taste experience. You probably don't want to know any more about how they're made, however.

Vegamót INTERNATIONAL This is a good consensus choice. The location is central, the prices affordable. The food is eclectic (with an emphasis on Tex-Mex, Italian, and Indian) but very approachable, almost too bland by Nordic tastes. Surroundings are elegant and bustling, suggesting the beginning of an evening rather than the end of one. Portions are generous, but the menu offers plenty of light meal options. Good choices are the steak sandwich, the garlic fried beef strips with onion, mushrooms, and béarnaise sauce on a baguette; or any of the reliable burgers, pizza, and panini sandwiches. Late at night Vegamót transforms into one of the city's hippest bars. The popular "Luxury" brunch (weekends until 4:30pm) includes pancakes, maple syrup, eggs, bacon, and mango yogurt.

Vegamótastígur 4, just below Laugavegur. ✆ **511-3040.** www.vegamot.is. Reservations recommended. Main courses 1,690kr–3,690kr. AE, MC, V. Mon–Thurs 11am–1am; Fri–Sat 11am–5am; Sun noon–1am. Minimum age 22 after 10pm (when kitchen closes).

INEXPENSIVE

Bæjarins Bestu ★ HOT-DOGS This little shack facing a parking lot near the waterfront is nothing short of a national landmark: since 1935 it has served the country's best hot-dog in the world's best hot-dog country (see "Hot-Dog Utopia," above). Any other business would add a second employee and sell T-shirts, but the only change in recent times is the addition of a framed photo of Bill Clinton, posing with the proprietor and holding a hot-dog. (He ordered it with mustard only, which isn't advised, but if that's what you want, ask for a "Clinton.") Seating is limited to one outdoor picnic table. Britain's *Guardian* newspaper, voting this place "Best Hot-Dog Stand in Europe," credited the rémoulade sauce, but locals believe it's the secret cooking fluid (most think beer is involved).

Tryggvagata 101, corner of Pósthússtræti. No phone. Hot-dogs 280kr. Daily 10am–3am.

Eldsmiðjan ★ PIZZA Tucked away from the tourist byways, this first-rate pizzeria is great for a casual meal and can also deliver to your hotel. Pizzas are thin-crusted but hearty, with no fewer than 51 toppings to choose from (perhaps you've always wanted a pizza combining alfalfa and mussels). They tell us the most popular combo is the "pepperoni special" with jalapeños, cream cheese, pineapple, olives, garlic, mushrooms, and spices—but we couldn't bring ourselves to try it.

Bragagata 38A, at Freyjugata. ✆ **562-3838.** Reservation recommended only for groups of 6 or more. Main courses 1,255kr-2,875kr. AE, DC, MC, V. Daily 11am-11pm.

Krúa Thai ★ THAI Students on a budget have long relied on this authentic hole-in-the-wall run by a Thai family in the old port area. Service is fast and perfunctory, and the food is hearty and richly seasoned if not exactly delicate. You might expect the spiciness to be toned down for Nordic taste buds, but they do it their way unless you specify otherwise. The pad Thai is particularly spicy and delicious—heavy with chunky peanuts. You can ask for a free rice refill. Lunches are even cheaper.

Tryggvagata 14. ✆ **561-0039.** Main courses 1,200kr-1,800kr. MC, V. Mon-Fri 11:30am-9:30pm; Sat noon-9:30pm; Sun 5-9:30pm.

Sægreifinn ★ SEAFOOD Run by three local fisherman and crammed inside a small warehouse by the old port, "The Sea Baron" has the city's best value seafood and its best ramshackle ambience. You order at the counter, then sit on a fish-packing container until the food arrives in a foam container with plastic utensils. Many tourists sample whale here, as suggested by the restaurant's hilariously shameless logo, "Moby Dick on a Stick." Cod, scallops, and seasonal fish and seabirds also appear in kebab form, but the restaurant's most famous concoction is the *humarsupa* (lobster soup): sweet and creamy, with suggestions of celery, red pepper, tomato, cinnamon, clove, and coriander—and a decent portion of lobster.

Geirsgata 8 between Ægisgata and Tryggvagata. ✆ **553-1500.** Main courses 850kr-1,800kr MC, V. Summer (usually May 15-Sept 15) daily 11:30am-11pm; off season daily 11:30am-10pm.

Cafes & A Bakery

Various explanations are given for why Iceland runs on coffee: the former prohibition of beer, the high cost of alcohol, the long and dark winters, all the sudden downpours of rain, the need to digest heavy diets. Whatever the cause, Icelandic coffee is fine and strong, and coffeehouse culture thrives in Reykjavík where international chains have yet to gain a foothold. Cafes are a great place to meet locals, second only to the pools. Magazines are usually lying around, refills are often free, and you can linger for hours without being glared at. Many cafes serve food by day and function as bars and clubs at night, closing at 1am or later on weekends. The number of cafes opening before 11am is steadily increasing, to cater to an emerging breakfast trend.

C is for Cookie★ is a great new place which serves light meals at very reasonable prices. The soup of the day is delicious and the tasty tofu sandwich is surprisingly good. While you are sipping your coffee, artistically decorated with chocolate syrup, and nibbling on a tasty home-baked cookie or cake, look out for cute surprises in the decor here and there.

Týsgata 8, ✆ **578 5914.** Light meals 450kr-1,190kr. AE, MC, V. Mon-Sat 8am-8pm.

Cafe Paris Spilling onto Austurvöllur Square, this is Reykjavík's closest approximation of a Parisian brasserie, complete with good streetside people-watching. The menu serves fish and lamb dishes which, typical of Iceland, are always good. The Cajun halibut with cognac-spiced creamy mushroom sauce is very good. There are burgers and pasta too. For dessert try the fabulous French chocolate cake.

Austurstræti 14, on Austurvöllur Square. ✆ **551-1020.** Reservations recommended for dinner. Main courses 990kr-3,450kr. MC, V. Daily 9am-1am. Closed Dec 24-25.

Grái Kötturinn ★ The Icelandic artists running this bohemian, book-lined, basement-level hideout returned from a stint in New York and grieved to find no Reykjavík cafes serving pancakes and bacon at a nice early hour. The result is "The Grey Cat," which prepares coffee, bagels, and light meals. Taxi drivers often deliver North Americans here straight off the red-eye.

Hverfisgata 16a. ✆ **551-1544.** Main courses 550kr-1,450kr. AE, MC, V. Mon-Fri 7am-3pm (only sandwiches are available from 2-3pm); Sat-Sun 8am-3pm.

Kaffitár ★ is one of Iceland's two main coffee chains (the other is **Té og Kaffi,** below) and has a cafe towards the bottom of the main shopping street. It supports direct trade with coffee farmers and holds the Nordic Eco Label for environmental responsibility. The main attraction, though, is the excellent coffee, thanks to the Icelandic champion baristas (including siblings Ingibjörg and Tumi Ferrer) on the staff. To go with your coffee you can choose from cakes, pastries, or the tasty banana bread.

Bankastræti 8, ✆ **511 4540.** Sandwiches and cakes 320kr-1,150kr. AE, MC, V. Mid-June-mid-Aug Mon-Sat 7:30am-10pm, Sun 10am-10pm. Mid-Aug-mid-June Mon-Sat 7:30am-6pm, Sun 10am-6pm.

Mokka Kaffi ★ Nothing splashy here, not a place to be seen, just great coffee and good prices at the oldest cafe in town (since 1958). The interior is a bit dark, cramped, and worn, but it might appeal to you for those reasons. You may wonder why your book or conversation is so absorbing, and then notice no music is playing, the enlightened house policy. The small menu is most famous for its fabulous waffles with jam and whipped cream, but the toasted sandwiches are excellent, too.

Skólavörðustígur 3a. ✆ **552-1174.** Sandwiches and waffles around 700kr. MC, V. Daily 9am-6:30pm.

Sandholt Bakarí Head baker Ásegir Sandholt studied painting before turning his artistic skills to baked goods, eventually earning the title of "Nordic Champion of Cake Decorating." One of his brilliant creations is a cake in the form of an aging, hardbound Icelandic saga, opened in the middle, with yellowed frosting "pages" curling at the edges. In the pleasant coffeehouse in the back, you can order a marvelously creamy pastry, as well as soups, salads, and sandwiches.

Laugavegur 36. ✆ **551-3524.** Sandwiches around 900kr; pastries or cake 520kr-680kr. MC, V. Mon-Sat 6:30am-6:30pm; Sun 7:30am-5:30pm.

Skólavörðustígur ★ Pretty in pastiche, this little place with great rooftop seating is an attraction for visitors, but also has a loyal following of locals, charmed by the fabulous staff, welcoming atmosphere, and tasty breakfasts. It's especially famous for its cheesecake, made by the owner who hails from New York. If you happen to be in the area on Halloween, this place is a must, if only to check out the wicked decorations.

Skólavörðustígur 22, ✆ **555-8845.** Light meals 680kr-980kr. MC, V. June-Aug daily 10am-11pm, Sept-May 11am-11pm.

Té og Kaffi ★ is almost always located within Eymundsson bookstores (see p. 138). This one has great street views and great coffee, especially if prepared by Gerða or Steinar, who make the best cappuccinos. The soup of the day is also consistently good.

Skólavörðustígur 11, ✆ **820 8371.** Light meals and sandwiches 250kr-1,190kr. AE, MC, V. Mon-Fri 9am-10pm, Sat-Sun 10am-10pm.

Tíu Dropar Loungers and caffeine addicts come for the quiet atmosphere and free coffee refills at this pleasant retreat from the commotion on Laugavegur. This is one of the few cafes to offer hearty breakfasts of eggs, bacon, and waffles. The grilled sandwiches, based mostly on ham, bacon, and gouda, are reliable. A good deal is the smoked salmon open sandwich with cream cheese and greens; and the Belgian waffles with rhubarb jam, syrup, whipped cream, Nutella, and bananas.

Laugavegur 27. ✆ **551-9380.** Breakfast items 1,090kr–1,690kr; sandwiches and waffles 750kr–840kr. MC, V. Mon–Fri 9am–6pm; Sat 10am–5pm.

WHAT TO SEE & DO

In many ways, comparisons between Reykjavík and other European cities are best left alone. It boasts no castles, skyscrapers, grand squares, or monuments; the oldest house dates from 1764. Reykjavík's grandeur resides in its people, landscape, and culture: the museums, the music, the burgeoning restaurant and bistro culture, the geothermal pools, the style and attitude, the bustle and nightlife, and the cultivation of civic space.

As you survey the sights, keep some architectural notes in mind. Many Reykjavík buildings, largely from 1910 to 1930 but extending to the present, have corrugated iron siding, a distinctly Icelandic architectural trademark. Whatever its aesthetic merit, it was born of necessity: wood is scarce and rots in the driving wind and rain, and iron is more stable in earthquakes. Since World War II, residents have brightened the cityscape with sidings and trims in cheerful reds, blues, and greens. Almost no traditional turf structures (see box, p. 237) survive within city limits, but the tradition survives in modern Icelandic architecture and strolling around the residential areas off the main street downtown you will stumble across the occasional turf-roofed house or garage (such as at the corner of Fjólugata and Njarðargata).

Other Icelandic style innovations date from the Nationalist period of architecture, roughly 1920 to 1950, and often have to do with using native materials and invoking native landscapes. Look for interior and exterior walls made from solid or crushed Icelandic rock varieties, such as gabbro, rhyolite, basalt and, sometimes, lava.

Old City

The **tourist information office** at Aðalstræti 2 (p. 99) is a good starting point. **Aðalstræti** is the oldest street in Reykjavík, and the point from which all street numbers begin: the higher the number, the greater the distance from Aðalstræti. On the footpath across the road (Vesturgata) from the information office, the official hub of Reykjavík is marked, the perfect if clichéd place to stand a moment before you launch your journey around the city. **Ingólfstorg** ("Ingólfur's Square") takes up most of Aðalstræti's eastern edge. Ingólfur Arnarson, traditionally regarded as Iceland's first permanent settler, is thought to have settled here around 870—though Reykjavík didn't have a proper street until the 18th century. For most of its history, Reykjavík was just one of many hereditary coastal estates. In 1613 the Danish monarch, who had imposed an oppressive trade monopoly on its Iceland colony, bought the settlement under threat of force. Reykjavík then grew into a kind of shanty town for seasonal workers assisting Danish merchants, mostly associated with the fishing trade. The **oldest house** in Reykjavík, from 1764, is at Aðalstræti 10; plans are afoot to open the house for tours. (The 871±2 Settlement Museum, at Aðalstræti 16, is listed below.)

The Reykjavík Welcome Card

This little gem can save you a bundle. The card includes admission to most major museums and galleries, along with access to public transport and the city's pools (p. 133). Cards come in three varieties: 24-hour (1,500kr), 48-hour (2,000kr), and 72-hour (2,500kr). To calculate how soon you'll break even, consider that museums are routinely 700kr, pools 360kr, and buses 280kr. Most museums are free 1 day of the week, so patient and flexible schedulers can do without the card. It is active from the first time you use it until your 24-, 48-, or 72-hour period expires. Cards are available all around Reykjavík (check website for list) including at the Tourist Information Office (p. 99), BSÍ and Hlemmur bus terminals (p. 100), the City Hostel (p. 111), and the three branches of the Reykjavík Art Museum (p. 126, p. 129 and p. 130), but not online.

A block east of Aðalstræti is **Austurvöllur Square**, an important outdoor gathering place and potent national symbol to every Icelander. During the early days of the financial crisis in 2008 (p. 14) this is where people gathered to protest. In December a Christmas tree arrives here, a gift from the people of Oslo, as Iceland produces no adequately tall specimens. By European standards the square has little architectural distinction, but Austurvöllur has only been a public green since 1930. In the middle is a **statue of Jón Sigurðsson** (1811–1879), the hero of Iceland's independence movement from Denmark. His birthday, June 17, was designated "National Day" after Icelandic independence in 1944. On the pedestal is a relief called "The Pioneer," depicting an early settler, amid cliffs and basalt columns, forging a trail for later generations, who are lined up waiting to follow. Both the statue and relief are by Iceland's best known sculptor Einar Jónsson (p. 128).

Jón Sigurðsson looks approvingly at **Alþingishús (Parliament House),** an 1880 stone building with a glass and stone annex added in 2002. From October to May you can watch parliamentary proceedings from the visitors' gallery (Mon 3pm; Tues–Wed 1:30pm; Thurs 10:30am). The Alþingishús (or Alþingi) and City Cathedral next door represent Icelandic independence and Reykjavík's coming of age in the late 18th century. In 1797, the Danish king consolidated Iceland's northern and southern bishoprics into a single diocese in Reykjavík, just as the cathedral was being completed. The following year, the Icelandic parliament (Alþing) was moved here from Þingvellir, only to be abolished 2 years later. It was reinstated in 1845 in an advisory role to the Danish authorities. Behind the Alþingi is the **Parliament House Garden,** the country's oldest park maintaining its original design: a traditional, formal layout with paths emanating from a circular lawn.

The elegant, understated **City Cathedral (Dómkirkjan)** ★ (✆ **520-9700;** Monday to Friday 10am to 4:30pm unless in use for services; Sat–Sun often busy for weddings, but open before or after; high mass Sunday 11am; various masses Sunday evenings; prayer mass Tuesday 12:10 to 12:30pm followed by light lunch [500kr]) is a good counterweight to the grandiosity of Hallgrímskirkja. National independence received its first religious blessing here, and annual sessions of parliament start here with a prayer service. Completed in 1796 and enlarged in 1848, the cathedral was designed by Copenhagen's royal architect A. Winstrup, with a conventional blend of

What to See & Do in Reykjavík

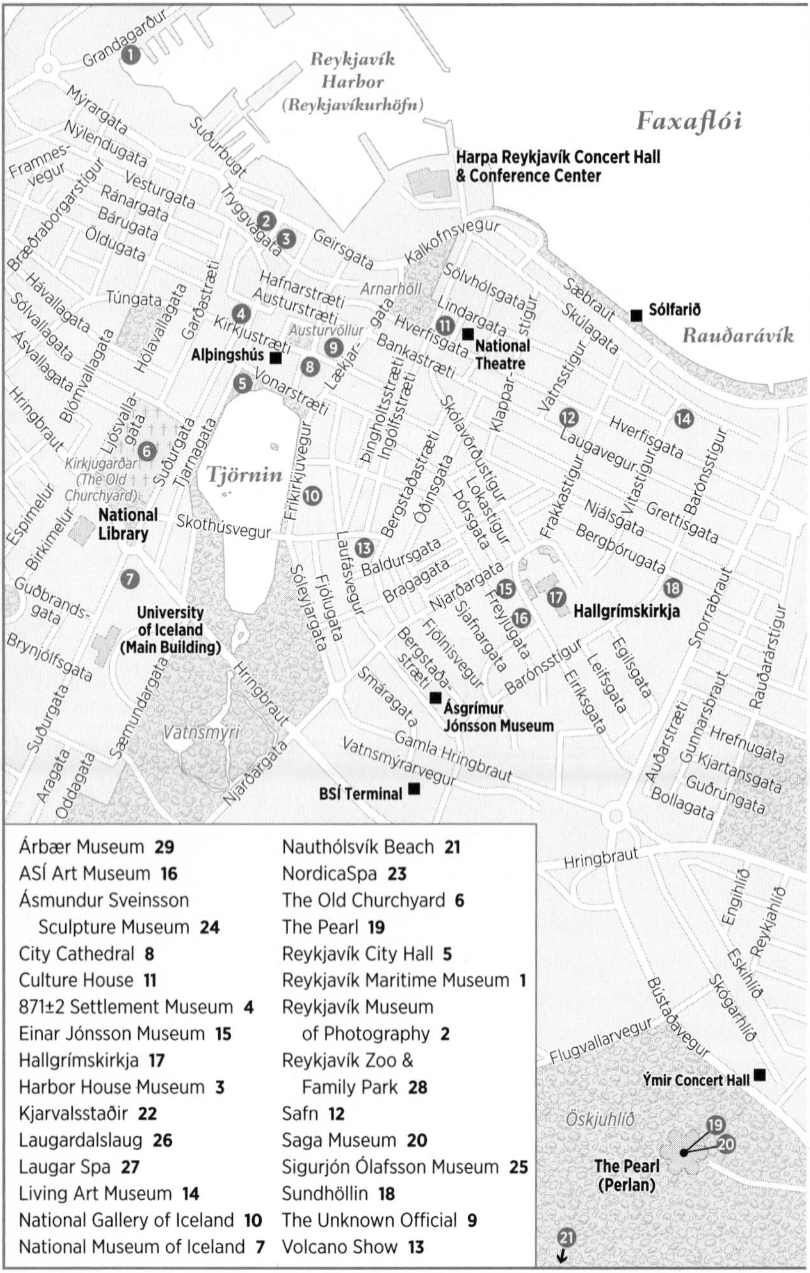

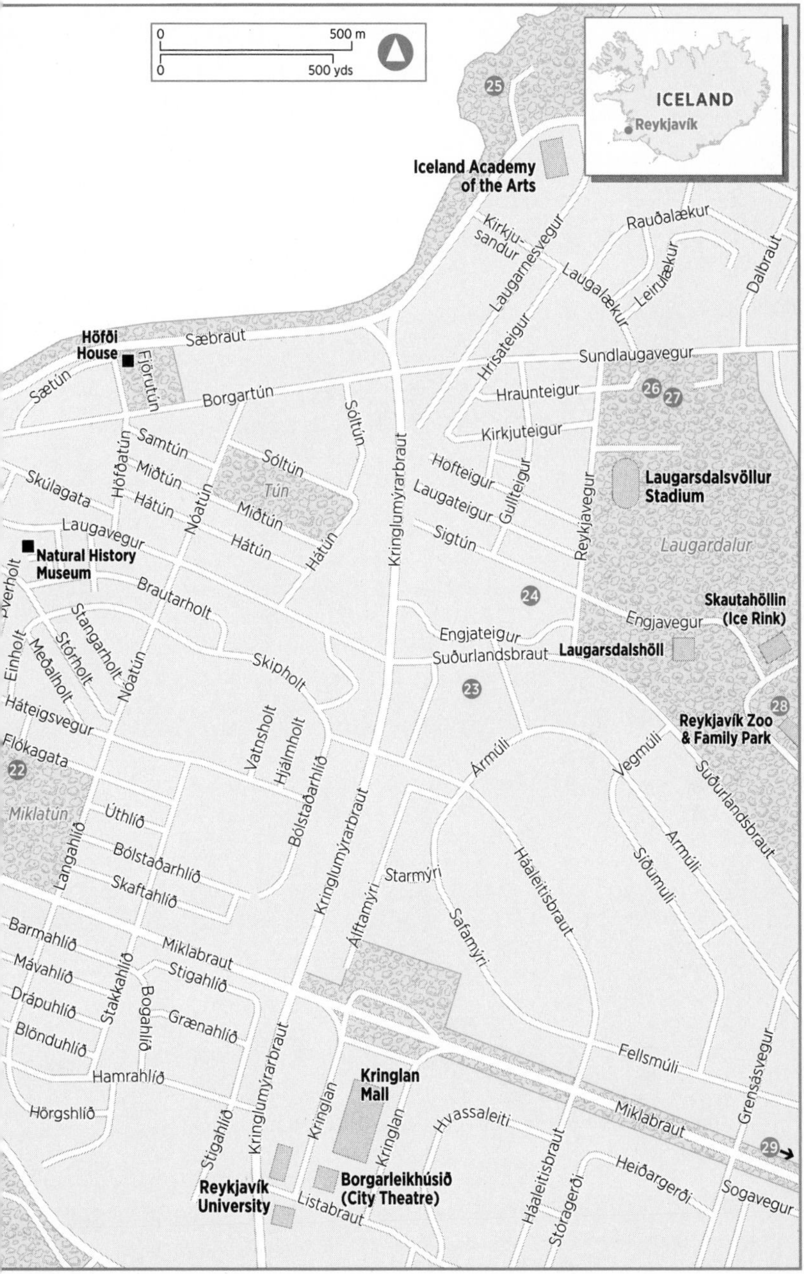
0
500 m
0
500 yds
ICELAND
Reykjavík
Iceland Academy of the Arts
Höfði House
Natural History Museum
Laugarsdalsvöllur Stadium
Laugardalur
Skautahöllin (Ice Rink)
Laugarsdalshöll
Reykjavík Zoo & Family Park
Kringlan Mall
Borgarleikhúsið (City Theatre)
Reykjavík University
Miklatún
Tún
Sæbraut
Sætún
Fjörutún
Borgartún
Samtún
Sóltún
Höfðatún
Miðtún
Hátún
Nóatún
Skúlagata
Laugavegur
Brautarholt
Stangarholt
Stórholt
Meðalholt
Einholt
Háteigsvegur
Flókagata
Skipholt
Vatnsholt
Hjálmholt
Bólstaðarhlíð
Úthlíð
Langahlíð
Skaftahlíð
Barmahlíð
Mávahlíð
Drápuhlíð
Blönduhlíð
Stakkahlíð
Bogahlíð
Stigahlíð
Grænahlíð
Hamrahlíð
Hörgshlíð
Miklabraut
Kringlumýrarbraut
Kringlan
Listabraut
Kirkjusandur
Laugarnesvegur
Rauðalækur
Laugalækur
Leirulækur
Dalbraut
Hrísateigur
Sundlaugavegur
Hraunteigur
Kirkjuteigur
Hofteigur
Laugateigur
Gullteigur
Sigtún
Reykjavegur
Engjateigur
Engjavegur
Suðurlandsbraut
Ármúli
Vegmúli
Síðumúli
Háaleitisbraut
Safamýri
Starmýri
Álftamýri
Fellsmúli
Grensásvegur
Hvassaleiti
Heiðargerði
Sogavegur
Stóragerði
22
23
24
25
26
27
28
29

neoclassical and baroque features. The loft was the original site of the National Museum and Archives, and still has an interesting photo exhibit. Check the information box outside the church for concerts and events, listed in Icelandic but often discernible anyway.

Also in Austurvöllur Square is the **Hótel Borg,** Iceland's first luxury hotel, built in 1930 to accommodate foreign guests for the millennial celebration of Iceland's first parliamentary assembly at Þingvellir. It's been an important cultural landmark ever since: public dances for Allied soldiers were held here during World War II; foreign visitors suffering under prohibition laws have found refuge at the bar; and Iceland's punk rockers performed here in the 1980s. Come in the morning to breakfast among parliament members, or visit for a drink in the small, wildly decorated lounge tucked between the lobby and the Borg's restaurant, **Silfur.**

One long block east of Austurvöllur is **Lækjargata,** a broad avenue dividing the western and eastern halves of the city. Originally there was a brook here, and Tjörnin pond still drains to sea underneath the pavement.

In the courtyard behind Lækjargata 6 is **The Unknown Official ★**. Several countries have monuments to the Unknown Soldier, but perhaps only Iceland has a sculpture paying tribute to—in light-hearted manner—the thankless, anonymous job of the bureaucrat. The 1994 sculpture by Magnús Tómasson depicts a man in a suit holding a briefcase, with his head and shoulders subsumed in a slab of unsculpted stone.

Reykjavík's geographical heart, **Lækjartorg Square,** has an important history of public meetings. From the square, look northeast to the **statue of Ingólfur Arnarson** holding his spear aloft and the grassy slope of **Arnarhóll,** which was named for him. According to the Icelandic sagas, Ingólfur became Iceland's first permanent settler in 874. After his exile from Norway on murder charges, he wintered for 3 years on the south coast of Iceland. Arnarson decided on Reykjavík after following a pagan ritual that involved throwing his high-seat pillars (carved wooden columns set at the corner of a chieftain's chair) into the sea and trusting the gods to guide him to the right spot. Ingólfur's slaves, so the story goes, found the pillars 3 years later right at Arnarhóll. The statue by Einar Jónsson (p. 128) was unveiled in 1924.

Austurstræti leads from Ingólfstorg to Lækjargata, then changes name to **Bankastræti**, which proceeds east from Lækjartorg Square, and after 3 small blocks divides into two busy commercial streets, **Laugavegur** and **Skólavörðustígur.** Austurstræti, Bankastræti, and Laugavegur form a fairly straight line, and many assume Laugavegur covers this whole stretch. A block north of Laugavegur is **Hverfisgata,** another good street for strolling and people-watching.

Laugavegur (Hot Spring Path), Iceland's busiest and most prestigious commercial street, was originally built as a trail for maids walking to Laugardalur to wash laundry in the natural springs. The street's odd jumble of buildings reflects the emergent needs of commerce and benign neglect of architectural planners.

One important hub of experimental and contemporary art, free for visitors, is **Safn,** Laugavegur 37 (✆ **561-8777;** www.safn.is). Safn rotates works from a large private collection in addition to hosting short-term installations (Wed–Fri 2–6pm, Sat–Sun 2–5pm; free guided tour Sat 2pm). Another nearby is the **Living Art Museum** (**Nýlistasafnið,** or Nýló), Skúlagata 28 (✆ **551-4350;** www.nylo.is), which focuses on young, emerging artists and holds temporary exhibitions (Tues–Sat noon–5pm).

871±2 Settlement Museum ★ In 2001, on the southern end of Aðalstræti, workers excavating an underground parking garage stumbled upon the remains of a Viking longhouse. It turned out to be the oldest known evidence of human habitation in Reykjavík, dating from 871 plus or minus 2 years—thus the name of this engaging new museum. The excavated ruin lies amid a large room, surrounded by high-tech panoramic displays that tackle the larger questions of why the Vikings came to Reykjavík, how they adapted to the conditions, and what the landscape originally looked like. The ruin itself is basically just a wall foundation, and the museum's greatest feat is to bring the longhouse back to life using digital projectors.

Aðalstræti 16. ✆ **411-6370.** www.reykjavikmuseum.is. Daily 10am–5pm. Adults 600kr; seniors/children aged 13–18 300kr; children aged 12 and under free.

Culture House (Þjóðmenningarhúsið) ★ An old Icelandic proverb states, "It's better to be barefoot than without books," and Icelanders are indeed the most avid book readers and publishers in the world. The main attraction at this museum is the ground-floor exhibition of bound medieval books, where Iceland has its formative history embodied in literature on calfskin paper.

Most of the books were transcribed and bound in the 14th and 15th centuries, and are stored behind glass in low light to preserve the fragile materials. Famous treasures include several saga manuscripts, the *Book of Settlement* (an early census from the 12th century), and the earliest-known edition of the *Codex Regius of the Elder Edda,* a scholarly work largely responsible for our modern-day understanding of Norse cosmology and poetic traditions. Some of the most captivating objects are the most primitive and obscure, for example a booklet of magic spells written in runic symbols. The exhibit explains the context and value of these books effectively, and a re-created scriptorium relates the bookmaker's craft and unenviable life of medieval scribes. Culture House displays a temporary exhibit as well.

Hverfisgata 15, east of Ingólfsstræti ("Landsbókasafn" is etched over the door). ✆ **545-1400.** www.thjodmenning.is. Admission 400kr adults; 200kr seniors/students; children under 18 free. Free admission Wed. Daily 11am–5pm. Free guided tours in English Mon and Fri 3pm, group tours by request.

Old Port (Hafn)

The port north and west of the old city, built from 1913 to 1917, was the largest construction project to that point in Icelandic history. (Before then most ships had to drop anchor well out to sea and transport goods in by rowboat.) Dredged rocks were hauled away by a locomotive, which is still on display along the shoreline east of the harbor. Today, most boat traffic has moved east to Sundahöfn port, but the old port isn't a museum yet. It's perfect for an evening stroll when the breeze isn't too chilly.

The area most visited by tourists is the eastern pier, where Reykjavík's four remaining whale-hunting ships are absurdly lined up right across from the whale-watching tours (p. 135). The irony is not lost on the Icelanders, since the whale-watching industry has been leading the campaign against commercial whaling. The whalers are painted black on the hull and white above, with "Hvalur" written across the bow and stern. You can actually climb aboard and poke around.

Furthest to the east of the downtown harbor area is **Harpa,** Reykjavík's new concert hall and conference center, opening in spring 2011. The building became a landmark on the waterfront well before 2011, with a dramatic honeycomb glass casing—

designed by renowned Icelandic-Danish artist Ólafur Elíasson—being constructed piece by piece. With state-of-the-art acoustics, Harpa encompasses a variety of halls and is set to become the country's premier concert venue (www.harpa.is, see p. 145, "Performing Arts: Music & Dance").

The western piers have the most fishing vessels, as well as the **Óðinn**, a grey Coast Guard vessel with a vertical stripe in blue, white, and red. These ships are the closest thing Iceland has to a military, and they defend the country's territorial fishing waters. They were sent out to slice British fishing nets in the so-called "Cod Wars," which date back to 1432 but culminated in the 1970s, when Britain broke off diplomatic relations. (Icelanders like to say this was the only war the British Navy ever lost.)

Harbor House Museum (Hafnarhús) ★★ This renovated 1930s warehouse, one of three branches of the Reykjavík Art Museum, houses two or three temporary exhibitions of Icelandic and international contemporary art along with the permanent collection—dominated by the works of Erró, an Icelandic-born artist who was based in Paris and best known for his large-scale comic-book-styled dreamscapes and montages. The second floor has a cafe with excellent soups and a wonderful reading room with hundreds of art books, children's toys, and a view over the waterfront.

Tryggvagata 17. ✆ **590-1200.** www.artmuseum.is. Admission free. Daily 10am–5pm, Thurs 10am–10pm.

Reykjavík Maritime Museum (Víkin) Iceland still derives most of its export income from fish, and this museum, opened in 2005 in a converted fish-freezing plant, takes an in-depth look at the country's 20th-century seafaring heritage. The permanent exhibit shares many features with local maritime museums across the country, such as well-crafted ship models and dummies in very uncomfortable-looking raincoats. The exhibit shows real curatorial professionalism but is best for those with a pre-existing fascination for objects like buoy lights and engine controls. However, the re-created captain's room and claustrophobic sleeping quarters are standouts.

Grandagarður 8. ✆ **517-9400.** www.sjominjasafn.is. Jun–Sept 11am–5pm. Admission adults 1,000kr; seniors/students/children 13–18 700kr; children 12 and younger free. Bus 14.

Reykjavík Museum of Photography ★ 🎁 This free museum and archive above the City Library surpasses most photographic collections in two respects. First, it has meticulously collected photographs of the Reykjavík area from every viewpoint: professional and amateur, public and personal, journalistic and aesthetic. Second, you can leaf through thousands of contact sheets in a side room full of binders; the shots are print-size, not negative-size, and the staff can even process your choice in their own lab.

Tryggvagata 15, 6th floor. ✆ **411-6930.** www.photomuseum.is. Free admission. Mon–Fri noon–7pm; Sat–Sun 1–5pm.

Around The Pond

Tjörnin, the city's central pond, makes for a great circular walk. Several early 20th-century timber houses, built for the newly-emergent middle class, are clustered along Tjarnargata on the western shore. It's worth strolling by to appreciate their gingerbread-house flourishes.

National Gallery of Iceland (Listasafn Íslands) ★ Iceland's endless variations of light and natural formation have always been a boon to painters, and many

Reykjavík with Children

Children in Iceland are noticeably well-integrated into adult life, and you'll feel welcome bringing them just about anywhere. They are often seen feeding the voracious waterfowl in **Tjörnin pond** (p. 126) by City Hall, and the opposite end of the pond has a climbing apparatus. The **Volcano Show** (p. 146) has enough geological violence and destruction to be entertaining, even if the film quality is quite outdated. **Whale-watching** (p. 135), **puffin-watching** (p. 135), and the **Reykjavík Park and Zoo** (p. 130) are all pretty foolproof. **Horseback riding** and other activities are outlined in "Pools, Spas, Outdoor Activities & Spectator Sports" (p. 133). The most engaging museums for children are the open-air **Árbær Museum** (p. 132) and the **Saga Museum** (p. 131). Perhaps best of all are the **outdoor thermal pools,** a family institution throughout the country (see "Pool Guide," p. 134). The deluxe **Laugar Spa** (p. 133) can entertain your children while you pamper yourself, and the Kringlan mall has a child-minding service for while you shop. See p. 93 for a full 5-day family holiday itinerary.

of the greatest results are on display at this museum, the largest and probably the most important repository of 19th- and 20th-century Icelandic art. The gallery has no permanent exhibit, only revolving exhibits from the permanent collection. The basement level has a nice area for keeping children occupied, and the top floor has a pleasant cafe with slow service but pretty good coffee.

Fríkirkjuvegur 7. ✆ **515-9600.** www.listasafn.is. Tues–Sun 11am–5pm. Free admission to permanent collection exhibit; otherwise 500kr adults, 300kr elderly or disabled (all exhibitions free for people under 18). Free guided tours Tues and Fri 12:10pm.

The Old Churchyard (Suðurgata or Hólavallagarður Cemetery) This cemetery 1 block west of the pond, between Ljosvallagata and Suðurgata, has plenty of informational panels and makes for an interesting stroll. The grave of Jón Sigurðsson, the most important leader of Iceland's independence movement, is found here: walk from the main entrance on Ljosvallagata straight down the center, past the old chapel bell, and it's the beige obelisk on the left, a few plots before you reach the outer wall. Its lack of ostentation speaks volumes about Iceland's egalitarian ideals.

✆ **562-2510.** www.kirkjugardar.is. Cemetery open 24 hr; office weekdays 9am–1pm.

Reykjavík City Hall (Ráðhús) This modern gray structure inaugurated in 1992 has many detractors, but its strengths are under-appreciated. Design elements such as dripping, moss-covered walls add nicely organic touches to the concrete, metal, and glass. The building seems to float at water level, humbly absorbing the lapping waves. The usual pomposity and self-importance of city halls is absent, replaced by democratic symbolism: the ground floor looks almost like a natural extension of the public street. Inside is a wonderful, enormous 3-D relief map of Iceland, which took four men 4 years to construct. City Hall has a tourist information desk, an exhibition area, and a pleasant cafe with free Internet and huge windows overlooking the pond.

North end of Tjörnin pond. ✆ **411-1111.** Free admission. Mon–Fri 8am–7pm; Sat–Sun noon–6pm. Cafe daily weekdays 11am–6pm; Sat–Sun noon–6pm.

South of the Pond

National Museum of Iceland ★★ Iceland's museums are all of manageable size; even this relatively large exhibition condensing Iceland's entire history and culture won't wear out your legs or attention. "The Making of a Nation" selects specific figures, objects, and vignettes to represent stages and themes of Icelandic history: a charming, old instant-photo booth, for example, signals the onset of modernity. Interactive elements are cutesy but effective: you can pick up a phone and have a one-way conversation with a medieval chieftain from 1117, or Guðriður the nun in her convent in 1323. The exhibit begins with a pagan burial site and ends with a traditional Icelandic dress refashioned by contemporary artist Ásdís Elva Pétursdóttir in transparent plastic. Everything in between is worth seeing for yourself.

The ground floor houses the free **National Gallery of Photography ★**, which, in keeping with the exhibit upstairs, features the Iceland of yore. The cafe on the ground floor is best for morning or afternoon tea, with little for lunch. The museum shop has more interesting souvenirs than many of the bigger tourist shops.

Suðurgata 41. ✆ **530-2200.** www.natmus.is. National Museum admission adults 1,000kr; senior/students 500kr; children under 18 free. Free admission Wed. Museum and Gallery May–Sept 15 daily 10am–5pm; Sept 16–Apr Tues–Sun 11am–5pm; first Thurs of month until 9pm. Bus: 1, 3, 4, 5, 6, 11, 12, or 14.

East of the Old City

ASÍ Art Museum (Ásmundarsalur) This small selective contemporary art museum, run by the Icelandic workers union, fits several Icelandic artists into each monthly exhibition. Selections from the permanent collection are featured in July and August, usually including Jóhannes S. Kjarval's lovely painting *Fjallamjölk* (Mountain Milk) inspired by the landscape of Þingvellir.

Freyjugata 41. ✆ **553-2155.** Free admission. May–Sept daily 10am–4pm; Oct–Apr weekends 1–4pm.

Einar Jónsson Museum ★★ The former home and studio of Iceland's best-known sculptor, Einar Jónsson (1874–1954), holds most of his life's work. Einar was often inspired by Icelandic folklore, and his sculptures depict classical human and mythological figures in wildly imaginative and unorthodox poses. He identified with the romantic symbolists, and his sculptures speak in allegories, personifications, and ciphers. In the 1930s, W. H. Auden mockingly summed up his work as "Time pulling off the boots of Eternity with one hand while keeping the wolf from the door with the other." But these remarkable creations have become only more mystical and revelatory over time—even people not typically drawn to art will find themselves gawking in admiration and wonder. Outside is a small park with 26 bronze castings of his work, well worth a look even if the rest of the museum is closed.

Eiríksgata. ✆ **551-3797.** www.skulptur.is. Admission 500kr adults; 300kr senior/students; children under 16 free. Free admission to sculpture park. Jun–Sept 15 Tues–Sun 2–5pm; Sept 16–Nov and Feb–May Sat–Sun 2–5pm. Closed Dec–Jan.

Hallgrímskirkja (Hallgríms Church) ★ Hallgrímskirkja, the tallest and largest church in Iceland, is Reykjavík's most photographed emblem by far, visible from everywhere in the city. It was designed by state architect Guðjón Samúelsson (1887–1950), who never saw it completed: work began in 1945 and continued for 49 years. The church is named for Reverend Hallgrímur Pétursson (1614–1674), Iceland's foremost hymn writer, and also an ecclesiastical scholar and poet. His best-known work, *Hymns* *of the Passion,* is still sung and recited as verse in homes throughout Iceland (an English translation is available in the gift shop). For a fee you can ascend the 75m (246ft.) steeple by elevator for great views over the city. At the top are three bells representing Hallgrímur, his wife, and his daughter who died young.

The distinctive exterior, with its prominent steeple, is often described in terms both primordial and futuristic—as if the church were some kind of volcano or glacier transformed into a rocket ship. Guðjón was indeed inspired by the Icelandic landscape, and the frontal columns are meant to resemble the hexagonal basalt formed by cooling lava. The interior is quite traditional in contrast, with its Gothic high-pointed vaults and tall, narrow windows. The uniform, textured-concrete surfaces can seem pedestrian, even to those accustomed to Lutheran principles of simplicity, and the altar is so ordinary as to resemble a hotel lobby. It could have been very different: a photograph hung in the entry hall depicts Einar Jónsson's proposed alternative design, a fantastical creation to rival Gaudí's cathedral in Barcelona. An Art Deco spire supports human figures in relief trudging upward amidst Middle Eastern-inspired domes. In 2010 a new bronze and blue glass door for the church was unveiled. Designed by Leifur Breiðfjörð, the door draws a connection with the windows, especially when lit up by the late evening sun.

Concerts here often involve the church's most popular interior feature: a gigantic organ built in Germany in 1992. It's about 15m (50 ft) tall, with 72 stops, 5,275 pipes, and remarkable sound projection. The church also hosts drama, art exhibitions, even public debates. Especially recommended are choral performances, a form in which Icelanders have always excelled.

A **statue of Leifur (Leif) Eiríksson** is aligned directly in front of the church, as if he's about to lead it down the hill. The statue was a gift from the U.S. to commemorate the 1,000th anniversary of the founding of Iceland's parliament. It was also a tacit acknowledgment that Leifur beat Christopher Columbus to North America by almost 500 years. (Excavations in Newfoundland have settled this question beyond a doubt.) He certainly strikes a heroic pose, but looks rather like a comic-book figure once you've seen the Viking statues in the Einar Jónsson museum next door.

Skólavörðuholt, at southeastern end of Skólavörðustígur. ✆ **510-1000.** www.hallgrimskirkja.is. Daily 9am–8pm. Suggested donation 100kr. Elevator to tower 500kr adults; 200kr children. Holy Communion sung Sun 11am and Wed 8am. Prayers Tues 10:30am. Meditation with organ music Thurs at noon. Anglican service in English usually last Sun of each month at 2pm. Organ concerts mid-Jun to mid-Aug at noon on Thurs and Sat; longer performances Sun 8pm.

Kjarvalsstaðir ★ Jóhannes Sveinsson Kjarval (1885–1972) is the most highly regarded painter in Icelandic history, and this branch of the Reykjavík Art Museum is named in tribute. The Sixties-era modernist building holds three galleries: two with temporary exhibits and one drawing from the museum's large collection of Kjarval's paintings. Deeply inspired by native landscapes and folklore, his work is too varied to pigeonhole stylistically, but "expressionist" approximates the thick, paint-laden brushstrokes and abstract arrangements of tone and shape.

Flókagata. ✆ **517-1290.** www.artmuseum.is. Admission free. Daily 10am–5pm. Bus: 1, 3, 4, 5, 6, or 13.

Laugardalur

According to legend, Ingólfur Arnarson chose the name Reykjavík, or "Smoky Bay," when he saw distant steam rising from what is now Laugardalur (Hot Spring Valley), thinking it to be smoke. Those hot springs still heat the Laugardalslaug pool, and Icelandic families are also drawn by the zoo, family park, botanical garden, sports stadiums, and luxury Laugar Spa (see also "Pools, Spas, Outdoor Activities & Spectator Sports," below).

Ásmundur Sveinsson Sculpture Museum (Ásmundarsafn) In the 1940s, modernist sculptor Ásmundur Sveinsson (1893–1982) designed and built this futuristic home and studio, now a branch of the Reykjavík Art Museum. The sphinx-like design was inspired by Turkish and Egyptian models, which he thought fitting for Iceland's treeless environment. The museum focuses almost entirely on his work, influenced by Henry Moore and the cubists. Often drawing from Icelandic folklore, his pieces range from recognizable human forms to pure abstract shapes. The small outdoor sculpture park, which is free and accessible at all times, features more of Ásmundur's work.

Sigtún, near the sports complex in Laugardalur Park. © **553-2155.** www.artmuseum.is. Admission free. May–Sept daily 10am–4pm; Oct–Apr 1–4pm. Bus: 2, 14, 15, 17, or 19.

Reykjavík Zoo & Family Park ☺ No attempt was made here to import exotic species; this zoo is just for families to have fun and interact with the animals Icelanders know and love: sheep, horses, cattle, pigs, goats, reindeer, mink, seals, and the Arctic fox, the only indigenous land mammal. An animal petting schedule is posted each day—foxes at midday—and pony rides begin at 2pm. The aquarium, opened in 2004, holds seals and fish native to the North Atlantic. The Family Park is surefire children's entertainment, with a trampoline, bumper boats, a go-cart driving school complete with traffic lights, and a "science world," where little ones can measure their screams in big decibels. Next door is a botanical garden with a pleasant greenhouse cafe in summer.

Hafrafell (at Engjaveg, Laugardalur Park, behind sports complex). © **411-5900.** www.mu.is. May 15 to mid-Aug daily 10am–6pm; mid-Aug to May 14 daily 10am–5pm. Admission Mon–Fri 500kr adults; 400kr children 5–12; 4 and under free. Sat–Sun add 100kr to ticket prices. Rides cost extra. Bus: S2, 14, 15, 17, or 19.

Sigurjón Ólafsson Museum The sculptures of Sigurjón Ólafsson (1908–1982) span multiple developments in 20th-century art and range from formal busts to primitivist metal totems to wood pieces haphazardly stuck together. This museum inside his former oceanside studio is devoted exclusively to his work, and has a pleasant cafe with homemade pies and cakes and peaceful waterfront views.

Laugarnestangi 70. © **553-2906**. www.lso.is. Jun–Aug Tues–Sun 2–5pm; Sept–May Sat–Sun 2–5pm, but closed intermittently for long periods, check website. Admission 500kr adults; free for ages 12 and under. Bus: 12 or 15.

Öskjuhlíð Hill

This wooded area to the south of the city is a perfectly nice walking, jogging, or biking retreat, but, aside from the **Pearl (Perlan),** holds little to entice visitors.

Nauthólsvík Beach It's often said Iceland has everything the world has . . . but only one of them. Nowhere is this truer than Nauthólsvík, where runoff hot water from the city's geothermal heating system is pumped into the ocean through a beach of imported yellow sand. The ocean temperature is brought to about 18°C (64.4°F), and Icelandic families flock here on warm days to sunbathe and splash around in the almost-hot tubs. **Kaffi (Cafe) Nauthóll** is close by, and you can rent towels or store valuables for 200kr; coffee, soda, ice-cream, and hot-dogs are on offer all day.

Nauthólsvegur, directly south of the Pearl. ✆ **511-6630.** May 15–Aug daily 10am–7pm. Bus: 16.

The Pearl (Perlan) Rivaling Hallgrímskirkja for domination of the Reykjavík skyline, this futuristic glass dome, built in 1991, sits atop six enormous cylindrical tanks storing 24,000 tons of the city's geothermally heated water. The first floor "Winter Garden" is leased for various expos, and features a fountain lamely mimicking a geyser. On the grass outside is a more impressive spectacle: another artificial geyser, but one designed to replicate the actual geyser mechanism (p. 160); eruptions are every 15 minutes or so between 1 and 5pm. The fourth floor is ringed by a free viewing deck with fabulous views over the city and beyond; inside is a cafe whose main strength is its ice-cream. The top floor, which makes a complete circular revolution every 2 hours, contains a pricey restaurant (dinner only), and is accessible only to diners.

Öskjuhlíð. ✆ **562-0200.** www.perlan.is. Free admission. Daily June–Aug 10am–11:30pm; Sept–May 10am–9pm. Free admission. Cafe daily 10am–9pm. Restaurant daily 6:30–10:30pm. Bus: 18.

Saga Museum ★ ☺ This privately run museum conveys Icelandic history and saga lore with an expert blend of entertainment and educational value. Listening to mini-lectures on iPods, visitors move among installations enlivened by eerily lifelike silica human figures and gore aplenty: feuding Vikings, witches burned at the stake, the beheading of Iceland's last Catholic bishop. If the kids get fidgety, send them to watch the creepy video showing the designer crafting the heads from face casts of his friends and family, and then stitching the hair on. (Ingólfur Arnarson has the face of the museum's owner.)

Inside the Pearl, Öskjuhlíð. ✆ **511-1517.** www.sagamuseum.is. Admission 1,500kr adults; seniors/students 1,000kr; children 800kr. Apr–Sept daily 10am–6pm; Oct–Mar daily noon–5pm. Bus: 18.

Outskirts & Nearby

VIÐEY ISLAND ★

Viðey is hardly the most dramatically situated island off the Icelandic coast, but it provides a very nice afternoon escape from Reykjavík. The island has a surprisingly grand history, and is now a showcase for environmental art.

Viðey was inhabited as early as 900. From 1225 to 1539 it was the site of a prestigious Augustine monastery, which at one point owned 116 Reykjavík estates. In 1539 the Danish king appropriated the land in the name of the Protestant Reformation. Eleven years later, Iceland's last Catholic bishop, Jón Arason, took the island by force, but he was beheaded a few months later. At the beginning of the 20th century, the country's first harbor for ocean-going vessels was built on Viðey's eastern coast, but it was soon outmoded by Reykjavík's port. Viðey's population peaked in 1930 with 138 people, but by the 1950s the only inhabitants were birds enjoying the peace. In 1983 Viðey became city property.

Viðey has no cars and is only 1 square mile in area. It consists of **Heimæy (Home Island)** and **Vesturey (West Island),** linked by a narrow isthmus. You can bring a bike, but several free bikes are left out for any takers; some have baby seats and all have helmets. Visitors spend most of their time strolling along the easy trails. (Pick up the free trail map in the ferry ticket office.) Thirty bird species have been counted here. The most populous is the *eider,* the seafaring duck harvested on farms all over Iceland for down feathers. Many birds nest in the grasses, so it's best to stick to the paths.

Visitors disembarking the **Viðeyjarferju ferry** (✆ **533-5055**) won't miss **Viðey House (Viðeyjarstofa)** (✆ **533-5055;** Jun–Aug daily 1–5pm), the country's first stone-and-cement structure, dating from 1755. It was originally home to Skúli Magnússon (1711–1794), who was appointed Royal Superintendent of Iceland by the Danish crown; now it's a cafe serving coffee and waffles in summer. Close by is **Viðeyjarkirkja,** the second-oldest church in Iceland, consecrated in 1774, with Skúli's tomb beneath the altar.

Vesturey's only man-made feature is Áfangar (Stages) ★, a vast yet understated work, erected in 1990, by American minimalist sculptor Richard Serra (b.1959). Nine pairs of vertical basalt columns are spread across the land, their proportions determined by strict mathematical criteria. If you climb to the high point you can see all nine pairs, as well as a grand view of the surrounding mountains. Viðey is also home to the **"Imagine Peace Tower"** designed by Yoko Ono, featuring peace prayers in 24 languages, and—during late fall and significant Lennon dates—a shaft of light visible from the mainland.

The 7-minute ferry from the port of Sundahöfn, east of the city, has seven departures per day (mid-May–Sept; 11:15am–5:15pm; last ferry back at 6:30pm). Buses depart Reykjavík's old port 15 minutes before each ferry departure. Sundahöfn can be also reached by Bus 16. In July and August, a noon ferry goes directly from the old port to Viðey, returning at 3:30pm. Round-trip tickets, which include the bus, are 1,000kr adults; 900kr seniors/students; 500kr children aged 6 to 18; those under 6 go free.

ELLIÐAÁR VALLEY

Árbær Museum (or Árbæjarsafn) ★ This open-air folk museum, a 15-minute drive east of the city, is a division of the Reykjavík City Museum. It is a re-created historic village built around a traditional farm and many buildings slated for demolition in Reykjavík found refuge here; an 1842 church was transported from the north coast. Árbær was a working farm until 1948, and interior decorations are meant to represent a typical 1920s farmhouse. (Look for a marvelous piece of homegrown artwork on the wall: a bird and bouquet constructed entirely from human hair.) From June to August, staff in period costume milk cows, weave wool, and cook chewy pancakes *(lummur)* on the farmhouse stove for visitors. What really makes a visit worthwhile is a guided tour (free with paid admission) of the original turf-roofed farmhouses, so time your visit accordingly. Without a guide you won't learn how to spin yarn, how meat was smoked (with sheep manure, a method still used today), and how everyone washed their hair (in urine).

Kistuhylur, in Artunsholt. ✆ **411-6300.** www.arbaejarsafn.is. Admission 600kr adults; seniors/children under 18 free. Ticket valid for 2 visits. Free admission Fri, but guided tour requires full ticket price. June–Aug daily 10am–5pm; 90-min. guided tours at 11am and 2pm; Sept–May Mon, Wed, and Fri open only for guided tour at 1pm. Bus: 5 (to Strengur, a short walk from museum).

POOLS, SPAS, OUTDOOR ACTIVITIES & SPECTATOR SPORTS

For a thorough exploration of outdoor activities in Iceland, see chapter 4.

Thermal Pools

The city operates seven **thermal pools** (**www.spacity.is**), all with changing rooms, lockers, showers, wading pools for small children, and "hot pots" (hot tubs), usually in a row with successively higher water temperatures. All but one have water slides and other delights for children. Entrance fees are typically 360kr for adults and 110kr for children aged 6 to 15. Swimsuit and towel rental are typically 350kr apiece.

Don't be dissuaded by poor weather. Icelanders still show up in the rain, and believe the combination of cold air and hot water greatly beneficial to health. (They have very long life spans to show for it.) For a side of the city few tourists witness, show up at 7am, when Icelanders have a dip before work. For more on **pool etiquette,** see "Pools & Spas," in chapter 4.

Spas

A few Reykjavík hotels offer fitness rooms, saunas, massages, and health and beauty treatments, but only at Hilton Reykjavík Nordica's **NordicaSpa,** Suðurlandsbraut 2 (✆ **444-5090;** www.nordicaspa.is; Mon–Fri 6am–8pm, Sat 9am–6pm, Sun 10am–3pm), do these combined services truly amount to "spa" status. NordicaSpa is especially adept at treatments featuring Iceland's natural resources, from geothermal mud massages to seaweed wraps. Non-guests of the hotel are welcome.

Laugar Spa This mammoth complex, opened in 2004, has spared no expense to wow patrons with the latest in super-deluxe spa and fitness technology. Features include indoor and outdoor pools, exhaustive beauty and massage treatments, and a

When in Iceland

Visiting a genuine Icelandic thermal pool is the best antidote for culture shock. Lounging in a hot tub with Icelanders, who are quite blasé about this everyday ritual, provides a tamer way to interact with locals than Reykjavík's famed wild nightlife. If you're lucky enough to be visiting during winter, one of the most magical Reykjavík experiences is to sit in a hot pot watching the falling snow vanish as it melts in the steam just above your head.

REYKJAVÍK thermal POOL GUIDE

- **Árbæjarlaug,** Fylkisvegur 9, Árbær, near Elliðaár River (✆ **411-5200;** Mon–Fri 6:30am–10pm; Sat–Sun 8am–9pm all year round. Bus: 19), is a kiddie wonderland full of water toys, but has plenty for adults, too. A 15-minute bus ride from the city's heart, this pool is one of the less touristy. Reykjavík's largest public Jacuzzi is here, but you won't find anywhere to do laps.
- **Laugardalslaug,** Sundlaugavegur 30, at the north end of Laugardalur Park (✆ **411-5100;** Mon–Fri 6:30am–10:30pm; Sat–Sun 8am–10pm. Bus: 14), in the eastern part of the city, is the biggest and most populated pool, with several outdoor swimming areas, an Olympic-size indoor pool, a steam room reminiscent of a whale's belly, and a massage room. In 2010 this pool started offering late night fun, celebrating mid-summer by staying open 24 hours a day for a few weeks.
- **Sundhöllin,** Bergþórugata 16, at Bergþórugata, behind Hallgrímskirkja (✆ **411-5350;** Mon–Fri 6:30am–9:30pm; Sat–Sun 8am–7pm. Bus: 1, 6, or 13), is mostly indoors, so you may feel you're missing out on a true Icelandic experience (plus the kids will lament the lack of water slide). The hot pools are outside, however, with views of the city. The historic pool building was designed by the architect of Hallgrímskirkja, and each locker in the labyrinthine facilities has a fold-out dresser with mirror and stool.
- **Seltjarnarneslaug,** Suðurströnd 8, Seltjarnarnes (✆ **561-1551;** Mon–Fri 6:30am–10pm; Sat–Sun 8am–8pm. Bus: 11), is the least touristy pool listed here (no signs in English), and the only one featuring saltwater. You may find yourself sharing the big hot tub with brave souls just in from a cold swim in the ocean. In Seltjarnarnes, Reykjavík's suburb to the west, it's not far by car or bike.
- **Vesturbæjarlaug,** Hofsvallagata, at Melhagi (✆ **411-5150;** Mon–Fri 6:30am–10pm; Sat–Sun 8am–8pm. Bus: 11 or 15), is a 15-minute walk from Tjörnin Pond, on the southwestern edge of the city, near the university and just a short distance from good shoreline strolling on Ægisiða. Nauthólsvík Beach is nearby, and you can pay extra to sit under sun lamps, a nice splurge on a gloomy day.

health food restaurant. The six steam rooms are set at different temperatures, and each has a thematic fragrance. Among the spa baths, choose freshwater or seawater. One pool is designed exclusively for foot-soaking. To visit the "relaxation cave," you must have your retina scanned at reception; then at the cave entrance, your eye-print is acknowledged and the doors snap open. Children can be left in their own playrooms or watching movies while you attend to yourself.

Sundlaugavegur 30a, at the north end of Laugardalur park, next to Laugardalslaug pool. ✆ **553-0000.** www.laugarspa.com. Gym and spa Mon–Fri 6am–11:30pm; Sat 8am–10pm; Sun 8am–8pm. Beauty salon Mon–Fri 9am–7pm; Sat 11am–6pm. Massage salon Mon–Fri 9am–9pm; Sat 11am–6pm. Bus: 14.

Whale-Watching

Reykjavík's **Faxaflói Bay** is a prime whale-watching area (though visitors headed to Húsavík on the north coast should probably wait and head out from there). The smaller and less dramatic minke whales are the most common sightings, but you stand a good chance of spying humpback whales, harbor porpoise, white-beaked dolphins, and orcas as well. From May to mid-August, whale tours also stop at **Lundey Island,** a puffin nesting site (see below). Trips last 2½ to 3 hours and leave from Ægisgarður, the easternmost pier of the old port.

All the tour companies are reputable, but a solid choice is **Elding** (**© 555-3565;** www.elding.is), the largest operator, boasting a 98% whale-sighting success rate. Tickets are 8,000kr adults, 3,500kr children aged 7 to 15, and free for children aged 6 and under. Boats depart June through August at 9am, 1pm, and 5pm; also 10am and 2pm July through early August; April, May, and September at 9am and 1pm; October at 1pm; and November through March at 1pm Friday to Sunday. The price includes warm overalls and raincoats, plus admission to the "Nature Center" with a simple exhibition on marine life in Faxaflói. Most boats have a play area for kids. If you want to throw in some sea angling with your whale- and puffin-watching, **Hvalalíf** (**© 562-2300;** www.hvalalif.is) combines all three activities for just about the same prices as above, with departures April through October at 8:55am, 12:55pm, and 4:55pm. They will even grill your catch for you as your sail back.

Puffin-Watching

West of Reykjavík, the small islands of **Lundey** and **Akurey** are home to some 50,000 puffins during breeding season. Many whale-watching tours include a puffin stop; but **Puffin Express** (**© 892-0099**) offers a shorter, less-costly tour for puffin fanatics (for more on puffins, see p. 296), and their boats are better designed for drawing close to the bird cliffs. Tours, which last 1 hour, leave from Ægisgarður pier at the old port. Tickets are 2,800kr for adults, 1,400kr for children under 12. Boats sail May to mid-August, five times daily between 8:30am and 4:30pm.

Fishing

Not many world capitals have good salmon fishing within city limits. The season for Reykjavík's **Elliðaár River** extends from June 1 to August 31, and opens with the mayor throwing the first cast. Contact the **Angling Club of Reykjavík** (**© 568-6050;** www.svfr.is) for information on permits and procedures. Also ask about trout and Arctic char fishing in nearby lakes. For tackle and equipment, try **Veiðihornið,** Síðumúli 8 (**© 568-8410**).

For **sea fishing, Hvalalíf** (see "Whale-Watching," above) has a 3-hour evening tour that leaves at 5pm, May until September, and culminates with their chef serving up your catch on board. Tickets for the trip are 9,100kr. **Elding** (**© 555-3565;** www.elding.is), has a 3-hour sea-angling tour for 8,400kr from May to September, leaving daily at 11am, with grills on board.

Other Outdoor Activities

Many local farms offer 2- to 4-hour **horseback-riding tours,** which may include lunch and hotel pickup. Two excellent companies near Reykjavík are **Laxnes Horse**

Farm, in Mosfellsdalur (✆ **566-6197;** www.laxnes.is) and **Íshestar,** in Hafnarfjörður (✆ **555-7000;** www.ishestar.is).

Reykjavík has three **golf courses.** The **Reykjavík Golf Club** (✆ **585-0200;** www.grgolf.is) runs two 18-hole courses: the oceanside **Korpúlfsstaðir** to the northeast (Thorsvegur, via Korpúlfsstaðir; Bus: 24) and the difficult **Grafarholt,** Iceland's premier championship course, to the east (Grafarholtsvegur, off Route 1; Bus: 15 or 18). Both are about a 15-minute drive from the city center and stay open during summer evenings. Course fees are 7,500kr, club rental is 3,500kr, cart rental is 4,500kr, and trolley rental is 500kr. Closer to the center, in Seltjarnarnes, west of Reykjavík, is the casual 9-hole **Golfklúbbur Ness,** at the end of Suðurströnd (✆ **561-1930**), with good ocean views (Bus: 11).

See chapter 4 for information on scuba diving, glacier tours, hiking, Jeep tours, aerial tours, and rafting.

Spectator Sports

The unique Icelandic form of wrestling known as ***glíma*** dates back to the Viking era. The main season for competitions is from September to April. For more information, contact the **Icelandic Glíma Association** (✆ **514-4064**). Also keep an eye out for historical reenactments at museums or special events like the **Viking Festival** in Hafnarfjörður (p. 34).

Icelanders are fanatical about the unusual and exciting sport of **handball,** once described as "water polo without the water." Iceland finished fourth in the 1992 Barcelona Olympics, and eighth in the 2007 World Cup, but their moment of glory was at the 2008 Beijing Olympics when they won silver—the smallest nation ever to win an Olympic silver medal in a team sport. The height of the season is September until April. For more information, contact the **Icelandic Handball Federation** (✆ **514-4200;** www.hsi.is).

The Icelandic national **soccer** team was ranked 37th in the world in 1994, and fell to as low as 117th position in 2007, before climbing up to 79th position in 2010, just below China and Belarus. If you'd like to attend a game, you can check out a match at **Laugardalsvöllur Stadium,** Laugardalur Park (✆ **510-2900**).

SHOPPING

Reykjavík is not the shopping mecca that is Paris or London, but a new wave of boldly conceptual storeowners is gaining almost as much attention as the restaurateurs. Most shops are concentrated on **Laugavegur** and **Skólavörðustígur** —with some of the best discoveries in the network of streets in between. The two streets which extend the bottom of Laugavegur—**Austurstræti** and **Bankastræti**—are also good shopping streets.

Reykjavík is a good place to buy supplies before hitting the rest of the country, where goods are even more expensive. General shopping hours are 9am to 6pm weekdays, and 10am to 4pm Saturdays. Almost everything is closed Sunday except for a few shops, particularly those selling knitted things and puffin snow globes. ***Note:*** Store listings below do not indicate opening hours unless they deviate from the norm.

Save up to 15% with a VAT Refund

Iceland Refund (✆ **564-6400; www.eurorefund.com/iceland**) reimburses you the **Value-Added Tax** you pay (about 15% of purchase price) under the following four conditions: 1) purchases must be taken out of the country; 2) each sales receipt must total at least 4,000kr—for less expensive items you can consolidate purchases at a single store; 3) purchases must be from an accredited store; and 4) you must leave the country within 3 months of purchase. When you make a purchase, request a **Tax Free form,** which must be signed by the salesperson. Your refund can be claimed from the following places: Keflavík Airport, at the Landsbanki Íslands Bank at the far end of the departure hall; the Seyðisfjörður ferry to Europe, onboard prior to departure; and Reykjavík's Tourist Information Office (p. 99). If the total value of your *refund* is less than 5,000kr (that is, if your total purchases amount to about 33,000kr or less), you can receive the refund directly in cash or have it credited to your credit card at the airport or the ferry; at the Tourist Information Office, you can only have it applied to your credit card. If the refund is more than 5,000kr, your only option is to have the refund applied to your credit card no matter where you claim it—and all goods (except wool goods) need to be shown at customs before check-in for your departing flight.

Arts, Crafts & Photography

Fótógrafí This gallery sells work by over 40 Icelandic photographers, from journalists to landscape specialists. You can buy fine-art prints, posters, and photo books, or just admire the art. Skólavörðustígur 22. ✆ **821-5600.**

Gallery KSK Kolbrún S. Kjarval's shop and studio offers graceful ceramic wares in all shapes and sizes, often decorated with bird themes. Locals particularly covet her tiny bowls designed to hold toothpicks or coins, a unique souvenir or gift. Skólavörðustígur 22. ✆ **511-1197**. www.ksk.kk5.org

Kirsuberjatréð Ten Icelandic women artists run the "Cherry Tree" collective, where you'll find fish-skin wallets, pig-bladder boxes, mugs for left-handers, "paper" bowls made of sliced radish and zucchini, clothes embroidered with mini pom-poms, and much more. Rather expensive but not unjustifiably so. Vesturgata 4. ✆ **562-8990.** www.kirs.is.

Listaselið Founded in 2000, this collectively run art and crafts store and gallery sells textiles, glass-art, handmade books, ceramics and paintings, straight from the artists themselves. Skólavörðustígur 17b. ✆ **551-5675**. www.listaselid.is.

Reykjavík Museum of Photography The only independent museum of photography in Iceland, this gem is hidden on the sixth floor of Grófarhús by the harbor. You can buy photography publications, and copies of your choice from their many collections, picking the size and photographic paper to be used. See p. 126 for details.

Books & Music

English-language books are not hard to come by, as many Icelanders prefer them to translated editions. (See p. 21 in chapter 2 for book recommendations.)

Bad Taste (Smekkleysa) After many relocations, this legendary music store/label/gallery has settled on the main street. Inspired by the maxim, "Good taste is the enemy of art," the label boasts Icelandic supernovae Björk, Sigur Rós, and Múm along with lesser-known homegrown acts. An entertaining "Lobster or Fame" exhibit documents the label's history. Laugavegur 35. ✆ **551-3730.** www.smekkleysa.net.

Eymundsson This bookstore chain started up in 1872 and now has branches all over Iceland. Most branches have a foreign-language (mostly English) section of Icelandic literature—both modern and going back to the sagas. Both of the central Reykjavík branches have cafes serving light fare and decent coffee. Open daily until 10pm. Skólavörðustígur 11. ✆ **515-2510**. www.eymundsson.is.

Fornbókabúðin This antiquarian bookseller has some English-language items (for example, out-of-print travel accounts) among the dusty Icelandic tomes. You can browse old prints, maps and postcards; and saga lovers are sure to find some precious treasure—at a price, of course. Klapparstígur 25–27 (at Hverfisgata). ✆ **552-1710.** www.bokin.is.

Mál og Menning This respected Icelandic bookstore chain has late hours and plenty of books in English. This branch is right in the heart of things, and you can take books, newspapers, and magazines to the upstairs cafe until 10pm. Laugavegur 18. ✆ **552-3740.** Bankastræti 2. www.malogmenning.is.

Sangitamiya—The Nectar Music A music store featuring instruments of the world, many made to order by local craftsmen. They also offer presentations about the instruments and the musical traditions to which they belong. Here you can find the traditional Icelandic Langspil—a simple but lovely string instrument. Grettisgata 7. ✆ **551-8080**. www.sangitamiya.is.

12 Tónar This store, boasting its own rock/alternative label, stocks eclectic, international, home-grown—whatever music the connoisseur owners like. You'll probably be offered coffee, and you can sample CDs while hanging out on the couch. Live performances are usually held every other Friday. Skólavörðustígur 15. ✆ **511-5656.** www.12tonar.is. Also open Sun 1–4pm in summer.

Clothing

Einstakar Ostakökur "Unique Cheesecakes" is a unique little store with clothing from various classically-influenced designers, combining modern fabrics with the glamour of the golden era. The clothing has a '30s to '60s feel, but there's nothing grandmotherish about these curve-hugging classics. The John Fluevog shoes are especially hard to resist. Laugavegur 20b (enter from Klapparstígur). ✆ **551-5200.**

ELM Three women with respective backgrounds in art, textile design, and drama therapy started this wildly-popular store. (Oprah often wears ELM clothing on her show.) The high-grade cotton and wool garments hug in only the right places, exuding comfort and flexibility. The designs, mostly black and white with the odd bright burst, feature tasteful frills amid linear simplicity. Laugavegur 1. ✆ **511-0991.** www.elm.is.

Forynja The main designer of the renowned Naked Ape brand is back under her own label. Sara María has put her own stamp on street-culture wear and is still going strong. A burst of geometric forms and random textures, the design most resembles canvas art transformed into clothing. Laugavegur 12.

Gyllti Kötturinn For lovers of bright, secondhand clothing, this little shop is one of the hottest used-clothing stores in Reykjavík. Austurstræti 8. ✆ **534-0005**.

KronKron This large boutique has a flair for combining the cream of the upstart designer crop with established names like Vivienne Westwood and Fred Perry. Think candy stores, cabarets, and circuses: anything from vintage Nikes to party dresses to embroidered long johns (with plenty of gear for the men, too). Sister shoe store **Kron** with its own fabulous brand is down the street at Laugavegur 48. Laugavegur 63b (around the corner on Vitastígur). ✆ **562-8388.** www.kron.is.

Spaksmannsspjarir This well-established high-end women's boutique, with grown-up styles for all ages, has a gift for striking, sexy, and original combos: feminine skirts with masculine vests, or classic cuts in modern materials. Unlike most Reykjavík fashion, the clothes actually bear Icelandic weather in mind. Bankastræti 11 (at Laugavegur). ✆ **551-2090.** www.spaksmannsspjarir.is.

STEiNUNN Steinunn Sigurðardóttir takes inspiration from Iceland's wilderness (think endless twilights, cloud vaults, and sub-Arctic flora) and goes for pure, unmixed soft materials like silk and lambswool. The cuts are minimalist yet very feminine and textural with ruffles, bunches, and unexpected uses of fur or tulle. Bankastræti 9. ✆ **588-8849.** www.steinunn.com.

Concept Stores

Aurum This unique store has everything from an award-winning small-space designer coffee table to an antique tea set to hair accessories, and all in a crisp setting reminiscent of an art museum. Bankastræti 4. ✆ **551-2770.** www.aurum.is.

Kisan This store is about sensory comfort, charm, and nostalgia, like walking through Amelie's imagination. Toy livestock bones, art books, fake moustache variety sets, children's clothes from the Petit Bateau label—everyone is bound to find something they don't need but must have. Laugavegur 7. ✆ **561-6262.** www.kisan.is.

SPARK Design Space A platform for various design projects with a focus on collaboration between designers and other professions—perfumers, potters, and even chefs. SPARK fosters projects and events that play with your sense of touch, sight, smell, and taste, and the best part is that you can purchase the items on display. Klapparstígur 33. ✆ **552-2656**. www.sparkdesignspace.com.

Jewelry

Jewelry is relatively less expensive in Iceland, especially gold and silver. You'll find countless items inspired by the country's natural features and pagan history, often made from lava stones and native minerals. Most makers eagerly make up what you want, a good way to bring home a little piece of Iceland (especially since it's illegal to collect minerals yourself). For classic designs, try the well-stocked **Gull & Silfur,** Laugavegur 52 (✆ **552-0620**).

Hringa This find is great for some fun designs and custom-made pieces. A great variety of nameplate items in many shapes and forms. Laugavegur 33. ✆ **551-1610.**

Mariella Each piece at the very-offbeat Mariella deals with the question, "What is Icelandic?" "The Icelandic interior is like this one," says owner Maria, pointing to a string of lava beads interrupted by glass jewels. "Very boring and rough, but then maybe you find a flower." Skólavörðustigur 12. ✆ **561-4500.**

Markets & Malls

Kolaportið Reykjavík's enormous flea market takes you back to the "old days"—say, 25 years ago—when Reykjavík was far less wealthy. Stalls are crammed with books, antiques, crafts and clothes, with hardly any tourist schlock, though you'll have to hunt for treasures. In the back is a well-priced fish market, where you can snack on pickled salmon, fulmar eggs, and shark. An ATM is on the premises. Tryggvagata 19. ✆ **562-5030.** Sat–Sun 11am–5pm. Bus 1, 3, 4, 5, 6, 11, 12, or 13.

Kringlan This 150-store mall is usually too far away to reach on foot, but features free parking, Wi-Fi, a taxi stand, and a play area where you can leave your 3- to 9-year-olds while you shop—**Adventureland** (✆ **517-9025;** maximum 2 hours (950kr); Mon–Wed noon–6:30pm; Thurs, Fri noon–7pm; Sat 11am–6pm; Sun 1–5pm) . Most stores are European chain fashion and homeware, but there are some nice quirky places, too, plus a liquor store, food court, cinema, and grocery store. The restaurants and cinema stay open after hours. Kringlan 4-12. ✆ **517-9000.** www.kringlan.is. Mon–Wed 10am–6:30pm; Thurs 10am–9pm; Fri 10am–7pm; Sat 10am–6pm; Sun 1–5pm. Bus 1, 3, 4, or 6.

Smáralind Away from the heart of the city, this is the newer of the two malls and the biggest mall in Iceland. The stores are mostly major chains, and the restaurants and cinema stay open after hours. Hagasmári 1, 201 Kópavogur. ✆ **528-8000.** www.smaralind.is. Mon–Wed and Fri 11am–7pm; Thurs 11am–9pm; Sat 11am–6pm; Sun 1–6pm. Bus 2.

Outdoor Gear

Cintamani, Laugavegur 11 (✆ **517-8088;** www.cintamani.is), the upstart competitor of fashionable 66° North (see below), has slightly lower prices, more camping gear (tents, boots, maps, and so on), and a travel agency for adventure tours. **Útilíf** (www.utilif.is) is the best place for technical outdoor equipment, especially for camping, climbing, cycling, and fishing—or if you just forgot your swimsuit. Útilíf is found in both major shopping malls: Kringlan (✆ **545-1580**) and Smáralind (✆ **545-1550**).

66° North This Icelandic outerwear line, which began by serving fishermen, unites fashion and outdoor readiness so well as to make brands like Patagonia and REI look dowdy and utilitarian. Iceland has eight branches—including in both Kringlan and Smáralind malls (see above)—and they've reached retailers in North America and all over Europe. Pricey, but a great place to pick up waterproofs, fleeces, and ski gear for all ages. Bankastræti 5. ✆ **535-6680.** www.66north.com.

Wool Garments

Over centuries of harsh weather, Icelandic sheep evolved a dual-layered wool: inner fibers are soft and insulating; the outer ones water and dirt repellent. These qualities combine for knitwear that is surprisingly light, resilient, and wearable in all kinds of weather. Sweaters in traditional Icelandic patterns are well-known, and you'll also find wonderful hats, mittens, socks, and blankets. Don't wait until your return to Keflavík Airport to buy your sweaters; the selection isn't near what it used to be.

A miniature branch of the discount outlet in suburban Mosfellsbær (see p. 150), **Álafoss,** Laugavegur 1 (✆ **562-6303;** www.alafoss.is), offers marginal savings over its competitors, and has a decent selection of sweaters and handicrafts. Clothing line **Farmer's Market** (www.farmersmarket.is) doesn't have its own shop, but the brand is worth seeking out for its sexier, lighter, less bulky take on traditional Icelandic sweater patterns. The sweaters are made from Icelandic wool, but don't wear one into the Handknitting Association store—they're manufactured abroad. They're available at Kisan (see above), the Keflavík airport, the Blue Lagoon (p. 164), and Geysir (p. 160).

Handknitting Association of Iceland (Handprjónasamband Íslands) This well-stocked store, with three branches across the city, is owned, run, and supplied by a cooperative of about 200 Icelandic women handknitters. The main branch is on Skólavörðustígur, but you'll find longer hours at the Saga Hotel branch (daily 8am–2pm and 4–10pm). The branch at Laugavegur 64 keeps normal hours. Skólavörðustígur 19. ✆ **552-1890.** www.handknit.is.

REYKJAVÍK NIGHTLIFE

The fastest-growing tourist demographic in Iceland are long-weekenders who don't come *just* to party . . . but if there were no party they wouldn't come. Reykjavík rocks like a city 10 times its size, with more than 50 bars and clubs in the throbbing heart of the city. Thankfully there's much more to Reykjavík's famous nightlife than bar-hopping, and any evening in the city is full of cultural activity. For a current schedule of events, see "Visitor Information," at the beginning of this chapter.

BARS & NIGHTCLUBS

Until 1989, beer with an alcohol content above 2.2% was illegal, and other forms of booze were tightly restricted. Alcohol consumption in Iceland is actually lower than in most European countries, but when Icelanders do drink, they tend to make up for lost time. Late Friday or Saturday night, you'll likely witness dancing on every available surface, public urination, the occasional brawl, sexual goings-on, and so on. At least the 2007 smoking ban has made the air more hospitable.

The legal drinking age is 20, but it's not heavily policed. Some bars and clubs have a 22-and-over policy. Drinking on the street is prohibited, but the law isn't enforced—some bars will even give you a to-go cup. Drug laws are stricter, but recent years have seen a troubling surge in cocaine and amphetamine use. Reykjavík is a safe place, but as always, women should beware of accepting drinks which may have been tampered with. Many foreigners, usually men, come in search of reputedly loose Icelandic women and are disappointed.

Fashion in the club scene is surprisingly dressy for laid-back Iceland, though admittedly you don't see many Icelanders shopping downtown in their sweatpants during the day either. Sneakers are usually frowned upon, and—though jeans are "in"—they'd better be hot. A certain divide has opened up between spiffier joints (b5, Thorvaldsen, Oliver) and hangouts with too many hipsters, rockers, and bohemians for any sort of dress code (Bakkus, Kaffibarinn, Boston).

On weekends, not much gets started before midnight, and clubs stay open as late as 6am. (Until a few years ago all bars had to close at 3am on weekends, but this created such mayhem in the streets that the authorities thought better of it.) Weeknights,

Joining the Party

- **Freaky Friday** The first Friday or so of every month (call to be sure), all day and into the evening, the trendy and adventurous line up and surrender their hair to the creative whims of the talented stylists of **Gallerí Gel,** Hverfisgata 37 (✆ **551-7733**), while regulars chat and onlookers line the walls and couches drinking beer and wine. Book ahead (beauticians take only two victims at a time).
- **Night Circle Tour** Nightlife comes in a package tour, starting Friday and Saturday nights at 10pm at **Bar 11,** Hverfisgata 18 (✆ **847-5337**). For an extremely good value 3,000kr you get an hour of free drinks at Bar 11, shots at two different bars, a cocktail at a nightclub, and—to complete the ritual—a hot-dog. Around 40 others are along for the ride, Icelanders and tourists alike.
- **Professional Partier** Jón Kari Hilmarsson of **Nightlife Friend** (✆ **822-6600;** www.nightlifefriend.is) has a lot of friends in Reykjavík, and (for a fee) you can be one of them. For $450, he'll design a nightlife tour for half a dozen or so people, and then take you around to the hotspots, introduce you to locals, and help you cut some lines. When he started the business, he envisioned his clients as timid nerdy types, but the majority are 30-plus American males working in business/finance who see no stigma in getting professional assistance for social events.

when bars are required to close at 1am, are far more relaxed. On Thursday nights, DJs and live music often take it up a notch. Most of the clubs are cafes by day and serve food until 10pm. Bars or clubs only have cover charges when there's live music.

Many locals save money by drinking at home and then heading out around 1am, when the boisterous lines start forming. At the end of the evening, many partiers wind down in Austurvöllur Square, near the biggest late-night taxi stand at Tjörnin Pond.

Reykjavík bars change constantly, and listings are quickly outdated. If you're not sure where to go, trust your instincts, keep on the move, and ask locals for advice. Icelanders are very accessible, especially when they're in party mode, and the nightlife scene is nowhere near as snobby as it is trendy.

For some American-style sports bar action, complete with large-screen TVs, Risið Bar, Tryggvagata 20 (✆ **552-6868**), is known for its loud music and late-night partying on weekends. Then there's **Sportbar.is,** Hverfisgata 46 (✆ **552-5300**). Self-explanatory: bar, TV, sports, pool tables. For a bit more sophistication, try the only dedicated wine bar in Iceland: **Vinbarinn,** Kirkjutorg 4 (✆ **552-4120**), in a tasteful spot behind the City Cathedral. Many locals consider it the primo place for over-30s to meet after 11pm.

b5 Housed in a former bank, this cafe-bar is popular among natty young professionals savoring their mango mojitos. (You'll feel out of place in frumpy travel clothes.) The basement bank vaults have been converted into private lounges with expensive bottle service. Bankastræti 5. ✆ **552-9600.** www.b5.is.

Bakkus Despite its flimsy set, this pub has become central in the Reykjavík nightlife over the past few months. An unusually large selection of vodka brands, cheap (and flat) beer, table football, and a photo booth (!) will ensure you don't leave the place until early in the morning. If that's not enough, access to next door

Venue is direct from Bakkus, in case you feel like having a wild time on the dance floor. Tryggvagata 22. ✆ **770-1517.**

Barinn Formerly "Bar 22," this no-dress-code cafe and nightspot is rapidly gaining a reputation for wild partying. It's one of the few bars hosting DJs 5 nights a week, but they leave the top floor free for conversation. Laugavegur 22 (at Klapparstígur). ✆ **578-7800.** www.barinn.is.

Boston Owner Sigga Boston, former proprietor of the iconic Sirkus (a much mourned venue that closed down in 2007 despite lengthy local protest), earns this bar automatic hipster cachet. It's a notch more laid-back, roomy, and loungy than its peers, with comfortable seating and music played at a less intrusive volume. Laugavegur 28b. ✆ **517-7816.**

Cafe Oliver Dress well for this trendy and slick nightspot, jam-packed on weekends with 25 and ups. By day Oliver is a cafe/bistro, and when they make way for the DJ and dance floor, they leave some tables out for patrons who want bottle service. Laugavegur 20a. ✆ **552-2300.** www.cafeoliver.is.

Dillon The buzzwords for this dark English-style pub are rock, students, tattoos, and beer. It's busy weeknights, with occasional live music. The DJ on Saturday is white-haired local fave Andrea Jóns, the so-called "grandmother of Icelandic rock." Laugavegur 30. ✆ **511-2400.** www.dillon.is.

Hemmi & Valdi Opening shortly after the building was saved from destruction, this comfy cafe and bar has become one of Reykjavík's hotspots. Whether for a cup of tea or to kick off a good party night, Hemmi & Valdi will always make you feel welcome with their cheap drinks and snug sofas. Laugavegur 21. ✆ **551-6464.**

House of Guinness 🎁 Just a good, regular pub most of the time, this place is a must visit for amateur musicians on a Thursday night. From about 9pm musicians start rocking up for a whole-of-pub jam session—guitars, violins, banjos, voices, everyone and everything welcome. The style of music varies but tends to err on the side of folksy Irish. Lækjargata 10. ✆ **578-0440.**

Hressingarskálinn Known locally as "Hresso," this long-established Austurstræti landmark is a good consensus choice: not too glamorous, a nicely mixed crowd, plenty of space and outdoor seating, good bistro food to 10pm, live music Thursdays, and plenty of Eighties and Nineties hits from the DJs. Austurstræti 20. ✆ **561-2240.** www.hresso.is.

Kaffibarinn A bit of celebrity cachet here—Björk stops in, scenes from the cult film *101 Reykjavík* were shot here, and Britpop entrepreneur Damon Albarn owned a share—but celebrity cachet doesn't go far in Reykjavík. Artists, musicians, filmmakers, and, of course, tourists are the core clientele. DJs spin Wednesday to Saturday, but you can converse upstairs on weekends. Bergstaðstræti 1. ✆ **551-1588.** www.kaffibarinn.is.

Ölstofan The place to go if you enjoy discussing poetry over a pint of Guinness. This is where Icelandic intellectuals and artists meet when they're in the mood for a nice chat with friends or perfect strangers. Vegamótastígur 4. ✆ **552-4687.**

Restaurant Reykjavík This cafe, restaurant, and endearingly unhip live music venue (mostly cover bands) is best known for its **Ice Bar,** where the walls, tables, bar, and glasses are all made from glacial ice and the room is kept at 21°F (–6°C). For 1,500kr, visitors are handed gloves, a parka, and a welcome cocktail. Tube lighting and vodka bottles frozen into the walls set the tone. Some love it; for others it's an overpriced, touristy walk-in freezer. Vesturgata 2. ✆ **552-3030.** www.restaurantreykjavik.is.

Rex This weekend-only nightclub, with its velvet couches and chandeliers, walks a compelling line between seediness and glamour, so dress stylishly if not properly. The crowd tends toward well-groomed 30-somethings, but you wouldn't be surprised to come across an aged movie star in furs. Austurstræti 9. ✆ **552-5599.** www.rex.is.

Gay & Lesbian Nightlife

The perception among Reykjavík's gays and lesbians is that the city's wild nightlife doesn't extend as much to them. The population is just too small to support a major "scene." On the upside, gay and lesbian visitors feel personally welcomed, not lost in the crowd. Reykjavík is also more integrated than you might expect; there's no gay area, and only one bar has an officially gay identity. **Barbara,** Laugavegur 22, welcomes visitors into a small bar (if you manage to get yourself through the blindingly pink doorway) that can quickly turn into a flaming dance floor on weekends. Upstairs is a quieter room with tables and an outside smoking area.

For more info and activities, the website **www.gayice.is** posts a schedule of events. The **Reykjavík Gay Pride Festival** (www.gaypride.is) usually takes place in the first week of August. The gay and lesbian community center, **Samtökin '78,** Laugavegur 3, 4th floor (✆ **552-7878;** www.samtokin78.is), holds open-house social gatherings at their **Rainbow Cafe** Mondays and Thursdays 8 to 11:30pm and Saturdays 9pm to 1am (Thurs nights are especially popular among lesbians). Their library is open during these gatherings and on weekdays from 1 to 5pm. The Icelandic lesbian group **Konur Með Konum** (www.kmk.is) posts events and useful information, like where to join the KMK gals for a game of volleyball. **MSC Ísland** (www.msc.is) is Iceland's gay men's association with special attention paid to dress code (casual, leather, latex). The association owns a private club open Friday and Saturday nights from 11pm (see website for details). Gay and lesbian student visitors are usually welcome at parties sponsored by the University of Iceland's GLB group, **Q Félag** (www.queer.is), every week at Samtökin '78 (above).

Live Music

Since the late 1980s, especially since Björk's solo career took off, Iceland has enjoyed an outsized reputation as an incubator of alternative popular music. The **Iceland Airwaves Festival** (p. 35) attracts more visitors to Iceland than any other single event. Good music can be heard virtually every night, often in galleries, stores, and other unpredictable venues, so check listings in the free circular ***The Reykjavík Grapevine*** (www.grapevine.is). Reykjavík's two alternative music store/labels ***12 Tonar*** and ***Smekkleysa*** (p. 138) are also prime places to tap into local happenings.

Why Iceland? Many look no further than Iceland's strong singing traditions. Others point to Reykjavík's ideal size: big enough to constitute a "scene," yet small enough that—with no real record industry or celebrity culture—the scene stays down to earth. Everyone is influenced by everyone else, styles easily cross-fertilize, and no one raises an eyebrow at the most outlandishly clashing double bills. Every record is reviewed in the press, though ironically many bands have risen only after gaining foreign attention.

The alternative scene roughly divides into three camps: hard rock, indie rock, and electronica. But don't mistake the hippest, edgiest alternative bands like Sigur Rós,

Múm and Gus Gus for the entire popular music scene. Iceland's version of *American Idol, Idol Stjörnuleit* (Idol Starsearch) is watched by half the country and is as unabashedly "pop" as its American forebear.

Nasa, Austurvöllur Square (✆ **511-1313;** www.nasa.is; daily 10pm–5:30am), Reykjavík's largest club venue, hosts every style imaginable. Another prestigious and diverse club venue, where you can usually catch two bands for less than the price of a movie ticket is **Sódóma Reykjavík,** Tryggvagata 22, (✆ **821-6921).**

A more intimate club than NASA, **Faktóry Bar,** Smiðjustígur 6 (✆ **865-2360;** www.faktory.is), showcases some of the best new acts on the Reykjavík scene. By contrast, the arena-size **Laugardalshöll,** Engjavegi 8 (✆ **553-8990;** www.laugardalsholl.is), on a soccer ground in Laugardalur Park, hosts the biggest international acts. **Cafe Rosenberg,** Klapparstígur 25-27 (✆ **551-2442**), is a dimly lit place to catch a jazz or folk band while sipping a glass of wine.

Performing Arts: Music & Dance

CLASSICAL MUSIC

Although overshadowed by Reykjavík's popular music scene, classical music thrives here and even has its own celebrities: Vladimir Ashkenazy has been an Icelandic citizen since 1972, and best-selling operatic tenor Garðar Thór Cortes is regularly voted sexiest man in Iceland. As with popular music, concerts have unpredictable schedules and play in unpredictable venues, so check daily listings. A highly recommended experience is to see an organ recital or choral music in **Hallgrímskirkja** (p. 128) or the more intimate **Fríkirkjan (Free Church),** Laufásvegur 13 (✆ **552-7270;** www.frikirkjan.is), on the east side of Tjörnin Pond.

In July and August the **Sigurjón Ólafsson Museum** (p. 130) moves aside the sculptures in its main hall for a discriminating series of classical and jazz concerts Tuesday evenings at 8:30pm. Each concert is 1 hour with no interval. **Salurinn,** Hamraborg 6 (✆ **570-0400;** www.salurinn.is), is a state-of-the-art classical venue in the nearby suburb of Kópavogur. The hall is made from Icelandic materials (driftwood, spruce, crushed stone) and has fabulous acoustics.

The **Icelandic Symphony Orchestra** (✆ **545-2500;** www.sinfonia.is), founded in 1950, is quite accomplished despite its short history. Sixty performances run each season from September to June. The most regular performance time is Thursday at 7:30pm. Currently they perform at **Háskólabíó,** aka the University Cinema, on Hagatorg Square at the university complex, but in 2011 they move into **Harpa,** the flashy new performance complex by the old harbor (see p. 125).

The Icelandic Opera, Ingólfsstræti 101, between Laugavegur and Hverfisgata (✆ **511-4200;** www.opera.is), was founded in 1978 and stages international and Icelandic operas. It will also soon have a new home at **Harpa.** Unfortunately for summer tourists, the northernmost opera house in the world only opens its doors in the spring and fall.

JAZZ

Reykjavík has no full-time jazz club—the closest approximation, Cafe Rósenberg, burned down in 2007—so devotees will just have to scour the listings. The **Reykjavík Jazz Festival** (✆ **862-1402;** www.reykjavikjazz.com) usually runs from late September to early October.

DANCE & THEATER

Most drama in Iceland is in Icelandic, but there are occasional shows put on with a tourist audience in mind, and these performances often provide a great (and amusing) insight into Icelandic culture. Ask at the Tourist Information Office and check listings in *The Reykjavík Grapevine*.

The **Icelandic Dance Company,** Listabraut 3 (✆ **568-8000;** www.id.is), focuses exclusively on contemporary dance and performs at the City Theatre (see below). The **Reykjavík Dance Festival** (www.dancefestival.is) includes choreographers from around the world and runs for 4 days in early September.

The **National Theater,** Hverfisgata 19 (✆ **551-1200;** www.leikhusid.is), hosts everything from Shakespeare and Chekhov to Rodgers and Hammerstein; but most productions are in Icelandic and the whole place shuts down in July and August.

The **Reykjavík City Theatre,** Listabraut 3, behind Kringlan shopping mall (✆ **568-8000;** www.borgarleikhus.is), is also unseen by most tourists, since most plays are in Icelandic and the season lasts from late September to May.

The **Travelling Theatre Company,** Vonarstræti 3, **Iðnó Theater,** near City Hall (✆ **551-9181;** www.lightnights.com), performs "Light Nights" for most of July and August, Monday and Tuesday nights at 8:30pm. The 90-minute mélange of Icelandic folk dancing, saga scenes, ghost stories, wrestling, and so on is aimed at tourists, and is a bit amateurish but genuine. Sometimes only available to pre-booked tour groups. Performances not suitable for children aged under 7.

Cinema

Instead of a full-time arty cinema, Reykjavík has a dedicated alternative distributor, **Græna Ljósið** (Green Light Films). Otherwise films are largely restricted to American blockbusters. Movies are subtitled, except for some children's films which are dubbed. Tickets are generally 1,000kr. The daily newspaper *Morgunblaðið* has film listings in English, or go to www.kvikmyndir.is and click the "Í Bíó" tab. As for cinema etiquette, Icelanders are strangely averse to watching film credits; most rise from their seats even before credits start to roll and ushers become impatient with any lingerers. Films have an intermission which abruptly cuts the film mid-sentence, unless distributed by Græna Ljósið (look for the green band on posters).

Volcano Show Since the 1950s, quasi-suicidal filmmakers Ósvaldur and Villi Knudsen have set out by 'copter, car, and foot to capture all of Iceland's volcanic eruptions. The presentation is disappointingly low-tech (this is no IMAX cinema) but some footage is unforgettable, notably the aerial view of a glacial waterburst after the 1996 Grímsvotn eruption and views of the 2010 eruptions (see p. 306). A second 1-hour film, which focuses on two major eruptions in the Westman Islands, is optional. The amiable Villi will likely be there to welcome you and ask where you're from.

The Red Rock Cinema. Hellusund 6A. ✆ **845-9548**. Tickets available at box office 30 min. before showtime, or at Tourist Information Office (p. 99). For 1-hr. program: 1800kr adults; 900kr students; 500kr children aged 10–16. For 2-hr. program: 2000kr adults; 1100kr students; 600kr children. Showtimes in English Jul–Aug 11am, 3 and 8pm; Apr–Jun and Sept, 3 and 8pm; Oct–Mar 8pm. AE, MC, V.

NEAR REYKJAVÍK

Visitors using Reykjavík as a home base will find an incredible wealth of scenery and activities within easy reach. Typical highlights of Icelandic nature and culture are only a day trip away. If you have limited time, or are taking advantage of Icelandair's free stopover on flights between North America and Europe, this southwest chunk of Iceland will provide you with more than enough waterfalls, geysers, lava fields, activities, and museums. There are plenty of good bus tours, but we recommend renting a car (even just for a day) because many sights are otherwise inaccessible. Keep in mind that parts of West and South Iceland (Chapters 8 and 10) are also only an hour or two away, in case you'd like to add a glacier or recent volcanic eruption to your itinerary too.

HAFNARFJÖRÐUR

10km (6 miles) S of Reykjavík.

From the main road, it's easy not to notice Hafnarfjörður, even though it's Iceland's third-largest town (pop. 26,000) and second-busiest port. Once you've reached the waterfront, however, it's clear Hafnarfjörður has a distinct identity. Its port has been trading continuously since the 14th century and by the early 15th century it had become a major trading hub, first with the British, then the Germans, before the Danish king imposed a trade monopoly on Iceland in 1602. This history, combined with the shape of the port and its effect on centuries of town planning, gives Hafnarfjörður more the ambience of a Northern European seaside town than Reykjavík. Also unlike Reykjavík, the town is carved out of the surrounding lava field.

Icelanders are often subjected to two stereotypes: 1) that they are modern-day Vikings, and 2) that they still believe in elves. Icelanders hardly disown these stereotypes, but may cringe when confronted with them in crude forms. Two of Hafnarfjörður's biggest tourist draws—the **Viking Village** and **Hidden Worlds elf tours**—play up these stereotypes outrageously. If you're visiting in June and want kitsch overload, come to Hafnarfjörður for the **Viking Festival** (p. 34).

Essentials

GETTING THERE The drive from Reykjavík is only 15 minutes; take Route 40 south to the Hafnarfjörður turnoff. Bus 1 runs every 30 minutes (more regularly from September to May) from Hlemmur and Lækjartorg bus stations in Reykjavík to Hafnarfjörður's shopping area, near the tourist information office (and a 10-minute walk from the Viking Village). The trip takes about 25 minutes. Buses connecting Reykjavík and Keflavík often stop in Hafnarfjörður. For a taxi, call **A-Stöðin** (✆ **555-0888**).

VISITOR INFORMATION The **tourist office,** Strandgata 6, inside the Town Hall (✆ **585-5780;** www.visithafnarfjordur.is), is open Monday to Thursday 8am to 5pm, Fridays 9am to 5pm; from June to August it's also open weekends, from 10am to 3pm.

What to See & Do

Fjörukráin Viking Village ☺ Hafnarfjörður's biggest tourist draw is this over-the-top, Viking-themed restaurant and hotel. The Viking Restaurant dining hall is based on a Norwegian church, with dragon heads carved on the roof, and the interior is festooned with shields, tapestries, horse hides, and runic symbols. Dinner is the main event, as actors in Viking and Valkyrie costumes sing, dance, and tell stories. Friday and Saturday nights are especially raucous. The secret of Fjörukráin's success is the combination of shameless kitsch (Viking employees storm arriving tour buses to "kidnap" visitors, who are later presented with "honorary Viking" certificates) with earnest historicism (they'll have you know *real* Vikings never had tusks sticking out of their helmets). Keep an eye on the tour groups. They've probably paid extra for combat demonstrations and the like, and you can eavesdrop. The popular "Viking menu" includes fish soup, dried haddock, lamb shank, and *skyr* for dessert—plus a

NOTES ON entering THE COUNTRYSIDE

You don't need to venture far from Reykjavík to feel as though you're in the countryside, or perhaps on another planet. Mossy lava fields abound, cliff tops swarm with thousands of squawking birds, and thin ribbons of waterfall are haphazardly strewn about mountainsides. But if you're leaving downtown Reykjavík for the first time since you arrived in Iceland, the dramatic landscape is an invigorating shock to the system. The land feels strangely unformed, caught in geological transition. Without trees or thick vegetation obscuring the view, the ever-distant horizon seems impossibly close, yet the tops of mountains impossibly high. Iceland's original settlers found no natives to subdue, and never had to group their homes on hilltops in defensive clusters. Farmsteads, evenly spread throughout the land, have been the basis of Icelandic society until relatively recent history. Every farm has a name—often the same name it had 1,000 years ago—and its own road sign. The name is usually derived from its surrounding geography. Still today, each farm and its natural environs merge personalities.

Near Reykjavík

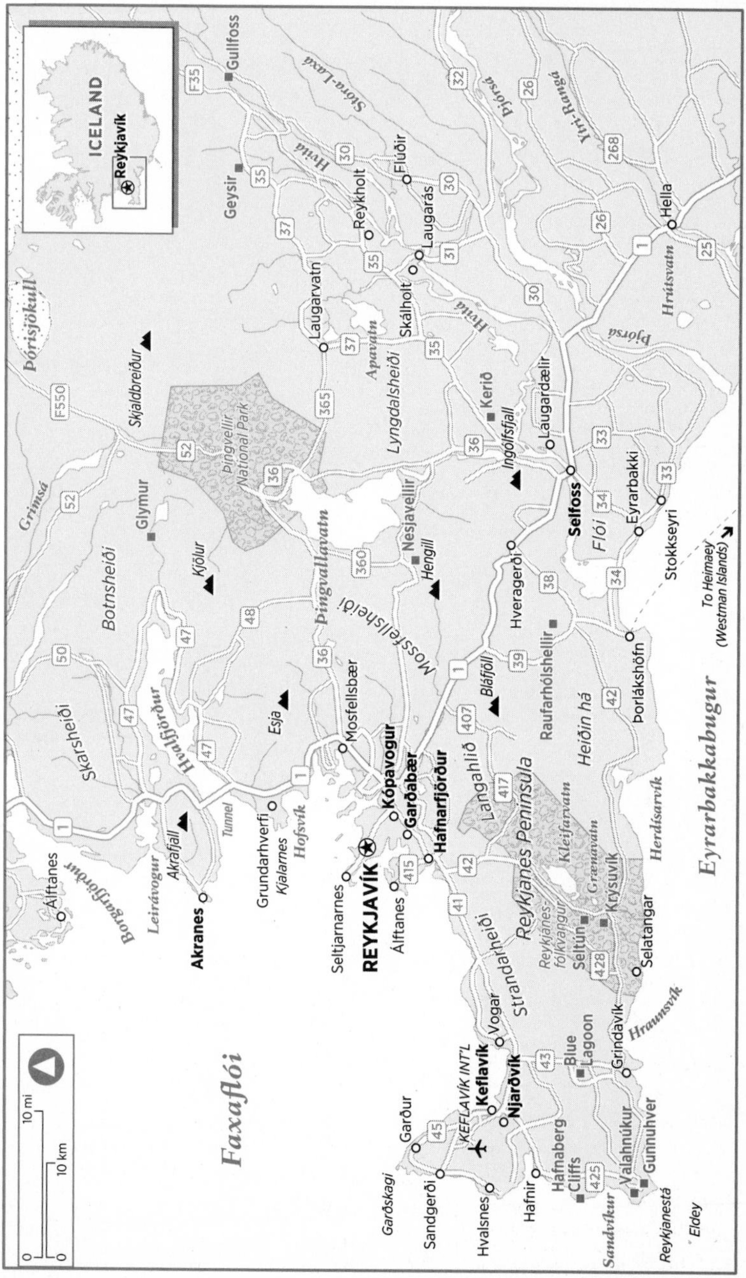

cube of putrefied sharkmeat speared with an Icelandic flag (get your napkin or a shot of *Brennivín* ready). Plenty of conventional dishes are offered, too, and no one will make you consume raw horsemeat. For the Viking Hotel, see below.

Strandgata 55 (at Viking Village). ✆ **565-1213.** www.vikingvillage.is. Reservations recommended. Main courses 2,150kr-6,150kr; Viking menu 8,700kr including drinks. MC, V. Lunch Thurs-Sat noon-3pm; dinner daily 6-10pm; bar open late Fri-Sat.

Hidden Worlds ☺ Hafnarfjörður is famous for its large population of "hidden people" (see p. 148), particularly elves, and local medium Sigurbjörg "Sibba" Karlsdóttir can help you find them. Hidden people pop up along the tour route, which should intrigue young kids, even if the costumes aren't terribly convincing. Afternoon tours leave twice per week all year around and last 1½ to 2 hours.

✆ **694-2785.** www.alfar.is. Tickets 3,600kr including a "Hidden Worlds" map. Tues and Fri 2:30pm.

Where to Stay & Dine

Hafnarfjörður has plenty of places to stay (listed at www.visithafnarfjordur.is) and some decent food, but most dinnertime visitors are here to experience the Viking Village.

Fjörukráin Viking Village Hotel While the adjoining restaurant is crammed with Viking paraphernalia, the hotel's pleasant, modern rooms are sparingly adorned with Viking motifs—tree-stump tables, some beds with chariot wheels. The deck is perfect for a sunset cocktail. The Viking Village's second restaurant, **Fjaran,** shares the same menu as the Viking Restaurant (above) but with a more subdued atmosphere.

Strandgata 55. ✆ **565-1213.** Fax 565-1891. www.vikingvillage.is. 42 units. Apr-Sept 17,500kr double; 23,500kr mini suite. Rates around 30% lower Oct-Mar. Rates include breakfast. MC, V. **Amenities:** Hot tub; sauna. *In room:* TV, Wi-Fi.

Súfistinn This friendly, local hangout is a good place to relax and recharge with a cup of the best coffee in town. The cafe menu offers salads, sandwiches, quiche, and a good selection of cakes, crepes, and other sweet treats. The outdoor seating is pleasant in fine weather.

Strandgata 9. ✆ **565-3740.** Small dishes 790kr-2,490kr. DC, MC, V. Mon-Thurs 8:15am-11:30pm; Fri 8:15am-midnight; Sat 10am-midnight; Sun noon-11:30pm.

MOSFELLSBÆR

15km (9¼ miles) NE of Reykjavík.

This town hasn't been swallowed up by the overflowing city, but its day may soon come. Even Kópavogur, now closer to the middle of Reykjavík than its outer reaches, was once a distinct town. The outskirts of Mosfellsbær yield to beautiful pastureland, where you'll find the town's main attraction: the former home of Halldór Laxness (below), Iceland's greatest modern writer.

The **tourist office** (✆ **525-6700;** www.mos.is) is at the library in the Kjarni shopping mall (Þverholt 2).

Halldór Laxness Museum (Gljúfrasteinn) ★ Gljúfrasteinn, which became a museum in 2004, should interest most fans of the Nobel Prize-winning author. Halldór spent most of his adult life in this mid-20th-century country home, full of original furniture and artwork by close friends Jóhannes Kjarval, Svavar Guðnason, and Nina Tryggvadóttir. Halldór's well-polished 1968 Jaguar still sits in the driveway.

The recommended 25-minute audio tour includes interview clips with Halldór and his wife, voiced over in English. Halldór was a fine pianist, and concerts are still held on his grand piano every Sunday at 4pm from June through August; tickets are only 500kr. Guests are encouraged to bring picnics and walk along the river.

It's no longer easy to reach Gljúfrasteinn without a car. Bus 15 takes you from Reykjavík to central Mosfellsbær; from there bus 27 is scheduled to take you to near the museum, but now this is effectively a taxi service run by the bus company which you need to order at least an hour in advance—and the same again in reverse for the "bus" back. If you combine the museum visit with horseback riding at Laxnes Farm, you may be able to strike a deal with them as they offer hotel pickup (for not much more than a bus fare) anyway.

✆ **586-8066.** www.gljufrasteinn.is. Admission 800kr adults, children aged under 18 free. June–Aug daily 9am–5pm; Sept–May Tues–Sun 10am–5pm. From Reykjavík by car, take Rte. 1 through Mosfellsbær, then turn right on Rte. 36; the museum is marked a few km ahead.

HORSEBACK RIDING Across the road from the Laxness Museum (above)—but no longer connected with Halldór Laxness' family—is **Laxnes Horse Farm** (**✆ 566-6179;** www.laxnes.is). A visit to the farm is recommended for those who would like a short ride near the premises or a longer tour of the area. 6,000kr for a 2-hour ride, leaving daily 9:30am and 1:30pm (hotel pickup at 9am or 1pm usually available); generally not for children under 6.

SHOPPING Prices on the large selection of wool clothing and handicrafts at **Álafoss Factory Outlet,** Álafossvegur 23 (**✆ 566-6303;** www.alafoss.is), are 15–20% below Reykjavík levels. Coming by bus (15 from Hlemmur, then 27 or 57) involves a 400m (¼ mile) walk from the nearest stop. By car, follow Route 1 north through three traffic circles in Mosfellsbær, then turn right off the fourth traffic circle onto Álafossvegur. The store is 320m (1,050 ft.) ahead on the left. Hours are Monday through Friday 9am to 6pm and Saturday 9am to 4pm. Other stores in this hub include **Knives of Distinction,** Álafossvegur 29 (**✆566-7408**; www.knifemaker.is), where you can watch Páll Kristjánsson at work carving knife handles and other trinkets from whale teeth and reindeer antlers.

ESJA, HVALFJÖRÐUR & AKRANES

Esja is 22km (14 miles) N of Reykjavík; Hvalfjörður is 25km (16 miles) N of Reykjavík; Akranes is 48km (30 miles) N of Reykjavík.

This coastal area north of Reykjavík is often bypassed by visitors, but the scenery is up to Iceland's high standard, particularly Iceland's tallest waterfall, **Glymur.**

Essentials

GETTING THERE Route 1 leads north from Reykjavík, passing Esja before reaching the tunnel across Hvalfjörður to Akranes. For Akranes, turn left after the tunnel on Route 51, then left again on Route 509. Nine buses make the trip from Reykjavík to Akranes on weekdays (six on weekends); the route—bus 15 from BSÍ or Hlemmur stations, connecting with bus 57 in Mosfellsbær—goes right past the Esja trailhead (tell the driver if that's your destination) but bypasses the coastline of Hvalfjörður by taking the tunnel.

VISITOR INFORMATION Questions about Esja should be directed to the tourist information office in Reykjavík (p. 99). Hvalfjörður is in Akranes township. The **Akranes Tourist Information Office,** at the Akranes Museum, Garðar, (**© 431-5566;** www.visitakranes.is), is open daily mid-May to mid-September from 10am to 5pm, and daily 1pm to 5pm the rest of the year. The **Borgarnes Tourist Information Office** (**© 437-2214;** www.westiceland.is; p. 181), is also helpful.

Exploring the Area

Climbing **Esja ★** all the way to the top is formidable but rewarding, and the mountain's main trails are well-marked and negotiable. Many opt to linger on the gentle slopes at Esja's base, especially those with children. Several routes lead up Esja, which is more of a volcanic range than a single peak. The recommended and most popular trail starts at a parking area along Route 1. (Heading north from Reykjavík, it's at the base of the mountain; look for the sign "Gönguleiðir á Esju" just after a driveway marked "Mógilsá.") From there it's a 780m (2,559-ft.), 4km (2½-mile) ascent to the marvelous Þverfellshorn lookout. Allow at least 5 hours for the return trip. The tallest peak (914m/2,999 ft.) is 3km (2 miles), but only tempts very devoted hikers. The excellent Myndkort "photomap," compiled from aerial satellite photographs, details all of Esja's trail routes.

North of Esja, drivers on Route 1 pass through a very deep, 6km (3¾-mile) **tunnel beneath Hvalfjörður,** completed in 1998. (***Beware:*** It's a speed trap.) On the far side are Iceland's only toll booths, which collect 900kr (Visa/MasterCard accepted) per car. The tunnel shortened the drive by 47km (29 miles), but the old route around the fjord is a scenic drive and the only way to reach Glymur.

Hvalfjörður means "whale fjord," and, if you keep your eyes fastened on it, you might see why. At 30km (19 miles) it's the longest fjord in southwest Iceland, and was an important naval base for the Allies in World War II.

Glymur ★★ is the tallest waterfall in Iceland (200m/656 ft.) and what it lacks in raw power, it makes up for in lithe beauty. Getting there is half the fun, with great views out to the fjord and surrounding countryside, and into a dramatic gorge filled with nesting birds in late spring and early summer. When the flow is substantial, Glymur is as breathtaking as Gullfoss (p. 161), but with 99% fewer tourists, thanks to its inaccessibility to cars. Glymur is also relatively unknown because the path is somewhat dangerous: the trail requires real caution, good balance, and agility. Also, the waterfall is less spectacular when the flow tapers off; ask around at local hotels and information offices to get an educated guess based on rain and meltoff.

To reach the trail to Glymur, turn off the main road at the head of Hvalfjörður. The parking area is a few minutes ahead. From the car park, a fenced-off dirt road bears toward the right, but the trail bears slightly left, marked with yellow-painted stones. In 2 to 3 minutes the trail divides, again without posted signs, though both routes are still marked with yellow rocks. The trail bearing left takes you up the west side of the gorge. This trail is shorter and easier but you don't get a good view of the waterfall. The right-hand path takes you across the river and up the east side of the gorge and is fully worth the extra effort. It reaches the river in 20 minutes or so; you have to wind through a cavity in the cliff to reach the shore, and then cross the river on a round wooden beam, while holding on to a steel suspension cable. Allow 2½ hours round-trip for the hike up the east side of the river.

Continuing west on Route 47 along the north shore of Hvalfjörður, you'll soon pass a deserted **whaling station.** At the tip of the peninsula is **Akranes,** a fishing and cement-factory town of around 6,000. The first settlers, who came as early as 880, are believed to have been Irish hermits. Akranes commemorates its founding with the **Irish Days festival** on the second weekend in July; events include a sandcastle competition, beach barbecue, and a contest to see who has the reddest hair. Just east of town is **Akrafjall,** the town's twin-peaked patron mountain. At 555m (1,804 ft.), Akrafjall's southern peak **Háihnúkur ★** is a less exhausting climb than Esja. A well-marked trail to the top runs along the edge of a cliff full of great black-backed gulls and other birds. The parking area is along Route 51, at the Akranes hot water utility.

Akranes Museum Iceland has many small-town folk museums. While this is one of the better and larger ones, it's typically hit or miss. In the **Icelandic Sport Museum,** one of several installations in the complex, you'll find entertaining artifacts such as a bike hand-twisted by Jón Páll Sigmarsson, Iceland's three-time winner of the "World's Strongest Man" competition. Even better than the extensive **rock and mineral collection** is the cartography exhibit, which has good English captions explaining the old surveying equipment and the personalities of all the sea monsters on 17th-century maps. Several old fishing vessels lie outside on the lawn.

Garðar. ✆ **431-5566.** www.museum.is. Admission 500kr adults; 300kr seniors; children under 16 free. June–Aug daily 10am–5pm; Sept–May daily 1–5pm. Entering Akranes on Rte. 509, turn left at first traffic circle onto Esjubraut; at next roundabout turn left onto Garðagrund; then take second left on Safnasvæði, and the museum is ahead on the left.

Where to Stay

Most day trippers from Reykjavík won't find reason to stay overnight, but Hvalfjörður offers a few beautifully situated accommodations.

Guesthouse Kiðafell This pleasant, down-home accommodation near the south shore of Hvalfjörður, 38km (24 miles) from Reykjavík, consists of four tidy, woody guest rooms on the upper floor of the farmer's house. Dinner is served on request, access to an Internet terminal is free, and short horseback riding tours are available.

✆ **566-6096.** www.dagfinnur.is/kidafell. 4 units w/shared bathroom. 13,800kr double, 8,500kr single. Rates include breakfast. Sleeping-bag accommodation from 4,500kr per person, not including breakfast (1,400kr). MC, V. From the southern junction of Rte. 1 and Rte. 47 (the junction south of the tunnel), take Rte. 47 east for about 4km (2½ miles), then turn right on Rte. 460 and the farm is 200m (656 ft.) ahead. *In room:* No phone.

Hotel Glymur ★★ Perhaps instead of staying in Reykjavík for your first or last night in Iceland, you'd prefer communing peacefully with coastal fjord scenery—and getting some luxury and style, too. This place more than fits the bill, with views out to the fjord.

Rte. 47. ✆ **430-3100.** Fax 430-3101. www.hotelglymur.is. 22 units. May–Sept from 3,640kr double; from 5,500kr for suite. Rates around 25% lower Oct–Apr. Children under 12 840kr for an extra bed. Rates include breakfast. Package offers available online. MC, V. From the northern junction of Rte. 1 and Rte. 47 (the junction north of the tunnel), take Rte. 47 east for 12km (7½ miles). **Amenities:** Restaurant, bar; outdoor hot tub. *In room:* TV, minibar, hair dryer, Wi-Fi.

Where to Dine

For an excellent "country chic" dinner in Hvalfjörður, make a reservation at **Hotel Glymur** (above). The menu includes catch of the day, trout, lamb, chicken and a vegetarian dish, for a set rate of 4,590kr. From noon to five it's a less expensive cafe, serving fish soup, fresh salad, and hot waffles.

In **Akranes,** the **Galito Restaurant,** Stillholt 16–18 (✆ **430-6767;** main courses 1,490kr–4,990kr; DC, MC, V; Sun–Thurs 11am–9pm, Fri–Sat 11am–10pm), has a typical small-town menu with a touch of pizzazz—possibly a reindeer special alongside the fish, lamb, burgers and pizza. The local bakery, **Brauða- og Kökugerðin**, Suðurgata 50a (✆ **431-1644**), makes sandwiches and serves coffee for those wanting a quick and easy lunch.

GOLDEN CIRCLE: ÞINGVELLIR, GEYSIR & GULLFOSS

Þingvellir is 49km (30 miles) NE of Reykjavík; Geysir is 118km (73 miles) NE of Reykjavík; Gullfoss is 125km (78 miles) NE of Reykjavík.

Each Golden Circle tour has its minor variations, but all include three major sights: **Þingvellir ★★**, meaning "Parliament Fields," where the Icelandic parliament first convened in 930; **Geysir ★**, a geothermal hotspot from which the English word geyser is derived; and **Gullfoss ★**, a majestic waterfall, whose name means "golden falls." The "Golden Circle" route as a whole isn't notably golden or circular, but "Mossy Green Triangle" is a less marketable title for the most popular day tour in Iceland. Nearby sights are often incorporated into the route, particularly the **Nesjavellir power plant, Kerið crater,** and **Skálholt,** once the most dominant settlement in south Iceland.

Essentials

GETTING THERE Bus tours are popular and convenient, especially in less than perfect weather or for when you're in the mood to sit back and relax, keeping your eyes wandering across the landscape while a local provides insights about the geography and history of the area. Even so, many visitors prefer the flexibility of a rental car. This allows time for a hike into the valley at Þingvellir, and you might fit in **Hveragerði** (p. 174) or the **Þjórsárdalur valley** (p. 298). The roads are open all year but can be very slippery and dangerous in winter. ***Note:*** If you plan on taking the interior Kjölur Route (p. 367) to Akureyri, you can see Geysir and Gullfoss then.

By car, Þingvellir is less than an hour from Reykjavík; take Route 1 north of Mosfellsbær, then turn right on Route 36. From Þingvellir, continue east on Route 36, turn left on Route 365, and turn left again on Route 37 in Laugarvatn; when Route 37 ends, turn left on Route 35. From there it's a short way to Geysir, and another 10 minutes to Gullfoss.

Regular service from **Reykjavík Excursions** (✆ **580-5400;** www.re.is) costs a bit less than a formal tour and is an economical way to spend all day at Þingvellir. Bus 6 leaves from the BSÍ terminal in Reykjavík daily mid-June through August at 8:00am, stopping at Þingvellir (8:55–9:40am), Laugarvatn (10:15am), Geysir (10:45am–12:45pm), and Gullfoss (1–1:45pm). Bus 6a does the reverse route without extended stops, except half an hour at the Þingvellir Service Station, arriving back at Reykjavík at 4:45pm. A one-way ticket to/from Þingvellir costs 1,900kr; to/from Gullfoss 3,900kr. Children up to age 11 free; ages 12 to 15 get 50% off.

Bus 2 on **Sterna** (✆ **551-1166;** www.sterna.is), leaving Reykjavík's BSÍ terminal daily at 8am from mid-May through August, stops at Þingvellir, Laugarvatn, Geysir, and Gullfoss—and on the return trip, Reykholt, Minniborg, and Selfoss—allowing time for sightseeing at Geysir and Gullfoss. Alternatively, you can take the 8:30am bus (confusingly called Bus 2 as well) which makes the same stops in the reverse order, again stopping for sightseeing at Geysir and Gullfoss. In both cases, there is a later return bus for those wanting to take a longer hike from Gullfoss or Geysir. The round-trip costs 7,200kr.

Bus tours leave from Reykjavík's BSÍ terminal, and prices include free hotel pickup and dropoff. Standard tours generally last 8 hours and leave at 8:30 or 9am. **Reykjavík Excursions** (✆ **580-5400;** www.re.is) charges 9,800kr for the standard Golden Circle tour, which includes Kerið Crater and Hveragerði. For Gullfoss and Geysir only, the "Gullfoss Geysir Direct" tour costs 8,600kr, lasts 5½ hours, and runs both during the day and as an evening tour. Children aged 12 to 15 get 50% off; ages 11 and under ride free. The Golden Circle tour from **Iceland Excursions** (✆ **540-1313;** www.icelandexcursions.is) costs 840kr and includes Nesjavellir geothermal power plant, Skálholt, Kerið Crater, and Hveragerði. "Golden Circle Afternoon" and "Golden Circle Evening" tours costs 800kr and last 6 hours. The **Netbus** (✆ **511-2600;** www.netbus.is) "Grand Golden Circle" tour will pick you up at your accommodation in Reykjavík daily at 8am from June until August, heading in an anti-clockwise direction to all the sites, stopping at Hveragerði, Geysir, Gullfoss, and Þingvellir for 8,000kr. **Iceland Total** (✆ **585-4300;** www.icelandtotal.is) has a Golden Circle tour focusing exclusively on the big three destinations for 860kr. If you want to make an even bigger day of it, there are also combination tours, taking in a museum or a glacier; check tour operator websites for details.

VISITOR INFORMATION Þingvellir has two **tourist offices** (www.thingvellir.is). Approaching from Reykjavík, the first you come to is **the interpretive center,** at the top of the Almannagjá fault; the turnoff from Route 36 is marked "Fræðslumiðstöð" (June–Aug daily 9am–7pm; Apr–May and Sept–Oct daily 9am–5pm; Nov–Mar Sat–Sun 9am–5pm). It has fun and informative video displays explaining the area's natural and cultural history, and sells books and maps. Along Route 36 is the **information office** (✆ **482-2660;** May–Sept daily 8:30am–8pm; the cafe is also open Apr and Oct 8:30am–8pm and Nov–Mar Sat–Sun 9am–5pm) with bookshop.

The **Geysir Center** (✆ **480-6800;** www.geysircenter.com; June–Aug daily 9am–10pm, May and Sept daily 9am–8pm, Oct and Apr daily 10am–4pm), across the street from the geothermal area, has an information desk, cafe, and extensive souvenir shop.

The unstaffed **Gullfoss visitor center** (Mon–Fri 9am–6pm; Sat–Sun 9–7pm) is right next to a **cafe and gift shop** (✆ **486-6500;** Oct–Apr daily 8am–6pm; May–Sept 8am to as late as 10pm), where questions can be directed.

Þingvellir ★★

Þingvellir, a rift valley bounded by cliffs to the east and west, about 6km (3¾ miles) apart, is the symbolic heart of the Icelandic nation, though it's hardly clear why at first glance. Without obvious historical markers, such as significant ruins, knowing a little of the area's history beforehand makes a visit much more interesting, and for the ultimate level of appreciation, reading an Icelandic saga or two will enable you to experience Þingvellir in the company of its many legendary ghosts. The first Icelandic parliament (or *Alþing*) convened here in 930, and remained here off and on through

Þingvellir National Park

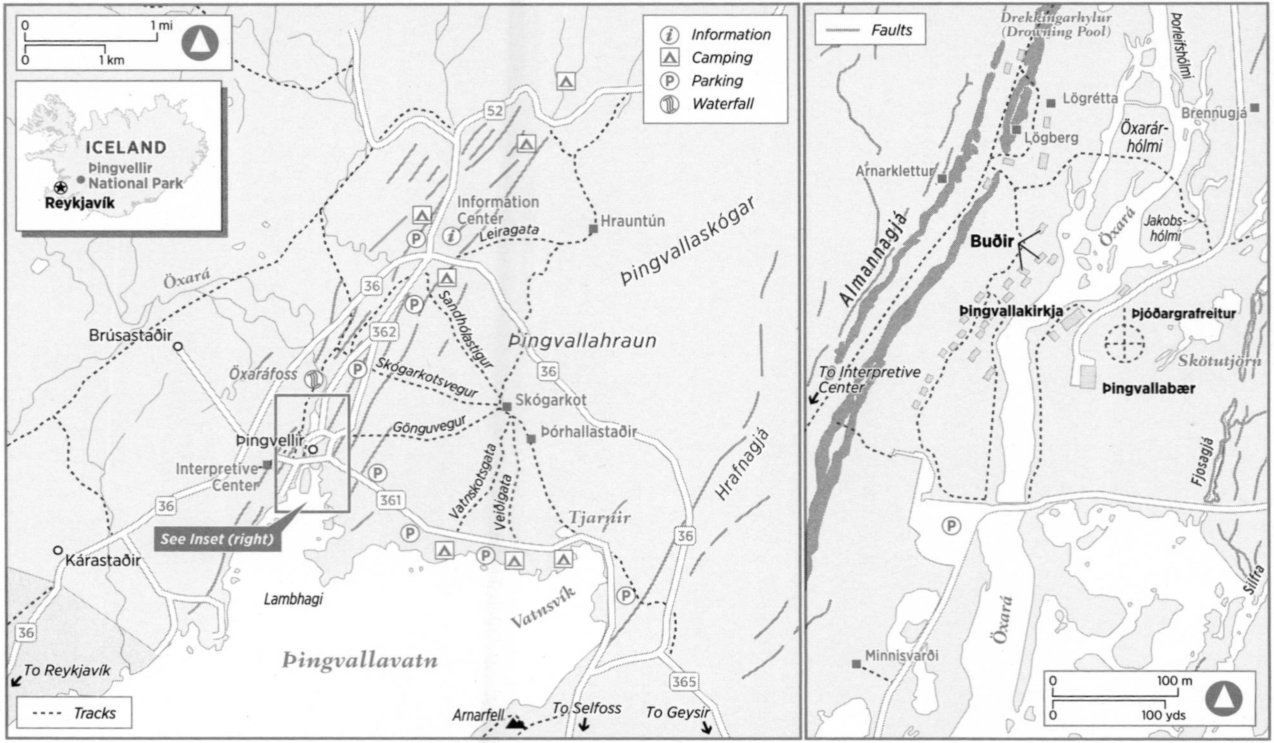

1798. (The Alþing, now in Reykjavík, is widely considered the oldest continuously-operating parliamentary institution in the world; it was actually disbanded for many years by Iceland's colonial rulers, so the Isle of Man has its own claim to this streak.) Þingvellir's annual parliamentary meetings were hardly limited to legislative sessions and court proceedings, however. They were also a news conference, trade fair, singles event, poetry reading, and circus ring all rolled into one. To Icelanders, Þingvellir is not only where their political independence originated, but also where their oral and literary traditions were passed on, and where their very sense of peoplehood formed. In the 19th and early-20th centuries, Þingvellir became a potent symbol and meeting place for the growing nationalist movement for independence from Denmark. In 1930, marking the millennium of the first Alþing, Þingvellir became Iceland's first national park. When Iceland gained formal independence in 1944, 20,000 people—one-sixth of the country's population—gathered at Þingvellir. The proclamation of independence was read in the pouring rain, followed by 2 minutes of silence, and then the peal of church bells. In 2004 Þingvellir became a UNESCO World Heritage site. It's still used for national commemorations.

Þingvallavatn, the largest natural lake in Iceland, forms Þingvellir's southern boundary; 90% of its water comes from underground springs and fissures. Þingvellir sits directly on the continental rift: land west of the **Almannagjá (Everyman's Gorge)** is moving west, and land east of the **Hrafnagjá (Raven Gorge)** is moving east. These borders have moved about 70m (230 ft.) apart in the last 10,000 years and continue to separate at about 8mm (⅓ in.) per year. The broad, lava-covered plain in the middle has fallen about 40m (131 ft.) in the same time span, forming the cliffs on either side. (In other words, 10,000 years ago the top of Almannagjá was level with what is now the valley floor.) In 1789, after an earthquake, the valley floor fell 5 feet in 10 days. The entire plain is riven with small crevices from all this geological stretching. ***Note:*** The tourist industry will tell you that the land to the west is "North America," tectonically speaking, and the land to the east is "Europe" or "Eurasia;" but the land to the east can't really be called Eurasia, because there's another major rift line farther east, running from Hella and Hvolsvöllur in the south to Mývatn in the north.

EXPLORING ÞINGVELLIR

Þingvellir is no Versailles; the only visible remnants of the old parliamentary gatherings are hardly more than lumps in the ground. All the main historical sites are clustered in the southwest corner of the park, and the vast majority of visitors never venture farther. This area was a good assembly site because the cliffs served as a natural amphitheater, the river provided fish and drinking water, and the plains held plenty of room for encampments. The rest of the park is undeveloped except for walking trails.

The parking areas closest to the sights are at the interpretive center and down in the valley off Route 362, about 150m (492 ft.) from the church. From the former there's a nice view of the latter, and a broad, well-tended path leads a short distance down through the **Almannagjá (Everyman's Fault)** to the designated **Lögberg (Law Rock),** marked by a flagpole. (No one knows for certain where the original rock was.) The **Lögsögumaður (Law Speaker),** the only salaried official at the Alþing, recited the laws from this podium by memory. Christianity was proclaimed the national religion at the Law Rock in the year 1000. (All Icelanders had to get baptized, but they were allowed to wait and find a warm geothermal spring on their way home.) Facing toward the south and the river, you can see bulges of earth and stone, the remains of temporary encampments called **búðir (booths).** The fault of **Flosagjá** forms the eastern border of the assembly. Northeast of the Law Rock, across the river, are the **Neðrivellir (Low Fields),** thought to be the meeting place for the **Lögretta (Law Council).**

The **Öxará (Axe River)**—so named, according to Icelandic folk legend, because this is where the axe that killed Jóra the troll washed up, an event predicted by the Norwegian king who had told Icelanders to set up their parliament wherever the axe was found—was probably diverted from its original course to provide drinking water for the assembly. North along the river is the **Drekkingarhylur (Drowning Pool),** where at least 18 women convicted of incest, infanticide, witchcraft, or adultery were tied in sacks and held under water. An informational panel marks the supposed spot. In the Christian millennial celebrations of 2000, a wreath was placed here in atonement for the executions. (Capital punishment was never widely practised in Iceland, and was phased out entirely by the mid-19th century. Even in the sagas, murderers are simply banished from Iceland for 3 years without imprisonment.) A short walk farther north is a pretty waterfall, **Öxaráfoss.**

Walking east from the Law Rock, you'll cross an islet in the river where duels were fought in the first decades of the Alþing. Dueling came to be known as *hólmganga,* which means "island-going." Duels drew big crowds, but were outlawed in 1008.

Across the river is the simple and charming **Þingvellir Church (Þingvallakirkja)** (Jun–Aug 9am–7pm), which seats about 35. The first church at the site was built around 1016, with a bell and timbers sent by King Olaf of Norway. The current church was consecrated in 1859 and restored in 1970 to something close to its original condition, with the notable exception of the new copper roof.

Next to the church is the unremarkable farmhouse **Þingvallabær,** a summer residence for the Prime Minister—no security fence necessary. It was built in 1930 to

WHY DOES ÞINGVELLIR church HAVE TWO ALTARPIECES?

Inside the church are two altarpieces. One depicts the Last Supper, and was painted on driftwood by local farmer and artisan Ófeigur Jónsson in 1834. The other, "Christ Healing the Blind Man," from 1896, is by Danish painter Niels Anker Lund (1840–1922). Ófeigur's painting was the original altarpiece, but it was deemed too primitive and amateurish by church authorities and replaced by Lund's painting at great expense. Ófeigur's painting was bought for a pittance by a Victorian heiress named Mary Disney Leith (1840–1926). Leith, who had a lifelong fascination with Iceland, journeyed there 18 times, wrote travel memoirs, and translated some sagas. The piece ended up in the collection of St. Peter's Church, Shorwell, on the Isle of Wight, near Leith's estate. When Þingvellir church was renovated in 1970, Magnus Magnusson—the prolific author, saga translator, and longtime "Quizmaster" on BBC1's *Mastermind*—tracked it down with the help of Mrs. Leith's granddaughter. The congregation in Shorwell Church returned it in exchange for a replica made at Iceland's National Museum.

commemorate the millennium of the first Alþing, and is not open to the public. Behind the church is **Þjóðargrafreitur,** a raised circular **graveyard.** Burial at this spot has been bestowed to only two men, Jónas Hallgrímsson (1807–1845) and Einar Benediktsson (1864–1940), both poets and key figures in Iceland's nationalist revival.

By the nearest parking area is a bridge overlooking the **Peningagjá (Money Fault).** Inside the fault is a clear, glistening pool that makes every child dream of diving down to collect all the coins. Throwing coins in pools all over the park is frowned upon by the wardens.

OUTDOOR ACTIVITIES

HIKING Simplistic trail maps are available for 350kr from the visitor offices, but trails are well-marked and you can probably just remember or jot down your route from signboards. More serious maps, including one called *The Golden Circle* (1,450kr) covering this whole region, are available at book stores and information offices.

Apart from the historical sites, and the north–south trails connecting the sites to the information office, all trails extend east into the **Þingvallahraun** lava field. All the field's lava flowed about 9,000 years ago from **Skjaldbreiður (Shield Volcano),** a perfectly rounded, squat cone visible to the north once you're out in the field. Named for its shape, Skjaldbreiður then lent its name (in translation) to all other shield volcanoes, just as Geysir lent its name to all geysers.

Virtually all the trails leaving from the western edge of the park converge halfway across the valley at the ruins of **Skógarkot,** a sheep farm abandoned since the 1930s. Each trail takes about 30 to 40 minutes. Skógarkot is now just a pleasant, grassy spot on a high point in the field, with a few stone foundations. Further east lies **Þórhallastaðir**, another farm ruin, but Skógarkot is more picturesque and enough to satisfy most day walkers. It's also an ideal picnic spot, with a great view over the lake to Hengill (p. 175) and the Nesjavellir geothermal power plant (below).

A **recommended loop itinerary** starts and ends at the information office. If you have 3 hours, head south along the fault to the historical sites, then take the trail east from the church to Skógarkot, cutting directly back to the office. With only two hours to spare, park near the historical sites and squeeze in a hike to Skógarkot and back. If you have just 1 hour, stick to the historical sites and venture north along the fault. Remember that you can time your trip to take advantage of the **free 1-hour guided tours** of the historical sites, leaving from **Þingvellir Church** (**Þingvallakirkja**) at 10am and 3pm weekdays, June through August. Serious hikers can follow a trail all the way to the eastern edge of the rift—near to where Route 36 climbs the eastern rift wall at Hrafnagjá—but it's too long for a return trip in 1 day, so you'd want to arrange a ride one way.

Forty percent of all Icelandic flora can be found in Þingvellir, but nothing is taller than a dwarf birch. It's especially pretty late in the year. As you walk through the valley, be careful not to step into the many fissures along the trail, and keep a close eye on children.

SCUBA DIVING **Diving** in Þingvallavatn has taken off recently. Dives focus on dramatic fissures on the lake bottom, up to 40m (131 ft.) below the surface. Þingvallavatn is not recommended for beginners, given the cold temperatures and currents inside the fissures. **Silfra** is the most renowned of these otherworldly ravines in Þingvallavatn. Dives must be reserved in advanced; see p. 80 for more information.

South of Þingvellir

Near the southwest shore of lake Þingvallavatn are the Nesjavellir power plant and the Hengill hiking area (p. 175), which is also accessible from Hveragerði to the south. The brochure *Hiking Trails in the Hengill Area* can be found at Nesjavellir and book stores.

Nesjavellir Geothermal Power Plant Iceland's renewable energy sources, hydropower and geothermal power, are the envy of fossil fuel-guzzling nations around the world. Nesjavellir, which produces municipal hot water and electricity from geothermal hot springs, was built in 1987 and attracts 20,000 visitors a year. Exhibits are informative, and the glassed-in observation platform affords a good view of the plant's gleaming pipery, but visitors expecting something out of a sci-fi movie may be disappointed. **Reykjavík Excursions** (✆ **580-5400;** www.re.is) and **Iceland Excursions** (✆ **540-1313;** www.icelandexcursions.is) include Nesjavellir in day-long bus tours, often combined with Þingvellir (above) and the geothermal greenhouses of Hveragerði (p. 174).

Off Rte. 360, around 12km (7½ miles) south of the Rte. 36/Rte. 360 junction. ✆ **480-2408.** Free admission. Jun–Aug Mon–Sat 9am–5pm, Sun 1–6pm; Sept–May no regular hours; call to inquire about group tours.

Geysir ★

The word "geyser" derives from this fascinating geothermal area full of hot springs, steaming creeks, mud marbled in mineral shades, turquoise pools encrusted with silica, and one reliable geyser. Access is always open.

Geysir (*gay-seerr*), discovered and named in 1294, refers to both this general area and a specific geyser, which once spouted as high as 80m (262 ft.), but is now just a calm, steamy vent with occasional hisses and gurgles. Rocks and soap were often dumped into Geysir to make it erupt on demand, only accelerating its demise. Recent research has shown that if the water level were lowered 2m (6½ ft.), Geysir would again erupt every 30 to 60 minutes to a height of 8 to 10m (26–33 ft.). Thankfully **Strokkur (The Churn),** another geyser next to *the* Geysir, spouts reliably every 5 minutes or so. Each spout varies in size, so wait to see at least two or three.

The geyser mechanism is not completely understood, but scientists agree that the eruptions are basically caused by a pressure buildup formed when hot water and gas is trapped beneath a cooler layer of water. Strokkur's eruptions reach as high as 35m (115 ft.). (Americans can be seen affecting nonchalance, since Old Faithful reaches 25–55m/82–180 ft., and Steamboat reaches 90–120m/295–394 ft.) The spouting water is around 257°F (125°C), so be careful not to stand downwind. Geysir is no doubt a natural wonder, but leaving Strokkur aside, there are several other Icelandic geothermal fields of equal or greater interest.

Geysir Museum (Geysisstofa) This catch-all museum has lighted panel displays on geysers, geothermal energy, hydropower, and earthquakes; and a video screen showing stock volcano footage. The earthquake simulator is quite fun if you've not experienced an earthquake before, but otherwise we'd recommend using the time instead to climb the hill overlooking the geothermal area.

Rte. 35, across from Geysir. ✆ **480-6800.** www.geysircenter.com. Admission 1000kr adults, 800kr seniors and children aged 6–12, free for children under 6. For opening hours, see Geysir Center, above.

Gullfoss ★★

Along the Hvitá river, just 7km (4 miles) from Geysir, Gullfoss is Iceland's most iconic and visited waterfall, as elegant as it is massive. The waterfall is a 5-minute walk from the parking area, and you'll hear it well before you see it. Two smaller falls at the top lead to an L-shaped curtain cascade dropping another 21m (69 ft.) into a 2.5km-long (1½-mile) gorge. The viewing angle doesn't quite let you see where the water hits bottom, but the spray (bring a raincoat) would conceal it anyway. When it's sunny, you can always expect a rainbow; in winter the falls are filigreed in beautiful ice formations.

Near the falls is a **monument to Sigríður Tómasdóttir,** who probably saved Gullfoss from being submerged by a hydroelectric dam in the 1920s. The daughter of the farmer who owned the property, Sigríður threatened to throw herself over the falls if the project went through. The courts ruled against her, but the hydroelectric company gave in to public pressure, and the contract simply expired in 1928.

The **visitor center** (Mon–Fri 9am–6pm; Sat–Sun 9am–7pm) is right next to a **cafe and gift shop** (Oct–Apr daily 8am–6pm; May–Sept 8am to as late as 10pm).

Near the Golden Circle

The sights below are listed in the order you would encounter them in a return trip from Gullfoss to Reykjavík. Kerið Crater and Skálholt are included in some Golden Circle tours. With your own car, you might also consider a side trip to the Þjórsárdalur Valley (p. 298) or Hveragerði (p. 174).

SKÁLHOLT

Skálholt, about 40km (25 miles) from the town of Selfoss, is off Route 31, a short detour south from Route 35, which connects Gullfoss and Selfoss. Though few visible remnants exist today, Skálholt was once the most wealthy, populated, and influential settlement in Iceland. In 1056 it became the seat of Iceland's first Catholic bishop. A church built at Skálholt in the mid-12th century from two shiploads of Norwegian timber was the largest wooden structure in medieval Scandinavia (and twice the length of the current church). The clerical class got rich from land tenants, but was also an important force in bringing education for all: laypersons of both sexes were enrolled, and classes were conducted in Icelandic as well as Latin. By the early 13th century Skálholt was Iceland's largest settlement, with 200 people; just before the Reformation it owned 10% of all land holdings in the country.

In 1550 Jón Arason, Iceland's last Catholic bishop—in fact, the last Catholic bishop of any Nordic country—was beheaded here along with his sons, after leading a rebellion against the Danish king's order to Lutheranize the country. They were buried without coffins at the back of the church, and by the following year, the monarchy had appropriated all church lands. Eighty meters (262 ft.) from the current church lies a crude relief on two slabs of stone, **a monument to Jón Arason,** to whom most Icelanders today can trace their ancestry.

The current **neo-Romanesque church** was inaugurated in 1956. The altarpiece, by prominent Icelandic artist Nína Tryggvadóttir (1913–1968), is an enormous mosaic of Christ with arms outstretched. The pulpit, which long predates the church, has a panel featuring the old Icelandic coat of arms: a filet of cod.

As you enter the church, a door to your left leads to a **museum** (✆ **486-8872;** admission 500kr; children under 12 free; mid-May to Aug daily 9am–8pm; Sept to mid-May; ask for key from the office building during working hours) in an underground passage that once connected the medieval church with its school buildings. Skálholt's history is well annotated here, but the centerpieces are the bishops' tombstones and the sarcophagus of Bishop Páll Jónsson (1196–1211), carved from a solid block of sandstone. The sarcophagus was discovered in a 1956 excavation, and the lid was raised in a formal ceremony. Páll's head lay on a stone pillow, his crosier (staff) still on his shoulder, but his Episcopal ring had been stolen by grave robbers.

Skálholt Summer Concerts Festival ★ Running since 1975, this free classical music festival features both contemporary music and early Icelandic music (mostly Baroque) with period instruments. The festival, which is held in the church, begins the first week of July and continues for 5 weeks.

✆ **486-8824.** www.sumartonleikar.is. Free admission. Concerts are usually Thurs 8pm, Sat 3 and 5pm, and Sun 3pm. There's also a Sun 5pm performance as part of a church service.

KERIÐ CRATER

Passersby on Route 35 (15km/9¼ miles northeast of Selfoss) should hop out to see this small but shapely scoria crater, formed 6,500 years ago by a collapsing magma chamber at the end of a volcanic eruption. Kerið is 55m (180 ft.) deep, including the stagnant water at the bottom, and the sides are nicely streaked in red, black, and ochre. Björk once did a concert from a raft in the middle, but the acoustics weren't ideal. A path runs around the rim, but watch your footing.

Outdoor Activities

RIVER RAFTING The Hvitá is Iceland's most popular river for white-water rafting, with fabulous scenery and easy to medium-difficulty rapids that don't require previous experience. Every afternoon from June through August, the recommended tour operator **Arctic Adventures** (Laugavegur 11; ✆ **562-7000;** www.adventures.is) sets out from its Drumbóbase camp, signposted from Rte. 35 about a 10-minute drive south of Geysir. The three-hour tour—with breaks for cocoa and cliff jumping—is 7,990kr per person, or 10,990kr with pickup/dropoff in Reykjavík (minimum age 12). For 9,990kr per person (12,990kr from Reykjavík), more daring paddlers can tackle the river in two-person inflatable canoes.

Where to Stay Along the Golden Circle

ÞINGVELLIR & NEARBY

Hótel Hengill This new Icelandair hotel with views of Lake Þingvallavatn is now the only non-camping option in the area, since Þingvellir's Hótel Valhöll was destroyed by fire in 2009. Rooms are bright and comfortable, and the hotel has the atmosphere of a relaxing country retreat.

✆ **444-4000** or 482-3415. Fax 444-4001. www.icelandairhotels.com. 22 units. June–Aug from 21,800kr double. May and Sept from 19,000kr; Oct–April from 14,000kr. Special offers available online. Rates include breakfast. AE, DC, MC, V. **Amenities:** Restaurant; bar; hot tubs; sauna. *In room:* Free Wi-Fi. From the Rte. 36/Rte. 360 junction, take Rte. 360 for 12km (7½ miles) and exit at the Nesjavellir turnoff for a further 4km (2½ miles) to the hotel.

GEYSIR

Geysir Guesthouse This simple, clean, and dependable guesthouse tends to fill up, so book early. Dinner is served on request, and the hot tub is a great spot for winding down.

Rte. 35 (Haukurdalur 3) just east of the Geysir Center. ✆ **486-8733** or 893-8733. Fax 872-1537. agustath@visir.is. 12 units w/shared bathroom. June–Sept 16,200kr double. Oct–Apr 13,900kr. Breakfast available for 1,200kr. MC, V. **Amenities:** Guest kitchen; hot tub.

Hótel Geysir Despite being right across the road from the geothermal field, very few rooms in this comfortable hotel have a view of the erupting geyser. Luxury doubles have king-size beds and Jacuzzis, and apartments and cabins are also available.

At the Geysir Center. ✆ **480-6800.** Fax 480-6801. www.geysircenter.is. May–Sept 19,900kr double. Discounts for children under 13. Rates around 10% lower Oct–Apr. Breakfast available for 1,400kr. **Amenities:** Restaurant; outdoor pool and hot tub; activities desk; horse rental. *In room:* TV, no phone, Wi-Fi.

GULLFOSS

Hótel Gullfoss This hotel is slightly more tasteful than others in the area, with medium-size rooms and an outdoor hot tub. With its strategic position at the northeast corner of the Golden Circle area, Hotel Gullfoss is well positioned for travelers heading into the interior.

On Brattholt farm, Rte. 35 between Geysir and Gullfoss. ✆ **486-8979.** www.hotelgullfoss.is. 16 units. Mid-Jun–Aug 31 22,500kr double; 33,750kr triple. Rates around 25% lower Sept–mid-June. Rates include breakfast. **Amenities:** Restaurant; bar; outdoor hot tub. *In room:* No phone.

FLÚÐIR

Icelandair Hótel Flúðir ★ The pretty town of Flúðir, known for its dairy farms and mushroom greenhouses, is ideal for exploring the Golden Circle and Þjórsárdalur Valley. This not-quite-upscale hotel has the usual single-story pre-fab look, but the medium-size rooms feel unusually relaxing. The village geothermal pool and fitness hall are close by, and the restaurant is exceptional (see "Where to Dine" below).

Vesterbrún 1, just off Rte. 30. ✆ **444-4000** or 486-6630. Fax 486-6530. www.icelandairhotels.is. 32 units. June–Aug from 21,800kr double. May and Sept from 19,000kr; Oct–April from 14,000kr. Special offers available online. Breakfast available (1,500kr). AE, MC, V. **Amenities:** Restaurant; bar. *In room:* TV, hair dryer, free Wi-Fi.

REYKHOLT

Guesthouse Húsið This friendly, low-key guesthouse with outdoor hot tub is a good economical option, perfect for exploring the area. Reykholt (not to be confused with the better-known Reykholt in west Iceland, see p. 181) is on Route 35, about 30km (19 miles) northeast of Selfoss.

Bjarkarbraut 26. ✆ **486-8680.** husid@best.is. 8 units w/shared bathrooms. June–Sept 15 8,400kr double. Rates around 15% lower mid-Sept to May. Sleeping-bag accommodation 3,000kr per person. Breakfast available on request (900kr). No credit cards. **Amenities:** Guest kitchen; Internet access; Wi-Fi. *In room:* No phone.

Where to Dine

Þingvellir's tourist office has a basic **cafe** (✆ **482-2660;** Apr–Oct daily 8:30am–8pm; Nov–Mar Sat–Sun 9am–5pm). The Geysir Center has a bigger **cafeteria** (✆ **480-6800;** June–Aug daily 9am–10pm, May–Sept daily 9am–8pm, Oct–Apr daily 10am–4pm) and Hotel Geysir (see above) has a good **restaurant** (main courses 2,200kr–3,700kr). Gullfoss has **Gullfoss Kaffi** (✆ **486-6500;** Mon–Fri 9am–6pm; Sat–Sun 9am–7pm), suitable for light meals.

Hótel Flúðir ★ FRENCH/ICELANDIC The menu at Flúðir is short and sweet, with just five main courses to get maximum benefit from the fresh ingredients, many of which are locally grown and organic. The mains could include a slowly baked cod with potato mousse, roast vegetables, and beurre noisette (hazelnut butter). The lunch menu always includes a burger or two, but also more traditional options such as "plokkfish" (a creamy fish and potato dish).

In Hótel Flúðir (see above). ✆ **486-6630.** Reservations recommended. Main courses 3,500kr–5,500kr. Daily 11:30am–9pm.

Hótel Hengill ★ ICELANDIC It may be another Icelandair hotel, but you'd be lucky to find food anywhere near this good on a plane. The fish is your best bet and is one of the few places in Iceland where you can taste Þingvallavatn char. The three-course "chef's pick" is great value for 5,200kr, especially compared with similar quality places in Reykjavík.

In Hótel Hengill (see above). ✆ **482-3415.** Main courses 3,200kr–4,200kr. Daily 11am–9pm.

Lindin ★ ICELANDIC This is the only standout restaurant in the Þingvellir to Gullfoss stretch of the Golden Circle itinerary and is much cheerier than the two Icelandair hotel restaurants (above). Look for seasonal offerings such as reindeer, goose, and guillemot, and the chocolate mousse which has earned an all-year-round place on the menu. Laugarvatn is a tiny resort town popular with Reykjavíkians, but Lindin restaurant is one of the few attractions it holds for tourists—others being sailboat rental at the lake and a geothermal sauna at the town pool.

Lindarbraut 2, 1 block from Rte. 37, Laugarvatn. ✆ **486-1262.** www.laugarvatn.is. Reservations recommended. Main courses 2,200kr–4,890kr. May–Aug daily 11:30am–10pm.

THE BLUE LAGOON (BLÁA LÓNIÐ)

50km (31 miles) SW of Reykjavík.

The **Blue Lagoon** ★★ (✆ **420-8800;** www.bluelagoon.com; June–Aug daily 9am–9pm; Sept–May daily 10am–8pm) is the most popular tourist attraction in Iceland, with around 360,000 visitors each year—20% more than Iceland's entire population. The surreal image of bathers in milky blue water, faces smeared with white mud, backgrounded by a power plant amid an expanse of black lava, may be the most common photographic emblem of an Iceland visit. Not everyone sees what the fuss is about, but all are guaranteed to walk out with that fresh mineral tingle.

WHAT IS THE BLUE LAGOON? Well, not the age-old hot pool you might imagine. It's actually the by-product of the geothermal power plant, when deep boreholes were drilled to extract blazing-hot, mineral-rich water under pressure from thousands of feet underground. This water produces electricity by driving steam turbines. The runoff water, still very hot, is too salty to provide central heating for homes, so it was piped into the lagoon, which was dug out of the lava field. The water gets its pearly, bluish hue from the combination of algae, silica, and other minerals. (In high summer, when the algae is in full bloom, the water is more green than blue.) The fuss all started when an Icelander suffering from psoriasis popped in for a swim. He noticed an immediate improvement in his skin condition, and the rest is a textbook marketing success story. (The "Blue Lagoon" was named not long after the 1980 Brooke Shields movie.) Recently a bank of lava was added, to shelter swimmers from the wind and to block views of the power plant. Sadly, some of the sci-fi ambience has been lost.

The spa has drilled its own water boreholes to regulate the temperature and balance the mineral and salt content. The salinity matches ocean water and reduces the eggy smell normally associated with geothermal water. Other spas have mimicked the Blue Lagoon's success, but none can quite duplicate its water formula. Studies have apparently confirmed the water's effectiveness for psoriasis, and the public health system even covers some visits here. Claims made for curing arthritis, baldness, negative karma, and the like are less reliable. In reality the two most common ailments treated by the Blue Lagoon are jetlag and hangovers.

Getting There

BY CAR The Blue Lagoon is less than an hour from Reykjavík, and just 15 minutes from Keflavík International Airport. From Route 41, which connects Reykjavík and Keflavík, turn south on Route 43. After about 8km (5 miles), turn right on Route 426 and follow the signs.

BY BUS A **public bus** goes to the Blue Lagoon from the BSÍ terminal (p. 100) in Reykjavík, but **bus tours** (see below) include the entrance fee and work out to almost the same price, plus they'll pick you up at your hotel.

TOURS Tours to the Blue Lagoon usually don't include a guide and are really just shepherding. **Netbus** (✆ **511-2600;** www.netbus.is) has the best deal: 5,500kr includes Reykjavík hotel pickup and dropoff plus admission to the Lagoon. There are five round-trips daily leaving between 9am and 5:15pm, plus four trips from the Lagoon to the airport. **Reykjavík Excursions** (✆ **580-5400;** www.re.is) has the same offer for 6,300kr; children aged 11 to 15 are half-price, under 11 free. They also have an evening tour that leaves Reykjavík at 6pm and gets you back at 10pm—order dinner from the restaurant before you jump in.

The Lagoon Experience

No orientation lecture here—basically you're just handed a locker key and sent off to shower and jump in a hot lake. (Make sure to remove rings, bracelets, and such; the water damages precious metals, especially silver.) White silica mud, which conditions and exfoliates the skin, is scraped from the bottom and left in buckets for guests to smear all over themselves. The water is around 100°F (36°–39°C), but the temperature can change abruptly as you move around. Watch out for the rectangular wood structures, where hot water is introduced. One billows steam just for effect.

Minerals in the lagoon water will temporarily coarsen and harden your hair. Conditioner—provided free in the showers—should be left in while you soak, and long hair should be tied up.

It's a very mixed scene: Icelanders are interspersed among visitors—some of whom aren't sure they want to share a bath with so many strangers. (Be reassured: the water is completely replaced by natural flow every 40 hours.) Private locker rooms are being added for those who don't like showering en masse.

Any time of year is great for a visit. Winter nights may be best of all, since you can watch the northern lights in complete comfort with icicles forming in your hair.

Basic admission (3,900kr adults; 1,180kr seniors (67+) and teenagers aged 14 to 15; 13 and under free) includes entrance to the lagoon, sauna rooms, and a pummeling waterfall. BYOT, unless you've booked a massage (in which case a towel is included in the price), otherwise towel rental is 830kr, and suit rental is 830kr.

Once you've had an **in-water massage,** you might never go back to on-land ones. You lie floating on your back with a blanket over you, while the masseuse's hands slide between your back and the floating mat. A 30-minute massage (6,000kr) is ideal; the shortest is 10 minutes (2,250kr). Call or check the website for a full menu of fabulous **spa treatments.** Book well in advance.

Where to Stay & Dine

The Blue Lagoon's 15-room "Clinic" is quite the undiscovered gem and has anything but an antiseptic hospital atmosphere. It is intended primarily for psoriasis patients, but accepts other guests when space is available. The luxurious rooms all have verandas, and guests enjoy a private section of the lagoon. Rates range from 30,800kr for a double in high season, to 18,200kr over winter. The Blue Lagoon has a push-your-tray **cafeteria** and the sit-down **Lava Restaurant,** which is surprisingly good and fairly priced, given the captive clientele. The broad menu has an international range, and several main courses are under 2,500kr. Reservations are recommended for dinner.

The Blue Lagoon had planned to open a luxury hotel in 2010, however this was put on hold indefinitely after Iceland's economic crisis in 2008 (see p. 14). In the meantime, your other dining and accommodation options are the nearby Northern Light Inn (below) and several places in Grindavík (6km/3¾ miles away) and Keflavík (20km/12 miles away; below).

Guesthouse Borg This convivial guesthouse in central Grindavík (p. 172) is 5 minutes from the Blue Lagoon and won't break the bank. Rooms are snug, and breakfast is an array of cereal and cold cuts.

Borgarhraun 2 (by Víkarbraut). ✆ **895-8686.** Fax 462-8696. www.guesthouseborg.com. 7 units w/ shared bathroom. May 15–Sept 15 11,000kr double. Rates around 25% lower off season. Rates include breakfast. MC, V. **Amenities:** Guest kitchen; Internet terminal.

Northern Light Inn ★ This hotel's prices somewhat reflect its perceived monopoly, but it's an appealing and welcoming place nonetheless, with handknits by the proprietor for sale in the lobby. The glass-walled dining room and sun porch are great for gazing across the stunning lava field. Rooms are simple and sizeable. The **restaurant,** open daily from 7am to 9pm, delivers what it calls "hearty Nordic soul food," but it has a more healthy and refined touch than the label implies (main courses 2,500kr–5,900kr).

Rte. 426, just east of Blue Lagoon. ✆ **426-8650.** Fax 426-8651. www.nli.is. 20 units. June–Aug 26,600kr double; 32,900kr triple. Rates around 15% lower May and Sept, 30% lower Oct–Apr. Rates include breakfast. MC, V. **Amenities:** Restaurant; free airport & Blue Lagoon transfers. *In room:* TV, fridge, free Wi-Fi.

KEFLAVÍK

47km (29 miles) SW of Reykjavík.

For many visitors, one look down from their descending plane on to Keflavík's sprawling Lego housing is all they need to know. But **Keflavík ★** is an underrated town, and you could do much worse than spend your first or last night here. It's also a good base for all of Reykjanes Peninsula. In early September, the sea cliffs are dramatically lit up for the "Night of Lights," with live music, family entertainment, and a fireworks show.

After World War II, Keflavík prospered from providing services for the nearby NATO base, but September 30, 2006, marked the end of an era when the base was officially abandoned. In an understated ceremony, the U.S. flag was lowered, and the Icelandic flag was raised in its place. Iceland now has no armed forces on its territory. Since then the base has been in a state of transformation, offering student accommodation and hosting a variety of businesses focusing on green energy, health, and logistics. Keflavík maintains a strong fishing economy and has merged with Njarðvík to the east, to form a single municipal entity called Reykjanesbær. The joint population is more than 10,000—by far the largest settlement on the peninsula.

Essentials

GETTING THERE Route 41 connects Reykjavík to Keflavík. **SBK** (✆ **420-6000;** www.sbk.is) links Reykjavík and Keflavík with five to seven scheduled buses each weekday, and three on weekends (1,600kr; ages 4–11 half-price). The bus leaves from BSÍ terminal in Reykjavík, stopping at Kringlan Mall, and makes several stops in Keflavík.

VISITOR INFORMATION The Reykjanes Peninsula **tourist office** is at Krossmói 4, Reykjanesbær (✆ **421-3520;** www.visitreykjanes.is; Mon–Fri 9am–5pm, Sat 10am–2pm).

Exploring Keflavík

If it's your last day in Iceland, and you'd like one last stroll to commune with the ocean, proceed north from the Duus Hús on the well-worn **path along the clifftop.** On a clear day you can see Reykjavík or even Snæfellsnes Peninsula 100km (62 miles) away.

For contemporary art incorporating sound and space, Suðsuðvestur, Hafnargata 22 (✆ **421-2225** or **662-8785;** www.sudsudvestur.is), right on the main strip, is among Iceland's best exhibition venues. Admission is free, and the space is open weekends (2–5pm) or by calling ahead.

Duus Hús ★ This large warehouse contains an art museum and cultural exhibit—both very competently run—but is best known for its collection of almost 100 ship models, all built by local skipper Grímur Karlsson. Since his 1984 retirement, Grímur has constructed over 200 .6m to 1.5m (2–5 ft.) models of actual, midsize Icelandic fishing vessels. The models are meticulously detailed but also beautifully capture the vessels' various characters. In 2009, Grímur was awarded the Knight's Cross, Iceland's highest medal, in recognition of the cultural value of his work.

A small concert space hosts everything from piano recitals to juggling performances (call for schedule). You can wander in anytime to see an original work by Iceland's best known painter, Jóhannes Kjarval, on the side wall.

Duusgata 2-10. ✆ **421-3796.** www.listasafn.reykjanesbaer.is. Free admission. Weekdays 11am–5pm; weekends 1–5pm.

Where to Stay

As the closest town to the airport, Keflavík has many lodging options, most of which offer free airport transfers.

Keflavík

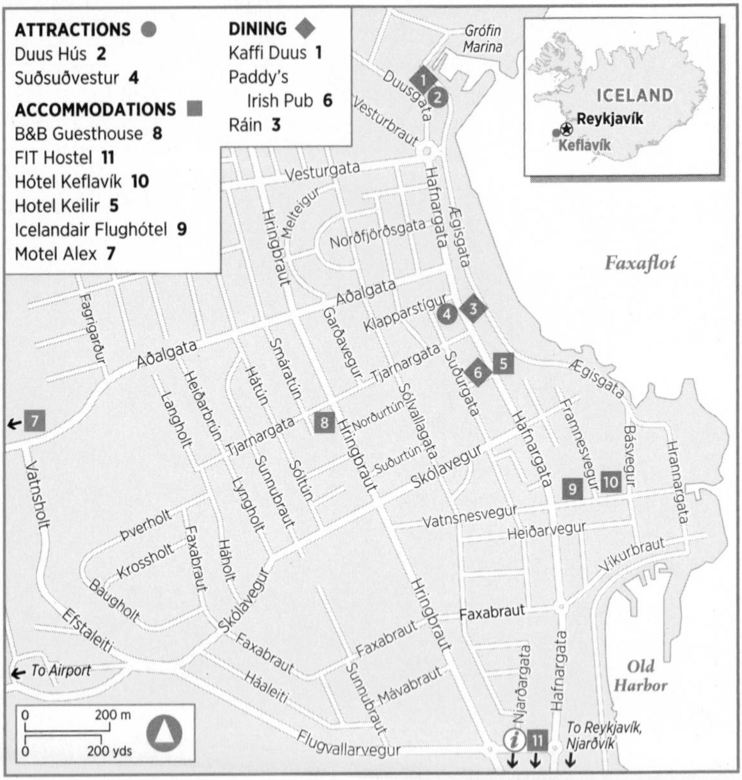

EXPENSIVE

Hótel Keflavík ★ Compared to the Flughótel below, this hotel is frumpier but has more character, celebrating its 25th anniversary in 2011. Make sure to ask for an ocean view. Standard rooms are not great value; deluxe rooms are significantly more spacious, with desks and bathtubs, and suites have hot tubs. Booking online is key, because you'll probably get at least 20% off published rates. Two good **restaurants** are on the premises: Café Iðnó—very reasonably priced dishes such as "health sandwiches" and grilled trout—and the Sunset, with more of an emphasis on traditional Icelandic food. The hotel also maintains a six-room **guesthouse** across the street. The rooms are perfectly acceptable, and you get the same access to hotel facilities for around half the price.

Vatnsnesvegur 12–14. ✆ **420-7000.** Fax 420-7002. www.kef.is. Hotel: 68 units. 27,800kr–29,800kr double; 31,800kr family room; 32,800kr–33,800kr suite. Guesthouse: 6 units w/shared bathroom. 12,800kr double. Rates include breakfast. MC, V. **Amenities:** Restaurants; bar; health club; sauna; solarium; free airport transfer; room service. *In room:* Hotel: TV/DVD, DVDs on request, CD player, minibar, hair dryer, free Wi-Fi. Guesthouse: TV, no phone.

Icelandair Flughótel ★ Right next door to the Hótel Keflavík, this modern business-class hotel meets the usual smart and efficient Icelandair standard. Rooms in the newer wing have better soundproofing. Deluxe rooms are not much larger and probably not worth the extra money, but booking online will usually save you 10–40% off published rates.

Hafnargata 57. ✆ **421-5222.** Fax 421-5223. www.icelandairhotels.com. 62 units. 26,400kr–31,400kr double; 36,400kr junior suite. Rates around 25% lower Apr–May and mid-Sept to Oct, and around 40% lower Nov–Mar. Rates include breakfast. AE, MC, V. **Amenities:** Restaurant; spa; free airport transfer. *In room:* TV, minibar, hair dryer, free Wi-Fi.

MODERATE

Hotel Keilir This downtown hotel offers good, personal service—if you phone, it will probably be the owner who answers and it's possible to negotiate the rate during quieter times. Half the rooms, which are all minimalist, have good ocean views from cement balconies; the other half overlook the main drag. Bathrooms are more spacious than average.

Hafnargata 37. ✆ **420-9800.** Fax 422-7941. http://eng.hotelkeilir.is. 40 units. May 15–Sept 15 17,900kr double; 19,000kr deluxe double/family room. Rates around 40% lower Sept 16–May 14. Rates include breakfast. MC, V. **Amenities:** Bar. *In room:* TV, minibar, free Wi-Fi.

INEXPENSIVE

If you need inexpensive options, **B&B Guesthouse,** Hringbraut 92 (✆ **421-8989;** www.bbguesthouse.is), a short walk from Keflavík's main drag, has 10 comfortable and clean (if not cheery) doubles with shared bathroom for 10,400kr including breakfast. Amenities include a guest kitchen and free airport transfer. Your cheapest option is **FIT Hostel,** Fitjabraut 6a (✆ **421-8889;** www.hostel.is), in Njarðvík, where basic doubles start at 10,100kr (8,100kr for the room, plus bed linen 1,000kr per person) and dorm beds are 3,100kr. Amenities include Internet access and a hot tub.

Motel Alex On the outskirts of town, and just 2 minutes from the airport, this functional and spotless choice has camping grounds, sleeping-bag accommodation in a 10-bed dorm, guesthouse doubles, and 19 self-contained mini-huts with kitchenette, fridge, coffeemaker, and a tiny bathroom all squeezed in . . . and there's a hot tub. For the increasing number of cycling tourists, if you spend your first and last night's camping here, Motel Alex will store your bike box in between for free.

Aðalgata 60. ✆ **421-2800.** Fax 421-4285. www.alex.is. 26 units, 7 w/shared bathroom. June 15–Aug 9,900kr double in guesthouse w/shared bathroom; 11,900kr hut for 2 persons w/private bathroom; 2,000kr sleeping-bag accommodation—Jun–mid-Sept only. Children aged 9 and under free. Guesthouse/hut rates include breakfast. Guesthouse closed Dec–mid-Apr; huts closed Nov–mid-Apr. AE, MC, V. **Amenities:** Hot tub; bike rental; free airport transfer for guesthouse/hut guests, otherwise 300kr; guest kitchen; free Internet.

Where to Dine/Nightlife

Keflavík's best down-to-earth local bar, **Paddy's Irish Pub,** Hafnargata 38 (✆ **421-8900;** Sun–Thurs 5pm–1am; Fri–Sat 5pm–5am), has live music Friday and Saturday with no cover—and, of course, Guinness by the pint.

Kaffi Duus CAFE/SEAFOOD This charmer tucked away on the north end of town has nice harbor views, outdoor seating, and fishing paraphernalia adorning the walls. By day it's a casual cafe, by night it's fine dining, and after dinner it's an energetic bar with occasional live music. Fish specials are reliably exceptional.

Duusgata 10. ✆ **421-7080.** Reservations required for dinner. Main courses 1,900kr–4,700kr; lunch 1,200kr–1,800kr. Daily 10am–10pm; bar open late Fri–Sat.

Ráin ICELANDIC The huge dining area, with great ocean views, arcs around a dance floor and stage, where live bands cover oldies but goodies on weekends, and locals sing karaoke on Thursdays after 10pm. LPs lining the walls of the bar hark back to the 50s and 60s, when Keflavík was at the vanguard of the rock 'n' roll revolution, thanks to radio broadcasts from the U.S. military base. Ráin—*row-inn*, meaning crosstree, not precipitation—is very appealingly unhip and the menu, especially its extensive seafood offerings, is easily recommended.

Hafnargata 19a. ✆ **421-4601.** www.rain.is. Reservations recommended. Main courses 3,390kr–4,600kr. Sun–Thurs 11am–1am; Fri–Sat 11am–3am.

REYKJANES PENINSULA

47km (29 miles) NE of Reykjavík.

From Keflavík airport, this southwestern extremity of Iceland appears to be a bleak and uniform expanse of lava rock. But however barren and austere, Reykjanes is a wondrous and geologically varied landscape. The north coast is indeed flat and contains most of the peninsula's population. The western, southern, and interior regions, on the other hand, contain striking volcanic ranges, geothermal hotspots, and sea cliffs full of nesting birds. Some parts are so remote that only a few local farmers in search of stray sheep have ever set foot in them. A trail system is well developed, but hiking routes are often unmarked, and it can be difficult to find drinking water or a soft place to pitch a tent.

Essentials

GETTING AROUND Reykjanes is really best accessed by car or tour. Regular bus routes do extend to Garður and Sandgerði in the northeast and Grindavík on the south coast, but stops aren't spaced with tourists in mind. **SBK** (✆ **420-6000;** www.sbk.is) connects Garður, Sandgerði, Grindavík, and Vogar to Keflavík and Reykjavík several times a day. **Reykjavík Excursions** (✆ **580-5400;** www.re.is) connects Reykjavík and Grindavík three times a day, stopping at the Blue Lagoon.

TOURS **Iceland Excursions** (✆ **540-1313;** www.icelandexcursions.is) has a half-day Super Jeep tour of the wilds of Reykjanes Peninsula for 7,500kr and a bus tour around the coast, with optional dropoff at the Blue Lagoon.

VISITOR INFORMATION The **Reykjanes tourist office,** Krossmói 4, Reykjanesbær (✆ **421-3520;** www.visitreykjanes.is; Mon–Fri 9am–5pm, Sat 10am–2pm) and Grindavík's **Saltfish Museum** (p. 172) are the best bets.

The Icelandic Touring Association's *Reykjanes Myndkort* ("picture map"), assembled from aerial satellite photographs, is an essential resource for identifying walking and hiking routes.

Exploring Reykjanes

The sights listed below follow a counterclockwise loop around the peninsula, but you can also follow the route in reverse.

GARÐUR & GARÐSKAGI

Garður, 15 minutes' drive northwest from Keflavík, is the northernmost town on the peninsula. Its main tourist draw is **Garðskagi,** a rocky point with two lighthouses and a quirky folk museum. To reach Garðskagi, drive through Garður and follow the coast toward the lighthouse in the distance. (As you leave town, consider stopping at **Útskálakirkja,** the lovely church visible from the road on your right.) The larger lighthouse, **Garðskagaviti,** is the tallest in Iceland; the outmoded 1897 lighthouse still stands close by. Built in 1944, Garðskagaviti was a gift from American servicemen grateful for being rescued from a sinking U.S. Coast Guard vessel. Visitors can climb all the way to the 360-degree lookout platform at the top. (If it's locked, ask for a key in the museum.) The last stretch of the climb involves steep, narrow steps and a trap door. Garðskagi offers a broad, flat ocean vista, bird sightings, and lots of wind.

Garður Peninsula Historical Museum (Byggðasafnið á Garðskaga) ★ This small-town folk museum next to the lighthouse features mid-century boat engines. Nothing super exciting, but admission is free, and the back rooms—full of old radios, sewing machines, and antiquated domestic knickknacks—sweetly conjure another era. Also look for the homemade organ. The upstairs **Flösin cafeteria** (✆ **422-7214**) is open from 1pm to midnight daily from April through October.

By Garðskagi lighthouse. ✆ **422-7220.** Free admission. Apr–Oct daily 1–5pm.

SANDGERÐI

Sandgerði is a busy fishing village 5km (3 miles) south of Garður on Route 45. The Nature Center, below, is on the north end of town, in a cluster that also includes two art galleries, the Mamma Mía pizzeria and the Vitinn restaurant.

Hallgrímur Pétursson, Iceland's most revered clergyman, had his first parish at **Hvalsneskirkja ★**, 5km (3 miles) south of Sandgerði. Hallgrímur's only child, Steinunn Hallgrímsdóttir, died here in 1649, profoundly affecting his religious mission. Her gravestone was found in 1964 when the church's stone walkway was built. It now sits near the altar of the beautifully restored church, its crude lettering remarkably intact. Someone should be around to let you in during the summer from 8am to 4pm, but if not, you can borrow a key from the Nature Center, below. The area around the church has only one full-time resident, now in his late 80s.

Fræðasetrið Nature Center Iceland is rife with local natural history museums that amount to little more than displays of stuffed animals. This museum adds some unusual specimens—barnacles, shark eggs, and a walrus, for instance—and also hosts research on marine invertebrates. Children can go to the beach, gather seawater and bugs, and examine them under microscopes. A new permanent exhibit on Jean-Baptiste Charcot (1867–1936), a French explorer who reached the South Pole in 1910 and died near Sandgerði in a 1936 shipwreck, does not yet have English translations.

Garðvegur 1, off Rte. 45, Sandgerði. ✆ **423-7551.** www.sandgerdi.is. Admission 400kr adults; 300kr children ages 6–12; ages 5 and under free. Mon–Fri 9am–5pm; Sat–Sun 1–5pm.

THE WESTERN COAST

Two kilometers (1¼ miles) south of Hvalsneskirkja is a junction. The road bearing right dead ends at a bright yellow lighthouse. The new road bearing left continues along the coast until it joins Route 44 near Hafnir. Until 2006, when the nearby

NATO base was abandoned (p. 24), this connecting road could not be built because of security concerns.

Hafnir is a sleepy town without much to see. Proceeding south along Route 425, the landscape is suddenly dominated by harsh black lava with little vegetation. This was one of three areas in Iceland used by the Apollo flight crew to practise moon-walking. About 5km (3 miles) south of Hafnir is a parking area on the right, with a small sign indicating the trailhead for the **Hafnaberg Cliffs,** a prime nesting site for guillemots, kittiwakes, fulmars, and razorbills. The 1½-hour round-trip hike is recommended for birders, but you'll find more visually dramatic seacliffs at Reykjanes, below. If you do walk to Hafnaberg, keep an eye out for whales.

Another 2km (1¼ miles) farther south is a turnoff for the **Bridge Between Two Continents,** a 15m (49-ft.) footbridge spanning a rift in the rock which is part of the jagged division between the North American and Eurasian tectonic plates. It serves as a reminder of where Iceland sits geologically, but there are similar rifts are all over the Reykjanes Peninsula without gimmicky bridges built across them.

REYKJANES

"Reykjanes" means "Smoky Point." The name originally referred only to this southwest corner of the peninsula, with its steamy geothermal hotspots. The highlight is **Valahnúkur ★★**, a magical stretch of coastline where you can clamber up grassy banks and peer over the indented cliffsides at crashing waves, while thousands of birds bob around in the wind currents. To get to Valahnúkur, turn right off Route 425 just before the power plant, and make your way past the lighthouse on the unsurfaced roads. The area can be fully explored in an hour or so. Be very careful at the cliff edges: winds can be extremely gusty, and some grass-tufted patches of earth may not support your weight. The striking, near-cylindrical island **Eldey,** a bird preserve 15km (9¼ miles) offshore, is part of the same volcanic rift line that formed Valahnúkur.

You can return to Route 425 by a different dirt road, which runs south of the power plant and its runoff lake. Once you've passed the lighthouse, just head for the steam rising from a small hill. This is **Gunnuhver,** a typical geothermal field swathed with mineral shades and thick, eggy smells. Gunnuhver is named for Gunna, a woman who, according to legend, was accused of murder and thrown into the boiling hot spring. ***Warning:*** Tread carefully and stick to the trails—one false step could melt the rubber right off your soles. The area is well monitored but is constantly changing. It was re-opened to the public in 2010 after three years when access was prohibited due to safety concerns.

GRINDAVÍK

The 17km (11-mile) stretch on Route 425 east from Reykjanes is practically deserted, so it's arresting to suddenly encounter Grindavík's clustered mass of prefab houses and difficult-to-navigate port. With its technologically advanced fish-processing plant, the town gives off an industrious and forward-looking air. Reykjanes has little arable land, so local economies are especially dependent on fishing. A helpful **visitor information desk** is inside the Saltfish Museum, below.

Arctic Horses, Hestabrekka 2, Grindavík (✆ **696-1919;** www.arctichorses.com), leads 90-minute rides around the scenic peninsula southeast of Grindavík (8,000kr per person).

The Icelandic Saltfish Museum (Saltfisksetur Íslands) In his novel *Salka Valka,* Halldór Laxness (see p. 25) famously wrote with deadpan irony, "When all is said and done, life is first and foremost salt fish." The motto "Life is saltfish" was adopted by this museum, which attempts to re-create the taste and feel of a fishing village in the 1930s, the heyday of the salt cod industry. No doubt Iceland was built on saltfish, and every effort is made here to convey that history through text, costumed dummies, sound effects, photos, and an affecting film of Icelanders on fish-processing assembly lines. You can even pick up a few recipes to try back home.

Hafnargata 12a (between Ránargata and Mánagata). ✆ **420-1190.** www.saltfisksetur.is. Admission 750kr adults; 500kr children aged 8–16. Daily 11am–6pm.

SELATANGAR

Route 427 proceeds east from Grindavík to Krýsuvík, fairly close to the south coast. This road will soon be paved, but if you continue directly back to Reykjavik, the route can be a bit rough. This has discouraged tourism to this eastern region of Reykjanes Peninsula, which feels wonderfully remote.

Twelve kilometers (7 miles) east of Grindavík, a small brown sign on the right points to **Selatangar ★**, a fishing settlement abandoned since 1880. The gravel road proceeds 1.7km (1 mile) to a small parking area near the shore. From there it's a 10-minute walk east, mostly on black sand, to an assortment of crude stone foundations for huts and storehouses. The setting is stark, poignant, and a little spooky. (Residents claimed they were chased out by a ghost named "Tumi.") Looking east, you can see this was the first decent place to land a boat for quite a stretch.

ROUTE 428

Returning to Route 427 and continuing east, the junction with Route 428 is 3km (2 miles) ahead. **Route 428 ★★**, a spectacularly scenic drive across an interior highland plateau, can be tackled in a conventional car in summer, but only by proceeding slowly and carefully. You'll need at least an hour to get to the Route 42 junction north of Kleifarvatn Lake. Along the way are several opportunities for short hikes to viewpoints on the ridges east of the road. The Myndkort photomap (see "Visitor Information," p. 170) is particularly useful for tracking a route.

KRÝSUVÍK

If instead of turning on to Route 428, you continue straight on Route 427, you'll reach **Krýsuvík Church (Krýsuvíkurkirkja)** in 9km (5½ miles). This tiny, brown, 1857 wood church once served the surrounding farm, which is now abandoned. A priest from Hafnarfjörður, who visits twice a year to conduct services, calls it "the most modest church in Iceland." Leave a note in the guestbook; he likes to read it aloud to the congregation. The church is always open, even in the off season. The altarpiece, mounted in summer only, is an abstract work in broad swaths of primary colors by **Sveinn Björnsson** (1925–1997). Sveinn, a sailor inspired by Picasso, primitivism, and the local scenery, lived in the blue house with the red roof visible to the north along Route 42. This house, crammed with Sveinn's paintings, turns into a **museum** (www.sveinssafn.is) on the first Sunday of each summer month (noon–5pm).

Across Route 427, opposite the church, is **Arnarfell,** a large, distinct hill with a rocky crest. Clint Eastwood, in his World War II movie *Flags of Our Fathers,* used Arnarholl to film the climactic scene, which reenacts the famous photograph of U.S. Marines raising the flag at Iwo Jima.

Just east of the church, Route 427 ends at Route 42. Turning right leads you on another beautiful drive to Þorlákshöfn and Hveragerði. Turning left takes you north toward Reykjavík through the Reykjanesfólkvangur wilderness reserve.

REYKJANESFÓLKVANGUR

Only 40km (25 miles) from Reykjavík, **Reykjanesfólkvangur** ★ was designated a nature reserve in 1975 to protect the region's lava formations around ridge volcanoes. Heading north from Krýsuvík on Route 42, the first notable landmark is **Grænavatn,** an oddly-tinted green lake inside an explosion crater. A parking area is on the right, and it's worth popping out for a quick look. Another kilometer (¾ mile) north is the **Seltún geothermic field** ★. A short loop trail proceeds through the chemical smells and bubbling mud cauldrons.

Slightly farther north is **Kleifarvatn** ★, a large, deep, and starkly beautiful lake with black sand beaches. Intake and outflow of water is very limited, and in 2000, water levels dropped considerably after earthquakes opened fissures on the lake bottom. The scenery is well enjoyed from the spit of **Lambatangi,** a short walk from the road on the southern end of the lake. Watch out for Kleifarvatn's resident monster, which is shaped like a worm but large as a whale.

Where to Stay & Dine

For nearby places to stay, see the Keflavík and Blue Lagoon sections earlier in this chapter.

Garður's folk museum has a **cafeteria,** and Sandgerði has two **restaurants.** In Grindavík, **Lukku Láki,** Hafnargata 6, where it dead-ends past Ægisgata (✆ **426-9999;** Sun–Thurs 6pm–1am; Fri–Sat 6pm–3am), is an eclectically designed restaurant and sports bar with main courses in the 1,100kr to 3,000kr range. **Salthúsið,** Stamphólsvegur 2 (✆ **426-9700;** Mon–Fri 5–9pm; Sat–Sun 11:30am–9pm; mains 1,800kr–4,500kr), is a bit more upscale and, as its name suggests, features salted cod.

HVERAGERÐI, SELFOSS & NEARBY

Hveragerði is 45km (28 miles) SE of Reykjavík; Selfoss is 57km (35 miles) SE of Reykjavík.

Unless you're planning a hiking expedition into Hengill, this region is usually more of an operational base or stopover than a destination in itself. Nonetheless, don't pass through on the Ring Road without considering a hike into the geothermally active valley **Reykjadalur,** an exploration of the cave **Raufarhólshellir,** or a gluttonous lobster dinner at **Fjöruborðið** in Stokkseyri (all below).

Essentials

GETTING THERE Hveragerði and Selfoss are both along Route 1. Frequent buses run daily from BSÍ terminal in Reykjavík to both towns, which are routine stops in many southern itineraries. A ticket to Selfoss is around 1,700kr, and from there buses run to and from Eyrarbakki and Stokkseyri.

VISITOR INFORMATION The **regional tourist office** (✆ **483-4601;** www.southiceland.is; Mon–Fri 9am–5pm, Sat 10am–2pm) for all of south Iceland is in Hveragerði, at Sunnumörk 2–4.

Exploring the Area

HVERAGERÐI

Hveragerði is at the southern end of an active geothermal region that extends north through Hengill to Lake Þingvallavatn. (One Hveragerði family recently discovered that a hot spring had erupted into their living room.) Since the 1920s, the town has harnessed this energy to grow fruits and vegetables in **geothermal greenhouses.** At night the greenhouses lend the town an orangey glow.

The horse farm **Eldhestar** (✆ **480-4800;** www.eldhestar.is), on Route 1, about 2km (1¼ miles) east of Hveragerði, is highly recommended for short local rides or longer trips on horseback into the Hengill hiking area. Beginners are welcome.

Eden This geothermal greenhouse is worked into several bus tour itineraries. The plants include bananas, papayas, and other unlikely specimens, but the novelty wears off rather quickly. Eden mostly exists to sell troll figurines and puffin snow-domes.

Austurmörk 25. ✆ **527-3300.** Mid-June to Aug daily 9am–8pm; Sept to mid-June daily 9am–7pm. Free admission.

NLFÍ Rehabilitation and Health Clinic Those who take their spa treatments very seriously should book a deep-heat mud bath—or even an extended stay—at this well-regarded clinic. NLFÍ developed innovative treatments for arthritis and other medical conditions using natural materials, and recently branched into the general spa market.

Frænmörk 10. ✆ **483-0300.** www.hnlfi.is.

HENGILL HIKING AREA ★★

Hengill is not Iceland's most dramatic or well-known hiking and camping region, but the mountain's august slopes and steaming geothermal valleys have a quiet authority and devoted following. The most common access points are Hveragerði to the south and Nesjavellir (p. 160) at lake Þingvallavatn to the north. Hengill itself is an 803m (2,634-ft.) active volcano, though its last eruption was about 2,000 years ago. Trail information is well mapped at all access points, and trails are well pegged in varied colors.

RAUFARHÓLSHELLIR ★★

Of all the lava tube caves in Iceland, this one perhaps best combines accessibility and mystique. Raufarhólshellir is essentially an empty riverbed of lava, formed about 3,700 years ago. At 1,350m (4,429 ft.), it's Iceland's second-longest cave, with over 1km (¾ mile) of complete blackness. The cave ceiling reaches as high as 10m (33 ft.) and averages 12m (39 ft.) in thickness. The ground is strewn with boulders and ice, making some passages difficult to traverse. The most spectacular lava contortions are at the very end, but fascinating ice formations can be seen throughout the route year-round. Entering the cave should not be attempted without a strong flashlight, warm clothing, and good shoes. A helmet and knee pads would be ideal. Exploring the full length of the cave should take around 2 hours. The unmarked parking area is just off Route 39, about 2km (1¼ mile) west of the Route 39/Route 38 intersection, between Hveragerði and Þorlákshöfn.

A DAY hike IN HENGILL

A hike to **Reykjadalur ★★**, or "Smoky Valley," is a great way to experience the Hengill area's best scenery—capped off with a swim in a natural hot spring—in as little as 2½ hours. It can be as gentle a hike as you choose.

From Hveragerði, head north on the main street, Breiðamörk, ascending to a level expanse surrounded by mountains. At a division in the road, bear left onto the gravel road marked "Reykjadalur." The road ends at a parking area at the base of the mountains, next to the Varmá River. Across the bridge is a signboard with a trail map of the area. The trail you're looking for is called Rjúpnabrekkur (Ptarmigan Slopes). It proceeds directly from the signboard and is marked with stakes painted like matchsticks.

After an initial ascent, a lesser descent leads into the Reykjadalur valley. The trail then crosses the stream and passes several gurgling mud pools. In just over an hour, you'll reach the head of the valley, with Ökelduhnúkur mountain straight ahead of you. A hot, steaming stream leads uphill to the left (west) along the Klambragil Valley. A cold stream leads uphill to the right (east), where a camping hut is visible. Where the waters merge is the place to swim. If it's too hot, head back downstream to find a suitable temperature. Don't forget your bathing suit.

An enjoyable hour-long trail circumnavigates Ökelduhnúkur. Several trails branch off from this loop trail, but if you stick with the inside route, you'll end up back at the swimming spot. The circuit is spoiled a bit by power lines but has several more geothermal hotspots. Ambitious hikers could continue all the way to Þingvallavatn in a day (after arranging transport on both ends).

SELFOSS

With over 6,000 residents, Selfoss is an important trade hub and the largest town in south Iceland. Selfoss sprang into existence in 1891, when a bridge was built over the river Öfulsá, replacing ferry transport across the river to the south. The town itself doesn't really compel a visitor's attention, but the tourist office (p. 174) provides information and maps for all surrounding towns as well, and the **geothermal pool** (✆ **480-1960**; all year round, weekdays 6:45am–8:45pm; weekends 9am–7pm; admission 390kr) makes a relaxing stop.

EYRARBAKKI

From Selfoss, the coastal towns of Eyrarbakki and Stokkseyri can be reached in about 10 minutes by car. The route proceeds across the Floí marshland, an important breeding ground for birds. Both towns were once prominent fishing and trading centers, but neither had a natural port, so they were eclipsed by the bridge at Selfoss and a new harbor at Þorlákshöfn to the west.

Eyrarbakki was once the largest community in southwestern Iceland, and has an unusual concentration of turn-of-the-last-century houses. As you enter town, the dominant white building is the **Litla-Hraun jail,** Iceland's largest. The country's total prison population is under 200, so there should be more than enough room.

Kayakaferðir Stokkseyri, Heiðarbrún 24 (✆ **896-5716;** www.kajak.is; closed Nov–Mar), runs 1- to 2-hour kayak tours (from 3,750kr) in nearby coastal lagoons and marshland canals full of birdlife.

Museums of Eyrarbakki This complex of buildings on the western edge of town is dedicated to documenting and preserving local history. The main feature is The House **(Húsið),** a restored 1765 home ordered from a Scandinavian catalog, and the town's only wooden structure at that time. Period-themed rooms have hit-or-miss artifacts—spoons carved from whale teeth, an old loom, products from a defunct drugstore. (The oddest juxtaposition is a club for battering baby seals next to a photo of Brigitte Bardot cuddling one.) The small **Egg House** in back has a nice collection of bird eggs and taxidermy. The **Maritime Museum,** included in the admission price, is 100m (328 ft.) away across a field; look for the flagpole. Items on display include leather seaman outfits softened with fish oil, shark hooks and porpoise harpoons, and a 1915 fishing boat for 16 sailors.

Eyrargata. ✆ **483-1504.** www.husid.com. Admission 700kr; seniors 67+ 500kr; children under 12 free. 15 May–15 Sept daily 11am–6pm; other times by arrangement.

STOKKSEYRI

Stokkseyri has a bizarre mix of tourist attractions, though most visitors are here for the excellent lobster restaurant (see "Where to Dine," below).

The Ghost Center Visitors here don headphones, and for 40 minutes proceed from one creepy installation to the next listening to traditional Icelandic ghost stories. The props are decent, if low-budget. (The smoke machine produces an eggy sulfur smell, which somehow ruins the illusion.) Not all the stories will resonate with non-Icelanders, but the tour may still produce a few goose bumps and is not recommended for children under 12.

Hafnargata 9. ✆ **483-1202.** www.draugasetrid.is. Admission 1,500kr adults; 990kr seniors and children aged 12–16. June–Aug daily 1–6pm; Sept–May Sat–Sun 1–6pm or by arrangement.

Hunting Museum This shrine to trophy hunting is on the right as you enter town. The museum has an enormous private collection of stuffed victims shot by a man-and-woman team; it includes a polar bear, lion, zebra, and hyena. Exhibits even include racks of hunting handguns and framed displays of bullets.

Eyrarbraut 49. ✆ **483-1558.** www.hunting.is. Admission 1,250kr adults; 650kr children aged 6–12. Mar–Oct daily 11am–6pm; Nov and Feb Sat–Sun 11am–6pm; closed Dec–Jan.

Icelandic Wonders Also known as "Elves, Trolls, and Northern Lights," this museum is a good place to have a northern lights experience if you're here in summer. The "Aurora Experience" film explains and shows footage of this phenomenon, and an ice cave—kept frozen all through summer by ice from the Vatnajökull glacier—projects northern lights in their more typical setting. Children will enjoy the elf and troll exhibits. The second floor affords a good view of the town and out to sea, and can be used by groups to hold a feast.

Hafnargata 9. ✆ **483-1202** or 895-0020**.** www.icelandicwonders.com. Admission 1,500kr adults; 990kr seniors and children aged 12–16; 500kr aged 6–11; aged 6 and under free. Jun–Aug daily 10am–8pm, Sept–May by prior arrangement.

Töfragarðurinn Magic Garden This theme park and zoo is good value for families with young children needing to expend some energy. There's mini golf, giant play equipment, and a stack of cute Icelandic animals—cats, goats, sheep, and horses among them—to pet.

Route 314 (Stjörnusteinar). ✆ **483-1590** or **896-5716.** Admission 500kr; free for children under 3. Jun–Aug daily 10am–8pm.

Where to Stay

HVERAGERÐI

The South Iceland tourist office in Hveragerði (see "Visitor Information," above) can help you book a place to stay for a 300kr fee.

Guesthouse Frost and Fire ★ This is one of the surprisingly few Icelandic guesthouses that are well landscaped into a river bend. Views over the Varmá river can be enjoyed from guest rooms, the two hot tubs, and the light-filled dining room, where organic breakfasts are served. Each room is named for the artist whose work boldly lines the walls. (You can preview each artist through the "Art Gallery" link at the website; we'd go for the Óskar Magnússon.)

Hverhamar (just off Breiðamörk, at the northern end of town). ✆ **483-4959.** Fax 483-4914. www.frostandfire.is. 14 units. June–Aug 20,000kr double. Rates around 10% lower May & Sept; around 30% lower at other times. Rates include breakfast. **Amenities:** Small outdoor pool and hot tubs; sauna. *In room:* TV, Wi-Fi.

Guesthouse Frumskógar This is a cheap and functional option that will not arouse any complaints about comfort or cleanliness. The family-friendly studio apartments sleep two to four and have kitchenettes, fridge, coffeemaker, and Wi-Fi.

Frumskógar 3 (off Heiðmörk, 2 blocks west of Breiðamörk). ✆ **896-2780.** www.frumskogar.is. 10 units. 8,000kr double w/shared bathroom; 16,000kr studio apartment w/private bathroom. Apt. rates 18% lower Mar–May and Sept–Oct, 27% lower Nov–Feb. Discounts on longer stays. Breakfast available for 1,100kr. **Amenities:** Hot tub. *In room:* TV, no phone. Studios have TV/DVD, CD player, fridge, Wi-Fi.

Hótel Eldhestar You don't have to be an equestrian to stay at this smart country hotel on one of Iceland's best horse farms. Rooms have a slightly softer and more personal touch than the Icelandic standard, and the hotel has been approved by the eco-certification association Nordic Swan for its environmentally-sound practices.

On Rte. 1, about 2km (1¼ miles) east of Hveragerði. ✆ **480-4800.** Fax 480-4801. www.hoteleldhestar.is. 26 units. June–Aug 22,600kr double. Rates around 30% lower Apr–May and Sept–Oct, and 45% lower Nov–Mar. Rates include breakfast. **Amenities:** Bar; hot tub. *In room:* TV, Wi-Fi.

Hótel Örk Rooms all have bathtubs, but otherwise arouse little excitement. The main draw here is the wealth of facilities, including tennis courts, golf course, ping-pong table, sauna, and swimming pool area, with hot tubs, kiddie pool, and water-slide. Superior doubles give you lots of extra space and a bigger TV.

Breiðamörk 1. ✆ **483-4700.** Fax 483-4775. www.hotel-ork.is. 85 units. May–Sept 22,700kr–30,900kr double; 26,500kr triple. Rates around 37% lower Oct–Apr. Rates include breakfast. MC, V. **Amenities:** Restaurant; outdoor pool; golf course; tennis courts; sauna; hot tubs; room service. *In room:* TV, fridge, hair dryer, Wi-Fi.

SELFOSS

Hotel Selfoss This upmarket hotel is clearly the place to make an important business deal followed by a wind-down in the sauna and "rainwater shower" at the brand-new in-house Northern Light Spa. But the only way to lend character to the d (if comfortable) rooms is to get one facing the river.

2. ✆ **480-2500.** www.hotelselfoss.is. 99 units. 29,260kr double. Rates around 28% lower lower Oct–Dec. Rates include breakfast. **Amenities:** Restaurant; spa; Wi-Fi. *In room:* TV, yer, Internet.

Menam Guesthouse Perched above a mediocre Thai restaurant of the same name, these well-priced rooms are clean and well-maintained, albeit with a bit of traffic noise. The common TV lounge, which is musty and worn, still manages to be both comfortable and welcoming.

Eyrarvegur (Rte. 34), just off the central roundabout. ✆ **482-4099.** www.menam.is. 5 units w/shared bathrooms. 9,900kr double; 12,900kr triple. MC, V. *In room:* No phone.

Where to Dine

Hveragerði's greenhouse products can be sampled at town markets; try the *hverabrauð,* a dark, cakey rye bread cooked in a geothermal oven. **Eden** (see above) has a basic cafeteria-style restaurant.

Fjöruborðið ★★ SEAFOOD This restaurant is a destination in itself. Many Reykjavíkians trek all the way to this famed lobster house just for dinner. An Icelandic lobster, more accurately termed a *langoustine,* is hardly larger than a jumbo shrimp, and extracting the meat doesn't require the usual heroics with tiny forks or shell-cracking implements. Fish, beef, lamb, and vegetarian dishes are also on hand, but most guests end their meal slurping their garlic and butter-drenched fingers.

Eyrarbraut 3a, Stokkseyri. ✆ **483-1550.** www.fjorubordid.is. Reservations recommended. Main courses 1,700kr–3,800kr. June–Sept Mon–Thurs, Sun noon–9pm; Fri–Sat noon–10pm; Oct–May not open for lunch on weekdays.

Hótel Örk (Árgerði) ★ ICELANDIC This is your best option in town for finer dining. The menu is small and focused and seasonal, adding a fine touch to standard Icelandic preparations of lamb—peppered rack of lamb with roast vegetable perhaps—beef and seafood.

Breiðamörk 1, Hveragerði's. ✆ **483-4700.** Main courses 1,900kr–3,900kr. MC, V. Daily 10am–10pm.

Hotel Selfoss ICELANDIC The food here is as good as at Hveragerði's Hótel Örk (above) but it's more expensive and the atmosphere is rather corporate.

Eyrarvegur 2, Selfoss. ✆ **480-2500.** Main courses 3,200kr–5,500kr. MC, V. Daily 11am–10pm.

Kaffi Krús ★ CAFE/BISTRO The town's most appealing hangout has excellent cakes and satisfying light meals. You won't go wrong with the tandoori chicken breast or the bagels and smoked salmon. Some nights the cafe features live music, which is usually on the mellow, acoustic side.

Austurvegur 7 (Rte. 1, opposite the library), Selfoss. ✆ **482-1266.** Main courses 1,500kr–3,200kr. MC, V. Sun–Thurs 10am–11pm; Fri–Sat 10am–midnight; kitchen closes at 9pm.

Rauða Húsið ★ ICELANDIC Settle in for a leisurely, classy dinner at "The Red House," a respected Eyrarbakki institution with local history lessons on the menu. The house special is seafood soup—creamy yet delicate with plenty of vegetables. For a main course, try the cod in basil and garlic with polenta, and for dessert the Rauða Húsið version of Icelandic *skyr* pudding. Afterward, retire to the cellar pub decorated with wooden casks.

Búðarstíg 4 (coastal Rd., at Bakarísstígur), Eyrarbakki. ✆ **483-3330.** www.raudahusid.is. Main courses 3,400kr–5,700kr . Sun–Thurs11am–9pm; Fri–Sat 11am–10:30pm.

WEST ICELAND

8

The Snæfellsnes Peninsula is a breathtaking combination of rugged peaks, ambling waterfalls, and the Snæfellsjökull glacier itself growing in magnificence as it ducks in and out of sight along the coast-hugging road. Across the bay—in fact, a fjord by name—to the Westfjords and the scenery becomes at once more girdled and more expansive as one's attention is drawn upwards along the stony steps of the mountain tops. The area comprises a tenth of Iceland's landmass and a third of its coastline, and round every bend is some new variation on how mountains can tumble to the sea. Fjord after fjord provides a calming contrast, stretching out to the distant Atlantic horizon.

On a clear day, the Snæfellsjökull glacier is visible from Reykjavík. Visitors arriving at Keflavík airport should scan the northern horizon as they head toward Reykjavík, because for most this is the closest they will come to witnessing Iceland's beautiful western corner.

It's easy to imagine that a region such as this created the cliché "rugged beauty." Yet, while many places such as the Snæfellsnes Peninsula make a worthwhile day trip from Reykjavík, they tend to suffer the fate of being all too often seen en route rather than being destinations in themselves. The Westfjords are even more neglected, despite boasting some of Iceland's grandest bird cliffs, loveliest sand beaches, and loneliest upland moors. Winters are relatively long and harsh, and the population is around 7,400—less than one inhabitant per square kilometer, compared with the national average of three. The image of the Westfjords as inaccessible, however, is exaggerated. The main road to Ísafjörður is now paved all the way to the Ring Road, and daily flights to Ísafjörður take just 40 minutes from Reykjavík. The next morning you could board a boat for Hornstrandir Nature Reserve, one of Iceland's most ruggedly beautiful and pristine hiking areas. By afternoon you might be staring down at an Arctic fox, or peering over a dizzying bird cliff at the crashing surf, with the world left completely behind.

West Iceland has other oft-neglected gems, some sitting right on the Ring Road. Snæfellsnes, a 70km-long (43 mile) finger of land pointing westward, is closely identified with the Snæfellsjökull glacier near its tip, but the peninsula has plenty more to offer and can easily sustain 2 or 3 days of exploring. Circling it is one of Iceland's most enjoyable road trips, especially if outdoor activities are tacked on. Possibilities include some splendid coastal walks; whale-watching from Ólafsvík; horseback riding along beaches on the south coast; snowmobile trips to the glacier; and kayak or boat tours among the low-lying islands and mudflats of Breiðafjörður, a thriving habitat for birds and seals.

BORGARNES, REYKHOLT & FARTHER INLAND

Overland routes from Reykjavík to all points in west Iceland pass through this region, which draws many historically-minded visitors. Borgarnes has an engaging museum on the twin themes of the first settlers in Iceland and *Egil's Saga,* a classic of medieval European literature. Saga enthusiasts also make pilgrimages to Reykholt, once the residence of Snorri Sturluson, the most prominent historical figure of Iceland's saga-writing age. There is ongoing work towards improving the land in this area, especially reforestation, and in recognition of this work, Reykholt was nominated for a national environmental award in 2009. Further inland are two of Iceland's most extensive lava caves: Surtshellir and Víðgelmir. From here, an alternate route south to Þingvellir passes between glacier-capped mountains for a taste of Iceland's starkly beautiful interior.

Essentials

GETTING THERE Borgarnes is on the Ring Road, 74km (46 miles) north of Reykjavík. Reykholt is on Route 518, 39km (24 miles) inland from Borgarnes.

Sterna buses (✆ **553-3737;** www.sterna.is) connect Reykjavík and **Borgarnes** two to five times daily depending on the time of year. The trip costs 2,200kr one-way and is 55 minutes, or 75 minutes with a stop at Akranes. From mid-May to mid-September, buses from Reykjavík to **Reykholt** leave daily at 8:30am, returning at 7pm or 7:45pm, with a one-way fare of 2,800kr. The bus stops at Borgarnes and makes several local stops between Borgarnes and Reykholt. See also "Bus Tours," p. 185.

VISITOR INFORMATION Regional **tourist information** for West Iceland is in Borgarnes at the **Hyrnan service station,** Brúartorg 1 (✆ **437-2214;** www.westiceland.is; Jun–Aug Mon–Fri 9am–6pm, Sat–Sun 10am–3pm; Sept–May Mon–Fri 9am–4pm), which is also the town's main bus stop. The reception office at **Snorrastofa** (✆ **433-8008;** gestastofa@snorrastofa.is; May–Sept daily 10am–6pm; Oct–Apr Mon–Fri 10am–5pm) provides information on Reykholt and nearby areas.

Exploring the Area

BORGARNES

Visitors tracing the footsteps of Egil Skallagrímsson, the warrior-poet hero of *Egil's Saga,* should pick up the free "Saga Trails of Iceland" brochure at the Settlement Center museum. The museum leads guided tours for groups by arrangement, and individuals can sometimes sign on by calling ahead.

West Iceland

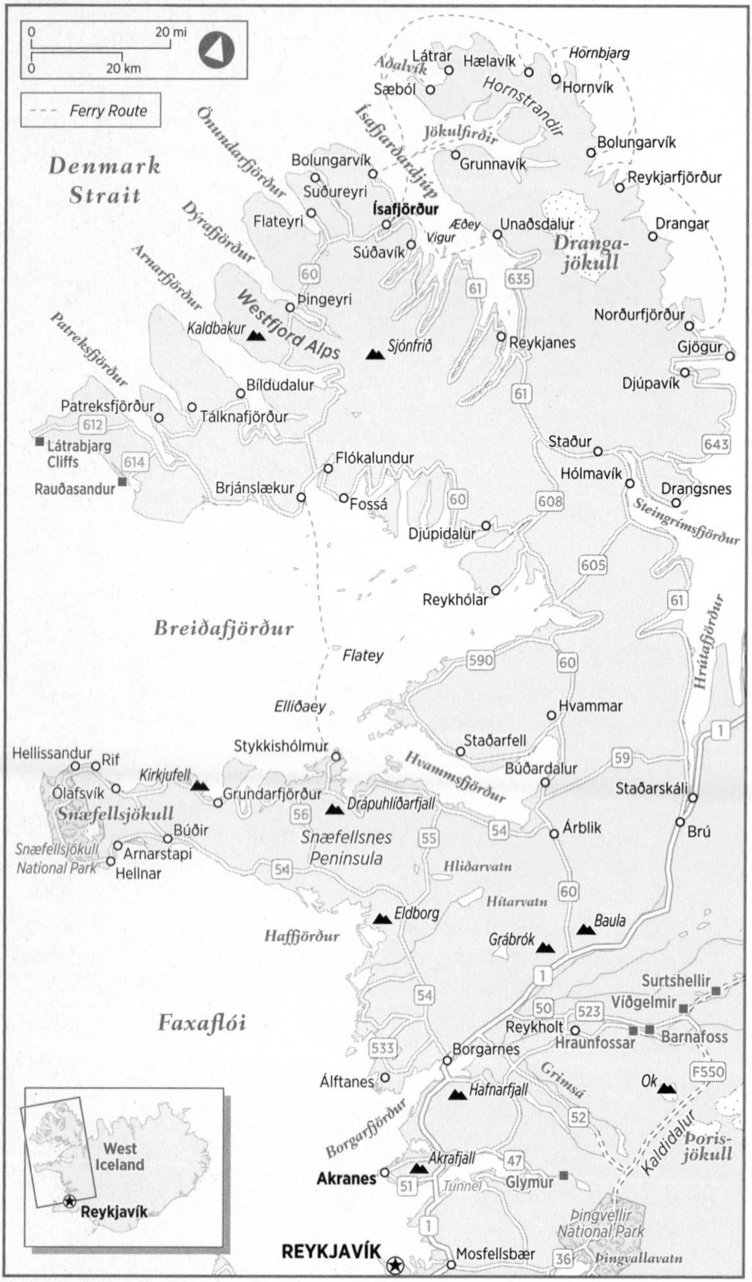

8

WEST ICELAND | Borgarnes, Reykholt & Farther Inland

The focal point of **Skallagrímsgarður Park,** a public garden on Skallagrímsgata downtown, is a burial mound thought to contain the remains of Egil's father and son. Facing the mound is a relief sculpture of Egil on horseback, his face twisted by grief, as he carries his dead 17-year-old son to the burial site.

Center for Puppet Arts (Brúðuheimar) ★ This interactive museum opened in 2010 and is especially worthwhile for pint-sized visitors. The extraordinary puppets—mostly wooden—are enough of an attraction in themselves, but trying one's hand at puppeteering and watching performances, both for children and adults, is simply a lot of fun, especially if you've just come from the more serious Settlement Center. There's a small gift shop and cafe serving light fare, coffee, and cakes.

Skúlugata 17. ✆ **530-5000.** www.bruduheimar.is. Admission 1,600kr. Children aged 7–12 1,000kr; aged 2–6 600kr; aged 0–1 free. June–Aug daily 10am–10pm; Sept–May 11am–5pm.

The Settlement Center ★ Visitors to this expensive but worthwhile museum, founded in 2006, strap on headphones for two 30-minute audio exhibits (choose just one if you're strapped for time or cash), one on the first 60 years of Icelandic settlement (around 870–930) and the other on *Egil's Saga*. The settlement exhibit is a basic primer and may feel a bit remedial to those well-versed in the subject. The successes of its interactive and multimedia features, such as a video of a recreated Viking ship, are perhaps a tribute to the background of the founders: an actor/playwright and a television reporter. The exhibit's only serious flaw is that folkloric narratives handed down over the centuries are often presented as established fact, blurring the line between history and fable.

Egil's Saga is among the five most celebrated literary achievements of medieval Iceland. Egil is a volatile and ambiguous character, capable of masterful poetry and merciless barbarity. While *Njál's Saga* has more passages illustrative of everyday life in 10th-century Iceland, *Egil's Saga* has every dramatic hallmark, from pagan sorcery to bitter love triangles to gory battle scenes featuring outlaws and berserkers. The exhibit ably conveys the strangeness and horror of the story. Be warned, however, that the installations may frighten young children. The life-size witch queen of Norway, rocking and grumbling over a fire, with a decomposed beast's head impaled on a pole, could give even grownups nightmares.

Brákarbraut 13–15. ✆ **437-1600.** www.landnam.is. Admission 1,500kr for one exhibit; 2,000kr for both. 1000kr seniors/children 6 to 14 for one exhibit; 1,600kr for both. Free for children under 6, but the *Egil's Saga* exhibition is not suitable for young children. June–Sept daily 10am–9pm; Oct–May daily 11am–5pm.

REYKHOLT

The historic settlement of Reykholt, less than an hour inland from Borgarnes, sits within the fertile, well-forested, and geothermally active Reykholtsdalur Valley. As the former home of chieftain, politician, scholar, and author Snorri Sturluson (1178–1241), Reykholt holds deep cultural resonance for Icelanders. Today the settlement is a cluster of buildings anchored by Snorrastofa, a research institute and museum dealing in medieval Iceland and Snorri's literary works. An 1887 church is charmingly restored, though a 1996 church has taken over its functions, including the annual Reykholt Music Festival (mainly classical) held on and around the last weekend of July (visit www.reykholtshatid.is for a schedule).

During the 1986 Reagan–Gorbachev summit in Reykjavík, a step toward ending the Cold War, Icelandic Prime Minister Steingrímur Hermannsson spoke to international reporters while relaxing in a hot tub at his local pool. Likewise, in the early 13th century, Snorri apparently held political powwows at Reykholt in an outdoor bath with crude taps for regulating hot and cold water flow. The exact site of the original **Snorralaug (Snorri's Pool)** is unknown, but in 1959 the National Museum settled on the current spot and built a reconstruction, 4m (13 ft.) in diameter, with hewn blocks of silica stone and stone piping found during excavations. Next to the pool is an underground passageway, perhaps leading to the basement where Snorri was murdered. Snorralaug is well marked on maps posted around Reykholt.

Snorrastofa ★ The permanent exhibit, "Snorri Sturluson and His Time," covers Snorri's life and oeuvres while examining specific facets of 13th-century Icelandic society, from education, language, religion, and music to the use of geothermal heat. Snorri was the likely author of *Egil's Saga,* and his own life story, packed with political intrigue and concluding in murder, is of saga-esque proportions. Snorri's other works include the *Prose Edda,* also known as *Snorri's Edda* or *Snorra Edda,* a kind of handbook for poets writing in the traditional skaldic style inherited from Iceland's pre-Christian past. This book provided a systematic account of Norse mythology, much of which might otherwise have been lost to history. The oldest calfskin copies of Snorri's works are held at the Culture House in Reykjavík (p. 125).

Rte. 518, 5km (3 miles) from the junction with Rte. 50. ✆ **433-8000.** www.snorrastofa.is. Admission 700kr, free for children. May–Sept daily 10am–6pm; Oct–Apr Mon–Fri 10am–5pm.

INLAND

Hraunfossar (Lava Falls) is a kilometer-long succession of small waterfalls that drape over the lava rock on the north bank of the Hvitá River. The falls originate from cold springs and gush out from beneath trees, creating the impression of a giant water sculpture. From Hraunfossar, a short path leads upstream to **Barnafoss** (Children's Falls), a raging ravine renamed (from Bjarnafoss, or Bjarni's Foss) by the mother of two children who went missing and were presumed to have drowned there. Hraunfossar is marked from the southern branch of Route 518, about 18km (11 miles) east of Reykholt.

Plunging into the monstrous **Surtshellir** ★ lava tube cave is an exhilarating adventure but should not be attempted without good shoes, warm clothes, and a strong flashlight; helmet and gloves are also recommended. Proceed with extreme caution: the cave floor can be slippery or strewn with loose boulders, and the complete darkness can be disorienting. The main tube extends nearly 2km (1 mile), but narrow side passageways are the most fun to explore. To reach Surtshellir, take Route F578 for about 8km (5 miles) from the easternmost point of Route 518. Regular cars should have no trouble reaching the marked parking area, which is a five-minute walk from the cave entrance.

Víðgelmir ★ is 148,000 cubic meters (5,226,571 cubic feet), making it the biggest lava cave in Iceland and one of the biggest in the world. Among its dramatic rock, ice, and mineral formations, its smoothed, icy stalagmites create the impression of a Moomintroll-populated underground. The cave is close to Surtshellir but can only be accessed on guided tours led by Fljótstunga Farm (✆ **435-1198;** www.fljotstunga.is). Tours leave from May until September (11am, 4pm, and by request), and some weekends off-season. The basic 1-hour tour is 2,000kr per person, with a minimum of four people; and a 3- to 4-hour tour is 4,500kr. Note that these tours are not suitable for young children. In 1993, Viking-era artifacts were found inside

Víðgelmir, including a fireplace and animal bones (leftovers from an ancient meal), and are now on display at the National Museum in Reykjavík.

From Route 518, east of Reykholt and close to Surtshellir and Víðgelmir, Route 550 cuts southwest through **Kaldidalur valley,** passing between the volcano Ok and the Þórisjökull and Langjökull glaciers before joining Route 52, which continues south to Þingvellir. Regular cars proceeding slowly and carefully usually will not encounter problems between mid-June and mid-September. (The road is sometimes mistakenly identified as mountain road "F550," and "F" usually signifies "4WD only.") However, all drivers should beware of sandstorms in high winds. Kaldidalur is recommended to those who will not otherwise experience Iceland's gritty and desolate interior highlands. The road's highest point, at 727m (2,385 ft.) above sea level, is marked by a huge cairn and has a marvelous view of a rhyolite peak to the east.

Tours & Activities

BUS TOURS **Reykjavík Excursions** (© **580-5400;** www.re.is) offers a guided "Saga Circle" tour from Reykjavík on Sundays year-round, and Tuesdays from May 15 through August. The tour visits Borgarnes and the Settlement Center, Reykholt and Snorrastofa, Hraunfossar and Barnafoss, Deildartunguhver hot spring, and Hvalfjörður. Tours last 8 to 9 hours and cost 14,500kr, including entrance to museums. **Iceland Excursions** (© **540-1313;** www.icelandexcursions.is) offers a similar "Saga Trail" tour from Reykjavík three times a week from early June to early September for 11,500kr.

CAVING See "Surtshellir" and "Víðgelmir," above.

GLACIER TOURS From May to August, **The Activity Group** (© **580-9900;** www.activity.is) has a full-day "Glacial Vistas–Langjökull Glacier Tour" for 34,200kr, including 4WD transport from Reykjavík to Þingvellir, Kaldidalur, and Hraunfossar, and an hour-long snowmobile ride on Langjökull, Iceland's second-largest glacier.

GOLF Borgarnes has an excellent 18-hole course, **Hamarsvöllur,** run by Golfklúbbur Borgarness (© **437-1663;** gbgolf@simnet.is). The course fee is 3,500kr–4,000kr, depending on the day and time.

KAYAKING **Arctic Adventures** (© **562-7000;** www.adventures.is) offers a kayaking tour of Hvalfjörður—almost certainly the best way to see this beautiful fjord—suitable for beginners; leaving from Reykjavík for 12,990kr.

JEEP TOURS **Mountain Taxi** (© **544-5252;** www.arcticsafari.is) has a year-round "Iceland in a Nutshell" tour from 33,000kr, which includes Þingvellir, Kaldidalur, Langjökull Glacier, Surtshellir, Hraunfossar, and Reykholt and many optional activities such as riding snowmobiles. The "Silver Circle" tour with **Touris** (© **517-8290**; www.tour.is) is nearly identical, but does not visit caves and costs 21,500kr (10,750kr for children aged 12–17; free for children under 12).

Where to Stay

Both located between Borgarnes and Reykholt, two recommended guesthouse alternatives to the Fosshótel are **Brennistaðir** (Rte. 515, 15km/9⅓ miles) from Reykholt; © **435-1193;** brennist@islandia.is; 10,000kr double including breakfast) and **Guesthouse Milli Vina** (Rte. 514; © **435-1530;** www.millivina.is; 13,000kr double, including breakfast, cash only), which is sometimes identified by its farm name, Hvítárbakki. Of the many farmsteads in the region which have been converted into guesthouses, we also recommend **Húsafell** (Rte. 518, 66km/41 miles) from Borgarnes; ✆ **895-1342;** sveitasetrid@simnet.is; 12,900kr double), popular for its proximity to walking trails, fishing spots, and a golf course, and also the site of very popular camping grounds and summerhouses for rent.

EXPENSIVE

Fosshótel Reykholt ★ With the Snorrastofa research institute next door, this hotel adopts the themes of medieval Icelandic literature and Norse mythology but also includes more modern themes such as the "Lord of the Rings lounge" (JRR Tolkien was inspired by the *Snorra Edda*). Rooms are spacious, and 24 "wellness rooms" include a bathtub but are more expensive than a standard room. The extensive well-being facilities include massage chair, lavender aromatherapy room, hot tubs with water jets, and an on-site masseuse.

Rte. 518, Reykholt. ✆ **435-1260.** www.fosshotel.is. 57 units. June–Aug 24,500kr double. Rates around 30% lower Oct–Dec, and around 40% lower Jan–Apr. Rates include breakfast. AE, DC, MC, V. **Amenities:** Restaurant; bar; spa; hot tubs; bike rental. *In room:* TV, Wi-Fi.

Hótel Hamar ★★ This Icelandair hotel has a modern, minimalist Scandinavian style, with neutral tones. Half the rooms have glacier views, but all have decks with outdoor seating; the rooms are sizeable with plush bedding, firm mattresses, and underfloor heating. The hotel is next to Hamarsvöllur golf course (though guests get no special access or discount).

Rte. 1, 3km (2 miles) north of Borgarnes. ✆ **433-6600.** Fax 433-6601. www.icehotels.is. 30 units. June–Aug 23,600kr double. Rates 25% lower May and Sept; around 35% lower Oct–Apr. Rates include breakfast. AE, DC, MC, V. **Amenities:** Restaurant; hot tubs. *In room:* TV, hair dryer, Wi-Fi.

MODERATE

Ensku Húsin ★ 🎁 Built in 1884 by an Icelandic cabinet-maker, but later used by English fishermen for almost a century, this "Old English Lodge" by the Langá River, 6km (3¾ miles) outside Borgarnes is the oldest surviving fishing lodge in Iceland. With its nostalgic photos and quirky old furniture, Ensku Húsin was restored in 2007 and exudes genuine old-world charm. The **restaurant** (p. 187) has a set three-course menu, reasonably priced and usually consisting of meat soup, fish, and dessert.

Rte. 533 (just off Rte. 54, 6km/3¾ miles from Rte. 1), Borgarnes. ✆ **437-1826.** Fax 437-1734. www.enskuhusin.is. 19 units, 11 w/bathroom. May 15–Sept 15 17,700kr double; 14,200kr double without bathroom. Rates around 10% lower Sept 16–May 14. Breakfast available (1,200kr). MC, V. Closed over Christmas. **Amenities:** Restaurant. *In room:* No phone, Wi-Fi.

Hotel Borgarnes Boasting a convenient location in town, this hotel is rather worn and bland, but it meets the basic comfort standards of a business-class hotel. Some doubles are big enough to bring in an extra bed, and children under 12 stay free.

Egilsgata 16, Borgarnes. ✆ **437-1119.** Fax 437-1443. www.hotelborgarnes.is. 75 units. June–Sept 16,500kr double. Rates around 40% lower Apr–May and Oct. Rates include breakfast. AE, DC, MC, V. Closed mid-Oct–Mar. **Amenities:** Restaurant; Internet terminal. *In room:* TV, minibar, hair dryer.

INEXPENSIVE

Bjarg Handily placed at the edge of town but in a rustic setting overlooking the fjord. The simple rooms at this farm are warm and spotless. If visiting in winter, be careful on the steep-sided narrow section of road as you approach the car park. (No connection with Hótel Bjarg on the other side of Iceland in Fáskrúðsfjörður.)

Off Rte. 1, about 1km (¾ miles) northeast of Borgarnes. ✆ **437-1925** or 864-1325. bjarg@simnet.is. 3 units, none w/bathroom, 1 apt. Mid-May—mid-Sept 14,400kr double; 22,000kr triple; 27,200kr quadruple. Rates around 25% lower w/sleeping-bag. Rates include breakfast. Rates around 25% lower mid-Sept-mid-May. AE, MC, V. **Amenities:** Guest kitchen. *In room:* TV, no phone.

Borgarnes B&B This bright, basic guesthouse in the old heart of town is walking distance from most attractions and a pleasant beach.

Skulagata 21, Borgarnes. ✆ **434-15666** (or 842-5866) www.borgarnesbb.is. 4 units. May-Sept 15,200kr double; 12,900 double without bathroom. Rates include breakfast. Rates around 30% lower Oct-May. AE, MC, V. **Amenities:** Guest kitchen, Internet terminal. *In room:* No phone.

Venus Guesthouse In a nice spot on the Ring Road across the fjord from Borgarnes, Venus has well-priced, functional rooms, eight of which overlook the fjord. There's also a big sign saying Motel Venus, with Route 66-style logo and passable **pizza restaurant,** yet no American 1950s retro theme is at play.

Rte. 1, 4km (2½ miles) south of Borgarnes. ✆ **437-2345.** Fax 437-2344. motel@emax.is. 17 units, 8 w/ bathroom. June-Aug 12,600kr double; 9,800kr double without bathroom; 2,900kr per person w/sleeping bag. Rates around 40% lower Sept-May. Breakfast available (950kr). AE, DC, MC, V. **Amenities:** Restaurant. *In room:* No phone.

Where to Dine

Hótel Hamar ★★ (above) is the area's best restaurant (main courses 3,500–6,900kr; AE, DC, MC, V; daily 11:30am–9:30pm; reservations recommended in summer), with a menu heavy with fish, lamb, and other local produce. Catch of the day—served with a basil risotto, perhaps—is very reasonable.

Other places to consider are **Ensku Húsin** (✆ **437-1826;** daily menu 4,500kr; June–Aug 7–9pm) for a home-cooked set menu, or **Venus Guesthouse (or Motel, see above)** (✆ **437-2345;** main courses 2,200–3,900kr; June–Aug daily noon–10pm, Sept–May 5–9:30pm) for a casual meal of fish or lamb or pizza. See "Where to Stay" for locations.

Fosshótel Reykhólt ★★ ICELANDIC This reliable restaurant, next to the Snorrastofa institute and en route to a couple of spectacular lava tube caves (p. 184), offers an excellent lunch buffet (4800kr), combining Icelandic dishes such as baked salmon and roast leg of lamb with an assortment of pastas and salads, as well as a good a la carte menu offering traditional Icelandic soups, local trout, and beef.

Rte. 518, Reykholt. ✆ **435-1260.** www.fosshotel.is. Main courses 3,290kr-4,190kr. AE, DC, MC, V. Daily noon-2pm and 6:30-9:30pm, coffee and light fare also available throughout the day.

Settlement Center Restaurant ★ ICELANDIC This restaurant, often called by its old name Búðarklettur, is the best option in central Borgarnes. With an upbeat, contemporary setting, it offers a soup menu at lunchtime and a good range of fish, lamb, and pasta dishes in the evenings, including several Icelandic specials. The menu even includes a local history lesson.

Brákarbraut 13, Borgarnes. ✆ **437-1600.** Reservations recommended for dinner in summer. Main courses 1,900kr-3,900kr. AE, DC, MC, V. June-Aug daily 10am-9pm; Sept-May Mon-Thurs 11am-5pm, Fri-Sun 11am-9pm.

SNÆFELLSNES

The jagged outline of the peaks of **Snæfellsnes ★★**, seen from Reykjavík on a clear day, lead one's gaze westwards along the horizon to the glistening white cone of Snæfellsjökull glacier, the peninsula's star attraction. With its mountainous and glacier-carved spine, black and golden sand beaches, and lava fields blanketed in luminescent moss, Snæfellsnes is almost an Iceland unto itself. An outdoor activity tour is an ideal complement to a Snæfellsnes road trip, so before setting out, consider signing up for whale-watching, horseback riding, or an expedition on the glacier. Another possibility is a boat tour of Breiðafjörður, leaving from Stykkishólmur, the largest town on Snæfellsnes. (Stykkishólmur and Breiðafjörður are covered in section three of this chapter, p. 199.)

The five municipalities of Snæfellsnes jointly hold a Green Globe certification for their commitment to environmentally responsible tourism, sustainable development, and cultural preservation. No other extended community in the Northern Hemisphere has received this tribute.

Essentials

GETTING THERE & AROUND Snæfellsnes can be done in a day trip from Reykjavík, but staying 2 days or longer is preferable. The peninsula has relatively good roads, and—with so many widely dispersed attractions—coming **by car** really pays off. (See p. 42 for more on renting a car in Reykjavík.)

The **bus service** is relatively extensive. **Sterna** (✆ **553-3737;** www.sterna.is) has a daily route between Reykjavík and Hellissandur from mid-June until August, and almost daily during the off-season (3–3¼ hr.; 5,700kr one-way) stopping at Akranes, Borgarnes, Vegamót (the southern junction of Rte. 54 and Rte. 56), Vatnaleið (where other Sterna buses connect to and from Stykkishólmur), Grundarfjörður, and Ólafsvík. From mid-June through August, the bus connects to the Snæfellsjökull **Circle bus,** which makes a clockwise run around the glacier and makes half-hour stops at Arnarstapi, Hellnar, and Djúpalónssandur, for a total cost of 3,700kr. (This makes for a very rushed "tour," if treated as such, but there is just enough time for the Arnarstapi–Hellnar trail, p. 192.) Another connecting bus continues back to Reykjavík.

Sterna offers **Snæfellsjökull National Park** day tours from Reykjavík for 15,000kr, but with more time to spare, Sterna also offers "The Snæfellsnes Peninsula and National Park" **bus passport** for 24,000kr, valid from June 15 to August 31, with unlimited travel on the Reykjavík–Hellissandur, Stykkishólmur–Hellissandur, and "Snæfellsjökull Circle" routes.

VISITOR INFORMATION On the north coast, local information offices are in **Ólafsvík,** at Pakkhúsið, Route 574 (✆ **433-9930;** May–Sept daily 11am–5pm) and **Grundarfjörður,** at Eyrbyggja Heritage Center, Grundargata 35 (✆ **438-1881;** daily 10am–6pm). For **Snæfellsjökull National Park,** which includes the entire western tip of the peninsula, there's the Gestastofa tourist office in **Hellnar** (✆ **436-6888;** mid-May–mid-Sept daily 10am–6pm) on the main road through the village. A good resource outside Snæfellsnes is in **Borgarnes,** Brúartorg 1 (✆ **437-2214;** www.west.is; Jun–Aug Mon–Fri 9am–6pm, Sat–Sun 10am–3pm; Sept–May Mon–Fri 9am–4pm).

The free brochure map *Snæfellsnes: Magical Iceland* is available at information offices. A more detailed map, *Snæfellsnes,* published by Mal og Menning, is available at

Snæfellsnes Peninsula

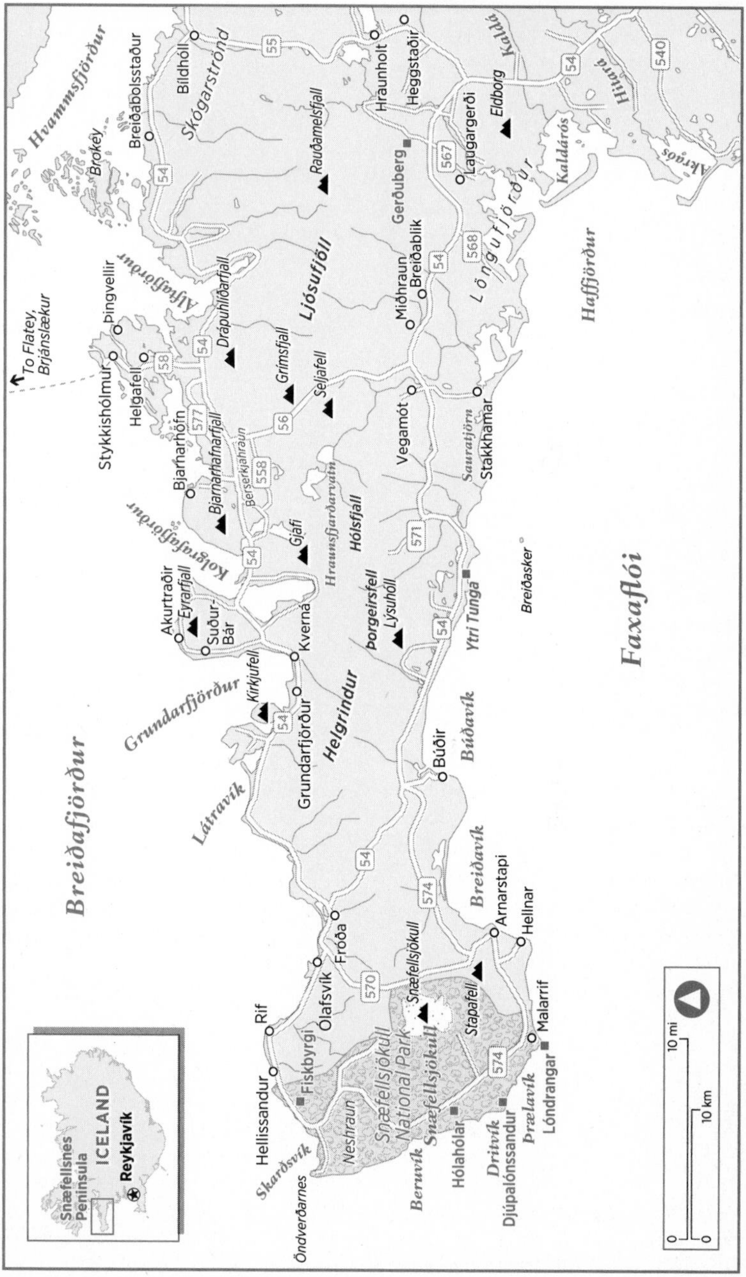

bookstores, service stations and tourist information offices. Online, **www.snaefellsnes.com** has thorough service listings.

Exploring the Area

The peninsula's southern coast has the most level land between mountains and sea, the best beaches for horseback riding and seal-spotting, and the most rain. The western tip is dominated by Snæfellsjökull and the lava that spouted from the volcano beneath it. The indented northern coastline has the best ports, and thus the vast majority of the population. The following sights are laid out in a clockwise pattern around the peninsula, but travel can, of course, commence in any direction.

BUS TOURS **Reykjavík Excursions** (✆ **580-5400;** www.re.is) offers a guided, 10-hour "Wonders of Snæfellsnes with Cruise" tour. Stops include Arnarstapi, Djúpalónssandur, and Ólafsvík. The tour costs 24,000kr, not including lunch, and leaves Reykjavík three times a week from June to August. **Iceland Excursions** (✆ **540-1313;** www.icelandexcursions.is) has a similar tour for 23,000kr, departing 3 days a week from June through August.

Reykjavík Excursions also offers a 17,500kr day package from Reykjavík to Ólafsvík, including a whale-watching tour and a visit to the shark-curing operation at Bjarnarhöfn Farm. The most common sightings here are minke whales, which are 7m to 8m (23–26 ft.) long and only flash their backs for a few quick breaths. Dolphins turn up on two out of three occasions and put on a better show. Lucky passengers see orcas (aka killer whales), sperm whales, or blue whales.

SOUTHERN SNÆFELLSNES

Eldborg, a 200m-long (656 ft.) crater at the southeast base of the peninsula, has an elegantly symmetrical, oblong shape rising from the lava field it spawned some 5,000 to 8,000 years ago. More dramatic scoria craters are found elsewhere in Iceland—Hverfell at Lake Mývatn, for example—but for visitors sticking close to Reykjavík, Eldborg is a fairly interesting 2-hour round-trip hike. The best approach is from Snorrastaðir Farm (see box below); the turnoff from Route 54 is 35km (22 miles) from Borgarnes.

Gerðuberg, an escarpment of hexagonal basalt columns, is strikingly broad and rectilinear. Gerðuberg is a 1km (¾ mile) detour from Route 54; the turnoff is about 46km (29 miles) from Borgarnes, on a dirt road almost directly opposite Route 567 to Hótel Eldborg.

Proceeding west, Route 54 passes Route 571 78km (48½ miles) from Borgarnes, and then moves close to the shoreline. Six and a half kilometers (4 miles) after the Route 571 junction is a turnoff for **Ytri-Tunga Farm** on the left, and past the farmhouse is a beach with a seal colony. The farm is private property, so be respectful of any signs, and do not disturb or try to feed the seals.

Iceland loves converting hot springs to swimming pools, however unlikely the location. The **Lýsuhóll geothermal pool** (✆ **433-9917;** mid-June to Aug 10am–10pm; admission 300kr) is so natural that you may find clumps of algae bobbing on the surface. To Icelanders, this is all the more healthful. The turnoff is on the north side of Route 54, 8.5km (5¼ miles) west of Ytri-Tunga.

Just west of Lýsuhóll, Route 54 passes **Búðavík,** a bay with lovely, broad sandbanks, and the glacier as a backdrop. After Búðavík, Route 54 cuts overland to the north coast, while Route 574 continues along the south coast. Off Route 574, less than a kilometer from the Route 54 junction, a turnoff leads to Búðir, once a thriving

HORSEBACK riding ON SNÆFELLSNES

The south coast of Snæfellsnes, with its sand beaches, lava fields, and sightings of birds and seals, is a wonderful setting for riders of all levels.

Snorrastaðir Farm (✆ **435-6628;** www.snorrastadir.is), at the base of the peninsula, leads rides on the picturesque sands of Löngufjörur at an hourly rate of around 4,500kr. Accommodation, if needed, is in functional up-to-six-person private cabins (set at a weekly rate of 15,500kr per person) or on floor mattresses in a large shared farmhouse (4,500kr per person with sleeping bag). The turnoff from Route 54 is 35km (22 miles) from Borgarnes, and the farm is 2km (1¼ miles) farther ahead.

Hótel Eldborg (✆ **435-6602;** www.hoteleldborg.is) has a 19,900kr package that includes a 4-hour ride on Löngufjörur, a night's lodging (before or after the ride), three-course dinner, and breakfast. The hotel is in a school building and operates only from June 5 to August 20; rooms are simple, with shared facilities. To get there, exit Route 54 on to Route 567, about 46km (29 miles) from Borgarnes, and proceed 4km (2½ miles).

Lýsuhóll Farm (✆ **435-6716;** www.lysuholl.is), the leading horse tour operator on the south coast, is based further west, about 9km (5½ miles) east of the southern junction of Route 54 and Route 574 (next to the Lýsuhóll geothermal swimming pool). Tours range from 90-minute rides (4,500kr) or day trips (17,000kr) to 7-day explorations of Snæfellsnes (210,000kr with full room and board).

Kverná (✆ **438-6813**; www.simnet.is/kverna), a farm 1km (½ mile) east of Grundarfjörður with 30 horses ready to be ridden, is the best horseback riding outfit on the north coast. Tours vary from 1 hour to 14 days and can range all over Snæfellsnes. A compelling nearby destination for a shorter ride is Kirkjufell Mountain (9,000kr; 2 hours).

fishing village and now just an 1848 church and an exclusive country hotel (see "Hótel Búðir," p. 196). West of Búðir along the coast is the **Búðahraun lava field,** a protected nature reserve. Route 574 passes north of Búðahraun to **Breiðavík,** another idyllic bay for strolling beachcombers. The free brochure *Snæfellsnes: Magical Iceland* lays out walking routes in these areas.

For centuries **Búðir** was the most active trading hub on the south coast of Snæfellsnes. A hundred people lived here in 1703, the year Iceland's first census was taken. The **church** is well restored and worth a look; ask for the key in the hotel lobby. Búðir is the best starting point for walks across Búðahraun. A 2km (1¼-mile) trail heads southwest along the coast to **Frambúðir,** an anchorage dating back to the Settlement Age. Ruins of fishermen's huts, fish-drying sheds, and trading booths are still visible, and whales are often spotted offshore. From Frambúðir, a trail cuts inland across the lava field to **Búðaklettur,** a volcanic crater 88 meters (289 ft.) deep. The surrounding lava flowed from here 5,000 to 8,000 years ago, and has since revegetated with mosses, wildflowers, heather, birch, and 11 varieties of fern. Unusual shade variations are found in the rock. To reach Búðaklettur from the hotel, allow 3 hours round-trip.

Arnarstapi, just a small cluster of houses on the western end of Breiðavík, is near a small, rocky cove. The village's coastline is popular with birdwatchers, though they could face attacks by Arctic terns, especially during the May–June nesting season.

Snjófell (p. 197), the leading tour operator for glacier expeditions, is based here. The clunky **stone sculpture** set back from the sea cliffs represents Bárður Snæfellsás, a half-human, half-giant saga hero and local guardian spirit. Just outside Arnarstapi, Route 574 skirts the base of **Stapafell,** a mountain long thought to be an elf domicile, hence the doorways painted on the rocks.

The 2.5km (1½-mile) **Arnarstapi–Hellnar trail ★★** between Arnarstapi and Hellnar, the next village to the west, falls within a protected nature reserve and is understandably the most popular seaside hiking route on Snæfellsnes. Of all the unusual forms of lava erosion seen from the clifftop trail, the most striking is **Gatklettur,** a natural arch extending into the sea.

Situated on a blissful stretch of rocky coast, the tiny fishing village of **Hellnar** (year-round population: 9) is a perfect rest stop, even for those not hiking the Arnarstapi–Hellnar trail. The Fjöruhúsið Café (see "Where to Dine," p. 198) has an outdoor deck overlooking some amazing layered lava rock formations and the **Baðstofa (Bathhouse),** a sea cave resounding with bird cacophony.

SNÆFELLSJÖKULL NATIONAL PARK (ÞJÓÐGARÐURINN SNÆFELLSJÖKULL)

Snæfellsjökull glacier lies atop a 1,446m-high (4,744-ft.) volcano that last erupted around the year 250. The national park, inaugurated in 2001, extends down from the glacier and volcano to cover the entire western tip of Snæfellsnes Peninsula.

The **Snæfellsjökull National Park Visitor Center** (✆ **436-6888** or 855-4260; www.ust.is; 20 May–10 Sept daily 10am–6pm) is in Hellnar, on the main road leading into the village. A second visitor center in Hellissandur, on the north coast, is scheduled to open in June 2011 in celebration of the National Park's tenth anniversary. Park information is also found inÓlafsvík, at the **Pakkhúsið** on Route 574 (✆ **433-6930;** May–Sept daily 11am–5pm). All these offices carry good topographical hiking maps of the park.

When seen from Reykjavík, 115km (71½ miles) away, **Snæfellsjökull** is a prominent knoll on the northern horizon, glittering by day and glowing red at dusk. With its near-symmetrical white cone and iconic stature, Snæfellsjökull could be compared to another dormant volcano: Japan's Mt. Fuji. Both mountains have exerted an unusual grip on artists, writers, and spiritualists. Jules Verne, in his 1864 sci-fi novel *Journey to the Center of the Earth,* made Snæfellsjökull the entry portal for a scientific expedition to the Earth's core. In the Halldór Laxness novel *Under the Glacier,* Snæfellsjökull inspires an almost hallucinatory religious transformation in a small Snæfellsnes community. New Agers make pilgrimages to the glacier, believing it to be one of the Earth's primary "energy points." Snæfellsjökull was exceptional even to the Vikings, who thought trolls lived inside it. (Trolls normally prefer rock dwellings.) Sadly, Snæfellsjökull—already one of Iceland's smallest glaciers—is shrinking rapidly. Since 1996, the icecap has dwindled from 14 sq. km to 11 sq. km (5¼ sq. miles–4¼ sq. miles), and more and more rocks poke through.

ACTIVITIES ON THE GLACIER Glacier conditions vary, and the visitor center should be consulted before you do any **climbing.** Generally, the best access is from Route 570, which skirts the eastern side of the glacier and connects with Route 574 on the south and north coasts, near Arnarstapi and Ólafsvík. Regular cars can usually traverse Route 570 in summer. (Snjófell, the tour operator listed below, can take you from Arnarstapi to the glacier's edge for 1,500kr round-trip.) Continuing 1.3km north on

Route 570, you will come to a parking area near the **Sönghellir** "singing cave." About 100m (330 feet) along the walking path is the tiny cave, and if you have a torch, peek inside at the graffiti dating back centuries. It took us a while to work out that the cave's famous echoing potential is best exploited when you stand outside the entrance and sing.

Hiking routes from Route 570 to the summit are inconsistent from year to year. The usual advice is to walk on tracks formed by snowmobiles and snow tractors, lessening the chances of falling into a hidden crevasse. ***Warning:*** Conditions are worsening as the glacier melts, and as a rule no one should climb Snæfellsjökull on foot before mid-February or after late July. The best time for an ascent is from March to May. Always be prepared for a sudden onslaught of rough weather. No technical equipment is necessary, except at the spire of rock at the final summit, which is sometimes coated in ice, necessitating an ice axe and crampons. The crater, about 1km (¾ miles) in diameter, is filled in with ice, and two lesser summits are along the ring.

Snowmobile and "snow cat" tours up Snæfellsjökull are arranged by **Snjófell** (✆ **435-6783;** www.snjofell.is), based in Arnarstapi. Scheduled trips run throughout the day from mid-February to mid-August, with additional 9pm and 11pm departures in summer to enjoy the midnight sun. Snowcats are tractor-like behemoths with bench space for up to 20 passengers. A snowmobile tour is 6,500kr per person (6 person minimum), and snowcat tours are 10,500kr or 15,500kr if you ride solo. Prices include snow suit, gloves, and helmet.

THE WESTERN COAST

The park map, available at all nearby tourist information offices, details many excellent alternatives to ascending Snæfellsjökull. The wild-looking peaks northwest of the glacier are particularly intriguing, with almost no tourist traffic.

NORTHERN lights: AURORA BOREALIS

A brightly-hued fog creeps across the night sky, shape-shifts into a solid green and red swirl stretching out from horizon to horizon, then suddenly breaks into dozens of daggers of light, piercing downward until they seem within reach. This is just one example of the *aurora borealis*, or Northern Lights (*norðurljós*), that we witnessed in Snæfellsnes; nature at its most magical. If you haven't witnessed this phenomenon before, Iceland is a great place to do so because the small population and big distances between towns make it easy to escape light pollution, even close to Reykjavík. If you need a lift to a more likely Northern Lights sighting than your hotel in the midst of town, the closest tourist information office will be able to provide details of tours. Northern Lights tours operate from mid-March to mid-April when they are best seen, but there are usually a few sightings up to early May, and occasionally even as early as late August, just keep an eye out. It seems that the *aurora borealis* occurs when Earth's magnetic field is intercepted by energy particles from the sun, which ionize atoms in the upper atmosphere. This is why solar activity is a good predictor of the intensity and duration of these auroral displays.

Bring a tripod if you have an SLR camera (or at least one that lets you leave the shutter open for 30 seconds or more) so your friends back home might believe your description of what you saw. The exact performance schedule is random, but admission is free!

At the peninsula's southwest end, **Malarrif ★** (Pebble Reef) is the starting point for a rewarding 40-minute round-trip walk east along the shore to Lóndrangar, a pair of beautiful sea pillars from a long-extinct volcano. The turnoff from Route 574 is 8km (5 miles) west of Arnarstapi, and the parking area is next to a lighthouse that looks like a rocket.

About 4km (2½ miles) northwest from Malarrif, Route 572 branches off from Route 574 and leads 2km (1¼ miles) to **Djúpalónssandur ★**, a black-sand beach set amid strangely eroded clumps of lava. The partial remains of a British fishing trawler shipwrecked in 1948 lie scattered on the beach, with an information sign. The wreckage looks simply like litter, but may resonate as a symbol of Iceland's historic struggles with the British over territorial fishing waters. From Djúpalónssandur, a 15-minute trail leads to **Dritvík ★**, an equally scenic cove to the north. Remarkably, Dritvík was the largest seasonal fishing station in all of Iceland from the mid-16th to the mid-19th centuries, with as many as 600 men camped out there during spring and summer. Some remains of stone walls can still be seen.

Hólahólar, a crater cluster that is clearly visible from Route 574, can be reached by a marked turnoff 3km (2 miles) north of the Route 572 junction. The road proceeds right into the largest crater, Berudalur, which forms a natural amphitheater. A wonderful, easy seaside trail proceeds from Hólahólar 4km (2½ miles) north to Beruvík.

The northwest corner of Snæfellsnes is accessed via Route 579, a bumpy road extending 7km (4¼ miles) from Route 574. Within 2km (1¼ miles) the road passes Skarðsvík, an alluring golden-sand beach with a sign marking the Viking grave site discovered there. One kilometer (½ mile) farther is a parking area on the left, with trails heading through the **Neshraun** lava field to Vatnsborg—a small crater with vertical walls descending to a captivating fern-filled hollow—and Grashólshellir, a small cave. Vatnsborg is 2km (1¼ miles) one-way, and the Grashólshellir is another kilometer (½ mile), but don't worry about either if time is limited. **Öndverðarnes** is the small peninsula at the very northwest tip, a scene of multiple shipwrecks and bleak cliffs known as **Svörtuloft (The Black Skies).** The lighthouse here is disappointingly stubby, and the sad ruins of a well lie 200m (656 ft.) away.

At **Fiskbyrgi,** the ruins of fish-drying sheds, simple structures of lava rock, are up to 600 years old and have taken on an eerie stateliness over the centuries. The 5-minute trail to the site starts at a parking area on the south side of Route 574, about 1km (½ mile) east of the Route 579 junction and just west of a 420m-high (1,378 ft.) radio transmitter once used by the U.S. Navy to position ships and aircraft.

THE NORTH COAST

One of Iceland's oldest fishing villages, **Hellissandur,** is home to **Sjómannagarður** (✆ **481-3295;** admission by donation; Jun–Aug Tues–Sun 10am–noon and 1–6pm), a humble maritime museum with a re-creation of a typical, turf-roofed fisherman's hut from the early 1900s. Sjómannagarður is on Route 574, across the road from and just west of the N1 filling station.

Ólafsvík is one of Iceland's oldest trade hubs, and today nets the most fish of any village in Snæfellsnes. The **Snæfellsbær Regional Museum** (**Byggðasafn Snæfellsbæjar**, the upper floor at Pakkhúsið), Route 574 at the corner with Kirkjtún 2 (✆ **433-6930;** admission 300kr adults, free for seniors and children under 12; May–Sept 11am–5pm), is inside an 1841 warehouse that also houses the tourist information office on the ground floor. The exhibits are mostly just antiquated household items and farm

A SHORT HISTORY OF GOING berserk IN ICELAND

The berserkers, from whom "gone berserk" originates, were a faction of Norse mercenaries known for their savage battle frenzy. In Old Icelandic, *berserkr* meant "bear-shirted," so they may have worn bear pelts; but *berr* also meant "bare," so the name may have only signified fighting without protective clothing. Berserkers disappeared by the 1100s, leaving a wake of mystery for future scholars. Some maintain they were merely symbolic archetypes to be invoked in wartime and as literary figures in the sagas.

The **Berserkjahraun** was named after a famous incident in the *Eyrbyggja Saga*. In the late 10th century, Vermundur the Slender of Bjarnarhöfn—a farm located just beyond the northwest boundary of the lava field—returned from Norway with two berserkers. They were difficult to handle, so Vermundur gave them to his brother Víga-Styrr (Killer-Styrr) at Hraun, now Hraunháls farm, at the northeast end of the lava field. One of the berserkers fell in love with Víga-Styrr's daughter Ásdís and demanded her hand. Víga-Styrr agreed, on the condition that the suitor clear a path through the lava field from Hraun to Bjarnarhöfn. The berserkers quickly finished this Herculean task, but Víga-Styrr reneged on the deal and killed them instead (by locking them inside a scalding hot sauna and spearing them as they tried to escape). In the saga, the berserkers are laid to rest in a hollow along the path.

The story could indeed have some basis in truth. A path through the lava field can still be found, and in a late-19th-century excavation alongside it, researchers uncovered the skeletons of two men—both of average height but powerfully built. To reach this path, exit Route 54 at its western junction with Route 577, marked "Bjarnarhöfn." After about 2km (1¼ miles), the road to Bjarnarhöfn branches off to the left. Stay on Route 577, and a sign for the "Berserkjargata" trail is shortly ahead. The trail extends about 1km (½ mile) through the lava field, and halfway along is the hollow, now marked only by a stone cairn and a blank, weather-beaten sign. The best Berserkjahraun scenery, however, is south of Route 54, where the lava looks like a stormy sea frozen in time. Three access points lead from Route 54; the westernmost and easternmost are marked as Route 558, and the one in the middle is unmarked. The roads are heavily rutted but passable in regular cars. Walking trails appear here and there, but the lava can be difficult to traverse.

The same farm that figures in the *Eyrbyggja Saga* (above), **Bjarnarhöfn,** off Route 577, near the western junction of Route 577 and Route 54 (✆ **438-1581**), now produces Iceland's most indelicate delicacy: cured and putrefied Greenland shark, or *hákarl* (p. 28). Visitors see a shark exhibit, tour the facilities, and sample the goods if they dare. **Hákarlasafn** has been featured on several TV cooking shows in the "revolting foreign custom" segment. Admission is 500kr adults, free for children under 14 (June to mid-Sept daily 9am–6pm or call ahead).

implements. The **Sjávarsafnið Ólafsvík** (admission 300kr adults, free for children 15 and under; June–Aug daily noon–5pm) is a recently renovated maritime museum by the dock featuring tanks full of marine specimens.

Grundarfjörður is the most picturesque town on the north coast. Kirkjufell, its oblong signature mountain, pokes up from a promontory west of town, while good trails lead south from town into the peninsula's mountainous spine. The **Eyrbyggja Heritage Center,** Route 54 at Hrannarstígur (✆ **438-1881;** admission 700kr; June–Aug daily 10am–6pm), which doubles as the tourist information office, has exhibits on the history of fishing and rural life on the peninsula and nonstop screenings of short Icelandic documentaries and fascinating feature films with English subtitles.

Meaning "Berserkers Lava Field," the gloriously weird **Berserkjahraun ★★** lies halfway between Grundarfjörður and Stykkishólmur. The lava flowed some 3,000 to 4,000 years ago and is young enough to retain all kinds of convoluted shapes, with fascinating hues and textural contrasts in the rock and thick mosses.

Where to Stay

The listings below—all excellent bases for exploring the entire peninsula—follow a clockwise pattern around the periphery. Places to stay in Stykkishólmur, the largest town on Snæfellsnes, are listed on p. 202.

SOUTH COAST

Guesthouse Hof ★ ☺ A long log cabin, with views of Snæfellsjökull glacier 30km (19 miles) away. The interior is modern and unfancy, but has plenty of communal space and feels like a real home. Families and self-caterers are particularly well served by the apartment-style lodgings.

Off Rte. 54, east of Búðavík Bay and just west of Ytri-Tunga Farm about 80km from Borgarnes. ✆ **435-6802** or 820-3897. www.gistihof.is. 6 units. May–Sept 11,000kr double; 9,000kr double w/sleeping bag. Rates about 40% lower Oct–Apr. Breakfast available (1,800kr). MC, V. **Amenities:** Hot tubs. *In room:* TV, kitchenette, no phone.

Guesthouse Langaholt This guesthouse has been running for more than 30 years (1978) and tourist services in the area, such as the 9-hole golf course on the premises, have grown around it. Rooms here have a simple, tasteful simplicity that lets the nearby beach, mountains, and glacier speak for themselves. The website is in Icelandic and German only, but icons help you navigate at least to view some photos and a map.

Rte. 54, at Garðar Farm, east of Búðavík Bay about 89km from Borgarnes. ✆ **435-6789.** Fax 435-6889. www.langaholt.is. 21 units, 12 with private shower. 19,000kr double. Rates include breakfast. MC, V. **Amenities:** Restaurant; golf course. *In room:* No phone.

Lýsuhóll Located on the eastern end of Búðavík Bay, next to the Lýsuhóll geothermal pool (p. 190), this horse farm has three adorably rustic cabins that sleep up to four, each has two or three single beds, a pullout couch in the living room, and a glacier view. In addition to the horse tours run by the owners, guests are entitled to fish for trout in the local rivulet. Sheets and towels are an extra 1,000kr per person, unless you bring your own. Set **dinner menus** are served on request from 2,900kr. Children (6–12) half price.

Off Rte. 54, about 9km (5½ miles) east of the southern junction of Rte. 54 and Rte. 574. ✆ **435-6716.** Fax 435-6816. www.lysuholl.is. 3 cottages. May–Sept 16,000kr cottage. 2 additional cottages offer separate rooms all year round at 16,000kr double, 10,000kr single. Breakfast available (1500kr). MC, V. Closed Sept–May. *In room:* kitchenette, no phone.

Hótel Búðir ★★ Just 2 hours from Reykjavík, Hótel Búðir may be the most hyped "romantic getaway" lodging in Iceland, creating expectations that are not always fair to visitors or the hotel. Some rooms have a less than ideal view and loud office parties from Reykjavík can pervade the hotel. All that aside, Búðir's hip country elegance is unsurpassed outside the capital. Rooms are individually designed, so ask to look around before choosing. The least expensive room, in the loft, is small but recommended for snugness and great views. The spacious deluxe rooms are a good insurance policy if everything needs to be perfect. No one is disappointed by the spectacular, isolated setting.

At Búðir, off Rte. 574, near the southern junction of Rte. 574 and Rte. 54. ✆ **435-6700.** Fax 435-6701. www.budir.is. 28 units. May–Sept 26,000kr–44,500kr double; 44,500kr suite. Rates around 30% lower Oct–Apr. Rates include breakfast. AE, DC, MC, V. **Amenities:** Restaurant; bar. *In room:* TV/DVD, hair dryer, Wi-Fi.

Snjófell Run by the company leading snowmobile and snow cat tours on Snæfellsjökull (p. 193), this guesthouse is a good option for travelers who just need a comfortable, well-maintained room and can suppress their desire for views until reemerging outdoors.

Arnarstapi, along the main road into the village. ✆ **435-6783** or 865-3459. 15 units, none w/bathroom. www.snjofell.is. Mar–June 10 7,400kr double; 5,900kr double w/sleeping bag. Breakfast available (2,000kr). MC, V. **Amenities:** Restaurant; guest kitchen. *In room:* No phone.

Hotel Hellnar ★ Nearby the Snæfellsjökull visitor center, Hotel Hellnar is an eco-hotel and as of 2010 is the sole Icelandic recipient of a Green Globe "gold" certification. It serves organic food, buys fair trade, and washing up is done with green detergents. Rooms are spare but dignified, and walls are a bit thin. All that distinguishes the more expensive doubles is the ocean view. The cottages have kitchens and sleep four to six. Since 2010 the hotel has been run by the Hringhótel chain.

Hellnar, off Rte. 574. ✆ **435-6820.** www.hellnar.is. 20 units. June–Aug 18,000kr–21,000kr double. Rates around 10% lower May and Sept. Rates include breakfast except cottages. MC, V. Closed Oct–Apr. **Amenities:** Restaurant; bar. *In room:* TV, hair dryer, no phone.

NORTH COAST

A very basic eco-conscious hostel in a cute, old, red house, **Grundarfjörður Hostel,** Hlíðarvegur 15, Grundarfjörður (✆ **562-6533** or 895-6533; fax 438-6433; www.hostel.is; 7 units, none w/bathroom; May–Sept 6,200kr double; 5,200kr double w/sleeping bag; 2,500kr per person sleeping-bag accommodation in 4–6 person room; rates around 10% lower Oct–Dec 15 and Jan 15–Apr; AE, DC, MC, V; closed Dec 16–Jan 14), has 34 beds but only one single and one double, so most guests stay in four- to six-person rooms. Bike rental is available for exploring the town environs, and the village geothermal pool is just down the block.

Hótel Hellissandur Service is thorough and rooms are smart if smallish and nondescript at this well-run hotel. Bathrooms have nice large sinks, a rarity in Iceland. Rooms facing south have mountain views, and three rooms glimpse the glacier. Prices include free admission to the Snæfellsbær geothermal pool in Ólafsvík, 10km (6¼ miles) away.

Klettsbúð 9, Hellissandur. ✆ **430-8600.** www.hotelhellissandur.is. 20 units. June–Aug 22,600kr double. Rates around 30% lower Sept–Dec and May; 40% lower Jan–Apr. Rates include breakfast. MC, V. **Amenities:** Restaurant; bar. *In room:* TV, Wi-Fi.

Hótel Ólafsvík Located right in the village center, Hótel Ólafsvík has reasonably sized, peach-hued rooms and the basic comforts expected of a mid-scale hotel. The 19 studios each have a sofa bed, fridge, microwave, and private bathroom but cost the same as the en suite doubles.

Ólafsbraut 19–20 (Rte. 574), Ólafsvík. ✆ **436-1650.** Fax 436-1651. www.hotelolafsvik.is. 29 units, 18 w/ bathroom, 19 studio apts. May–Sept 18,900kr double/studio apt; 10,900kr double without bathroom. Rates around 20% lower Mar–Apr. Rates include breakfast. MC, V. Closed Oct–Apr. **Amenities:** Restaurant; bar; Wi-Fi in bar. *In room:* TV.

Hótel Framnes ★ Extensive 2007 renovations by the owners—Gisli, a former seaman, and Shelagh, a craniosacral therapist from South Africa—have breathed fresh life into this former fishermen's hostel in Grundarfjörður. Not only are the showers powerful, but there's a mechanical massage chair for guests on the first floor. Most rooms have excellent mountain views.

Nesvegur 8, Grundarfjörður. ✆ **438-6893.** www.hotelframnes.is. 27 units. June–Aug 19,000kr double; 24,000kr triple; 280,000kr quadruple. Rates around 10% lower May and Sept; around 30% lower Oct–Apr. Rates include breakfast. AE, DC, MC, V. **Amenities:** Restaurant. *In room:* TV, Wi-Fi.

Kverná This idyllically-located horse farm just east of Grundarfjörður offers no-nonsense accommodation in three guesthouse rooms, plus three cabins for groups of four to six, and camping. The smaller cottage, with roof lines mimicking a Viking longhouse, is snazzier and more expensive. Icelandic farm **dinner** (fish, lamb) available on request for 4,000kr. Breakfasts include delicious Icelandic *skyr*.

Rte. 54, 1km (½ mile) east of Grundarfjörður. ✆ **438-6813.** Fax 438-6514. www.simnet.is/kverna. 3 units, none w/bathroom, and 3 cottages for up to 6 people. 12,000kr double; 18,000kr–20,000kr cottages. Breakfast available for 1,500kr. MC, V. *In room:* No phone.

Suður-Bár Situated on a promontory 7km (4¼ miles) from Grundarfjörður, this cheerful guesthouse has a glassed-in dining room to take in the stunning scenery. There is a golf course, and horseback riding can be arranged.

Rte. 576, 4km (2½ miles) north of Rte. 54. ✆ **438-6815.** www.sudur-bar.is. 6 units, 1 w/bathroom. June–Sept 15 16,000kr double; 14,000kr double without bathroom; 18,000kr triple. Rates include breakfast. AE, MC, V. *In room:* No phone.

Where to Dine

SOUTH COAST

Choices are limited in this sparsely populated region, and many visitors stock up on groceries in Borgarnes. The **Vegamót service station** (✆ **435-6690;** daily to 9pm), at the southern junction of Route 54 and Route 56, is a common fast-food pit-stop. Between Vegamót and Búðir, the best dinner option is the buffet at **Guesthouse Langaholt,** Route 54, at Garðar Farm, east of Búðavík Bay (✆ **435-6789;** 5,000–7,900kr; MC, V; May–Sept 7–9pm), with a large selection of fish dishes; make sure to call ahead, especially in May or September, so they know to expect you.

The most gourmet option by far is **Hótel Búðir ★★**, off Route 574, near the southern junction of Route 574 and Route 54 (✆ **435-6700;** reservations recommended; main courses 3,900–5,100kr; AE, DC, MC, V; Mar–Oct daily 6–10pm, Nov–Feb Fri–Sun 6–10pm), with a pared-down, seasonal menu strong on fresh, local ingredients—even the salad oil is made using local flowers. On the main road into Arnarstapi, **Arnarbær** (✆ **435-6783;** main courses 1,500–3,500kr; MC, V; daily 10am–10pm) is a reliable and unpretentious choice, with lamb and seafood specials as well as the usual burgers. In Hellnar, **Hotel Hellnar ★** (✆ **435-6820;** reservations recommended; main courses 3,490–4,990kr; MC, V; Sept–May daily 7–9pm) uses almost all organic ingredients in traditional dishes—perhaps a simple choice between lamb, cod, and hashed fish with brown bread. **Fjöruhúsið** (✆ **435-6844;** light fare 600kr–2,200kr;

MC, V; May 15–Sept 15 daily 10am–10pm) is a tiny seaside cafe with limited indoor and outdoor seating, but the atmosphere is sublime and their fish soup is famed.

NORTH COAST

The north coast has a greater array of dining options, but nothing worth planning your trip around—an array of hotel restaurants serving simple, good quality dishes, the village restaurant-bar (a couple of fish and lamb plates with burger/pizza fall-backs), and fast food at the filling station.

In Hellissandur, the **Hótel Hellissandur,** Klettsbúð 7 (✆ **430-8600;** reservations recommended; main courses 3,200–4,900kr; MC, V; mid-May to mid-Sept daily 7:30am–9pm), has the best of the Icelandic mainstays such as fresh fish or lamb soup, a vegetarian option or two, and reasonable prices, with light fare available all day.

In Ólafsvík, **Hótel Ólafsvík,** Ólafsbraut 19–20 (Rte. 574) (✆ **436-1650;** reservations recommended; main courses 2,990kr–5, 290kr; MC, V; daily noon–10pm), has a stately ambience and emphasizes fresh catches from the port next door.

In Grundarfjörður, **Hótel Framnes ★**, Nesvegur 8 (✆ **438-6893;** main courses 2,900–3,900kr; AE, DC, MC, V; mid-May to Sept daily 7–10pm), is the preferred choice, with a small menu; call in advance, especially in May or September. **Kaffi 59,** Route 54 (✆ **438-6446;** main courses 1,250–3,100kr; AE, DC, MC, V; Mon–Thurs 10am–10pm, Fri 9am–1am, Sat 11am–1am, Sun 11am–10pm, kitchen always shuts at 10pm), offering *bacalao* (salted cod) and lamb, as well as burgers and pizza, is also a good option.

STYKKISHÓLMUR & BREIÐAFJÖRÐUR

As the largest town on Snæfellsnes Peninsula—and with a ferry link to the Westfjords—Stykkishólmur is often the presumed base or transit hub for any trip in west Iceland. Actually, any place on Snæfellsnes is a good base if you have a car, and most visitors headed to the Westfjords drive or fly, bypassing Stykkishólmur altogether. Yet Stykkishólmur is an attractive place in its own right, at the tip of a peninsula amid Breiðafjörður's scattering of mirage-like islands. Despite its name, Breiðafjörður is more bay than fjord, and its extensive shallows, mudflats, and rocky coastlines sustain one of the most flourishing and diverse ecosystems in Iceland. Breiðafjörður has around 2,500 islands, but its pronounced tidal fluctuations make the final tally unknown. Most of Breiðafjörður falls within a strictly regulated nature reserve, and tours from Stykkishólmur provide opportunities for kayaking, fishing, birding, seal-spotting, and shellfish-slurping. The car ferry *Baldur* links Stykkishólmur to the south coast of the Westfjords, docking along the way at Flatey Island, an historic settlement that is the only populated island in Breiðafjörður.

Essentials

GETTING THERE & AROUND Stykkishólmur is 172km (107 miles) from Reykjavík, with good roads the entire way. **Sterna buses** (✆ **587-6000;** www.sterna.is) connect Reykjavík and Stykkishólmur (2½ hours; 4,900kr one-way), with one or two departures almost daily (not always on Wednesdays) in each direction year-round. Another route—also with one or two departures daily—covers the north coast of Snæfellsnes from Stykkishólmur to Hellissandur (65 min.; 2,200kr one-way), with stops at Vatnaleið (the northern junction of Rte. 54 and Rte. 56), Grundarfjörður, and Ólafsvík.

The car ferry ***Baldur*** (✆ **433-2254;** www.seatours.is/ferrybaldur) makes a scenic crossing of Breiðafjörður, linking Stykkishólmur to Brjánslækur in the Westfjords, with a stop at Flatey Island. For detailed information, see p. 201.

VISITOR INFORMATION Stykkishólmur's **travel information center,** Borgarbraut 4 (✆ **438-1750;** www.stykkisholmur.is; June–Aug Mon–Fri 9am–10pm, Sat–Sun 10am–7pm), marked from the main road into town, is in the sports/swimming hall. The office of the tour operator **Seatours,** Smiðjustígur 3 (✆ **433-2254;** www.saeferdir.is; June–Aug 8am–8pm, Sep–May 8am–5pm) is also helpful with planning.

Exploring the Area

STYKKISHÓLMUR

The **downtown waterfront** is worth a stroll, as Stykkishólmur has admirably preserved and maintained its older buildings. Those interested in architectural history should pick up the free brochure *Old Stykkishólmur* at the tourist office. To continue the walk, head past the ferry landing along a narrow causeway to **Súgandisey Island,** which protects the port and has wonderful views of Stykkishólmur's brightly-painted buildings and the islands of Breiðafjörður.

Four kilometers (2½ miles) due south of Stykkishólmur is **Helgafell,** a conspicuous, knobby hill of columnar basalt, 73m (240 ft.) high. Helgafell was held so sacred by early pagan settlers—who believed they would enter it upon death—that a decree forbade anyone to gaze upon it unwashed. Meaning "Holy Mountain," Helgafell figures prominently in two of Iceland's best-known sagas, *Eyrbyggja Saga* and *Laxdæla Saga*. A steep, 10 minute trail leads to the top, which affords great views of Breiðafjörður and surrounding mountains. At the summit are remains of a small stone structure, which may have been a chapel. According to tradition, you are granted three wishes for climbing Helgafell, but only by adhering strictly to these four rules: 1) Don't talk or look back during the climb; 2) Face east while making the wishes; 3) Don't tell anyone what you wished for; and 4) Make your wishes with a true heart. The 1903 church near Helgafell's base is also worth a peek. The turnoff to Helgafell is marked from Route 58.

Norwegian House (Norska Húsið) A prosperous trader imported Norwegian timber for this 1832 building, a palace in its time, and now the folk museum for the Stykkishólmur area. Exhibits recount town history, assemble artifacts from saddles to sewing machines, and re-create the domestic sphere of the original owner—all nicely presented. The gift shop is gorgeous with more Icelandic ware than mainstream tourist shops.

Hafnargata 5. ✆ **438-1640.** Admission 700kr adults; 400kr seniors and children 6–16. June–Aug daily 11am–5pm or by arrangement.

Library of Water (Vatnasafn) Twenty-four floor-to-ceiling transparent columns, each filled with water from a different Icelandic glacier or glacial river embody this collection. English and Icelandic adjectives associated with weather are inscribed on the rubber floor. In 2007, New York-based artist Roni Horn—who has toured widely in Iceland for more than 30 years—unveiled this permanent architectural installation inside a former library on a hill overlooking Breiðafjörður. With Iceland's glaciers rapidly shrinking, Vatnasafn may yet become an important environmental archive. Vatnasafn is also a community hub for local reading groups and chess players; check the website for concerts, film screenings, or other events.

Bókhlöðustígur 17. www.libraryofwater.is. Free admission. June 1–Sept 1 daily 1–6pm; May & Sept weekends 1–6pm; Oct–April Saturdays 2–6pm.

FLATEY ISLAND

For most of Icelandic history, Flatey—measuring a mere 1 x 2 kilometers—was the commercial hub of Breiðafjörður, peaking in the mid-19th century. Today the island has around 25 gaily-painted homes but only five year-round residents, who like to feel time has passed them by (though it's nice to have modern, satellite-fuelled phone coverage, too). Visitors simply take in views of Snæfellsnes and the Westfjords, stroll along the low bird cliffs, and keep the world at a manageable distance. The 1926 church is adorned with frescoes painted in the 1960s by Kristjana and Baltasar Samper; the side walls depict scenes from island life, complete with ducks and puffins, while the altarpiece portrays Jesus in a white Icelandic sweater standing over two sheep farmers. The yellow building behind the church, from 1864, is Iceland's oldest, smallest and cutest library. Visitors in early summer should remain on the lookout for divebomb attacks by arctic terns defending their nesting grounds.

The ferry ***Baldur*** (**✆ 433-2254;** www.seatours.is/ferrybaldur), which connects Stykkishólmur to Brjánslækur on the southern coast of the Westfjords, docks at Flatey four times per day (twice in each direction) from around June 10 to August 22. A visitor could, for instance, board the 9am ferry from Stykkishólmur, arriving at Flatey at 10:30am, and head back to Stykkishólmur at 1:15pm or 8pm. Departures are more limited outside of summer, but continue year-round. The one-way fare to Flatey is 2,700kr. Passengers taking the full route between Stykkishólmur and Brjánslækur may disembark at Flatey and re-embark later that day—or the next day—at no extra cost, even with a car. The ferry has an acceptable restaurant.

Flatey's two places to stay are **Hótel Flatey** (✆/fax **422-7610;** www.hotelflatey.is; June–Aug 19,900kr double including breakfast; MC, V; closed Sept–May), with snug, old-fashioned en suite rooms inside restored warehouses; and the guesthouse run by **Ólína Jónsdóttir** (**✆ 438-1476;** 15,000kr house for up to eight people; 5,000kr per person made-up bed; 3,500kr per person sleeping-bag accommodation; no credit cards; closed Oct–Apr), which has a guest kitchen and breakfast on request. The only **restaurant** is at Hótel Flatey (Jun–Aug Sun–Thurs 8:30am–10pm; Fri–Sat 8:30am–midnight), but serves up fresh catch, puffin, and light fare.

Tours & Activities

The dominant tour operator in Stykkishólmur is **Seatours,** Smiðjustígur 3 (**✆ 433-2254;** www.seatours.is), whose most deservedly popular offering is a 2-hour cruise called the **Unique Adventure Tour** (departures daily May 15–Sept 15; 5,950kr, free for children under 15). Breiðafjörður's endless islands, abundant birds and seals, and unusually strong tides are encountered aboard a 120-passenger catamaran with a serviceable restaurant. Nets are dropped overboard so that passengers can slurp the celebrated local scallops straight from the shell. For visitors based in Reykjavík, **Reykjavík Excursions** (**✆ 580-5400;** www.re.is) and **Iceland Excursions** (**✆ 540-1313;** www.icelandexcursions.is) incorporate the Unique Adventure Tour into bus tours of Snæfellsnes, while **Eagle Air** (✆ **562-4200;** www.eagleair.is) combines the tour with aerial sightseeing.

BIRD-WATCHING Breiðafjörður has 65% of Iceland's rocky shores and 40% of its mudflats, attracting a rich concentration of seabirds, waders, geese, and—the most coveted sighting of all—white-tailed eagles. Flatey Island and Seatours' "Unique Adventure Tour," both detailed above, are sure to please bird-lovers. Seatours also schedules 3-day nature cruises of Breiðafjörður, departing from Reykjavík, with two nights on Flatey.

SEA ANGLING **Seatours** (✆ **433-2254;** www.seatours.is) leads 2-hour fishing trips for 6,700kr, with daily departures from June to August. Seatours also rents equipment for fishing from the pier.

KAYAKING Breiðafjörður's countless islands and shallow waters are kayak heaven. Arctic Adventures (✆ **562-7000**; www.adventures.is) offers a 6-day combination kayaking, hiking, sightseeing tour on Breiðafjörður for 199,990kr.

WHALE-WATCHING Whale-watching tours depart from Ólafsvík; see p. 190.

Where to Stay

Sjónarhóll Youth Hostel, Höfðagata 1 (✆ **438-1417** or 861-2517. Fax 438-1417. www.hostel.is. 11 units, none w/bathroom; May–Oct 10,800kr double; 3,100kr per person; 1,000kr bed linen for whole stay; AE, DC, MC, V; closed Nov–Apr), occupies one of Stykkishólmur's oldest buildings and is understandably popular. Try to book far in advance, especially if trying to secure one of the three doubles. The owner arranges fishing excursions, followed by a barbecue on the patio. Reception is open from 11am–1pm and 5:30–10pm.

Höfðagata Guesthouse This inexpensive guesthouse has simple attic rooms, a central location, a satisfying breakfast and a bay view from the veranda.

Höfðagata 11. ✆ **694-6569.** 4 units, none w/bathroom. 11,000kr double; 14,000kr triple. Rates include breakfast. MC, V. **Amenities:** Guest kitchen. *In room:* No phone.

Hótel Breiðafjörður Hotel Stykkishólmur may have better views, but this smaller hotel is more intimate and has a more central location, near the restaurants and the waterfront. Rooms are simple but more than adequate for the price. Not to be outdone by Hotel Stykkishólmur, guests have free access to the local golf course.

Aðalgata 8. ✆ **433-2200.** Fax 433-2201. www.hotelbreidafjordur.is. 11 units. June–Aug 22,000kr double; 25,000kr triple or family room. Rates 20%–25% lower Sept–May. Rates include breakfast. MC, V. **Amenities:** Cafe; Internet terminal. *In room:* No phone.

Hotel Stykkishólmur ★ With its faded concrete exterior and chain hotel ambience, Hotel Stykkishólmur seems easy to snub. Yet, rooms are more spacious than the norm, with plenty of light, and have great views. The 45 rooms added in 2005 cost the same but have more space and panache, particularly on the third floor, while the old rooms tend to have better views. Guests have free access to the 9-hole golf course next door.

Borgarbraut 8. ✆ **430-2100.** Fax 430-2101. www.hotelstykkisholmur.is. 78 units. Mid-June–Aug 24,000kr double; 28,000kr triple. Rates include breakfast. Rates staggered from around 15-40% lower Sept–mid-June. AE, DC, MC, V. **Amenities:** Restaurant; bar; room service; Internet terminal; Wi-Fi (lobby only). *In room:* TV, hair dryer.

Where to Dine

Hótel Stykkishólmur's **Perspectives Ocean View Restaurant,** Borgarbraut 8 (✆ **430-2100;** reservations recommended; main courses 2,400kr–5,400kr; AE, DC, MC, V; daily 6–10pm) serves a fine selection of Icelandic cuisine.

Fimm Fiskar ★ ICELANDIC Meaning "Five Fish"—a reference to the variety of species in the feted house soup—this respectable backup to Narfeyrarstofa (below) features plenty of fish, guillemot, and puffin. The Icelandic catfish, identified here as wolffish and complemented with honey and Dijon; is especially tender and clean-tasting. There's also homemade pasta.

Frúarstígur 1. ✆ **436-1600.** Reservations recommended. Main courses 1,900–4,900kr. MC, V. May 15–Sept 15 daily noon–9:30pm.

Narfeyrarstofa ★★ ICELANDIC With its enticing menu and knack for atmosphere, this lively restaurant is popular with tourists—reservations are a necessity in summer. Fish soup and smoked guillemot with port wine sauce are the perennial house starters, and main courses include Breiðafjörður's famous scallops, grilled with garlic and lemon oil. Upstairs seating is more subdued, with an improved waterfront view.

Aðalgata 3. ✆ **438-1119.** Reservations recommended. Main courses 2,300–4,850kr. MC, V. Sun–Thurs 11:30am–10pm; Fri–Sat 11:30am–1am.

WESTFJORDS: THE SOUTHWEST COAST

The Westfjords region feels almost like an island—which would be the case, if not for a 7km (4 1 /4-mile) bridge of land at its base. The Ring Road bypasses the area altogether, though Westfjorders like to say they have a ring road of their own (comprised of Routes 60 and 61). To other Icelanders, the Westfjords conjure historic images of fugitives, shipwrecks, and remote villages hemmed in by pack ice through long winters. Westfjorders are sometimes stereotyped as resilient, hard-nosed survivors; as eccentrics; and—having contributed a disproportionate share of Iceland's prominent statesmen—as natural-born leaders.

To set priorities for visitors, this book bypasses the west coast of Iceland between Stykkishólmur (on Snæfellsnes) and Látrabjarg Peninsula (at the southwest corner of the Westfjords). The entire drive is lovely, though rough patches in the roads can be wearying. For help with places to stay en route, see "Where to Stay," p. 208.

Látrabjarg proper, at the southwestern tip of Látrabjarg Peninsula, is Iceland's largest sea cliff, stretching 14km (8¾ miles) and peaking at a height of 441m (1,447 ft.). Many visitors walk along the rim for an hour or two and zoom off again, but the entire peninsula, with its wonderful beaches and trails, handsomely rewards those who linger. May is optimal for birdwatchers since access to Látrabjarg is unrestricted during nesting season, and few other tourists are around. Most birds are gone by September, but after that visitors can bask in the solitude and ponder the *aurora borealis*.

For drivers continuing northeast from Látrabjarg Peninsula, this section also covers the next three coastal villages—Patreksfjörður, Tálknafjörður, and Bíldudalur—and their enviable surroundings.

Westfjords

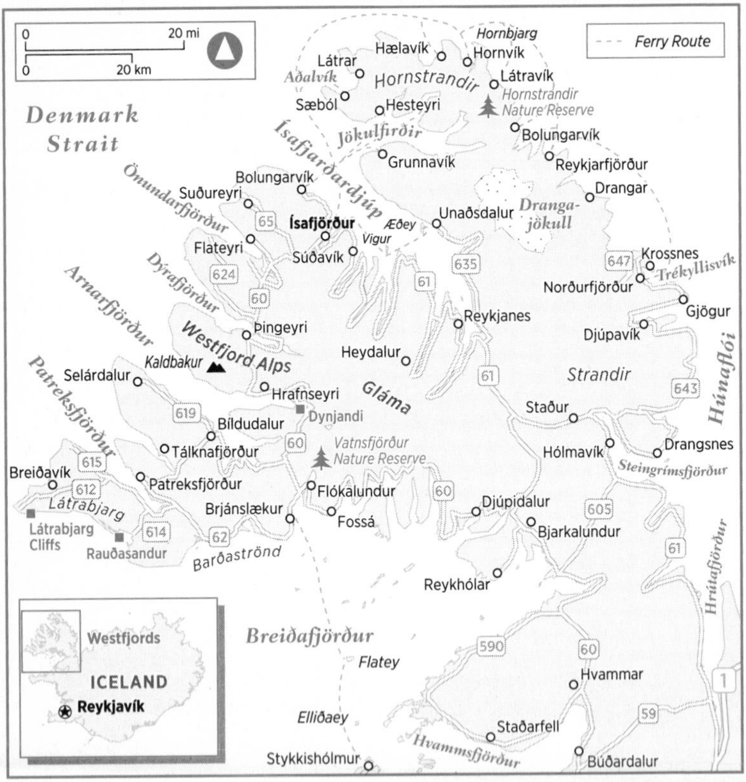

Essentials

GETTING THERE & AROUND

Many visitors tour the Westfjords by flying to Ísafjörður and renting a car from there.

BY CAR The condition of the main road to Ísafjörður has improved substantially in the past few years and is now paved all the way to the Ring Road, but the terrifyingly steep and unfenced drops remain and the secondary roads remain quite rough. With forbearance and caution, however, drivers in regular cars can get around as much as elsewhere. Drivers coming from north Iceland have a choice of shortcuts from the Ring Road over to Route 60, which follows the south coast of the Westfjords. Currently the best all-year link is Route 59, but the summer road Route 605 (via Route 61) is better when weather permits.

BY FERRY The car ferry ***Baldur*** (**© 433-2254;** www.seatours.is/ferrybaldur) links Stykkishólmur (on Snæfellsnes Peninsula) to Brjánslækur (on the south coast of the Westfjords) in a 2½-hour trip with a stop at Flatey island (p. 201); a restaurant is on board. Drivers headed from Reykjavík straight to the Westfjords do not save time by taking the ferry, but can enjoy the Breiðafjörður views and bypass some bumpy roads. Drivers coming from Snæfellsnes may save a short amount of time. From around June 10 to August 22, the ferry departs Stykkishólmur daily at 9am and 3:45pm, returning from Brjánslækur at 12:15pm and 7pm. For the rest of the year, the ferry departs Stykkishólmur at 3pm Sunday to Friday and 11am some Saturdays, returning from Brjánslækur 3 hours later. One-way tickets are 3,950kr adults, 3,160kr seniors, 1,975kr children aged 12 to 15, and free for children under 12, plus 3,950kr per car. Passengers with cars are advised to book in advance.

BY BUS **Sterna** (© **587-6000;** www.sterna.is) connects Reykjavík and Króksfjarðarnes (3½ hr; 5,600kr), at the eastern base of the Westfjords, 3 or 4 days per week, extending another 50 minutes to Reykhólar on Sundays. This route is a dead-end in terms of public transport, however.

From June through August, on Mondays, Wednesdays, and Saturdays, **Stjörnubílar** (© **456-5518;** www.stjornubilar.is) runs a bus from Ísafjörður to the **Látrabjarg cliffs** and back, with stops at Brjánslækur (ferry terminal), Patreksfjörður, and Örlygshöfn (Látrabjarg Peninsula). The bus continues to Látrabjarg only if passengers book in advance; otherwise, it turns back at Patreksfjörður. The full route, which is 4½ to 5 hours each way, can be taken as a round-trip day tour from Ísafjörður (8,500kr), with 90 minutes to walk along the clifftop. The bus stops at Brjánslækur at 12:15pm (on the way to Látrabjarg) and 6:45pm (on the way back) for ferry connections. Guesthouse Breiðavík (p. 209) can supply van transport all around Látrabjarg Peninsula for overnight guests.

Torfi Elís Andrésson (© **456-2636** or 893-2636) runs a short "flybus" route between Patreksfjörður and **Bíldudalur airport** to meet Eagle Air flights (below), with stops at Patreksfjörður, Tálknafjörður, and Bíldudalur in both directions.

Sterna's **Full Circle and Westfjords Bus Passport,** valid from June through August, costs 50,000kr and includes a complete circuit of Iceland, plus the ferry across Breiðafjörður and the Stjörnubílar bus to Látrabjarg Peninsula.

BY PLANE **Eagle Air** (© **562-2640;** www.eagleair.is) flies between Reykjavík and Bíldudalur, a village on the southwest coast of the Westfjords, every day but Saturday. Flights take 40 minutes and one-way fares start at 11,700kr. Although flights to Ísafjörður are generally cheaper, Bíldudalur is closer to Látrabjarg, so if planned carefully, flying to Bíldudalur in conjunction with the Torfi Elís Andrésson and Stjörnubílar buses (above) could allow for a visit to Látrabjarg en route to Ísafjörður without as much back-tracking.

Flower Gazing & Blueberry Picking

While out exploring in the Westfjords it's easy to be distracted by the magnificent views and large-scale landmarks, but don't forget to look down at the lovely mossy earth too. The ground is an oft overlooked trove of tiny wildflowers—ideal for those packing a macro lens—and carpeted with blueberries, best picked in late summer. Icelandic law stipulates that a person may pick enough blueberries on public land for private consumption, and blueberries seem to be particularly abundant in the Westfjords without even having to venture far from the road.

VISITOR INFORMATION

The tourist information office in **Ísafjörður** (p. 213) can provide help for any destination in the Westfjords. On **Látrabjarg Peninsula,** information is provided at the **Egill Ólafsson Folk Museum** (✆ **456-1511;** June–Sept 10 daily 10am–6pm). The **local pools** in **Patreksfjörður** (✆ **456-1301**) and **Tálknafjörður** (✆ **456-2639;** mid-June to Aug Mon–Fri 9am–9pm, Sat–Sun 10am–6pm; Sept to mid-June Mon–Fri 5–9pm, Sat–Sun noon–6pm) double as tourist information offices.

Exploring the Area

LÁTRABJARG PENINSULA

Entering the peninsula along Route 612, the landscape's allure is soon apparent. Three kilometers (2 miles) from the Route 62 junction is a picnic table, where the fjord view opens up, extending past a stranded ship, a lovely waterfall, and a mountain alley to the ocean.

From Route 612, Route 614 works its way south over the spine of the peninsula to **Rauðisandur ★**, a tiny and spellbindingly beautiful settlement, named for its broad, red-tinted sandbanks sheltering a large lagoon. Once Route 614 winds down from the mountains, an unnumbered road branches to the right and leads west along the coast for a few kilometers. At the end, past Saurbær church, is **Kaffihús Rauðasandi,** Iceland's most absurdly remote cafe, serving coffee, cake, and waffles (late June/early July–Aug 10 daily 1–6pm). The cafe has no telephone, so the only way to confirm it's open is to contact the folk museum, below. Rauðisandur is situated just beyond the eastern boundary of the Látrabjarg cliffs, and makes a great starting point for a coastal hike; see "Hiking Routes," below.

Local history is admirably and painstakingly preserved at **Egill Ólafsson Folk Museum,** Route 612, at Hnjótur Farm, by the waterfront at Örlygshöfn on the north coast (✆ **456-1511**; www.hnjotur.is). However, old saw blades, drill bits, and other trifles overwhelm the more deserving artifacts. The most unusual holding is a Russian plane that was stranded in Iceland in 1993 (admission 600kr adults; 400kr seniors; free for children under 16; June–Sept 10 daily 10am–6pm).

Each summer, **Látrabjarg ★★**, the largest if not the tallest sea cliff in Iceland, hosts about four nesting birds for every living Icelander. Every major Icelandic cliff-nesting species is found here. Puffins, sure to be the avian stars of your photos, start arriving at the end of April and disappear en masse in mid-August. Látrabjarg is the world's largest nesting area for razor-billed auks, identified by their black head and back, white breast, raven-like beak, and long tail. In May and June, locals rappel down the cliffsides to collect eggs, a skill that came in handy for the *Dhoon* rescue of 1947 (see the "Cliff-Scaling Icelanders to the Rescue" box, below).

The usual way to see Látrabjarg is to park at the end of Route 612, by the lighthouse, and walk east on the well-established trail along the clifftop. The highest point of the cliffs is reached in about an hour. Beware of overhanging grass tufts that may not support your weight. To hike the full length of Látrabjarg, see "Hiking Routes," below.

HIKING ROUTES The south coast of the peninsula from Látrabjarg cliffs to Rauðisandur makes for a memorable **one-way hike** over 1 or 2 days. The shorter route starts along the un-numbered road to Keflavík, a small bay at the eastern edge of the cliffs, and leads 10km (6 miles) west to the lighthouse at the end of Route 612. The road to Keflavík branches off from Route 612 a short way south of Breiðavík, and

CLIFF-SCALING ICELANDERS TO THE rescue

As you gaze over Látrabjarg, think of December 12, 1947, when the British fishing trawler *Dhoon* ran aground 500m (1,640 ft.) from the base of the cliff, prompting the most famous and dramatic rescue of shipwrecked sailors in Iceland's history. No roads reached Látrabjarg in 1947, and it took the first rescuers several hours to walk to the cliff's edge in the dark with one pack horse. (In December the Westfjords region has only 4 hours of daylight.) When the sky lightened on the following day, 12 men descended the 120m (394 ft.) cliff by rope, while three remained on top to hold the rope fast. A rescue line was fired over to the boat, and all 12 British sailors were brought to land suspended on a flotation buoy. When darkness and the tide set in, only seven sailors and one rescuer had been hoisted up the cliff. The rest spent the night huddled together on a small outcrop. It took all the next day, in heavy winds and rain, to hoist up the remaining men, who then had to spend the night in tents near the clifftop. The next morning, they turned down the horses that were brought over to transport them—after the 75-hour ordeal, they were too cold not to walk.

should be negotiable in a regular car up to the trailhead. The equally enticing **2-day route** begins in Rauðisandur, with an overnight in the Keflavík mountain hut, which sleeps nine on a first-come, first-served basis; there is no way to reserve.

Guesthouse Breiðavík (p. 209), with advance notice, can arrange transportation at one or both ends of the journey, and can also drop off or pick up supplies at Keflavík. The cost is usually around 8,000kr per trip, regardless of the number of passengers. The hut almost never fills up, but having Guesthouse Breiðavík deliver supplies could be a good insurance measure. The hut has no formal price, only instructions on how to make a voluntary contribution later. For other worthwhile hiking routes on the peninsula, consult Guesthouse Breiðavík and the *Vestfirðir & Dalir* hiking map of Látrabjarg. The map is widely available on the peninsula, and can be ordered in advance from www.galdrasyning.is (click "Magi-craft online store").

PATREKSFJÖRÐUR TO BÍLDUDALUR

The coastal route north from Látrabjarg Peninsula soon passes through or near the villages of Patreksfjörður, Tálknafjörður, and Bíldudalur. All three are stunningly situated and have restaurants, places to stay, and other basic services (including free Wi-Fi within village limits). Patreksfjörður is the third-largest village in the Westfjords, with about 700 residents.

Tálknafjörður has a standard geothermal village pool, 25m (82 ft.) long, with hot tubs, but **Pollurinn**—a little spring-fed beauty overlooking the fjord—is outside of town, completely unmarked, unadvertised, and disguised from the road. To get there, take Route 617 northwest from the village for 2 or 3km (1–2 miles); a driveway on the right leads to the pool, just uphill round the bend. The tiny facilities include showers, changing rooms, a shallow tub shaped like a recliner, and a deeper tub, often too hot for all but the most intrepid soakers. Admission is free all year round.

The Sea Monster Museum, Strangata 7, Bíldudalur (✆ **456-6666;** www.skrimsli.is; admission 500kr; June–early Sept daily 11am–6pm) is the latest reason to visit this cute village on the shores of Arnarfjörður. The museum entertains visitors with the history of sea monster sightings in Icelandic history, folk culture, and literature. A disproportionate number of such sightings have occurred in and around Arnarfjörður, which makes it very difficult to keep your eyes off the surface of the fjord as you leave town—was that definitely a seal you just saw?

Jón Kr. Ólafsson, a middle-aged Icelandic pop singer with a long performing career, runs **Tónlistarsafn,** Tjarnarbraut 5, Bíldudalur (© **456-2186;** admission 700kr; mid-June to Sept Mon–Fri 2–6pm), an informal museum of music memorabilia out of his Bíldudalur home. Jón's tastes are proudly stuck in the 1950s and 1960s, and his own singing is reminiscent of Engelbert Humperdinck. The mounted LP covers and stage outfits vividly evoke the Icelandic tangent of pop music history, but the collection is poorly arranged, with no English guidance and nowhere to sample recordings. You can ask Jón to put on some records—just don't request anything by Björk.

From Bíldudalur, Route 619 extends 25km (16 miles) northwest along a wondrous stretch of coast to Selárdalur, a remote settlement with one remaining farm, a church, and **Listasafn Samúels,** a museum devoted to the painter, sculptor, and former resident Samúel Jónsson (1884–1969). Since the church didn't need a new altarpiece, Samúel built his own makeshift church to display his work. Outside are several crude concrete sculptures, including a statue of Leifur Eiríksson and a replica of the Alhambra Palace in Granada, Spain. While his works could be dismissed as amateurish, his life sets a compelling example of how to reconcile artistic pursuits with poverty and seclusion. Samúel's church is left open from mid-June to August, with a sign requesting a small donation in a sealed box.

Where to Stay

The tourist office in Ísafjörður (p. 213) can help locate hotels and provides comprehensive listings on its website.

THE SOUTH COAST OF THE WESTFJORDS

The few hotels scattered along this barely populated stretch of coast sometimes come in handy for those en route to Látrabjarg.

Hótel Bjarkalundur, Route 60, about 100km/62 miles from Route 1 (© **434-7762;** www.bjarkalundur.is; 11,500kr double without bathroom, including breakfast; MC, V; closed Oct–Apr), has 11 presentable, well-priced rooms with sinks, and is part of an all-around pit-stop with a restaurant, bar, fuel, and small store.

Proceeding west, the next option is **Djúpidalur,** Route 60, about 122km (76 miles) from Route 1 (© **434-7853;** 8,000kr double without bathroom; no credit cards), in a geothermal valley popular among trout and salmon fishermen. Lodgings are straightforward, with a guest kitchen and indoor geothermal swimming pool.

The next place on Route 60—located 100km (62 miles) west of Djúpidalur, near the Route 62 junction, and 6km (4 miles) from the Brjánslækur ferry terminal—is **Hótel Flókalundur** (© **456-2011;** www.flokalundur.is; 12,500kr double, including breakfast; AE, DC, MC, V; closed mid-Sept to mid-May), with 15 small en suite rooms and a serviceable restaurant. A 5-minute walk from the hotel is a fabulous outdoor geothermal pool, lined with natural stones and overlooking the fjord. **Rauðsdalur** (© **456-2041;** raudsdal@vortex.is; 6,600kr double without bathroom; 5,600kr double with sleeping bag; MC, V), 8km (5 miles) southwest of the Brjánslækur ferry terminal on Route 62, has acceptable rooms, a guest kitchen, and a beautiful beach across the road.

LÁTRABJARG PENINSULA

Hotel Breiðavík ★★ Location is paramount here. Breiðavík, near the westernmost tip of Iceland, is a wonderfully serene and lovely bay, with a vast golden beach and a broad, sheltering arc of mountains—with the Látrabjarg cliffs just a short drive away. Guesthouse rooms are rustic, while en suite rooms are in a prefab row of identical units, nicer from the inside. The owners know the territory inside and out, and run a transportation service.

Rte. 612. ✆ **456-1575.** www.breidavik.is. 30 units, 14 w/bathroom. May 15–Sept 15 18,000kr double; 12,000kr double without bathroom; 6,000kr sleeping-bag accommodation. Rates include breakfast (except for sleeping-bag accommodation). MC, V. Closed Sept 16–May 14. **Amenities:** Restaurant; bar. *In room:* No phone, Wi-Fi.

Hótel Látrabjarg ★ An idyllic setting on the peninsula's north coast makes up for this former school's drab exterior. Fishing trips can be arranged, and horses are on call for rides along the picturesque beach. **Dinner** is served on advance request.

Rte. 615, 3km (2 miles) from the Rte. 612 intersection. ✆ **825-0025.** www.latrabjarg.com. 10 units, 4 w/bathroom. May–Aug 170,000kr double; 145,000kr double without bathroom; 200,000kr triple; 180,000kr triple without bathroom; 200,000kr family room. Rates include breakfast. AE, DC, MC, V. Closed Sept–Apr. *In room:* No phone.

PATREKSFJÖRÐUR & TÁLKNAFJÖRÐUR

Patreksfjörður boasts the new boutique hotel **Ráðagerði**, Aðalstræti 31 (✆ **456-0181**; radagerdi.com; 16,900kr double; AE, DC, MC, V) which opened during summer 2010. The hotel, renovated over three years by a designer-architect duo, boasts a beautiful interior and equally stunning views across the fjord. **Patreksfjörður** also has three inexpensive choices, all equipped with guest kitchens. **Guesthouse Erla,** Urðargata 2 (✆ **456-1227;** 8,000kr double without bathroom including breakfast; no credit cards), has clean, agreeable rooms. **Guesthouse Eyrar,** Aðalstræti 8 (✆ **456-4565;** handradinn@simnet.is; 11,000kr double with bathroom; MC, V), which shares a building with the local cafe and bakery, is great value for private facilities. **Stekkaból,** Stekkur 19 (✆ **456-1675;** stekkabol@snerpa.is; 8,000kr double without bathroom; 5,400kr per person sleeping-bag accommodation; MC, V), is a standard guesthouse spread over three buildings.

In **Tálknafjörður,** the cheery, welcoming **Skrúðhamrar Guesthouse,** Strandgata 20 (✆ **456-0200;** skrudhamar@visir.is; 8,000kr double without bathroom; MC, V), has TVs and Wi-Fi in each room. The backup is **Guesthouse Bjarmaland,** Túngata 42 (✆ **891-8038;** bjarmaland06@simnet.is; 8,800kr double without bathroom; MC, V), with a guest kitchen and one en suite room out of 11.

Where to Dine

LÁTRABJARG PENINSULA

The restaurant at **Guesthouse Breiðavík** is open daily in summer, with soup and bread starting at noon, cakes and waffles at tea time, and, from 7 to 9pm, a tasty, wholesome set dinner menu for around 4,000kr; reservations are advised. **Hótel Látrabjarg** also serves dinner by advance request. **Egils Ólafsson Folk Museum** (p. 206) has a cafe, and there's also the cafe **Völlurinn** (no telephone; hours vary) at the airfield along Route 612, about 10km (6 miles) from Route 62. See also **Kaffihús Rauðasandi** in Rauðisandur (p. 206).

PATREKSFJÖRÐUR TO BÍLDUDALUR

In Patreksfjörður, **Söluturninn Albína,** Aðalstræti 89 (✆ **456-1667**), has snacks and fast food, while **Eyrar,** Aðalstræti 8 (✆ **456-4565;** Mon–Fri 9am–6pm), is the resident cafe and bakery. Patreksfjörður and Tálknafjörður each have a restaurant on the standard small-town Icelandic model: local fresh fish, plenty of lamb, plus pasta burgers, pizzas, and sandwiches. The nod goes to the well-priced **Þorpið,** Aðalstræti 73, Patreksfjörður (✆ **456-1295;** main courses 990kr–2,290kr; MC, V; June–Sept 15 Mon–Fri 11am–9pm, Sat–Sun 12:30–9pm; Sept 16–May 31 daily 11am–2pm and 6–9pm), followed by **Hópið,** Hrafnadalsvegur in Tálknafjörður (✆ **456-2777;** main courses 1,500kr–3,900kr; MC, V; Mon–Wed noon–10pm, Thurs–Sun noon–11pm). **Vegamót/Siggi Ben,** Route 619 in Bíldudalur (✆ **456-2232;** MC, V; mid-June to Aug Mon–Fri 9am–10pm, Sat–Sun 10am–10pm; Sept to mid-June daily 11am–8pm), varies its menu by the season, but the most expensive item, for around 2,800kr, could be an overloaded pizza or chicken korma.

CENTRAL WESTFJORDS

The Westfjords are Iceland's oldest landmass, with no active volcanoes for the last 10 million years. Glaciation created more than half of Iceland's fjords but little lowland suitable for agriculture. The central coastal region of the Westfjords—with Arnarfjörður to the south and Ísafjarðardjúp to the north—is particularly mountainous and, in winter, roads to nearby towns can be cut off for days at a time. Highlights of this area include Dynjandi, the largest and most resplendent waterfall in the Westfjords; the "Westfjords Alps," a prime hiking area; and the village of Suðureyri, where locals invite visitors to experience the fishing life.

Essentials

GETTING THERE & AROUND Route 60 is the main artery of the central Westfjords. The distance from Bíldudalur to Ísafjörður, the Westfjords capital, is 145km (90 miles), and the road is now paved all the way. Thanks to a long, three-pronged tunnel built in 1996, Ísafjörður is only 25 minutes from Suðureyri, 20 minutes from Flateyri, and 45 minutes from Þingeyri.

Two **airports** with scheduled flights from Reykjavík are just outside the central Westfjords; to the south is Bíldudalur (p. 207), and to the north is Ísafjörður (p. 213).

From June until August, **Stjörnubílar** (✆ **456-5518;** www.stjornubilar.is) runs a **bus** from Ísafjörður to Látrabjarg peninsula and back (4,000kr one way), with **ferry connections** to Snæfellsnes Peninsula at Brjánslækur; in addition to scheduled stops along the way, a pickup or dropoff along Route 60 can usually be arranged informally.

F&S Hópferðabílar (✆ **893-1058** or 847-0285) operates the municipal buses that connect Ísafjörður to **Suðureyri, Flateyri,** and **Þingeyri** on weekdays year-round. The schedule is posted at www.isafjordur.is/ferdamadurinn/samgongur in Icelandic only, but you shouldn't have trouble figuring it out. One-way fares are only 280kr, and buses leave Ísafjörður from the N1 gas station on Pollgata, behind Hótel Ísafjörður.

VISITOR INFORMATION The tourist information office in **Ísafjörður** (p. 213) covers the entire Westfjords, though most towns have an ad hoc information kiosk, such as at service stations, museums, or guesthouses.

Exploring the Central Westfjords

Dynjandi ★, meaning "booming" or "resounding," comprises six waterfalls. The tallest is Fjallfoss, an astonishing 100m (328-ft.) waterfall that drapes its way down ever-broadening cascades in the shape of a tiered wedding cake. The five smaller falls beneath—Hundafoss, Strokkur, Göngumannafoss, Hrísvaðsfoss, and Sjóarfoss—add to the charm of the area, an ideal picnic stop. Dynjandi is clearly marked from Route 60, near the head of Dynjandisvogur, an inlet of Arnarfjörður. Heading south on a clear day you will see it from the road before the turnoff. A short scenic trail leads from the parking area to the base of the waterfall.

A settlement on the north shore of Arnarfjörður, **Hrafnseyri** was the childhood home of nationalist hero Jón Sigurðsson (1811–1879). **Byggðasafnið Hrafnseyri** (**✆ 456-8260** or 845-5518; www.hrafnseyri.is; admission 600kr; Jun–Aug daily 10am–8pm) focuses on Jón, but is also an excellent museum to give visitors a sense of 19th-century Icelandic life. There's also a pleasant cafe if you need a rest stop. Exact opening dates vary from year to year, and in 2011 the museum will open with a new exhibition on June 17, Iceland's National Day, the 200th anniversary of Jón's birth. Phone to arrange visits outside opening hours/dates.

In aerial photos, the Westfjords region is often identified by successions of table-topped mountains, formed by eruptions beneath the crushing weight of thick icecaps. The **Westfjords Alps ★★**, on the peninsula between Arnarfjörður and Dýrafjörður, were so named by breaking this pattern: not only are these "Alps" particularly tall—Kaldbakur, at 998m (3,274 ft.), is the highest peak in the Westfjords—but they're topped with razorback ridges that delight photographers and entice every hiker's inner tightrope walker.

The *Vestfirðir & Dalir* series provides the best map of **hiking routes** in the Alps. Given the vertiginous ridges, loose scree, and exposure to the weather, it's a good idea to review and register your route with the tourist information office in Ísafjörður. **Kaldbakur** is the most challenging and rewarding climb, with stunning panoramic views extending to Snæfellsnes Peninsula. Trails approach the peak from both the north and south. At the summit is a 2m (6½ ft.) cairn—with a guestbook inside—artificially raising Kaldbakur's height to four digits.

Iceland's Only Castles

All are welcome to participate in an annual sandcastle competition held the first Saturday of August at a beach on Önundarfjörður (from Route 60, head just over a kilometer northwest on Route 625). A pair of Brits won in 2006, proving that the hometown judges aren't biased.

In 1995 an avalanche crashed into the small fishing village of **Flateyri** on Önundarfjörður, killing 20 people and damaging or destroying 30 homes. As a result, the slope behind Flateyri now has a colossal, A-shaped barricade—1.5km long, 15 to 20m high, and 45 to 60m thick (1 mile x 49–66 ft. x 148–197 ft.)—designed to deflect tumbling boulders and snow into the fjord. The barricade is now being cultivated with vegetation.

From 1889 to 1901, Flateyri was the largest whaling station in the North Atlantic, with most trade controlled by Norwegians. The old Flateyri bookstore, **Gamla Bókabúðin,** Hafnarstræti 3–5 (daily 1–6pm) has a small exhibit on village history, and the local handicraft workshop **Handverkshúsið Purka,** Hafnarstræti 11 (✆ **456-7710;** daily 1–6pm), contains a curious collection of dolls from around the world.

When the fishermen of **Suðureyri ★** began taking steps to ensure an environmentally sustainable future, they were hardly scheming to lure tourists. Later came the knowledge that tourism revenue, together with carrying the banner of environmental responsibility, could form a virtuous circle. The aptly named **Fisherman company** (Skipagata 3, Suðureyri; ✆ **450-9000** or 862-6200) sets up fishing trips for visitors, including the opportunity to accompany and assist professional fisherman out at sea. If you catch something, you can choose to have it cooked at Talisman restaurant (see "Where to Dine," below). Prices from 5,000kr an hour.

The fishermen make short, fuel-efficient trips in fiberglass boats. All fish are caught by hook and bait, a method far less harmful to marine ecosystems than the practice of dragging weighted nets across the ocean floor. No fish parts are wasted; bones are powdered for animal food, and heads are dried and shipped to Nigeria to be ground into meal. All Suðureyri homes are heated by underground hot springs piped through radiators, and all power comes from a hydroelectric facility.

The Route 65 causeway entering the village created a lagoon, now full of cod accustomed to being fed by humans. Fish food is sold at the N1 service station. You can even pet the cod if you like—just don't let them bite you.

Where to Stay

The welcoming and idyllic **Korpudalur Kirkjuból Hostel** (✆ **456-7808** or 893-2030**;** www.korpudalur.is; 6 units, none w/bathroom; June–Aug 10,000kr double; 3,700kr per person w/sleeping-bag; breakfast available for 1,450kr; MC, V; closed Sept–May) is a 1912 farmhouse at the head of Önundarfjörður (on Route 627, 5km/3 miles southeast of Route 60). Ísafjörður is only 17km (11 miles) away, and airport or bus pickup can be arranged. The hostel is also an excellent resource for arranging kayaking, sailing, and sea-angling trips.

Kirkjuból With a fabulous mountain backdrop, this hospitable farmstay offers well-maintained, mid-sized rooms with a warm yet modern look. **Dinner** is served on request. Kirkjuból is right on Route 60, in Bjarnadalur Valley just south of Önundarfjörður.

Rte. 60. ✆ **456-7679.** www.kirkjubol.is. 5 units, 1 w/bathroom. Early June–late Aug; 13,000kr double; 8,500kr double without bathroom. Breakfast available (1,200kr). MC, V. Closed late Aug–early June. **Amenities:** Guest kitchen; Internet terminal. *In room:* No phone.

VEG-Gisting The owners of this sparkling-clean and comfortable modern hotel are also behind Talisman (see "Where to Dine," below) and Suðureyri's scheme to give visitors a window on the fishing life (above). The staff is extremely welcoming, and rooms have a spare yet cheerful Scandinavian look with simple furnishings.

Aðalgata 14, Suðureyri. ✆ **450-9000.** www.sudureyri.is/gistiheimili. 15 units, 13 w/bathroom. 14,900kr double; 10,900kr double without bathroom. Rates include breakfast. MC, V. **Amenities:** Restaurant; guest kitchen. *In room:* TV, hair dryer, Wi-Fi.

Við Fjörðinn Like most Icelandic guesthouses, Við Fjörðinn assumes you came for the outdoor scenery and just attends to basic comforts, but it does the latter very well. The two apartments, with bathrooms, kitchens, TVs, and private entrances, plus one new studio apartment, are nicer than the guesthouse rooms. **Dinner** and **packed lunches** are available on request. Breakfasts including homemade jams and breads are enjoyed in a bright, glass room next to the owner's house.

Aðalstræti 26, Þingeyri. ✆ **456-8172** or 847-0285. www.vidfjordinn.is. 10 units, none w/bathroom; 3 apts. from 9,000kr double; 3,000kr sleeping-bag accommodation; 13,000kr apts for 3–4 persons. Breakfast available (1,200kr). MC, V. **Amenities:** Guest kitchen. *In room:* No phone.

Where to Dine

The only food between Þingeyri and Bíldudalur (in the southwest Westfjords) or Flókalundur (on the south coast) is at the **Byggðasafnið Hrafnseyri cafe** (p. 211). Þingeyri is just 45 minutes from Ísafjörður, so many drivers headed north aim to reach the Westfjords capital by dinnertime. The N1 service stations in **Þingeyri** and **Flateyri** have fast food grills to tide you over. **Sandafell** is a low-key eatery at Þingeyri, Hafnarstræti 7 (✆ **456-1600;** June–Aug daily 10am–10pm; closed Sept–May) with soups, sandwiches, cakes, and a dish of the day.

Talisman ★ ICELANDIC In Suðureyri, just 25 minutes from Ísafjörður, Talisman is perhaps the only restaurant worth actively seeking out in the central Westfjords. The ambience is classy, with fishskin mats on tables. Starters include *bacalao* carpaccio with roasted pine nuts and cucumber, while main courses depend on the fishermen's daily haul. Plenty of non-fish choices are available, and portions are generous.

Aðalgata 14, Suðureyri. ✆ **450-9000.** Main courses 2,200kr–3,000kr. MC, V. Daily 6–10pm.

ÍSAFJÖRÐUR & ÍSAFJARÐARDJÚP

Icelandic towns present a compelling contrast of isolation and worldliness, with no better example than **Ísafjörður** ★, the likeable and sophisticated hub of the Westfjords. Even in such a remote and unlikely setting, you'll find nice restaurants, trendy shops, and cafes full of laptop users. Built on a gravel spit in a fjord within a fjord, Ísafjörður possesses an ideal natural port and has been one of Iceland's busiest trading hubs since the late-18th century. In the late-19th century, it was the same oasis it is today, with two hotels, several gaming clubs, and a drama club. The current population is around 4,100, more than half the Westfjords total. Its steep, mountainous backdrop and conscientiously preserved architecture encourage relaxing strolls around town.

Boats leaving Ísafjörður soon enter **Ísafjarðardjúp,** the enormous fjord that nearly cleaves the Westfjords in half; the lovely, winding drive east along its southern shore is also the fastest route to Reykjavík.

Essentials

GETTING THERE & AROUND

BY PLANE **Air Iceland** (✆ **570-3030;** www.airiceland.is) connects Reykjavík and Ísafjörður two or three times daily year-round. The flight is 40 minutes, and ticket prices are from around 9,000kr (check website for specials—sometimes almost 50% less). Sitting on the left side of the plane grants views of Snæfellsjökull and the most picturesque Westfjords coastline. All flights from Akureyri to Ísafjörður connect through Reykjavík.

An **airport shuttle** operated by **Valdimar Lúðvík Gíslason** (✆ **456-7195** or 892-1417; 500kr starts from Bolungarvík and stops at Hótel Ísafjörður approximately 45 minutes before flight departure times. The shuttle also picks up arriving passengers and stops at the hotel on the way back to Bolungarvík. The driver will stop at other hotels in Ísafjörður on request.

Ísafjörður

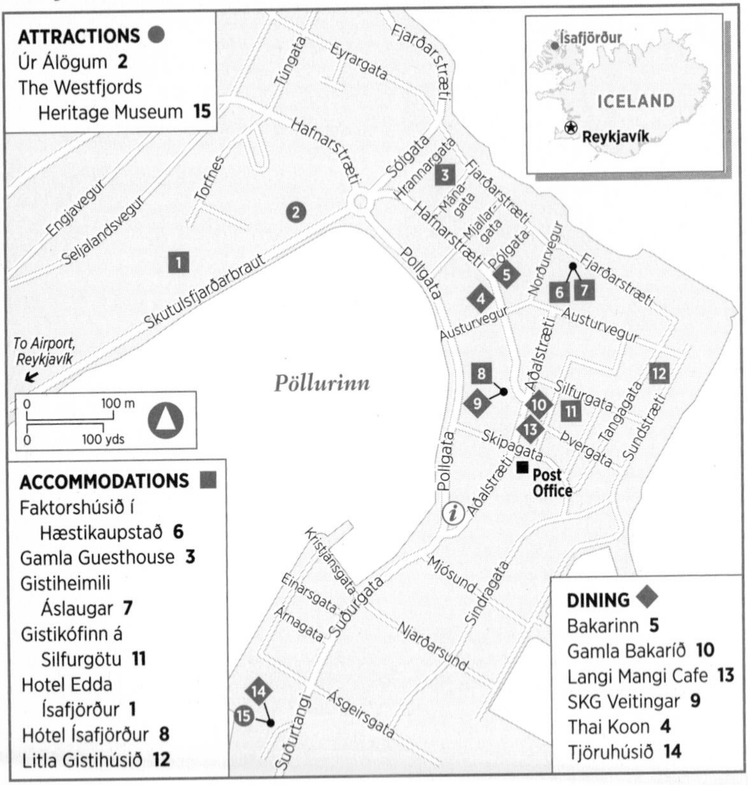

BY CAR Drivers heading from Reykjavík to Ísafjörður have three main options. The fastest route (441km/273 miles; 6½ hr.) follows this road sequence: Ring Road (Route 1)—Route 60—Route 608—Route 61. The entire route is paved, and has been further streamlined by a new bridge over Mjóifjörður. Another route (455km/283 miles; 7½ hr.) follows Route 60 from the Ring Road all the way to Ísafjörður. This route is more scenic and provides access to the southwest and central Westfjords. About a third of the route is unpaved, however, and the rutted sections can be nerve-wracking. The third option is to take the ***Baldur* car ferry** (p. 201) from Stykkishólmur (on Snæfellsnes Peninsula) to Brjánslaekur (in the Westfjords), and then continue to Ísafjörður on Route 62 and Route 60. The total travel time is around 8 hours, but the driving distance is cut to 294km (183 miles). Drivers headed to Ísafjörður from north Iceland should simply take Route 61 from the Ring Road.

Ísafjörður has two **rental** agencies, **National/Bílaleiga Akureyrar** (✆ **461-6000;** www.holdur.is) and **Hertz** (✆ **522-4400;** www.hertz.is). Both are airport-based, but deliver cars anywhere in town for no charge.

BY BUS Bus travel is usually not a convenient or cost-efficient means of getting to Ísafjörður from outside the Westfjords, though if you're coming from Reykjavík or Snæfellsnes, combining the bus with the car ferry has some sightseeing advantages.

Three connecting buses lead from Reykjavík or Akureyri to Ísafjörður. The first leg, with **Sterna** (✆ **553-3737;** www.sterna.is) leads to Brú, on the Ring Road. Morning buses approach Brú both from the south, starting in Reykjavík, and from the north, starting in Akureyri. The next leg, also with Sterna, goes from Brú to Hólmavík. The final leg from Hólmavík to Ísafjörður—which runs only from June to August on Tuesdays, Fridays, and Sundays—is serviced by **Stjörnubílar** (✆ **456-5518;** www.stjornubilar.is).

For the bus–ferry route from Reykjavík, the first leg is the morning **Sterna** bus from Reykjavík to Stykkishólmur, arriving at 11:10am from June 1 to 15, or 10:35am from mid-June through August. The ferry then goes from Stykkishólmur to Brjánslækur in the Westfjords. The ferry does not leave Stykkishólmur until 3:45pm, so you'll have some time to kill there; from mid-June until August you might throw in the 11am "Unique Adventure Tour" (p. 201). The connecting bus from Brjánslækur to Ísafjörður—with service only from June to August on Mondays, Wednesdays, and Saturdays—is handled by Stjörnubílar (4,000kr; see p. 205 for other connections to the southwest Westfjords). The total travel time is 12 hours from Reykjavík to Ísafjörður, or 7¾ hours on the way back (except the first half of June, when visitors need to overnight in Stykkishólmur).

Sterna's **Full Circle and Westfjords Bus Passport** (p. 205), valid from June through August, includes a complete circuit of Iceland, including the ferry *Baldur.*

For buses connecting Ísafjörður to the southwest Westfjords, see p. 205. For municipal buses connecting Ísafjörður to Suðureyri, Flateyri, and Þingeyri, see p. 210.

The main bus stop in Ísafjörður is the N1 service station on Pollgata.

BY TAXI **Leigubílar Ísafirði** (✆ **456-3518**) is on call 24/7.

BY BIKE **West Tours,** Aðalstræti 7 (✆ **456-5111;** www.westtours.is) rents good mountain bikes for 3,500kr per day.

VISITOR INFORMATION

Ísafjörður's **tourist office,** Aðalstræti 9 (✆ **450-8060;** www.westfjords.is and www.isafjordur.is; Jun–Aug Mon–Fri 8.15am–6pm, Sat–Sun 11am–2pm; Sept–June Mon–Fri 11am–4pm) is very efficient and provides information and hotel assistance for the Westfjords.

Exploring Ísafjörður

Ísafjörður is laid out on a coastal spit shaped like the number "7" in a small fjord called Skutulsfjörður. The northernmost part of town—from the mainland to the elbow of the "7"—is known as ***Hæstikaupstaður,*** which loosely translates to "Uptown." Hæstikaupstaður has most of Ísafjörður's historic homes, built by fish merchants in the 19th and early-20th centuries. Before walking around town, pick up the ***Ísafjörður History* map** at the tourist office, or visit the Heritage Museum (below), which has an accessible exhibit on town history. **West Tours** (below) offers a 2- to 3-hour town walking tour on request (around 4,000kr, including admission to Heritage Museum; minimum two people), which smartly combines historical sites with introductions to local characters—including Ísafjörður's accordion-playing barber.

Miðkaupstaður (Midtown), boundaried by Silfurgata to the north and Mjósund to the south, is Ísafjörður's commercial hub. The main drags are Hafnarstræti and Aðalstræti, which converge at Silfurtorg, the town square. The information office is on Aðalstræti, at Miðkaupstaður's south end. The Heritage Museum, the waterfront, and most of the warehouses and industrial buildings are in ***Neðstikaupstaður*** (Downtown), the southernmost section of Ísafjörður.

Set back from the roundabout where Ísafjörður meets the mainland, **Úr Álögum (Breaking the Spell II)** is a provocative and intricate rendering of St. George and the dragon, by Iceland's foremost sculptor Einar Jónsson (p. 128). The naked woman curled on George's arm is the Libyan princess he spared from being sacrificed to the dragon. A shriveled female figure, a symbol of the dragon's curse, is morphed into a cloak that the princess casts off as the dragon's head is pierced by George's sword.

What to See & Do

While Iceland Airwaves (p. 35) in Reykjavík each October is the country's reigning alternative/indie music festival, Ísafjörður's **Aldrei fór ég suður** ★(www.aldrei.is), on the Friday and Saturday before Easter, is a more intimate though very well-attended festival held since 2004. Its name means "I never went south," an expression used by locals who have resisted the waves of migration to the city. Like Airwaves, international acts are included; but, unlike Airwaves, every performance is free. Flight and accommodation packages are sold by **West Tours** (below).

Other events during Easter Week include art exhibitions and **Ski Week (Skíðavikan),** featuring trail competitions, snowboard jumps, and a family day. Check with the Ísafjörður tourist office for details.

Ísafjörður's annual **Act Alone Theater Festival** (www.actalone.net), held over 3 days in mid-August, is devoted to solo performances by Icelandic and international "monodramatists." Admission is free.

Swamp soccer, a sport recently invented in Finland, is basically what it sounds like: soccer on a muddy field, with some rule modifications. Ísafjörður is a swamp soccer hotbed, with a tournament held the first weekend of August, Iceland's Labor Day Weekend (see p. 34); for more information, visit www.myrarbolti.com.

The Westfjords Heritage Museum (Byggðasafn Vestfjarða) Housed in a 1784 warehouse near Ísafjörður's southern tip, this engaging if esoteric folk museum features an intelligently laid out maritime exhibit of fishing and nautical paraphernalia, plus an informative primer on Westfjords regional history. An engaging documentary on open rowboat fishing is screened continuously, with English subtitles. Film screenings and other events are held from mid-June to mid-August on Monday and Thursday evenings; call or check with tourist information for schedules.

Suðurgata, near southern tip of Ísafjörður (look for flagpoles). ✆ **456-3291.** Admission 550kr adults; 450kr seniors; free for children aged 15 and under. June Mon–Fri 10am–5pm, Sat–Sun 1–5pm; July Mon–Fri 10am–6pm, Sat–Sun 10am–5pm; Aug daily 10am–5pm.

Tours & Activities

West Tours, Aðalstræti 7 (✆ **456-5111;** www.westtours.is), the dominant tour operator in the Westfjords, is highly recommended and has an imaginative range of offerings, from birdwatching and sea kayaking to fox-spotting and berry picking. A particularly exciting **day tour** is the 12-hour boat and hiking excursion to Hornvík in

Hornstrandir Nature Reserve. (For tours to Hornstrandir, see p. 225.) West Tours rents **mountain bikes** and can suggest fantastic routes, such as the coastal road around the peninsula between Arnarfjörður and Dýrafjörður. Some tours are for groups only, but it's worth asking about any scheduled group tours you could sign on with.

In winter, options are abundant, particularly for cross-country or backcountry skiers.

HIKING The *Ísafjörður-Dýrafjörður* trail map (part of the *Vestfirðir & Dalir* map series), on sale for 1,100kr at bookstores and the tourist office, thoroughly outlines local trails. A pleasant short hike (about an hour round-trip) starts from Route 61, directly across the fjord from the southern tip of Ísafjörður and ascends 220m (722 ft.) along a creek to **Naustahvilft,** a bowl-like indentation in the mountainside (Icelanders call such formations "troll seats"). A recommended **all-day hike** (20km/12 miles; 8 hr.) starts from Ísafjörður's northern suburb Hnífsdalur, ascending Hnífsdalur Valley before descending through Seljalandsdalur valley and back into town. A municipal bus goes to Hnífsdalur roughly once an hour on weekdays (7:15am–6:45pm; schedule at www.isafjordur.is/ferdamadurinn/samgongur). An equally recommended and somewhat less exhausting hike (16km/10 miles; 6½ hr.) starts by a bridge at the base of Skutulsfjörður and ascends through **Engidalur valley** along the Langá river past a hydroelectric power station, with a detour to Fossavatn lake.

Where to Stay in Ísafjörður

For places to stay in Suðureyri and Önundarfjörður (within a 25-minute drive of Ísafjörður), see p. 212.

EXPENSIVE

Faktorshúsið í Hæstikaupstað ★★ This 1788 house, among the oldest in Iceland, has been lovingly restored. Book early, as there's only one guest apartment, with two double beds and a child's bed in a single bedroom, plus a small kitchen and bathroom with tub. But if you miss out, you can still take the chance to admire the building's beautifully restored interior since it also hosts a small, inexpensive restaurant/cafe serving everything from waffles to whale.

Aðalstræti 7. ✆ **456-3868** or 899-0742. Fax 456-4075. gistias@snerpa.is. 1 unit. 16,900kr double. Breakfast available (1,100kr). MC, V. *In room:* Kitchen, no phone, Wi-Fi.

Hótel Ísafjörður ★ Visitors looking for a spacious, comfortable, modern, en-suite hotel room in the heart of town need look no further. Most rooms have nice views over the water. The only deluxe double has a CD player, bathtub, minibar, and a bigger TV. Sleeping-bag accommodation is available October through April (6,500kr double).

Silfurtorg 2. ✆ **456-4111.** Fax 456-4767. www.hotelisafjordur.is. 36 units. June–Aug 24,000kr–36,000kr double. Rates 30%–40% lower Sept–May. Rates include breakfast. Internet specials available. AE, DC, MC, V. **Amenities:** Restaurant; bar. *In room:* TV, fridge, hair dryer, Wi-Fi.

MODERATE/INEXPENSIVE

Gamla Guesthouse This 1896 ex-nursing-home on a historic residential block has nine decent-size, simple, and serene rooms. Corridors are lined with old photos, and the breakfast room is bright and inviting. Sleeping-bag accommodation (the other five rooms) is in a separate house, 100m (328 ft.) down the street, with a TV lounge and large guest kitchen.

Mánagata 5. ✆ **456-4146** or 897-4146. Fax 456-4446. www.gistihus.is. 14 rooms, none w/bathroom. May-Sept 13,100kr double; 9,400kr; double w/sleeping bag; 16,600kr triple; 3,300kr sleeping-bag accommodation in room for 4-6 people. Rates around 20% lower Oct-Apr. Rates include breakfast, except sleeping-bag accommodation (1,200kr). MC, V. **Amenities:** Guest kitchen; Internet terminal. *In room:* TV, Wi-Fi.

Gistiheimili Áslaugar This is the oldest guesthouse in Ísafjörður, having been open since 1989. Manager Áslaug Jensdóttir's ship-builder grandfather built the house in 1942.

Austurvegur 7. ✆ **899-0742**. Fax 456-4075. Double from 21,000kr; single from 7,500kr. Family rooms and sleeping-bag places also available. Common bathroom. AE, MC, V. **Amenities:** Guest kitchen, TV, phone. *In room:* Wash basin, no phone.

Gistikófinn á Silfurgötu This studio apartment is a basic but very cheap option especially suited to couples or families of three or four wanting to stay a few nights.

Silfurgata 12. ✆ **862-5669** or 863-5669. massi@massi.is. Studio apartment, double plus loft. 1-2 people 14,000kr; 3 people 16,000kr; 4 people 18,000kr; 2-5 extra nights 11,000kr per night. Rates around 20% lower Oct-mid-May. MC, V. **Amenities:** TV, Internet. *In room:* No phone.

Hotel Edda Ísafjörður A dormitory during the school year, this practical and rather generic summer lodging offers both sleeping-bag accommodation—the super-cheap beds are in the classrooms—and 10 renovated doubles with modern fittings and private facilities. The town is a 15-minute walk away.

Off Skutulsfjarðarbraut (Rte. 61). ✆ **444-4960.** Fax 456-4767. www.hoteledda.is. 42 units, 10 w/bathroom. Early June-Aug 20 17,600kr double; 11,000kr double without bathroom. Breakfast available (1,500kr). AE, DC, MC, V. *In room:* No phone.

Litla Gistihúsið The decorated stairway is enlivened by a mural of exotic animals, and there's an appealing vintage look throughout, including a relaxing living room with fireplace. Rooms are hospitable if not luxurious. The two ground floor rooms have tiny private bathrooms at no extra cost, but the two upstairs rooms have more space and character. Another two rooms in an adjoining house are more neutral and functional.

Sundstræti 43. ✆ **474-1455.** reginasc@simnet.is. 6 units, 2 w/bathroom. 9,800kr double. MC, V. **Amenities:** Guest kitchen. *In room:* TV, no phone.

Where to Dine in Ísafjörður

EXPENSIVE

SKG Veitingar ICELANDIC Hotel Ísafjörður has the town's only smart restaurant, with specials such as salted cod au gratin with garlic potatoes, and pan-fried puffin from Vigur Island with blue cheese sauce.

In Hótel Ísafjörður, Silfurtorg 2. ✆ **456-3360.** Main courses 2,450kr-4,150kr. AE, DC, MC, V. Sun-Thurs 7:30am-10pm, Fri-Sat 7:30am-10:30pm.

MODERATE

Tjöruhúsið ★★ SEAFOOD Nestled inside a 1781 fish warehouse next to the Heritage Museum, with bench seating and long wooden tables, this fabulous seafood restaurant would earn three stars if wine and dessert were available to cap things off. The waiter simply points to a sheet of fish illustrations to indicate which species are freshly available that day. The fish arrives still sizzling in the pan and seasoned to perfection, with potatoes, tomatoes, lettuce, grapes, and lemon slices. Single portions are usually enough to satisfy two.

Suðurgata. ✆ **456-4419**. Reservations recommended. Main courses 2,190kr-3,490kr. AE, DC, MC, V. June to mid-Sept daily noon-2:30pm and 6-10pm.

INEXPENSIVE

Thai Koon ★ THAI This casual, cafeteria-style eatery in Ísafjörður's shopping arcade is a welcome break from the interchangeability of most provincial Icelandic restaurants—and the food is genuinely good. Combo plates are generous, with eight or 10 dishes to choose from.

Neisti Shopping Center, Hafnarstræti 9-11. ✆ **456-0123.** Main courses 990kr-1,990kr. DC, MC, V. Mon-Sat 11:30am-9pm; Sun 5-9pm.

CAFES & BAKERIES

Bakarinn This local staple has an honest, workaday ambience and offers good crepes, pizza, and other light fare as well as baked goodies.

Hafnarstræti 14. ✆ **456-4771.** Pastries and light dishes 70kr-980kr. AE, DC, MC, V. Mon-Fri 7:30am-6pm; Sun 9am-4:30pm.

Gamla Bakaríð A perfect spot for a rainy afternoon, this atmospheric patisserie with an embossed tin ceiling has seating space and soft, cozy lighting.

Aðalstræti 24. ✆ **456-3226.** Pastries 110kr-670kr. AE, DC, MC, V. Daily 7am-6pm.

Langi Mangi Café Ísafjörður's coolest after-hours hangout offers panini and other light fare, as well as drinks.

Aðalstræti 22. ✆ **445-6031**. Sandwiches 950kr-1150kr. MC, V. Mon-Wed 11am-11pm; Thurs 11am-1am; Fri 11am-3am; Sat noon-3am; Sun 1-11pm.

Shopping/Nightlife

Ísafjörður's boutique stores and souvenir shops are all arrayed along Aðalstræti and Hafnarstræti. The best **bookstore and newsstand** is **Bókhlaðan Penninn,** Hafnarstræti 2 (✆ **456-3123;** Mon–Fri 9am–6pm; Sat 10am–1pm), right off Silfurtorg square. For **outdoor gear,** head downtown to **Hafnarbúðin,** Suðurgata (✆ **456-3245;** Mon–Fri 9am–6pm, Sat 10am–2pm), near the Heritage Museum.

The only dance club in town is **Krúsin** (no phone; Fri–Sat nights only), but **Langi Mangi Café,** Aðalstræti 22 (✆ **445-6031**), is the ever-reliable hangout and bar.

Ísafjarðardjúp

BOLUNGARVÍK

14km (9 miles) northwest of Ísafjörður, Bolungarvík—the second-largest town in the Westfjords—braves exposure to raw weather conditions to lie close to fertile fishing grounds. The only eateries are the **service station grill** and **Kjallarinn Krá,** Hafnargata 41 (✆ **456-7901;** main courses 2,200kr–3,900kr; Jun–Aug daily 11am–11pm, Sept–May Fri–Sat 6–11pm), where the menu focuses on fresh catch from the waterfront. Bolungarvík's **tourist office,** Vitastígur 1 (✆ **450-7010;** bolungarvik@bolungarvik.is; June–Aug Mon–Fri 9am–4:30pm; Sat 2–5pm) is next to a crafts shop and the Natural History Museum.

Natural History Museum (Náttúrugripasafn Bolungarvíkur) Displays of stuffed animals, bird eggs, and minerals are found all over Iceland. While this one is more professional and extensive than usual, not enough context is in English. The most poignant specimens came to Iceland by accident: a polar bear, shot 64km (40 miles) offshore after drifting from Greenland on pack ice, and a poor lost flamingo.

Vitastígur 3. ✆ **456-7005.** www.nave.is. Admission 700kr adults; children under 16 free. Mon–Fri 9–11:45am and 1–4:45pm; June 15–Aug 15 also Sat–Sun 1–4:45pm.

Ósvör Museum Visitors to this re-creation of a seasonal fishing station from a century ago are greeted by the resident fisherman, who remains in character, hang-drying and salting cod in a sheepskin outfit. (Growing a long beard also seems to be in the job description.) The primitive encampment includes a turf-insulated stone hut, an authentically odorous salting shed, and a restored rowboat with a capstan for hauling it ashore. It's an expensive few minutes, but touchingly earnest nonetheless and worth a quick stop even out of hours to peer through the cod-drying shack and soak up the olden-days atmosphere.

Rte. 61, 1km (½ mile) east of Bolungarvík. ✆ **892-1616.** www.osvor.is. Admission 600kr adults; 450kr seniors; children under 16 free. Early June–mid-Aug daily 10am–5pm.

SÚÐAVÍK

Around 20km (12½ miles) southeast of Ísafjörður, the main attraction of Súðavík is its **Arctic Fox Center,** or **Melrakkasetur Íslands** (✆ **862-8219**; June–Aug 10am–10pm; 800kr admission). This nonprofit place holds exhibitions, screens films, and doubles as a research station focusing on Iceland's only native land mammal, the Arctic fox.

VIGUR ISLAND

Owned and occupied by the same family for four generations, Vigur is not the most scenically compelling island in Iceland, but most visitors are pleased enough gazing at birds—especially puffins—and vicariously experiencing the solitary island life (which in this case, we notice, has satellite TV). The family has 25 sheep and also earns money from puffin-hunting and harvesting down feathers from eider-duck nests.

Every afternoon from mid-June through late August, **West Tours** (p. 216) offers a 3-hour tour of Vigur for 6,100kr, starting with a 35-minute boat ride from Ísafjörður. The walking is very leisurely, as photographers loiter to inch their way closer to puffins on the low cliff ledges. (Be aware that puffins fly south en masse in mid-Aug, and on sunny days they often go off fishing for sand eels.) Other notable sights include seals and an 1830 windmill, the only one left standing in Iceland. Tours end with coffee and cake at the farmhouse.

HEYDALUR ★

This picturesque valley near the head of Mjóifjörður, about 135km (84 miles) southeast of Ísafjörður, provides a wonderful interlude in any journey along the Ísafjarðardjúp coast on Route 61. Tours organized by the **Heydalur Country Hotel** (✆ **456-4824;** www.heydalur.is) include horseback riding (90 min.; 5,000kr); sea kayaking in Mjóifjörður, usually accompanied by curious seals (3 hr.; 8,000kr); and an hour's hike up the valley to a trout fishing lake (2,000kr rod rental). All activities wind down with a soak in a fabulous outdoor geothermal pool. Heydalur is also a good spot for mingling with locals, as there are plenty of Icelandic clientele.

The hotel has nine simple, pleasant en-suite **guest rooms** (11,900kr) double; 5,000kr double with sleeping bag; AE, DC, MC, V) and an atmospheric **restaurant** (main courses 1,900kr–3,750kr; June–Aug daily 11am–10pm) inside a restored barn. (A parrot named Kobbi lives in the corner, but he only speaks Icelandic.) Order the home-caught salmon with pesto, then bathe in the pool while it's cooking.

THE STRANDIR COAST

Flanking Húnaflói bay, at the northeast edge of the Westfjords, the Strandir coast has a mysterious allure that's difficult to account for. In many ways, the region accentuates what is already exceptional about the Westfjords. Winters are unusually harsh, and pack ice often remains into late spring. Lowland is scarce, and inhabitants are especially dependent on the sea; even the sheep have been known to taste like seaweed, their backup diet. Strandir's topography is more varied than most of the Westfjords, and the abundance of driftwood lends an enchanting and melancholic cast to the shoreline. Historically Strandir's villages have been among the most isolated in the country, and outlaws have sought refuge on its austerely beautiful upland moors. Whatever the cause, visitors often describe the Strandir coast in quasi-mystical terms, as if they've escaped time or recovered some lost part of themselves.

One day is not enough time for Strandir to work its way into your system; 2 to 4 nights are better, ideally followed by an excursion north to Hornstrandir Nature Reserve. Those not keen on roughing it in Hornstrandir—or without the time to spare—can still reach the astonishing sea cliffs at Hornbjarg on day tours from Norðurfjörður twice a week in summer (see p. 223).

Essentials

GETTING THERE No public buses venture up the Strandir coast past Hólmavík and Drangsnes, so a rental car is indispensable. Car rental is not available in Hólmavík or Gjögur, Strandir's only airport, so drivers usually arrive from Reykjavík, Ísafjörður, or Akureyri. Hólmavík, a village at the base of Strandir, is along Route 61, 224km (139 miles) from Ísafjörður and 274km (170 miles) from Reykjavík. A few kilometers north of Hólmavík, Route 643 branches off from Route 61 and heads up the coast, ending 96km (60 miles) later at Norðurfjörður.

Eagle Air (✆ **562-2640;** www.eagleair.is) flies twice a week from Reykjavík to Gjögur (from 11,700kr one-way; 40 min.), 16km (10 miles) southeast of Norðurfjörður.

Buses connecting Ísafjörður to towns outside the Westfjords stop at Hólmavík; see p. 215. On Fridays, the **Sterna** (✆ **587-6000;** www.sterna.is) bus from Brú (on the Ring Road) to Hólmavík extends up Strandir to Drangsnes.

For information on the **ferry** connecting Norðurfjörður to Hornstrandir, see p. 225.

VISITOR INFORMATION The tourist office for all of Strandir is in **Hólmavík,** Norðurtún 1 (✆ **451-3111**; June 10–Aug daily 9am–5pm), at the community center. Off season, rely on the tourist office in Ísafjörður (p. 213).

Exploring the Strandir Coast

The coastal route from Hólmavík to Norðurfjörður on Route 643 is among the most scenic, rugged, and hypnotic drives in all of Iceland. Norðurfjörður has a general store with basic groceries, fuel (operable 24 hr. by credit card) and a bank (open weekdays 1–4pm, but no ATM; stock up in Hólmavík accordingly). Also make sure to pick up a hiking map at the Hólmavík tourist office (above).

HÓLMAVÍK

Museum of Icelandic Sorcery and Witchcraft (Galdrasýning á Ströndum)

Mass hysteria about witches and sorcerers never really took hold in Iceland, at least relative to the rest of Europe. However, from 1625 to 1685, around 120 alleged sorcerers were tried across the country, with 25 burned at the stake (23 of them men) and many more flogged. The Strandir coast had more than its share of trials—and more than its share of expert sorcerers, according to this gleefully morbid museum.

Admission includes a 30-minute audio tour through several installations relating the sorcerer's craft. The exhibit is genuinely educational, but doesn't take pains to separate history from folklore. (No historian really knows, for instance, whether Icelandic sorcerers ever skinned a human corpse from the waist down to make "necropants.") Most convicted sorcerers were too poor to leave any historical record, and the only real artifact here is an ancient "blood stone" used for animal sacrifices. In any case, you'll learn plenty of useful formulas, including which symbols to carve on a hunk of cheese before it's eaten by the object of your affection.

An accompanying exhibit called "The Sorcerer's Cottage" is in Bjarnarfjörður, 20 minutes north on Route 643, but it's very dispensable—basically all you see is a turf hut filled with dummy figures casting spells, without explanations in English.

Höfðagata 8–10. (Sorcerer's Cottage ✆ **451-3525.**) www.galdrasyning.is. Admission 700kr adults; children under 12 free. June–Sept 15 daily 10am–6pm; rest of year by request.

DJÚPAVÍK ★★

The soulful hotel at Djúpavík, a stunningly beautiful inlet of Reykjarfjörður, is the ideal base for exploring Strandir. Activities arranged by the hotel (see "Where to Stay," below) include sea fishing and sea kayaking—no experience necessary—and touring the ruins of a herring factory next door.

Djúpavík's first houses went up in 1917, soon after herring were discovered in Reykjarfjörður. The factory, finished in 1935, was an engineering marvel and the largest concrete structure in Europe. The herring trade was so lucrative that the factory paid for itself in a single five-month season. During peak summers, 200 workers—mostly teenage girls—worked the machinery round the clock. In the early 1950s the herring simply failed to show up, and in 1971 Reykjarfjörður was completely abandoned. Today the only winter residents are the couple who have run the hotel since 1985—and their adorable Icelandic sheepdog Tína.

Guided 45-minute tours of the factory ruins start at 2pm daily from mid-June through August; the 950kr cost includes an informative photo-and-text exhibit in an anteroom. The factory is certainly atmospheric, but interest will vary; for some it's just crumbling concrete and rusting metal, while for others it's equal to the Roman Coliseum. Exploring on your own is prohibited for safety reasons.

For further information on Djúpavík, and an extensive online photo gallery of the Strandir coast, visit the hotel's website www.djupavik.com.

GJÖGUR, TRÉKYLLISVÍK & NORÐURFJÖRÐUR

Gjögur, near the tip of the peninsula north of Reykjarfjörður, has a cluster of summer homes. A crude road winds past Gjögur's minuscule airport to **Gjögurstrond ★**, an evocative stretch of beach and rocky coastline, with steam drifting from underground hot springs.

The next bay to the north is **Trékyllisvík,** and on its south shore is the 19th-century church at **Árnes.** In February 1991, during a severe windstorm, the church was lifted off its foundation and deposited a few feet over, but nothing inside was damaged. Next to the church is the small museum **Minja-og Handverkshúsið Kört** (✆ **451-4025;** kort@trekyllisvik.is; admission 300kr; June–Aug daily 10am–6pm), with a haphazard, regional collection of textiles, dolls, and various fishing and farming artifacts. Without paying admission, you could still visit the **handicrafts shop,** which has locally knit woolens plus bowls, vases, and candleholders sculpted from driftwood and whalebone.

Norðurfjörður, a tiny village at the north end of Trékyllisvík, has the only market and fuel beyond Hólmavík. From late June to mid-August, a boat departs from here three times a week for Hornstrandir Nature Reserve (p. 225). Route 643 ends at Norðurfjörður, but a coastal road continues another 4km (2½ miles) to Krossnes farm. Shortly after passing the farm, a driveway on the right leads downhill to **Krossneslaug ★**, one of Iceland's most sublime geothermal pools. A gorgeous stone beach is just a few feet away, and some intrepid souls brave the freezing ocean water before scrambling back to the heated pool. (Do not attempt this without shoes for traversing the rocks.) The pool is large enough to swim laps, and the temperature is perfect—though the water is a tad over-chlorinated. The pool is open anytime, but twilight is especially idyllic.

OUTDOOR ACTIVITIES

HIKING The *Vestfirðir and Dalir* ("Westfjords and Valleys") hiking map series, available at the Hólmavík tourist office (and sold online at www.strandir.is/hikingmaps), includes several maps covering the Strandir area and details the most worthwhile hikes, with thorough directions, distances, and difficulty ratings. The hikes recommended below are of moderate difficulty.

A 5km (3 mile) **loop hike** from Hótel Djúpavík heads up a steep cleft behind the hotel, then east along a plateau with fabulous fjord views before descending to meet Route 643; allow 3 hours to stop and smell the mosses.

Starting from Naustvík on the north shore of Reykjarfjörður, an ancient footpath heads through a scenic mountain pass to **Árnes** on Trékyllisvík Bay; the route is 3.5km (2 miles) and about 90 minutes each way.

Just north of Gjögur is **Reykjaneshyrna,** a small mountain and sea cliff rising conspicuously between the road and the ocean. You can either approach from the Gjögur airfield, or park much closer—at a blue sign for Reykjaneshyrna along Route 643—to make the 90-minute round-trip climb. The top has great views in all directions.

Another excellent hike is a 4 to 5-hour clockwise loop starting from **Krossneslaug.** Walk back to Norðurfjörður, then turn right on Route 647, which heads overland to Munaðarnes Farm, on the coast of Ingólfsfjörður. Then continue around the peninsular coastline—first on an unmarked trail, then along a road—back to Krossnes for a triumphal dip in the pool.

Where to Stay

Djúpavík and Norðurfjörður, on the northern stretch of the Strandir coast, are the most memorable places to stay. Heading south, one good option is the **Kirkjubol** guesthouse (✆ **451-3474**; kirkjubol@strandir.is; 10,400kr double with breakfast), especially if you want to break the drive between Ísafjörður and Akureyri. If you need lodging anywhere else in Strandir's southern portion, contact the Hólmavík information center (p. 221) or visit www.westfjords.is.

Djúpavík Hotel ★ Built in 1938, this former boarding house for herring workers celebrated its 25th anniversary as a hotel in 2010. It is the most characterful and beautifully situated accommodation on the Strandir coast. Rooms aren't big, beds aren't wide, and sheets and towels aren't plush; but in such an inviting refuge none of that seems to matter. (If you feel cramped, think of the herring days, when eight girls shared each room.) Ever-mindful of local history, the proprietors include herring in the breakfast spread. The hotel also offers additional rooms and sleeping-bag accommodation at Lækjarkot and Álfasteinn Cottages, with space for up to 18 people.

Ⓒ **451-4037.** Fax 451-4035. www.djupavik.com. 8 double rooms, none w/bathroom. 9,400kr double; family room from 11,900kr. Breakfast available (1,200kr). MC, V. **Amenities:** Restaurant. *In room:* No phone.

NORÐURFJÖRÐUR

Gistiheimili Norðurfjarðar (Ⓒ **554-4089;** gulledda@simnet.is; 4,200kr per person made-up bed, 2,500kr per person sleeping-bag accommodation; no credit cards), in the same building as the general store, has three very straightforward rooms: two doubles and a triple. Very close by is the village's only other guesthouse, **Gistiheimilið Bergistanga** (Ⓒ **451-4003;** arneshreppur@simnet.is; 2,500kr sleeping-bag accommodation; no credit cards), with equally serviceable rooms but sleeping-bag accommodation only. Both lodgings have guest kitchens, but only Bergistanga serves breakfast, and only on request (1,100kr). A 10-minute walk from the general store is **Valgeirsstaðir mountain hut (Gistiskáli Ferðafélag Íslands)** (Ⓒ **451-4017;** 3,200kr per person sleeping-bag accommodation; closed Sept–June), with a well-equipped kitchen, a hot shower, and eight rooms, each accommodating up to six people in sleeping-bags. Booking must be done online through the hiking group **Ferðafélag Íslands** (Ⓒ **568-2533;** www.fi.is; MC, V); they mail you a voucher, which you bring along to show the warden. If you show up and space is available, you won't be turned away. Note, however, that sleeping-bag accommodation is cheaper in the guesthouses, where you can have a private room.

Where to Dine

Hólmavík has a large **supermarket** for stocking up on supplies; Norðurfjörður has a far more rudimentary one. Hólmavík's only other dining option besides Cafe Riis (below) is fast food at the **service station.** No restaurants are north of Hótel Djúpavík.

Cafe Riis ICELANDIC Housed inside Hólmavík's oldest building, with driftwood floorboards and a welcoming air, Cafe Riis has above-average food at reasonable prices. Delicious local fish, mussels, puffin with blueberry sauce, lamb. Who could want more? Well, if you do there are burritos and pizza.

Hafnarbraut 39, Hólmavík. Ⓒ **451-3567.** Main courses 1,400kr–2,990kr. Sun–Thurs 11:30am–11:30pm; Fri–Sat 11:30am–3am; kitchen closes daily 10pm.

Hotel Djúpavík ICELANDIC In summer the hotel's restaurant stays open all day, but lunch is restricted to light meals—fish soup, sandwiches, and cake—and dinner is a simple choice between lamb and fish. The food says "home cooking" more than "fine dining;" but out in Strandir, it hits the spot. In August you're likely to get a fabulous dessert of freshly picked berries with *skyr* and cream. Call ahead so they know you're coming.

Rte. 643, Djúpavík. Ⓒ **451-4037.** Dinner menu 4,000kr per person. MC, V. Mid-June to Aug daily 8am–9:30pm, with dinner starting at 6pm; other times of year call ahead.

HORNSTRANDIR NATURE RESERVE

Among Iceland's coastal areas, **Hornstrandir ★★★** —the spiky peninsula at the northern tip of the Westfjords—is the truest wilderness. Because of its harsh climate, few Icelanders ever settled here, and the last full-time residents left in 1952. There are no roads, no airstrips, no powerful rivers for hydroelectricity, and just one hot spring for geothermal heat. Hornstrandir was designated a nature reserve in 1975; since grazing by horses and sheep is forbidden, the vegetation—from mossy tundra to meadows full of wildflowers—now resembles that from when the Vikings first arrived. Arctic foxes, seen scurrying by day and heard cackling at night, are also protected. The coast is lined with idyllic sandy bays, spooky abandoned homes, and rugged sea cliffs teeming with birdlife. Other visitors are few and far between.

Visiting Hornstrandir can require careful planning, but the logistics are not as difficult as they're often made out to be. The best time to come is from late June to mid-August; but, to cut weather risks, most visitors arrive the second half of July or the first week of August.

Essentials

VISITOR INFORMATION The best source is the tourist office in Ísafjörður (p. 213). The Environment and Food Agency website **www.ust.is** (click "Protected Areas," "Nature Reserves," then "Hornstrandir") has a very useful general profile of the nature reserve.

GETTING THERE & AROUND For those not taking a tour, the general procedure is to sketch out an itinerary in sync with ferry schedules. Most visitors take **ferries** to Hornstrandir from Ísafjörður or Bolungarvík, the village 14km (9 miles) northwest of Ísafjörður. The other ferry connection is from Norðurfjörður (p. 223), on the Strandir coast. You could start in Ísafjörður and end up in Norðurfjörður, or vice-versa, but Norðurfjörður is a tiny settlement with no scheduled buses or car rentals. A few people **walk** the 16km (10 miles) between Norðurfjörður and the tiny Gjögur airport (p. 222), which has weekly **flights** to and from Reykjavík. Hardcore hikers sometimes walk into Hornstrandir over several days, starting from Unaðsdalur, at the end of Route 635 on the north shore of Ísafjarðardjúp.

Contrary to what many have heard, camping is not necessary in Hornstrandir (see "Where to Stay," below). If you like to camp but don't enjoy lugging your tent and gear around in a heavy backpack, the ferry system allows you to set up base camps from which to explore. **West Tours** (below) acts as an agent for all ferries below, and can even arrange for packages to be sent in. Their website lists schedules.

Sjóferðir (✆ **456-3879;** www.sjoferdir.is), based in Ísafjörður, has a weekly ferry service to Grunnavík, Hesteyri, Aðalvík, Veiðileysufjörður, Hrafnfjörður, and Hornvík from late June to late August. The schedule at the website is misleading, because many listed departures are only for arranged tours with West Tours (below).

The ferry run by **Ferðaþjónustan Grunnavík** (✆ **456-4664;** www.grunnavik.is) leaves from Bolungarvík and has irregular service (phone to check or book) to Grunnavík, Hesteyri, and Aðalvík from mid-June through August (all prices one-way).

Freydís (✆ **893-6926** or 852-9367; www.freydis.is) operates the ferry from Norðurfjörður three times a week from mid-June to mid-August, stopping at guesthouses in Reykjarfjörður (not to be confused with the other fjord of the same name south of Norðurfjörður) (6,500kr); Bolungarvík Eystri (7,000kr); and Látravík (near Hornbjargsviti lighthouse) (8,000kr); en route to Hornvík (8,500kr); and back to Norðurfjörður (all prices one-way). Taking the round-trip route as a sightseeing day trip is 8,000kr. A fourth weekly trip extends only from Norðurfjörður to Reykjarfjörður.

> **Don't Stand Up the Ferry Man**
>
> **If you're touring independently in the Nature Reserve, your ferry operator will ask when and where you expect to be picked up. If your plans change, relay a message to the boat operator through a guesthouse or another visitor. Otherwise an expensive search and rescue mission will probably be launched.**

Tours

If you'd like a private guide instead of a group tour, contact the Ísafjörður tourist office, which keeps a list of licensed guides.

West Tours, Aðalstræti 7, Ísafjörður (✆ **456-5111;** www.westtours.is), the most reputable tour operator in the Westfjords, offers scheduled day tours to Hesteyri (4–5 hr.; 6,200kr) and Hornvík (12 hr.; 21,500kr), guided day hikes from Sæból (in Aðalvík) to Hesteyri (12 hr.; 15,300kr), and spectacular 4-day, 3-night camping expeditions to Hornvík (69,000kr).

Iceland's premier hiking group, **Ferðafélag Íslands,** Mörkin 6, Reykjavík (✆ **568-2533;** www.fi.is), leads a variety of Hornstrandir trips even into October.

Borea Adventures, Hlíðarvegur 38, Ísafjörður (✆ **899-3817;** www.boreaadventures.com), offers marvelous 5- to 6-day Hornstrandir trips aboard its 18m (60-ft.) racing yacht. Participants alight from the yacht for kayaking, observing wildlife, or, in winter, backcountry skiing. Prices range from 190,000kr to 220,000kr, including food and equipment.

Hiking Hornstrandir

The *Vestfirðir and Dalir* series (p. 223) includes the best Hornstrandir map. The maps indicate which trails are passable only at low tide, and the Ísafjörður information office can supply tide tables. Also make sure to bring a compass, shoes for fording streams, and plenty of warm clothing. Most clear running water is safe to drink, unless it passed through bird nesting areas. Hiking alone is not a good idea.

When sketching out an itinerary, always allow extra time to get from one place to another. Harsh weather or thick fog could roll in, and even the few marked trails can be difficult to follow. (It never gets completely dark, so you can always take your time.) Trails at higher altitudes may have deep snow even in July. Take note of nearby emergency huts, which have radios, heaters, and food. Check weather reports and review the challenges of your route with the Ísafjörður tourist office.

No one itinerary stands out in Hornstrandir, but one sight is decidedly worth putting at the top of your list. **Hornbjarg ★★★**, a sea cliff on Hornstrandir's north coast, just east of Hornvík bay, is the most spectacular landmark on Iceland's coastline. From its narrow summit, the inland slope descends in a surreal parabolic curve. Gazing down at the birds and surf from the 534m (1,752-ft.) ledge—which is also the highest point on Hornstrandir—is exhilarating and unforgettable. Campers stationed in **Hornvík ★★**, the bay just west of Hornbjarg, should venture to the sea cliff **Hælavíkurbjarg ★★**, the canyon river **Gljúfurá ★**, and **Hornbjargsviti ★**, the lighthouse at Látravík. The guesthouse connected to the lighthouse is almost as convenient a base as Hornvík.

On the south side of Hornstrandir, which is more accessible from Ísafjörður, the ghost town of **Hesteyri ★** is another excellent base camp for hikes. Hesteyri's population peaked at 80 in the 1930s, when the herring trade was in full swing, and a forlorn long-abandoned whaling station lies close by. Hornstrandir's other main settlement was at **Aðalvík ★★**, a 6-hour hike overland from Hesteyri. Some hikers continue from Aðalvík to Straumnes lighthouse, the Rekavíkurvatn lagoon, Fljótsvatn lake, and back to Hesteyri in a memorable, 3-day clockwise loop. The hike between Hesteyri and Hornvík is somewhat demanding and takes 2 days, with an overnight in Hælavík.

This brief overview hardly exhausts the endless hiking and camping possibilities in Hornstrandir, not to mention the equally pristine wilderness south of the nature reserve, including Snæfjallaströnd peninsula and the uplands surrounding Drangajökull, the biggest glacier in the northern half of Iceland.

Campers are trusted to respect the land and pick up after themselves. The truly responsible don't even leave a trace of their toilet paper. Fires are prohibited. Make sure to keep food inside your tent at night so the foxes don't steal it.

Where to Stay

All guesthouses in Hornstrandir require you to bring your own sleeping bag. All have guest kitchens and are open from around mid-June to mid-August. If any guesthouse proves difficult to reach, **West Tours** (p. 216) can act as a booking agent. ***Note:*** No Hornstrandir guesthouses accept credit cards.

Within the nature reserve, the most accessible guesthouse from Ísafjörður is **Læknishúsið** (✆ **456-1123** or 845-5075 (after July 1 call Hesteyri directly on 853-5034); 4,000kr per person); this former doctor's house is in Hesteyri, an abandoned village on Hornstrandir's south coast. On the north coast, a few kilometers east of Hornvík,**Óvissuferðir** (✆ **566-6752** or 892-5219; www.ovissuferd.is; 3,300kr per person) sleeps 50 in a building adjoined to Hornbjargsviti, the lighthouse at Látravík.

Two rudimentary guesthouses—neither of which have private doubles—lie on the east coast of Hornstrandir, along the Freydís ferry route (p. 225) from Norðurfjörður to Hælavík. The first is **Reykjarfjörður** (✆ **456-7215** or 853-1615; reykjarfjordur@simnet.is; 3,000kr per person), in the fjord of the same name, just outside the nature reserve. Reykjarfjörður's best asset is a large, outdoor geothermal pool. The second guesthouse is **Ferðaþjónustan Mávaberg,** (✆ **852-8267;** mavaberg@freydis.is; 3,000kr per person) in Bolungarvík Eystri, three fjords west of Reykjarfjörður.

Grunnavík, at the tip of the Snæfjallaströnd Peninsula south of Hornstrandir, is included in some ferry routes and has the guesthouse **Ferðaþjónustan Grunnavík** (✆ **862-8411** or 866-5491; grunnavik@grunnavik.is; 3,000kr per person).

Wild camping in the nature reserve is free. All the above have tent sites for around 1,000kr per person, including use of facilities.

NORTH ICELAND

9

The north of Iceland is tucked just beneath the Arctic Circle and Greenland Sea, but enjoys relatively hospitable weather and forgiving land. Northerners gloat about their climate, which is sunnier and drier than the southwest in summer. The multiform northern coast bears little resemblance to the south coast, which is dominated by glaciers and worked over by the flow of glacial sediments. The north has the highest population of any region outside the southwest corner; even cod are migrating to the north coast as the oceans warm.

Most visitors cluster in the near northeast region comprising Akureyri, Iceland's thriving northern capital; Mývatn, a wonderland of lava forms, multi-hued geothermal fields, and birdlife; Húsavík, Iceland's whale-watching mecca; and Jökulsárgljúfur, an extensive canyon full of magisterial rock formations and waterfalls.

Touring within this so-called "Diamond Circle"—a bit of marketing one-upmanship based on the popular "Golden Circle" in the southwest—you may keep seeing the same tourists, who can access all these sights by day from the same accommodation. Venture west of Akureyri or east of Jökulsárgljúfur and the tourist sightings quickly diminish. Visitors zoom past Húnaflói on the Ring Road, but would not regret an excursion to a seal colony on its Vatnsnes peninsula, or the stone church at Þingeyrar.

The Skagafjörður region offers Glaumbær, Iceland's best museum of preserved 19th-century farm buildings; Hólar, seat of Iceland's northern bishopric in the Catholic era; and Siglufjörður, a fjord town as scenically situated as any in the country. The Arctic Circle cuts right through the tiny island of Grímsey, which exerts a mystical pull on those visitors who can't resist remote islands. The northeast corner of Iceland, with its driftwood beaches, sea cliffs, lonely moors, and misty lakes and lagoons, is a wonderful place to forget about hectic, goal-oriented travel.

Online, www.northiceland.is has a good search engine for places to stay and other services throughout the region—though visitor information offices and websites listed in each section below are more thorough.

HÚNAFLÓI

Húnaflói (Bear Cub Bay) lies between the Westfjords and Skagi Peninsula, and its environs are among the least tourist-trodden in the country. Drivers heading from Reykjavík to Akureyri on the Ring Road mostly see undulating agricultural land, but few dramatic landmarks to beckon them off course. Anyone passing through, however, should consider a daytime or overnight detour, particularly for **seal-watching** on Vatnsnes peninsula or visiting the **19th-century stone church** at Þingeyrar. For a dinner excursion, consider a side trip to Texas courtesy of the **Kántrýbær restaurant,** run by Icelandic country-and-western impresario Hallbjörn Hjartarson (see box, "The Cowboy of Skagaströnd," p. 235). Tune your car radio to FM 96.7, 102.2, or 107.0 to catch Hallbjörn's radio show.

Essentials

GETTING THERE The main hubs in Húnaflói are Hvammstangi and Blönduós. Hvammstangi is 6km (3¾ miles) north of the Ring Road on Route 72, 197km (122 miles) north of Reykjavík, and 203km (126 miles) west of Akureyri. Blönduós is along the Ring Road, 243km (151 miles) from Reykjavík and 145km (90 miles) from Akureyri.

Sterna (✆ **553-3737;** www.sterna.is) runs at least one **bus** daily year-round between Reykjavík and Akureyri, stopping at Hvammstangi and Blönduós. Reykjavík to Hvammstangi is 3 hours and 20 minutes; a ticket costs 5,600kr; Akureyri to Hvammstangi is 3 hours and 5,700kr; Reykjavík to Blönduós is 4 hours and 6,800kr; Akureyri to Blönduós is 2 hours and 10 minutes and 4,200kr. Blönduós has a bus connection to Skagaströnd, but make sure to notify the driver.

VISITOR INFORMATION The best tourist info for Húnaflói is in **Blönduós** (✆ **452-4520;** www.northwest.is; June 1–Aug 23 daily 8am–8pm), just off the Ring Road on Brautarhvammur; look for the international flagpoles. In **Hvammstangi,** tourist info is at the Icelandic Seal Center (Selasetur Íslands), Brekkugata 2 (✆ **451-2345;** www.selasetur.is; June–Aug daily 9am–6pm, Sept 1–15 Mon–Fri 10am–4pm). Off season, rely on the regional tourist office at **Varmahlíð** (✆ **455-6161;** www.visitskagafjordur.is; June 1–14 and September daily 9am–5pm; June 15–Aug daily 9am–7pm; Oct–May daily 10am–3pm) in nearby Skagafjörður.

Exploring Húnaflói

VATNSNES PENINSULA

Húnaflói is home to the majority of **Icelandic harbor seals** (plus a few gray seals), and the best place to spot them is on this nubby peninsula west of Blönduós. The peninsula's only town, **Hvammstangi,** is at its southwestern base. Vatnsnes has a mountainous interior, but its shores blend wild coastline with fertile grazing land for horses and sheep. Seals can be viewed any time of year, though they often disappear unpredictably in search of fish. Centuries of hunting have not made the seals any less curious about humans, and they like to shadow your movements from a distance. The seal population is just a third of what it was in 1980, but not because of the viral disease that has affected seal populations in Europe; it is extremely important not to disturb them or try to feed them.

The "World of the Sea People" exhibit at Hvammstangi's **Icelandic Seal Center (Selasetur Íslands),** at Brekkugata 2 (✆ **451-2345;** www.selasetur.is; June–Aug

North Iceland

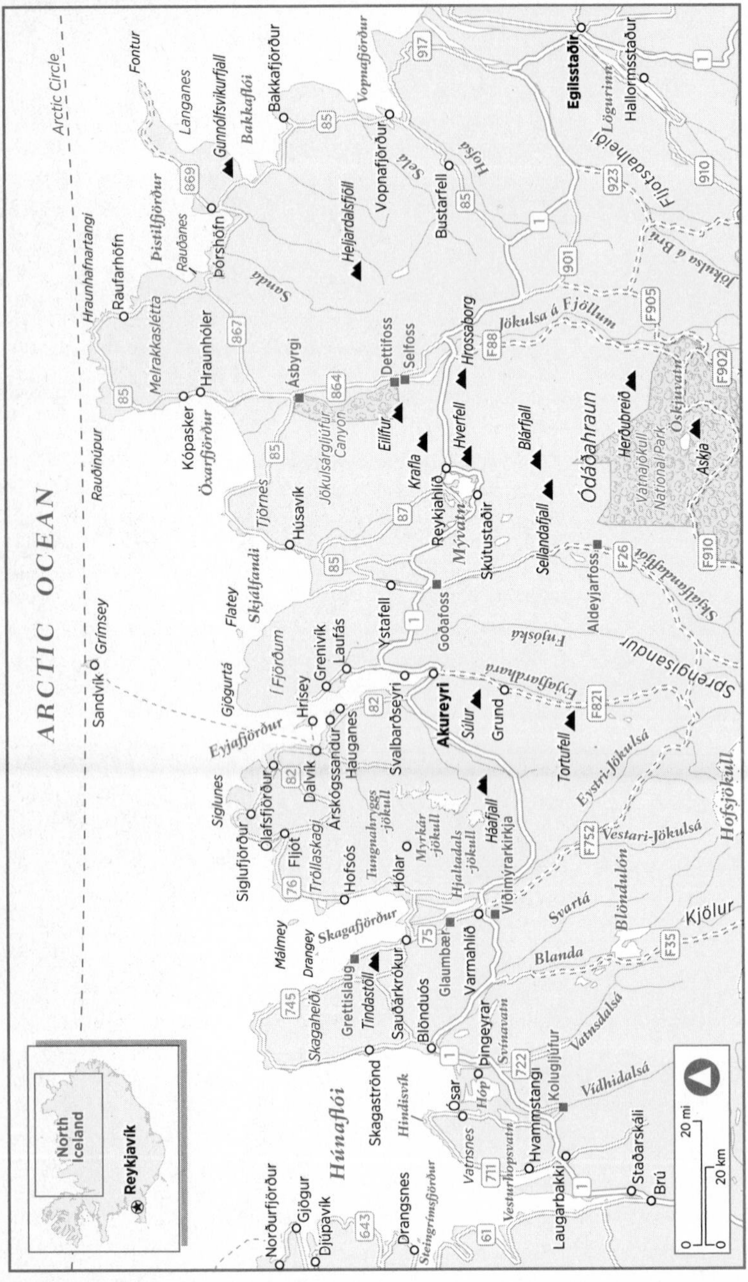

daily 9am–5pm, Sept 1–30 Mon–Fri 10am–2pm) is a good primer on seal biology, seal–human relations and seal-related folklore, and the staff is very helpful and give updates on current seal-viewing locations. Admission is 900kr adults and 450kr for children aged 6–16.

From Hvammstangi, Route 711 follows the periphery of Vatnsnes. On clear days, the west side of the peninsula has **great views** of the Strandir coast. Signs are sometimes posted at turnoffs for viewing seal colonies. A particularly accessible **seal colony** is on the peninsula's western shore, about 15km (9 miles) north of Hvammstangi and just north of the Hamarsrétt sheep round-up pen, which is marked from the road.

Illugastaður About 26 km (16 miles) further along the western coastal road of the Vatnsnes peninsula on Route 711 from Hvammstangir is Illugastaðir, currently the best place to view the seal colonies. From the main car park, a trail leads about 900m to a viewing platform with superb views of Strandir. Illugustaðir also has a coffee shop (✆ **451-2664**; June 20–Aug 20 daily 2pm–6pm) with camping (750kr adults, free for children under 16) and bathroom facilities. The area is closed during the nesting season from April 25 to June 23; ask at the **Icelandic Seal Center** (above) for other places to view the seals.

Ósar ★ is the most idyllic spot on Vatnsnes for an overnight stay and another great place to watch the seals (see Ósar Youth Hostel, below). **Hvítserkur** ★, just off the shoreline near Ósar, is a bizarre, M-shaped, 15m-high (49-ft.) basalt crag with its own bird population. To reach this requisite photo stop, turn off Route 711 a short distance north of Ósar and proceed to the parking area. Scramble down to the black sand beach and, if the tide is low, walk into Hvítserkur's arches. Walk south along the beach for 20 minutes, past the resident ducks, jellyfish, and harbor seals that will probably be seen lounging on the sands across the channel (one or two seals will probably swim over to investigate). From this part of the beach, it's a 10-minute walk uphill to Ósar.

KOLUGLJÚFUR

This picturesque 1km-long (½ mile) gorge on the Viðidalsá river makes for an enjoyable half-hour diversion or picnic spot near the Ring Road. Kolugljúfur plunges 50m (164 ft.) and was named for Kola, the troll who dug it out. To reach the gorge, exit the Ring Road onto Route 715 at either junction (Rte. 715 forms a "V," meeting the Ring Road at both ends). From the bottom of the "V," turn off Route 715 and continue south to the sign that reads "Litla-Hlið/Bakki/Kolugljúfur;" turn right and park just before the bridge. Paths head downstream along either side.

ÞINGEYRAR

The distinctive stone **Þingeyrar Church** ★ (✆ **452-4473;** free admission. Jun–Aug daily 10am–5pm) lies on pastureland east of Vatnsnes peninsula. It was built between 1864 and 1877, and financed entirely by Ásgeir Einarsson, a local farmer and member of parliament. While most Icelandic churches from this time are sided with sheets of corrugated iron made to resemble painted wood, Þingeyrar was constructed at great expense from hewn basalt and limestone. The interior layout varies from the ultra-rectangular Icelandic norm. The apse—the semicircular projection on the eastern end of the church that normally holds just the altar—is deepened and broadened to encircle everything in front of the pews ("apsidal choir" is the technical term). Many Icelandic church ceilings have a few hundred gold stars mounted on square panels; Þingeyrar church has about a thousand gold stars on a smooth, dark-blue ceiling, which is half-domed over the apsidal choir.

The altarpiece, made in England (Nottingham) in the 15th century, illustrates Biblical scenes with appealingly crude alabaster figures in relief. (A similar altarpiece at Hólar is more compelling; see p. 239). It once had wing panels, lost during a failed attempt to sell the altarpiece abroad. The Baroque-style canopied pulpit and matching baptismal font were made in the Netherlands in the late-17th century. The church's best-known feature is the "Apostles Collection:" small, painted oak-wood figurines, placed between the railings of the gallery. The originals were made in Germany in the late-16th century, sold from Þingeyrar in the early 20th century, and then donated to the National Museum. What you see here are expert 1983 replicas.

To reach Þingeyrar Church, exit on to Route 721 from the Ring Road, 20km (12 miles) west of Blönduós, and proceed 7km (4¼ miles) to the end.

BLÖNDUÓS

This coastal town and agricultural trading hub is the largest settlement in Húnaflói, with nearly 1,000 residents. Visitors have little reason to dawdle for long.

Textile Museum (Heimilisiðnaðarsafnið) ★ Not everyone will be captivated by century-old crocheted nightgowns and exquisitely-embroidered undergarments, but it's hard not to be impressed by the dedication put into this nationwide textile collection. One room is full of mannequins sporting the national costume in several late-19th century variations—the best such display in Iceland. Another section hosts temporary exhibits by contemporary Icelandic textile artists. Guests can weave wool on the loom downstairs, or grab a pair of gloves at reception to fondle specimens at will. Make sure to find the portrait made from lint.

Árbraut 29. ✆ **452-4067.** www.simnet.is/textile. Admission 600kr adults, 500kr seniors, free for ages 16 and under. Jun–Aug daily 10am–5pm. From the Ring Road, turn on to Húnabraut, then bear left on Árbraut, following the northeast side of the river Blanda.

SKAGASTRÖND

Thanks to Icelandic cowboy Hallbjörn Hjartarson (p. 235), this tiny town 23km (14 miles) north of Blönduós is a bastion of country-and-western culture. See "Where to Dine," below.

Outdoor Activities

HORSEBACK RIDING **Gauksmýri** (✆ **451-2927;** www.gauksmyri.is), about 50km (31 miles) west of Blönduós, is a reputable horse farm that offers short tours of the Húnaflói area. Rides start at 7,500kr for 1 hour and can include introductory lessons. Gauksmýri is also an eco-minded guesthouse and restaurant; see "Where to Stay," below.

Arinbjörn Jóhannson at **Brekkulækur Farm** (✆ **451-2938;** www.abbi-island.is) has been putting together epic 3- to 15-day riding adventures for three decades. Tour itineraries, outlined on the website, usually include highlands, coastal regions, and some mingling with locals.

Where to Stay

VATNSNES PENINSULA & NEARBY

Gauksmýri Many guests are here for horseback riding, but non-riders should be equally content. The 18 new en-suite rooms are somewhat small and typically featureless, but bright and comfortable nonetheless. Heated towel rails are a welcome perk.

Plenty of horse-motifed lounging space is on hand, and a glassed-in dining room overlooks the farm. **Dinner** is available on request: meals include a grill buffet (4,000kr) and homemade bread and vegetables from the farm's own greenhouse.

Rte. 1, about 50km (31 miles) west of Blönduós and 4km (2½ miles) east of the Rte. 1/Rte. 72 junction. ✆ **451-2927.** Fax 451-3427. www.gauksmyri.is. 27 units, 18 w/bathroom. June–Sept 20,000kr double; 13,500kr double without bathroom. Rates around 15% lower Oct–May. Rates include breakfast. MC, V. **Amenities:** Restaurant; bar; Internet terminal. *In room:* No phone, Wi-Fi.

Hanna Sigga Guesthouse (Gistiheimili Hönnu Siggu) It can take some visitors a while to get used to the custom of staying in other people's houses. This friendly, family-run guesthouse in Hvammstangi makes the transition easy, with bright and spacious rooms, board games in the living room, and a hot tub overlooking the fjord.

Garðarvegur 26, Hvammstangi. ✆ **451-2407.** www.simnet.is/gistihs. 6 units, none w/bathroom. May–Sept 10,500kr double; 3,500kr sleeping-bag accommodation. Rates 10–15% lower Oct–Apr. Breakfast available (1,200kr). AE, DC, MC, V. **Amenities:** Guest kitchen; hot tub; Internet access. *In room:* No phone.

Ósar Youth Hostel ★ This alluring retreat on Vatnsnes peninsula—25 or 30km (16–19 miles) north of the Ring Road, depending which direction you're coming from—lies close to Hvítserkur (p. 231) and a large seal colony. Though pickup from the Ring Road can be arranged, Ósar is reachable only by car and tends to attract nature lovers who are a tad more sedate than the typical hostel crowd. Guests can stay in the farmhouse or one of three new cabins; the house has more common space and a TV room, while the cabins are a little more private. The nearest market and restaurant is in Hvammstangi, 25 minutes away, but breakfast can be ordered and eaten inside a Mongolian-style yurt. Book well ahead for the summer.

Rte. 711. ✆ **862-2778.** www.simnet.is/osar. 10 units without bathroom. 8,500kr double; 3.300kr sleeping-bag accommodation; 11,100kr triple; 3,300kr sleeping-bag accommodation in dorm bed; 1,200kr sheet rental for entire stay. Breakfast available (1,500kr). AE, DC, MC, V. Closed Dec–Apr. Coming from the west, turn left from the Ring Road onto Rte. 711 and proceed about 30km (19 miles). Coming from the east, turn right from the Ring Road onto Rte. 716, then turn right again on Rte. 711 and proceed about 19km (12 miles). **Amenities:** Guest kitchen; Internet terminal. *In room:* No phone, Wi-Fi.

BLÖNDUÓS

Guesthouse Glaðheimar Run by Hótel Blönduós, this straightforward and efficient guesthouse in a former post office building has a range of rooming options. Superior doubles have more space and TVs but still no private bathroom. Cottages vary from 15 to 58 sq. m (49–190 sq. ft.) and sleep two to eight. Most of the large cottages have their own hot tub and sauna.

Blöndubyggð 10. ✆ **452-4205.** Fax 452-4208. www.gladheimar.is. 20 units, 1 w/bathroom. May–Sept 9,900kr–10,500kr double without bathroom; 9,900kr persons. Rates around 25% lower Oct–Apr. MC, V. **Amenities:** Guest kitchen. *In room:* No phone, Wi-Fi (main building only).

Hótel Blönduós ★ The town's top hotel, restaurant and bar are all under this roof. The homey, welcoming rooms—though unlikely to form any lasting impression—are painted in hot sunset shades and touch on the eccentric. Superior doubles mean extra lounging space. ***Note:*** Summer weekends fill up early.

Aðalgata 6. ✆ **452-4205.** Fax 452-4208. www.gladheimar.is. 16 units. May–Sept 19,900kr double. Rates about 20% lower Oct–Apr. MC, V. **Amenities:** Restaurant; bar. *In room:* TV, hair dryer, Wi-Fi.

Where to Dine

See also **Gauksmýri** in "Where to Stay," above.

HVAMMSTANGI

Café Sirop ICELANDIC As the resident restaurant-bar for Hvammstangi and environs, Sirop has the expected provincial menu of burgers, pizzas, fish, and peppered lamb. Yet the food—and ambience—have a touch more class and finesse than is strictly necessary to get by.

Norðurbraut 1. ✆ **451-2266.** Main courses 1,490kr–3,290kr. MC, V. Mon–Thurs 11am–10pm; Fri–Sat 11am–3am; Sun noon–10pm.

BLÖNDUÓS

Hótel Blönduós ★ ICELANDIC This restaurant inside the Hótel Blönduós is the best in town, and the traditional lamb and fish menu has few disappointments—or surprises. Tables fill up with locals and visitors alike on summer weekends, but the restaurant sometimes closes between 2 and 5pm.

Aðalgata 6. ✆ **452-4205.** Reservations recommended. Main courses 2,700kr–3,800kr. MC, V. Late Apr–early Oct daily 11am–10pm; mid-Oct to mid-Apr call in advance.

Potturinn Og Pannan ☺ ICELANDIC Eating at this chain restaurant is not a memorable experience but is also unlikely to disappoint. The menu's star feature is seal steak, although most people go for the local fish and lamb, and the even less adventurous stick to burgers and pasta. Kids get their own AstroTurf hut to watch TV and play games in. The hot chocolate is superb.

Norðurlandsvegur 4. ✆ **453-5060.** Reservations recommended weekends. Main courses 1,880kr–5,400kr. MC, V. Daily 11am–10pm.

Við Árbakkann CAFE/LIGHT FARE This casual roadside cafe with outdoor terrace seating gets a fair amount of Ring Road tourist traffic. Choices include a fine fish soup, meat and fish dinner specials, plus salads, sandwiches, bagels, waffles, and cakes.

Húnabraut 2. ✆ **452-4678.** Main courses 1,200kr–2,600kr; light meals 620kr–1,100kr. AE, MC, V. June 1–Sept 7 Sun–Thurs 11am–9pm, Fri–Sat 11am–3am.

SKAGASTRÖND

Kántrýbær TEXAN/ICELANDIC This saloon-style restaurant in remote Skagaströnd is the inspiration of Hallbjörn Hjartarson (p. 235), Iceland's avatar of all things country-and-western. The menu is more Icelandic with Texan twists than vice-versa, though Tex-Mex burgers, steak sandwiches, chicken fingers, and pecan or apple pie a la mode are hard to come by elsewhere. If you've already eaten, drop in for a beer adorned with Kántrýbær's custom label, and check out Hallbjörn's outlandish exhibit of C&W memorabilia—including his jackets with fringes and rhinestones to spare. The dance floor—country music only, of course!—opens up weekend nights in summer.

Hólanesvegur. ✆ **452-2829.** www.kantry.is. Main courses 1,100kr–2,990kr. AE, DC, MC, V. June 1–Aug 31 daily 11:30am–10pm.

SKAGAFJÖRÐUR

About 4,100 people live along this broad fjord or in the fertile valley at its head: Sauðarkrókur, 25km (16 miles) north of the Ring Road, is a likable coastal town with over half of the region's population. Near Sauðarkrókur, Glaumbær Folk Museum is the most engaging of Iceland's many 19th-century turf-roofed farmsteads. Inside the fjord are the strangely-shaped islands of Drangey and Málmey. Hólar, home to Iceland's northern bishop from 1106 to 1798, retains some vestiges of its former glory.

THE cowboy OF SKAGASTRÖND

The youngest of 16 children, Hallbjörn Hjartarson developed his mania for country music in the late 1950s, while working at the American military base in Keflavík. In 1963 he returned home to tiny Skagaströnd and, in 1983, after singing in various bands, founded Kántrýbær (Country Town), his restaurant, bar, radio studio, and all-around country-and-western shrine. (He lives across the street, and is rarely seen without a cowboy hat.) He has only visited the U.S. once—in 1988, to record an album in Nashville—but never ventured outside Tennessee. For several years he put on a C&W festival in Skagaströnd, complete with barn dancing, rodeo stunts, and can-shootin' competitions, but it's been on hiatus since 2002. Hallbjörn's 24-hour radio show, usually hosted live from 2 to 6pm and 8pm to midnight, airs on FM 96.7, 102.2, and 107.0; it can be heard from as far as Akureyri and the Strandir coast. On air he insists on thanking Johnny Cash, Dwight Yoakam, and other stars each time their music is played. The request line is ✆ **452-4774.** To listen online, visit www.kantry.is and find the "Útvarpið Á Netinu...Smelldu" link.

Hofsós, halfway up Skagafjörður's eastern shore, was a launch point for Icelandic emigrants to North America, and many of their descendants return there to visit the Emigration Museum and genealogical center. Siglufjörður, the most beautifully situated town in north Iceland, is 55km (35 miles) northeast of Hofsós: the main draws here are the Herring Era museum and the surrounding mountains. Skagafjörður is famous across Iceland for its horse breeding and horsemanship, and for adrenaline-seekers, the Eystri-Jökulsá is one of Iceland's fiercest rivers for white-water rafting.

Essentials

GETTING THERE

BY PLANE **Eagle Air** (✆ **562-2640;** www.eagleair.is) connects Reykjavík to Sauðarkrókur six times weekly from June until August (twice Tues and Thurs, once Fri and Sun). Check the website for information on the winter schedule. Flights are approximately 40 minutes and 11,700kr one-way.

BY CAR The Ring Road passes to the south of Skagafjörður's major sights. Route 75 meets the Ring Road at Varmahlíð—294km (183 miles) from Reykjavík and 94km (58 miles) from Akureyri—and proceeds north to the Glaumbær Folk Museum, Sauðarkrókur, and western Skagafjörður. From the Ring Road 5km (3 miles) east of Varmahlíð, Route 76 leads 97km (60 miles) to Siglufjörður, along the east side of Skagafjörður, past the roads to Hólar and Hofsós.

The only **car rental agency** in Sauðárkrókur is **National/Bílaleiga Akureyrar** (✆ **840-6079** and 461-6000; www.holdur.is).

BY BUS **Sterna** (✆ **551-1166;** www.sterna.is) runs at least one bus daily year-round between Reykjavík and Akureyri, stopping at Varmahlíð (twice daily during the summer). Reykjavík to Varmahlíð takes 5 hours and costs 8,100kr; Akureyri to Varmahlíð takes 85 minutes and costs 2,800kr. A bus between Varmahlíð and Sauðárkrókur runs at least twice daily, May to September, and is timed to connect with the Reykjavík–Akureyri bus. Another bus running between Sauðárkrókur and

Siglufjörður stops at Hólar and Hofsós and Fljót. Departures are every day but Saturday, from June until September, and are timed to connect with flights from Reykjavík. Always check their website before leaving.

VISITOR INFORMATION

Skagafjörður's tourist information office is in **Varmahlíð** (✆ **455-6161;** www.visitskagafjordur.is; June 1–June 15 daily 9am–5pm, June 16–Aug 15 daily 9am–7pm, Sept 1–May 31 daily 10am–3pm), in a turf-roofed building next to the N1 gas station, and has a free Internet terminal. The website **www.northwest.is** has good listings of local services. For Siglufjörður, tourist information is at the Herring Era museum (p. 241).

Exploring Skagafjörður

NEAR VARMAHLÍÐ

Glaumbær (Skagafjörður Folk Museum) ★★ Iceland has several museums inside preserved 19th-century turf buildings, and Glaumbær can be a good stand-in for all of them. These farmsteads are reminders of how dramatically Icelandic life has changed within a single lifespan. They are also vital repositories of cultural memory: with no coffeehouses or village squares, Icelanders were once homebound in residences such as this through long, dark winters.

Like most of the more prosperous farms of the time, Glaumbær has several buildings, constructed at different times but accessed from a central corridor. Aside from the usual fishskin shoes and toys made from animal bones, Glaumbær's more unique holdings include driftwood desks, primitive brainteasers, and a snuff box made of a whale tooth. For Icelanders, the most treasured piece is a basket allegedly made by Fjalla-Eyvindur, the beloved 18th-century outlaw. The near-waterproof basket, expertly woven from willow roots, is inside an unmarked glass case at the back of room #5. The church next door is worth a quick look to see the six disassembled panels from a 1685 Danish pulpit.

Áskaffi, in an adjoining 1886 clapboard house, serves hot drinks, cakes, sandwiches, old-fashioned pancakes, and *skyr* cake.

Rte. 75, between Varmahlíð and Sauðárkrókur. ✆ **453-6173.** www.glaumbaer.is. Admission 600kr adults, 300kr students, free for children aged 15 and under. June–Sept 10 daily 9am–6pm, other times by appointment.

Víðimýrarkirkja This 1834 church with wooden gables, turf roof, and thick sod walls has a simple, elemental quality that charms many visitors. The interior has little architectural detail to speak of, however, beyond some ornamental carving and closed pews up front for prominent families. The 1616 altar painting, probably Danish, is a Last Supper exhibiting the character exaggeration of folk art: Judas holds a moneybag. The pulpit is probably from the 17th century, but the paint has mostly worn off.

Off Rte. 1, 5km (3 miles) west of Varmahlíð. ✆ **453-5095.** Admission 400kr adults; free for children under 16. Daily 9am–6pm.

SAUÐARKRÓKUR ★

This town of 2,550 inhabitants is more than a convenient regional base with good dining and places to stay. It's also an agreeable base to come back to at the end of the day and enjoy an after-dinner stroll in the older part of town. Consider unwinding at the **town pool,** which has two large whirlpools (ask to have the bubbles turned on).

WHY BUILD A house WITH TURF?

By the mid-12th century, Iceland's climate had cooled considerably, and most of the country had been deforested. Turf housing became the norm and remained so even into the 20th century. Wood was scarce and expensive, and Icelanders roamed the coasts monogramming driftwood to claim it. Roof sod was supported by grids of flat stones and wood rafters. Icelandic grass, which is very thick, with enduring roots, held the turf together. A turf house could last as long as 100 years in areas with moderate rainfall. The roof slope was critical: too flat and it would leak, too steep and the grass would dry out. Glass was costly, too, so windows were often stretched animal skins or abdominal membranes. Turf construction lent itself to small rooms, maze-like interiors and easy lateral expansion, but required constant repair. Even the best turf house was leaky, damp, dark, cold, and unventilated, with lingering smoke from the burning of peat and dried manure. Sleeping quarters were often directly over the stables, to take advantage of the animals' body heat.

Gestastofa Sútarans Did you say fishleather? This tannery in Sauðárkrókur is the only tannery in Europe that makes fishleather. A guided tour of the tannery, where fishskin is processed to make high-quality leather costs 1,000kr. This unusual material has caught the imagination of internationally known fashion houses and brands such as Prada, Dior, and Nike. Leather and hides can also be bought directly from the tannery, but you might also find a variety of them dangling in tourist shops in Reykjavík. Tours of the tannery start at 2pm on weekdays or by arrangement.

Borgarmýri 5. ✆ **512-8025.** www.sutarinn.is. Admission 1,000kr June–Sept 15 Mon–Fri 11am–5pm, Sat 11am–3pm.

Minjahús The permanent exhibit features the outmoded workshops of a local blacksmith, watchmaker, carpenter, and several saddlers. Of more interest is the temporary exhibit, which lingers a few years. The current exhibit on regional archaeological digs does a fine job of imparting the thrill of discovery and explaining what can be deduced from artifacts. In addition, the Minjahús is the new home of a polar bear that in 2008 caught a ride with an iceberg and disembarked close to Sauðárkrókur only to meet its destiny.

Aðalgata 16b. ✆ **453-6870.** Free Admission. June–Aug 21 daily 1–6pm.

DRANGEY ★ & MÁLMEY ★

These two uninhabited, bird-rich islands—whose fantastical shapes look like artists' creations—make for an ideal joint tour. Drangey is surrounded by vertical cliffs reaching 180m (591 ft.). From a distance it appears cylindrical, but a closer look reveals strange contortions and indentations in the rock face. It's the ultimate fortress, and in *The Saga of Grettir the Strong* (aka *Grettis Saga*), one of Iceland's best-known legends, the outlaw Grettir spends the last three years of his life here. Sheep once grazed on Drangey's smooth top and had to be hoisted up and down with ropes. From the single landing spot, a steep path ascends to the top with ladders and cable handrails. Málmey is larger, with an elegant S-shaped contour, and reaches 156m (512 ft.) high. A family farm prospered here before burning down in 1950.

Jón Eiríksson, "the Earl of Drangey" (✆ **453-6503** or 846-8150; fagri@simnet.is), leads tours of both islands on request. Tours can leave from Sauðárkrókur, though he prefers setting off from Fagranes Farm or Reykir on Skagafjörður's west coast. The price is 7,000kr per person, but could be higher if the group numbers fewer than six. If you'd like to include fishing, let him know. Jón's English is limited; if you have trouble, call his daughter Ásta (✆ **453-6073**), who often leads the tours. If a tour with Jón doesn't work out, contact visitor information at Varmahlíð and ask them to find a guide in Hofsós.

GRETTISLAUG ★

In *Grettis Saga,* Grettir swims from Drangey to the western shore of Skagafjörður, where he bathes in a geothermal spring and then fetches some glowing embers to bring back to the island. In 1992, 962 years later, Jón Eiríksson built **Grettislaug,** a pool in open surroundings at Grettir's legendary bathing spot. An adjacent pool was added in 2006. Both are constructed with natural stones and remain at bathwater temperature. For a memorable swim at Grettislaug, drive north from Sauðárkrókur on Route 748 to the end of the road. The pools do not yet have toilets or changing rooms, and bathers are asked to contribute 500kr into a metal box.

Jón's house is close by, and uphill is a shed with a fluorescent tube over the door. This is Jón's homemade hydroelectric power station, which uses the stream toppling from the mountain 500m (1,640 ft.) away. On a clear day, you could walk further up the mountain for a view over the fjord.

HÓLAR ★

Hólar (✆ **455-6333;** free admission; all sites open daily 9am–6pm unless otherwise specified), also known as Hólar Í Hjaltadalur, was the northern seat of power in Iceland's Catholic era. Today's visitors see little direct connection to its bygone prestige, but the present cathedral **Hóladómkirkja** displays perhaps the best artifacts of any church in Iceland.

In 1056, Iceland's first Catholic bishop was installed at Skálholt in the southwest. Northern Icelanders complained he was too far away, and 50 years later a second diocese was added at Hólar. Just before the Reformation, the Hólar bishopric owned a 70-ton ship, invaluable manuscripts, stockpiles of gold and silver, and large holdings of land and livestock—all ripe for confiscation by the Danish king, who, like other European monarchs of the time, understood Protestantism would ease his financial problems. Hólar's last Catholic bishop, Jón Arason (1484–1550) was beheaded at Skálholt, after leading a rebellion against the king. Lutheran bishops remained at Hólar until 1798, when the two bishoprics were consolidated and relocated to Reykjavík. Hólar is now home to about 110 people and Hólaskóli, a small university with courses in equine sciences, rural tourism, and aquaculture.

Hólaskóli's main building holds a restaurant, pool, and guesthouse. In the lobby you'll find the free brochure *Hólar History Trail,* which lays out the nearby sights in walking tour format. **Nýibær** is a preserved 19th-century turf farmhouse, but it's empty and hardly worth visiting with Glaumbær (p. 236) so close by. **Auðun's House (Auðunarstofa)** is a reconstruction of a bishop's residence from the early 14th century, built in 2002 with only 14th-century building methods. A 13th-century chalice, vestments, and medieval manuscripts are stored in the basement, which may by now be open as an exhibit.

Built in 1763, the current cathedral, though large by Icelandic standards, is the smallest ever built at Hólar. It's also Iceland's oldest stone church, built with local red sandstone and basalt. The detached bell tower was consecrated in 1950; just inside the entrance is a 1957 mosaic of Jón Arason by the well-known contemporary artist Erró, then barely out of art school.

Inside the cathedral, a glass case holds a 1584 Bible, the first printing in Icelandic. A painting of a Hólar bishop, from 1620, is the oldest known portrait of any Icelander. On the side wall is a crucifix from the early 16th century. Its large size is uncharacteristic of Lutheran churches, and it's surprising to learn it was imported in the mid-17th century after the Reformation, probably from southern Europe. The 1674 baptismal font is made of soapstone, which—according to popular lore—drifted to Iceland on an ice floe from Greenland. More likely, it was imported from Norway.

The **altarpiece ★★**, made around 1500, is an impressive, painted wooden sculpture depicting the Crucifixion story with apostles and saints on the wings. Jón Arason bought the piece in Holland, though it's thought to be German. Both side panels swivel inward, revealing paintings on their back sides; on the right side, St. Sebastian spurts blood from several arrow wounds, while St. Lucy is indifferent to a sword through her neck. Make sure to ask the attendant to draw out these back panels for you. An even older English altarpiece, from Nottingham, made of alabaster and also in sculpted storybook form, hangs over the side entrance.

An attendant is always on hand for questions, but tours (300kr) are only given for groups; so call ahead. A concert series is held in the cathedral from June to August, and the schedule is posted online at www.kirkjan.is/holar, but only in Icelandic. Evening prayers are at 6pm Monday to Saturday, and Sunday services are at 11am. A single Catholic ceremony is held each summer.

HOFSÓS & NEARBY

Hofsós, a trading post dating back to the 16th century, has maintained its throwback feel by preserving some of its 18th-century buildings and replicating others. Built in 2010, the new swimming pool in Hofsós (☺ 🎁 ✆ **455-6070;** admission 380kr adults, 180kr children aged 6–16; open Mon–Fri 9:15am–9:15pm, Sat–Sun 10:15am–7:15pm), sits on the cliff tops, with superb views of the fjord and Mount Tindastóll. Whilst swimming you feel like you could swim directly to the Islands in the fjord.

Icelandic Emigration Center (Vesturfarasetrið) North Americans of Icelandic descent often head straight for this museum and genealogical research facility, founded in 1996 and spread across three buildings. The permanent *New Land, New Life* exhibit details Icelandic emigration in the late-19th and early-20th centuries, including the fate of various settlements from Utah to Brazil. (In "New Iceland," a settlement founded in 1875 on Lake Winnipeg, Manitoba, many older people still speak Icelandic as a first language.) By 1914, 15,000 Icelanders—almost 20% of the population—had left for the New World. A temporary exhibit takes on a specific emigration sub-theme. Visitors researching their family roots should contact the museum in advance at hofsos@hofsos.is; general inquiries are free, and more intensive archival research can be hired at an hourly rate.

✆ **453-7935.** www.hofsos.is. Admission 1,500kr adults for all three exhibits, or 700kr for individual; 1,200kr for seniors; free for children under 12; free admission for genealogy room. Jun–Aug daily 11am–6pm; other times by arrangement.

Skagafjörður Transportation Museum (Samgönguminjasafn) Located off Route 76, about 12km (7½ miles) south of Hofsós at Stóragerði Farm, this is basically a vintage car collection, and 75% of visitors are "car guys" asking to peek under the hoods. The range of models is impressive. The owner's favorite is a huge, white, 1947 modified Chevy pickup.

✆ **845-7400.** Admission 700kr adults; free for children under 11. Mid-June to Sept daily 11am–6pm.

FLJÓT ★★

Just 30 km (19 miles) northeast of Hofsós on the coast road to Siglufjörður (Route 76) is one of Iceland's best-kept secrets. Sparsely populated Fljót is the northernmost settlement in Skagafjörður and certainly stunning across all seasons. In the summer the wild Icelandic flowers still reign and green pastures contrast perfectly with the snow-capped, convoluted mountains of Tröllaskagi. The valley is divided by one of Iceland's best fishing rivers, Fljótaá, where the salmon are so superior the rights to fish in it were snapped up quickly by a fishing club in Siglufjörður. The abundant snowfall in the winter transforms the area into a wonderland of snow illuminated with hues of purple, pink, and gold by the winter sun. The stars and northern lights are much clearer in this area because of its northerly location.

Ask at **Bjarnargil** (p. 243) about places to explore, including: Stiflavatn, Haganesvik, and day hikes to Siglufjörður,Ólafsfjörður, and Hólar; but don't forget either to ask about the legend of Blákápa or the history of Hrafnaflóki. There's a filling station and small grocery store, **Ketilás** (✆ **467-1000**), at the junction of Route 76/82.

SIGLUFJÖRÐUR ★★

Lovingly dubbed 'Sigló' by the locals, the impossibly picturesque town of Siglufjörður, with a steady population of 1,300, was for many years only accessible by a single road that winds along a pretty stretch of remote coastline. In December 2010 a tunnel east to Ólafsfjörður increased access to Siglufjörður, also cutting two hours off the road trip to Akureyri. Visitors experience disbelief that such an established community would be deposited here, inside a short, steep-sided fjord less than 40km (25 miles) from the Arctic Circle.

Siglufjörður, which still runs on fish, was a herring-boom town in the early- and mid-20th century. During the town's herring heyday, hundreds of ships were docked, and hordes of girls came for the summer to gut, salt, and pack the fish in barrels for export. Herring populations plummeted after World War II, because of overfishing aided by sonar equipment, and, in 1969, the herring failed to show up entirely. Since then, thanks to better management, numbers have largely recovered.

A walk around the docks is a good window on the fishing life. Any pungent odor emanating from the fish factory is what Icelanders call "the smell of money." The town has preserved its older buildings well, and its faded glory is worn gracefully.

Besides strolling around town, or perhaps a round on the **nine-hole golf course,** the main activities for visitors are the **Herring Era Museum** and the fine hiking nearby. From July to the first week in August, you might time your visit for a Saturday, when **herring-salting demonstrations** are presented at 3pm, complete with costumes, song, dance, and accordions. Tickets are 1,200kr and include museum admission. On the first weekend of August, a celebratory holiday across the country, Siglufjörður draws hundreds of visitors for its nostalgic **Herring Adventure Festival**, with musical performances, family entertainment and yet more fish preparation demos. In early July, a 5-day **folk music festival** (www.siglo.is/festival) includes workshops as well as concerts day and night by Icelandic and international artists.

The Siglufjörður area offers several first-rate **hiking routes.** Avid hikers can sustain themselves for two full-day trips, one to the west of the fjord and one to the east. Routes are listed at http://www.fjallabyggd.is/is/page/gonguleidir (not translated into English).

The excellent and widely-available trail map *Gönguleiðir á Tröllaskaga II: Fljót, Siglufjörður, Ólafsfjörður, Svarfaðardalur* has no descriptions in English, but you can still deduce estimated walking times and altitudes. A short hike on the fjord's eastern shore leads to the Evanger herring factory, destroyed by an avalanche in 1919. Two routes head east overland to Héðinsfjörður, a wild and beautiful fjord abandoned in 1951; the shorter route is at least 4 hours one-way. A popular hike follows the old road leading west through the 630m (2,067 ft.) Siglufjörðarskarð Pass; this road is usually free of snowdrifts and passable in 4WD vehicles from early July to late August. Instead of taking the full 15km (9-mile) route one-way, and having to arrange transportation back, you could cut north along the ridge and then descend into town in a strenuous but very rewarding 6–7 hour loop.

Folk Musik Center (Þjóðlagasetur) This museum inside the home of a late 19th-century reverend and folk music collector features unique Icelandic instruments and videos of traditional musical, from *rímur* chanting to nursery rhymes. Concerts are held Saturday evenings in July and August.

Norðurgata 1. ✆ **467-2300.** www.folkmusik.is. Admission 600kr adults; free for children under 16. June 20–Aug 20 daily 10am–6pm, June 1–June 19 and Aug 21–Aug 31 daily 1–5pm.

Herring Era Museum (Síldarminjasafnið) If a museum about herring sounds faintly ridiculous, keep in mind that the herring trade was for Icelanders what the California Gold Rush was for Americans. At various times herring alone accounted for more than a quarter of Iceland's export income, and Siglufjörður was the country's largest herring production base. This award-winning, ambitious museum is spread across three buildings; one replicates an entire 1950s quayside, complete with 9 herring vessels of various types and sizes, and another reconstructs a processing factory for herring meal and oil. Most affecting are the old living quarters for the herring girls; with tiny beds that each slept two. Information posted in English increases every year, and the staff is very helpful and informative. The admission fee here includes access to the Folk Musik Center and the Ura Museum (a watch and silversmith workshop).

Snorragata 15. ✆ **467-1604.** www.sild.is. Admission 1,200kr adults; 600kr seniors and for ages 16–20; free for children under 16. Mid-June to Aug 20 daily 10am–6pm; May 15–June 15 and Aug 21–Sept 15 daily 1–5pm.

Outdoor Activities

HORSEBACK RIDING The three farms below offer lessons and short rides as well as multi-day adventures for all ability levels. In September you can participate in round-ups (p. 36), retrieving sheep and horses that have run wild in the highlands all summer; all-night parties follow. Dates are posted at www.northwest.is.

Flugumýri (✆ **453-8814;** www.flugumyri.com), on Route 76, 3km (2 miles) off the Ring Road, presents exhibitions for groups, showing off the talents of the Icelandic horse; call ahead, and, if an exhibition is scheduled, you can sign up for 2,500kr, including coffee and cake.

Hestasport (✆ **453-8383;** www.riding.is), a respected outfit just outside Varmahlíð, has several good route options for summer including the Hofsós and Hólar area, the Kjölur Route (p. 367) through the interior to Gullfoss and Geysir, and local sheep round-ups. This company also offers winter tours with snowmobiling and skiing options.

Lýtingsstaðir (✆ **453-8064;** www.lythorse.com; lythorse@simnet.is), on Route 752, 20km (12 miles) south of Varmahlíð, has a good range of highland tours, including horse and sheep round-ups. The tours vary in length and theme depending on the time of year; the longer tours include full board and accommodation. They also have horses for sale.

RIVER RAFTING The rivers feeding Skagafjörður provide the best river rafting in North Iceland. The Eystri-Jökulsá has difficult class III and IV+ rapids, while the Vestari-Jökulsá has easier class II rapids, as well as a cliff-jumping ledge and a hot spring (where rafters gather to make cocoa).

Activity Tours (✆ **453-8383;** www.activitytours.is), affiliated with the horse tour company Hestasport (above), is the best operator. It also offers super-tame trips on the Blanda River (ages 6 and up), and an exciting 3-day adventure down the Eystri-Jökulsá, starting deep within the desert interior. The Eystri-Jökulsá trip lasts 6–7 hours and costs around 12,900kr all-inclusive, with a minimum age of 18. The Vestari-Jökulsá trip lasts 4–5 hours and costs about 7,900kr, minimum age 12. Trips run from May to early October.

Where to Stay

The best backup source for accommodation is Icelandic Farm Holidays (✆ **570-2700;** www.farmholidays.is), which has several member farms in the Skagafjörður Valley south of the Ring Road. Also try the tourist information office at Varmahlíð.

VARMAHLÍÐ

Flugumýri This budget-friendly horse farm has three basic, agreeable bedrooms sharing a bathroom, guest kitchen, and TV room; plenty of occupants are non-equestrians. A small apartment is also available for rent.

Rte. 76, 3km (2 miles) off the Ring Road. ✆ **453-8814**/fax 453-8814. www.flugumyri.com. 5 units, none w/bathroom. 12,000kr double. Rates 10% lower Oct–Apr. Rates include breakfast. MC, V. **Amenities:** Guest kitchen. *In room:* No phone.

Hestasport Cottages These fetching, spacious, woody cottages are clustered around a stone-lined hot tub. The cottages, which vary in size and may accommodate up to seven, are particularly convenient for families or large parties.

Varmahlíð, just off the Ring Road. ✆ **453-8383.** Fax 453-8384. www.riding.is. 5 cottages. June–Sept 18,000kr double; 3,000kr each additional person in same cottage. Rates around 30% lower Oct–May. Breakfast available (1,500kr). MC, V. **Amenities:** Hot tub. *In room:* Kitchenette, no phone.

Hótel Varmahlíð This convenient stopover for those passing through on the Ring Road offers spacious, nondescript en suite rooms and a good **restaurant** (see "Where to Dine," below). Anyone actually exploring the area, however, would probably be better served by a stay in Sauðarkrókur.

Rte. 1. ✆ **453-8170.** Fax 453-8870. www.hotelvarmahlid.is. 19 units. May–Sept 23,900kr double; 32,500kr family room. Rates around 30% lower May–June 14 and Sept; around 45% lower Oct–Apr. Rates include breakfast. AE, DC, MC, V. **Amenities:** Restaurant. *In room:* TV, hair dryer, Wi-Fi.

SAUÐÁRKRÓKUR

Hótel Mikligarður This large summer-only hotel is a school dormitory during the school year—it's hard to miss as it resembles a stack of bright orange Lego blocks. It has ample lounge space and the rooms are warm and bright. The location is quiet, but not far (1km/ 1/2 mile) from the shops or the inviting, older part of town.

Skagfirdingabraut (by Sæmundarhlíð). ✆ **453-6880.** www.mikligardur.is; mikligardur@mikligardur.is 65 units, 61 w/bathroom. June–Aug 18,000kr double; 5,000kr sleeping-bag accommodation. Rates include breakfast. AE, DC, MC, V. Closed Sept–May. **Amenities:** Restaurant; bar; Internet terminal. *In room:* No phone, Wi-Fi.

Hótel Tindastóll ★★ Compared to the rest of Europe, Icelandic hotels outside Reykjavík are rather antiseptic and featureless, with every furnishing conspicuously mass-produced. Tindastóll, a distinctive, characterful, old-fashioned hotel, gets extra kudos just for being different. The building is an 1884 Norwegian kit home, with many original beams intact and sea-stone walls lining the atmospheric downstairs bar-lounge. Rooms are dominated by natural wood. Deluxe doubles have a DVD player and more space, with room for extra beds. Bathrobes come standard for the round, natural-stone hot pool in back. Guests can get a 10% discount at **Þrek Sport** the local health club (a short distance away), which includes massage, solarium, and hair salon.

Lindargata 3. ✆ **453-5002.** Fax 453-5388. www.hoteltindastoll.com. 11 units. June–Aug 24,400kr double. Rates 10–30% lower May and Sept; 20–40% lower Oct–Apr. Rates include breakfast. AE, DC, MC, V. **Amenities:** Bar; hot tub. *In room:* TV, hair dryer, Wi-Fi.

Guesthouse Mikligarður This well-managed guesthouse is ideally located just off the central church square. Rooms #13 and #14 face east so the sun can be a problem when it comes up at 3am in June and July. The choice rooms are #1 (with bathroom), or #5, #8, and #9, without. Sleeping-bag accommodation is available off season.

Kirkjutorg 3. ✆ **453-6880.** www.skagafjordur.com/mikligardur. 14 units, 2 w/bathroom. May 1–Sept 30 18,000kr double w/bathroom; 14,000kr double without bathroom; 17,000kr triple without bathroom. Rates 5%–20% lower Sept 16–May 14. Rates include breakfast (May 15–Sept 15 only). AE, DC, MC, V. **Amenities:** Guest kitchen. *In room:* TV, No phone, Wi-Fi.

HOFSÓS

If researching your family tree keeps you in Hofsós overnight, the **Icelandic Emigration Center** (p. 239) can find you accommodation. **Gistiheimilið Sunnuberg,** Suðurbraut 8 (✆ **453-7310;** June–Aug 11,000kr double; Sept–May 6,600kr double) has five acceptable rooms with private bathroom. **Lónkot,** 13km (8 miles) north of Hofsós, does not have private bathrooms but is a nicer place to stay, with beds going for 5,500kr per person; see "Where to Dine," below.

FLJÓT

Bjarnargil Guesthouse Located 2km (1 mile) along Route 82 just off Route 76, this modest home accommodation is run by an exceptionally lovely pair named Sibba and Trausti, and is the only guesthouse in the area. The summer nights are pleasant, with an exceptional view of the midnight sun. Guests are invited to share their travel experiences over dinner (served on request), sometimes cooked in a turf oven in the garden. The owners can also help arrange hiking and fishing trips.

Fljót. ✆ **467-1030.** Fax 467-1077. www.northwest.is. 6 units, none w/bathroom. June 15–Aug 31 4,500kr made-up beds. *In room:* No phone, Wi-Fi.

SIGLUFJÖRÐUR

Hvanneyri Guesthouse This hotel-sized guesthouse is not particularly fashionable or up-to-date, but the rooms are warm and welcoming enough. You may even find the dated lounge furniture and satiny bedspreads endearing.

Aðalgata 10. ✆ **467-1506.** Fax 467-1526. www.hvanneyri.com. 19 units, 1 w/bathroom. May 15–Sept 15 9,600kr double without bathroom; 12,600kr triple without bathroom; 16,000kr suite; 3,100kr per person sleeping-bag accommodation. Rates include breakfast (May 15–June 15 only). AE, DC, MC, V. **Amenities:** Guest kitchen. *In room:* TV, no phone, Wi-Fi.

Where to Dine

VARMAHLÍÐ

The **N1 filling station** on the Ring Road, open daily to 9pm, is a step up from the usual pit-stop cafeteria, with lamb chops and fish dishes as well as burgers and hot-dogs.

Hótel Varmahlíð ★ ICELANDIC Inside a white hotel easily spotted from the Ring Road, this restaurant is committed to fresh, local, and environmentally-friendly ingredients. The manager is married to a farmer, and the lamb comes fresh from their own flock.

Rte. 1. ✆ **453-8170.** Main courses 3,350kr–4,500kr. AE, DC, MC, V. June–Aug daily 6–9:30pm; May and Sept daily 7–9pm; Oct–Apr (by request in advance).

SAUÐÁRKRÓKUR

The bakery, **Sauðárkróksbakari,** Aðalgata 5 (✆ **455-5000;** Jun–Aug 7am–6pm, Sept–May 8am–4pm), is perfect for breakfast, a soup and sandwich lunch or a pastry: try the chocolate cake with coconut sprinkles.

Kaffi Krókur ★ ICELANDIC This restaurant-bar is in an 1887 house across the street from Ólafshús, and the dishes include pan-fried lamb and fish. The most popular options are the puffin and the lobster/shrimp sandwiches. It's closed during the winter apart from Friday/Saturday, when it opens as a bar from 9pm–3am.

Aðalgata 16b, Sauðárkrókur. ✆ **453-6299.** Main courses 1,190kr–2,690kr. AE, DC, MC, V. June–Aug daily 11:30am–11:00pm.

Ólafshús ★ ICELANDIC This unpretentious, reliable restaurant in the old town is popular among local families. Main courses include all-you-can-eat at the soup and salad bar. If you can bear it, this is a good time to try foal, which is almost indistinguishable from beef but harder to overcook. It's served here with mushroom sauce, leeks, and grapes. If not, stick with the fish, lamb, pizzas, or BBQ ribs.

Aðalgata 15. ✆ **453-6454.** Main courses 770kr–2,770kr. AE, DC, MC, V. June–Aug Sun–Thurs 11am–2pm and 5:30–10:30pm, Fri–Sat 11am–11pm; Sept–May daily 11am–2pm and 5:30–10pm.

HOFSÓS & NEARBY

Within the village, your choices are **Solvík** (✆ **453-7930;** June 1–Aug 31 daily 11am–9pm) a pleasant, summer-only restaurant-cafe next to the Emigration Center.

Lónkot ★ ICELANDIC Lónkot is a worthwhile dinner destination from anywhere in Skagafjörður, especially because it's on the fjord north of Hofsós, where you'd never expect to find a gourmet restaurant. If you pass through by day, stop for coffee or snacks in the viewing tower, a converted silo overlooking the fjord. The set dinner menu, usually around 4,500kr, is based on whatever's fresh and available; call ahead to see if it appeals. Chef's specials include puffin, marinated cod, lamb, trout, and ice-cream made with wild violets. Lónkot also has a charming **guesthouse,** and a nine-hole golf course.

Rte. 76, 11km (7 miles) north of Hofsós. ✆ **453-7432** or 848-2182. Reservations recommended for dinner. AE, DC, MC, V. Jun–Sept 15 8am–midnight; kitchen closes at 10pm.

SIGLUFJÖRÐUR

The latest culinary delight of Siglufjörður is **Hannes Boy Café** Gránugata 23 (✆ **461-7730;** AE, DC, MC, V; June–Aug Sun–Thurs 11:30am–10pm, Fri–Sat 11:30am–11pm) a restaurant inspired by the herring fishing tradition of Siglufjörður. It focuses on herring and seafood dishes (freshly caught in the area), but also has very good lamb plus an unusual, but tasty, pork belly and langoustine combo; the lobster soup is also very good! The specially-designed furniture, with an old herring barrel theme, is a nice touch.

The bakery **Aðalbakari,** Aðalgata 36 (✆ **467-1720;** MC, V; daily 7am–5pm), serves breakfast and lunch, with sandwiches, pastries, and cakes. **Torgið,** Aðalgata 32 (✆ **467-2323;** AE, DC, MC, V; June–Sept daily 11am–10pm; Oct–May daily 5–9pm) is a fun Reykjavík-based chain that serves salads, burgers, fish, pizza, and chicken. The restaurant **Allin** complete with stage, was once a movie house (said to be the first ever in Iceland), and can seat 200 people. Aðalgata 30 (✆ **467-1111;** MC, V. Daily 11am–9pm). It has well-priced pizza, burgers, fish, and lamb, and is also the best local bar.

AKUREYRI

Nestled at the head of Eyjafjörður, Iceland's longest fjord, **Akureyri** ★ is north Iceland's largest fishing port, and its cultural, industrial, and trade hub. It's often called Iceland's "second city," but residents don't seem to take this the wrong way. Akureyri has only 17,000 people, so just reaching the status of "city" is an unrivaled achievement outside the Reykjavík metropolitan area. (Technically, Akureyri is Iceland's fourth-largest city, after the Reykjavík suburbs of Kópavogur and Hafnarfjörður.) Akureyri is a sophisticated and thriving place, and Akureyrians boast of their superior weather, warmer and drier than drizzly Reykjavík in summer, with more frost and snow in the winter. You can't help feeling anything but admiration for the town; even the experience of waiting at traffic signals has been turned into an attraction, with love-heart-shaped red lights.

Akureyri's first known settler was Helgi the Lean, who arrived around 890. By 1602 it was an active trading post, and by 1900 had 1,370 residents. The trade cooperative KEA, formed in 1886, still owns large shares of several Eyjafjörður businesses, and in 1915 Akureyri had the country's first social-democratic government. The University of Akureyri, established in 1987, is the only state-run university outside of Reykjavík.

Akureyri sees about 180,000 visitors a year, and has no shortage of restaurants and museums. The annual Summer Arts Festival, which includes concerts, exhibitions, dance, and plays, lasts from mid-June to late August, with a street party finale.

Essentials

GETTING THERE & AROUND

Akureyri is on Route 1 (the Ring Road), 388km (241 miles) from Reykjavík and 265km (165 miles) from Egilsstaðir. The downtown, clustered around Hafnarstræti, with Ráðhústorg Square at its northern end, is easily navigable **on foot.** Much of Akureyri is spread along a steep incline, however, so a car is helpful. Akureyri's one bike rental company has closed; check with tourist information to see if it's been replaced.

Akureyri

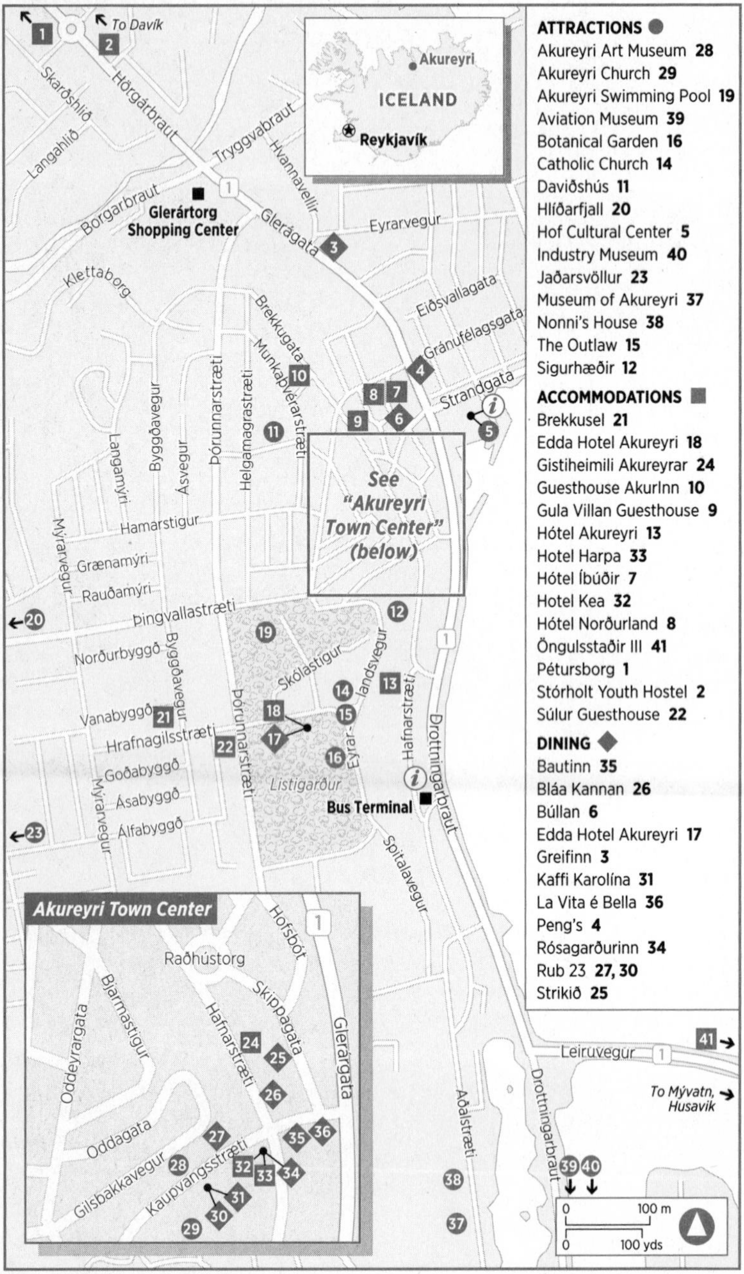
ATTRACTIONS
Akureyri Art Museum 28
Akureyri Church 29
Akureyri Swimming Pool 19
Aviation Museum 39
Botanical Garden 16
Catholic Church 14
Daviðshús 11
Hlíðarfjall 20
Hof Cultural Center 5
Industry Museum 40
Jaðarsvöllur 23
Museum of Akureyri 37
Nonni's House 38
The Outlaw 15
Sigurhæðir 12
ACCOMMODATIONS
Brekkusel 21
Edda Hotel Akureyri 18
Gistiheimili Akureyrar 24
Guesthouse AkurInn 10
Gula Villan Guesthouse 9
Hótel Akureyri 13
Hotel Harpa 33
Hótel Íbúðir 7
Hotel Kea 32
Hótel Norðurland 8
Öngulsstaðir III 41
Pétursborg 1
Stórholt Youth Hostel 2
Súlur Guesthouse 22
DINING
Bautinn 35
Bláa Kannan 26
Búllan 6
Edda Hotel Akureyri 17
Greifinn 3
Kaffi Karolína 31
La Vita é Bella 36
Peng's 4
Rósagarðurinn 34
Rub 23 27, 30
Strikið 25
ICELAND
Akureyri
Reykjavík
To Davík
Glerártorg Shopping Center
See "Akureyri Town Center" (below)
Akureyri Town Center
Bus Terminal
Listigarður
To Mývatn, Husavík
0 100 m
0 100 yds
Skarðshlíð
Hörgárbraut
Langahlíð
Tryggvabraut
Hvannavellir
Borgarbraut
Glerágata
Eyrarvegur
Klettaborg
Brekkugata
Munkaþverárstræti
Eiðsvallagata
Gránufélagsgata
Strandgata
Þórunnarstræti
Helgamagrastræti
Byggðavegur
Ásvegur
Langamýri
Hamarstigur
Mýrarvegur
Grænamýri
Rauðamýri
Þingvallastræti
Norðurbyggð
Skólastígur
Eyrarlandsvegur
Hafnarstræti
Drottningarbraut
Vanabyggð
Hrafnagilsstræti
Goðabyggð
Ásabyggð
Álfabyggð
Spítalavegur
Hofsbót
Raðhústorg
Skipagata
Bjarmastígur
Oddeyrargata
Glerárgata
Oddagata
Gilsbakkavegur
Kaupvangsstræti
Leiruvegur
Aðalstræti

BSO taxi (© **461-1010**) is on call 24 hours and operates a **taxi stand** on Strandgata at Hofsbót, with at least one wheelchair-accessible car.

BY PLANE **Air Iceland** (© **460-7000;** www.airiceland.is) has eight 45-minute flights daily between Reykjavík and Akureyri. One-way tickets average 9,600kr, but go as high as 14,630kr and as low as 5,990kr with early booking online. From Akureyri, direct flights go to Vopnafjörður and Grímsey Island; all other destinations are routed through Reykjavík. From June until August, **Iceland Express** (© **550-0600;** www.icelandexpress.com) has a weekly flight to Copenhagen. Akureyri Airport (AEY) is on the Ring Road, 3km (2 miles) south of town.

BY CAR Rental agencies at the airport are **Budget** (© **562-6060;** www.budget.is), **Avis** (© **824-4010;** www.avis.is), **Europcar** (© **461-6000;** www.europcar.is), **Hertz** (© **522-4440;** www.hertz.is), and **Bílaleiga Akureyrar** (© **461-6000;** www.holdur.is), which has another office at Tryggvabraut 12. All agencies should offer to pick you up anywhere in town. If you rent in Akureyri and leave the car in Reykjavík, the dropoff fee will likely be 8,000kr to 10,000kr.

Parking—clustered along Skipagata, one block east of the pedestrian-only stretch of Hafnarstræti—is free, but during working hours you need to dash into a store or bank and ask for a "parking disc," a windshield sticker with attached clock hands. Signs indicate how long the parking spot is good for, from 15 minutes to 2 hours. Set the clock hands ahead to the time the spot expires. You can park all day if you keep returning to the car to reset the disc.

BY BUS Sterna (© **550-3737;** www.sterna.is) connects Reykjavík and Akureyri twice daily in summer via the Ring Road (6 hr.; 10,400kr), and once daily via the Kjölur interior route (10 hours; 11,400kr). Sterna also has daily summer connections between Akureyri and Dalvík (45 min.; 1,600kr), and Egilsstaðir (4 hours; 7,300kr).

SBA-Norðurleid (© **550-0700;** www.sba.is) includes sightseeing stops in its routes, often with guides. One bus connects Reykjavík and Akureyri daily in summer through the Kjölur route (9 hours; 8,600kr), with brief stops at Geysir, Gullfoss, and Hveravellir. Other daily summer routes connect Akureyri to Mývatn, Húsavík, and Jökulsárgljúfur Park in various combinations. The winter tour to Mývatn is 10,000kr, where the snow and frost transforms the lake into a scene from a fairytale.

Buses within Akureyri are free—yes, free—with four routes (numbered 1, 2, 3, 4) that run hourly on weekdays from 6am to as late as 10:30pm. No buses run on weekends or holidays. All routes leave from Ráðhústorg Square, by the shop named *Nætursalan.* No routes go to the airport. For schedule and route information, pick up a brochure at the tourist information office, call © **462-4929,** or visit www.akureyri.is/ferdamenn/samgongur/straetisvagnar.

VISITOR INFORMATION

The very competent **tourist information office** (© **553-5999;** www.visitakureyri.is or www.nordurland.is; June 15–Sept 6 Mon–Fri 7:30am–7pm) is in the new **Hof Cultural Center** (p. 253) at Strandgata 12, a five-minute walk east from Ráðhústorg Square. The office is useful for all of north Iceland, and the staff will find and book places to stay for a 500kr fee.

Anyone planning a hiking adventure in north Iceland or the interior can buy maps and get free advice from the local hiking club, **Ferðafélag Akureyrar,** Strandgata 23 (© **462-2720;** www.ffa.is; ffa@ffa.is; June–Aug Mon–Thurs 3–7pm, Fri 4–7pm;

Feb–May Fri 4–7pm). This is also where to register your itinerary, so that if you don't return, they'll know where to come looking for you.

[FastFACTS] AKUREYRI

Banks/Currency Exchange Banks are generally open weekdays from 9:15am to 4pm and have commission-free currency exchange and 24-hour ATMs. The main bank is **Landsbanki** (✆ **460-4000**) at Strandgata 1, open weekdays from 9am to 4pm. Hótel KEA exchanges currency but charges an outrageous 10% commission.

Cellphones For thorough information, see p. 59. Phones and calling plans are available at **Síminn,** (✆ **800-7000**), Nova (✆ **519-1000**), or **Vodafone,** (✆ **599-9000**) all located in the Glerátorg Mall, open: Mon–Fri 10am–6:30pm, Sat 10am–5pm, Sun 1–5pm.

Doctors & Dentists see "Medical Help," below.

Drugstores **Apótekarinn** (✆ **460-3456;** Mon–Fri 9am–5:30pm) is downtown at Hafnarstræti 95. Drugstores with extended hours are **Apótekið,** Furuvellir 17, Hagkaup Market (✆ **461-3920;** Mon–Fri 10am–7pm, Sat 10am–4pm, Sun noon–4pm) and **Lyf & heilsa,** Glerártorg Mall (✆ **461-5800;** Mon–Fri 10am–6:30pm, Sat 10am–5pm, Sun 1–5pm).

Emergencies Dial ✆ **112** for ambulance, fire, or police. See also "Medical Help," below.

Hospitals See "Medical Help," below.

Internet Access **Akureyri Library** (see "Libraries," below), has multiple terminals, a cafe, and the best price (300kr per hour). The **tourist information office** (see "Visitor Information," above) has two terminals for 150kr every 15 minutes. Both places, plus several cafes and the Penninn bookstore/cafe (Hafnarstræti 91-93), are **Wi-Fi hot spots.**

Laundry **Þvottahúsið Höfði,** Hafnarstræti 34 (✆ **462-2580;** Mon–Fri 8am–6pm), a full-service laundry, 2,500kr for up to 5kg/11 lb.

Libraries **Akureyri Library,** Brekkugata 17 (✆ **460-1250;** June–Sept Mon–Fri 10am–7pm; Sept–May Mon–Fri 10am–7pm, Sat 12am–5pm), has cheap Internet access and a decent collection of English-language books and magazines; tourists can borrow books for free.

Lost & Found See "Police," below.

Luggage Storage The **tourist information office** (see "Visitor Information," above) can hold bags for up to one night, but does not have a secure room.

Mail See "Post Office," below.

Medical Help For an ambulance, call ✆ **112. Akureyri Hospital** (Spítalavegur, by Eyrarlandsvegur; main number ✆ **463-0100,** emergency room ✆ **463-0800,** 24-hour telephone service, consultation ✆ **848-2600;** Mon–Fri 5am–9pm, Sat–Sun 7am–noon and 2–4pm) is just south of the botanical garden. **Heilsugæslustöðin Clinic,** Hafnarstræti 99 (✆ **460-4600;** daily 8am–4pm), is downtown.

Pharmacies See "Drugstores," above.

Police For emergencies, dial ✆ **112.** The police station (✆ **464-7700**) is at Þórunnarstræti 138.

Post Office/Mail The **post office** (✆ **580-1000;** Mon–Fri 9am–6:00pm) is at Standgata 3, in the middle of the city.

Supermarkets Supermarkets include **Bónus** (Langhólt 1), **Haugkaup** (Furuvellir, near Hjalteyrargata), and **Nettó** (Glerártorg Mall). Supermarkets open late include **10-11** (Þingvallastræti at Mýrarvegur; 24 hours), **Samkaup Strax** (Borgarbraut at Hlíðarbraut; 24 hours), and another **Samkaup Strax** (Byggðavegur at Hrafnagilsstræti; Mon–Fri

9am–11pm; Sat–Sun 10am–11pm).

Taxis See "Getting There & Around," above.

Telephone Public phones are available at the **tourist information office** (see "Visitor Information," above), **Akureyri Hospital** (see "Medical Help," above), Spítalavegur (by Eyrarlandsvegur), the **city pool** (p. 256), and the **Penninn Eymundsson** bookstore on Hafnarstræti 91–93. See also "Cellphones," above.

Where to Stay

EXPENSIVE

Hótel Akureyri ★ Ideally located a short walk from downtown, and right across from the tourist information office, this hotel isn't aiming for much character distinction; but rooms feel sumptuous, and the staff is obliging. Rooms facing the fjord are booked out first. Breakfast gets extra credit for the waffle iron and whipped cream. Hótel Akureyri also offers six snazzy apartments with kitchens, sleeping five to 10 people. ***Note:*** The hotel has four floors but only stairs.

Hafnarstræti 67. ✆ **462-5600.** Fax 462-5601. www.hotelakureyri.is. 19 units, 6 apts. May–Sept 22,700kr double; 32,300kr apt. Rates around 25% lower Oct–Apr. Rates include breakfast, except apts. AE, DC, MC, V. *In room:* TV, fridge, Wi-Fi.

Hótel Harpa The plain but upstanding Hótel Harpa shares management with the glitzy Hótel Kea next door, and Harpa's high prices reflect the shared service and amenities. Harpa's rooms are bright and renovated but much less smartly-appointed. The one "superior" double has extra space, and a bathtub.

Hafnarstræti 83–85. ✆ **460-2000.** Fax 460-2060. www.keahotels.is. 25 units. June–Aug 23,000kr double; 30,300kr triple. Rates 20% lower May and Sept; 30% lower Oct–Apr. Rates include breakfast. AE, DC, MC, V. **Amenities:** Restaurant; bar; room service; same-day laundry/dry-cleaning service; Wi-Fi in lobby. *In room:* TV, hair dryer, pay Internet (via cable).

Hótel Kea ★★ Built in 1944—and clearly tops in town—this central, four-star hotel presides over the base of the long stairway to Akureyri Church. Renovations in 2006 added handsome dark-wood furnishings and plush beds but bypassed the small bathrooms. Some 4th floor rooms open on to a large balcony. "Superior" doubles on the 5th floor have great views, big TVs, and nice bathrooms but not much more space.

Hafnarstræti 87–89. ✆ **460-2000.** Fax 460-2060. www.keahotels.is. 74 units. June–Aug 27,500kr double; 35,800kr triple. Rates around 20% lower May and Sept, 30% lower Oct–Apr. Rates include breakfast. AE, DC, MC, V. **Amenities:** Restaurant; bar; room service, Wi-Fi in lobby. *In room:* TV, minibar, hair dryer, pay Internet (via cable).

Hótel Norðurland Norðurland is in the same chain as the Harpa and Kea, and is equally central. Rooms are well-appointed but a bit dated, spiritless, and small, with tiny TVs. Four rooms have balconies with an unremarkable view over the street. "Superior" doubles on the second floor get you more space.

Geislagata 7. ✆ **462-2600.** Fax 462-2601. www.keahotels.is. 34 units. June–Aug 23,400kr double; 30,300kr triple. Rates around 20% lower May and Sept, 30% lower Oct–Apr. Rates include breakfast. AE, DC, MC, V. **Amenities:** Wi-Fi in lobby. *In room:* TV, fridge, hair dryer.

MODERATE

Edda Hótel Akureyri ★ Edda hotels get a lot of bad press for being student dormitories during the school year, but in this case you'll wonder how such nice rooms could be lavished on students. The more expensive doubles are in a separate new building, and have spiffier furniture, balconies (with good views on floors 4–6), more space, and a mini-kitchen with sink, microwave, and fridge but no utensils. The location is close to the botanical garden but a steep walk uphill from town.

Hrafnagilsstræti, just west of Eyrarlandsvegur. ✆ **444-4900.** Fax 444-4901. www.hoteledda.is. 204 units, 132 w/bathroom. Mid-June to late-Aug 16,000kr–18,300kr double; 10,000kr double without bathroom. Breakfast available. AE, DC, MC, V. Closed late-Aug to mid-June. **Amenities:** Restaurant; bar; Internet terminal. *In room:* TV (rooms w/bathroom only).

Hótel Íbúðir ★★ Just off Ráðhústorg in the heart of the city, this excellent mid-range choice has attentive staff, a communal kitchen, and classy, understated rooms with excellent, adjustable "health beds." The apartments have balconies, spacious living rooms, and fully-equipped kitchens.

Reception and apts at Geislagata 10 ✆ **462-3727.** Fax 462-3200. www.hotelibudir.is. 3 units, 6 apts. May–Sept 18,900kr double; 18,900kr studio double; 18,900kr 1-bedroom apt; 26,900kr–33,900kr 2-3 bedroom apts. Rates 15%–25% lower Oct–Apr. AE, MC, V. **Amenities:** Guest kitchen. *In room:* TV, hair dryer, no phone, Wi-Fi.

Öngulsstaðir III If you have a car and enjoy ending the day in a hot tub overlooking a pastoral scene, consider staying at this hospitable guesthouse 10km (6¼ miles) south of Akureyri. The rooms are short on rustic character, but you'll find nothing dreary about them either. Dinner is available on request.

Rte. 829, 10km (6¼ miles) south of Akureyri. ✆ **463-1500.** www.ongulsstadir.is. 17 units w/bathroom. June–Aug 16,500kr double; 20,300kr triple; 22,800kr family room. Rates around 10% lower Oct–Apr. Rates include breakfast. AE, DC, MC, V. **Amenities:** Hot tub. *In room:* No phone.

INEXPENSIVE

Brekkusel ★ The location isn't the most central, but for basic value, comfort and relaxation, this guesthouse is hard to beat. The bathroom floor tiles are heated, and with 2 hours' notice they'll fill the hot tub.

Byggðavegur 97. ✆ **461-2660.** www.brekkusel.is. 10 units, 2 w/bathroom. 2 apts. 12,900kr double; 10,900kr double without bathroom; 13,500kr triple; 39,000kr 3 bedroom apts. **Amenities:** Guest kitchen; hot tub; washer/dryer access (300kr). *In room:* No phone, Wi-Fi.

Gistiheimili Akureyrar All three buildings of this guesthouse are dead central, with not much to choose among them; Hafnarstræti 108 has slightly larger rooms, but the other two have sinks in each room, and Hafnarstræti 104 has desks. Rooms are spare, with TVs but not even a token framed print on the wall. Ask for an inside room if you're sensitive to noise, especially on weekends. Reception is at Hafnarstræti 104 in July and August, and at Hótel Akureyri from September to June.

Hafnarstræti 104, Hafnarstræti 108, and Skipagata 4. ✆ **462-5600.** Fax 462-5601. www.guesthouseakureyri.is. 44 units, 8 w/bathroom. May–Sept 12,500kr double; 10,700kr double without bathroom; 12,500kr triple; 15,000kr quadruple. Rates around 20% lower Oct–Apr. *In room:* TV.

Guesthouse AkurInn ★ This sweet old house, a 2-minute walk from the city's heart, has low-key, tasteful rooms and a charming TV lounge but no guest kitchen.

Brekkugata 27a. ✆ **461-2500.** Fax 461-2502. www.akurinn.is. 4 units, none w/bathroom. May–Sept 10,000kr double; 13,000kr triple; 15,000kr quadruple. Rates about 13% lower Oct–Apr. Breakfast available (1,500kr). AE, DC, MC, V. *In room:* No phone, Wi-Fi.

Gula Villan Guesthouse This no-complaints guesthouse is about basic habitable rooms and friendly service. In summer a second location opens up at Þingvallastræti

14; the main house is more centrally located, while the Þingvallastræti house is right by Akureyri's fabulous geothermal pool and has Wi-Fi.

Brekkugata 8. ✆ **896-8464.** Fax 461-3040. www.gulavillan.is. 40 units, 1 w/bathroom. May 15–Sept 12,600kr double; 10,600 double without bathroom; 8,000kr double with sleeping bag; 14,800kr triple; 11,800kr triple with sleeping bag; 18,000kr quadruple; 15,200kr quadruple with sleeping bag. Rates around 10% lower Sept–May 14. Rates do not include breakfast. MC, V. **Amenities:** Guest kitchen. *In room:* No phone.

Pétursborg ★ This is the pick of local farm stays bordering the city. Akureyri is only 5km (3 miles) away, but horses graze across the road, the hot tub is always at the ready, and the house pets—Pookie the cat and Primo the Labrador retriever—are cute and friendly. A short trail leads to the fjord, where you can walk along the shore. Rooms in the two cabins are most inviting, but all are comfortable and unassuming.

Rte. 817 (1.5km/1 mile off Rte. 1, 5km/3 miles north of Akureyri). ✆ **461-1811.** Fax 461-1333. www.petursborg.com. 8 units, 3 w/bathroom. June–Aug 12,900kr double; 9,400kr double without bathroom; 13,650kr triple without bathroom; 16,800kr quadruple without bathroom. Rates include breakfast. MC, V. **Amenities:** Guest kitchen; hot tub. *In room:* No phone, Wi-Fi.

Stórholt Youth Hostel If your image of a hostel is a grubby dorm room full of bunk beds and unkempt, snoring backpackers, Stórholt will inspire a drastic revision. Most rooms have two or three beds, plus TVs, and guests include families and tourists of all ages. There are two cottages for three and eight people. The location is quiet and residential; the city is a 15-minute walk, or there's a free hourly bus. Book far in advance if you can. Tour operators for whale-watching and river rafting offer good discounts through the front desk.

Stórholt 1, just east of Rte. 1. ✆ **894-4299** or 462-3657. Fax 461-2549. www.akureyrihostel.com. 18 units, 1 w/bathroom. 10,000kr double w/bathroom; 5,600kr double without bathroom; 9,500kr triple; 2,700kr dorm bed. Cottages 10,000kr–28,000kr. AE, DC, MC, V. **Amenities:** Guest kitchen. *In room:* No phone, Wi-Fi.

Súlur Guesthouse ★ Not much distinguishes this guesthouse from its competitors, and neither of its two locations are particularly convenient, but both are likable, livable, and good value. Reception is at the house on Þórunnarstræti, which has TVs in every room; the Klettastígur house, with larger rooms, is open in summer only.

Þórunnarstræti 93 and Klettastígur 6. ✆ **461-1160.** sulur@islandia.is. 20 units, none w/bathroom. May–Sept 10,400kr double; 14,400kr triple; 6,000kr sleeping-bag accommodation. Rates 10% lower Oct–Apr. MC, V. **Amenities:** Guest kitchen. *In room:* No phone, Wi-Fi.

Where to Dine

Reykjavík's restaurants are hard to match, but Akureyri makes a respectable showing and makes the most of local strengths. The Eyjafjörður Valley is a big beef and dairy-producing region, and *skyr*—Iceland's famous whipped whey concoction—was invented here. Delicious blue mussels are cultivated in Eyjafjörður. Perhaps we shouldn't tell you that Eyjafjörður's excellent smoked lamb is smoked "the traditional way"—with dried manure. Iceland's first and only microbrewery, *Kaldi,* is in the tiny village of Árskógssandur, although the beer is made with grain from the Czech Republic. On the workaday side, locals like their burgers with béarnaise sauce and stuffed with fries. In a stroke of genius, this burger concept has been transferred to create the popular *Bókullupizza:* Yes, that would be pizza topped with beef, béarnaise sauce, cheese, and fries.

If the options below are full, consider the first-rate **Rósagarðurinn** (Rose Garden) at Hótel Kea, with traditional Icelandic main courses around 2,000kr to 3,500kr.

Rub 23 ★ INTERNATIONAL Confusingly Rub 23 has two restaurants of the same name, one on either side of Kaupvangsstræti. The steakhouse is at number 23 above Café Karólína and the other is at number 6, a little further down the main road (on the left looking towards the sea), which is seafood and sushi made from fresh Icelandic fish. Decorated in line with current trends in Iceland's high-end restaurant business, both have bright, modern interiors, wooden floors, and smooth furniture. The owners are award-winning Icelandic chefs and both establishments serve quality food. What makes the food interesting, though, is the spice mixtures, which customers can pick, and which are rubbed into the food, hence the name. The kitchens close in both places at 10pm but customers can stay drinking until 4am.

Kaupvangsstræti 23 and 6. ✆ **462-4423** (23) and 462-2223 (6). www.rub23.is. Main courses 3,750kr–6,250kr. AE, DC, MC, V. Daily 5:30–10pm.

Strikið ★ ICELANDIC Perched on a fourth floor overlooking the sea, this buzzing restaurant is better than the casual atmosphere might suggest. Familiar dishes come with twists: béarnaise sauce on the beef tenderloin tastes of curry and coconut; lobster soup has a hint of cognac; and the chocolate cake comes with meringue and vanilla ice cream. Pizzas are excellent if you like thin crust, sharp tomato sauce, and lots of Parmesan in the cheese mix. Service can be slow, but you can wait outside on the roof patio under a heat lamp.

Skipagata 14. ✆ **462-7100.** www.strikid.is. Reservations recommended. Main courses 2,090kr–6,290kr. AE, DC, MC, V. Sun–Thurs 11am–10pm; Fri–Sat 11am–11pm.

MODERATE

Those staying up the hill should consider the **Edda hotel's** quality dinner buffet, which costs 4,450kr, with a la carte options available.

Bautinn ☺ ICELANDIC Right on Akureyri's busiest corner, this crowd-pleaser is reasonably priced and the food is comfortingly predictable. The ambience is more for families than a date, unless your companion enjoys playrooms. All main courses, which come with fried vegetables and potatoes, also include the soup and salad bar.

Hafnarstræti 92. ✆ **462-1818.** www.bautinn.is. Main courses 2,360kr–4,850kr. MC, V. Daily 9am–11pm.

Greifinn ☺ ICELANDIC This family-oriented restaurant lacks Bautinn's central location, but outdoes it in most other respects: prices are slightly lower, the huge menu branches into Italian and Tex-Mex, and the playroom has video games. Tables have electric buzzers for service; small children find them irresistible and harass the waiting staff. Greifinn was the originator of saltfish pizza, an Eyjafjörður must-try. The 1,290kr lunch special, weekdays from 11:30am to 2pm, is a steal.

Glerárgata 20 (Rte. 1). ✆ **460-1600.** www.greifinn.is. Main courses 1,510kr–5,690kr. AE, DC, MC, V. Daily 11:30am–11pm.

La Vita é Bella ITALIAN Food here tends to be less-than-authentic and flooded in creamy sauces, but if you just need a change of pace, you might work around these limitations with a salad or the freshly-made pesto. The "Mussolini" pizza, which combines pepperoni, blue cheese, and bananas, achieves bad taste on multiple levels. Half portions are substantial enough for all but the famished.

Hafnarstræti 92 (behind Bautinn). © **461-5858.** Reservations recommended. Main courses 1,950kr–6,150kr. MC, V. Daily 6–11pm.

Peng's CHINESE The food is what you'd expect from the one Chinese restaurant in a place like Akureyri: none of it is particularly authentic or subtle, but most customers get the grease-heavy fix they've come for. The daily 1,590kr lunch buffet is a great deal.

Gránufélagsgata 10. © **466-1001.** Reservations recommended for dinner. Main courses 1,090kr–1,990kr. MC, V. Mon–Thurs 11:30am–2pm and 5pm–9:30pm; Fri 11:30 -2pm and 5–10pm, Sat 5–10pm, Sun 5–9:30pm.

INEXPENSIVE

Búllan BURGERS This low-key joint with American Route 66-style decor serves burgers (including veggie burgers) a notch above standard—and proper milkshakes, too.

Strandgata 11. © **462-1800.** Burgers 750kr–1,750kr. AE, MC, V. Daily 11:45am–10pm.

CAFES & A DELI

Bláa Kannan This cheerful, roomy hangout, spilling on to Akureyri's main pedestrian street, is ideal for writing postcards over cake and coffee. Meal options are limited to soups, salads, sandwiches, quiche, spinach pie, and a daily pasta dish.

Hafnarstræti 96. © **461-4600.** Main courses 950kr–1,150kr. MC, V. Mon–Sat 9am–11pm; Sun 10am–11pm.

Kaffi Karólína This fashionable cafe-bar, adjoining the upscale restaurant Rub 23, serves tasty bagels and sandwiches.

Kaupvangsstræti 23. © **461-2755.** AE, DC, MC, V. Daily Sun–Thurs 5pm–1am, Fri–Sat 5pm–4am.

What to See & Do

HEART OF THE CITY

The latest attraction in Akureyri is the **Hof Cultural Center** (**Menningarhúsið Hof**) on Strangata 12 (© **450-1000;** www.menningarhus.is; info@mennigarhus.is), which opened officially in August 2010. Unfortunately the real-life basalt-covered monster is not quite as pretty at the digital version projected in the plans. As with many Icelandic buildings, the beauty is rather on the inside, where the modern, acoustically-designed hall hosts concerts, conferences, and performances in dance and drama.

Akureyri maintains museums in the former homes of Davíð Stefánsson (1895–1964), a novelist, playwright, and poet laureate, and Matthías Jochumsson (1835–1920), a poet, playwright, and translator. These museums—**Daviðshús** and **Sigurhæðir**—do an admirable job of preserving their legacies, but most information is presented in Icelandic, and neither writer has anything in print in English.

Akureyri Art Museum (Listasafníð á Akureyri) ★ The main area for gallery enthusiasts is Kaupvangsstræti, which winds uphill from the middle of the city, just north of Akureyri Church. Artists and art enthusiasts, with the city's help, appropriated several disused industrial buildings and converted them to exhibition and performance spaces, an art school and studios for resident and visiting artists. The umbrella arts-sponsoring group is **Listagil** (© **466-2609;** listagil@listagil.is), and its main showcases are this museum and the **Summer Festival of the Arts,** which lasts from mid-June to late August and uses several spaces clustered near the museum. Pick up a *Listasumar* brochure anywhere in town, or check the schedule at www.akureyri.is. Founded in 1993, the well-designed museum has no permanent collection and is devoted mostly to contemporary Icelandic art, with international shows on occasion.

Kaupvangsstræti 12. © **461-2610.** www.listagil.akureyri.is. Admission free. Tues–Sun noon–5pm.

Akureyri Church ★ A long stairway extends from the city's midst up to this bravura concrete church, whose Art Deco twin spires have drawn mixed critical responses but rarely fail to make an impression. The hilltop location, face-forward design, and beckoning, outstretched spires lend the frontal exterior a Batman-like animal vitality. The church was consecrated in 1940 and designed by Guðjón Samúelsson, the state architect responsible for the even larger Hallgrímskirkja in Reykjavík. However distinctive his bold geometric outlines, Guðjón's signature is just as evident in the fine details, such as the basalt-inspired hexagonal columns above the doorway, and the obsessive tiering in the ceiling, archways, and surrounding lawn. Make sure to inspect the lovely tilework in Iceland spar—a native crystal used to make light prisms—on the pulpit and the illuminated cross hanging from the ceiling. The midsection of the stained glass window directly behind the altar comes from the original Coventry cathedral, one of England's great casualties in World War II.

Off Eyrarlandsvegur ✆ **462-7700.** Mon-Fri 8:30am-10pm; until 8:30pm Wed. June-Sept Sun service 11am; Oct-May Sun service 11pm. Prayers Thurs noon.

BOTANICAL GARDEN & NEARBY

The riveting 1901 sculpture **The Outlaw (Útlaginn) ★**—easy to miss amid the greenery in the traffic island formed by Eyrarlandsvegur and Hrafnagilsstræti—established the reputation of Iceland's best-known sculptor, Einar Jónsson. A wild-looking outlaw dressed in skins carries his dead wife over his back, a spade in one hand and his little boy asleep on his other arm. He wants to bury her in consecrated ground, but would be put to death if captured, so he comes secretly at night. This cast metal version conveys tension and detail lacking in the plaster model at the Einar Jónsson Museum in Reykjavík (p. 128).

Botanical Garden (Lystigarður Akureyrar) This is Iceland's best outdoor botanical garden, with remarkable variety for such a northerly latitude, but for most visitors it's not what they came all this way for.

Eyrarlandsvegur (by Hrafnagilsstræti). Free admission. June-Oct daily 8am-10pm; Nov-May Mon-Fri 8am-10pm.

Catholic Church (Kaþólska Kirkjan) This inviting church near the Botanical Garden holds mass in English, Icelandic, and Polish on Saturdays at 6pm and Sundays at 11am. After Sunday mass, attendees are invited downstairs for coffee with Father Patrick Breen, from Ireland, and the Carmelite order of nuns.

Eyrarlandsvegur 26 (at Hrafnagilsstræti). ✆ **462-1119.** June-Aug 8am-10pm; Sept-May 8am-8pm.

SOUTH OF THE CITY CENTER

Aviation Museum (Flugsafn Íslands) ★ Devoted fans of antique planes will delight in this museum inside an airplane hangar. One display holds the remains of a British warplane that crashed into a glacier in 1941 and was regurgitated at the glacier's edge 58 years later. The funniest contraption—affectionately known as "the stick"—is a homemade, one-man Icelandic plane powered by bike pedals and a small engine.

At south end of Akureyri airport. ✆ **461-4400.** www.flugsafn.is. Admission 800kr adults; free for children aged 11 and under. June-Aug daily 11am-5pm; Sept-May Sat 2-5pm, or by appointment.

Industry Museum (Iðnaðarsafn) This endearing curiosity tells the tale of 72 20th-century companies of the Akureyri area, most of them now defunct. Products on display include everything from clothing to paint cans to canned hot-dogs; connoisseurs, take note of the outmoded advertising aesthetics and charming packaging designs.

Krókeyri (off Drottníngarbraut). ✆ **462-3600.** www.idnadarsafnid.is. Admission 600kr adults; 300kr seniors; free for children under 16. Jun–Sept 14 daily 10am–5pm; Sept 15–May Sat 2–4pm.

Museum of Akureyri (Minjasafn Á Akureyri) This museum is in the oldest section of town, a 15-minute walk south of the modern part, and holds a permanent exhibit on the cultural history of Akureyri and environs, plus a temporary exhibit on a sub-theme, such as the art of Icelandic headboard carving. Strong points include elaborate woodcarvings and a charming pulpit from Kaupvangur Church, painted with hearts and flowers, but those without a particular interest in the Eyjafjörður area will get that heavy feeling in their legs.

Aðalstræti 58. ✆ **462-4162.** www.akmus.is. Admission 600kr adults; 250kr seniors; free for children aged 15 and under. June–Sept 15 daily 10am–5pm; Sept 16–May Sat 2–4pm.

Nonni's House (Nonnahús) This museum is squeezed inside the tiny childhood home of Jón Sveinsson (1857–1944), author of a semi-autobiographical children's book series famous throughout Iceland and Germany. ("Nonni" applies to Jón *and* his fictional boy-hero.) Sveinsson studied abroad and became a Jesuit priest and missionary. The fictional Nonni, along with his younger brother Manni, live on an isolated north Iceland farm and run into all kinds of family drama and adventure, including a brush with polar bears. The books were written in German, but English translations were recently published, and are sold at reception. The museum, founded in 1957, is full of manuscripts and personal items. Nonnahús and the Museum of Akureyri offer discounted joint admission.

Aðalstræti 54. ✆ **462-3555.** www.nonni.is. Admission 600kr adults; 300kr seniors; children under 16 free. Jun–Aug daily 10am–5pm.

Outdoor Activities

Akureyri's best travel agency for booking tours is **Nonni Travel,** Brekkugata 5 (✆ **461-1841;** www.nonnitravel.is; Mon–Fri 9am–5pm). The **tourist information office** (p. 247) can also book many tours.

AERIAL TOURS Seeing Iceland from an airplane may seem decadent or extravagant, but few regret this memorable and exhilarating experience. **Mýflug Air** (✆ **464-4400;** www.myflug.is) offers sightseeing trips from 20 minutes up to 2 hours; prices range from 9,000kr–27,000kr. Logical destinations include Mývatn, Jökulsárgljúfur, Herðubreið, Askja, and Kverkfjöll; for all these places, however, it's cheaper to take off from Mývatn. Eagle Air and Mýflug flights can be booked through the tourist office.

GOLF **Golfklúbbur Akureyrar** (✆ **462-2974;** www.gagolf.is; gagolf@gagolf.is) runs the world-class course **Jaðarsvöllur** (course fee 4,900kr; club rental 2,000kr; cart rental 4,000kr; June–Aug 8am–10pm), which hosts the 36-hole **Arctic Open** (www.arcticopen.is; entry fee 46,600kr) in late June; contestants tee off into the morning hours under the midnight sun. Tournament slots fill up by February or March. The course is up the hill southwest of the city, off Eikarlundur.

HIKING The best local hiking is southwest of Akureyri in and around Glerárdalur Valley, which is surrounded by small glaciers and some of north Iceland's tallest mountains. Most routes are strenuous, and hikers should be aware that harsh weather, even snowstorms, could set in without warning. The best place to start is **Ferðafélag Akureyrar** Strandgata 23, Akureyri (✆ **462-2720;** www.ffa.is), which maintains the **Lambi mountain hut** in Glerárdalur, and publishes the *Glerárdalur* hiking map (300kr), also available at the tourist office.

HORSEBACK RIDING **Pólar Hestar** (✆ **463-3179;** www.polarhestar.is), one of Iceland's most established horse tour companies, is recommended for everything from 1-hour rides (3,500kr) to multi-day pack trips through the interior. Pickup from Akureyri can be arranged.

SEA FISHING **Haffari Seatours** (✆ **860-3890;** www.haffari.is; tickets 4,900kr adults, 2,450kr children aged 8–15, free for children aged 7 and under, minimum charge 10,000kr; June 1–Aug 31 daily departures at noon, 3:30pm, and 8pm) offers 3-hour fishing and sightseeing tours in 10-passenger boats leaving from Akureyri. More intense anglers could head 44km (27 miles) north to Dalvík, where **Bátaferðir** (✆ **771-7600;** www.bataferdir.is) has 3-hour fishing trips in a bigger boat for 7,000kr (four person minimum).

SKIING **Hlíðarfjall** (✆ **462-2280;** www.hlidarfjall.is;) is Iceland's premier ski area, sitting on the banks of the fjord with lovely watery views. Best conditions are usually in February and March, and the slopes are floodlit during the darkest winter days. The longest run is 2.5km (1½ miles) with a 500m (1,640 ft.) vertical drop, and the area is served by six lifts including four-man chairs. Hlíðarfjall also offers cross-country trails, a snowboarding course, a ski school, equipment rental, and a restaurant. Hlíðarfjall is 7km (4¼ miles) west of town; take Hlíðarbraut or Þingvallastræti to Hlíðarfjallsvegur. There's no bus service, and a taxi costs about 2,500kr each way.

SWIMMING The **Akureyri Swimming Pool ★**, Þingvallastræti 21 (✆ **461-4455;** admission 450kr adults; free for children under 16; June–Aug Mon–Fri 6:45am–10pm; Sat–Sun 8am–7:30pm; Sept–May Mon–Fri 6:45am–9pm, Sat–Sun 10am–4:30pm), is a water wonderland, with indoor and outdoor pools, a children's pool, two waterslides, hot tubs, massaging water jets, a steam bath, fitness equipment, an ice-cream stand, and, for an extra charge, a sauna. Bring a towel to avoid the 450kr rental fee.

WHALE-WATCHING Whale-watching in Eyjafjörður is based at Hauganes and Dalvík, north of Akureyri (p. 258). **SBA Norðurleid** (✆ **550-0700;** www.sba.is) offers day tours that include bus transport to Húsavik (p. 272) and a whale-watching trip from there for 11,000kr in summer.

Shopping

Most Akureyri shopping can be quickly scanned by perusing Hafnarstræti (especially the northern, pedestrian-only stretch), Skipagata, and Ráðhústorg Square, where the two streets meet. Along Glerárgata, just north of the Glerá River, is **Glerártorg Mall** (✆ **461-5770;** Mon–Fri 10am–6:30pm; Sat 10am–5pm; Sun 1–5pm), two restaurants, a drugstore, a supermarket, and 37 stores; including the trendy Icelandic outerwear company 66° North (p. 140) which also has a store across the street.

Fold-Anna Check here if you're seeking the perfect Icelandic woolens for your next trip to the ski slopes or souvenirs for folks back home. Hafnarstræti 100. ✆ **461-4120.** Mon–Fri 9am–7pm; Sat 10am–2pm.

Frúin í Hamborg This curious second-hand store sells furniture, clothing, and sundries sourced from Iceland, Holland, and Belgium. There's no shortage of reasonably priced grandma-chic dresses or gowns embroidered with sequins and pearls. Hafnarstræti 90. ✆ **461-5577.** Mon–Fri 11am–6pm; Sat 11am–4pm.

Gallerí Svartfugl og Hvítspói This engrossing gallery-cum-shop is run by two local artists, one producing nature-themed prints on paper, the other textiles—including, of late, clothes made from salmon skin. Brekkugata 3a (behind Nonni Travel). ✆ **461-3449.** June to mid-Sept Mon–Fri 1–5pm, Sat 1–4pm; mid-Sept to May Mon–Fri 1–5pm.

Penninn Eymundsson This bright, inviting bookstore on Akureyri's busiest corner has a variety of English-language books, plus maps, souvenirs, Wi-Fi, and a cafe. Hafnarstræti 91–93. ✆ **540-2180.** Mon–Fri 9am–10pm; Sat–Sun 10am–10pm.

Sirka This stylish boutique sells housewares, jewelry, and women's clothing with an intriguing mishmash of nostalgic and modern design. Skipagata 5. ✆ **461-3606.** Mon–Fri 10am–6pm; Sat 11am–4pm.

The Viking This is Iceland's largest souvenir shop, with a good selection of knitwear, crafts, and kitsch. Hafnarstræti 104. ✆ **461-5551.** Mid-May through Aug daily 8am–10pm; Sept to mid-June Mon–Fri 10am–6pm, Sat–Sun 10am–4pm.

Akureyri Nightlife

Most nights in summer, activities are not limited to loud bars and clubs; the ***Listasumar*** brochure delineates everything from Thursday night jazz sets to choral concerts and evening "history sailing" in the fjord. Akureyri's bars and nightclubs are within a 10-minute walk of each other, so roam (as Icelanders do) until you find a scene to your liking. Only live music commands a cover charge, and you'll never be pressured to buy drinks. As elsewhere in Iceland, Akureyri's young people work hard, and work even harder at partying. On Friday and Saturday nights teenagers drive around town at a crawl, dressed as if they're cruising Miami Beach in a 50s convertible, honking and gabbing at each other out the car windows.

The main nightspots are **Café Amour,** Ráðhústorg 9 (✆ **461-3030**), which has a wine bar downstairs and small DJ room upstairs with holographic bordello wallpaper; **Græni Hatturinn,** Hafnarstræti 96 (✆ **461-4646**), is a dedicated music venue inside one of Akureyri's oldest houses; **Kaffi Akureyri,** Strandgata 7 (✆ **461-3999**), whose back room is turned over to DJs on weekends; **Kaffi Karólína,** Kaupvangsstræti 23 (✆ **461-2755**), a bar where the knowingly cool and sophisticated cliques hang out; and **Sjallinn,** Geislagata 14 (✆ **462-2770**), loud, raucous and packed.

NEAR AKUREYRI

Akureyri is a great base for excursions fanning out in several directions. Eyjafjörður, with its broad, smoothly-sloping bowl shape and rich farmland, seems to welcome human habitation more than other Icelandic fjords. Safnasafnið and Smámunasafn are two of Iceland's most offbeat and inspiring museums. The inhabited islands of Hrísey and Grímsey, both full of birdlife, are fascinating worlds unto themselves.

Farther afield, Goðafoss and Aldeyjarfoss are among Iceland's most exquisite waterfalls. Some sights, notably Safnasafnið and Goðafoss, are on the Ring Road and can fit into trips to Mývatn, Húsavík, and Jökulsárgljúfur.

Dalvík

This fishing town of just under 2,000 people, on the western shore of Eyjafjörður 44km (27 miles) north of Akureyri, may provide a diversion worth adding to a ferry trip to Hrísey or Grímsey.

ESSENTIALS

BY CAR Take Route 82 from the Ring Road 10km (6¼ miles) north of Akureyri. **Sterna** (✆ **533-3737;** www.Sterna.is) runs three **buses** between Akureyri and Dalvík on weekdays year-round; the ride is 45 minutes and costs 1,600kr.

Dalvík's **tourist office,** Svarfaðarbraut (✆ **466-3233;** www.dalvik.is; June–Aug Mon–Fri 6:15am–8pm, Sat–Sun 10am–9pm; Sept–May Mon–Fri 6:15am–8pm, Sat–Sun 10am–4:30pm), is at the local swimming pool, and the website has information in English. **Pizza Vero,** Goðabraut 3 (✆ **466-2041**), is the best place to grab a meal.

EXPLORING DALVÍK

Little known among tourists, **"The Great Fish Day" (Fiskidagurinn)** is a huge, outdoor festival that takes place on the first or second weekend of August. Everything is free: food, soft drinks, live music, folk-dancing in traditional costume, short films, and, of course, exhibitions of fish in tubs full of ice. The local fish factory is the main sponsor, and all workers are volunteers. On Saturday from 11am to 5pm, the largest grill in Iceland cooks up cod, haddock, salmon, and about 12,000 fish burgers. The night before, around 70 Dalvík families place two torches outside their doors, a signal that anyone is welcome to stop in for fish soup.

Dalvík Folk Museum (Byggðasafnið Hvoll) This better-than-average local museum displays minerals, taxidermy (including a polar bear), farm artifacts, and a tribute to native son Jóhann Pétursson (1913–1984), who during his lifetime was the world's second-tallest person. Standing at 2.34m (7 ft. 8 in.) in U.S. size 24 (62 European) boots, he appeared in Viking costume as "Jóhann the Giant" in U.S. and European circuses, and made several Hollywood cameos. He was understandably ambivalent about his work and stage name, and returned to Dalvík in his final years. The museum displays his circus costumes and shows a video documentary, mostly in Icelandic but gripping nonetheless.

Karlsrauðatorg. ✆ **466-1497.** www.dalvik.is/byggdasafn. Admission 500kr adults; 200kr seniors; 200kr children aged 6–16. Jun–Aug daily 11am–6pm; Sept–May Sat 2–5pm.

OUTDOOR ACTIVITIES

Hestaþjónustan Tvistur (✆ **466-1679** or 861-9631; ebu@ismennt.is) based in Dalvík arranges **horseback riding** in the lovely Svarfaðardalur Valley south of town. Golf club **Hamar** (✆ **466-1679**) has a new 9-hole course in the same valley. **Bergmenn Mountain Guides** (✆ **698 9870;** www.bergmenn.is; info@bergmenn.com) are the best agents in the area for **hiking tours** and ski mountaineering on the beautiful Tröllaskagi Peninsula (including the fabulous 2- to 3-day route from Dalvík west to Hólar). **Guesthouse Skeið** (✆ **466 1636;** www.thule-tours.com; mail@thule-tours.com) in Svarfaðardalur Valley is a great base for hiking in the area.

Most visitors to north Iceland save their **whale-watching** for Húsavík, which has better infrastructure—more scheduled departures, waterfront coffee houses, the whale museum—but only a marginal advantage in whale sightings. **Bátaferðir** (✆ **771-7600;** www.batarferdir.is), based in Dalvík, leads 3-hour whale-watching tours (7,000kr adults, 5,000kr children aged 7–16; June 1–June 30daily 9am, 7pm; July–Aug 26 9am, 7pm, 11pm), and sea-angling trips by arrangement. **Whale-Watching Eyjafjörður** (✆ **867-0000;** www.niels.is), based in Hauganes, 30km (19 miles) north of Akureyri and 14km (8¾ miles) south of Dalvík, has comparable services.

Hrísey Island ★

Heimaey (Home Island) in the Westman Islands is Iceland's largest and most populated offshore island; Hrísey is second on both counts, with about 180 residents. With its paved roads, well-tended homes, and geothermal swimming pool, the village does not feel particularly marginal. Hrísey has been inhabited since the 10th century but sprouted rapidly in the 19th century as a base for processing and exporting herring. The herring vanished at the end of the 1960s, and in 1999 the fish-freezing plant closed, forcing many residents to leave.

Hrísey has a clear view to the northern horizon, and is perfect for witnessing the scooping midnight sun in early summer. Fjord views on the island are heart-stirring if not heart-stopping. In mid-July, Hrísey plays at being a sovereign nation during its "Independence Day" family festival: guests pass through customs, get their Hrísey passport stamped, then enjoy tractor and fishing trips, dancing, and a children's singing competition.

ESSENTIALS

The main **ferry** to Hrísey, **Sævar** (✆ **695-5544;** round-trip ticket 1,000kr adults, free for children 11 and under; departures every 2 hours daily from 9:30am–11pm), leaves from Árskógssandur, a small village on the western shore of Eyjafjörður, 35km (22 miles) north of Akureyri. The ride lasts 15 minutes.

Hrísey's **information office** is inside a shark museum called **"The House of Shark Jörundur,"** the oldest house on the island, on Norðuvegur 5, (✆ **695-0077;** www.northiceland.is or www.hrisey.net; mid-June to mid-Aug daily 10am–4pm). There's a crafts store by the ferry landing named Pearl Gallery. The Akureyri tourist office (p. 247) is also helpful.

EXPLORING HRÍSEY ISLAND

In summer, as you disembark the ferry, you'll likely see **Tractor Trips** in action (✆ **695-0077**) where tourists take **birdwatching tours** in a tractor-pulled trailer, which has seats and a loudspeaker so the driver can commentate. Call in advance to make reservations.

Free **trail maps** are available on the ferry. The main trail ascends to Hrísey's highest point in a 2.3-km (1.4-mile) loop, but the longer trails are best for bird sightings. The far northern section of Hrísey, **Ystabæjarland,** is a private nature reserve accessible only with the owner's permission; consult the information office if you hope to hike all the way there. Permission is usually not granted until mid-July, to protect birds during nesting season.

Hrísey's **bird populations** chose their residence well. Hunting is prohibited, and no foxes or mink have made it out to the island. Hrísey is a quarantine station for imported pigs and cattle, so Icelandic horses and sheep—that never interbreed with foreigners, at least not in Iceland—are kept off the island to keep them safe from species-hopping diseases. This leaves more vegetation for ground-nesting bird species.

⚠ Arctic terns, which harass and sometimes attack anything that comes near their eggs, are a serious menace and can turn a Hrísey walk into a Hitchcockian nightmare. Terns are very agile and the attack comes in a quick swoop, with furious flapping and hideous shrieks. (The Icelandic word for tern, *kría,* comes from the shrieking sound.) The worst time is June, when walkers should carry some sort of stick, pole, or umbrella over their heads for protection.

Ptarmigans, on the other hand, haven't the slightest fear of people, and in early September waddle right into village streets and yards seeking protection from falcons. The spindly-legged and needle-billed godwits, around from mid-May to mid-August, are another endearing sight.

WHERE TO STAY & DINE

The market **Verslun Hrísey** (✆ **466-1213;** Mon–Fri 11am–6pm; Sat–Sun noon–5pm), a short walk from the waterfront, has seating for snacks such as skyr and hot-dogs. The only restaurant and lodgings are at **Brekka** (✆ **466-1751;** brekkahrisey@brekkahrisey.is; AE, MC, V; restaurant Jun–Aug daily 11:30am–9pm, Sept–May Fri–Sat dinner only), a yellow building visible from the water's edge. The restaurant is far better than you might anticipate, with first-rate fish, lobster, and lamb dishes (2,590kr–5,900kr) as well as burgers, pizzas, and sandwiches. Four basic doubles with shared bathroom and ocean views go for 7,000kr.

Grímsey Island ★

Many visitors studying a map of Iceland notice an obscure speck, 41km (25 miles) north of the mainland and bisected by the Arctic Circle, and feel strangely compelled to go there. Grímsey is indeed a worthwhile and exotic destination (more for the Arctic location than any exceptional topography) with 85 hardy inhabitants, basalt cliffs reaching 105m (344 ft.), and abundant birdlife.

Many visitors come in late June to see the midnight sun "bounce" off the horizon, but this involves a tradeoff. June and early July is also when Arctic terns most aggressively defend their nests, sometimes drawing blood from the scalps of unwitting tourists (see "Warning," above).

ESSENTIALS

GETTING THERE Until 1931, the only way to get to Grímsey was on a mail boat that came twice a year. Today, **Air Iceland** (✆ **570-3030;** www.airiceland.is) flies from Akureyri daily at 7:30pm (1pm Saturdays) and returns to Akureyri at 3:15pm. The flight is 25 minutes and costs around 11,800kr one-way; a connection to or from Reykjavík is around 15,465kr one-way. From June 10 to August 20 Air Iceland offers an evening tour—round-trip airfare with a 1-hour guided walk, but no dinner—for 20,880kr from Akureyri or 32,720kr from Reykjavík (clearly a much better deal from Akureyri). **Mýflug Air** (www.myflug.is; ✆ **464-4400**) does the same tour for 27,500kr, but leaves from Mývatn in a smaller plane that does aerial sightseeing along the way.

From May 15 until the end of August, the **Sæfari ferry** (✆ **853-2211;** www.landflutningar.is; round-trip from Dalvík, 6,480kr adults; 3,249kr seniors and children aged 12–15; free for children aged 11 and under) sails from Dalvík to Grímsey on Mondays, Wednesdays, and Fridays. A bus leaves Akureyri at 7:50am and connects with the ferry, which leaves at 9am and arrives at noon. The return trip is at 4pm, reaching Dalvík at 7pm, where another bus bound for Akureyri awaits. From September until mid-May, the ferry departs for Grímsey at the same times, but heads right back to Dalvík after unloading.

One-way tickets for Air Iceland flights and the ferry are half-price, so it makes sense to mix and match. Taking the ferry there and the flight back, for instance, gives you more than 8 hours on Grímsey.

VISITOR INFORMATION Consult **Akureyri's tourist information office** (p. 247), or either guesthouse listed below.

EXPLORING GRÍMSEY ISLAND

Grímsey is flat-topped and only 5.3sq. km (3⅓ sq. mile), with the highest cliffs on the east side, and walks are a straightforward matter. The island is home to more than 60 **bird species.** The most popular are puffins, which can be observed from May to mid-August.

For the right price, someone is always willing to take you **sea fishing, bird hunting,** or, in May or June, **egg-collecting;** contact either guesthouse listed below.

Gallery Sól, Sólberg (✆ **467-3190**), a gallery and souvenir shop, opens up to greet arriving and departing visitors from the ferry or plane. The community hall has a library endowed by David William Fiske (1831–1904), a wealthy American who never set foot in Grímsey but was touched by how much the locals were dedicated to chess.

WHERE TO STAY & DINE

Most of Grímsey's houses are in the village of Sandvík, which has a small market.

Guesthouse Básar This simple and warm guesthouse, newly renovated, is right by the airport and just a few steps from the Arctic Circle. Reasonably-priced dinners are served by advance request: 2,200kr for fish and 3,000kr for bird or lamb. Some rooms accommodate up to three or four.

Básar ✆ **467-3103.** 8 units, none w/bathroom. ,9,000kr double; 2,500kr per person sleeping-bag accommodation. Breakfast available (1,000kr). MC, V. **Amenities:** Guest kitchen. *In room:* No phone.

Guesthouse Gullsól These six elemental guest rooms with a shared TV lounge and guest kitchen are attached to the Gallery Sól handicraft store; the friendly proprietors can help arrange any kind of local activity.

Sólberg. ✆ **467-3190** or 467-3150. grimsey@simnet.is. 6 units, none w/bathroom. 7,800kr double; 4,400kr double with sleeping bag. AE, DC, MC, V. **Amenities:** Guest kitchen. *In room:* No phone.

Restaurant Kría Grímsey's hangout by default, Kría serves up burgers, sandwiches, crepes, fish, lamb, and puffin. No pizza, surprisingly; locals with pizza cravings have to get it delivered from Akureyri on the evening flight.

Nýja-sjáland. ✆ **467-3112.** Main courses 1,500kr-3,000kr. MC, V. May–early Sept daily noon–9pm; bar open late Fri–Sat. Early Sept–Apr usually closed, but call ahead.

Upper Eyjafjörður

Icelanders tolerate and even nurture their single-minded eccentrics, as evidenced by the three sights below. All are on Route 821, which heads directly south from Akureyri. A few kilometers past the Akureyri Airport, you also pass a tiny gift shop, **Álfaland,** selling Icelandic crafts and woolens, where the surrounding land has been transforming into an elven enclave since 2010.

Christmas House (Jólagarðurinn) ★ ☺ Giant pieces of candy sit atop this Christmas fanatics' dreamhouse, complete with Santa's suit hanging on the washing line. All things Christmassy are on sale inside, while outside you'll find an enormous advent calendar inside a faux medieval turret and perhaps the most festive restroom in the world. Beware Grýla the troll who lives downstairs.

Rte. 821, 11km (6¾ miles) south of Akureyri. ✆ **463-1433.** Free admission. June–Aug daily 10am–10pm; Sept–Dec 2–10pm (until 6pm on Christmas Eve); Jan–May daily 2–6pm.

Grund Church This curious 1905 church, atypically aligned north to south, has several Romanesque spires, an onion dome, and a balconied interior reminiscent of an opera house (although unfortunately you can no longer see inside). It's the largest Icelandic church financed by an individual, and is atypical of most Icelandic churches of the late-19th and early-20th centuries, which tend to be simple structures with square belfries, sometimes elongated, and topped by a kind of narrow-brimmed hat.

Rte. 821, 18km (11 miles) south of Akureyri.

Museum of Small Exhibits (Smámunasafn) ★ 🎁 This oddball museum is essentially a junk collection meticulously sorted and arranged by master carpenter Sverrir Hermannsson (1928–2008). Exhibits include mounted arrays of nails, cocktail napkins, perfume bottles, fake teeth, hair elastics, waffle irons, and unbroken spirals of pencil shavings. You'll have to decide for yourself whether the patterns and repetitions are artistic or simply obsessive. Sverrir marked most items with the initials of the original owner, and many bear the word *gámur* meaning they were rescued after being thrown out. A cafe is on-hand, and up the hill is **Saurbær Church,** a typical turf church from 1858.

Rte. 821, 27km (16¾ miles) south of Akureyri. ✆ **463-1261.** www.smamunasafnid.is. Admission 600kr adults; 350kr seniors; free for children 15 and under. May 15–Sept 15 daily 1–6pm.

Northeast of Akureyri

Laufás Of the many 19th-century turf-covered farms that are now museums, Laufás—a parsonage built in the 1860s, in a meadow overlooking Eyjafjörður—was the most prosperous. Twenty to thirty people lived in the labyrinthine interior, with rooms designated for weaving, cleaning birds, and dressing brides. The damp and claustrophobic rooms have only thin shafts of light from high windows, but contemporaries would have envied the wood floors and crafting of the walls, with their alternating layers of stone and tweed-patterned sod. The scene would be complete with some peat smoke wafting toward an open chimney, the smell of oil lamps, and household members spinning yarn and churning butter. Unfortunately the museum has no guided tours and little information in English.

Laufás earned money harvesting eider down, which explains a gable carving of a woman's head crowned by a duck. The 1865 church is well-restored and typical of its time; the most endearing feature is the 1698 pulpit, with unschooled but talented carvings of five saints grinning like dolls. An old-fashioned cafe next door serves flatbread with smoked trout, rhubarb pie, and bread with mountain moss baked inside (originally eaten to keep Icelanders from dying of scurvy). On a Sunday in mid-July, Laufás hosts a historical event with staff in period costume carving wood, cooking pancakes, and mowing with scythes.

Rte. 83 (about 10km/6¼ miles from Rte. 1 and 30km/19 miles from Akureyri). ✆ **463-3196.** www.akmus.is. Admission 600kr adults; free for children 16 and under. May 15–Sept 15 daily 10am–6pm.

Safnasafnið ★★ The admirable concept behind this enjoyable and penetrating museum is to erase boundaries between folk art, "outsider" art, and contemporary art—and the results here are highly successful. Established artists are included, but curators also scour the country in search of compelling work by anyone, including those with no formal training. Safnasafnið expanded in 2007 and puts on 14 exhibitions a year, in any conceivable artistic genre. The two constants are a rotating exhibit from the Icelandic Doll Museum, and a hands-on toy exhibit inspired by optical illusions. Wondering about that blue-and-yellow cube on the wall? Stare at it for a minute, then focus on the white wall and its inverse image appears. The museum has a wonderful reading room and a birch grove outside with picnic tables.

Rte. 1, 11km (7 miles) northeast of Akureyri. ✆ **461-4066.** www.safnasafnid.is. Admission 500kr adults, 400kr seniors; free for children under 14. Early May to mid-Aug daily 10am–6pm; Apr–Oct by appointment.

Between Akureyri & Mývatn

GOÐAFOSS ★

Located right off the Ring Road, about 50km (31 miles) east of Akureyri and 53km (33 miles) west of Reykjahlíð, Goðafoss (Waterfall of the Gods) is not very tall or powerful, but admirers point to the separate cascades forming an elegant semicircular arc, the swirling patterns in the blue-green (or sometimes brown) water, and the strange bubbliness of the surrounding lava. According to legend, Goðafoss was named in the year 1000 when the Law Speaker of the Icelandic parliament, after proclaiming Iceland a Christian country, tossed his pagan statuettes into the falls.

Just downstream is the restaurant and guesthouse **Fosshóll** (✆ **464-3108;** www.nett.is/fossholl; 17,800kr–22,800kr double; May 15–Sept daily 6–10pm; closed Oct–May 14), which serves local trout on top of the usual road-stop fare. You can park right by the falls, but walking upstream from Fosshóll is a more satisfying approach.

ALDEYJARFOSS ★★

This stunning waterfall is worth the substantial detour from the Ring Road. The falls have a powerful churning force, and the freakish basalt formations are enough to make spectators wonder what planet they've been transported to. To reach Aldeyjarfoss, turn south on Route 842 from the Ring Road, just west of Goðafoss, and proceed 41km (25 miles) to the marked turnoff. Buses on the Sprengisandur route from Mývatn to Landmannalaugar all make a sightseeing stop.

MÝVATN & KRAFLA

Iceland's president Ólafur Ragnar Grímsson wrote: "The Old Testament teaches us that God created the world in 6 days and then rested. This is not altogether true. Iceland was forgotten when He went to rest." The **Mývatn–Krafla region** ★★★—a volcanic smorgasbord of surreal lava fields, boiling and burping mud pools, sulfurous steam vents, explosion craters, and pseudocraters—is Iceland's most varied place to see the earth in mid-formation. Lake Mývatn is also a unique ecosystem and the largest migratory bird sanctuary in Europe, with thousands of waterfowl feeding on bugs and algae in the warm shallow waters.

Lake Mývatn

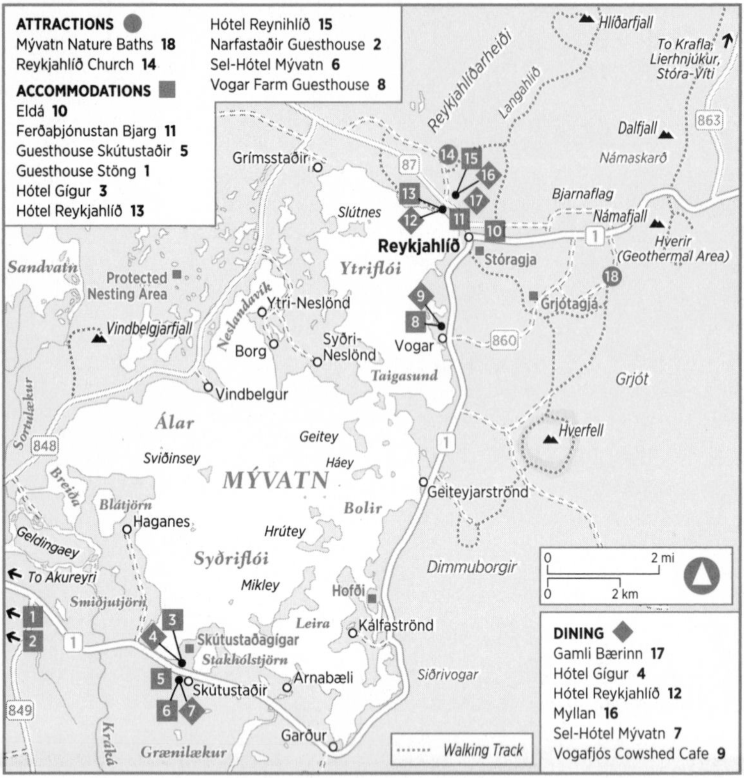

Mývatn is part of the greater Krafla volcanic system, a swath of faults and fissures 4 to 10km (2.5–6 miles) wide and 80km (50 miles) north to south, with Krafla caldera at its center. Krafla's last two eruption periods were 1724–1729 and 1975–1984. Both times, multiple fissures shifted and dilated, with sporadic eruptions and lava fountains, but much of the magma never surfaced, petering out laterally underground. Today the most active geothermal areas are Krafla and Bjarnarflag, each with a geothermal power plant. Two new plants have been proposed for close by, pitting power companies and some locals against conservationists and the increasingly influential tourist industry. The Krafla region is ideal for plants harnessing geothermal energy, because eruptions are infrequent and foreshadowed by a year of tectonic grumbling.

Mývatn–Krafla is well-touristed, and places to stay fill up quickly in summer, so the May or September shoulder season is advantageous. In high season, it may be a good idea to visit here early in your itinerary, before you've been spoiled by solitude elsewhere. On June weekends there may be choral concerts in the church or at Dimmuborgir; contact tourist information (below) for details. Mývatn–Krafla is also a compelling winter destination; see "Iceland in the Off Season," p. 35. Despite the multitude of sights, 2 days here is enough for the vast majority of visitors.

Mývatn sounds much less inviting in translation: "Midge Lake." Most of these pests don't bite, but they're attracted to carbon dioxide and may fly right into your nose and mouth. Head nets and insect repellent are available in the market at the N1 filling station. A head net may look ridiculous, but on warm, calm days you'll be glad to have one.

Essentials

GETTING THERE & AROUND

The only village in the area is **Reykjahlíð,** on the northeast shore of Mývatn. **Skútustaðir,** on the south side of the lake, has a small cluster of tourist services.

BY CAR Reykjahlíð, along Route 87 just off the Ring Road, is 103km (64 miles) east of Akureyri and 166km (103 miles) west of Egilsstaðir. The only place to arrange **car rental** is **Hótel Reynihlíð** (✆ **464-4170;** www.myvatnhotel.is).

BY BUS The **Sterna bus** (✆ **553-3737;** www.sterna.is) connecting Akureyri and Egilsstaðir stops at Skútustaðir and Reykjahlíð. It runs daily from June until August. The cost is 2,900kr from Akureyri or 4,700kr from Egilsstaðir. **SBA Norðurleið** (✆ **550-0700;** www.sba.is) has Mývatn–Krafla **sightseeing day tours** departing from Akureyri and Mývatn; they are detailed in the widely-available brochure *Iceland On Your Own*. The tour from Akureyri (10,500kr) hits Goðafoss (p. 263), Stóra-Víti, Hverir, Grjótagjá, and Dimmuborgir. From Reykjahlíð, the main daily tour (5,200kr; 3¼ hr.) hits Dimmuborgir, Grjótagjá, Stóra-Víti, Hverir, and the Mývatn Nature Baths. Unforgivably, neither tour goes to Leirhnjúkur (p. 268). All Sterna and SBA buses leaving Reykjahlíð board at the tourist information office (below) next to the N1 filling station.

Unfortunately there's no "hop-on hop-off" bus circling the lake on a regular basis, and SBA Norðurleið's tours generally decline to take passengers on short rides.

BY BIKE **Bike rental** is available from **Hótel Reynihlíð** (✆ **464-4170;** www.myvatnhotel.is), **Ferðaþjónustan Bjarg** (✆ **464-3800;** ferdabjarg@simnet.is) rents out bikes for 2,200kr a day, but like cows and horses they must be returned to the shed every evening by 9pm. **Hlíð campsite** (✆ **464-4103;** hlid@isholf.is) has bikes for 2,000kr a day; you can ride as long as you like before you return it.

ON FOOT Touring the sights by foot is possible, but most visitors find bus tours, car rental, or bike rental more practical. All hotels, restaurants, and services in Reykjahlíð are within walking distance of each other.

VISITOR INFORMATION

Mývatn's **tourist information office** is at Hraunvegur 8 (✆ **464-4390;** www.visitmyvatn.is; June–Aug daily 9am–6pm; call for off-season opening hours).

Exploring the Area

AROUND MÝVATN

The following sights form a clockwise route around the lake, starting in Reykjahlíð. The distance around the lake is 36km (22 miles) by car.

In 1729, at the height of the Krafla eruption, a lava stream gobbled up two farmhouses and was headed straight for **Reykjahlíð Church.** At the last moment, the stream split and flowed into the lake. The church site is slightly elevated, but prayer was credited for averting disaster. The current church dates from 1962, and the vivid pulpit carving depicts the old church with the eruption in the background and "27 August, 1729" written in psychedelic font. All that remains of the old church is a foundation wall in the graveyard, and menacing heaves of lava are still clearly visible just beyond the graveyard wall.

The road to the church (and campsite and airfield) leads uphill from Hótel Reynihlíð. Near the end of the road, a pleasant trail leads west over the Eldhraun lava field, before crossing Route 87 and heading back to town along the north shore of the lake; allow 2½ to 3 hours round trip.

Stóragjá, Grjótagjá, Hverfell, and **Dimmuborgir** (below) are connected by a recommended and well-marked trail, 7km (4.3 miles) or 2½ to 3 hours in each direction. The **trail** begins from the Ring Road near Reykjahlíð, a few meters east of the Route 87 junction. Between Grjótagjá and Hverfell, the trail has two marked junctures—one coinciding with the Hverfell parking area—where you can detour to **Mývatn Nature Baths** (p. 268).

The **Storagjá fissure** is not directly on the trail, but it's only a short detour, right from the trailhead. Partway along Stóragjá is a staircase into the narrow fissure, descending about 5m (16 ft.) to a grassy floor. From there, assisted by a chain and rope, you can peer through a crack at a limpid, turquoise geothermal pool. The pool has recently cooled, attracting too many bacteria for safe swimming.

The steamy **Grjótagjá fissure** ★ is set amid a geothermal valley of red and black gravel. Grjótagjá is 2km (1¼ miles) from the Stóragjá–Dimmuborgir trailhead, and also reachable by car on Route 860, which connects with the Ring Road at two points. (Approaching from the west requires opening a sheep gate.) Near the parking area, two portals in the heaving lava lead to an enticing hot spring and pool. You can climb down and sit by the water, but it's too hot for swimming and fogs up camera lenses.

Hverfell ★★ The striated black mound shaped like a dog-bowl is unmistakable. The name 'Hverfell' is a controversial subject—for the past 150 years it's been Hverfjall (*fjall* meaning mountain). However, a local man took the matter to court and won his case to have it returned to its original Hverfell (*fell* meaning small hill). Hence signs that say Hverfell (Hverfjall). Either way, it was formed between 2,500 and 2,900 years ago, when rising magma met with groundwater, forcing a massive explosion of steam, ash, and rock. The rim is 1km (½ mile) in diameter, and the crater is 140m (459 ft.) deep, with a round nub in the middle.

Hverfell's solemn, elemental grandeur cannot be fully appreciated without walking up to the crater rim. It's a 3km (1.9-mile) walk south from Grjótagjá, but you can also drive from the Ring Road to a parking area on Hverfell's north side. From there it's a 25-minute ascent. The trail loops completely around the rim, and the descent of the southern slope toward Dimmuborgir is steep and more challenging.

Meaning "Dark Castles," **Dimmuborgir** is a surreal lava field 1km (½ mile) in diameter. Its most distinctive features are the contorted crags and pillars reaching 20m (66 ft.) in height; nothing quite like them exists elsewhere, except on the ocean floor. Dimmuborgir was formed around 2,200 years ago, when molten lava formed a lava lake on the site. Eventually the lava found an outlet and drained into Mývatn, but hardened pillars had formed around steam vents (lava finds steam chilling) and were left behind. The surface of the lava lake had half-congealed, and left all kinds of crusty "watermarks" on its way out. The best time of year to visit is at the end of summer when the fiery hues of the birch contrast spectacularly with the black lava formations; plus the air is free of midges.

Dimmuborgir is a 2km (1 mile) walk from the southern face of Hverfell, and can also be reached by car off the Ring Road. Plan on walking for an hour or two among the well-marked loop trails. The recommended **Kirkjuvegur trail** leads to **Kirkjan** (Church), a lava chute forming an archway. The more hazardous **Krókastígur trail** cuts through the middle of the site, past some of the most bizarre formations. Take care not to step into a fissure, and keep a close eye on children.

Höfði, a lakeside park on a small promontory, makes for a nice hour-long stroll along peaceful forested pathways. The fragrant spruce and other trees were planted by Höfði's former owner. After entering the park, the trail branching off to the right leads to another juncture where you can detour uphill to a fantastic viewpoint. If instead you bear left after the park entrance and circle the promontory clockwise, you'll pass a clearing that overlooks Kálfarströnd. (The walk at Kálfarströnd farm, below, gives you a far better view.) Near the middle of Höfði is a rectangular lawn with benches—a good picnic spot, if the midges aren't too bothersome.

The name **Kálfarströnd ★** refers to a farm on a grassy peninsula extending into Mývatn, and also to a series of lava columns *(klasar)* rising like strange mushrooms in a cove between the peninsula and Höfði Park. The turnoff from the Ring Road is 1km (½ mile) south of Höfði. After parking, pass through the farm gate, and the 30-minute, staked loop trail past the klasar is shortly ahead on the right. Kálfarströnd is sublime on a calm, soft-lit evening, with the klasar looming, the sky reflected in the aquamarine shallows, Höfði's evergreens in the background, and Mývatn's trim green islands etched in the distance. Bring your head net.

If Mývatn had a visual trademark, it would be **Skútustaðagígar,** the cluster of pseudocraters surrounding Stakhólstjörn pond, at the southwest shore of the lake. Pseudocraters, found primarily in Iceland (and on Mars), are so named because they were never conduits for emerging lava. They're formed when lava flowing above ground heats sub-surface water, causing explosions from steam and gas buildup. The Skútustaðagígar pseudocraters, each around 20m (66 ft.) deep, are quite striking from the road (or from Vindbelgjarfjall, below); but when viewed from the rims, they're simply grassy bowls. The walk around Stakhólstjörn takes an hour, or a 30-minute circuit begins opposite the Skútustaðir gas station or from Hótel Gígur (p. 270).

The best all-around vista of Mývatn is from the top of **Vindbelgjarfjall mountain ★**, near the northwest shore. The 2-hour round-trip hike to the summit leaves from Vagnbrekka farm, off Route 848, 4km (2½ miles) from the junction with the Ring Road. From the farm to the base of the mountain, the trail traverses a protected nesting area for waterfowl. The protected area is off-limits from May 15 to July 20, but does not extend to the trail. The ascent is all scree and a bit slippery, but manageable.

THE KRAFLA GEOTHERMAL AREA

The Krafla central volcano crater is difficult to see from the ground because its shape is broken and irregular, yet its overall diameter is as large as that of Mývatn. Krafla is the name of a small mountain in the area, just east of the Víti crater but is not to be confused with the Krafla central volcano. The Krafla Geothermal Area is within the Krafla central volcano and includes the areas Leirhnjúkur and Stóra-Víti, while Mývatn Nature Baths, Hverir, Námafjall Ridge and Bjarnarflag are the geothermal areas south of the Krafla Geothermal Area.

Hverir ★, a large geothermal field, full of bubbling mud cauldrons and hissing steam vents, is 7km (4¼ miles) east of Reykjahlíð and easy to spot from the Ring

Road. Walking through Hverir feels unreal, as minerals and chemicals in the earth form an exotic spectrum unlike anything normally associated with nature. Some patches of ground are hot enough to cause severe burns, so stick to the paths. From Hverir, an hour-long trail ascends Námafjall, then cuts north to a parking area off the Ring Road at Námaskarð Pass, and then loops back to Hverir. Views are fabulous; but, again, be cautious, stay on the trail, and look out for scalding-hot patches of pale earth. The crust might look solid and is not particularly hot on the surface, but there may lie underneath a pocket of boiling mud, and people have been known to get their feet stuck in them. The walk can be seriously gloppy after rain.

Just east of Hverir, Route 863 branches off the Ring Road and leads north into the Krafla caldera. After about 8km (5 miles), the road passes under a pipeline arch at **Krafla Geothermal Power Station (Kröflustöð),** built in the 1970s. The **visitor building** (✆ **515-9000;** www.landsvirkjun.is; daily 1–5pm) has an informative free exhibit for those interested in the process of converting geothermal heat to electricity.

Gritty as burnt toast, **Leirhnjúkur lava field ★★★** is the best place to witness remnants of the 1975 to 1984 eruptions, and may be the most surreal landscape you will ever see. The parking area is clearly marked from Route 863, and from there it's a 15-minute walk to a geothermal field at the edge. Some visitors make the drastic mistake of looking at the boiling gray mud pots and color-streaked earth, and then heading back to their cars. Allow at least another hour for circling the trails, peering at the subtle range of color, texture, and moss inside each steamy rift. A good way to start is by proceeding from the geothermal field toward a bowl-shaped pseudocrater visible to the north. A recommended trail known as the **Krafla Route** leads straight from here to Reykjahlíð, and takes 3 to 4 hours one-way. ***Remember:*** Stick to the paths, watch your step, and beware of light-colored earth.

Route 863 dead-ends at a parking area by the rim of **Stóra-Víti,** a steep-sided explosion crater, formed in 1724, with a blue-green lake at the bottom. A trail circles the rim and descends on the far side to an interesting hot spring area. The route, which is worthwhile but not essential, takes about an hour round-trip and is not advised during muddy conditions.

Mývatn Nature Baths (Jarðböðin Við Mývatn) ★ It's tempting to tout this nature bath as the undiscovered alternative to the crowded and touristy Blue Lagoon, but it has some catching up to do. Both spas make extravagant claims about the health benefits of their water and sell a full line of beauty products. The waters at each bath are a unique solution of minerals, silicates, and microorganisms; only the Blue Lagoon includes seawater. Yet, while the Blue Lagoon blocks views of its surrounding lava field, bathers at Mývatn commune with the steaming hills. Though it may seem like a lot of money for a swim, it's the best way to unwind after a strenuous day of touristing, and saunas are included in the admission price. The water remains at a comfortable bath temperature, between 36°C and 39°C (96.8°F–102.2°F). Remove any copper or silver you might be wearing, as it will be damaged by sulfur in the water. Bring your own towel and swimsuit—rental for each is 500kr.

Rte. 1, 3km (2 miles) east of Reykjahlíð; turn right at blue sign for "Jarðböðin við Mývatn." ✆ **464-4411.** www.jardbodin.is. Admission 2,500kr adults; 2,000kr seniors/students; 1,000kr children aged 12–15, children under 12 free. June–Aug daily 9am–midnight, no entry after 11:30pm; Sept–May daily noon-10pm, no entry after 9:30pm.

Magma Essentials, Birkihraun 11 (✆ **464-3740** or 898-9964; www.magmaessentials.com or www.massage.is) is a holistic health offering everything from 90-minute therapeutic massages to yoga instruction and aromatherapy.

Outdoor Activities

Mývatn is a common launch point for tours of the interior, especially to Askja Caldera and Kverkfjöll. The bus that takes the Sprengisandur route across the interior highlands to Landmannalaugar also leaves from Mývatn. Askja, Kverkfjöll, and Sprengisandur are covered in chapter 12.

AERIAL TOURS **Mýflug Air** (✆ **464-4400;** www.myflug.is), based at the small airfield just outside Reykjahlíð, runs sightseeing tours of Mývatn–Krafla, Jökulsárgljúfur, Askja, Kverkfjöll, Vatnajökull, Grímsey and other natural spectacles with a fleet of two six-seaters and a ten-seater. Tours range from 20 minutes and 9,500kr to 2 hours and 19,000kr to 27,500kr with a minimum of two passengers, or three for Grímsey. Flights are weather-dependent, and departure times are by agreement.

CAVING **Sagatravel** (✆ **659-8888;** www.sagatravel.is) arranges 5-hour guided tours of **Lofthellir,** a lava cave alive with lustrous and ghostly ice formations. The cost is 17,500kr adults or 8,750kr children aged 6 to 12, with a four-person or 52,500kr minimum. Gloves, helmets, flashlights, and studded boots are provided. Tours run June until September. Dress warmly.

4WD TOURS **Sagatravel** (✆ **659-8888;** www.sagatravel.is) offers a 6- to 7-hour excursion covering Krafla and Jökulsárgljúfur (23,000kr adults, 11,500kr children aged 6–12). The tour includes **Gjástykki,** a starkly-beautiful volcanic area north of Krafla caldera and inaccessible to regular cars. Gjástykki is under consideration for a new geothermal power plant, so enjoy the scenery while you can. Departures, by reservation only, are from June 15 until September at 8am, with a four-person minimum. Trips to Dettifoss and Jökulsárgljúfur run year round. From September until May, **Sel-Hótel Mývatn** (✆ **464-4164;** www.myvatn.is) runs a 4WD tour of Mývatn, and other off-road tours; call in advance for bookings and prices.

HORSEBACK RIDING **Safari Hestar** (✆ **464-4164;** www.myvatn.is or www.safarihestar.is) has 1-hour tours with a choice of destinations for 4,000kr per person; a 2-hour excursion is 7,000kr. **Saltvík** (✆ **847-9515;** www.skarpur.is/saltvik), based 5km (3 miles) outside Húsavík, leads unforgettable multi-day tours in Saltvík and the Mývatn–Krafla area.

Where to Stay

All options below are around Mývatn, mostly in Reykjahlíð, the village on the northeast corner of the lake, and Skútustaðir, a small settlement on the south side. On short notice, the information office can tell you which have vacancies, but in July and early August every single room could well be occupied. Two guesthouses west of Mývatn are good, relatively-inexpensive backups: **Guesthouse Stöng** (✆ **464-4252;** www.stong.is) and **Narfastaðir Guesthouse** (✆ **464-3300;** www.farmhotel.is).

VERY EXPENSIVE

Hótel Reynihlíð ★ The standard doubles here—identified as "deluxe"—are decent-sized but not as smart as expected from an upscale hotel. The "superior" doubles, often corner rooms, are worth the upgrade, with more space, swankier furnishings, and bathrooms with short bathtubs. Ask for a lake view. Service is exceptional, and the front desk is helpful with travel arrangements.

Rte. 87, Reykjahlíð. ✆ **464-4170.** Fax 464-4371. www.reynihlid.is. 41 units. June–Aug 33,600kr double. Rates around 30% lower Sept–May. Rates include breakfast. AE, DC, MC, V. **Amenities:** Restaurant; room service. *In room:* TV, hair dryer, Wi-Fi.

EXPENSIVE

Hótel Gígur ★ Rooms at this summer-only hotel are a bit faded and small, but the dining area, overlooking the lake and the Skútustaðagígar pseudocraters, is the perfect spot for morning coffee. Rooms with lake views are scarce and book quickly.

Rte. 1 at Skútustaðir. ✆ **464-4455.** Fax 464-4279. www.keahotels.is. 37 units. May 15–Aug 26,900kr double; 32,800kr triple. Rates include breakfast. AE, DC, MC, V. Closed Sept–May 14. **Amenities:** Restaurant; bar; Internet terminal. *In room:* TV.

Hótel Reykjahlíð ★★ This small lakeside hotel is one of Iceland's most appealing country accommodations. The nine rooms are tasteful and pleasant if not purring with luxury. In 2007 new beds were imported and bathrooms were renovated to include tubs. All rooms have lake views except for #5, which has the biggest bathroom. Top-floor rooms—including #11 and #14, the picks of the litter—are slightly larger. The hotel's small size keeps service personal and attentive; the downside is that the entire summer is booked out by April.

Rte. 87, Reykjahlíð, on lake side of road. ✆ **464-4142.** Fax 464-4336. www.reykjahlid.is. 9 units. Jul–Aug 20 30,600kr double; 37,100kr triple. Rates around 5% lower June and Aug 21–31; 35% lower May, Sept, and Dec 15–Jan 15; and 40% lower Jan 16–Apr and Oct–Dec 14. Rates include breakfast. MC, V. **Amenities:** Restaurant. *In room:* Hair dryer, no phone, Wi-Fi.

Sel-Hótel Mývatn ★ Rooms in this mid-grade hotel, across the road from the Skútustaðagígar pseudocraters, have just enough of an antiqued look to set them apart from the cold impersonal standard. The hot tub and sauna operate all winter, but in high season *might* be turned on by advance request. In winter Sel-Hótel has outrageous discounts and puts together a panoply of enticing tours.

Rte. 1, Skútustaðir. ✆ **464-4164.** Fax 464-4364. www.myvatn.is. 35 units. June–Aug 29,500kr double. Rates around 37% lower May and Sept; 50% lower Oct–Apr. Rates include breakfast. AE, MC, V. **Amenities:** Restaurants; bar; hot tub; sauna. *In room:* TV, hair dryer, Wi-Fi.

MODERATE

Eldá This guesthouse operates in four different houses in Reykjahlíð. All have extremely basic and functional rooms, though the house at Birkihraun 11 has a more personal touch. The breakfast buffet is bounteous no matter where you stay and includes freshly-baked bread. All guests check in at Helluhraun 15.

Helluhraun 15, Reykjahlíð. ✆ **464-4220.** Fax 464-4321. www.elda.is. 27 units, none w/bathroom. June 21–Aug 31 16,700kr double, 23,600kr triple. Rates 10%–20% lower off season. Rates include breakfast in summer. MC, V. Just north of the N1 filling station, turn on Hlíðarvegur, then make first right on Helluhraun. At the T junction, turn right; Eldá is shortly ahead on the left. **Amenities:** Guest kitchen. *In room:* No phone, Wi-Fi.

Guesthouse Skútustaðir This friendly and dependable place in the Farm Holidays Network has spacious but otherwise standard guesthouse rooms, and a nice lake view from the breakfast area. The five en-suite rooms are in a prefab block that looks like a row of lockers, but from the inside you shouldn't be disappointed.

Rte. 1, Skútustaðir, next to Sel-Hótel Mývatn. ✆ **464-4212.** Fax 464-4322. 13 units, 5 w/bathroom. June–Aug 20 17,300kr double w/bathroom; 12,600kr double without bathroom. May and August 21–31 12,000kr double w/bathroom; 9,600kr double without bathroom. Rates include breakfast. MC, V. Closed Oct–Apr. **Amenities:** Guest kitchen. *In room:* No phone, Wi-Fi.

Vogar Farm Guesthouse These efficient, identical, wood-lined rooms are comfortable, with a Scandinavian touch. If you get to breakfast at 7:30am you can look through a glass partition at cows being milked (see "Vogafjós Cowshed Cafe," below). It sits 3km (2 miles) south of Reykjahlíð, far from any bus stop. Reception is at the cafe.

Rte. 1, 3km (2 miles) south of Reykjahlíð. ✆ **464-4303.** Fax 464-4341. www.vogarholidays.is. 20 units. June–Aug 26,400kr double. Rates up to 50% lower Sept–May. Rates include breakfast. **Amenities:** Cafe. *In room:* No phone.

INEXPENSIVE

Ferðaþjónustan Bjarg This campground with good facilities also has two utilitarian guest rooms with fair views. The soft-spoken proprietor knows everything there is to know about the area and is also a one-man travel agency.

Reykjahlíð; exit Rte. 1 on to Rte. 87 and take first left turn. ✆ **464-4240.** Fax 464-4341. ferdabjarg@simnet.is. 2 units without bathroom. May–Oct 14,000kr double; 19,000kr triple. AE, DC, MC, V. Closed Oct–April. **Amenities:** Guest kitchen. *In room:* No phone.

Where to Dine

Fast food can be found at the **N1 filling station** in Reykjahlíð and at the **cafeteria** adjoining the restaurant at the Sel-Hótel Mývatn in Skútustaðir (below).

EXPENSIVE

Hótel Gígur ★ ICELANDIC This snazzy restaurant is perfectly attuned to its surroundings, with floor-to-ceiling windows overlooking the lake and Skútustaðagígar pseudocraters, and decorated with clear vases of lava rock and moss. The menu reaches beyond the usual fish and lamb—but quality is hard to predict, due to frequent chef turnover.

Rte. 1 at Skútustaðir. ✆ **464-4455.** Reservations recommended. Main courses 3,250kr–3,990kr. AE, DC, MC, V. May 15–Aug daily 6–10pm.

Hótel Reykjahlíð ★★ ICELANDIC This is the region's best restaurant, both for cooking and ambience, especially if you're seated near a window. Outside, horses graze, ducks paddle, and waves lap the lake shore. The menu ranges from traditional to daring, with a vegetarian option, but always relies on lamb, salmon, and Arctic char. The *skyr* dessert with fresh fruit and cream is utter perfection. Reserve at least a day in advance.

Rte. 87, Reykjahlíð, on lake side of road. ✆ **464-4142.** Reservations recommended. Main courses 3,600kr–4,900kr. MC, V. June–Aug 7:30am–10am and 7–10pm; May and Sept daily 7–10pm; Oct–Apr on request in advance.

Myllan ICELANDIC This restaurant at the up-market Hótel Reynihlíð is serviceable but hardly a standout. Stay with the lamb or trout, or perhaps the breast of duck with mango chutney.

Rte. 87, Reykjahlíð. ✆ **464-4170.** Reservations recommended. Main courses 4,900kr–6,900kr. AE, DC, MC, V. Daily 11am–midnight.

Sel-Hótel Mývatn ICELANDIC Big eaters can take advantage of the lunch and dinner buffets at this plainly decorated, traditional Icelandic restaurant—even if they have to work around Icelandic "specials" such as putrefied shark, blood pudding, and sheep's head jelly. The a la carte menu has plenty of palatable alternatives.

Rte. 1, Skútustaðir. ✆ **464-4164.** Reservations recommended. Main courses 1,400kr–4,990kr; lunch buffet 1,550kr, dinner buffet 5,250kr. June–Aug daily 7:30–10am, noon–2pm and 6:30–9pm; Sept–May 7–9pm.

MODERATE

Gamli Bærinn ICELANDIC As the only casual restaurant in Reykjahlíð that doesn't serve fast food, Gamli Bærinn is overrun in summer. Prepare to be overlooked for a while by the harried teenage wait staff. Lamb and trout supplement a long roster of sandwiches, burgers, and vegetarian plates. The food is not quite as good as the with-it tavern atmosphere seems to promise. Musicians might just take the stage—and then exit just as unceremoniously. Make sure to reserve a table.

Rte. 87, next to Hótel Reynihlíð. ✆ **464-4270.** Reservations recommended. Main courses 1,700kr–2,900kr. AE, DC, MC, V. Daily 10am–11pm.

Vogafjós Cowshed Cafe ☺ CAFE Bedrooms in old Icelandic turf farms were often placed directly over the cowsheds for sharing body heat. Cow intimacy carries on at this cafe, which looks directly into a milking shed. (Thankfully the barn smell doesn't seep through the glass partition.) Milking times are 7:30am and 5:30 or 6pm, and warm milk is passed around; otherwise the cows are usually outside the shed. The cafe-style menu has sandwiches, crepes, and dishes featuring homemade products such as mozzarella, feta, smoked lamb, and very creamy ice-cream.

Rte. 1, 3km (2 miles) south of Reykjahlíð; look for cow-shaped sign. ✆ **464-4303.** Reservations required for dinner. Breakfast 2,000kr; main courses 900kr–5,300kr. MC, V. May 15–Sept daily 7:30am–11:30pm; other times call ahead.

HÚSAVÍK & NEARBY

Húsavík, once a busy whale-hunting port, is now Exhibit A in making the case that whale-watching tours are a better source of income. Packaging itself as the "European Capital of Whale-Watching," this pretty fishing town of 2,300 complements the tours with pleasant waterfront eateries and a compelling whale museum. Húsavík's regional folk museum is also a standout, but far more visitors choose to gain a deeper scientific understanding of penises at the Icelandic Phallological Museum, a collection of 235 mammalian male members.

Húsavík is usually just a 1-day wonder in travel itineraries that dwell longer in Akureyri, Mývatn, and Jökulsárgljúfur. Scan the sights and activities below, however, to see if a second day would be worth your time.

Essentials

GETTING THERE Húsavík is on Route 85, 92km (57 miles) from Akureyri, 54km (34 miles) from Mývatn, and 65km (40 miles) from Ásbyrgi in Jökulsárgljúfur. The only **car rental agency** in town is **Húsavík Car Rental,** Garðarsbraut 66 (✆ **464-2500;** b.h@simnet.is).

SBA Norðurleið (✆ **550-0700;** www.sba.is) has a daily direct bus from Akureyri to Húsavík and Húsavík to Akureyri from mid-June through August; the cost is 2,800kr one-way and 1,400kr for children aged between 4 and 11. The service from Akureyri

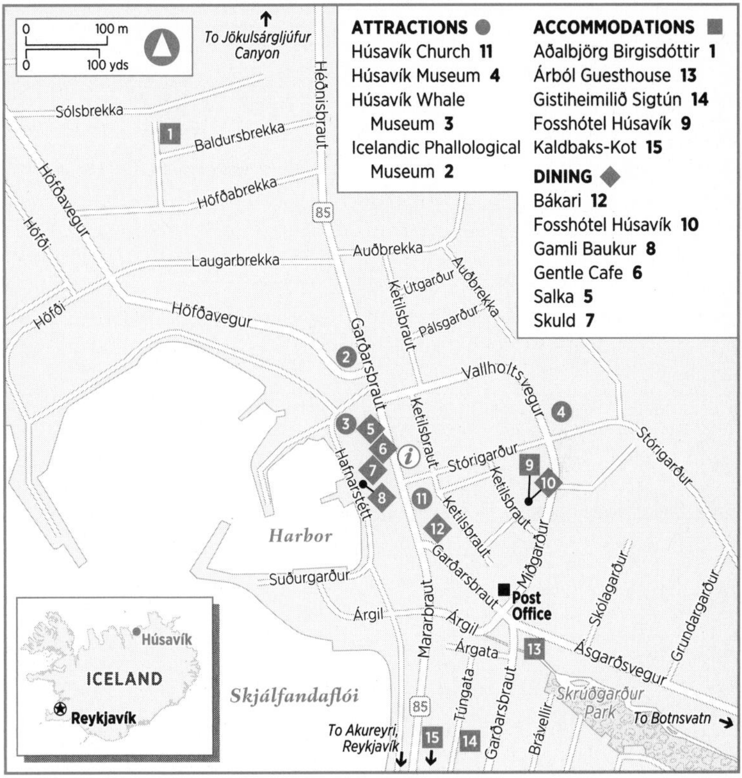

to Dettifoss and back also stops in Húsavík and Ásbyrgi; the cost is 6,600kr one-way. From Dettifoss a connecting bus goes on to Mývatn (2,800kr), and another bus connects Mývatn and Húsavík twice daily (2,200kr).

SBA also provides **day tours of Húsavík** from Akureyri, including a whale-watching tour. The day trip from Akureyri costs 11,000kr in high season, 500kr more than buying bus tickets and a whale-watching tour independently.

VISITOR INFORMATION Húsavík's **tourist office,** Garðarsbraut 5 (✆ **464-4300;** www.nordausturland.is; June–Sept Mon–Sat 9am–7pm, Sun 10am–6pm), is on the main street in the middle of town and can assist with finding places to stay.

Exploring the Area

BETWEEN AKUREYRI & HÚSAVÍK

Transportation Museum at Ystafell (Samgönguminjasafnið Ystafelli) Vintage car junkies should enjoy this collection of 100 vehicles, all veterans of Icelandic roads. Curator Sverrir Ingólfsson, who restored the magnificent 1969 Ford Mustang

WAS ICELAND'S first SETTLER NOT A VIKING?

Húsavík's beginnings pose a vital challenge to the way Icelandic history is told. In the 860s, a few years before the Norse settlement of Reykjavík, a Swede named Garðar Svavarsson spent a winter at Húsavík. According to later accounts, one of Garðar's men, Nattfari, escaped with two slaves—a man and a woman—and stayed behind, settling across the bay and then farther inland. Nattfari's identity, motives, and ultimate fate remain a mystery. He may have been a slave himself. His name isn't Norse, and probably means "Night Traveler," but his origins are unknown. Still, Nattfari may well have been Iceland's first permanent settler—not Ingólfur Arnarson, who is traditionally assigned this role.

Why was Nattfari left out of the picture? The introduction to the *Book of Settlements,* a key Icelandic text from the 13th century, suggests a motive: " . . . we think we can better meet the criticism of foreigners when they accuse us of being descended from slaves or scoundrels if we know for certain the truth about our ancestors." Ingólfur was Norse, with superior class status, and his emigration to Iceland seemed more deliberate and heroic. In 1974, Iceland held its official 1,100-year celebration of Icelandic settlement. Four years before, the people of Húsavík held their own ceremony for Nattfari and his two companions.

with crimson velvet upholstery and window tassels, can lift hoods for inspection. Recently added to the collection is a 1919 Dixie Flyer, one of only three in the world.

Rte. 85, 9km (5½ miles) north of Rte. 1 and 37km (23 miles) south of Húsavík. ✆ **464-3133.** www.ystafell.is. Admission 500kr adults; free for children aged 12 and under. May 15–Sept daily 10am–8pm; Oct–May 14 call ahead.

HÚSAVÍK

Most tourist activity—including the whale-watching ticket booths, four eateries, a bookstore, a market, a handknit woolens store, the Whale Museum, and the Phallological Museum—are clustered on two parallel streets: Hafnarstétt, which runs right along the waterfront, and Garðarsbraut, just uphill.

The German- and Swiss-inspired design of **Húsavík Church (Húsavíkurkirkja)**—located along Garðarsbraut—stands out in Iceland, as do the 1907 church's cruciform shape and absence of a pulpit. The lovely patterns painted on the interior walls are from 1924 and feature the Lutheran symbol of a cross within a heart. The 1931 altarpiece depicts Jesus raising Lazarus from the dead, as an onlooker faints. The painter Sveinn Þórarinsson was raised nearby, and the mountains in the background look suspiciously Icelandic.

Húsavík Museum (Safnahúsið) ★ Icelandic museums based on regional histories are often too esoteric, but Safnahúsið has an unusually broad range of interesting artifacts. On the first floor the maritime exhibit screens old-time fishing documentaries, and just outside is an authentically stinky baiting-shack and the skull and chin bone of a blue whale. The natural history collection on the second floor includes a stuffed polar bear shot at Grímsey Island in 1969, and a rare albino eider duckling, normally stomped to death by its mother to protect its siblings from predators. Among the folk arts don't miss the whalebone carvings or the display case, marked "Hárfínt Handbragð," full of necklaces and collars made from ladies' hair. The third floor is dedicated to art and photo exhibitions. Signage in English is limited, but the staff is responsive to questions.

Stórigarður 17. ✆ **464-1860.** www.husmus.is. Admission 600kr adults; free for children under 16. June–Aug daily 10am–6pm; Sept–May Mon–Fri 10am–4pm.

THE saga OF ICELANDIC WHALING

Icelanders can be touchy about whaling. Mere mention of the subject could provoke an impassioned speech about how Iceland is unjustly judged by a sanctimonious and hypocritical outside world.

In 1986, the International Whaling Commission (IWC)—formed in 1946 to promote cooperation among whaling nations—placed a moratorium on commercial whaling. The moratorium had no legal authority, but Iceland withdrew its IWC membership in protest. Iceland rejoined in 2002, but two years later resumed whaling under the pretense of scientific research. This meant that studies were conducted on the whales' stomach contents—and on the resulting implications for fish stocks—before the meat was sold off. In 2006 Iceland dispensed with the scientific cover and set a commercial whaling quota in open defiance of the moratorium.

Whaling supporters point out that minke whales, which comprise the vast majority of victims, have a worldwide population of 900,000 and are not an endangered species. Evidence does suggest that minke whales reduce fish stocks, particularly cod, which alone account for as much as 20% of Iceland's export income.

Icelanders have hunted whales for over 300 years, and consider it part of their cultural heritage. From the time of settlement, beached whales were such a precious resource that the Icelandic word for beached whale, *hvalreki,* also means "windfall" or "godsend." Icelanders also feel they have fought too long and hard for control of their territorial waters to let foreigners once again meddle.

Opponents highlight the gruesome details of whale hunting; from the first harpoon strike, these noble and intelligent creatures can take a full hour to die. Whales may compete with fishermen for cod, but whaling provides only a few seasonal jobs, and demand for whalemeat is low. Tourists have shown some interest, but most Icelanders rarely eat whale. Whalemeat costs less than chicken in Icelandic supermarkets, and often ends up as animal food. The main foreign buyer, Japan, is increasingly wary of toxins found in the meat of North Atlantic whales.

Since Iceland resumed whaling, Greenpeace has led a tourist boycott. Within Iceland, however, most anti-whaling activists would prefer tourists to come and spend money on whale-watching tours. Decades ago, tourist buses took a 1-hour trip from Reykjavík to Hvalfjörður to watch whales being sliced up and processed. Now nearly 100,000 tourists a year watch Icelandic whales that are very much alive.

In August, 2007, Iceland's fisheries minister announced a halt to commercial whaling. In 2008 the ministry issued a new quota of 40 minke whales. Despite opposition from Icelanders, and diplomatic pressure from at least 26 countries, in 2009 commercial whaling was allowed to continue until 2012 with an extended quota of 150 fin whales and 100 minke.

Húsavík Whale Museum (Hvalasafnið á Húsavík) ★ ☺ This engaging and informative museum examines all things whale: whale biology, whale sociology, whale hunting, whale-watching. Full skeletons of 10 species hang from the ceiling. Screens show gripping footage of whales underwater, whales being hunted and processed, and Icelanders gathering to push stranded whales back into the ocean. The museum is sponsored by environmental groups, but wisely avoids any preachiness, letting the facts on whaling speak for themselves.

Garðarsbraut. ✆ **464-2520.** www.icewhale.is. Admission 1,000kr adults; 800kr seniors/students; 400kr children aged 6–14. June–Aug daily 9am–7pm; May and Sept 10am–5pm.

Icelandic Phallological Museum Sigurður Hjartarson began collecting dismembered mammal penises in the 1970s and began this exhibit in Reykjavík while working as a high-school teacher. The inventory, mostly ghost-white and jarred in formaldehyde, includes penises from 52 whales, 30 seals and walruses, 110 land mammals, and a polar bear. The largest, at five feet two inches, belonged to a sperm whale. A magnifying glass is provided for the smallest, which belonged to a hamster. No human specimen is on display, but four men have provided for the museum in their wills. (Two of the men sent plaster casts, so we can see what we have to look forward to.) Recently the museum added testicles and a sperm tube which were surgically removed from an anonymous 50-year-old Icelander. Also on hand are smoked horse penises, originally intended for eating, and lamps made from scrotal sacs of bulls and rams. Visitors are sure to find the scientific education they've come for, learning for instance about all of nature's mechanisms for producing erections. More interesting, and less gruesome, than you might imagine.

Héðinsbraut 3a (on main road, just north of the dock). ✆ **561-6663.** www.phallus.is. Admission 600kr. May 20–Sept 10 daily noon–6pm.

BOTNSVATN ★

This isolated, peaceful lake in the hills behind Húsavík is the perfect destination for an easy, after-dinner walk as the sun sets over the bay. Two routes lead to the lake, both starting along the Búðará stream at the eastern edge of town. On the north side of the stream, Ásgarðsvegur becomes a dirt road and leads directly to the lake, but walkers will prefer the path that follows the stream most of the way. Paths on both sides of the stream converge on the north side, and from there it's a 25-minute walk to a pebbly beach and picnic table on the lake's western side. Another path circles the lake.

TJÖRNES

Northeast from Húsavík, Route 85 follows the periphery of this stubby peninsula. Fossil devotees should stop for a look at the **Ytritunga Fossils:** millions of sea shells—deposited when sea levels and water temperatures were far higher—in steep banks where the Hallbjarnarstaðaá stream meets the ocean. The turnoff from Route 85 is about 12km (7½ miles) northeast of Húsavík, just past Ytritunga Farm, and marked by a sign with "fossils" in small lettering. Be careful on the road's final descent to the ocean; if it's washed out, you may never get back up. At the end of the road, walk ahead to the stream and turn the corner.

Mánárbakka Museum This quirky home museum would be much more fun as an antique store. The collection spans everything from vintage matchboxes to a hand-operated washing machine to a teacup designed to keep moustaches dry. Their most treasured piece, inside a glass case upstairs, is a pearl that supposedly originated in Turkestan and was brought from Norway by the Vikings.

Rte. 85, 23km (14 miles) northeast of Húsavík. ✆ **464-1957.** Admission 500kr adults; free for ages 12 and under. June–Aug daily 10am–6pm.

OUTDOOR ACTIVITIES

HORSEBACK RIDING **Saltvík** (✆ **847-9515;** www.skarpur.is/saltvik), 5km (3 miles) outside Húsavík, offers a popular 2-hour strut along the seashore for 7,000kr per person.

SAILING/BIRDWATCHING **North Sailing** (✆ **464-2350;** www.northsailing.is) offers the memorable 3½-hour tour "Whales, Puffins, and Sails" on a two-masted schooner, combining whale-watching with a visit to **Lundey,** an island bristling with puffins. Passengers can help set sails or even take the helm. Tickets are 10,300kr for adults, or half-price for children under 15, with one or two departures daily from early May to late August. (After Aug 15, you're unlikely to see puffins.)

SEA FISHING Húsavík's two whale-watching companies, **Gentle Giants** and **North Sailing** (see below) both offer fishing trips in pursuit of cod and haddock. Expect to pay around 11,000kr for a 2- to 3-hour tour, with all equipment provided and arrangements made for grilling the catch. The Gentle Giants schedules regular departures at 6pm in summer, but requires a four-person minimum.

WHALE-WATCHING Húsavík lies close to whale migratory lanes, and whale-watching prospects are somewhat better than elsewhere in Iceland; but visitors should keep expectations in check. Tour companies boast a 98% success rate, but "success" could be a fleeting glimpse of a minke whale, which is relatively small and doesn't put on much of a show. The most acrobatic performer is the humpback whale, whose feeding technique involves blowing a vertical spiral of bubbles—halting the fish within—and then launching itself open-mouthed up through the spiral and into the air. Humpbacks appear two times out of three. Odds of seeing a white-beaked dolphin are one in three; a harbor porpoise, one in five. The very lucky see the world's largest creature, the blue whale, whose heart is the size of a VW beetle. The very, very lucky encounter a whale so accustomed to people that it allows itself to be patted; though tour announcers do their best to pretend everyone has been lucky.

Húsavík has two whale-watching tour operators, **Gentle Giants** (✆ **464-1500;** www.gentlegiants.is) and **North Sailing** (✆ **464-2350;** www.northsailing.is). Despite the intense and sometimes silly advertising competition between the two companies—North Sailing is "The Original," while Gentle Giants is "The Truly Original"—differences are negligible. Gentle Giants charges 7,400kr, North Sailing 7,700kr. Gentle Giants is free for children under 16, while North Sailing is free for children under 7 and half price for children aged 8 to 16. Those who have difficulty making decisions might consider that Gentle Giants has snazzier jumpsuits and gives away twisted donuts called *kleina,* while North Sailing hands out cinnamon rolls. Each has a ticket kiosk easily spotted from the main road.

The season runs from late April until October, when whales start returning south to breed. From June to August, several tours depart daily from 8am to 8:15pm. In late April, May, and September, three tours depart daily, the latest at 1:30pm. In October, Gentle Giants has morning tours on Saturday and Sunday only. The standard tour lasts 3 hours.

Tours are sometimes cancelled in rough weather, so anyone coming from out of town should call ahead. Seasick pills are a good idea (ginger also works well), even if conditions seem calm. Take the insulated jumpsuits that are supplied to all passengers; we thought we could do without one, and learned otherwise.

Where to Stay

For those who don't like changing beds every night, Húsavik can be a base for exploring Jökulsárgljúfur and the Mývatn area. Húsavík's tourist information office (p. 273) can assist in finding vacancies.

The Aðaldalur Valley between Akureyri, Húsavík, and Mývatn is often overlooked, but also makes for good operational headquarters. **Icelandic Farm Holidays** (**✆ 570-2700;** www.farmholidays.is) lists several places in and around Aðaldalur; among the most peaceful and welcoming are **Hagi 1** (Rte. 853, off Route 845; **✆ 464-3526;** www.hagi-1.com; 13,000kr double without bathroom, including breakfast) and **Þinghúsið Hraunbær** (Route 845, 3km/2 miles south of Route 85 junction; **✆ 464-3695;** 12,600kr double without bathroom, including breakfast), both on the river Laxá, 20 minutes from Húsavík. The nicest hotel in Aðaldalur is **Hótel Rauðaskriða** (Route 85, around 18km/11 miles from Route 1; **✆ 464-3504;** www.hotelraudaskrida.is; 21,500kr double including breakfast), with a restaurant, bar, and hot tubs.

EXPENSIVE

Fosshótel Húsavík Standard doubles at this overpriced, whale-themed hotel are bland, while the 26 newer and more expensive rooms have extra space, white-suede chairs, elegant bathrooms with tubs, and photographic imaging of a pebble beach on the flooring. Rooms with ocean views also fall into the higher price bracket, but they don't seem quite worth it.

Ketilsbraut 22. **✆ 464-1220.** Fax 464-2161. www.fosshotel.is. 70 units. June–Aug 29,000kr double. Rates around 30% lower Sept–May. Rates include breakfast. AE, DC, MC, V. **Amenities:** Restaurant; bar; Internet terminal. *In room:* TV, hair dryer.

MODERATE

Kaldbaks-Kot ★ Freestanding mini-cabins are charmingly different to a proper hotel room, and in Iceland they're a common and convenient option, especially for self-caterers. These well-equipped cabins have a double bed, bathroom, living area with pullout sofa, kitchenette, and outstanding views across the bay. Two cabins add sleeping lofts. Unless you bring sheets and towels, they cost 800kr for the entire stay, and guests are expected to clean up after themselves or pay a 1,900kr cleaning fee.

Rte. 85 just south of Húsavík. **✆ 464-1504.** Fax 464-1503. www.cottages.is. 17 units. July to mid-Aug 14,000kr double cabin; 18,000kr cabin w/sleeping loft. Rates 10% lower June and late Aug; 20% lower Sept and May. MC, V. *In room:* TV, kitchenette, no phone, Wi-Fi.

INEXPENSIVE

Aðalbjörg Birgisdóttir Guests at this small, friendly and very inexpensive guesthouse feel quite aware of staying in someone's home. Not that the owners, a retired Hungarian fisherman and his Icelandic wife, disrespect anyone's privacy—in fact, their English is very limited. The feeling comes from the decorations, and from finding yourself gazing at framed photos of kids and grandkids in the hallway.

Baldursbrekka 20 (at Háhöfði). **✆ 464-1005.** 4 units, none w/bathroom. June–Aug 7,000kr double; 3,000kr sleeping-bag accommodation per person. Breakfast available. No credit cards. Closed Sept–May. *In room:* No phone, Wi-Fi.

Árból Guesthouse ★ Situated close to a pleasant stream and park, this former residence of the district governor is the nicest guesthouse in town. The best rooms are in the attic—#8 is particularly prized for its ocean view—if you don't mind showering downstairs.

Ásgarðsvegur 2. ✆ **464-2220.** Fax 464-1463. www.simnet.is/arbol. 10 units, none w/bathroom. 14,400kr double. Breakfast available (1,300kr). Rates 20% lower Oct-Apr. DC, MC, V. *In room:* No phone, Wi-Fi.

Gistiheimilið Sigtún Rooms here are matter-of-fact but comfortable, and guests have free use of a kitchen, Internet terminal, and washing machine. The owner has trouble with English, so e-mail (gsigtun@gsigtun.is) is probably the best way to make arrangements.

Túngata 13. ✆ **464-1674.** Fax 464-1671. www.gsigtun.is. 5 units, none w/bathroom. 13,500kr-8,700kr double; 23,000kr quadruple. Rates include breakfast. MC, V. **Amenities:** Guest kitchen; washer/dryer access; Internet terminal. *In room:* No phone, Wi-Fi.

Where to Dine

If other places are full, **Fosshótel Húsavík** (see "Where to Stay," above) has a standard-issue **restaurant.** The **Bákari** (Garðarsbraut, off Mararbraut; ✆ **464-2901;** Mon–Fri 8am–6pm, Sat 10am–2pm; 8am–6pm), indeed a bakery, has sandwiches as well as baked goods and could pass for lunch.

Gamli Baukur ICELANDIC This waterfront restaurant provides good maritime ambience for its heavily-tourist clientele—the best ocean view is from upstairs—and the food is slightly above expectation. The shellfish soup is predictably overloaded with butter and cream. The herring is prepared in-house, and served in pickled and spiced form, but it's an acquired taste. Grilled lamb is an excellent standby.

Hafnarstétt 9 (by stairs to Garðarsbraut). ✆ **464-2442.** Reservations recommended. Main courses 1,900kr-4,000kr. MC, V. Sun-Thurs 11:30am-10pm; Fri-Sat 11:30am-midnight; kitchen closes at 10pm.

Gentle Cafe LIGHT FARE Right next to the whale-watching ticket booths, this food kiosk, with outdoor tended seating, whips up grilled fresh fish, meat, soup, sandwiches, and a dish of the day—which can be anything from garlic-grilled trout to cured lamb.

Garðarsbraut. ✆ **864-6641.** Small dishes 600kr-1,900kr AE, DC, MC, V. June-Aug daily 9am-8pm; often closed in bad weather.

Salka ICELANDIC Compared to its competitor, Gamli Baukur, Salka has more of a living-room feel, but neither has any real edge in food, prices, or atmosphere. The smoked puffin is an interesting traditional dish and the grilled lamb or the cod with mashed potato and yellow beets served with vanilla-infused foamy sauce will do for a main course. The reliable pizzas have a deep-dish option and can be delivered to your accommodation.

Garðarsbraut 6. ✆ **464-2551.** Main courses 1,600kr-4,300kr. MC, V. Sun-Thurs 11:30am-9pm; Fri-Sat 11:30am-10pm.

Skuld CAFE With indoor and outdoor seating overlooking the harbor, this tiny coffeehouse and souvenir shop is a prime locale for whiling away some time over light bites like pastries and sandwiches.

Hafnarstétt 11, downstairs from North Sailing ticket booth. ✆ **464-7280.** Snacks 300kr-1,350kr. AE, DC, MC, V. Daily 8am-8pm.

VATNAJÖKULL NATIONAL PARK

Jökulsárgljúfur ★★★ is now part of Vatnajökull National Park (Europe's largest national park), which has extended to encompass the entirety of the Vatnajökull Glacier. **Jökulsárgljúfur Canyon** is Iceland's most celebrated canyon, which channels Iceland's second-longest river, the Jökulsá á Fjöllum. The river's opaque, gray water carries sediments from Iceland's largest glacier, Vatnajökull. A comparison to America's Grand Canyon and the Colorado River is tempting, but Jökulsárgljúfur does not register on such an instantly overwhelming scale. Rather, its treasures—including an extraordinary range of basalt formations, waterfalls, and plant life—unfold at each turn.

The ideal way to experience Jökulsárgljúfur is by taking a 2-day hike from bottom to top, but day hikes suffice for most. The busiest season is mid-June to mid-August, so if you crave solitude—and wish to avoid rowdy visitors at campsites—aim for late May to early June or late August and September.

Essentials

GETTING THERE & AROUND

BY CAR Jökulsárgljúfur—a mouthful that simply means "Glacial River Canyon"—is aligned north to south. Roads run along the east and west sides, connecting Route 85 in the north to the Ring Road in the south. In general, regular cars have more access to park sites from the north. On the west side of the canyon, you can navigate Route 862 from Route 85 as far south as the Vesturdalur campsite, near Hljóðaklettar—though potholes can be treacherous, especially in late summer. You might even get as far as the Hólmatungur parking area, but check with your car-rental company, as this could void your insurance. On the east side of the canyon, regular cars can take Route 864 between Route 85 and Dettifoss—and usually all the way to the Ring Road, depending on conditions. Those with 4WD vehicles can probably get from the Ring Road to Route 85 on either side of the canyon, but Route 864 on the east side is far easier.

BY BUS From mid-June into August, **SBA Norðurleið** (✆ **550-0700;** www.sba.is) has a daily morning bus from Akureyri to Dettifoss (on the west side of the canyon), stopping at Húsavík, Ásbyrgi, and Hlóðaklettar. A one-way trip is 6,600kr. The bus returns to Akureyri in the afternoon. Another bus, also daily from mid-June through August, starts at Mývatn and reaches Dettifoss from the opposite direction—that is, by taking Route 862 north from the Ring Road. These two buses connect with each other, so visitors can loop in either direction. From June 18 to August 31 SBA also has a marathon 13-hour "Jewels of the North" tour from Akureyri, covering both the Mývatn–Krafla region and Jökulsárgljúfur for 10,350kr, half price for children.

ON FOOT Park trails are well-marked and well-tended, with maps posted at trailheads, but it's still a good idea to secure maps and trail brochures at the information office before setting out. Visitors are asked not to venture off the trails, as sub-Arctic vegetation is fragile and slow to recover from trampling.

Hiking the full length of the park over two days can proceed in either direction, but almost everyone heads downstream, from south to north, starting at the parking area for Dettifoss (on the west side of the river) and ending at Ásbyrgi. The only legal campsite along the 34km (21-mile) route is at Vesturdalur. The warden at Vesturdalur

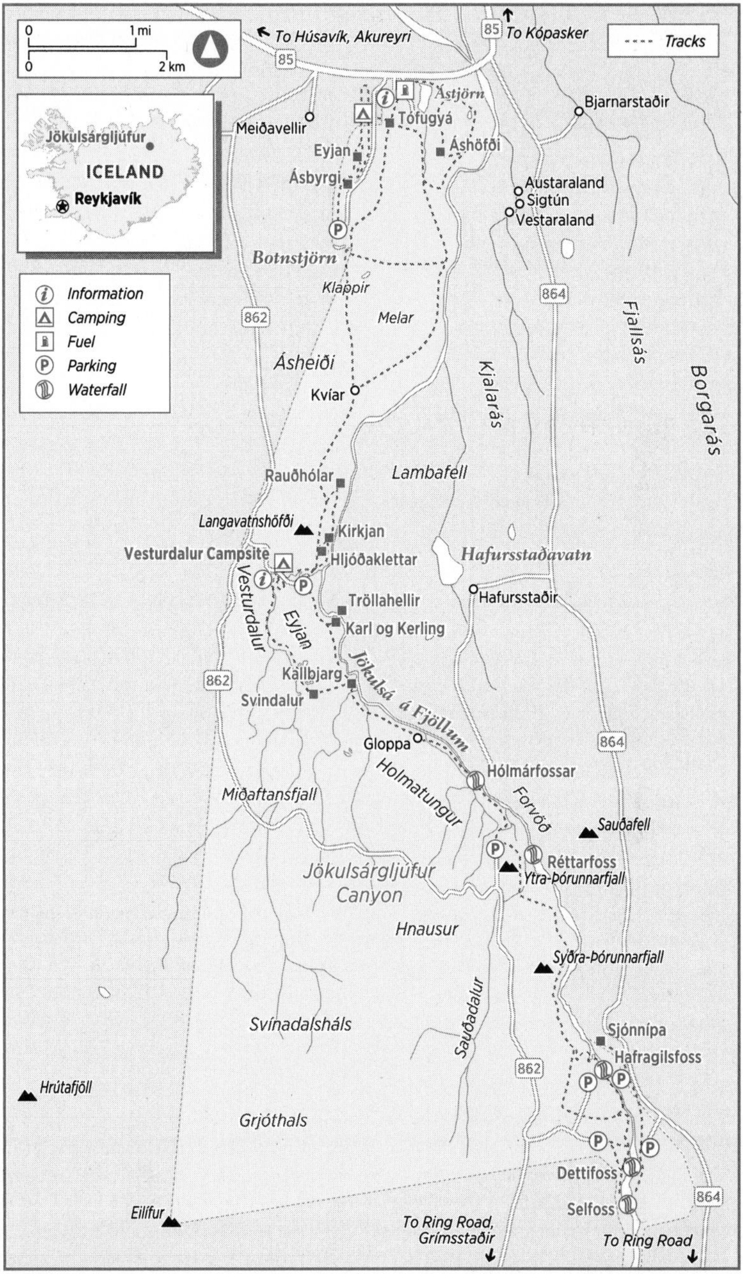
0
1 mi
0
2 km
To Húsavík, Akureyri
85
To Kópasker
Tracks
Jökulsárgljúfur
ICELAND
Reykjavík
Information
Camping
Fuel
Parking
Waterfall
Ástjörn
Bjarnarstaðir
Meiðavellir
Tófugyá
Eyjan
Áshöfði
Ásbyrgi
Austaraland
Sigtún
Vestaraland
Botnstjörn
Klappir
864
862
Melar
Fjallsás
Ásheiði
Kjalarás
Borgarás
Kvíar
Lambafell
Rauðhólar
Langavatnshöfði
Kirkjan
Vesturdalur Campsite
Hljóðaklettar
Hafursstaðavatn
Hafursstaðir
Vesturdalur
Tröllahellir
Eyjan
Karl og Kerling
Jökulsá á Fjöllum
Kallbjarg
Svindalur
Gloppa
Holmatungur
Hólmárfossar
Forvöð
Miðaftansfjall
Sauðafell
Réttarfoss
Ytra-Þórunnarfjall
Jökulsárgljúfur Canyon
Hnausur
Syðra-Þórunnarfjall
Sauðadalur
Svínadalsháls
Sjónnípa
Hafragilsfoss
Hrútafjöll
Grjóthals
Dettifoss
Eilífur
Selfoss
To Ring Road, Grímsstaðir
To Ring Road

is happy to store bags during the day, so clever planning can lighten your load. Visitors with cars could drop supplies at Vesturdalur, then park back at Ásbyrgi and take the daily SBA bus (which starts in Akureyri) from Ásbyrgi to Dettifoss, arriving around 1:20pm. (Make sure you can reach Vesturdalur before dark.) Those without cars can still jump off the bus at Vesturdalur and leave things with the warden before continuing on to Dettifoss. The hike has challenging segments and route variations, so make sure to review your plans with the park information office (above).

VISITOR INFORMATION

Tourist information can be found at the **visitor office** in **Ásbyrgi** (**✆ 470-7100;** www.vjp.is; May 1 to May 31 and Sept 1 to Sept 30 10am–4pm; June 1 to June 20 and Aug 16 to Aug 31 9am–7pm; June 21 to Aug 15 9am–9pm) which is on Route 861; exit Route 85 at the filling station, and it's shortly ahead on the left. The staff is accessible and helpful, and a free exhibit chronicles local geology, flora and fauna.

Exploring Jökulsárgljúfur

Our top three walking areas are: Ásbyrgi, the wooded horseshoe canyon at the park's northern end; Hljóðaklettar and Rauðhólar, in the middle of the park; and on the south end of the park, a triumvirate of waterfalls: Hafragilsfoss, Dettifoss, and Selfoss. All three areas could be crammed into one day, but two days or even three are preferable. Another prime walking area is **Hólmatungur ★★**, with its luxuriant cascades and vegetation, but access is more limited (see "Getting There & Around," above).

ÁSBYRGI ★

This broad canyon, near Route 85 and west of the Jökulsá á Fjöllum River, forms a "U" shape about 3.5km (2 miles) north-to-south and 1km (½ mile) across, with a forested plain on the bottom and a rock "island" called Eyjan in the middle. Geologists believe Ásbyrgi was gouged out by catastrophic flooding from Vatnajökull somewhere between 8,000 and 10,000 years ago, and again around 3,000 years ago. Apparently these flood bursts had 2,000 times the force of the Jökulsá á Fjöllum today. The river then shifted east to its current location, leaving Ásbyrgi dry. The Vikings had their own explanation for Ásbyrgi: clearly the god Óðinn's horse, Sleipnir, had left an enormous hoof print with one of his eight legs.

Walks in Ásbyrgi can start from the information office or from a parking area at the southern end of the "U," near the base of the cliffs. Route 861, which splits off from Route 85 at the N1 filling station, passes the information office and ends at the parking area. No one path asserts itself among the walking routes; so, if you have a car, it makes sense to drive to the parking area and scan the many options from there. Beautiful ferns and orange lichen inhabit the cliff walls, along with 1,200 pairs of nesting fulmars. If you decide to see Ásbyrgi from the rim above, backtrack to the information office and find the trail leading to Tófugjá, where you can ascend the rim with the aid of ropes.

HLJÓÐAKLETTAR & RAUÐHÓLAR

Hljóðaklettar (Echo Rocks) ★★ and **Rauðhólar (Red Hills) ★★** form an ideal 2-hour loop hike, starting from a parking area shortly past the Vesturdalur campsite on the west side of the canyon. The trail has tricky footing in spots, but is not otherwise difficult. The area is covered in the national park map ***Jökulsárgljúfur*** available at the visitor office (300kr). The trail weaves through some of Iceland's most intriguing basalt configurations, often eroded from below to form honeycomb patterns. The human-sized trees along the trail feel oddly companionable, and the woolly willow is easily noted by its light-green, fuzzy leaves. Hljóðaklettar earned its name from certain locations where the sound of the river echoes and seems to come from the wrong direction. The best spot to witness this phenomenon is right by the marked turnoff for Kirkjan (Church), a fabulous cave once sought out by sheep during storms. Rauðhólar, a crater row tinted with red gravel, marks the northern end of the loop and has great panoramic views. Some trekkers take the bus to Vesturdalur and continue all the way to Ásbyrgi.

HAFRAGILSFOSS, DETTIFOSS, & SELFOSS

Moving progressively upstream along the Jökulsá á Fjöllum River, the magnificent waterfalls **Hafragilsfoss, Dettifoss ★★**, and **Selfoss ★** are a kind of three-course meal. Hafragilsfoss, at 27m (89 ft.) high and 91m (299 ft.) across, is captivating and monstrously powerful. The best view is from the Sjónnípa lookout point, a 1km (½-mile) hike north from the parking area. Hafragilsfoss is overshadowed, however, by Dettifoss, Europe's mightiest waterfall. On average, the milky-gray glacial water cascades over the 44m (144 ft.) drop at a rate of 200 cubic meters (656 sq. ft.) per second. Selfoss is only 11m (36 ft.) high, but its unusual breadth and parabolic shape are well worth seeking out as a pleasing finale.

Most visitors see the waterfalls from the east side of the river, since the parking areas on the west side are not accessible to regular cars. Those in 4WD vehicles often approach Dettifoss from the west side, where the view is somewhat better. The SBA buses (p. 247) also stop on the west side. On the east side, however, views of Selfoss are slightly improved and Hafragilsfoss is much more accessible. The drive to the waterfalls from Ásbyrgi—on Route 864, down the eastern side of the canyon—takes about 40 minutes. Selfoss is reached by walking 1.5km (1 mile) south from the Dettifoss parking areas on either side of the river.

Where to Stay

PARK CAMPGROUNDS Camping within the park is restricted to three campgrounds on the west side of the river: Ásbyrgi, on the park's north end; Vesturdalur, in the middle; and Dettifoss, on the south end. Ásbyrgi and Vesturdalur are supervised from June through September 15 and accessible to regular cars. Ásbyrgi has showers, a shop and snack bar, laundry machines, and facilities for trailers and camper vans. Vesturdalur is for tents only and has no showers, so the party crowd gravitates to Ásbyrgi. Ásbyrgi can be a zoo late at night, especially on summer weekends, despite the quiet policy after 11pm. The Dettifoss campground has minimal facilities—just outhouses and a water tap—and is only meant for hikers who traverse the park north to south and then continue toward Mývatn. The campsites rarely if ever run out of tent space, but it's still a good idea to call in advance to see if the site is crowded through the information office (above).

Camping is 950kr per person per night, 500 for children aged 13–16 or free for children under 13. Showers at Ásbyrgi are 300kr and require six 50kr coins. Tents can be rented from the information office for 2,000kr per night.

OUTSIDE THE PARK The options below are all on Route 85, near Ásbyrgi.

Hóll ★ This snug farmhouse accommodation has homely charm, but may not appeal to those who dislike the feeling of being a houseguest. Rooms are simple, warm, and endearingly-decorated with old books and pastoral prints. For 4,000kr an hour guests can go horseback riding. A **two-course dinner** is available on request for 3,500kr.

Rte. 85, 9km west of Ásbyrgi. ✆ **465-2270** or 465-2353. hrunda@simnet.is. 4 units, none w/bathroom. 9,000kr double. Breakfast available (1,250kr). MC, V. *In room:* No phone.

Hótel Lundur ☺ This hotel is a school off season, with a run-down playground, stashes of toys and board games, kids' art displays, and the Icelandic touch: a heated pool and hot tub. Rooms are institutional but perfectly okay. Sleeping-bag accommodation is in classrooms and may revive memories of kindergarten nap time.

Rte. 865, just off Rte. 85, 9km (5½ miles) northeast of Ásbyrgi. ✆ **465-2247.** Fax 465-2311. lundur@dettifoss.is. 8 units, none w/bathroom. June–Aug 8,000kr double; 3,300kr sleeping-bag accommodation. Closed Sept–May. **Amenities:** Restaurant; heated pool; hot tub. *In room:* No phone, Wi-Fi.

Keldunes The six rooms in the main house are satisfactory, if sometimes small, while the two cabins outside have their own bathrooms, TVs, and kitchenettes, and can squeeze in a third or fourth person. Prices are higher than nearby competitors, justified only by free use of the washing machine and the hot tub, for which bathrobes are provided in each room. **Dinner** is available by arrangement for 3,900kr–4,200kr.

Rte. 85, 12km (7½ miles) west of Ásbyrgi. ✆ **465-2275.** www.keldunes.is. 8 units, 2 w/bathroom. 12,900kr double/cabin; 4,000kr sleeping-bag accommodation. Rates 15% lower Oct–Apr. Breakfast available (1,500kr). MC, V. **Amenities:** Guest kitchen; hot tub. *In room:* No phone, Wi-Fi.

Skúlagarður Inn The rooms in this former boarding school are thoroughly ordinary, but the building, with its **restaurant,** bar, dance hall, and theater, has some appealing community spirit.

Rte. 85, 14km (9 miles) west of Ásbyrgi. ✆ **465-2280.** Fax 465-2279. skulagardur@simnet.is. 21 units, none w/bathroom. May 15–Aug 9,200kr double; 11,000kr triple; 3,700kr per person sleeping-bag accommodation. Rates around 30% lower Sept–May 14. Breakfast available (1,200kr). MC, V. **Amenities:** Restaurant; bar; guest kitchen; Internet access. *In room:* No phone.

Where to Dine

The only dining option near Ásbyrgi is the shop/snack-bar (✆ **465-2260**) next to the **filling station** on Route 85, and in high season the few tables are often full. Some kind of fish plate is added to the usual burger and sandwich offerings. Hours are 9am to 10pm from mid-June through August, with earlier closing times in the off season. There's a small **market,** but you're better off bringing groceries from Húsavík or another town.

THE NORTHEAST CORNER

"Land of Fire and Ice," the number-one cliché of Iceland's travel industry, has little bearing on Iceland's peaceful and remote northeast corner, which has no fearsome volcanoes, no mighty glaciers, no one-of-a-kind geological marvels. No romantic villages are nestled in majestic fjords. Not a single restaurant, hotel, museum, church, or saga site exerts any significant pull. Yet visitors come here time and again, just to gaze at birds on misty moors and walk to lonely lighthouses. It may have no star attractions, but the northeast corner is an ideal meeting of pristine beauty and blessed solitude.

Essentials

GETTING THERE & AROUND

BY PLANE Every weekday, **Air Iceland** (✆ **570-3030/473-1121;** www.air iceland.is) connects Akureyri to Þórshöfn and Vopnafjörður; service may increase to two flights per weekday in summer. All flights from Reykjavík to Þórshöfn or Vopnafjörður connect through Akureyri, expect another stop in Vopnafjörður if traveling to Þórshöfn. Typical airfares to Þórshöfn or Vopnafjörður are between 14,000kr–29,000kr from Reykjavík or 12,000kr from Akureyri. Book online for a cheaper bonus fare.

BY CAR In September 2010 a new road cutting across Hólaheiði and Hófaskarð at the base of the peninsula was laid, shortening the 300km (186-mile) distance from Húsavík to Vopnafjöður by 53km (27 miles). The new road takes the number of the old coastal road (Route 85) and the old coastal road around Melrakkaslétta has a new number (Route 870). At the same time another new road was laid to Rauðarhöfn (Route 874), branching off the new Route 85 across Hólaheiði at Ormarsá. This road has shortened the distance to Raufahöfn by 21km (11miles).

In Vopnafjörður and Þórshöfn, the only car-rental agency is **National/Bílaleiga Akureyrar** (✆ **461-6000** or 840-6076; www.holdur.is).

BY BUS **SBA Norðurleið** (✆ **550-0700;** www.sba.is) operates one bus on weekdays year-round from Akureyri to Þórshöfn, with a change at Húsavík, and stops at Ásbyrgi, Kópasker, and Raufarhöfn. The bus departs Akureyri at 8:15am and reaches Þórshöfn at 12:30pm; the return trip is from 1:45pm to 6:30pm. A one-way ticket from Akureyri to Þórshöfn is 8,400kr. For 5,300kr (one-way) the same company runs a daily bus service between Akureyri and Vopnafjörður in the summer, making several stops on the way (including Dettifoss). The service is reduced to 4 times weekly from September to December. Another company may take over the service between January and May. Call ahead to check.

VISITOR INFORMATION

The tourist information office in Akureyri (p. 247) can offer general help. In **Raufarhöfn** the most knowledgeable figure is Erlingur Þoroddsen, proprietor of **Hótel Norðurljós** (✆ **465-1233;** hotelnordurljos@hotelnordurljos.is), and basic service information is listed at http://www.hotelnordurljos.is. In **Þórshöfn,** tourist information is at the local swimming pool, Langanesvegur (✆ **468-1515;** www. langanesbyggd.is.; mid-June to Aug Mon–Fri 8am–8pm, Sat–Sun 11am–5pm; Sept to mid-June Mon–Thurs 4–8pm, Fri 3–7pm, Sat 11am–2pm). In **Vopnafjörður,** tourist information is next to the fish factory at Hafnarbyggð 4 (✆ **473-1331;** Jun 20–Aug 20 10am–6pm).

Exploring the Northeast

For outdoor activities in this region, arrangements can be made informally. Someone is always willing to take you hiking, birdwatching, fishing, canoeing, or horseback riding, but no specific tours are advertised on websites or brochures. Birdwatchers should pick up the widely available brochure *Birds in the Coastal Areas of Thingeyjarsysla.* To download it, visit **http://norce.org** and click the links for "Wildlife" and then "Thingeyjarsysla."

The following sites form a clockwise route around the northeast corner.

MELRAKKASLÉTTA

Melrakkaslétta, which means "Arctic Fox Plains," is the only general name for the broad peninsula extending to the northernmost point of the Icelandic mainland. Shingle beaches full of driftwood and wading birds are seen along the mostly low-lying coastline, while small lakes, moors, boggy tundra, and eroded hills form the interior. Most farms on the peninsula have been abandoned.

An excellent new **hiking map** for Melrakkaslétta, the fifth in the *Útivist & Afþreying* series, is widely available in the region.

Rauðinúpur ★, the headland at the northwest tip of the peninsula has a lighthouse, sea stacks, bird cliffs tinted with red slag, and that end-of-the-Earth allure. The turnoff from Route 85 is roughly 22km (14 miles) north of the village of Kópasker (and 3.5km/2 miles *after* a turnoff which heads along the coast to Grjótnes). In 8km (5 miles) the road ends at Núpskatla crater, and Rauðinúpur is visible to the left. Walk along the rocky shore, which can be slow-going, then past the lighthouse to the sea cliffs.⚠ Beware of attacks by arctic terns, especially in early summer, and have a stick handy to raise over your head in defense. Puffins are seen in large numbers, and one of the sea stacks hosts a gannet colony. Allow 2 hours for the round-trip.

Hraunhafnartangi is a promontory at the peninsula's northeast corner, less than 3km (2 miles) from the Arctic Circle. (Hraunhafnartangi was once thought to be the northernmost point of the mainland, but Rifstangi, a few kilometers to the west, wins that title by a hair.) The solitary lighthouse is visible from the road, and a 1.7km (1-mile) 4WD track leads directly there along the shore (going toward the lighthouse, the ocean will be on your left). The dock by the lighthouse was active in the saga age, and a large cairn marks the gravesite of hero Þorgeir Havarsson. As with Rauðinúpur, be on the lookout for attacks from nesting birds.

The eastern region of Melrakkaslétta is dotted with endless **lakes** and ponds, treasured by a small coterie of fishermen and birdwatchers. A lovely, peaceful trail leads 5km (3 miles) from the village of Raufarhöfn to Ólafsvatn Lake; from Hotel Norðurljós, walk up to the power line and follow the staked route from there. A canoeing trail for fishermen is in the works. For further information on the lakes, or to plan a fishing trip, contact Erlingur at Hotel Norðurljós.

RAUFARHÖFN

Raufarhöfn, the **northernmost village on the Icelandic mainland,** was a major processing hub for herring into the 1960s but now numbers less than 250 inhabitants. Erlingur at Hotel Norðurljós is Raufarhöfn's one-man **tourist bureau,** and the best resource for any outdoor activities in Melrakkaslétta. He's also behind a scheme called **Arctic Henge** (www.arctichenge.com), a Stonehenge-inspired sundial structure, 54m (177 ft.) in diameter, on a hill just north of town. It's still under construction and awaiting further investment, but the government has promised matching grants.

If you're staying in Raufarhöfn, consider a walk along the Raufarhafnarhöfði headland, a pleasing locale for observing birds on sea cliffs and watching boats come in and out of the harbor. A 2km (1.2-mile) loop trail starts from the church.

RAUÐANES

The 7km (4-mile) circuit of this small cape halfway between Raufarhöfn and Þórshöfn is one of the best walks in the northeast corner. The route follows the bluffs, with views of sea pillars and archways, and one opportunity to clamber down to a beach. The turnoff from Route 85 is about 35km (22 miles) south of Raufarhöfn, and leads to a farm called Vellir. The trailhead is about 2km (1.2 miles) from the turnoff, on the right side of the road. After circling the periphery of Rauðanes counter-clockwise, the trail ends up farther down the road.

ÞÓRSHÖFN & LANGANES

Anyone with a taste for truly out-of-the-way places should look into **Langanes ★**, a 45km-long (28-mile) peninsula shaped like a duck's head. Much of the landscape is moorland full of lakes and ponds, with a few mountains reaching 719m (2,359 ft.) on the east side, some bird cliffs, and a good range of vegetation and wildflowers. The near-total solitude, abandoned farms, driftwood beaches, persistently foggy climate, and remote lighthouse at the narrow tip of the peninsula all give Langanes its own forlorn enchantment.

The village of **Þórshöfn** is the launch point for excursions into Langanes. A regular car can proceed about 33km (20½ miles) beyond Þórshöfn on Route 869, and a 4WD road extends 12km (7 ½ miles) along the northwest coast of the peninsula all the way to the lighthouse at Fontur, with side routes branching off to the southeast. Worthwhile destinations include the ruins of Skálar, a village abandoned since 1954; the bird cliffs of Skálabjarg, just southwest of Skálar; the staked trail at Hrollaugsstaðir, where Hrollaugsstaðafjall mountain meets the sea; and the Fontur lighthouse, which has a guestbook to sign. All the hiking and 4WD routes are detailed in English on an essential new hiking map, the seventh in the *Útivist & Afþreying* series.

To plan a trip to Langanes, start with tourist information at Þórshöfn (p. 285). The **Sauðaneshúsið museum** (✆ **468-1430;** June 10–Aug 31 daily 11am–5pm), 6km (3¾ miles) north of Þórshöfn on Route 869, is devoted to relics of Langanes, and the caretaker is very knowledgeable about the region. The farm hostel **Ytra-Lón** (✆ **468-1242** or 846-6448; www.visitlanganes.com) is located even farther into Langanes, and the website lists several great options for fishing, horseback riding, and participating in farm life. From May 15 to June 10, the **egg-collecting club of Þórshöfn** leads expeditions into Langanes where visitors can rappel down cliffsides snatching bird eggs. (Be prepared to feel like a wimp if you refuse to eat one raw.) The club leader is Halldór Halldórsson (✆ **862-2905**; fontur@isl.is); his English is limited, but the friendly staff at the **Ytra-Áland farm accommodation** (✆ **468-1290** or 863-1290; ytra-aland@simnet.is) can arrange trips with him, and can also set up 4WD expeditions to Langanes or take you on day tours.

VOPNAFJÖRÐUR & BUSTARFELL

Vopnafjörður is the largest town in the region, with around 680 people, an airport, and one police officer. Drivers continuing south along the coast on Route 917 toward Egilsstaðir are treated to incredible views as they pass through **Hellisheiði**, Iceland's highest coastal mountain pass (656m/2,152 ft.) on the steep descent into Fljótsdalshérað Valley. Anyone headed west from Vopnafjörður to Mývatn should be sure to fill up the gas tank. The two sights listed below are some distance outside of town.

Bustarfell Museum ★ Not all that much distinguishes this preserved 19th-century turf-farmhouse museum from others of its kind, but it does have a good range of artifacts and an unusually distinct identity from having remained in the same family for 400 years. Bustarfell's more unique holdings include hand-carved chess pieces, snuff boxes made from animal bones, a driftwood shoulder harness with sheep-horn hooks, granddad's winning dark-green bridegroom suit, and a pair of baby booties knitted from human hair. English signage is limited, and it's difficult to get the full import of the exhibit without asking staff. (Many visitors, for instance, see the short beds and assume Icelanders have become much taller—when in fact they slept partially upright to aid digestion of their low-fiber diets.) A guided tour could well be yours for the asking. For 1 day in early July, usually the second Sunday, staff in period costume demonstrate traditional farming chores. The museum's **Croft Cafe** serves old-fashioned cakes and cookies.

Rte. 85, about 20km (12 miles) southwest of Vopnafjörður. © **471-2211.** www.bustarfell.is Admission 700kr adults; 100kr for children aged 9-13; children under 9 free. Jun 10–Sept 10 daily 10am–6pm.

Vopnafjörður Pool Vopnafjörður is the rare Icelandic settlement without a geothermally-heated pool inside the village proper. Many residents, however, feel privileged to have this idyllic alternative next to the Selá, an elite salmon-fishing river once used by George H. W. Bush. The simple 12m pool is about 60 years old and at 32 to 33 degrees Celsius (90 °F–91.5 °F), it's warmer than most Icelandic pools. It has two hot tubs and changing rooms. The turnoff from Route 85, about 9km (5½ miles) north of Vopnafjörður, is marked by the usual swimming pool icon. The pool is 3km (2 miles) from the turnoff. It's possible to visit the pool out of hours, but there is no warden present and guests must observe the hygiene rules.

© **473-1499.** Admission 300kr adults; 150kr children; 10am–7pm daily.

Where to Stay

RAUFARHÖFN

Hótel Norðurljós This is the only game in town, though proprietor Erlingur Þoroddsen—the northeast corner's leading travel authority—can find guesthouse accommodation when the hotel is full. Rooms do the job, and a pleasant terrace overlooks the waterfront. Some rooms don't have TVs, so specify whether you'd like one.

Aðalbraut 2. © **465-1233.** Fax 465-1383. www.hotelnordurljos.is. 15 units. 16,200kr double. AE, DC, MC, V. **Amenities:** Restaurant; bar. *In room:* No phone, Wi-Fi.

ÞÓRSHÖFN & NEARBY

Guesthouse Lyngholt Rooms here are modern and clean-cut, with cheerful floral-patterned duvets. The common areas, with comfy furniture and lots of natural light, are especially relaxing and inviting.

Langanesvegur 12. © **468-1239** or 897-5064. www.lyngholt.is. 8 units, none w/bathroom. June 1–Aug 31 9,900kr double. Rates 40% lower Sept–May. AE, DC, MC, V. **Amenities:** Guest kitchen. *In room:* TV, hair dryer, no phone, Wi-Fi.

Hótel Jórvík Despite the "hotel" in the name, this is actually a small guesthouse in a cute private home. The rooms are comfortable and positively modest. Guests can relax in front of the open fire with the sound of breaking waves in the background. The views of the ocean are splendid. Breakfast is not available but the kitchen is open for guests.

Langanesvegur 31. © **468-1400.** Fax 468-1399. www.jorvik.vefur.com. 7 units, none w/bathroom. June 1–Aug 31 8,500kr double. Rates 40% lower Sept–May MC, V. *In room:* No phone, Wi-Fi.

Ytra-Áland This pleasing farm accommodation just west of Þórshöfn is run by an exceptionally nice family that can also arrange hiking and sightseeing tours with a guide and 4WD excursions throughout the northeast corner. **Dinner** is served on request.

Off Rte. 85, 18km (11 miles) west of Þórshöfn. ✆ **468-1290** or 863-1290. Fax 468-1390. www.ytra-aland.is. 6 units, 2 w/bathroom. 15,000kr double; 11,800kr double without bathroom; 3,500kr sleeping-bag accommodation per person; 9,000kr cottage for 3–8 persons. Rates include breakfast, except for cottage. MC, V. **Amenities:** Guest kitchen. *In room:* No phone.

VOPNAFJÖRÐUR

Hótel Tangi Rooms at this functional hotel meet modern standards but fail to make any further impression. En suite rooms also have a TV and a fridge, and rooms without private bathrooms compensate only with sinks.

Hafnarbyggð 17. ✆ **473-1840.** Fax 473-1841. hoteltangi@simnet.is. 17 units, 4 w/bathroom. 15,900kr double; 10,900kr double without bathroom. Rates include breakfast. AE, DC, MC, V. **Amenities:** Restaurant; bar. *In room:* No phone, Wi-Fi.

Mávahlíð Guesthouse This well-priced guesthouse, opened in 2007, has crisply white, utilitarian rooms. The guesthouse opens for advance bookings only during the winter season.

Hafnarbyggð 26. ✆ **695-2952.** www.123.is/mavahlid. 5 units, none w/bathroom. May–Sept 9,400kr double; 4,000kr sleeping-bag accommodation. Breakfast available (1,000kr). No credit cards. Closed Oct–Apr. **Amenities:** Guest kitchen. *In room:* No phone.

Where to Dine

The villages of Raufarhöfn, Þórshöfn, and Vopnafjörður each have one restaurant and an **N1 filling station** grill.

Eyrin ICELANDIC This restaurant-cum-bar by the dock is the one-and-only hangout for Þórshöfn's 450 residents. It serves up local clam chowder, alongside fish, lamb, burgers, and pizzas. A large-screen TV and a pool table sweeten the pot.

Eyrarvegur 3, Þórshöfn. ✆ **468-1250.** www.eyrin.is. Main courses 1,270kr–4,280kr. MC, V. Mon–Thurs 11am–10pm; Fri–Sat 11am–3am; Sun noon–10pm.

Hótel Norðurljós ICELANDIC The hotel's reliable restaurant overlooking the waterfront is a friendly respite in this remote corner of the world; you'll feel welcomed and rewarded just for coming this far. Stick with the lamb or a fresh catch.

Aðalbraut 2, Raufarhöfn. ✆ **465-1233.** Main courses 2,500kr–3,800kr. MC, V. Daily 7–10am and noon–10pm.

Hótel Tangi ICELANDIC Tangi admirably upholds its role as Vopnafjörður's gathering place, with a big screen for soccer games and a dependable menu of burgers, pizza, fish, and meat. The bar is open later on weekends.

Hafnarbyggð 17, Vopnafjörður. ✆ **473-1840.** Main courses 2,350kr–3,800kr. AE, DC, MC, V. Daily noon–2pm and 6–9pm.

SOUTH ICELAND

10

A masterpiece of nature and home to some of Iceland's most celebrated wonders, the south provides a dynamic feast for the visitor's senses. Presiding majestically over the region is Europe's greatest glacier, Vatnajökull, a multi-tongued monster stretching east and thrusting its force down upon 8% of the country. The frozen white mass—crowned by Iceland's highest peak, Hvannadalshnúker, which surfaces just above the sub-glacial tongue, Öræfajökull—creates a well-focused distinction against the black deserts to the south.

The area is also the location of Iceland's newest star Eyjafjallajökull (that's AY-YAH-FYATL-AH-YER-KUTL), the unpronounceable volcano which in April 2010 brought European air traffic to a standstill.

The Ring Road (Route 1) threads 374 km (235 miles) across this diverse landscape from Þjórsárdalur to Höfn, stitching together a progression of magnificent sights each with its own collections of folktales and legends.

In *Njáls Saga*-country around Hella and Hvolsvöllur, every rock, knoll, and crag seems to have a story. The 4-day trek connecting Landmannalaugar and Bórsmörk—each an unbeatable hiking area in its own right—is the most celebrated trail in Iceland. Active tour opportunities abound, from horseback riding to dog sledding. On the enchanting Westman Islands, you can explore dramatic bird cliffs by boat, or by sidling close to puffins on the ledges. No wonder the south is the busiest region for tourism outside the Reykjavík orbit.

The south was the last stretch of coastline to be fully claimed by settlers. Most early Norse arrivals took stock of the sand deserts, glaciers, and heavy surf, then moved on to better ports and more forgiving habitats. Even today, the largest town in southern Iceland is Heimaey (Home Island), on the Westman Islands, with a population of 4,500; no town on the mainland has even 1,000 residents.

Most of the south is well served by buses in summer, and the Ring Road bus extends at least to Höfn year-round. But if you're connecting a lot of dots, a rental car is the ideal transport.

Famous destinations such as Gullfoss, Geysir, and Kerið, though geographically located in the south, are covered in the "Near Reykjavík" chapter because so many people visit them as part of the Golden Circle day trip from the city (p. 154).

For the best visitor information online, consult **www.south.is**).

WESTMAN ISLANDS (VESTMANNAEYJAR)

In traditional annals, Norse settler Hjörleifur Hródmarsson was killed by his Irish slaves on Iceland's south coast, around the year 870. The slaves fled to the islands they could see offshore, but were later hunted down and killed by Ingólfur Arnarson, Reykjavík's first settler and Hjörleifur's brother-in-law. The Norse referred to Irishmen as "west men," and the islands have since been known as the **Westman Islands (Vestmannaeyjar) ★★★**. Herjólfur Bárðarson was thought to be the first Norse inhabitant of the Westmans around 900, but archaeological evidence points to a Norse settlement as early as the 7th century.

The Westmans became world famous in 1963, when a new island, **Surtsey,** was created by a series of volcanic eruptions 120m (394 ft.) beneath the ocean surface. As the magma fought its way out of the sea, huge clouds of steam and ash sailed into the stratosphere. New land was being cooked up right on television. Surtsey was 1.7sq. km (1 sq. mile) when the eruptions subsided, but has since eroded to half that area. It's now a nature reserve accessible only to scientists, who are studying how life takes root on barren foundations. (See "Tours & Activities," p. 297, for trips that circumnavigate Surtsey.)

Of the 15 Westman Islands, only the largest, **Heimaey (Home Island),** is inhabited. Westman Islanders have a strong local identity; a common joke refers to the mainland as "the sixteenth island." A few even dreamed of independence from Iceland, especially because the Westmans are relatively wealthy and contribute more in taxes than they receive in services. But their dependence on the Icelandic state became all too clear, when, on January 23, 1973, a volcano right next to Heimaey town erupted after 5,000 years of dormancy. When the molten rock finally stopped flowing on July 3, 30% of the town was buried in lava and ash, and 400 buildings were destroyed. Heimaey had also grown by 2.5sq. km (1 sq. mile).

One night in the Westmans will probably not feel like enough; 2 nights are ideal. The first weekend of August is a huge party in Heimaey, as Islanders join thousands of visitors at the campgrounds for live music, fireworks, and bonfires through the night. The ferry can sell out, and it's very difficult to find somewhere to stay.

Essentials

GETTING THERE

BY AIR Flying to Heimaey is an exciting and sometimes terrifying experience, as planes are often buffeted in the wind. Flights are regularly cancelled because of weather conditions, so if your itinerary is tight, take the ferry. The airline listed below offers day packages, which might include a bus tour of Heimaey or a round of golf. A taxi ride into town costs around 1,400kr, or you could walk there in about 20 minutes. Taxis often wait for flights, but if not, call **Eyjataxi** (**© 698-2038**) from the airport.

Eagle Air (**© 562-4200;** www.eagleair.is) has now taken over the service from Air Iceland and flies 20-minute flights twice daily to and from the Westman Islands.

South Iceland

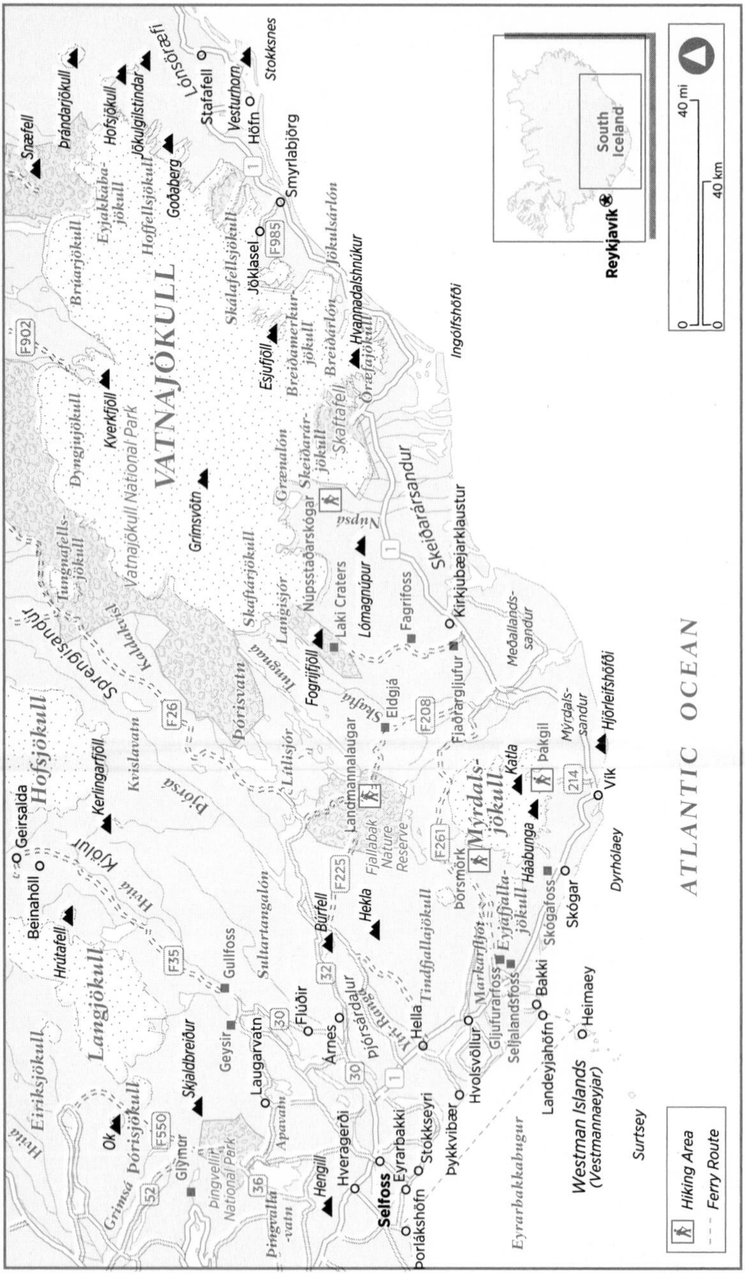

From June until August, the price is from 20,000kr. Check the website for the winter schedule and prices.

BY FERRY **Landeyjahöfn** (✆ **481-2800;** www.herjolfur.is), is a new port on the tip of Iceland's south coast. The new location, which is a model of environmentally-friendly architecture and engineering, has shortened the journey from the mainland to **Heimaey** from three hours to 30 minutes and doubled the number of daily trips. The ferry *Herjólfur* now makes 32 round-trips in summer (June–Aug) between Landeyjahöfn and Heimaey; five daily trips from Thursday to Sunday and four trips a day from Monday to Wednesday. One-way tickets are 1,000kr adults, 500kr seniors and children aged 12 to 15, and free for children aged 11 and under. For all schedules, call ahead or check the website. Weather cancellations occur only two or three times a year, and almost never in summer. The ferry sometimes sells out for cars, but never for passengers, except possibly the first weekend of August. Buses from Reykjavík to Landeyjahöfn on **Sterna** (✆ **553-3737;** www.sterna.is), are aligned with the ferry schedule and depart from the **BSÍ bus terminal** at Vatnsmýrarvegur 10. One-way bus fare from Reykjavík is 3,100kr for adults, 2,200kr for seniors, and 1,500kr for children aged between 4 and 12. Adult returns are 5,000kr.

It may seem indulgent to take a car, but it's not a bad idea. Transporting the car costs only 500kr more than buying a passenger ticket, and Heimaey has a good road system. If you do bring a car, make sure to reserve in advance. Even if car reservations are full, you have a decent chance of getting on on standby; register your name at the ticket office, which opens an hour before departure.

VISITOR INFORMATION

The **tourist information office** (✆ **481-3555;** www.vestmannaeyjar.is: click on the "i" at the bottom) is located in City Hall (*Ráðhús*). **Visit Westman Islands** (www.visitwestmanislands.com) is also useful. Make sure to pick up the free **walking map** from the tourist office, open May 15 to Sept 15 (Mon–Fri 10am–6pm, Sat–Sun 11am–5pm), Sept 16 to May 14 call ahead.

What to See & Do

HEIMAEY TOWN

Heimaey is the most profitable fishing port in Iceland, bringing in 12–13% of the country's annual catch, or about 200,000 tons of fish. During the 1973 eruption, lava threatened to cut the port off entirely, so Iceland's geologists proposed a novel and successful strategy: pumping seawater onto the molten rock, to create a hard outer layer and retard the flow. Ironically, the port ended up more sheltered than before. (The lava also took care of Heimaey's landfill shortage.)

On a cliff facing the innermost waterfront is a rope hanging from a cliff. This is where local children are trained in **spranga,** the "national sport" of the Westmans. The sport originated with egg-collecting and involves all sorts of daredevil cliff-scaling. Egg-collecting season is in May and June, and it's fun to watch. If you're interested in learning, ask the tourist information office; they might be able to find an instructor for you.

Aquarium & Natural History Museum (Fiska og Náttúrugripasafnið) ★ The special attraction here are the tanks full of unusual sea creatures donated by local fishermen. The collection of stuffed birds is above average too.

Heimaey Island (Home Island)

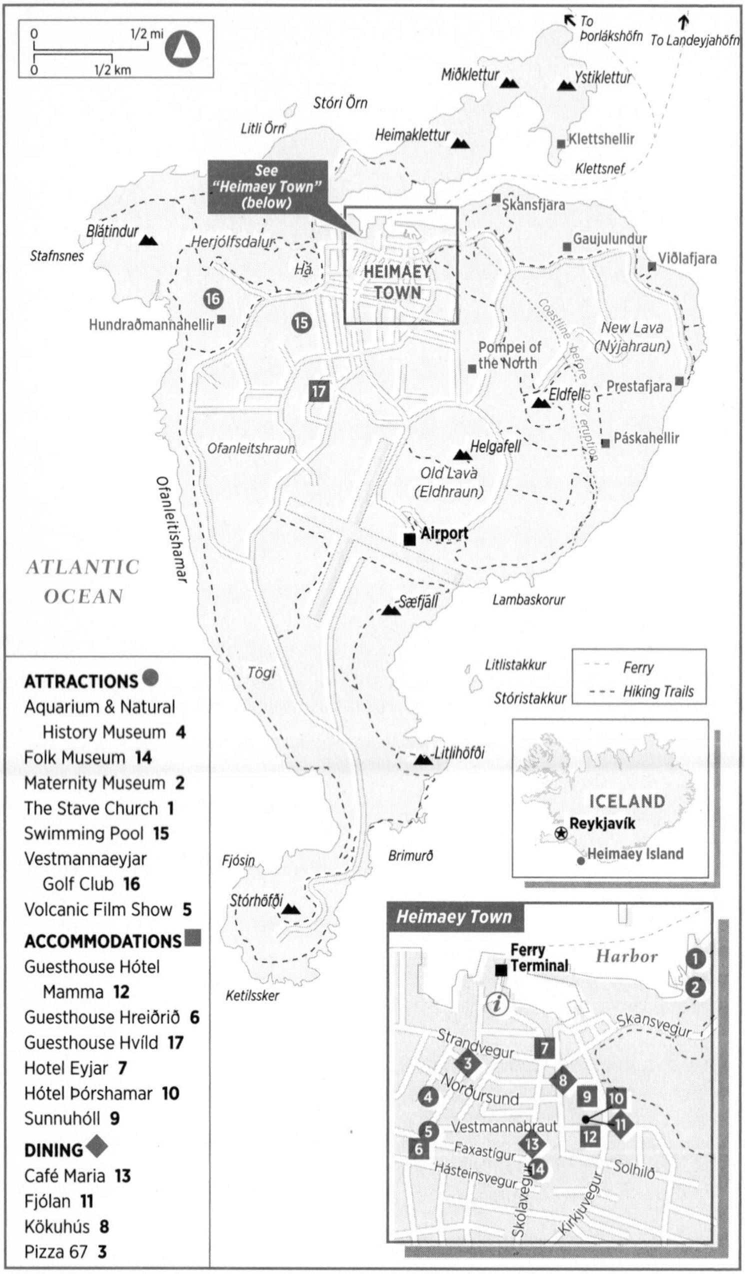

Heiðarvegur 12. ✆ **481-1997** and 863-8228. www.saeheimar.is . Admission 500kr adults; children under 14 free. May 15–Sept 15 daily 11am–5pm; Sept 16–May 14 Sat 1–4pm.

Folk Museum (Byggðasafn Vestmannaeyja) Located above the library and tourist information office, this large exhibit contains every local folk artifact you do and do not need to see. All annotations are in Icelandic. Renovations and translations are in progress.

Ráðhúströð (toward Skólavegur). ✆ **488-2045.** Admission 500kr adults; children under 16 free. May 15–Sept 15 11am–5pm; Sept 16–May 14 1–5pm; Sat 11am–2pm.

Volcanic Film Show This recommended hour-long film includes footage of the creation of Surtsey, the 1973 eruption, puffins, and egg-collecting. In July and August, the 9pm show tacks on a 30-minute documentary about the annual rescue of the pufflings (see "The Great Puffling Rescue," p. 296).

Eyjamyndir Félagsheimilinu (cinema), Heiðarvegur (at Vestmannabraut). ✆ **481-1045.** Admission 800kr adults; 600kr seniors; 400kr children aged 6–12; children under 6 free. Screenings in English May 15–June 15 3:30pm; June 15–Aug 31 2pm, 3:30pm and 9pm; Sept 1–Sept 15 3:30pm.

SKANSINN

Skansinn is on the east side of town, where the lava meets the port. A partially-crushed water tank at the lava's edge is a vivid illustration of the volcano's destructive power. The English built a fortification here in the 15th century, when they were Iceland's biggest trading partners. This was of little use in 1627, when Algerian pirates landed on Heimaey's southeast coast. Of the island's 500 inhabitants, about half were taken to Algiers and sold into slavery. Many others were herded into a storehouse and burned alive. The few remaining islanders survived by hiding in caves or rappelling down cliffs. Only 39 of the captives were eventually ransomed and returned to Copenhagen.

Maternity Museum (Landlyst) In 1874 Heimaey built Iceland's first maternity clinic to combat infant mortality. This re-creation would be more interesting if the ominous-looking medical implements—what's that hacksaw for?—and other artifacts were explained in English.

Skansinn. ✆ **481-1149.** Free admission. May 15–Sept 15 daily 11am–4pm.

The Stave Church (Stafkirkjan) The Norwegian government presented this building to Heimaey in 2000 to commemorate the millennium of Iceland's official adoption of Christianity. In the year 999 or 1000, the king of Norway sent emissaries to the annual Icelandic assembly *(Alþing)* to lobby against heathenism. According to saga accounts, their instructions were to build a church wherever they first set foot on land, which turned out to be Heimaey. The location of the original site is under dispute, and the new church is based on medieval Norwegian models. In keeping with the saga, the church was built in 2 days. The building process and architectural details are well-documented in a book on display in the Maternity Museum next door.

Skansinn. Free admission. May 15–Sept 15 daily 11am–5pm.

AROUND THE ISLAND

Eldfell & The "New Lava" Locals refer to the red volcanic cone created in 1973 as **Eldfell** (Fire Mountain), and the surrounding lava as **"the new lava,"** or *nýjahraun,* to distinguish it from the "old lava" *(eldhraun)* around Helgafell on the south side of town. Take a rambling drive or walk through the new lava to witness how islanders are improvising on and shaping their new landscape. Some have built lava gardens, or sculptures, or memorials for homes that are buried directly underneath.

The 5m (16 ft.) wooden cross at the base of Eldfell is a good starting point for an ascent. The cone is still steaming slightly, and the ground is still warm if you scratch beneath the surface. Just southeast of the cone is **Páskahellir,** a lava tube that should not be entered without a strong flashlight; the easiest trail access is near the airport. See also "Tours & Activities," (p. 297), for tips on hiking the new lava.

Pompei of the North (www.pompeiofthenorth.com) is a work-in-progress: a street with 10 homes covered in ash will be completely excavated to become a kind of time-capsule museum. Only one original occupant objected to the project; his house will stay buried. Others have already been able to pop into their upper-story windows for the first time in more than 30 years. Visitors can inspect the site anytime.

Other Walks A trip to the Westmans is not complete without a good walk. A thrilling, vertiginous, and somewhat dangerous **hiking trail** starts on a 4WD road behind the N1 service station by the port; it continues along Heimaey's northeastern cliffsides, eventually connecting with equally harrowing trails that ascend from Herjólfsdalur, near the golf course. Ropes and chains guide you up and down the steep sections. A gentler trail along **Ofanleitishamar** on the west coast is great for puffin close-ups. The lighthouse at **Stófjörði,** on the southern tip of the island, is officially the windiest spot in Iceland. In the southeast, the sea cliffs of **Litlihöfði** are another picturesque spot for puffin-watching.

THE GREAT puffling RESCUE

With their orange beaks and feet, tuxedoed 18cm (7-in.) tall bodies, and sad clown eyes, puffins are by common consent among the world's cutest creatures. Their air speed can reach 80kmph (50mph), yet they flap awkwardly and frantically, like animals in cartoons who suspend themselves momentarily before crashing to earth. For centuries, Icelanders have hunted puffins by waving a kind of giant butterfly net over cliff ledges to catch them in mid-air. Most puffins breed in Iceland, and the Westman Islands boast Iceland's largest puffin colony. In 2007, however, puffin numbers declined alarmingly; speculation is that warmer ocean waters have pushed their main food source, sand eels, farther north.

Puffins are usually monogamous for life, and—unless they end up on a dinner plate—have an average lifespan of 25 years. They usually return to the same breeding area, if not the same clifftop nesting burrow, and the females lay two eggs per year, but only one at a time. The pufflings hatch in around 42 days, and both parents gather fish for them. In mid-August the parents abandon the nest, and the pufflings are left to fend for themselves.

In late August, hundreds of hungry pufflings are attracted and disoriented by Heimaey's lights and end up crashing into yards and streets. Locals lock their cats inside, but let their children stay up late to gather the pufflings in cardboard boxes lined with soft fabric. The pufflings stay in the families' homes overnight. The next morning, the children take the pufflings to the sea and free them by tossing them high into the air. Visiting families are most welcome to participate.

A live Internet **"puffin cam"** stationed on Heimaey's northeast corner can be viewed all summer at http://puffin.eyjar.is.

Tours & Activities

Boat tours ★★ led by avian experts offer an entirely different viewpoint on coastal caves and bird cliffs around Heimaey. You might also see seals, dolphins, or even orcas, which populate the sea around the Westmans.

Viking Tours (✆ **488-4884;** www.vikingtours.is), headquartered at Cafe KRÓnear the ferry landing, offers a 90-minute circle tour of the island; the captain will likely enter a sea cave and demonstrate the acoustics by playing saxophone for an audience of thousands of nonplussed birds. Tickets are 3,900kr for adults, 2,900kr for children aged 9 to 14, and free for children aged 8 and under. Other options include bus tours (with plenty of walking), whale-watching, and dinner sailings. Viking also offers a tour of Surtsey, though the boat is not permitted to land.

Westman Islands Tours (✆ **481-1045;** http://tourist.eyjar.is) offers horseback riding, bus tours (Skansinn, Eldfell, a lava garden, Pompei of the North, and a puffin colony), and an inexpensive 3-hour "new lava" hiking tour, which includes exploring the lava cave Páskahellir and baking bread in the still-smoldering ash. **Vestmannaeyjavöllur** (✆ **481-2363;** www.gvgolf.is) is the only Icelandic golf course situated inside a volcano crater. It may also be Iceland's most scenic course, though you never know where the wind will take the ball. Course fees are 5,000kr, with inexpensive club rental, and tournaments take place most weekends in summer.

Where to Stay

If the recommended places below are full, a complete list of options is available at **www.vestmannaeyjar.is** via the tourist information link. Another option is **Sunnuhóll,** Vestmannabraut 28 (✆ **481-2900;** fax 481-2900; www.hotelvestmannaeyjar.is;7 units without bathroom; May–Sept 3100kr double; AE, MC, V), the spotless homey hostel owned by Hótel Þórshamar; it is generally indistinguishable from a rudimentary guesthouse—except for the fact that you rent the sheets (1,000kr for your entire stay).

EXPENSIVE

Hótel Þórshamar ★ This three-star hotel has plenty to recommend it—the excellent Fjólan restaurant, billiards lounge, hot tubs, and sauna. Go for one of the three snazzy suites, each a different size. The double rooms are ordinary and rather small.

Vestmannabraut 28. ✆ **481-2900.** Fax 481-1696. www.hotelvestmannaeyjar.is. 21 units. May–Sept 17,200kr double; 21,500kr triple; 19,800kr–22,000kr suites. Rates around 10% lower Oct–Apr. Rates include breakfast. AE, MC, V. **Amenities:** Restaurant; hot tubs; sauna. *In room:* TV, hair dryer, Wi-Fi.

MODERATE

Hótel Eyjar ★ Eyjar's straightforward and well-maintained doubles are more like small apartments with private bathrooms and well-equipped kitchens. The suites have even more space and nicer furnishings.

Bárustígur 2 (at Strandvegur). ✆ **481-3636.** Fax 481-3638. www.hoteleyjar.eyjar.is. 11 units. June–Aug 12,000kr double; 20,000kr suite for 2–4 people; 16,000kr family room. Rates around 10% lower Sept–May (except suites). Breakfast available (1,300kr adults, 750kr children under 13). AE, MC, V. *In room:* TV, kitchenette, fridge, coffeemaker, Wi-Fi.

INEXPENSIVE

Guesthouse Hótel Mamma ★ This cheerful, well-appointed guesthouse with sizeable rooms is run by the Hótel Þórshamar across the street. Both floors have a full kitchen, and only the family room has a double bed instead of twins. A slim staircase—not for bulky suitcases—leads to a lovely attic double.

Vestmannabraut 25. ✆ **481-2900.** Fax 481-1696. www.hotelvestmannaeyjar.is. 7 units, without bathroom. May–Sept 9,400kr double; 12,400kr triple; 15,300kr family room. Rates around 15% lower Sept–Apr. AE, MC, V. **Amenities:** 2 guest kitchens; washer/dryer. *In room:* TV/VCR, no phone.

Guesthouse Hreiðrið ★ The couple running this guesthouse also manage the Volcanic Film Show, Westman Island Tours, and Eydís Boat Tours; needless to say, they're very helpful. You'll find an orca mural, puffin stenciling, and an outdoor grill inside a gazebo. Student discounts available.

Faxastígur 33. ✆ **481-1045** or 699-8945. Fax 481-1414. http://tourist.eyjar.is. 10 units without bathroom. May–Aug 7,800kr double; 9,900,kr triple; 12,900kr family room; 2,900kr sleeping-bag accommodation. Rates around 10% lower Sept–Apr. Breakfast available (1,200kr). **Amenities:** Guest kitchen. *In room:* No phone.

Guesthouse Hvíld A little way out from the middle of town. All rooms meet basic comfort standards—but not all have TVs, so you may want to request one that does.

Höfðavegur 16. ✆ **481-1230** or 894-4480. www.simnet.is/hvild. 5 units without bathroom. May 16–Sept 8,500kr double; 12,000kr triple; 14,000kr room for 4 people; 3,000kr sleeping-bag accommodation. Rates around 25% lower Oct–May 15. MC, V. **Amenities:** Guest kitchen. *In room:* No phone.

Where to Dine

Café Maria ★ ICELANDIC Try the puffin—served rare, with an aromatic sauce that includes Icelandic malt. This welcoming restaurant with upstairs bar also has a good fish menu and decent pizza.

Skólavegur 1 (by Vestmannabraut). ✆ **481-3160.** Reservations recommended for dinner. Main courses 3,500kr–5,600kr. AE, DC, MC, V. Daily 11:30am–11pm; bar open to 3am Fri–Sat.

Fjólan ★ ICELANDIC Heimaey's best all-around restaurant, especially for seafood dishes. The catch of the day is usually excellent (not to mention a bargain), and you won't regret the mixed seafood plate either. Service is friendly and scrupulous.

At Hótel Þórshamar, Vestmannabraut 28. ✆ **481-3663.** Reservations recommended. Main courses 2,200kr–5,900kr. AE, MC, V. Daily 11:30am–9pm.

Kökuhús BAKERY/CAFE This popular cafe serves excellent Scandinavian-style pastries and cakes, and is great for a casual soup-and-sandwich lunch.

Bárustígur 7. ✆ **481-2664.** Small dishes 750kr–2,000kr. Mon–Fri 7:30am–5:30pm; Sat 7:30am–4pm; Sun 10am–4pm.

Pizza 67 PIZZA This Icelandic chain with an amusing 1967 theme has reliably satisfying pizza, with toppings ranging from the familiar to the psychedelic (smoked salmon, bananas, and so on . . .). Ask about student discounts.

Heiðarvegur 5. ✆ **481-1567.** Main courses 990kr–3,520kr. AE, DC, MC, V. Daily 11am–10pm.

ÞJÓRSÁRDALUR & HEKLA

Dominated by Iceland's legendary Mount Hekla, Þjórsá is Iceland's longest and mightiest river, and its valley—Þjórsárdalur—holds what is believed to be the world's most voluminous lava flow since the end of the last Ice Age. The flow is about 8,000 years old, and covers around 805sq. km (499 sq. miles). In the river's lower reaches, the lava has yielded to fertile grazing land. The upper reaches near

Hekla remain bleak, thanks to ash fallout from Hekla's periodic eruptions. The valley may be considered by some to be off-the-beaten-track, but plays host to many Icelandic campers during the summer.

Essentials

GETTING THERE Fifteen kilometers (9 miles) east of Selfoss, Route 30 branches off from Route 1 and follows the northwest side of the Þjórsá. At Árnes (your last chance for a hot-dog), turn on to Route 32 to continue along the river. Eventually Route 32 bridges the Þjórsá and dead-ends at Route 26. To the left are Hrauneyjar (p. 372) and the Sprengisandur route to the north (p. 370). A right turn leads back to Route 1 on the opposite side of the river, passing near the base of Hekla.

VISITOR INFORMATION The best resource is the regional tourist office at **Hveragerði** (p. 174). Þjórsárdalur's website is www.sveitir.is, which features a concise translation in English.

Exploring the Area

This region makes for an ideal day trip from Reykjavík or anywhere within reach. The highlights listed below follow a circular route up the northwest side of the Þjórsá on Route 32, and back down the southeast side on Route 26. No bus tours cover the area, so you'll need a car. Come prepared for a long stretch without food or facilities. If you're planning a hike in the Stöng/Gjáin/Háifoss area, bring a map. The annual updated brochure *Uppsveitir Árnessýlu* is widely available in the Hveragerði–Selfoss area, it's crude but adequate. Connoisseurs of unlikely bathing spots will want a swimsuit and towel.

ALONG ROUTE 32

Returning to Route 32 and continuing east for approximately 2km (1¼ miles), you'll see a marked turnoff for **Hjálparfoss,** a picturesque waterfall on the right, which breaks through the breadth of lava rock into a duel torrent. It's certainly worth the 1km (½-mile) detour. Clamber up to the vantage point above the cascade.

Return to Route 32 from Hjálparfoss, turn right, and immediately cross a bridge. Within another 1km (½ mile) you'll come to a gravel road (Route 327) on the left. It's marked with a small sign for the ancient site of Stöng, which is 7km (4⅓ miles) down the gravel road. The road is very rough, but usually passable—if only just—in a conventional car. From the parking area, look for the red-roofed building that houses the ruins. All that remains of **Stöng** are the simple stone foundations of a 12th-century Viking longhouse, but it's probably the most intact Saga Age building yet excavated. The ruins were preserved by ash from the first recorded Mt. Hekla eruption in 1104. As many as 20 farms once occupied this area, which is hard to believe from the bleak vistas seen today. Informative panels map the layout of the women's quarters, central fireplace, barn, smithy, and church, which has been reconstructed with driftwood.

The lush, peaceful gorge of **Gjáin ★★**, in the Rauðá (Red River), full of wildflowers and curious rock formations, is only a 10-minute walk from Stöng; the well-worn trail leaves right from the ruins. Gjáin (pronounced GYOW-in) is so lovely that several people are said to have had their ashes spread there.

A very short distance past the turnoff to Stöng and reached by a marked right turn off Route 32, **Þjóðveldisbærinn** (**✆ 488-7713;** www.thjodveldisbaer.is; admission

600kr adults, free for seniors and children under 13. Groups of 20 or over get a 30% discount; June–early Sept 10am–noon and 1–6pm) is an ambitious reconstruction of a Viking-era homestead—the only such project in Iceland. The longhall design is mostly based on the excavated ruins at Stöng, but is meant to represent all similar settlements from the 11th and 12th centuries. (Consider visiting Þjóðveldisbærinn before Stöng, to better understand what Stöng once looked like.) It's striking to compare the Vikings' commodious interiors to the damp, claustrophobic living quarters in 19th-century turf farmhouses preserved all over Iceland. Settlers had more access to wood for construction and were not as concerned with insulation since Iceland was warmer before the mid-12th century. The builders of Þjóðveldisbærinn restricted themselves to the same technology available to the Vikings 900 years ago. The exhibit also explains Viking home economics, such as how many kilometers a woman had to walk in circles to spin a length of cloth.

Háifoss ★, a slender and beautiful waterfall, the third tallest in Iceland at 122 meters (400 ft.), is reached by a very rough gravel road. The turnoff, marked "Háifoss" and "Hólaskógur," is on the left side of Route 32, roughly 10km (6 miles) past the turnoff for Þjóðveldisbærinn. (Soon after exiting for Háifoss, another road branches off to the left toward Gjáin and Stöng; this road should not be attempted without 4WD.) Hólaskógur is a mountain hut 2km (1¼ miles) from Route 32, and Háifoss is roughly 6km (3¾ miles) farther. The last stretch of the road may be too rough for a regular car; stop at Hólaskógur and ask about road conditions. In any case, Háifoss is a memorable sight and worth the hike (less than 8km/5 miles) even all the way from Route 32.

HEKLA & ENVIRONS

Shortly after the turnoff for Háifoss, Route 32 crosses the Þjórsá and dead-ends at Route 26. A right turn leads you back to the Ring Road, passing close to the base of **Hekla,** Iceland's most notorious volcano. After a few kilometers (about 2 miles), you'll pass the 4WD road F225 to Landmannalaugar on the left. About 4km (5 miles) later, look out to the right until you see **Tröllkonuhlaup,** a short but broad and commanding waterfall with an island in the middle; the turnoff is unmarked, but you can easily find your way to the stepladder that climbs over the fence.

At this point you're as close as the road will come to **Hekla,** the majestic, oblong, snow-crested peak rising distinctly from the plains. Hekla is the second most active volcano in Iceland, and its white collar masks its molten heart: *Hekla* means "hood," a name derived from the clouds that usually obscure the peak.

For most nationalities, natural disasters are just periodic intervals in their collective memory. In Iceland's national story, Hekla and its ilk are vital players. A 1585 map of Iceland pictures Hekla in mid-eruption, with the caption: "Hekla, cursed with eternal fires and snow, vomits rocks with a hideous sound." Hekla's first recorded eruption in 1104 blanketed every farm and village within a 50km (31-mile) radius. Since then it's erupted more than 100 times. Since the 1970s, Hekla has erupted about once a decade, with the last occurrence in 2000. An enormous reforestation project, covering 1% of Iceland's entire land surface, aims to surround Hekla with trees. The trees should survive the acrid precipitation better than low-lying vegetation, and can even absorb the flow of lava.

Hekla Center (Heklusetur) ★ This small but informative exhibit helps bring Hekla volcanically to life. Video screens display eruption footage, a seismometer keeps track of current grumblings, and screen saver-like software artistically renders

ASCENDING hekla

Hekla remained unclimbed until 1750—perhaps because in popular mythology, it was the gateway to hell. (The rumblings heard for months after each eruption were said to be tormented souls.) Climbing Hekla is no piece of cake: a round-trip hike to the 1,491m (4,892 ft.) summit takes at least 7 hours (4 hours up, 3 hours down). A trail on the north side is well marked, but don't attempt it without a good map and expert advice on current conditions. One good source is the **Hekla Center** (✆ **487-8700**) at Leirubakki Farm on Route 26, near the mountain (see above).

Toppferðir, in Hella (✆ **861-1662;** www.mmedia.is/toppbrenna), ascends Hekla by snow tractor from December to mid-June for around 15,000kr per person. **Mountain Taxi** (✆ **544-5252;** www.arcticsafari.is), based in Reykjavík, leads a 10- to 12-hour circuit of Hekla in Super Jeeps, with a stop for a dip in the Landmannalaugar hot spring.

the seismometer. At the end, Hekla itself is framed on the wall—through a window. To reach the exhibit, continue southwest on Route 26; it's at the Leirubakki Farm, opposite an N1 service station.

✆ **487-8700.** www.leirubakki.is. Admission 700kr, adults; 350kr children aged 7–11; 6 and under free. There is a 100kr per person discount on groups of 10 people or over. Daily 10am–10pm.

Where to Stay & Dine

For other options in the vicinity, see "Hella, Hvolsvöllur, & Markarfljót Valley," later in this chapter. **Rjúpnavellir** (✆ **892-0409;** rjupnavellir@simnet.is) is ideally located for access to Landmannalaugar, Veiðivötn (p. 372), and Fjallabaksleið. It offers basic but comfortable sleeping-bag accommodation for 2,600kr per person. Half price for children aged between 8–14, and under 7s can bunk for free. The resort, near the base of Hekla, comprises two cottages, providing room for a total of 44 people. A made-up bed is an option for those without a sleeping bag but will cost extra at 3,900kr.

Leirubakki ★ This farm and store in the shadow of Hekla hosts a volcano exhibit (p. 300), a hotel, and respectable Icelandic restaurant. A "Viking Pool" is cut right into the lava. Rooms are plain and functional. Horseback riding is available. The **dining room,** open from 10am to 10pm, has a splendid view of Hekla. Main courses range from 2,000kr to 7,000kr, and reservations are requested for dinner.

Rte. 26. ✆ **487-8700.** Fax 487-6692. www.leirubakki.is. 18 units, 14 w/bathroom. May–Sept 14 23,900kr double w/bathroom; 17,800kr double without bathroom; 14,100kr triple without bathroom; 26,800kr 4-person room without bathroom; 4,900kr sleeping-bag accommodation. Family rooms available for 4 and 6 people. Rates around 35% lower Sept 15–Apr. Rates include breakfast. MC, V. **Amenities:** Restaurant; heated outdoor pool; hot tub; sauna. *In room:* No phone, Wi-Fi.

LANDMANNALAUGAR, FJALLABAK & SURROUNDINGS

Naming Iceland's best hiking area is a pointless exercise, but if the proverbial gun were put to our heads, **Landmannalaugar ★★★** would edge out the competition. In photographs, this area is usually represented in two ways: by the rhyolite

Landmannalaugar & Rhyolite

Landmannalaugar holds Iceland's largest concentration of rhyolite. Rhyolite is one of more than 700 types of igneous rock formed by cooled magma. Rhyolite comes from relatively low-temperature magma that has erupted explosively and cooled rapidly. It looks somewhat glassy, and its components include quartz and mica. Obsidian, an even glassier black mineral found in the vicinity of Landmannalaugar, is a rhyolite that cooled especially quickly. Rhyolite mountains are not known for their vibrant hues, but Landmannalaugar's geothermal chemistry has cooked the rocks into subtle and infinite variations. What's more, these variations can completely change character from close-up and receded perspectives; use every megapixel at your disposal.

mountains, with their astonishing mineral spectra, and by deeply-contented bathers in the natural hot spring by the main camp. But Landmannalaugar is a much wider world unto itself—with glacial valleys, marshes, canyons, moss-covered lava fields, tephra desert, and plentiful geothermal hotspots—and can sustain several days of exploring. The ideal follow-up is the Laugavegurinn (p. 304), the world-famous 4-day trek to Þórsmörk.

Landmannalaugar proper is a flat, gravelly area 600m (1,969 ft.) above sea level, set between a glacial river and a lava flow dating from the 15th century. But the name Landmannalaugar is commonly applied to its surrounding area as well, all part of the **Fjallabak Nature Reserve.** Landmannalaugar is reached from the west by two mountain roads: F225 from Hekla, and F208 from the Hrauneyjar area. F208 continues east (on what is known as "the Fjallabak Route") past the volcanic rift Eldgjá and eventually joins the Ring Road west of Kirkjubæjarklaustur.

Essentials

GETTING THERE From June 15 to September 13, daily buses from **Reykjavík Excursions** (**© 580-5400;** www.re.is) connect Reykjavík and Skaftafell in both directions via Landmannalaugar and the Fjallabak route. The bus from Reykjavík leaves at 8:30am and from Skaftafell at 1:20pm. The bus from Reykjavík ends at Landmannalaugar and returns to Reykjavík the same day. Buses from Reykjavík—with stops at Hveragerði, Selfoss, Hella, and Leirubakki—arrive at Landmannalaugar at 12:45pm, and leave at 3pm. A one-way ticket between Reykjavík and Landmannalaugar is 7,100kr for adults and 3,500kr for children under 12.

From July 27 to August 24, another Reykjavík Excursions bus connects Landmannalaugar to Mývatn in the north, via the **Sprengisandur Route** through the interior (p. 370). The bus departs at 8:30am three times a week in each direction, and takes 10 hours, with some sightseeing stops.

It's possible to reach Landmannalaugar by **driving** a conventional car, but only from Hrauneyjar via Route F208, which opens up around the end of June. Insurance for rental cars is usually voided on "F" roads, however, so it's probably not worth the risk. The bus to Landmannalaugar uses Route F225 for scenic reasons, but even drivers with 4WD vehicles should check with the Landmannalaugar hut about road conditions before attempting this route; a particularly hazardous ford is close to

Landmannalaugar. Coming from the east, a car could take Route 208/F208 from the Ring Road as far as Eldgjá, but the same insurance problem applies. ***Note:*** Fuel stops are nonexistent between Hrauneyjar and Kirkjubæjarklaustur.

Where to Stay & Dine

Landmannalaugar has just one place to stay, a two-story mountain hut (✆ **854-1192;** open mid-June until early October and run by **Ferðafélag Íslands** (✆ **568-2533;** www.fi.is). Reservations must be made online, with advance payment. Vouchers are sent to you by mail and must be shown to the wardens. If you show up without a reservation and they have room, you can pay with cash, MasterCard, or Visa. The hut is perhaps the most overburdened in Iceland, and reservations should be made at least 6 months in advance if possible, especially for July and August.

The basic wooden structure has 78 sardine-style beds in four bedrooms, with kitchen, toilets, and showers, though showers cost 400kr. Beds are 4,200kr for adults, 2,100kr for ages 7 to 18, and free for ages 6 and under, but you must bring your own sleeping bag. Camping costs 1,000kr per person, and gives you access to the toilets and showers, but not the kitchen. Some visitors assume they'd prefer sleeping indoors, but the hut can get hot, and it's easy to be kept awake by a room full of rustlers, snorers, and chatterboxes, so bring earplugs.

From late June until the end of August, **Fjallafang, a café** housed inside a green bus, serves coffee, tea, beer, cake, and sandwiches from 11:30am to 6pm daily. Otherwise, all food must be brought in.

Exploring the Area

Landmannalaugar can be enjoyed in day tours, afternoon visits, and 2-hour bus layovers, but 2 to 4 nights is ideal. Arriving by bus one afternoon and leaving the next just doesn't allow time for hikes that take the better part of a day. **Fjallabak** is often drizzly, so it's smart to include an extra day for weather insurance. A surefire itinerary is to spend 3 nights in Landmannalaugar, 3 nights on the 4-day Laugavegurinn (see box, p. 304), and a final night or two in Þórsmörk (p. 311).

Available at the hut for 1,000kr, **maps** of the Landmannalaugar area lay out the trails in detail. Wardens and fellow hikers are happy to detail routes of any length or difficulty. Recommended destinations include Brandsgil Canyon, Frostastaðavatn Lake, the summits of Bláhnúkur and Brennisteinsalda, and the unjustly named Ljótipollur (Ugly Puddle), a red crater with a lake full of brown trout. Almost all visitors complete the day with a dip in the famous hot spring near the hut.

East of Landmannalaugar, the roughest stretch of Route F208 leads to **Eldgjá ★**, or the "Fire Canyon." This 30km-long (19-mile) volcanic fissure reaches a depth of 270m (886 ft.) and width of 600m (1,969 ft.), revealing reddish rockslides and a pretty waterfall named**Ófærufoss**. The buses heading both east and west stop at Eldgjá for around 45–60 minutes. Eldgjá is also included in some arranged tours.

Tours & Activities

Many tour companies in Reykjavík offer day trips to Landmannalaugar by 4WD, combined with some sightseeing around Þjórsárdalur and Mt. Hekla, but you'll probably feel cheated by having so little time. Also, 4WDs are prohibited from venturing off-road, so do not offer the freedom of access you might anticipate.

THE laugavegurinn ★★★

This 55km (34 mile) route between Landmannalaugar and Þórsmörk is Iceland's best-known trek, and for good reason. The scenery is breathtaking, endlessly varied—from ice caves and geothermal fields to glacial valleys and woodlands—and perfectly choreographed through each leg of the journey. Sleeping-bag huts with kitchens, toilets and (usually) showers are spaced at roughly 14km (9 mile) intervals. Some energetic hikers sprint the entire route in 2 days, but 4 or even 5 days is ideal for fully digesting your surroundings. The trail opens up anytime from late June to mid-July, and remains passable until some point in September. The season could be extended a little on either end by bringing an ice axe and crampons for the steep, icy sections of the trail.

Either bring a tent or book somewhere to stay well in advance. **Ferðafélag Íslands** (✆ **568-2533;** www.fi.is) runs the hut at Landmannalaugar, all three huts along the route, and one of the three huts at Þórsmörk (p. 313). The costs and payment procedures are the same as for the Landmannalaugar hut (p. 303). It's a great luxury to have your bags carried from hut to hut by 4WD; see "Tours and Activities," below. You must pack in all of your own food, unless provisions are part of your arranged tour.

You'll also want good hiking shoes, a full weatherproof outfit, extra footwear for fording rivers (supportive rubber sandals are best), and a map and compass, even though the trail is heavily-used and well-marked. The Landmannalaugar hut sells a standard hiking map of the route, as well as a small book (*The Laugavegurinn Hiking Trail,* by Leifur Þórsteinsson) with good detail on sights along the trail as well as potential side trips.

The route can be hiked in either direction, but most trekkers head from Landmannalaugar to Þórsmörk. This route evens out the strenuousness of each day, and has a slight net loss of altitude. Many hikers continue from Þórsmörk on the 2-day trek to Skógar (p. 314).

Enlisting in a **Laugavegurinn hiking tour** has several advantages. All tours include transportation to and from Reykjavík, huts with showers, a guide, and plenty of companionship, usually including Icelanders. Best of all, your bags are delivered from hut to hut.

From July into early September, **Ferðafélag Íslands (Icelandic Touring Association)** (✆ **568-2533;** www.fi.is) leads a few Laugavegurinn tours, with one exclusively for women. The cost is 53,000kr per person, which includes a final meal at Þórsmörk. Children under 18 pay half price.

Útivist (✆ **562-1000;** www.utivist.is), equally recommended, has even more Laugavegurinn departures for a slightly higher fee: 55,000kr per person, and half price for children between 6–16. As with Ferðafélag Íslands, a meal at Þórsmörk is included. Útivist also offers a choice between more strenuous 4-day trips and less strenuous 5-day trips. Cross-country skiing trips to Landmannalaugar leave in spring, and a 4WD tour of the Fjallabak reserve leaves in late August. Útivist also leads a few 4-day trips to **Sveinstindur–Skælingar ★★★** in July and August for 46,000kr (children between 6–16 half price). This remote and otherworldly landscape northeast of Eldgjá is far less known than Landmannalaugar and Þórsmörk.

The medium-difficulty trip features a mountain climb and long traverse of a lovely, river-braided glacial valley. Bags are transported by 4WD.

Icelandic Mountain Guides (© **587-9999;** www.mountainguide.is) hosts a Laugavegurinn tour for groups of 6 to 14 at 125,00kr per person. All meals are included and cooked for you, which accounts for the much higher price.

Dick Phillips Specialty Icelandic Travel Service (Whitehall House, Nenthead, Alston, Cumbria, CA9 3PS, England; from the U.K. © **0143/438-1440**; outside the U.K. © **44/1434-381440;** www.icelandic-travel.com) has been operating for 50 years and leads unforgettable, multi-day, off-the-beaten-track hiking trips through Fjallabak and surrounding areas. The success of this tour operator is driven by the owner's passion for Icelandic nature and his desire to share the wonders of the landscape with likeminded nature lovers. Trips are launched from the **Fljótsdalur Youth Hostel** (p. 309). Be prepared to carry a moderate backpack.

HORSEBACK RIDING

Riding in this area is spectacular, but may not be suitable for beginners. **Hraun Hestar** (© **566-6693** or 868-5577; www.hnakkur.com) offers horseback riding tours from Landmannalaugar, lasting anywhere from 1 hour to all day. ***Note:*** The service is available between July 1 and August 31. **Hekluhestar** (© **487-6598;** www.hekluhestar.is) arranges 6- and 8-day riding trips around Hekla, Landmannalaugar, and the Fjallabak reserve. The 6-day Hekla–Landmannalaugar pack trip, including horses, equipment, guide, and full board, costs 205,000kr per person.

HELLA, HVOLSVÖLLUR & MARKARFLJÓT VALLEY

Proceeding east from Reykjavík along the southern coast, this area represents the last broad expanse of agricultural land before mountains and glaciers press more tightly to the coast. The villages of Hella and Hvolsvöllur are right along the Ring Road; east of Hvolsvöllur, the broad Markarfljót river valley leads inland toward Þórsmörk. (For the lower route through the Markarfljót valley to Þórsmörk, see p. 313.)

Prior to the volcanic eruptions in spring 2010, this area was more famous for raising horses and as the home country of *Njáls Saga*, perhaps the most famous of Icelandic tales. Since the eruptions, the area has seen a huge increase in volcano tourism, with off-the-beaten-track areas such as Fljótshlíð suddenly being invaded with an army of traffic. There are a number of quality tour operators in the area leading various tours to the volcano site (p. 306). Míla, an Icelandic telecommunications network company, has installed three web-cams in the area for live viewing of Eyjafjallajökull; check: http://eldgos.mila.is/english.

Eyjafjallajökull might not be Iceland's biggest and best volcano, but it's certainly the one everyone wants to see. If you watched open-mouthed as the amazing images of Eyjafjallajökull erupting filled your TV screen for days if not weeks, now's your chance to see the celebrity in person. To get a close look at the now resting beast, the best place to view it is from Fljótshlíð, about 25km (13 ½ miles) east of Hvolsvöllur and a 130km (70-mile) drive from Reykjavík. To get there by car take the Ring Road (Route 1) to Hvolsvöllur and then turn left on to Route 261 and drive all the way to the end of the road, the last 7km (4 miles) of the road is unpaved. In good weather the volcano is clearly visible, with the white surface of the glacier emerging slowly from underneath a thick blanket of black ash. Every now and then the restless sleeper vents a plume of steam. To get even closer you need to take a tour (see below).

Essentials

GETTING THERE All buses headed from Reykjavík to Þórsmörk, Vík, and Höfn stop at Hella and Hvolsvöllur en route, with plenty of daily options; contact **Sterna** (✆ **553-3737;** www.sterna.is) or **Reykjavík Excursions** (✆ **562-1011;** www.re.is) and check bus schedules for the South.

VISITOR INFORMATION In **Hvolsvöllur,** tourist information (✆ **487-8043**; www.hvolsvollur.is) is located in the community hall **Hvoll (Félagsheimilið Hvoll)** on Austurvegi, just off the Ring Road. The free and widely-available brochure/map *Power and Purity* has very detailed information for the region.

Exploring the Area

HELLA

If you want to try out the manageable and good-tempered Icelandic horse in Iceland's premier horse-farming area, consider combining a ride with a **farm stay.** Some farms offer packages for anything from overnights to week-long pack trips. The Icelandic farm holidays brochure *Upp í Sveiit* provides comprehensive information on what's available and where. Bear in mind that many farms are open to visitors for a limited period each summer.

THE ring OF FIRE

On March 20, 2010 a new star of Icelandic tourism was born on the volcanic stage. The show started with the opening of a vent fissure in **Fimmvörðuháls.** The tourist companies in Iceland were quick to arrange an army of tourist pursuits, including helicopter trips and 4WD tours to the volcano site.

One of the more extravagant excursions, offered by **Hotel Holt** (p. 106), shuttled people by helicopter to the site and prepared for them a red carpet champagne dinner cooked on the newly-laid lava field! After three weeks of activity the show ended, only to be upstaged by an even bigger and more dangerous eruption underneath the glacier **Eyjafjallajökull** directly to the west of the first. After a protracted second act, the world was left waiting for the sleeping sister **Katla** to awake and perform the grand finale.

Since these eruptions took place the area has now been dubbed the "Ring of Fire." If you are lucky enough to be visiting Iceland during one of these spectacular performances of nature, the following tour operators are likely to host special volcano tours: **Glacier Guides** (✆ **571-2100;** www.glacierguides.is), a popular tour company with super truck rides to the best possible view at a safe distance. **Extreme Iceland** (✆ **565 9320;** www.extremeiceland.is) is a similar company with Super Jeep rides to the volcanic areas. For an entirely different perspective Norðurflug (✆ **562-2500;** www.nordurflug.is) operates unforgettable helicopter tours of active volcanoes. Tours are, of course, always changing depending on the level of volcanic activity.

Hekluhestar, on Austvaðsholt Farm, Route 272, 9km (5½ miles) northeast of Hella (✆ **487-6598;** www.hekluhestar.is), is mentioned above for its 6- and 8-day trips around Mt. Hekla and the Fjallabak reserve. Like many of the horse farms, they'll negotiate just about any trip in the vicinity. Hekluhestar welcomes you to take part in farm life, which could be especially delightful during lambing season in late April/early May, foaling season in late May, and the sheep roundup in September.

Herríðarhóll, is a lovely farm run by a German/Icelandic family on Route 284, about 5km (3 miles) north of Route 1, and 15km (9⅓ miles) from Hella (✆ **487-5252** or 899-1759; www.herridarholl.is). It offers anything from local beginners' tours to multi-day expeditions through the highlands. Destinations include Þjórsárdalur, Mt. Hekla, Dýrholaey, Skógar, Geysir, and Gullfoss. Look into package deals, for example lodging, dinner and breakfast, a day of riding, and a picnic for only 21,500kr. The farmhouse has five guest rooms and its own hot spring nearby.

Hestheimar, on Route 281, just off Route 26, 7km (4⅓ miles) northwest of Hella (✆ **487-6666;** www.hestheimar.is), is an appealing guesthouse with two cottages for up to six people that offers horseback riding and renowned home cooking. The guesthouse has four rooms, two with private bathroom, and a barn loft with sleeping-bag accommodation for up to 18; amenities include a guest kitchen and hot tub.

HVOLSVÖLLUR

THE SAGA CENTER Despite the sword embedded in a boulder outside the entrance, this is not a hokey theme park, but a serious (almost too serious) educational exhibit—it's like walking through the pages of a well-written textbook. Extensive information panels, illustrations, and props cogently explain the historical context and literary significance of the sagas, with a long synopsis of *Njáls Saga* (see box, "*Njál's Saga* & Its Sites," p. 308).

Rte. 261 (just off Rte. 1). ✆ **487-8781.** www.njala.is. Admission 500kr. Free for ages 16 and under. Audio tour included w/admission price. May 15–Sept 15 daily 9am–6pm; off season, call in advance.

MARKARFLJÓT VALLEY

Before the Markarfljót river was diked and bridged in the 1930s, it would swell with meltoff from Mýrdalsjökull and Eyjafjallajökull and change course, creating havoc downstream for farmers and tourists. From Hvolsvöllur, Route 261 proceeds east along the northern side of the Markarfljót valley for 27km (17 miles) to the Fljótsdalur Youth Hostel (see "Where to Stay," p. 309), where it turns into mountain road F261. The valley becomes progressively narrower, and Þórsmörk seems very close by, but the river is uncrossable, not even in a 4WD.

If you can't get to Þórsmörk, a day hike up **Þórólfsfell ★★** is a very worthy substitute. The 3-hour round-trip walk from the Fljótsdalur hostel isn't too strenuous, and wandering around the flat-topped peak yields fabulous views. With no single route or marked trail up Þórólfsfell, the best approach is from its northwest side, not from F261 to the south, which is much steeper. In good weather, your destination is clearly visible, but if fog rolls in it's best to have a map and compass. From the top, you could descend the east side of the mountain and walk back to the hostel along F261.

The most ambitious hikers tackle the 9-hour round-trip from Fljótsdalur to the **Tindfjallajökull icecap ★★**; ask at the youth hostel about trail conditions. The hostel is also used as a base for extensive treks run by Dick Phillips tours (p. 305).

NJÁL'S saga & ITS SITES

Of Iceland's medieval sagas, *Njál's Saga* is by critical consensus the most lasting literary achievement, and the only one set in south Iceland. It is a rampant tale of love, feuds, sword-wielding, and bloody murder; Conan the Barbarian eat your heart out. It has also been an invaluable historical resource, providing, for example, the most thorough account of Iceland's conversion to Christianity in the year 1000. The book was written around 1280 by an anonymous author, and purports to recount events almost 300 years earlier. The well-crafted story revolves around Njáll Þorgeirsson and his friend Gunnar Hámundarson, both actual historic figures.

Sites associated with *Njál's Saga* are heavily featured in tourist literature and roadside information panels: just look for the "S" icon. The history recounted in *Njál's Saga* has left almost no human trace on the landscape, but the vividly described natural settings are much the same as they were in Njál's time (below). Local farmers can usually recount any saga event that took place on their property as if it happened yesterday.

For a **horseback riding tour** of the *Njál's Saga* sites, try **Njála Tours** (✆ **487-8133** or 865-4655), which operates out of Miðhús farm on Route 262, 2km (1¼ miles) north of Hvolsvöllur.

For an oddball re-creation of a 19th-century turf house, see **Kaffi Langbrók** in "Where to Dine," below.

THE NJÁL'S SAGA TRAIL

Þingskálar In Njál's time this was the annual spring assembly site for the Rangá river district, and the scarce remains of 37 temporary encampments have been found. Several scenes are set here, including one in which Ámundi the Blind regains his eyesight just long enough to kill Lýtingur á Sámsstöðum. East of the ruins stands a large boulder named **The Sacrifice Stone (Blótsteinn);** according to folklore the stone was used to slaughter sentenced criminals.

From the Ring Road, 2km (1¼ miles) east of Hella, exit on to Rte. 264 heading north. In about 7km (4⅓ miles), turn left on Rte. 268 and proceed another 8km (5 miles); Þingskálar is on the left.

Keldur This ancient farm just northeast of Hvolsvöllur is said to be the location of the oldest buildings in Iceland. According to *Njál's Saga* it was the home of Ingjald Höskuldsson, the uncle of Njál's love child, around the year 1000. It is now a modern dairy farm with more than 20 preserved buildings from the 19th century. The most notable survival is a 15th-century hall with stave construction and a 12th-century hidden underground passageway. This kind of tunnel (Jarðhús) is mentioned in the sagas and was probably used as an escape route when the farm was under attack.

Keldur is at the easternmost point of Rte. 264, about 20km (12 miles) east of Hella. ✆ **487-8452.**

Gunnarssteinn In a savage battle scene, Gunnar Hámundarson and his allies are ambushed at this rock, which can be reached on foot from Keldur. Excavations turned up a skeleton and a bracelet engraved with two hearts. This bracelet might have come from Gunnar's brother Hjört (Heart), who in the saga was slain at Gunnarssteinn.

At Keldur, ask to be directed to the Gunnarssteinn trail, which leads 3km (2 miles) to the Rangá river, crosses a bridge, and follows the river south for 1km (½ mile).

Hlíðarendi Once Gunnar's home, this pretty spot overlooking the Markarfljót valley now holds a few farm buildings and a nicely restored country church. After Gunnar was killed here, he turned over in his grave and spoke cheerfully to his sons in verse. Ruins only amount to simple mounds in the earth. BergÞórshvoll (below) is barely discernible in the distance.

A sign for Hlíðarendi is marked on the left side of Rte. 261, about 17km (11 miles) from Hvolsvöllur.

Bergþórshvoll Once Njál's home, Bergþórshvoll is now just a low hill amid marshy land 3km (2 miles) from the ocean. In the saga account, Njál's family is burned alive inside the house in the year 1011. Excavations from 1927–28 and 1951–52 proved conclusively that there was indeed a fire around this time.

Exit the Ring Road onto Rte. 255, 4km (2½ miles) south of Hvolsvöllur. When 255 ends, turn left on Rte. 252. Bergþórshvoll is 5km (3 miles) ahead on the left.

Where to Stay

On Route 261, 27km (17 miles) east of Hvolsvöllur in Markarfljót valley, the remote **Fljótsdalur Youth Hostel** ★ (✆ **487-8498** or 487-8497; www.hostel.is; 2 units without bathroom; Apr 12–Oct 15 2,400kr bunk; 500kr sheet rental; AE, DC, MC, V; closed Oct 16–Apr 11) is practically a mountain hut. Yet, with its turf roof, beautifully tended garden, library full of yellowing travelogues, and incredible views towards Eyjafjallajökull, it could hardly offer more ramshackle appeal. Book well in advance, and remember that all food must be brought in.

Fosshótel Mosfell This is a privately owned guesthouse which is simply leased to the Fosshótel chain in summer, so the rooms are more charmingly old-fashioned (and a lot more green) than the hotel's. Tiny twin rooms with shared bathrooms are half the price of those with en suite. Sleeping-bag accommodation is even cheaper.

Þrúðvangur 6 (behind the service station), Hella. ✆ **487-5828.** Fax 562-4001. www.fosshotel.is. 53 units, 35 w/bathroom. June–Aug 24,000kr double w/bathroom; 13,000kr double without bathroom; 5,500kr sleeping-bag accommodation. Rates around 30% lower Sept–May. Rates include breakfast. AE, DC, MC, V. **Amenities:** Restaurant, lounge; Internet terminal. *In room:* No phone.

Hellishólar A compound with scattered cottages, a golf course, and an adjoining campground full of camper vans is not everyone's idea of an idyllic farmstay, but this recently renovated guesthouse is unpretentious, comfortable, and popular among Icelanders. Cottages, which come in different sizes, are economical for families or groups. All have kitchenettes, but bathrooms in the smallest cottages don't include showers, which are by the campsite. Horseback riding can be arranged with a nearby farm.

Rt. 261, 11km (7 miles) east of Hvolsvöllur, in Markarfljót Valley. ✆ **487-8360.** Fax 487-8364. www.hellisholar.is. 40 units. 13,000kr cottages for 3–5 persons; 16,000kr cottages for 4–6 persons; 19,500kr cottages for 6–8 persons; 25,000kr cottages for 13 persons .Rates around 38% lower off season. MC, V. **Amenities:** Restaurant; bar; hot tubs. *In room:* Kitchenette, no phone.

Hótel Hvolsvöllur ★ Don't expect country ambience or any view to speak of at this rather generic hotel; rooms are large however, the restaurant is excellent, the bar is inviting, and prices are reasonable considering this is Hvolsvöllur's only top-tier option. Ask for a room in the brand-new wing. No sleeping bag option available here.

Hlíðarvegur 7 (Rte. 261, just off Rte. 1), Hvolsvöllur. ✆ **487-8050.** Fax 487-8058. www.hotelhvolsvollur.is. 53 with bathroom units. May 1–June 15 18,200kr double w/bathroom; June 15–Aug 15 21,700 double w/bathroom. Rates around 33% lower Sept 16-May 14 (except Christmas season). Rates include breakfast. AE, DC, MC, V. **Amenities:** Restaurant; bar; hot tub. *In room:* TV, hair dryer, Wi-Fi.

Hótel Rangá ★★ Salmon fishing in Iceland's choicest rivers costs upwards of 93,750kr *a day,* so some of the classiest places to stay are private fishing lodges used by the likes of Prince Charles and Eric Clapton. This four-star hotel on the banks of the Rangá, a prime salmon river, is a mainstream luxury lodge—including the showy taxidermy and beautiful artwork. A new expansion ups the ante with themed suites, a rooftop pool, with massage rooms, hot tubs, and sauna. Within room classes, it's very hit and miss whether you get a balcony or hot tub, so make your wishes known. Also decide if you'd rather face the river or a distant Hekla.

Off Rte. 1, 7km (4⅓ miles) east of Hella. ✆ **487 5700.** Fax 487-5701. www.hotelranga.is 51 units. June-Aug 43,000kr double; 67,300kr-100,300kr 2-6 person suites. Rates around 23% lower Apr-May and Sept-Oct; 33-40% lower Jan 5-Feb and Nov-Dec 23. Rates include breakfast. AE, DC, MC, V. Closed Dec 24-25 and Dec 31-Jan 1. **Amenities:** Restaurant; 2 conference rooms; lounge; bar; hot tubs; in-room massage; tour desk; room service. *In room:* TV, minibar, hair dryer, Wi-Fi.

Smáratún Country Hotel ★ This sweet, peaceful, homely affair has a range of options, including camping, "chalets" (small cottages), "cottages" (cabins), rooms in the farmhouse, and a new wing of hotel rooms, one side of which has views of the horse ring. Chalets sleep four with two bunks, a double bed, bathroom, TV, and kitchenette. "Cottages" sleep six to ten, and all except one have a private hot tub. A shared hot tub and sauna is accessible to all guests. For chalets and cottages, bed linen must be rented for 1,400kr per stay. Horseback-riding tours and lake-fishing permits are available.

Rte. 261, 13km (8 mile) east of Hvolsvöllur, in Markarfljót Valley. ✆ **487-8471.** Fax 487-8373. www.smaratun.is. 14 units, with shared bathrooms. ,9,000kr guesthouse double; 3,000kr sleeping-bag accommodation; 9,000kr chalet; 10,500kr-20,000kr cottages; 15,400kr double in hotel wing. Rates 15% lower off season. Rates include breakfast (hotel guests only). MC, V. **Amenities:** Restaurant; hot tub; sauna; guest kitchen. *In-room:* TV (new wing and chalets only), no phone.

Where to Dine

Eldstó Café CAFE This excellent road stop serves traditional Icelandic soups with homemade bread, as well as good cakes and light meals. Local pottery made with volcanic glazes is for sale.

Rte. 1, across from the N1 service station, Hvolsvöllur. ✆ **482-1011.** Main courses 1,790kr-2,900kr. MC, V. Daily 10am-9pm, in summer.

Gallery Pizza PIZZA This popular hangout with snug dining booths and local artwork on the wall serves mainly pizza, but also subs, burgers, and fried fish. The pizzas are fluffy in the crust and heavy on the cheese. Each pizza on the menu is named after a famous painting—"The Scream" comes with pepperoni, pineapple, Tabasco, jalapeño, black pepper, and cayenne pepper—but thankfully you can design your own.

Hvolsvegur 29, Hvolsvöllur. ✆ **487-8440.** Reservations recommended. Pizzas 970kr-2,860kr. MC, V. Sun-Tues noon-9pm; Fri-Sat noon-10pm.

Hellishólar ICELANDIC This new restaurant offers grills and buffets and can cater for groups of up to 180 people; it's a popular venue for wedding parties. Top choice is the steak buffet (3,590kr) with seasoned lamb and chicken breast stuffed with sun-dried tomatoes, basil, and feta cheese. There's also an interesting selection of finger-food.

Fljótshlíð. ✆ **487-8360;** www.hellisholar.is. Reservations recommended. Main courses 1,900kr-4,490kr. MC, V. Sun-Tues noon-9pm; Fri-Sat noon-10pm.

Hótel Hvolsvöllur ★ ICELANDIC Seafood and lamb are the staples, such as, say, lightly fried scallops with creamy yogurt sauce and a thin crisp of fried parmesan, followed by lamb filet in red wine sauce with gratinéed potatoes and a vegetable mélange. The best option in town; and presentation and service are more than up to par.

Hlíðarvegur 7 (Rte. 261, just off Rte. 1), Hvolsvöllur. ✆ **487-8050.** Reservations recommended. Main courses 3,100kr-5,500kr. AE, DC, MC, V. Daily 6-9:30pm.

Hótel Rangá ★ SCANDINAVIAN/MEDITERRANEAN The hotel is styled as an elite hunting and fishing lodge, and the restaurant follows suit with a virtuoso menu of seasonal fish and game, plus a token vegetarian dish. There's an award-winning fish soup and a stunning vanilla cod dish, plus several different unique combination platters; the strawberry/champagne/salmon main course is sublime. Make sure to save room for the fabulous chocolate and *skyr* cake. The four-course chef's menu is excellent, and portions aren't so large that you'll be wiped out.

Off Rte. 1, 7km (3⅓ miles) east of Hella. ✆ **487-5700.** Reservations required. Main courses 2,700kr-6,000kr; four-course chef's menu 8,900kr per person. AE, DC, MC, V. Daily 6:30-10pm; closed Dec 24-25 and Dec 31-Jan 1.

Kaffi Langbrók 🎁 CAFE This little cabin cafe is a dream— note the unique hingeless door, the 200-year-old whale vertebra fashioned into the wall, the saga-inspired escape hatch and the basalt-stone xylophone, dampened by an old pair of long underwear. It keeps things simple with cakes, waffles, soup, and an evening meal: there's a TV, Internet access, and a campground outside.

Rt. 261 (about 12km/7½ miles from Rte. 1), in the Markarfljót Valley. ✆ **863-4662.** Daily noon-11:30pm; Sat-Sun11:30am-1am.

Kanslarinn ICELANDIC This non-touristy local joint in Hella has soccer on TV, occasional live music, and the only public pool table in south Iceland (or so they claim; the Westman Islands has another one). Lamb and fish, plus lasagna, pizza, and burgers.

Rte. 1, in the center of Hella. ✆ **487-5100.** Reservations recommended for dinner in summer. Main courses 1,350kr-3,990kr. MC, V. Daily 11am-10pm; bar open late Fri-Sat.

ÞÓRSMÖRK

Thór, the hammer-wielding Norse god of farmers and seafarers and pioneers, has always been especially revered by Icelanders, who see in him a personification of the persevering Icelandic character. **Þórsmörk** ★★★ (Thór's Wood) has an aura of enchantment in the minds of Icelanders, as its name suggests. Surrounded by broad, silt-covered river valleys and three towering glaciers, Þórsmörk is a kind of alpine oasis; ask any sheep which has sought shelter there. Scenic surprises lie around every corner, from waterfalls, twisted gorges, and dripping, moss-covered caves to wildflowers, mountain grasses, and birch trees.

Come prepared: only basic food supplies are available, and temperatures are colder than in coastal regions. Þórsmörk can be visited on day tours, but staying 1 to 3 nights is recommended.

Essentials

GETTING THERE Þórsmörk is accessed via Route 249/F249, which proceeds 30km (19 miles) east from the Ring Road along the southern edge of the Markarfljót Valley. Only 4WD vehicles with good clearance can reach one of Þórsmörk's three places to stay (Básar), and possibly another (Skagfjörðsskáli), though it's often safer to park and walk the final kilometer by crossing a pedestrian footbridge a short way downstream. Even 4WD vehicles should not drive directly to the third option, Húsadalur; drive to Skagfjörðsskáli (or the pedestrian bridge) and walk the 30 to 45 minutes to Húsadalur from there.

From June 15 until September 12, **Reykjavík Excursions** (✆ **580-5400;** www.re.is) has a daily bus that leaves Reykjavík at 8am and arrives at Húsadalur at noon, with stops in Hveragerði, Selfoss, Hella, and Hvolsvöllur. (The bus is cancelled only two or three times a year after surges of glacial meltwater.) At 1pm the bus leaves for Básar, arriving at 1:40pm and then continuing to Skagfjörðsskáli (called "Langidalur" on the schedule). The bus returns to Húsadalur at 4pm, and leaves straight away for Reykjavík. From June 15 until August, every day, a second excursion bus leaves Reykjavík at 4pm and arrives at Húsadalur at 7:10pm, returning to Reykjavík at 8:30am the following morning without stopping at the other lodgings. A one-way adult ticket from Reykjavík to Þórsmörk is 5,800kr.

VISITOR INFORMATION For general information, contact people where you'll be staying (see "Where to Stay," below). An excellent **hiking map,** *Þórsmörk og Goðaland,* is for sale at all the huts (1,000kr). An only slightly less detailed map can be downloaded free from **www.thorsmork.is**.

Where to Stay

All three places here have tent sites, guest kitchens, and showers. Húsidalur has options of made-up beds, sleeping-bag accommodation, or sheet rental. To beat the summer rush, make sure to book at least a few weeks in advance.

Básar (✆ **893-2910**), run by and booked through Útivist (✆ **562-1000;** www.utivist.is), comprises a small hut (sleeps 23) and a large hut (sleeps 60). Both are open May until October, and a warden is on hand. From November until April the smaller hut remains open, but you need to get a key in advance. Básar is notorious for late-night partying on summer weekends because it's most easily accessible to 4WD vehicles. Sleeping-bag accommodation is 2,500kr per night.

Húsadalur (✆ **546-4466;** www.hostel.is), maintained by Hostelling International, is open from June 1 to September 15. It has the best facilities of the three, with an extensive compound of huts, cabins, cafe lounge, and a geothermal pool and sauna. The cafe, open until 9pm, sells drinks, skyr, soup, and basic sandwich supplies. Unlike the other two options, some sleeping quarters have private doubles and made-up beds. Sleeping-bag accommodation in a twin room is 4,100kr per person per night, and cottages sleeping 1 to 5 people are 12,500kr. Sheets and towels are available for rent. The pool is included, but a sauna and shower is 500kr. Of the three huts, Húsadalur has the least picturesque location, but the best hiking areas are within easy reach. Húsadalur is also the most peaceful after hours, since quiet time is more strictly enforced.

Skagfjörðsskáli (© **893-1191**), also known as "Langidalur" or simply "Þórsmörk Hut," is run by and booked through **Ferðafélag Íslands** (© **568-2533;** www.fi.is). The hut, open from mid-May until the end of September, sleeps 75 people in three well-packed rooms. Sleeping-bag accommodation, at 4,200kr, is more expensive than the competition. A tiny store sells chocolate, soap and a few other necessities. Vehicles must cross the Krossá River (just by the hut) which can sometimes get quite deep; ask at the hut to view the photo album which contains an interesting history of vehicles getting stuck in the river.

Exploring Þórsmörk

Iceland Excursions (© **540-1313;** www.icelandexcursions.is) run day tours to Þórsmörk on Tuesdays, Fridays, and Sundays, including pickup from Reykjavík, setting out at 8:30am and returning at around 6pm. The trip costs 16,500kr per person. For a little more zip (and lunch), you could pay 33,000kr per person for a Super Jeep tour with **Mountain Taxi** (© **544-5252;** www.mountaintaxi.is), but the 4WDs can't go anywhere the buses can't.

See p. 303 for arranged tours of the Laugavegurinn trail between Þórsmörk and Landmannalaugar.

The Route To Þórsmörk Route 249/F249 to Þórsmörk from the Ring Road is fabulously scenic, with the Markarfljót Valley on one side, and waterfalls and glacial tongues on the other.

Seljalandfoss waterfall, just a short distance up Route 249, is easily spotted from the Ring Road by drivers heading east, and is accessible to regular cars. Buses to Þórsmörk often discharge passengers here for a few minutes to walk behind the falls, where spray fills the air and the roaring sound is dramatically magnified. This waterfall is brilliantly illuminated and especially enchanting in the evenings.

A short distance along Route 249, **Gljúfurárfoss ★** is lesser-known but more mysterious and alluring, as the water falls into an enclosed cavern. Park at the farm with the neat lawn and the turf-roofed houses. From there, it's a precarious 3-minute clamber, aided by a chain and ladder, to a good viewpoint. ***Warning:*** Once you've climbed the final stretch of rock, it can be very difficult to get back down. A safer alternative is to wade up the stream into the cavern.

Close to Þórsmörk, the bus usually makes a photo stop at the small azure lake **Lónið,** with floating icebergs calved from the glacial tongue **Gígjökull.**

HIKING The hiking map ***Þórsmörk og Goðaland,*** available at the huts, sorts out the dense tangle of trails and is essential for exploring the area. The map is less helpful for calculating the length of your hike, so get an estimate from the wardens.

Technically, only the area north of the Krossá River is Þórsmörk. The area south of the Krossá is called Goðaland (Land of the Gods), and the hiking there is generally harder and steeper. Þórsmörk and Goðaland are connected by a pedestrian bridge near the base of Valahnúkur, a short distance west of the Skagfjörðsskáli hut in Langidalur Valley. Climbing Valahnúkur is a good introduction to the area: reaching the summit takes less than an hour from Húsadalur or Langidalur. Most hikers stay north of the Krossá and fashion a loop trail to the east, starting and ending at Langidalur. A 6-hour loop will take you as far east as Búðarhamar and around the

THE FIMMVÖRÐUHÁLS trek ★★★

How many treks are there where you can actually walk on a steaming lava field and peer into crevices still glowing with brimstone? This spectacular 20km (12-mile) hike connecting Þórsmörk and Skógar, which traverses the 1,093m (3,586 ft.) Fimmvörðuháls Pass between Eyjafjallajökull and Mýrdalsjökull, has a new dimension added with compliments of Mother Nature. The trek was closed for a few months in 2010 after the vent fissure eruption spewed lava over a vast area with at least 200 meters of the famous trekking path consumed. Re-opening later in the summer of 2010 with a new path marked out around the lava, trekkers can now get close up and even walk on and explore the newly-laid lava field. A few sections are steep and vertiginous, but no special equipment is usually required between early July and early September. The entire route could be done in 1 exhausting day, but most trekkers spend the night in the **Fimmvörðuskáli hut,** a short detour west of the trail near the top of the pass and about 3km from the lava field. The hut sleeps 23 in snug double-bed sleeping-bag bunks, and must be reserved in advance through **Útivist** (✆ **562-1000;** www.utivist.is), at a cost of 2,500kr per person. Facilities include a kitchen but no showers. No camping is allowed outside the hut or anywhere along the trail. Always check weather forecasts before setting out.

The trek can be done in either direction. Hikers going north to south (Þórsmörk to Skógar) have often started on the Laugavegurinn (p. 304), forming a continuous 6-day journey from Landmannalaugar to Skógar. The north-to-south route has the advantage of a net loss of altitude, but the south-to-north route affords a dramatic descent into Þórsmörk.

Arranged tours all go from south to north, to give visitors the option of spending another 1 to 3 nights at the huts in Þórsmörk. The best tour leader is **Útivist** (✆ **562-1000;** www.utivist.is), which offers Fimmvörðuháls treks every few days in summer. The very reasonable 22,500kr cost includes transportation from Reykjavík to Skógar and Þórsmörk to Reykjavík, a group guide, and accommodation at the Fimmvörðuskáli hut, but no food.

peak Tindfjöll. An ambitious and rewarding 8-hour round-trip hike leads through Goðaland to the Tungnakvíslarjökull glacial tongue.

Iceland's most famous trail, the Laugavegurinn, connects Þórsmörk and Landmannalaugar in a 4-day hike (see box, p. 304).

SKÓGAR, VÍK & MÝRDALSJÖKULL

Here marks the opening stretch of the southern coast's most dramatic scenery. Tall mountains press against the Ring Road, and a long succession of waterfalls originates from the glaciers looming above. This region also boasts Iceland's best folk museum at Skógar, south Iceland's best coastal walks at Vík, and some lesser-known inland detours toward Mýrdalsjökull Glacier. If you are passing this way, add at least 2 nights to your itinerary to take in Vík's environs, including the Þakgil camp.

Essentials

GETTING THERE All sights in this section are arrayed on or near Route 1 and can be reached by regular car. Skógar is 155km (96 miles) from Reykjavík, and Vík is 31km (19 miles) farther. In summer, two daily buses connect Reykjavík and Skógar (4,400kr), and two daily buses connect Reykjavík and Vík (5,300kr). Service continues through the winter, with departures at least three times per week. For tickets contact **BSÍ** (✆ **562-1011**).

VISITOR INFORMATION The regional tourist office at **Hveragerði** (p. 174) covers this area; the local office in Hvolsvöllur (p. 306) also services the area but is only open during the summer . In **Skógar,** limited tourist information can be found at the **folk museum** (p. 315), and at the **Fossbúð market** en route to Skógafoss. In **Vík,** the information desk is in the **Brydebúð Museum,** Víkurbraut 28 (✆ **487-1395;** http://brydebud.vik.is), open June 15 to September 15 Mon–Fri from 10am to 8pm, Sat–Sun 1to 8pm. The free and widely-available **map** *Power and Purity* is detailed and useful.

What to See & Do

WEST OF SKÓGAR

Seljavallalaug ★ In this "only in Iceland" geothermal swimming pool, built in 1923, one wall is actually a mountainside from which the natural hot water trickles in. The pool is semi-abandoned and therefore free of charge. The pool is not monitored, but it is cleaned at regular intervals.

May–Sept. From the western junction of Rte. 1 and Rte. 242, take Rte. 242 for 1km (½ mile), and then continue straight as Rte. 242 curves off to the right. Seljavellir is about 2km (1¼ miles) ahead. Park at the farm's newer pool (now closed) and walk 15 min. to Seljavallalaug.

SKÓGAR

Skógar feels more like an outpost than a village, but it's been continuously settled since the 12th century. It is best known for its waterfall and folk museum, and as a launching point for the 2-day Fimmvörðuháls trek to Þórsmörk (p. 311).

For a wonderful day hike—especially if you like continuous and varied waterfalls—walk north from Skógafoss waterfall along the **Fimmvörðuháls trail ★★** for about 2 hours, then head back along the same route.

Clearly visible from the Ring Road, the powerful, 62m (203 ft.) **Skógafoss ★** waterfall looks ordinary from a distance but rewards closer inspection. Walk as close as you can on the gravel riverbed to be enveloped in the sound and spray and refracted light. A metal staircase leads to the top, where you can look down at nesting fulmars.

The prolific and affecting **Skógar Folk Museum (Skógasafn) ★★★** (✆ **487-8845.** www.skogasafn.is) is all the work of Þórður Tómasson, who has been gathering artifacts from local farms for almost 70 years. Since Þórður started the museum in 1949, countless imitations have sprung up all over Iceland, but none match the inspiration of the original. A pair of ice skates with blades made from old cow bones. A cask made from a hollowed out whale vertebra, another used as a kitchen stool. A barometer made from a cow's bladder, which shrivels at the approach of bad weather. Most displays are annotated in English, but guided tours are free with admission for groups. Þórður prowls around the museum most days and may sing for you while accompanying himself on an old harmonium or dulcimer.

Admission to Skógasafn is 1200kr adults, 900kr seniors and students, 600kr for children aged between 12–15, and free for children under 12. (June–Aug daily 9am–6pm; May and Sept daily 10am–5pm; Oct–Apr 11am–4pm). From Route 1, on the eastern side of Skógar, follow signs for "Byggðasafnið í Skógum."

MÝRDALSJÖKULL

A short distance east of Skógar, Routes 221 and 222 provide the easiest Ring Road access to **Mýrdalsjökull,** the country's fourth-largest glacier. **Sólheimajökull,** a projectile of Mýrdalsjökull, just 5km (3 miles) from the Ring Road via Route 221, is a worthwhile diversion if you are not bound for greater glories east at Skaftafell and Jökulsárlón. Sólheimajökull is retreating up to 100m (328 ft.) every year, a vivid demonstration of the effects of global warming. Some visitors walk atop the glacier, but taking a tour is much safer. Watch out for quicksand at the glacier's edge.

Icelandic Mountain Guides, Vagnhöfði 7, 110 Reykjavík (✆ **587-9999;** www.mountainguides.is), leads daily glacier walks of Sólheimajökull in summer, with explorations of crevasses and an introduction to basic climbing techniques. A 90-minute tour is 6,300kr per person, and a 3-hour tour is 9,500kr, not including transportation from Reykjavík or elsewhere. The children's price (8–15 years of age) is 3,900kr, the minimum age for the short tour is 8, the longer tour, 10.

Arcanum Adventure Tours (✆ **487-1500;** www.snow.is) is based at the Sólheimaskáli hut, 10km (6 miles) from the Ring Road on Route 222, and offers snowmobile, ice-climbing, and Super Jeep tours of Mýrdalsjökull. A snowmobile for two costs around 28,000kr for an hour. Road conditions on Route 222 vary, so ask if you'll need a ride from the Ytri-Sólheimar lodge at the base of the road.

DYRHÓLAEY ★★

This coastal bird sanctuary gets its name (meaning "doorway hill island") from a massive sea archway that photographers—and daredevil pilots—find irresistible. Dyrhólaey is not an island but a promontory, with a shallow inland lagoon full of wading birds, clifftops rife with puffins, and grassy slopes full of ground-nesting avian species. It's ideal walking territory, with some eye-catching sea stacks offshore. Dyrhólaey is closed during nesting season, from May 1 to June 25, though you can still take a guided tour with Dyrhólaeyjarferðir (see below).

Route 218 leads to Dyrhólaey from the Ring Road, crossing a narrow isthmus and rounding the sanctuary. Consider parking at the far end of the isthmus and walking clockwise around the perimeter to the lighthouse, then cutting through the middle back to the shallows. This circuit takes about 3 hours and has fabulous views in all directions. Those who want to cut to the chase can proceed directly to the famous doorway arch on the south side of the sanctuary.

Dyrhólaeyjarferðir (✆ **487-8500;** www.dyrholaey.com) offers a choice of 75-minute land or sea tours in amphibious vehicles. Only the sea trip passes through the arch, but the land trip—the only option in rough weather—includes refreshments. Tours cost 4,500kr for adults and 3,500kr for children aged 7 to 13.

Exploring Vík & Environs ★★

Almost at the southern tip of the mainland, the town of Vík (also known as Vík í Mýrdal) is quaintly poised between mountains, sea cliffs, and a long, beautiful black-sand beach. Vík's visual trademark is **Reynisdrangar,** a row of spiky basalt sea stacks that looks like a submerged stegosaurus and has long served as a navigational point for

TROLL tales

Trolls arrived in Iceland as stowaways on Viking ships and took to the local landscape, making their homes in caves and cliffs. Their boats are made of stone, and they can fish without line or bait. Most trolls never appear in sunlight, lest they turn into stone themselves.

To Icelanders, trolls are tough, menacing, ugly, and often lonesome—anything but *cute*. It's best not to cross them, though they'll keep their word if you reach an agreement. Trolls who live in bird cliffs are often a great danger to egg-collectors. In an emergency, Christianity can help drive trolls off.

Trolls have not survived in the modern age nearly as well as elves. In fact, many people believe them to be extinct. Electricity hasn't been good for hidden people: electric light makes the outer dark darker, diminishing the half-dark in which hidden people take form.

sailors. Lore has it that Reynisdrangar was formed when two trolls were unable to land their three-masted ship before dawn and turned to stone—as happens when trolls are caught in sunlight. The pillars reach up to 66m (217 ft.) in height and have their own bird populations. In good weather, the coastal walk along the Reynisfjall cliffs west of the town is spectacular.

Brydebúð The tourist information desk, Halldórs Cafe, and a local museum are concentrated in this 1831 timber house, which was actually transported to Vík from the Westman Islands in 1895. The museum has an art gallery and exhibitions on town history and shipwrecks.

Víkurbraut 28. © **487-1395.** http://brydebud.vik.is. Museum admission 500kr adults; free for children under 16. June 15–Sept 15 Mon–Fri from 10am to 8pm, Sat–Sun 1–8pm.

REYNISFJALL

On a clear day or summer evening, the cliffs along **Reynisfjall mountain ★★** west of Vík make for the most beautiful walk on Iceland's southern coastline. The most common approach is from Vík, where the ascent must be made inland along the 4WD road that winds its way up. If you have a 4WD vehicle and want to drive up, the road meets the Ring Road at the village's western border. In a regular car, you can shorten the trip a bit by driving to a parking area at the base of the ascent; turn off the Ring Road right next to the "Velkomin Til Vikur" sign.

To make the most of your trek, allow 3 hours in total so you can round the cliffs far enough to take in the views north toward the mountains and glaciers and west toward Reynisfjara Beach, Dyrhólaey, and the Westman Islands. The vibrant bird life includes a good many puffins. Reynisfjall can also be climbed from its western side, by driving south on Route 215 and following the trail that leads up from the Reyniskirkja church, near the power lines. You could also use this route to *descend* from Reynisfjall and extend your walk from Vík all the way to Reynisfjara.

REYNISFJARA

The black-pebble beach of **Reynisfjara ★★** at the southern end of Route 215 forms a 2.5km (1½ miles) spit, extending from Reynisfjall almost to Dýrholaey (p. 316), that divides the ocean from Dyrhólaós Lagoon. Reynisfjara is even more beautifully situated than the beach at Vík, but less frequented. On the eastern edge

ACTIVE volcanoes

The south of Iceland has the highest concentration of known sub-glacial volcanoes in the world. These spectacular forces of nature are a magnet for geo-tourists, but also produce a variety of potentially lethal hazards, such as: risk of lightning, tephra fallout (ash), and *Jöklahlaups:* sudden flood bursts of melted glacial ice mixed with ash, mud, huge chunks of ice, and toxic chemicals.

Since the eruption of Eyjafjallajökull in April 2010, all eyes have been focused on one of her angry sisters: Katla – a nearby sub-glacial volcano under the Mýrdalsjökull cap, directly north of Vík. This volcano has a history of erupting almost in unison with other local volcanoes and is long overdue. Since 1721, it has erupted five times at 34- to 78-year intervals, but there hasn't been an eruption since 1918.

Anyone visiting this area should be aware of the hazard areas and the evacuation procedures, especially in Vík, clearly set out in the widely available brochure *Eruption Emergency Guidelines.*

of the Reynisfjara, at the base of Reynisfjall, is the phenomenal basalt sea cave **Hálsanefshellir ★★**. It's inaccessible at high tide, so time your visit accordingly. For tidal schedules, ask around, call the **Icelandic Coast Guard** (**✆ 545-2000**), or use the "Marine Reports" link at www.myforecast.com. The Icelandic Maritime administration provides useful maps of the tides here: http://vs.en.sigling.is/.

ÞAKGIL & MÆLIFELL

Four kilometers (2½ miles) east of Vík, Route 214 extends 15km (9⅓ miles) north from the Ring Road to the Þakgil campground, situated in a sheltered enclave amid dramatic mountain scenery near Mýrdalsjökull Glacier. Route 214 itself is a fantastic drive, rough but passable in a regular car. At a high point halfway to Þakgil, the road passes some primitive wood shelters built for the movie set of *Beowulf and Grendel* (critics loved the scenery). A crude but serviceable **hiking map** is available at the campground or online at www.thakgil.is. One great hike follows a rough 4WD track, built for rounding-up sheep in September, to the base of Mýrdalsjökull in a 4-hour round-trip. Another recommended 4-hour loop includes the viewpoint at **Mælifell.** Two long but rewarding trails—about 7 hours apiece—lead to Þakgil all the way from Vík; the one further east, through Fagridalur and Bárðarfell, is slightly more picturesque.

MÝRDALSSANDUR & HJÖRLEIFSHÖFÐI

Shortly east of Vík is **Mýrdalssandur ★**, a vast expanse of black-sand desert. As you enter Mýrdalssandur, a 221m (725 ft.) mountain, just south of the Ring Road, rises eerily from the surrounding wasteland. This is Hjörleifshöfði, named for Hjörleifur Hródmarsson, who wintered here around the year 870 before being murdered by his Irish slaves.

Hjörleifshöfði makes for a memorable short climb. A rough gravel road leads south from the Ring Road along its western edge to an indentation where the trail ascends. The cliffs, which host a fulmar colony, show evidence of shoreline erosion. A farm was on Hjörleifshöfði until 1937, but all that remains are the farmers' gravestones.

Where to Stay

The stretch of coast from Markarfljót to Vík is teeming with idyllic farms to stay at, so **Icelandic Farm Holidays** (✆ **570-2700;** www.farmholidays.is) is a good backup resource to our recommendations below. Also look out for the farm holidays brochure *Upp Í Sveit*.

WEST OF SKÓGAR

Country Hótel Anna ★★ The interiors of Iceland's "country" hotels usually lack the kind of rustic character visitors hope for, but this three-star hotel (the smallest in Iceland) full of old furniture and embroidered bedspreads is a charmer. The hotel, which is named after the Icelandic travel writer Sigríður Anna Jónsdóttir, is also certified by Green Globe for responsible environmental practices. The seven rooms are all very similar in size. The two rooms on the upper floor are well suited to families.

Moldnúpur (easternmost farm on Rte. 246). ✆ **487-8950.** Fax 487-8955. www.hotelanna.is. 5 units. June–Sept 15 9,800kr double. Rates around 38% lower Sept 16–May. Rates include breakfast. MC, V. **Amenities:** Restaurant; hot tub; sauna. *In room:* TV, coffee/tea, Wi-Fi.

Drangshlíð This Farm Holidays spot near the base of a bird cliff has ample, comfortable en-suite rooms in three separate modern buildings. Nine brand-new family rooms sleep up to four. The restaurant gets high marks as well.

Drangshlíðð farm (Rte. 1, 4km/2½ miles west of Skógar). ✆ **487-8868.** www.drangshlid.is. 34 units. Jun–Sept 15 13,900kr double; 18,900kr family room. Rates 25% lower Sept 16–May. Rates include breakfast. *In-room:* No phone.

Guesthouse Edinborg Rooms at this Farm Holidays option are welcoming and decorated in warm hues. Eyjafjallajökull is within view and the Seljavallalaug thermal swimming pool is just up the road. The two cottages sleep four to six and have kitchenettes.

Lambafell farm (on Rte. 242, close to western junction of Rte. 242 and Rte. 1). ✆ **846-1384.** www.islandia.is/thorn. 6 double units (5 w/bathroom) and 2 cottages. May–Sept 17,700kr double; 18,900kr per person cottage, minimum two persons, 1,500kr for each extra person in the cottage. Rates include breakfast. MC, V. *In room:* No phone, Wi-Fi.

SKÓGAR

Hotel Edda Skógar This two-star hotel next to the folk museum has simple and serviceable rooms, and good dinner buffet for 4,450kr. Sleeping-bag accommodation is inside a gym on floor mattresses.

> **Reading the Weather Signs**
>
> **Illuminated road signs all over Iceland—including one just east of Vík—indicate wind conditions and temperature (in Celsius, of course) along the road. North, south, east, and west winds are indicated by N, S, A, and V respectively, and the number following the letter is the wind speed in meters per second. Anything above 20 is very severe, and flying sand could tear the paint right off your car. Thankfully, this rarely happens in summer.**

✆ **444-4830.** www.hoteledda.is. 34 units without bathroom. June–Aug 10,000kr double; 3,500kr sleeping-bag accommodation. Breakfast available (1,200kr). AE, DC, MC, V. Closed Sept 16–May. **Amenities:** Restaurant. *In room:* No phone.

Hotel Skógar The plain exterior masks a touch of class and a fine restaurant inside. Rooms are warmly and tastefully decorated, even if they offer no surprises. Let them know if you'd like one with a bathtub, otherwise you get a shower. Despite the location near Skógafoss, only the suite has a partial view.

Close to Skógafoss waterfall. ✆ **487-4880.** Fax 487-5436. www.allseasonhotels.is. 12 units. June–Sept 28,100kr double. Rates include breakfast. AE, MC, V. Closed Oct–Apr. **Amenities:** Restaurant; hot tub; sauna; Internet terminal. *In-room:* TV, no phone, Wi-Fi (in some rooms).

BETWEEN SKÓGAR & VÍK

Hótel Dyrhólaey The Farm Holidays network rates this as "Category IV," meaning all rooms have private bathrooms and meet basic hotel standards. The rooms are sizeable, and more importantly, Dyrhólaey and Reynisfjara are close by. Chose between a stunning coastal view or a view of the magnificent glacier.

Brekkur farm (Off Rte. 1, 2.5km/1½ miles) east of the Rte. 1/Rte. 218 junction). ✆ **487-1333.** Fax 487-1507. www.dyrholaey.is. 70 units. June–Sept 15 25,000kr double. Rates around 40% lower Sept 16–May. Rates include breakfast. AE, DC, MC, V. **Amenities:** Restaurant. *In room:* TV, Wi-Fi.

VÍK & ENVIRONS

On a slope with great views overlooking the town, the **Norður-Vík Youth Hostel,** Suðurvíkurvegur (✆ **487-1106** or 867-2389; fax 487-1303; www.hostel.is; 10 units, 36 beds, none w/bathroom; open all year round 3,200kr per bed per night; breakfast available for 1,000kr; MC, V; closed Nov 16–Mar 14), is a low-budget option that has more in common with a guesthouse.

Hótel Edda Vík This hotel meets the modern, comfortable and functional standard of the Edda chain, but it's in their "PLUS" category, meaning three-star accommodation, not the usual student-style housing. There are also 10 new cottages in hotel-room style.

Klettsvegur. ✆ **444-4840.** Fax 487-1418. www.hoteledda.is. 42 units. May–Sept 18,300kr double; cottage double 16,000kr. Breakfast available (1,200kr). AE, DC, MC, V. Closed Oct–Apr. **Amenities:** Restaurant; Internet terminal. *In room:* TV.

Hótel Höfðabrekka ★ A lovely, woody place near a cave and trout-fishing lake. Rooms, in four lodges, are comfortable and traditional, and there are four outdoor hot tubs. A Farm Holidays place, 5km (3 miles) east of Vík. It also has a good restaurant.

Höfðabrekka farm (Off Rte. 1, just east of Rte. 214). ✆ **487-1208.** Fax 487-1218. www.hofdabrekka.is. 62 units, w/bathroom. Jun–Aug 20,000kr double. May and Sept 14,000kr double. Rates include breakfast. AE, MC, V. Closed Nov–Mar. **Amenities:** Restaurant; hot tubs; guest kitchen. *In room:* TV, hair dryer, no phone.

Hótel Lundi ★ In the middle of the village, with a nicely worn-in feel and reasonable prices. Sleeping-bag accommodation is in the adjoining **Guesthouse Puffin,** which is thin-walled but pleasant, with good cooking facilities.

Víkurbraut 26 and 24a. ✆ **487-1212.** Fax 487-1404. www.hotelpuffin.is. 23 units, 12 w/bathroom. 16,500kr double; 19,500kr triple; 3,100kr sleeping-bag accommodation. Rates include breakfast, except for sleeping-bag accommodation. During peak season (July–Aug 15) the prices go up by 2,000kr. AE, MC, V. **Amenities:** Restaurant, bar. *In room:* Hair dryer.

Þakgil This is a wonderful campsite, with the chance to eat by candlelight in a cave—bring some charcoal for the grill. It has just added 10 cabins, each with kitchenette, toilet, and two double beds in bunks—but no hot water, so you'll need to venture outside to the showers. Accommodation is sleeping bag only, and no sheets are available for rent. You'll find it 15km (9⅓ miles) from the Ring Road.

✆ **893-4889,** 853-4889, and 487-1246. www.thakgil.is. June–Sept 15 14,000kr cabin; 850kr camping. MC, V. Closed Sept 16–May. 4km (2½ miles) east of Vík, take Rte. 214 from the Ring Road for 15km (9⅓ miles). *In room:* Cabins have kitchenettes, fridge, no phone.

Where to Dine

Several places listed above have good restaurants. **Country Hótel Anna,** west of Skógar, is open for dinner from mid-June until August, from 7 to 8:30pm; main two-course meals are 3,700kr to 4,500kr and include salmon, trout, and lamb. **Hótel Höfðabrekka,** east of Vík, has a dinner buffet from 7 to 9pm for 4,900kr; selections usually include whale, smoked and steam-boiled salmon, and lamb. No reservation is necessary for either spot. The kitchens of Höfðabrekka are also home to the famous Icelandic ghost Jóka.

In Skógar, the **cafeteria** at the folk museum (p. 315) is open daily from June 1 until September from 10am to 5pm. The restaurant at **Hótel Skógar** (above) is the choicest option, with a small menu of fish and lamb courses averaging 4,000kr. It's open from noon–3pm and 6–10pm; reservations are recommended for dinner.

Halldórskaffi ★ CAFE This appealing hangout adjoins the museum and tourist office. Unlike most Icelandic country cafes, it has a full range of coffee, even espresso. Food choices include a fish or lamb special, burgers, sandwiches, pizzas, and a tempting display of cakes and muffins.

Víkurbraut 28, Vík. ✆ **487-1202.** Reservations recommended for dinner. Main courses 2,690kr–4,250kr. MC, V. June–Aug daily 11am–10pm.

Hótel Lundi ICELANDIC This restaurant is the best in town, according to the locals. The menu is filled with traditional Icelandic food (the good stuff, not pickled testicles,) such as pan-fried puffin, marinated lamb, and grilled trout.

Víkurbraut 26, Vík. ✆ **487-1212.** Reservations recommended. Main courses 2,990kr–3,990kr. AE, MC, V. Daily 11am–4pm and 6–9pm.

Víkurskáli ICELANDIC Located inside the N1 station on the Ring Road, this restaurant is a small step up from a typical Icelandic filling station grill, both in seating and menu, which includes fish and lamb.

Rte. 1, Vík. ✆ **487-1230.** Main courses 750kr–2,150kr. MC, V. Mon–Fri 9am–9pm; Sat 10am–9pm; Sun 11am–9pm.

KIRKJUBÆJARKLAUSTUR & LAKI CRATERS

The 272km (169 miles) between Vík and Höfn—the most austerely beautiful stretch of the Ring Road—contain just one small village, Kirkjubæjarklaustur. (You can just call it "Klaustur," as locals do.) Klaustur means "cloister" and refers to a Benedictine convent located here from 1186 until the Reformation. Today the village is not much more than a few houses and a pit stop, but it also serves as a crossroads for the interior route to Landmannalaugar and the Fjallabak reserve (p. 301). Another road leads to the Laki Craters, one of Iceland's most awe-inspiring volcanic formations.

Essentials

GETTING THERE Kirkjubæjarklaustur lies along Route 1, 73km (45 miles) northeast of Vík and 259km (161 miles) from Reykjavík. This route with sightseeing stops is handled by **Reykjavík Excursions** (✆ **580-5400;** www.re.is). In summer, one **bus** per day connects Reykjavík and Höfn via the Ring Road, stopping at Kirkjubæjarklaustur. There is another **bus** from Vík to Höfn that runs daily. During the winter, the services are reduced to three times a week. From mid-June to early September, Reykjavík Excursions also connects Reykjavík to Kirkjubæjarklaustur and Skaftafell daily through the interior Landmannalaugar/Fjallabak route.

VISITOR INFORMATION Kirkjubæjarklaustur's **tourist information office** (✆ **487-4620**) is on Klaustuvegur 10 opposite the chapel. Opening times are June to August on Monday to Friday from 9am to 1pm and 3pm to 9pm, Sat and Sun 10am to 8pm.

Exploring the Area

A single road leads through town. It turns to gravel at **Systrafoss,** a pretty waterfall. At the top of Systrafoss is **Systravatn,** a pleasant lake surrounded by pasture. If you don't have a car to reach Fjaðrárgljúfur and just need a satisfying walk, a path ascends to Systravatn from the far side of the falls. Alternatively, the road continues past Systrafoss and soon ends at a parking area, where a path continues along the Skaftá River. Within a 15-minute walk is the **Systrastapa,** a freestanding crag that looks like a giant molar. According to local folklore, two nuns were buried on top of Systrastapa after being burned at the stake—thus the name, which means "Sisters' Crag." A steel cable and chain descend from opposite sides of the crag, but footing is dangerous.

Kirkjugólf (Church Floor), a designated national monument near Route 203 north of the central roundabout, is a kind of natural stone terrace formed by a cross-section of hexagonal basalt columns.

FJAÐRÁRGLJÚFUR

For a short hike or picnic spot along this stretch of the Ring Road, look no further than **Fjaðrárgljúfur ★★**, a 100m-deep (328-ft.) gorge formed during the Ice Age two million years ago. Its proportions aren't mind-boggling, but it wins high aesthetic marks for its indented cliffsides full of spikes, arches, and scary ledges. The walk along the eastern ledge is not challenging, and the most compelling views can be seen in a 1-hour round-trip.

To reach Fjaðrárgljúfur, turn on to Route 206 from the Ring Road, 6km (3¾ miles) west of Kirkjubæjarklaustur. In 2km (1¼ miles) or so, Route F206 branches off to the right; continue straight and the parking area is shortly ahead.

LAKI CRATERS (LAKAGÍGAR)

Those with an eye for beauty within bleakness should particularly admire the **Laki crater row ★★★**, formed during the largest lava eruption ever witnessed. Starting in 1783, and continuing for 8 months, an estimated 14.7 cubic km (3½ cubic miles) of lava emerged from over 100 craters along a 25km-long (16-mile) fissure, flowing as far as 60km (37 miles). The eruption could be seen all over Iceland and was followed by several earthquakes. The sun-obscuring haze lowered temperatures for the entire Northern Hemisphere by about 3°F (1°C–2°C), and reached as far as Asia and North Africa. Within 3 years 70% of Iceland's livestock had died, mostly from fluorine poisoning. Most water and food was not contaminated, but cold weather and famine, combined with an outbreak of smallpox, killed 22% of the population in the same time frame. Today, Lakagígar's splattered, scabby landscape has a forlorn grandeur, and the volcanic craters are carpeted in gray mosses that turn bright green after a rainfall.

The crater row could be explored for days, but all visitors should at least climb Mt. Laki, the tallest of the craters, for astounding 360-degree views of the boundless lava flows and distant glaciers. The climb is not difficult, and takes about 45 minutes one-way from the parking area. Bring a strong flashlight, in case you run into any lava tubes to explore.

Reykjavík Excursions (✆ **580-5400;** www.re.is) has one daily bus in July and August from Skaftafell to the Laki Craters and back, with a stop at Kirkjubæjarklaustur and 3½ hours to explore the crater row on foot. From Kirkjubæjarklaustur the price is 9,000kr. **Icelandic Mountain Guides** (✆ **587-9999;** www.mountainguide.is) is presently the only tour operator leading trekking tours of the Lakagígar area.

En route to Lakagígar, make sure to have a look at the aptly named **Fagrifoss ★** (Beautiful Waterfall). The turnoff is marked from Route F206, roughly 22km (14 miles) from the Ring Road.

The Laki Craters are reached via Route 206/F206, which joins the Ring Road 6km (3¾ miles) west of Kirkjubæjarklaustur. This route has difficult river crossings, and should only be attempted in 4WD vehicles with high clearance; always check road conditions in advance.

Where to Stay

Hótel Klaustur ★ As with most Icelandair hotels, everything is very professional, and once inside their modern rooms you'd hardly know whether you were at the airport or inside a volcano crater. "Superior" doubles have marginally more space, Nescafé packets, the option of a bathtub, and (drumroll) a hair dryer.

Klausturvegur 6. ✆ **487-4900.** Fax 487-4614. www.icehotels.is. 57 units. June–Aug 21,800kr–24,800kr double; 31,800kr junior suite. Rates about 18% lower Apr–May and Sept–Oct; about 33% lower Nov to mid-Dec and Feb. Breakfast available (1,400kr). AE, DC, MC, V. Closed mid-Dec–Jan. **Amenities:** Restaurant. *In room:* TV, phone, hair dryer, Wi-Fi.

Hótel Laki Efri-Vík ★ This ranch-like spread is quite a world unto itself, with a restaurant, fishing lake, and a nine-hole golf course. There are plenty of room options, including 15 economical cottages with kitchenettes and grills, which sleep four to eight. The restaurant has a nice dinner buffet in the summer from 7 to 9pm, usually including local trout for 4,500kr.

Efri-Vík 5km (3 miles) south of Kirkjubæjarklaustur on Rte. 204. ✆ **487-4694.** Fax 487-4894. www.hotellaki.is. 55 units. June–Aug 21,500kr hotel double; 14,000kr cottage double; 4,500kr sleeping-bag accommodation; 11,000kr and up for cottage single. Rates include breakfast, except for sleeping-bag accommodation. MC, V. **Amenities:** Restaurant; nine-hole golf course; spa; sauna. *In room:* TV, hair dryer.

Hörgsland ★ This friendly compound provides a combination of guesthouse and cottages, with the possibility of camping. The recently converted guesthouse has eight new rooms, five with showers. Each of the 13 cottages has a kitchen, porch, two bedrooms, and a sleeping loft with two beds (mind your head!). Each bedroom has a double bed with a single bed bunked above it, so eight guests can squeeze into each cottage. If you're only two, rates are 9,000kr in sleeping bags and 11,000kr in made-up beds, and you'll have the cottage to yourself. Rooms in the guesthouse are 12,000kr for a double and 15,400kr with a shower. A three-course dinner is available on request for 3,700kr, a two-course meal is 600kr cheaper. Hörgsland also sells fishing permits.

Rte. 1, 7km (4⅓ miles) east of Kirkjubæjarklaustur. © **487-6655.** www.horgsland.is. 21 units, 18 with bathroom. 15,400kr guesthouse double; 7,350kr–19,800kr cottages. Breakfast available (1,450kr). AE, DC, MC, V. **Amenities:** Cafe; hot tubs. *In room:* TV, CD player, no phone.

Where to Dine

Hótel Klaustur ★ ICELANDIC The hotel restaurant maintains very high standards for such a remote location; try the delicate local trout, or the tender lamb with demi-glace and herbed potatoes.

Klausturvegur 6. © **487-4900.** Reservations recommended. Main courses 3,200kr–5,000kr. AE, DC, MC, V. May–Sept daily 7:30–10am, noon–2pm, 7–9:30pm; Oct–Apr daily 8–10am, noon–2pm, 7–9pm.

Systrakaffi ★ ICELANDIC BISTRO This cafe-bar has little competition in this lonely territory, but takes this responsibility to heart with a morale-boosting ambience and surprisingly good bistro-style food. Choices include pan-fried Arctic char, smoked lamb, a tasty bagel plate with smoked trout, plus salads, pizzas, and burgers.

Klausturvegur 13. © **487-4848.** Main courses 2,050kr–3,600kr. Children's menu. MC, V. May 15–Oct Sun–Thurs 11am–11pm, Fri–Sat 11am–midnight; Oct–Dec and Mar–May 14 Sat–Sun 11am–11pm; closed Jan–Feb. Kitchen closes at 10pm.

VATNAJÖKULL, SKEIÐARÁRSANDUR & SKAFTAFELL

East of Kirkjubæjarklaustur, the Ring Road enters a long, townless stretch in the shadow of **Vatnajökull,** the largest icecap between the Arctic and Antarctic circles. South of Vatnajökull is a stupendously bleak glacial flood plain called **Skeiðarársandur,** or just "The Sandur." The main regional attraction is **Skaftafell** ★★, a popular hiking area bordering Vatnajökull. Most of Skaftafell's day hikes are on scrubby grassland, amid a panorama of spiky mountains and glistening ice.

Essentials

GETTING THERE Skaftafell is along the Ring Road, 327km (203 miles) east of Reykjavík. In summer, two buses a day connect Reykjavík and Skaftafell via the Ring Road, stopping at the park. Reykjavík to Skaftafell takes 6 hours, and the route continues to Höfn. The route with sightseeing stops is handled by **Sterna** (© **551-1166; www.sterna.is**) and takes almost 6½ hours, ending at Skaftafell. From mid-June to early September, Sterna and Reykjavík Excursions also connect Reykjavík and Skaftafell daily through the interior Landmannalaugar/Fjallabak route, which is more bumpy, expensive, scenic, and time-consuming. From mid-September until May, three weekly Þingvallaleið buses connect Reykjavík and Höfn, stopping at the Freysnes service station opposite Hótel Skaftafell (p. 328), 5km (3 miles) east of the park entrance.

VISITOR INFORMATION The **Skaftafell tourist office** (© **478-1627;** www.vatnajokulsthjodgardur.is) is well marked from the Ring Road. Basic **trail maps** are available there for 300kr, and can also be printed from the website. The

THE glacier MYSTIQUE

Those who have never seen a ***jökull*** (glacier) can find it hard to understand why these huge, dirty sheets of ice arouse so much interest. Part of the appeal is sheer magnitude, but the destructive power of glaciers also inspires respect. Only 10% of Iceland's land mass is covered by glaciers, but 60% of its volcanic eruptions occur beneath them, often causing catastrophic floods. In Icelandic folklore, someone crossing a glacier might plunge into a hidden crevasse, only to be heard singing hymns from the same spot for decades. But size and might are only part of the glacier mystique. Like an organism, its bodily matter replaces itself over time. Vatnajökull's oldest ice was formed around 1200, but rock, sediment, and human victims also churn through its messy digestive system. Stray airplane parts or ski poles from decades or centuries past often pop out from the glacier's edge. Glaciers also provide endless aesthetic variety. The same glacier can appear pink or white at a distance, brown- and black-streaked on nearer inspection, and a more translucent blue up close. Evidence suggests that glaciers aren't losing their hold on the Icelandic imagination: more than 150 living Icelandic men are named Jökull.

office is open daily from 9am to 7pm June 16 to August; daily from 9am to 6pm June 1 to 15 and September; and daily from 10am to 3pm October to April.

Exploring the Area

Halfway between Kirkjubæjarklaustur and Skaftafell, on the western edge of the Skeiðarársandur, **Núpsstaður**—a tiny, turf-roofed 17th-century chapel and collection of old farm buildings—is under the care of the National Museum. It was once home to the brave postmen and river guides who, until 1970, crossed the dangerous glaciers and rivers alone. Access is free at all hours, so consider a stop to contemplate this remote settlement between a waterfall, the table mountain Lómagnúpur, and the lifeless sands.

Núpsstaðarskógar ★★, near the western edge of Skeiðarárjökull along the Núpsá river, is a scrubland area rife with beautiful gorges, waterfalls, and glacier views; yet it remains one of Iceland's better-kept hiking secrets. The day-tour operator for Núpsstaðarskógar resigned in 2007. Until he is replaced, the only way to get there is via the very difficult 4WD road, by hiking there yourself, or—as we would advise—by signing up for a tour with **Icelandic Mountain Guides** (✆ **587-9999;** www.mountainguide.is). This recommended group leads 5-day hikes between Núpsstaðarskógar and the Laki Craters (p. 322), and a 4-day hike through Núpsstaðarskógar to Skaftafell, traversing the Skeiðarárjökull. Participants carry their own camping gear. Also check with **Útivist** (✆ **562-1000;** www.utivist.is); they don't operate scheduled tours, but they can arrange a group tour of the area.

A sandur is not just any desert. *Sandur* is the English as well as Icelandic term for a flood plain full of sand and sediment deposited by sub-glacial volcanoes. **Skeiðarársandur,** formed by flood bursts from Vatnajökull, is the largest sandur in the world. This flat, interminable expanse, braided in meltwater streams and drained of life and color, was impassable until the Ring Road was completed in 1974.

In 1996, after a volcanic eruption at Grímsvötn, underneath Vatnajökull, a huge floodburst was anticipated for several days. Shortly after the film crews from the foreign media got bored of waiting and went home, a torrent of water and sediment rivaling the Amazon in size and force crashed down into the Skeiðarársandur, with house-sized icebergs bobbing along like corks. Once the sediment had settled, Iceland was 7sq. km (2¾ sq. miles) larger. No one was killed or injured, and no communities were destroyed.

Approaching Skaftafell from the west, the Ring Road crosses three bridges. The first, Núpsvötn, was undamaged by the 1996 floodburst, even though water cascaded right over the roadway. The second bridge, Gígjukvísi, was pounded by icebergs and completely washed away. The third and longest bridge, Skeiðará, was partially demolished. A temporary road was ready in 3 weeks, and replacement bridges were completed in 9 months. A **monument** to the 1996 eruption, constructed from twisted hunks of the demolished bridges, lies between the new bridges and the Skaftafell park entrance.

SKAFTAFELL NATIONAL PARK ★★

Skaftafell is located in the southern territory of Vatnajökull National Park. The area has been conserved since 1967, and the variety of vegetation, wildflowers, and butterflies shows what can happen when grazing sheep are kept out for 40 years. The park's hiking trails for this area are mostly on the **Skaftafellsheiði** (Skaftafell heath), a scrubby green oasis wedged between Iceland's largest glacier and its flood plains. The glacier next door makes the weather milder and more hospitable to plant life. Most visitors, however, are not leafing through their field guides but gazing at the astonishing vistas, comprising some of Iceland's most imposing and picturesque mountainscapes, as well as the glacier and the vast black desert to the south.

GETTING THERE Visitors should park next to the tourist office. The walk from the official parking area leads you past three nice waterfalls (Þjófafoss, Hundafoss, and Magnúsarfoss). The office is essential if you don't have a trail map. It also has an exhibit on local flora and fauna, and continuous screenings of thrilling footage from the 1996 Grímsvötn eruption.

HIKING Skaftafell is most rewarding for those who penetrate farthest into the park. The easiest trail leads from the office to the glacial tongue **Skaftafellsjökull,** and takes about 30 minutes each way. The glacier has retreated for several years, as witnessed by moraines marking its old borders, and you can observe how vegetation reasserts itself in the glacier's wake. Some visitors poke around on the glacier itself, but they're taking a significant risk. This walk is perfectly nice but rather misses the point of the park, since you can drive right up to several equally interesting glacial tongues east of here. (**Svinafellsjökull** ★, a stranger, spikier, less touristy version of Skaftafellsjökull, is reached by leaving the park and turning left on a signposted gravel road, just east of the entrance. You can park 300m (984 ft.) away and walk right up to it, though climbing on it is unsafe.) (See also **Kvíárjökull,** p. 329.)

An ideal 2- to 3-hour hike takes in the magnificent Svartifoss waterfall, the Sjónarsker viewpoint, and the turf-roofed Sel farmhouse, built in 1912. **Svartifoss** ★★ (Black Waterfall) is a wonder of natural architecture and was named for its striking formation of black basalt columns. Eroded from below, it forms an overhang resembling a pipe organ. These unique characteristics inspired many of the 20th-century buildings by Guðjón Samúelsson, including the Icelandic National Theater. The

Sjónarsker viewpoint is about 20 minutes past Svartifoss. The farm site known as **Sel** (which simply means "Hut") was originally 100m (328 ft.) farther downhill, but was relocated in the mid-19th century to escape the encroaching sands.

Skaftafell's three premier hikes are much longer but worth the effort. One ascends through **Skaftafellsheiði** past Skerhóll and Nyrðrihnaukur and loops back along the eastern rim of Skaftafellsheiði, with incredible views throughout. An easier if slightly less recommended hike heads northwest, sloping down off the Skaftafellsheiði into **Morsárdalur** (the Morsá river valley). The trail then crosses a footbridge and leads to the Bæjarstaður, Iceland's tallest stand of birch trees. From there, continue southwest along the edge of Morsárdalur, past streams descending from the Réttargil and Vestragil gorges. On the far side of Vestragil, a trail leads uphill to a small, natural **geothermal pool** that's not shown on the park map. It's often perfect bathing temperature—and built for two. On the way back to the parking area, take the easier route through Morsárdalur without re-ascending Skaftafellsheiði.

The hike to **Kjós ★★** through the Morsárdalur is perhaps best of all, but takes at least 10 hours round-trip. Kjós is a steep-sided river valley surrounded by magisterial, spiky peaks and exotic mineral shades. **Camping** is permitted at a designated site, but only with a permit from the office. Bring extra footwear for fording streams.

TOURS **Icelandic Mountain Guides** (✆ **587-9999;** www.mountainguide.is) sets up a base camp at Skaftafell from March to October, and runs several recommended hiking and ice climbing tours on Svinafellsjökull and Vatnajökull. Another trip connects Skaftafell and Núpsstaðarskógar (p. 325).

From Coast To Mountains (✆ **894-0894;** www.oraefaferdir.is) offers a range of adventurous glacier excursions on Svinafellsjökull and Vatnajökull, including hikes, ski mountaineering, and ice climbing.

Eagle Air (✆ **562-4200;** www.eagleair.is), based in Reykjavík, takes unforgettable aerial tours of Skaftafell, from June to August, for around 30,000kr per person. The trips last 45 minutes and also fly over the Askja Volcano. Departures are upon request. It's also possible to create your own custom tour, for which prices are negotiable.

Where to Stay

For information on the **Skaftafell park campground** (where you might be kept up late by partiers and visited by pesky ptarmigans), contact the tourist office (p. 324).

The large **Hvoll Hostel,** Skatárhreppur (✆ **487-4785;** fax 487-4890; www.hostel.is; 25 units without bathrooms; Mar–Oct 4,750kr double; 7,300kr–8,500kr sleeping-bag accommodation; DC, MC, V; closed Nov–Feb), has clean and functional rooms at a pretty riverside location 25km (16 miles) east of Kirkjubæjarklaustur and 45km (28 miles) west of Skaftafell, on Route 201, 2.5km (1½ miles) south of the Ring Road; look for the Hvoll sign. You can call them up off-season and if you ask nicely they will accommodate you. If you're going by bus, you can arrange for the proprietors to pick you up at the junction, and then ask the bus driver to drop you there.

Bölti Guesthouse Bölti is sleeping-bag accommodation only, in cramped rooms with up to six bunks apiece; but it's the only guesthouse in the park and fills up faster than you can say Kirkjubæjarklaustur.

Skaftafell off Rte 998 ✆ **478-1626.** Fax 478-2426. 7 units without bathrooms. Mar–Oct 3,500kr sleeping-bag accommodation. MC, V. Closed Nov–Feb. **Amenities:** Guest kitchen. *In room:* No phone.

Foss Hótel Skaftafell This is an ordinary hotel in an extraordinary location 5km (3 miles) east of the park entrance, knows it has the only decent restaurant and en-suite guest rooms in the vicinity, and charges accordingly. The staff is very helpful with local travel arrangements.

Freysnes, on Rte. 1 opposite the Shell station. ✆ **478-1945.** Fax 478 1846 . www.fosshotel.is. 63 units. June–Aug ,29,000kr double. Rates around 25% lower May and Sept; around 50% lower Oct–Apr. Rates include breakfast. AE, DC, MC, V. **Amenities:** Restaurant; bar. *In room:* TV, Wi-Fi.

Where to Dine

The Skaftafell park visitor office has a small selection of snacks. **Söluskálinn** (✆ **478-2242;** Jun–Aug daily 9am–10pm, Sept–May 1–6pm) at the Shell station 5km (3 miles) east of the park entrance, has a mini-mart plus grill and seating area.

Foss Hótel Skaftafell This is your only choice for fine dining in the park vicinity, with dishes such as seared Arctic char served with a cool cucumber salsa and mixed wild rice. Icelandic lamb is a great alternative, and is here served with red wine sauce, fresh red cabbage, and rosemary potatoes. The glacier ice-cream is a must.

Rte. 1, 5km (3 miles) east of the park entrance. ✆ **478-1945.** Reservations recommended. Main courses 2,690kr-- 5,490kr. AE, DC, MC, V. May–Sept noon–2pm and 6–9pm.

BETWEEN SKAFTAFELL & HÖFN

In the 136km (85 miles) stretch from Skaftafell to Höfn, **Vatnajökull** is among mountains but the view is often blocked by clouds. Much of this area is considered part of the region known as Öræfi (Wasteland). This name was earned after a 1362 eruption under the Öræfajökull glacier, which explosively splattered ash, dust, and rock over a wide radius. The region's most famous attraction by far is **Jökulsárlón,** a fantastical lake full of icebergs calved from the glacier. **Ingólfshöfði,** a bird sanctuary on the cape, and glacier tours from Jöklasel earn some attention as well.

Essentials

GETTING THERE During the rest of the year, three buses travel in each direction weekly. From mid-June until August, **Reykjavík Excursions** (✆ **580-5400;** www.re.is) has departures twice daily from Skaftafell to Jökulsárlón and back, with 2 to 2½ hours at Jökulsárlón. See p. 333 for air travel to Höfn.

VISITOR INFORMATION No tourist information offices serve the area between Skaftafell and Höfn. The website **www.oraefi.is** has useful information on tours.

Exploring the Area

INGÓLFSHÖFÐI ★

This flat-topped wedge of coastal land seems to hover above the shimmering flats as you drive east from Skaftafell. Around the year 870, Reykjavík's founder, Ingólfur Arnarson, probably spent his first Iceland winter here—thus the name, which means "Ingólfur's Cape." It then had a sheltered port and was surrounded by grasslands and scrub; now it's separated from the mainland by an expanse of black volcanic sand. Ingólfshöfði is a nature reserve protected from everyone except seven local families, who have been hunting and egg-collecting the land for centuries. The birds most common to the reserve are puffin and skua, a large ground-nesting species.

The only way to visit Ingólfshöfði is on the bird-watching tour led by **From Coast To Mountains** (✆ **894-0894;** www.oraefaferdir.is). Tours last 2½ hours and run from May 1 to August 31, departing at noon from Hofsnes Farm, about 22km (14 miles) east of Skaftafell Park along the Ring Road. The cost is 4,000kr (cash or credit), and reservations are accepted. Bring sunglasses to protect your eyes from sand in high winds, and pack a lunch. If the weather is bad, at least be thankful that the puffins are more likely to be loitering on land.

This is no smooth bus tour—more of a 30-minute bumpy adventure in a tractor-drawn hay-cart. If the tide is right, you may see the sand flats covered with a thin layer of reflective water. The walking is leisurely on Ingólfshöfði, which peaks at 76m (249 ft.). The guide walks in front holding a walking pole aloft, in case of attack from a skua protecting its eggs. The tour group usually inspects a nest of these intimidating birds, while the mother squawks nearby.

INGÓLFSHÖFÐI TO JÖKULSÁRLÓN

Kvíárjökull ★ Thirty-nine kilometers (24 miles) east of Skaftafell, this glacial tongue and its scenic valley make for an easy, charmed hour-long hike minus the Skaftafell crowds. The turnoff from the Ring Road is marked "Kvíárjökulskambar," and a parking area is shortly ahead; Kvíárjökull is clearly visible in the distance.

Fjallsárlón ★ About 10km (6 miles) east is a marked turnoff for this lake—a kind of Jökulsárlón for loners. The waters are muddier and less sprinkled with icebergs, but the sight of Fjallsjökull calving into the lake is remarkable. The road to Fjallsárlón divides a few times, but all routes end up in the same place, within a 10-minute walk of the best glacier views.

Breiðárlón This lake is a similar variation on nearby Fjallsárlón and Jökulsárlón. The access road is well tended but unmarked from the Ring Road, about 3km (1½ miles) northeast of the Fjallsárlón turnoff. The number of icebergs can vary greatly, but on a good day you'll be glad you came.

JÖKULSÁRLÓN ★★

Nothing quite prepares you for the carnivalesque spectacle of a lake full of icebergs broken off from a glacier. "Calf ice" from glaciers takes on crazier shapes than "pack ice" in the sea. Calf ice is also marbled with photogenic streaks of sediment. Jökulsárlón's clear water creates a magical play of light and tints the icebergs blue. Glacial ice takes a long time to melt, and the icebergs here can last up to five years. The creaking, groaning, and crashing sounds at the glacier's edge are otherworldly. About 60 seals have established a colony at Jökulsárlón, and they can also be seen from the ocean side of the Ring Road especially in the winter.

Jökulsárlón did not exist 75 years ago, when Breiðamerkurjökull reached almost to the ocean. In the last few years, warming temperatures have accelerated the glacier's retreat and clogged the lake with growing numbers of smaller icebergs—an aesthetic demotion, unfortunately.

Glacier Lagoon Tours (✆ **478-2222;** www.jokulsarlon.is), which run May 15 to 30 (daily 10am–5pm), June to August (daily 9am–7pm), and September 1 to 15 (daily 10am–5pm), set out in amphibious vehicles and last 40 minutes. Tickets are 3,000kr for adults and 1,000kr for children aged 6 and over. Walking along the shore is almost as nice, but it's worth the money to float among the icebergs, view the glacier up close, and lick your very own ancient ice cube.

Vatnajökull Tours from Jöklasel ★

The vast **Vatnajökull glacier** covers about 8,000sq. km (3,089 sq. miles), with an average thickness of 400m (1,312 ft.) and a maximum thickness of 950m (3,117 ft.). Being atop Vatnajökull is truly transporting, and returning to sea level feels like re-entry from outer space. F985 dramatically ascends 16km (10 miles) to **Jöklasel** (✆ **478-1000**), a base camp at the edge of Vatnajökull, 840m (2,756 ft.) above sea level. Jöklasel is open from June 1 to September 10, from 11:15am to 5pm, and the small cafe there serves a daily lunch buffet from 11:15am to 2pm. Jöklasel can be reached in a good 4WD vehicle, but the road is nerve-racking and often thick with fog.

Most visitors come to Jöklasel for the snowmobile and Super Jeep tours based there. (Some visitors take walks on the glacier from Jöklasel, but they're at risk of falling into a crack or getting lost if fog closes in.) Jöklasel's two tour operators are **Glacier Jeeps** (✆ **478-1000;** www.glacierjeeps.is) and **Glacier Guides** (✆ **571-2100;** www.glacierguides.is). The most popular tour is the 3-hour snowmobile package, which costs between 18,000–20,000kr and includes pickup from the intersection of the Ring Road and Route F985 (about 35km/22 miles east of Jökulsárlón and 42km/26 miles west of Höfn), plus an hour on snowmobiles. **Glacier Jeeps** has scheduled departures at 9:30am and 2pm from late April to September 10 (reservations required). **Vatnajökull Travel** (see p. 334, chapter 11) runs a daily scheduled bus from Höfn to Jöklasel to Jökulsárlón and back; some of their tours combine snowmobiling with a boat trip at Jökulsárlón.

Snowmobile riders are outfitted with helmets, jumpsuits, rubber boots, and gloves. Make sure to bring sunglasses, since they don't supply goggles. Tours set out rain or shine and reach a height of 1,220m (4,003 ft.). Your views will depend entirely on the weather: you might see 100km (62 miles) in all directions, or just blankets of cloud. Normally you'll at least rise above the cloudline for clear views of the vicinity. Weather conditions are impossible to predict from sea level, so call ahead. Even snowmobile novices could find the riding too tame; everyone proceeds single file at the speed of the most cautious driver. Both tour companies also lead Super Jeep tours on Vatnajökull, from short joyrides to multi-day excursions.

Where to Stay & Dine

The recommended places below are listed in order of location, from west to east along the Ring Road.

The **cafe at Jökulsárlón** (✆ **478-2222** June–Aug daily 9am–7pm; May 15–30 and Sept 1–15 daily 10am–5pm) has good seafood soup, plus sandwiches and waffles. Two of the places listed have good restaurants. **Guesthouse Frost and Fire** serves a set-dinner menu of fish (4,100kr) or lamb (4,400kr) to non-guests who reserve in advance. **Smyrlabjörg's** enormous dinner buffet—with no less than nine fish dishes, plus lamb, pork, and beef—is open to non-guests from 6 to 8:30pm, June until mid-September; the cost is 5,400kr and no reservations are necessary. In the off season Smyrlabjörg serves set-dinner menus, but only with a day's advance notice.

Brunhóll Brunhóll is beautifully situated near Fláajökull, with a marked 6km (3¾ miles) trail leading to the glacier. Rooms are basic and mostly sizeable, some with views of Fláajökull. The Green Globe certification signifies sound environmental practices. We recommend their dinners, which are available on request.

Rte. 1 (30km/19 miles) west of Höfn. ✆ **478-1029.** Fax 478-1079. brunnhol@eldhorn.is. 20 units, 18 w/ bathroom. June 11–Aug 25 18,000kr double without bathroom; 19,900kr double w/bathroom; 28,000kr triple w/bathroom; 3,500kr sleeping-bag accommodation without bathroom; 4,500kr sleeping-bag accommodation w/bathroom (sleeping bag option is only available in the winter season). Rates around 15%–25% lower off season. Rates include breakfast (not for sleeping bag price, which is additional at 1,200kr). MC, V. Closed Nov–Mar. **Amenities:** Guest kitchen. *In room:* TV, no phone.

Guesthouse Frost and Fire (Frost og Funi) ★ Modern art and boldly-striped upholstery and bedspreads set the tone at this chic outpost. Try not to get stuck with one of the tiny rooms. Dinner is available on request; non-guests should call in advance. **Hofskirkja,** a wonderful 1884 turf-roofed church, is right next door.

Hof in Öræfi Farm (on Rte. 1, 18km/11 miles) east of Skaftafell Park). ✆ **478-2260.** Fax 478-2261. www.frostogfuni.is. 35 units, 14 w/bathroom. May 20–Sept 10 22,000kr double w/bathroom; 17,500kr double without bathroom. Rates include breakfast. MC, V. Closed Sept 11–May 19. **Amenities:** Restaurant; hot tub; sauna. *In room:* No phone.

Hólmur With a backdrop of the Fláajökull glacier tongue, this new farm stay offers simple and snug accommodation at good prices. The farm has a small animal park, which gives guests the opportunity to interact with the resident horses, sheep, bunnies, and a range of domestic birds such as chickens and ducks. The park is free for guests, 600kr for visitors. Dinner is available on request.

Rte. 1 (33km/21 miles) west of Höfn). ✆ **478-2063.** www.eldhorn.is/mg/gisting. 8 units without bathroom. June–Sept 9,600kr double; 3,700kr sleeping-bag accommodation. Rates around 30% lower Oct–May. Breakfast available. MC, V. **Amenities:** Guest kitchen. *In room:* No phone.

Smyrlabjörg Smyrlabjörg is a working farm with cattle, horses, and sheep. Look no further for a comfortable, no-nonsense, en-suite room in a motel block, with friendly service and a bounteous restaurant. The road to Jöklasel is only 2km (1¼ miles) away.

Rte. 1 (2km/1¼ miles) west of Rte. 1/Rte. F985 junction). ✆ **478-1074.** Fax 478-2043. www.smyrlabjorg.is. 45 units. May 20–Sept 1 21,240kr double; 30,000kr triple. Rates include breakfast. MC, V. **Amenities:** Restaurant; bar. *In room:* TV, hairdryer, no phone, Wi-Fi.

11 EAST ICELAND

The East has always been the domain of the dedicated explorer and a place for the tireless treasure hunter. Its remote location means that this quarter of Iceland is often left out of the regular tourist itineraries, which concentrate mainly on the areas near Reykjavík, the South, the North, and the Snæfellsnes Peninsula. Ferries from Europe arrive in the east, at Seyðisfjörður, but through-routes from there bypass some of Iceland's most stunning coastal scenery.

Visitors to the Eastfjords can expect to encounter a contrast of extremes, where the valleys are lush and greener, the lakes and fjords deeper, and the mountain slopes steeper. The east is at the forefront of reforestation efforts, and Iceland's reindeer herds are concentrated in its highlands.

Not surprisingly, local economies are dominated by fishing. In the heyday of the herring, cod, and whaling industries, the east's rich fishing grounds attracted many Norwegian and French-speaking fishermen. Today most fjords have their own fish-processing plant, and other fjords lie abandoned or near-abandoned in all their pristine majesty.

Two of Iceland's best hiking districts are in the east: Lónsöræfi, a mountainous reserve near Vatnajökull, and Borgarfjörður Eystri, the northernmost region of the Eastfjords. Seyðisfjörður is the region's prettiest and most culturally thriving coastal town. Southwest of Egilsstaðir are some of Iceland's most ruggedly beautiful highlands; the dam project in Kárahnúkur dominated Iceland's political debate for a while, though opposition has dwindled since the banking collapse of 2008. In summer, the east has the country's sunniest and warmest weather—though precipitation is actually higher, and winters are colder.

The main transit hubs for the east are Egilsstaðir and Höfn. During the summer, main bus services from Reykjavík reach the east through Akureyri and Höfn. During the winter, local companies continue to connect Höfn and Akureyri to Egilsstaðir and the Eastfjords.

www.east.is is an excellent regional resource for service listings, culture, and history.

HÖFN

Höfn (often used interchangeably with "Hornafjörður") simply means "dock." Höfn is a busy fishing port, lying on a narrow neck of land within

East Iceland

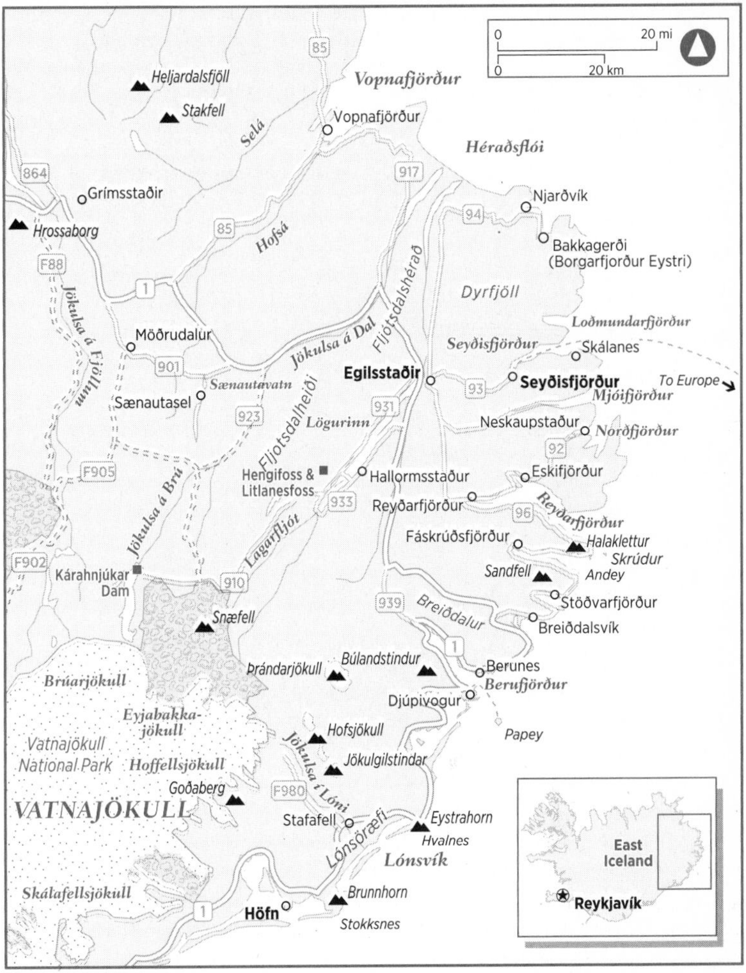

shallow, protected waters. The town has only just over 2,000 people, but that qualifies it for regional hub of the southeast. For tourists Höfn is simply a stopover, or a base for trips to Vatnajökull, Lónsöræfi, and elsewhere in the area. Höfn gets a major share of Iceland's lobster catch, and has a Lobster Festival (*Humarhátið*) the first weekend in July, with all sorts of family entertainment.

Essentials

GETTING THERE & AROUND

BY PLANE **Eagle Air** (✆ **562-2640;** www.eagleair.is) flies from Reykjavík to Hornafjörður (Höfn) twice daily on weekdays (once on Sat and Sun). The trip lasts

Höfn

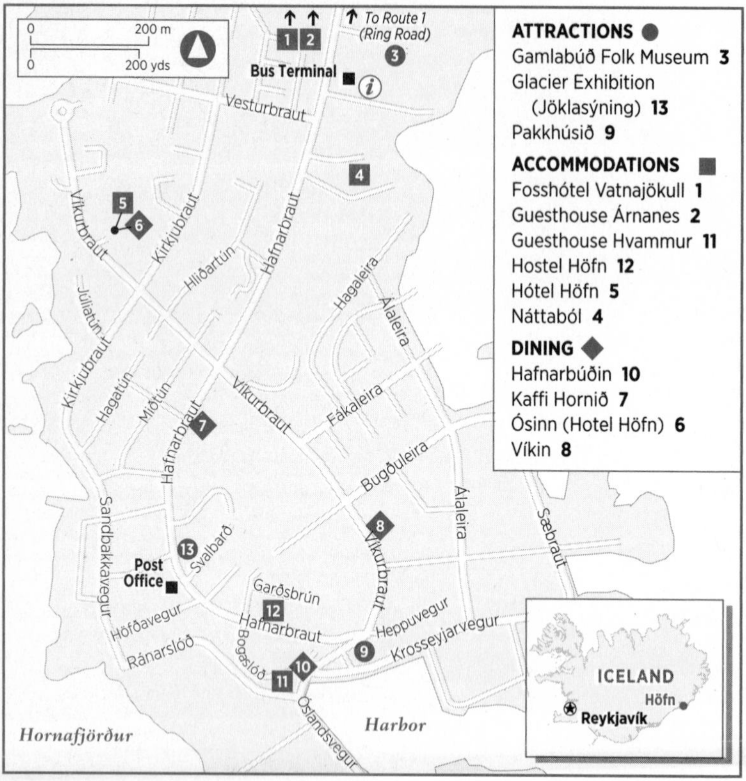

roughly an hour and costs around 13,900kr with discounts for children 2–11 years old (50%), students, and seniors (10%). **Hornafjörður Airport** (✆ **478-1250**) is a 10-minute drive northwest of town on Route 1, just off the Ring Road. Taxis do not wait at the airport, but you can call them on ✆ **865-4353.** The fare into town is typically 3,000kr.

BY CAR Car rental agencies at the airport are **National/Bílaleiga Akureyrar** (✆ **461-6000;** www.holdur.is), and **Hertz** (✆ **522-4470;** www.hertz.is).

BY BUS The Sterna bus line (✆ **551-1166;** www.sterna.is) connects Höfn to Reykjavík (8 hr.) and Egilsstaðir (3½ hr.). From May 15 until September 15, one bus travels daily between Reykjavík and Höfn in each direction, leaving Reykjavík at 8:30am and Höfn at 10am. For the rest of the year, the bus runs three times a week. From May until September 15, the daily bus between Höfn and Egilsstaðir stops at Djúpivogur, Berunes, and Breiðdalsvík. Haukur Elísson's bus service connects Djúpivogur and Höfn daily, except Tuesdays and Saturdays, all year round (✆ **893-4605**).

From June until August, **Vatnajökull Travel** (✆ **894-1616;** www.vatnajokull.is) runs a daily bus from Höfn to Jöklasel (p. 330) and Jökulsárlón (p. 329) and back to

Höfn, with sightseeing stops at both; the round-trip is 11,400kr for adults (half price for children 5 to 11 years, free for under 5s).

VISITOR INFORMATION

The **Höfn information office** is at the **Glacier Exhibition (Jöklasýning)** (✆ **478-1500;** www.ice-land.is; June–Aug daily 10am–6pm; May and Sept daily 1–6pm; Oct–Apr Mon–Fri 1–4pm) at Hafnarbraut 30.

What to See & Do

For glacier tours on Vatnajökull, see **Vatnajökull Tours from Jöklasel** (p. 330, chapter 9).

Pakkhúsið, Krosseyjarvegur, by the dock (✆ **478-1540;** free admission; Jun–Aug daily 1–6pm), is more of an arts and crafts store than a museum, but an unexceptional—and free—nautical exhibit is hosted downstairs.

Gamlabúð Folk Museum This is not Iceland's best folk museum, but it's free and represents what you'll find elsewhere: carved spoons, old medicine vials, the national costume, stuffed animals, and so on. Of particular interest, to some, are the ornamented bridles and saddles. Regular screenings of a 50-minute film from the 1960s are in Icelandic only, with demonstrations of traditional fishing and farming techniques.

Hafnarbraut (near campground). ✆ **478-1833.** Free admission. Jun–Aug 10 daily 1–5pm; closed weekends in June.

Glacier Exhibition (Jöklasýning) This museum in the tourist information office strays from glaciology to a variety of scientific subjects. The presentation alternates between earnest education (in the form of encyclopedic photo and text panels) and pure fun (in the form of videos of sub-glacial eruptions and a James Bond chase scene set in Jökulsárlón). Specimen types on display are centuries-old chunks of ice from Vatnajökull and "glacial mice"—pebbles that blow around on the glacier, growing moss on every surface.

Hafnarbraut 30. ✆ **478-2665.** www.ice-land.is. Admission 500kr adults, 350kr seniors; free for children aged 11 and under. May–Aug daily 10am–6pm; Sept–Apr open for bookings only.

EXPLORING HÖFN

For a view of Vatnajökull Glacier, take a short stroll along the water on the northwest side of town, behind Hótel Höfn (below). For an **easy 2-hour walk ★**, head to the Ring Road, drive 16km (10 miles) east, turn right shortly after exiting the tunnel, and proceed 2km (1¼ miles) beyond the farm buildings until the road ends. The walk south along the coast is uneventful for the first 30 minutes but eventually reaches a secluded and romantic expanse of sand, surf, and grassy tufts backed by steep mountains. Around the peak of Eystrahorn is another gorgeous beach.

Where to Stay

For backup options, click the "information center" link at **www.ice-land.is**. For farm accommodations between Höfn and Skaftafell Park, see p. 330.

EXPENSIVE

Fosshótel Vatnajökull Located 10km (6 miles) north of town, near the airport, this no-surprises three-star hotel is not as spiffy as the price would suggest, but has a friendly and helpful staff. Rooms are generally small but adequate, with spacious bathrooms. Some rooms and the dining room have great views of the glacier.

Route 1. ✆ **478-2555.** Fax 562-4001. www.fosshotel.is. 26 units. June–Aug 30,000kr double. Rates around 30% lower May 15–May 31 and Sept 1–Sept 25. Rates include breakfast. AE, DC, MC, V. Closed Sept 26–May 14. **Amenities:** Restaurant. *In room:* TV, hair dryer Wi-Fi.

Hótel Höfn A few minutes' walk from the town center, this modern hotel doesn't win any style awards, but the rooms are cheerfully decorated and spacious, and the staff and restaurant are professional. Make sure to ask for a glacier view.

Víkurbraut 24. ✆ **478-1240.** Fax 478-1996. www.hotelhofn.is. 68 units. May–Sept 26,500kr double; 45,320kr family room. Rates around 40% lower Oct–Apr. Rates include breakfast. MC, V. **Amenities:** Restaurant. *In room:* TV, hair dryer, Wi-Fi.

MODERATE

Guesthouse Árnanes Six kilometers (3¾ miles) west of Höfn, this guesthouse spread over a main house and three cottages is a great place to sit on the porch and take in views of the surrounding mountains and Vatnajökull. There's sleeping-bag accommodation in the basement. Dinner, by reservation only, is recommended and reasonably priced.

Route 1. ✆ **478-1550.** Fax 478-1819. www.arnanes.is. 18 units, 11 w/bathroom. Jun–Aug 22,900kr double w/ bathroom; 18,700kr double without bathroom; 30,900kr triple without bathroom; 4,700kr sleeping-bag accommodation. Rates around 15% lower May and Sept; around 30% lower Oct–Apr. Rates include breakfast. AE, DC, MC, V. **Amenities:** Restaurant. *In room:* No phone; Wi-Fi is being installed in some rooms.

INEXPENSIVE

Hostel Höfn, Hafnarbraut 8 (✆ **478-1736**; www.hostel.is; 10 units, 2 w/bathroom; 6,700kr double; MC, V), is crowded and a little shabby, but the location is central, and guests have access to kitchen facilities plus a washer/dryer.

Guesthouse Hvammur Right by the dock—and sometimes prone to fishy odors—this is all about basic rooms and practical facilities. The snazzy two-bedroom suite on the top floor goes for the same price as two doubles. If it's full there's always the annex on Hvannabraut, on the north side of town.

Ránarslóð 2. ✆ **478-1503.** www.hvammurinn.is. 20 units, none w/bathroom. May–Sept 10,800kr double; 13,800kr triple. Rates around 10% lower Oct–Apr. Breakfast available (1,200kr). MC, V. **Amenities:** Guest kitchen; Internet terminal. *In room:* TV, no phone, Wi-Fi.

Náttaból If you're in a group of four to six, you'll find no better value than this mundane campground, with small cabins splayed inartistically about. There are no bathrooms or showers; you have to use the campground facilities. The place is on the main road into town, on your left—you can't miss it.

Hafnarbraut 52. ✆ **478-1606.** Fax 478-1607. www.simnet.is/camping. 11 units. May–Sept 10,000kr cottage for 4–6 persons. Sheet rental 1,000kr. MC, V. Closed Oct–Apr. **Amenities:** Tour desk; Internet terminal. *In room:* Microwave, water heater, no phone.

Where to Dine

Hafnarbúðin, Ránarslóð 2 (✆ **478-1095;** main courses 240kr–1,450kr; MC, V; daily 9am–10:30pm; kitchen closes at 10pm), is an appealing hot-dog, burger, and fish-and-chips shack, right by the sea, with a handful of tables and a drive-in window.

Kaffi Hornið ★ CAFE The ambience in this casual, log-cabin restaurant wins you over immediately. Seafood specials include the popular local lobster, and burgers are above average. In summer, make reservations as Hornið is often packed and the staff are overworked.

Hafnarbraut 42. ✆ **478-2600.** Main courses 2,900–5,000kr. AE, DC, MC, V. May–Aug daily 10am–11:30pm; Sept–October 15 daily 10am–10pm; October 16–May Mon–Sat 10am–9pm.

Ósinn (Hótel Höfn) ★ ICELANDIC This is Höfn's finest dining, though many visitors prefer Kaffi Hornið's charisma over Ósinn's neutral atmosphere. The menu devotes a whole page to Icelandic lobster (the lobster soup can seem *too* creamy) but also includes beef, lamb, Arctic char, and duck. This wouldn't look like the time to order pizza, but it's awfully good here.

Víkurbraut 24. ✆ **478-1240.** Reservations recommended. Main courses 2,990kr–5,240kr. MC, V. May–Aug daily noon–10pm; Sept–Apr daily 6–9pm.

Víkin PIZZA Víkin is a stark contrast to Kaffi Hornið—the charmless interior will not set your heart aflutter—but if locals want to hang out over beer and pizza, this is where they usually converge. Prices are reasonable, the food is decent, and the menu also includes soups, salads, burgers, and seafood.

Víkurbraut 2. ✆ **478-2300.** Main courses 2,200kr–4,400kr. MC, V. Sun–Thurs 11am–1am, Fri–Sat 11am–3am; kitchen closes at 10pm July–Aug, 9pm Sept–May.

LÓNSÖRÆFI

The next bay east of Höfn—Lónsvík, or "Lagoon Bay"—is dominated by a large lagoon (Lón), fed by the Jökulsá í Lóni (Glacial River of the Lagoon). The mountainous interior region that feeds the Lón is called **Lónsöræfi** ★★★, or "Lagoon Wilderness." This striking and varied landscape, now a 320sq. km (124 sq. mile) private nature reserve, is easily one of Iceland's best hiking territories.

The best parts of Lónsöræfi are undeveloped. Glacial streams wind down steep valleys of subtle mineral spectra; yellow rhyolite rocks gleam from streambeds; and reindeer herds are occasionally seen grazing. Only one primitive road leads partly in, and accommodation is limited to basic mountain huts.

Essentials

GETTING THERE Forty kilometers (25 miles) east of Höfn, the Ring Road crosses the main branch of the Jökulsá í Lóni River. Northeast of the river valley, just past the main bridge, a road branches off inland and leads a few kilometers into Lónsöræfi, past several summer houses. Some short hikes can kick off from here, but the best routes are accessed by mountain road F980, which meets the Ring Road on the southwest side of the river valley. Route F980 is 25km (16 miles) long and ends at Illikambur, a 1-hour hike from the Múlaskáli mountain hut. The route is technically passable in a 4WD vehicle with good clearance, but definitely not advised, because the river crossings are volatile and dangerous. From June through August, **Bílar og fólk** (✆ **553-3737;** www.sterna.is) runs a daily bus between Höfn and Egilsstaðir that stops on request at Stafafell.

VISITOR INFORMATION The best source of information and advice is the **Stafafell Youth Hostel** (see below). Basic information can be found at **www.ust.is**; click "Protected Areas" and "Nature Reserves" then "Lónsöræfi." From July 1 to August 15 a **warden** is stationed at Múlaskáli hut, where there is no phone reception. Currently the warden is Helga Davids (✆ **470-8310;** helgadavids@vtj.is). The best **map** of Lónsöræfi is made by Mál og Menning, but a better, small-scale map is in the works.

Where to Stay & Dine

The main accommodation for this area is at the **Stafafell Youth Hostel ★** (✆ **478-1717;** www.eldhorn.is/stafafell; 14 units, 1 w/bathroom; June–Sept 15 11,000kr double w/bathroom; 8,000kr double without bathroom; 2,500kr sleeping-bag accommodation; rates 33% lower Sept 16–May; no breakfast available but there is a guest kitchen; AE, DC, MC, V.) Guests can stay either in two-bedroom cottages with kitchens, bathrooms, and living rooms, or in the owner's restored 19th-century farmhouse, which is humble and down-to-earth. Follow Route 1, 1km (.6 miles) east of the main bridge over Jökulsá í Lóni.

All food must be brought into the area. The nearest **markets** are in Höfn and Djúpivogur. Most of the mountain huts have kitchens.

Exploring the Area

HIKING **Stafafell Travel Service** (✆ **478-1717** or 478-2217; www.eldhorn.is/stafafell), based at the Stafafell Youth Hostel (above), is the best resource for planning your hiking trip. They can book the F980 bus, arrange transport from Höfn, reserve mountain huts, discuss your route and preparations, sell you a map—and sometimes even arrange to have food sent in.

Útivist (✆ **562-1000;** www.utivist.is) doesn't run scheduled trips but it's possible to book a group tour between May and September by sending an e-mail to **utivist@utivist.is**.

Several interesting **day hikes** are directly accessible from Stafafell, without taking the bus up Route F980. One particularly nice route leads through Seldalur to **Hvannagilshnúta,** a gorge surrounded by rockslides of brightly-streaked rhyolite. However, the scenery in these lower reaches of Lónsöræfi pales in comparison to the interior regions.

The Snæfell–Lónsöræfi Trek ★★

One of Iceland's better-known treks goes from Lónsöræfi to Snæfell (p. 351), a 1,833m (6,014 ft.) peak northeast of Vatnajökull. The hike takes at least 4 days, and can be extended to 7 days if the start or endpoint is Stafafell. Mountain huts are spaced along the route at intervals of no greater than 17km (11 miles). The trek's northern half is very different from Lónsöræfi, as it traverses the glacier Eyjabakkajökull and a more desolate, less mountainous landscape. This trek is for experienced outdoorspeople: hikes are fairly strenuous, trails are often poorly marked, and you may need rope, crampons, and an ice axe. The trek can head in either direction, but going from Snæfell to Lónsöræfi gives you a net loss of altitude and saves the most interesting scenery for last. The Stafafell Youth Hostel (above) is your best travel resource; make sure to review trail conditions beforehand. Snæfell is reached via Egilsstaðir by car, so be prepared for a long one-way trip to reconnect with your belongings.

It's possible to take the F980 bus in and out just for the day—this is even marketed as a "tour"—but you'd be cheating yourself. From mid-June to early September, the bus leaves Stafafell each day at 10am and reaches Illikambur, the end of the road, around noon. There is also another bus to Austurskógar on the east side of the river for 5,000kr. Weather cancellations are rare. A round-trip fare is 8,000kr. The bus returns from Illikambur at 2pm, reaching Stafafell at 4pm.

An ideal 2-night itinerary would involve taking the bus to Illikambur, spending the first night at Múlaskáli hut, another night at Egilssel hut, and then walking the 5 to 6 hours back to Illikambur the following morning, in time for the 2pm bus departure. Three nights is even better, and with 4 nights you'd hardly run out of routes to explore: make sure to see the Tröllakrókar (Troll Spires). With another 2 days, you could skip the Illikambur bus and instead hike from Stafafell to Múlaskáli, overnighting at the hut situated halfway.

Remember to bring extra shoes for stream crossings; the flow comes mostly from the glacier and is very unpredictable. Keep a map handy as trails can be poorly marked. Also bear in mind that Lónsöræfi has one of the country's highest precipitation rates.

LOWER EASTFJORDS: DJÚPIVOGUR TO FÁSKRÚÐSFJÖRÐUR

Djúpivogur is at the tip of a peninsula 104km (65 miles) northeast of Höfn. Proceeding further northeast, three more villages lie in this southern third of the Eastfjords, each with its own fjord or bay: Breiðdalsvík, Stöðvarfjörður, and Fáskrúðsfjörður. Tourism slackens off east of Höfn, and, after Djúpivogur, the coast is bypassed by the direct route to Egilsstaðir and the north.

Anyone passing this way, however, should not skip the Eastfjords entirely. On a road trip from the south, the scenery enters yet another glorious phase. The Eastfjords are steeper and less convoluted than the Westfjords, and each fjord has a kind of singular grandeur.

While activities are limited, you can spend a day or two hiking, horseback riding, or sea fishing, with perhaps a visit to Papey Island or Petra's mineral museum.

Essentials

GETTING AROUND Heading from Höfn toward Egilsstaðir, the Ring Road cuts inland at Breiðdalsvík, while the coastal Route 96 continues to Stöðvarfjörður and Fáskrúðsfjörður, then on through a 6km (3¾ mile) tunnel to Reyðarfjörður. However, the most direct route between Höfn and Egilsstaðir uses the Route 939 shortcut. Route 939 is being incorporated into the Ring Road and connects with it at the head of Berufjörður, northwest of Djúpivogur, and reconnects with it 43km (27 miles) south of Egilsstaðir. Although it is a rough gravel road, Route 939 is manageable, and the alternative stretch of the Ring Road is not entirely paved either. The Route 939 shortcut bypasses everything in this section except for Djúpivogur, which is also the gateway to Papey Island. From Egilsstaðir, the fastest route to Fáskrúðsfjörður and Stöðvarfjörður is via Routes 92 and 96, past Reyðarfjörður.

From June to August, **Sterna** (✆ **553-3737;** www.sterna.is) runs a daily bus connecting Höfn and Egilsstaðir via Djúpivogur, Berunes, and Breiðdalsvík. Haukur Elísson's bus service connects Djúpivogur and Höfn daily except Tuesdays and Saturdays all year round (✆ **893-4605**).

From Egilsstaðir, **Austfjarðaleid** (✆ **477-1713;** www.austfjardaleid.is) has buses between Breiðdalsvík and Egilsstaðir three times a week stopping in Stöðvarfjörður, Fáskrúðsfjörður, and Reyðarfjörður.

VISITOR INFORMATION The **Djúpivogur information office** (✆ **478-8288;** www.djupivogur.is; June–Aug daily 10am–6pm; weekends 10am–11.30am) is at the Langabúð museum by the port. **Breiðdalsvík's information office** (✆ **470-5560;** Mon–Fri 8am–noon and 1–4pm) is at Ásvegur 32; the **Hótel Bláfell,** Sólvellir 14 (✆ **475-6770;** www.blafell.is), is another good source. Tourist information for Stöðvarfjörður is handled at the regional information office in Egilstaður, Kaupvangur 10 (✆ **471-2320;** www.east.is). This office also covers the area further north, including Eskifjörður, Reyðarfjörður, Neskaupstaðir, and Mjóifjorður.

Exploring the Area

HIKING The trail map *Gönguleiðir á Suðurfjörðum Austfjarða,* the fourth in the *Gönguleiðir á Austurlandi* series (500kr), covers the coastal region from Berufjörður to Fáskrúðsfjörður, though trail descriptions are in Icelandic only. Two mountain climbs, Sandfell and Halaklettur, are especially recommended for their breathtaking coastal scenery; don't leave the peaks before signing the guestbook.

Sandfell is a distinctive 743m (2,438 ft.) rhyolite mountain between Stöðvarfjörður and Fáskrúðsfjörður. The best approach is from the south side of Fáskrúðsfjörður. The trail leaves the coastal road between Víkurgerði and Vík farms and proceeds along the Víkurgerðisá River before cutting west for the peak. (On the map, the trail begins as #13 and becomes #14.) The scenery is excellent en route, with views of Fáskrúðsfjörður and Andey and Skrúður islands. Allow 5 hours for the round trip.

The 573m (1,880 ft.) peak at the tip of the peninsula between Fáskrúðsfjörður and Reyðarfjörður is **Halaklettur.** Trail #7 starts at the north shore of Fáskrúðsfjörður, just east of the Kolfreyjustaður church. The ascent is less interesting than on Sandfell, but the superior view from the top takes in Fáskrúðsfjörður, Reyðarfjörður, the Vattarnestangi lighthouse, and Andey and Skrúður. Allow 4 hours for the round-trip. ⚠ Don't go if you're afraid of heights.

DJÚPIVOGUR ★

This small, charming fishing village dates from 1589, when merchants from Hamburg were licensed by the Danish king to trade here. After the Danish trade monopoly was imposed in 1602, Djúpivogur became the only commercial port in southeast Iceland. Today most visitors to Djúpivogur are primarily interested in tours to Papey Island.

Those who spend the night should know about the network of trails at the tip of the peninsula. It's a wonderfully peaceful area of shifting black sand dunes, active birdlife, and nice coastal views.

Langabúð This long red building on the seafront, which dates back to 1790, houses the tourist information office, a cafe, and the local folk museum. One wing is devoted to sculptor Ríkarður Jónsson (1888–1977), whose wood carvings and busts display real talent and delicacy. The folk history exhibit in the loft is like a country antiques store, with items such as old cash registers and typewriters, a butter churn, and a harmonium. The outdoor sculpture known as "Eggin í Gleðivík" (Eggs in Happy Bay), by the celebrated artist Sigurður Guðmundsson, is a must-see in Djúpivogur. The 34 different stone eggs can be seen on the coast, approximately 1 km (0.62m) from the village, an easy stroll.

Off Bakki ✆ **478-8220.** www.rikardssafn.is. Admission 500kr adults; 300kr seniors and children aged 11 and under. May 7–Sept 15 daily 10am–6pm.

PAPEY ★

Papey is not just another set of bird cliffs and a lighthouse; for centuries it was the only inhabited island off Iceland's east coast. Daily 4-hour tours with **Papeyjarferðir** (✆ **478-8838;** www.djupivogur.is/papey; tickets 5,500kr adults, 2,800kr children aged 7–12, free children under 7) leave Djúpivogur every day from June until September 15 if the weather permits.

Papey, a Celtic name, means "Friar's Island." Two 12th-century Icelandic sources affirm Irish monks founded a hermitage here, perhaps after being chased off the mainland by the Norse; but excavations have not yet discovered evidence of habitation predating the 10th century. Papey was quite independent of the mainland because of unstable and dangerous tidal currents. Settlers lived a mostly self-sufficient life growing potatoes, tending sheep, and eating birds, bird eggs, fish, seals, and sharks. Later generations earned income by harvesting down feathers from eider duck nests. Papey's population peaked in 1726, at 16. The last full-time resident was a man named Gisli, who bought the island in 1900, lived there 48 years, and lies buried there. The island still belongs to Gisli's family, and his granddaughter, now in her sixties, spends her summers there knitting and collecting eggs.

The best time to visit is June/July, when Papey is packed with guillemots, though puffins and other birds stay until mid-August. The seas are often choppy, so ask about conditions before your departure and have seasick pills at the ready. The 1-hour boat trip passes close to a rock shelf frequented by sunbathing or frolicking seals. Before docking at Papey, the boat enters a cove surrounded by low cliffs with chattering birds nesting on every ledge. The tour allows 2 hours for strolling around the island and visiting **Iceland's oldest wooden church,** which dates from 1807.

BREIÐDALSVÍK & BREIÐDALUR

Breiðdalsvík is a traditional coastal town of just over 200 people at the base of Breiðdalur (Broad Valley), a fertile enclave that attracts reindeer from the highlands in winter. The Ring Road cuts inland through Breiðdalur, and the surrounding mountains of sloping basalt strata are gorgeous at twilight. Breiðdalur is the longest and widest valley in the Eastfjords and surrounded by a spectacular view of towering mountains. It's popular for salmon fishing in Breiðdalsá and its waterfalls attract ice climbers in winter. Breiðdalsvík hosts an annual strongman competition called **Austfjarðatröllið (Eastfjords Troll)** during the second week of August.

STÖÐVARFJÖRÐUR

This sleepy town 18km (11 miles) from Breiðdalsvík is best-known for a great-grandmother's rock collection (see below). **Galleri Snæros,** Fjarðarbraut 42 (✆ **475-8931;** daily 10am–6pm), is an arts and crafts gallery that exhibits and sells paintings, ceramics, and textiles by regional artists. You can also arrange for a **cod-fishing trip** with the proprietor of Kirkjubær.

Steinasafn Petru ★ (✆ **475-8834;** www.steinapetra.is) This collection of rocks and minerals is magnificent, but what brings in 20,000 visitors a year is its personal story. Everything was gathered by Petra Sveinsdóttir, now in her mid-80s and living in a nursing home; the museum is in her house and garden. A gift shop sells rocks with googly eyes stuck on.

Sunnuhulið. ✆ **475-8834.** Admission 700kr adults; free for children aged 14 and under. Daily 9am–6pm; from Apr–Sept call ahead.

FÁSKRÚÐSFJÖRÐUR

Formerly known as Búðir, Fáskrúðsfjörður was settled by French-speaking sailors (mostly Belgian and Breton) in the 1800s as a fishing base for half the year. In the cod boom of 1880 to 1914, about 5,000 French and Belgian fishermen came to east Iceland each season. Cod fishing was one of the world's most dangerous professions; over 4,000 French-speaking fishermen alone died in Icelandic waters between 1825 and 1940. In Fáskrúðsfjörður, they introduced locals to cognac and chocolate, stole eggs and sheep, and built a local chapel and hospital. Street signs are in Icelandic and French, and a cemetery east of town along the shore holds the graves of 49 French and Belgian sailors. For 4 days in late July, Fáskrúðsfjörður celebrates its French heritage with the ***Franskir Dagar* (French Days)** family festival.

In 2005, a 6km (3¾-mile) tunnel opened up between Fáskrúðsfjörður and Reyðarfjörður, shortening the route by 34km (21 miles). Fáskrúðsfjörður became close enough to Reyðarfjörður's new aluminum smelter to share in its economic resurgence.

Einar Jónsson, Iceland's leading sculptor, designed the **Memorial to the Shipwreck of Dr. Charcot,** an intriguing tribute to arctic explorer Jean-Baptiste Charcot (1867–1936), shortly after Charcot's death in a shipwreck off the Icelandic coast. A guardian angel watches over a line of men, who ascend heavenward in a formation evoking a ship's prow. The sculpture is on Buðave, just east of the museum.

For **sea fishing,** contact the Hótel Bjarg, p. 343.

Fransmenn á Íslandi This small museum effectively tells the story of French-speaking fishermen in Iceland, with photos and a smattering of artifacts. If the guestbook is any indication, the exhibit is mostly of interest to the French.

Búðarvegur 8. ✆ **864-2728.** Admission 650kr adults; free for children aged 14 and under. June–Aug 10am–6pm.

ANDEY & SKRÚÐUR ISLANDS

These two islands near Fáskrúðsfjörður beckon, yet are not covered by tours. Skrúður is especially intriguing, with a large puffin colony, 160m (525 ft.) cliffs, and an enormous cave. If the weather permits, Skruður's owner occasionally offers a sightseeing tour by boat around the island; ask at the Hótel Bjarg (p. 343).

Where to Stay

The friendly, well managed **Berunes Youth Hostel ★** (✆ **478-8988;** fax 478-8902; www.hostel.is; 15 units, none w/bathroom; May–Sept 8,200kr double; breakfast available from 1,200kr; AE, DC, MC, V; closed Oct–Apr) is along the Ring Road 25km (16 miles) south of Breiðdalsvík, with comfortable rooms and great views of Berufjörður, and access to a guest kitchen and washer/dryer. Berunes itself is a very dignified-looking settlement: the house, farm buildings, church, and accommodations all blend harmoniously. The church is always open, and guests are welcome to play the organ.

Guesthouse Café Margrét Poised on a hillside overlooking the fjord, this log cabin guesthouse and restaurant—run by a German emigre has four attractive rooms decorated with German antiques and Persian rugs; two rooms have balconies.

Rte. 96, just east of the Ring Road junction, Breiðdalsvík. ✆ **475-6625.** cafemargret@simnet.is. 4 units w/shower. June–Aug 15,000kr double. Rates 15% lower Sept–May. Breakfast available (2,000kr). AE, DC, MC, V. **Amenities:** Restaurant. *In room:* TV.

Hótel Bjarg ☺ Guests are lulled to sleep by a tinkling stream that runs directly beneath the hotel. The smallish rooms have beautiful ocean views and come in assorted cheerful designs—you could have a painted fan depicting a palm beach over your bed. Children will appreciate the games room with table tennis, pool, foosball, and video games. Dinner is available on request. The entire hotel can be rented for weddings and parties.

Skólavegur 49, Fáskrúðsfjörður. ✆ **475-1466.** www.hotelbjarg.com. 8 units, 4 w/bathroom. 18,000kr double; 15,000kr double without bathroom; 25,000kr suite. Rates around 20% lower in winter. Rates include breakfast. MC, V. **Amenities:** Bar; hot tub. *In room:* Rooms w/bathroom have fridge, no phone, Wi-Fi.

Hótel Bláfell This timber hotel in the middle of town has a nice fishing lodge feel, with a clientele composed largely of tour groups. The guest rooms are snug and welcoming, and the lounge with its open fireplace is a perfect place to wind down.

Sólvellir 14, Breiðdalsvík. ✆ **475-6770.** Fax 475-6668. www.blafell.is. 25 units. June–Sept 15 16,100kr double. Rates 30% lower Sept 16–May. Rates include breakfast. MC, V. **Amenities:** Restaurant; bar; sauna; Wi-Fi in lobby/lounge. *In room:* TV.

Hótel Framtíð This cute waterfront hotel has a new wing added to a 1909 house. The new rooms are midsize, with a wood-cabin feel; the seaview rooms are booked out first. If you can do without a private bathroom, the rooms in the old house are appealing—especially #9—and far cheaper. The hotel owners also have 4 summerhouses and 3 apartments for rent.

Vogaland 4, Djúpivogur. ✆ **478-8887.** Fax 478-8187. www.simnet.is/framtid. 53 units, 22 w/bathroom. June–Aug 19,800kr double w/bathroom; 12,000kr double without bathroom; 8,500kr double sleeping-bag accommodation. Rates 25% lower Sept–May. AE, DC, MC, V. **Amenities:** Restaurants; bar; sauna; Wi-Fi in lobby. *In room:* TV, only en suite rooms have phones.

Hótel Staðarborg Opened in 2000, this former schoolhouse has comfortable if smallish and neutral rooms. Guests tend to spend more time fishing, horseback riding, or playing pool in the lounge than relaxing in their rooms anyway.

Rte. 1, 7km (4⅓ miles) west of Breiðdalsvík. ✆ **475-6760.** Fax 475-6761. www.stadarborg.is. 30 units. May–Sept 16,100kr double; 21,100kr family room; 4,500kr sleeping-bag accommodation. Rates 30% lower Jan–Apr. Rates include breakfast, except sleeping-bag accommodation. MC, V. **Amenities:** Restaurant; bar; Jacuzzi. *In-room:* TV, no phone, Wi-Fi in some rooms.

Kirkjubær This is Iceland's only public accommodation inside a former church (not every local was amused). The church is quite small and dates from 1925. The altar and pulpit are intact, pews are arranged around a dining table, and a kitchen was installed under the loft, which sleeps 10 people rather intimately. The owner can arrange everything from fishing to skiing to goose hunting.

Fjarðarbraut 37a, Stöðvarfjörður. ✆ **892-3319.** www.simnet.is/birgiral. 1 unit. 4,500kr sleeping-bag accommodation; 3,500kr made up bed. No credit cards. **Amenities:** Guest kitchen. *In room:* No phone.

Where to Dine

In Djúpivogur, the cafe at the **Langabúð** cultural building serves soup, sandwiches, and cake from 10am to 6pm daily, and **Við Voginn** at the service station dishes up basic fish plates as well as the usual hot-dogs and burgers until 8pm daily. All of your dining options are right on the waterfront.

Serving Breiðdalsvík, **Hótel Bláfell** and **Hótel Staðarborg,** listed above, both have restaurants as good as or better than Café Margrét. Bláfell's restaurant is a bit more traditional. Reservations are recommended at both places. **Fast food** is on hand at the N1 filling station.

Fransmenn á Íslandi, above, has a simple cafe serving soup, cakes, and quiche in Fáskrúðsfjörður during opening hours. **Hótel Bjarg** serves set fish dinners on request for 4,000kr to 5,000kr per person. The Shell station serves **fast food** daily until 9pm.

Berunes Youth Hostel ★ ICELANDIC Youth hostels may not be associated with great home cooking or dining ambience, but this restaurant overlooking Berufjörður has both in abundance. A traditional Icelandic dinner is around 3,000kr, with a simple choice between fish and lamb. Make sure to call ahead.

Rte. 1, 25km (16 miles) south of Breiðdalsvík, in Berufjörður. ✆ **478-8988** or 869-7227. AE, DC, MC, V. April to late Sept 8–10am and 6:30–10pm.

Brekkan FAST FOOD This basic burger, soup, and sandwich stop is simply a stomach-filler to get you to your next destination. Stöðvarfjörður has no further options, except for groceries at the small market next door.

Fjarðarbraut 44, Stöðvarfjörður. ✆ **475-8939.** Main courses 350kr–1,100kr. MC, V. Mon–Fri 9:30am–10pm; Sat 10am–10pm; Sun 11am–9pm.

Café Margrét GERMAN The decoration and fjord views outdo the food, but a pork schnitzel—or even a jellied pork chop or pickled pork knuckle—can be a nice change of pace. Beware the chicken schnitzel, which contains processed meat.

Rte. 96, just east of the Ring Road junction, Breiðdalsvík. ✆ **475-6625.** Reservations recommended. Main courses 1,400kr–3,900kr. AE, DC, MC, V. June–Aug daily 8am–11pm; Sept–May noon–9pm.

Café Sumarlína ICELANDIC This cafe-restaurant-bar with soccer on TV is clearly the place to be in the evening. If you happen to be around on ***Franskir Dagar*** **(French Days)** you will be treated to performances by what Icelanders call "troubadours"—that is, singers with guitars, playing as if they were sitting in front of a camp fire. Crepes with ham, bacon, salad, onion, or rice are a variation on the usual fare, or just stick with the battered salt cod with potatoes and veggies.

Búðavegur 59 (along Rte. 96, close to the dock), Fáskrúðsfjörður. ✆ **475-1575.** www.123.is/sumarlina. Main courses 1,500kr–2,900kr. AE, DC, MC, V. Daily 11am–9pm.

Hótel Framtíð ★ ICELANDIC The cooking and presentation are more refined than expected for a provincial hotel restaurant, and the dining room has a nice sea view. You can't go wrong with the locally-caught cod, haddock, and plaice.

Vogaland 4, on the harbor, Djúpivogur. ✆ **478-8887.** Reservations recommended. Main courses 3,900kr–5,300kr. AE, DC, MC, V. June–Aug noon–2pm and 6–9pm; Sept–May noon–1:30pm and 6:30–8:30pm.

MIDDLE EASTFJORDS: REYÐARFJÖRÐUR, ESKIFJÖRÐUR & NESKAUPSTAÐUR

In Iceland, Reyðarfjörður is now inescapably associated with Alcoa, the world's largest aluminum company, which in 2005 built a 2km-long (1¼-mile) smelting plant on the outskirts of town. The smelter, powered by new hydroelectric dams in the country's interior, remains a very contentious subject (p. 353). However short-sighted this project may turn out to be, Reyðarfjörður and its satellite towns are bustling with energy after years of economic stagnation and population decline. A housing boom is rushing to meet the needs of hundreds of foreign workers, and locals no longer have to drive to Egilsstaðir to go to the movies or a shopping arcade. Resident opinion runs strongly in support of the smelter; and the needs of tourists, whose fjord views have been blighted with power lines, factory buildings, and ugly housing developments, were left out of the equation. The three towns are the largest in the Eastfjords, and each still has a range of attractions, dining, and places to stay; an abundance of information can be found at **www.east.is**.

Essentials

Route 92 connects Egilsstaðir to Reyðarfjörður, Eskifjörður, and Neskaupstaður, a distance of 71km (44 miles). By bus, **Austfjarðaleið** (© **477-1713;** www.austfjardaleid.is) links all four towns (best to call and inquire as the schedule changes 3–4 times a year). **Regional tourist information** is in **Fáskrúðsfjörður's** City Hall ***Ráðhús***, Hafnargata 2 (© **470-9000;** www.fjardabyggd.is). The tourist office in Egilsstaðir (p. 347) is also helpful.

Exploring the Area

Neskaupstaður, the easternmost town in Iceland, is more picturesque and remote than Reyðarfjörður and Eskifjörður, and its surrounding coastline is full of wonderful bird cliffs, sea caves, inlets, and pebble beaches. **Fjarðaferðir** (© **864-7410;** www.fjardaferdir.is) offers sightseeing and sea-fishing tours, while **Kayakklúbburinn Kaj** (© **863-9939;** www.123.is/kaj) leads kayak trips.

As with all the Eastfjords, peninsular hiking trails offer great coastal scenery. A good **hiking map** with trail descriptions in English is *Gönguleiðir á Fjarðaslóðum*, number II in the *Gönguleiðir á Austurlandi* series.

If you have a strong flashlight and pass near Eskifjörður, consider poking around **Helgustaðanáma,** an abandoned spar quarry. **Iceland spar,** a type of calcite that can be cut along different planes to make light prisms, has been used in everything from microscopes to machines studying the emission of light from atoms. The shaft is 80m-long (62 ft.), and the calcites shimmer in the light. (Taking anything is illegal.) To get there from Eskifjörður, take the gravel road east of town along the coast. After 9km (5½ miles), there is a sign for Helgustaðir, and a marked trailhead, park at the quarry information sign and walk 10 minutes uphill.

Icelandic Wartime Museum (Íslenska Stríðsárasafnið) Reyðarfjörður was a military base for the Allies in World War II, and this museum is housed next to (and inside) some of the original barracks. The museum has plenty of artifacts, but the best way to bring the era alive is to reminisce with the old Icelanders who work there.

Spítalakampi, Reyðarfjörður. ✆ **470-9063.** www.fjardabyggd.is. Admission 550kr adults; free for children and seniors. June–Aug daily 1–6pm.

EGILSSTAÐIR

All roads in east Iceland fan out from Egilsstaðir, a hub for all the eastern towns. The regional airport is here, and ferry passengers from Europe pass through after docking at Seyðisfjörður. The town has expanded rapidly in the wake of the Kárahnjúkar hydroelectric project (p. 353). About 3,500 people live in greater Egilsstaðir, but most workers are here temporarily.

Egilsstaðir lies next to Lagarfljót (aka Lögurinn), Iceland's third-largest lake (53sq. km or 33sq. miles). Most services—supermarket, service stations, bus depot, bank, camping, tourist info, shops—are clumped together off the Ring Road. The store for **outdoor equipment** is **Verslunin Skógar,** Dynskógar 4 (✆ **471-1230**), near Fosshótel Valaskjálf.

Essentials

GETTING THERE & AROUND

Egilsstaðir is on the Ring Road (Route 1), 186km (116 miles) northeast of Höfn and 265km (165 miles) southeast of Akureyri. The distance from Egilsstaðir to Reykjavík is 653km (406 miles) by the northern route, or 635km (395 miles) by the southern route—though with the Route 939 shortcut, the difference is negligible.

BY PLANE Flights from Reykjavík are generally cheaper than bus tickets, and in good weather you get an aerial tour of Vatnajökull. **Air Iceland** (✆ **570-3030;** www.airiceland.is) flies from Reykjavík to Egilsstaðir six times daily in each direction. Typical airfare is 10,500kr–16,000kr one-way. **Taxis** are at the airport. Book flights online for a cheaper ticket.

BY CAR Car rental agencies at the Egilsstaðir airport are **National/Bílaleiga Akureyrar** (✆ **461-6070;** www.holdur.is), **Avis** (✆ **660-0623;** www.avis.is), and **Hertz** (✆ **522-4450;** www.hertz.is).

BY BUS Travel between Reykjavík and Egilsstaðir requires an overnight in Akureyri or Höfn, and costs more than flying unless you have a **bus passport** (p. 46). From June to September 15, **Sterna** (✆ **587-6000;** www.sterna.is) runs one bus daily between Reykajvík and Egilsstaðir. From June until December **SBA Norðurleið** (✆ **550-0700;** www.sba.is) runs a service both ways connecting Egilsstaðir to Akureyri. The service runs daily until Sept 15, but is reduced to four times weekly (Mon/Wed/Fri/Sun) in the winter. The winter service from January to May continues four times a week, but check with SBA for the right service provider.

Austfjarðaleið (✆ **477-1713;** www.austfjardaleid.is) connects Egilsstaðir to the surrounding towns of Breiðdalsvík, Stöðvarfjörður, Fáskrúðsfjörður, Reyðarfjörður, Eskifjörður, and Neskaupstaður (identified as "Norðfjörður") year-round Monday to Saturday. **Ferðaþjónusta Austurlands** (✆ **472-1515;** www.sfk.is) connects Egilsstaðir to Seyðisfjörður in summer (p. 354). **Jakob og Margrét** (✆ **472-9805**

Egilsstaðir

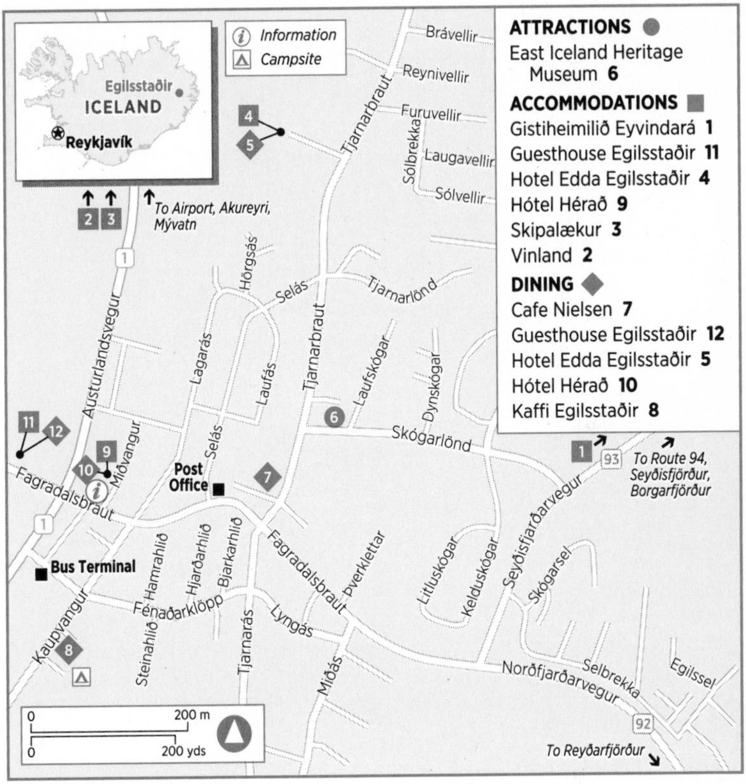

or 894-8305) takes passengers by van between Egilsstaðir and Borgarfjörður Eystri on weekdays (p. 359).

BY TAXI The two drivers to contact are Jón Björnsson (✆ **898-2625**) and Jón Eiður (✆ **892-9247**).

VISITOR INFORMATION

Egilsstaðir's excellent **tourist information office,** Miðvangur 1,(✆ **471-2320;** www.east.is; June 1–Sept 15 daily 8:30am–7:30pm; Mon–Fri 9am–5pm Sept 16–May 31 Mon–Fri 9am–5pm) serves all of east Iceland, and also offers Internet access.

Where to Stay

The tourist office (above) has a full list of what is available, or check the complete list of places to stay at **www.east.is**. There is also a good new campsite (✆ **471-2320**) on Kaupvangur, opposite Kaffi Egilsstaðir (p.349); another campsite sits beside the restaurant.

EXPENSIVE

Guesthouse Egilsstaðir ★★ This country estate along the lake is close to town but takes no part in Egilsstaðir's modernism. In fact, the town took its name from this farm, not vice versa. Rooms are warmly and tastefully decorated with antiques, a rarity outside the capital. Doubles vary in size, and those looking out on the lake and trees are in high demand. The restaurant has recently been extended.

Rte. 932, approx. 0.5km/(¼ mile .west of Rte. 1/Rte. 92 intersection). ✆ **471-1114.** Fax 471-1266. www.egilsstadir.com. 18 units. Jun-Aug 23,900kr double; 31,500kr triple. 50% discount for children aged 2-11. Rates around 30% lower Oct-Apr. Rates include breakfast. AE, MC, V. **Amenities:** Restaurant; bar; Internet terminal. *In room:* TV, hair dryer; Wi-Fi.

Hótel Hérað ★★ This three-star hotel in the Icelandair chain is in the middle of a modern town with no real focal point, so the setting and views are nothing to speak of. The rooms are up to business-class standards, however, and there's an excellent restaurant downstairs. A major expansion took place in 2004, but the new rooms are barely distinguishable from the old ones.

Miðvangur 5-7. ✆ **471-1500.** www.icehotels.is. 60 units. June–Sept 15 21,800kr double. Rates around 25% lower Apr-May and Sept 16-Oct 31; around 40% lower Nov-Mar. Rates include breakfast. AE, DC, MC, V. Closed Dec 23–Jan 3. **Amenities:** Restaurant, bar; room service. *In room:* TV, hair dryer.

MODERATE

Gistiheimilið Eyvindará This unfussy establishment 2km (1¼ miles) outside of Egilsstaðir is in a beautiful wooded area overlooking Lagarfljót, and has a range of options: guesthouse doubles without bathroom, a family room with bathroom, two cottages for two, one cottage for three, and one cottage for four. Some cottages only have bunk beds.

Rte. 94, 1km (½ mile) north of the Rte. 94/Rte. 93 junction. ✆ **471-1200.** Fax 471-1279. www.eyvindara.is. 16 units, 5 w/bathroom. 18,000kr double; 14,000kr double without bathroom; 16,000kr–25,000kr cottages for 2 to 4 persons. Rates include full breakfast. Rates discounted off season. MC, V. **Amenities:** Restaurant. *In room:* No phone, Wi-Fi.

Hótel Edda Egilsstaðir ☺ This hotel, like most in the Edda chain, uses student housing during summer, and the rooms and hallways have that slightly depressing institutional feel. Some rooms have nice lake views. Parents can take advantage of the enormous split-level family rooms and Egilsstaðir's excellent geothermal swimming pool.

Menntaskólinn (off Tjarnarbraut, across from pool). ✆ **444-4880.** Fax 471-2776. www.hoteledda.is. 52 units. June 1–Aug 20 16,000kr double. Breakfast available 1,200kr. AE, DC, MC, V. Closed Aug 21–May 30. **Amenities:** Restaurant; bar. *In room:* No phone.

Skipalækur Located in Fellabær, 3km (2 miles) northwest of Egilsstaðir, this multifaceted compound along the lake has beautiful views in both summer and winter. It offers camping, sleeping-bag accommodation, cottages with kitchens, and guesthouse rooms with and without bathrooms. The smaller cottage is ideal for parents with two children. Sleeping-bag accommodation is in double rooms, so it's an especially good deal. Horseback riding and fishing permits are available.

Rte. 931, off the Ring Road, and across the bridge from Egilsstaðir. ✆ **471-1324.** Fax 471-2413. www.skipalaekur.is. 20 units, 6 w/bathroom. 17,200kr double; 12,800kr double without bathroom; 16,500kr cottage for 2–4 people; 13,000kr cottage for 5–6 people; 3,600kr per person sleeping-bag accommodation. Rates around 10% lower off season. Rates include breakfast, except sleeping-bag accommodation. MC, V. **Amenities:** Guest kitchen. *In room:* No phone.

Vinland ★ Located across the bridge from Egilsstaðir in the satellite town of Fellabær, this new hotel somehow makes a pre-fab, metal-sided block of six identical rooms feel endearing on the outside and pleasing within. The pastel-mod rooms are well-appointed—with thoughtful extras like heated towel racks—and each has a private entrance.

Signposted off Rte. 1 in Fellabær. ✆ **615-1900.** www.vinlandhotel.com. 6 units. 16,600kr double. Rates 29% lower Sept–May. *In room:* TV/DVD, fridge, Internet cable.

Where to Dine

EXPENSIVE

Café Nielsen ★ ICELANDIC Situated in Egilstaðir's oldest house, this friendly cafe and restaurant has three intimate dining rooms on two floors and seating under the trees outdoors: Nielsen has a charming ambience even if the food doesn't quite keep pace. Many dishes over-rely on battering and deep frying, and not every dish is as exquisite as the renowned reindeer in wild game sauce.

Tjarnarbraut 1. ✆ **471-2626.** Reservations recommended. Main courses 3,000kr–6,200kr. MC, V. Mon–Thurs 11:30am–11:30pm; Fri 11:30am–2am; Sat 1pm–2am; Sun 1–11:30pm.

Guesthouse Egilsstaðir ★★ ICELANDIC This lovely restaurant in a 19th-century hotel is a unique culinary experience. The menu is simple, based on local products; beef and cheese from the farm, organic products grown on the lakeshore, and local trout. Due to a growing reputation, the restaurant has been renovated and doubled in size—remember to book especially on Wednesdays, the day before the ferry gets in.

Rte. 932 approx. 0.5km/(¼ mile .west of Rte. 1/Rte. 92 intersection). ✆ **471-1114.** www.egilsstadir.com. Reservations recommended. Main courses 2,700kr–4,900kr. AE, MC, V. Daily noon–9:30pm.

Hótel Hérað ★★ ICELANDIC This is perhaps the only restaurant in east Iceland that meets Reykjavík's cooking standards. The house special is reindeer steak in wild berry sauce: reindeer eat the same berries, and the sauce draws out the taste of the meat. The steak is seared for 30 seconds in brown butter and crystal sugar, then oven-roasted for 15 minutes.

Miðvangur 5–7. ✆ **471-1500.** Reservations recommended. Main courses 3,000kr–6,300kr. AE, DC, MC, V. Daily 11:30am–2pm and 6–9pm.

MODERATE

Hótel Edda Egilsstaðir ICELANDIC The restaurant on the upper floor of this utilitarian domicile offers a decent a la carte dinner. Expect dependable lamb and fish dishes and prices a notch below the competition.

Menntaskólinn (off Tjarnarbraut, across from pool). ✆ **444-4880.** Main courses 1,800kr–3,400k. AE, DC, MC, V. June 1–Aug 20 daily 7–9pm. Closed Aug 21–May 30.

INEXPENSIVE

Kaffi Egilsstaðir This new cafe and restaurant is opposite the new campsite. The pristine decor contrasts beautifully with the fire-red chairs and makes for a pleasant environment to enjoy a burger or a buffet. Although the kitchen closes at 10pm on Fridays and Saturdays the bar stays open late.

Kaupvangur 17 (across from the new campsite). ✆ **470-0200.** Main courses 1,390kr–2,600kr. AE, DC, MC, V. Sun–Thurs 10am–11.30pm; Fri–Sat 10am–10pm.

What to See & Do

For activities around Lake Lagarfljót (aka Lögurinn), see below.

East Iceland Heritage Museum (Minjasafn Austurlands) This above-average folk museum holds a diverse collection of local artifacts, including a restored turf farmhouse and a few pre-Christian relics. Information in English is limited, but the staff is usually eager to show visitors around. On summer weekends, the museum often holds spinning and weaving demos or offers horse-drawn carriage rides.

Laufskógar 1. ✆ **471-1412.** www.minjasafn.is. Admission 500kr adults; 200kr seniors and children aged 11 and under; free admission Wed. May 17–Aug daily 11am–5pm, 9pm Wed; Sept–May Mon–Fri 1–5pm.

INLAND FROM EGILSSTAÐIR: LÖGURINN, SNÆFELL & KÁRAHNJÚKAR

Southwest of Egilsstaðir, the Lagarfljót River widens into a 38km (24-mile), narrow lake known as Lögurinn—or still Lagarfljót, as "fljót" implies a very wide river. A round-the-lake drive is a popular and agreeable day trip, though much of its appeal derives from forestation projects and social campground retreats, both of which usually attract Icelanders more than visitors. Locals are especially fond of their changing foliage, but New Englanders might just take a pass and head for the Eastfjords instead.

Roads from Lögurinn branch off into the interior highlands, where reindeer roam through ruggedly beautiful scenery. Serious hikers are lured by Snæfell, the tallest Icelandic mountain not underneath Vatnajökull. A paved road leads to Kárahnjúkar dam, part of a controversial hydroelectric project (p. 353).

Essentials

GETTING THERE No scheduled buses head in this direction. Route 931—which meets the Ring Road both 10km (6 miles) south of Egilsstaðir and 3km (2 miles) north of Egilsstaðir—circumnavigates the lake, crossing a bridge near the southwest end. Route 933 branches off from Route 931 on both sides of that bridge, and forms its own loop via another bridge further southwest. Route 910 branches off from Route 933 (on the lake's northwest side) towards Snæfell, Kárahnjúkar, and elsewhere in the interior. Those headed directly from Egilsstaðir to Route 910 should take the north side of the lake for slightly less distance, or the south side for better roads.

VISITOR INFORMATION This entire area is covered by the **Egilsstaðir tourist information office** (p. 347). **Snæfellsstofa's** new tourist office (✆ **470-0840;** www.vjp.is; snæfellsstofa@vatnajokulsthjodgardur.is; May–Sept daily 9am–7pm) is in Skriðuklaustur off the main ring road on Route 933 *past* the Route 910 turnoff (about a 40-minute drive from Egilsstaðir). There's a souvenir shop and an innovative exhibition called Veraldarhjólið (the cycle of the world). It also serves as headquarters for the management of the national park's eastern territory.

Kárahnjúkar, the **Végarður tourist office** (✆ **470-2570;** vegardur@lv.is; June–Aug 31 daily 1–5pm) is about 2km further down the road. **Ferðafélag Fljótsdalshéraðs** (✆ **863-5813;** ferdafelag@egilsstadir.is), which runs the Snæfell mountain hut, is a great source of information for hiking in the highlands.

Exploring the Area

The following destinations follow a circular path around Lögurinn.

Hallormsstaðaskógur, 24km (15 miles) from Egilsstaðir on Lagarfljót's southeastern shore, is Iceland's largest forest—a fact which never fails to amuse passing tourists. Iceland, which was substantially forested when settlers first arrived, currently leads the world in annual per capita planting of trees. Hallormsstaðaskógur has far more diversity than Iceland's original forests, with larch, red spruce, and other species added to native birch, rowan, and willow. A free **trail map** of Hallormsstaðaskógur is available at the Shell station along Route 931. A more formal **arboretum**—the best in Iceland, for what it's worth—is on the lake side of the road, marked "Skógrækt Ríkisins/Trjásafn/Arboretum" on a brown wooden sign. A pleasant trail from the parking area leads to the lake.

Atlavík is a lakeshore campground that is extremely popular with Icelandic families and party types. To reserve a campsite place, call ✆ **470-2070** or 849-1461(mid-May to Sept). It is also the departure point for evening cruises on the **Lagarfljótsormurinn** (✆ **471-2900;** www.ormur.is). This 110-passenger ship, named for the Loch Ness-style sea monster supposedly dwelling in Lagarfljót, takes groups on lake cruises involving cookouts, fishing, or even live music (mid-June to Aug); call to see if an expedition is scheduled.

Gunnar Gunnarsson (1889–1975) didn't mean much in his native Iceland until late in his career, but from 1920 to 1946 he was Germany's second best-selling author, after Goethe. Gunnar was best-known for historical fiction—notably *The Black Cliffs (Svartfugl)*, based on a double murder case in the Westfjords along Route 933, 2km (1¼ miles) south of the Route 933/Route 910 junction. Gunnar's distinctive stone house, where he lived from 1935 to 1948, is now the **Gunnarstofnun cultural institute** (✆ **471-2990;** www.skriduklaustur.is; admission 700kr adults; 500kr students; 350kr seniors; free for children 16 and under; May 26–Aug 31 daily 10am–6pm; May 5–25 and Sep 1–16 daily noon–5pm), which includes a lovingly curated, permanent exhibit on the author (with some of his books for sale), temporary exhibits on local themes, an art gallery, and a first-rate cafe. Outside is an archeological excavation of **Skriðuklaustur,** an Augustinian monastery founded in 1500 A.D. Findings are exhibited inside, where bored children can make use of the playroom full of toys and art materials.

Located 3km (2 miles) southwest of Skriðuklaustur, the **Végarður Visitor Center** has free exhibits on the Kárahnjúkar hydroelectric project; see below for details.

A 90-minute round-trip hike with nice views over the lake leads along the Hengifossá River uphill for 2.5km (1½ miles) to two photogenic waterfalls: **Hengifoss ★ and Litlanesfoss ★**. The parking area is clearly marked from Route 933, between the junctions with Route 910 and 931. Hengifoss, at 118m (387 ft.), is Iceland's third highest waterfall and has a distinctive pattern of red clay stripes wedged between thick layers of black basalt. Unless the flow is especially strong, you can climb up to a cave behind the falls. Litlanesfoss, halfway along the trail, is no less beautiful, with fantastical formations of columnar basalt.

SNÆFELL, KÁRAHNJÚKAR & THE INTERIOR

From Lagarfljót, the newly paved Route 910 winds steeply up the hillside and finally levels off in **Fljótsdalsheiði ★**, a highland environment utterly distinct from the lake below. Chances are good you'll see a reindeer herd in this austerely beautiful landscape, dominated by rocky tundra, lakes, clumpy moss, lichen, and scrub. Compared to interior deserts such as Sprengisandur, it's positively lush. Route 910 reaches **Kárahnjúkar dam** within an hour's drive, passing close to the northern slopes of the imposing 1,833m (6,013 ft.) peak **Snæfell.**

The Kárahnjúkar project (p. 353) encompasses five dams, of which the Kárahnjúkar dam itself is the largest. Water is tunneled from the new reservoirs to a hydroelectric power station built into a mountainside substation on the northwest bank of the Jökulsá í Fljótsdal River, about 10km (6 miles) southwest of the Route 933/Route 910 junction.

The substation is open to visitors at certain hours through pre-booking. For accessibility to this high-tech wonder, contact the **Végarður tourist office** (see p. 350), on Route 933, about 5km (3 miles) southwest of the Route 933/Route 910 junction. Végarður is run by the Icelandic power company Landsvirkjun (www.landsvirkjun.com), and the video presentation on Kárahnjúkar's engineering marvels is very effective PR. If the screening is in Icelandic, ask for the English version. Visitors to **Kárahnjúkar** will probably be disappointed by how little there is to see.

The paved road ends at a viewpoint overlooking Hálslón Reservoir, which is as large as Lögurinn (Lagarfljót), covering 57sq. km (22 sq. miles). The more interesting and revealing viewpoint would look downstream from the dam, where the once-raging Dimmugljúfur Gorge has been reduced to a trickle. There are no tours of this area but **Tanni Travel** (**✆ 476-1399;** www.tannitravel.is), based in the Eastfjords town of Eskifjörð, will take group bookings on tours of Kárahnjúkar.

HIKING & CLIMBING The ***East Iceland Highlands*** **map,** produced by Iceland's national power company Landsvirkjun, details several rewarding hiking routes in the Snæfell–Kárahnjúkar area, with trail descriptions and difficulty ratings. (The map is not available online, but you can contact Végarður tourist office, above, and ask them to send you one.) Few trails are pegged, however, and some hikes require experience and advance planning.

Route 910 passes within 12km (7½ miles) of the **Snæfell mountain hut** (**✆ 860-1393**). A 4WD track leads all the way there, though you may encounter difficult river crossings. The hut is on Snæfell's western side, about 800m (2,625 ft.) above sea level, and sleeps 62, with a kitchen, tent sites, and showers. **Ferðafélag Fljótsdalshéraðs** (**✆ 863-5813;** www.fljotsdalsherad.is/ferdafelag; ferdafelag@egilsstadir.is) operates the hut, leads occasional hiking tours, and is the best source for information on regional hiking. The website provides information on tour dates, destinations, and activities: the more ambitious hiker can pursue their "Pearls" scheme which involves hiking to 9 of 18 locations of varying difficulty to be rewarded with a "Sprinter" certificate. **Snæfell** presides royally over its surroundings, and its spiky 1,833m (6,014 ft.) snow-capped peak tempts many climbers. A pegged trail leads up the western slope to the summit, but the climb requires some experience and equipment (crampons at the very least). Consult with the hut warden beforehand, and allow at least 7 to 9 hours round-trip. Hikes around the periphery of Snæfell are also recommended, and the full circuit is 29km (18 miles); check the *East Iceland Highlands* map for details.

For the glorious multi-day trek from **Snæfell to Lónsöræfi,** see p. 338.

KÁRAHNJÚKAR: ICELAND'S lost WILDERNESS

Among Iceland's natural resources, renewable energy—generated from geothermal heat and flowing water—is second only to fish. Aluminum smelting, which requires abundant energy and ready access to ports, seems the perfect fit.

Enter Kárahnjúkar—a $3-billion hydroelectric network of dams, reservoirs, water tunnels, generators, and 52km (32 miles) of monstrous power lines in the eastern interior highlands—all built to power the new aluminum plant at Reyðarfjörður in the Eastfjords. This mile-long behemoth is run by the American company Alcoa, the world's largest producer of aluminum products. Processed alumina powder is shipped in from as far away as Australia, and aluminum is produced in enormous vats cooked to 900°C (1,652°F).

Kárahnjúkar led to a worldwide protest campaign. In 2002, one in six Icelanders petitioned against the project, but the parliament approved it by a large majority. Many foreign activists staged protests near the construction sites, creating blockades or chaining themselves to the chassis of vehicles and obstructing workers.

Support for Kárahnjúkar still runs high in the east, where sagging local economies have already been boosted. Local fishermen were often idle after being outbid for fishing quotas. Iceland relies on dwindling fish stocks for most of its export income, and needs to diversify its economy. Kárahnjúkar's backers also stress that hydroelectric power is a "green" energy source: if aluminum plants were built elsewhere and powered by fossil fuels, they would produce 10 times the carbon emissions. Alcoa even has a relatively good environmental track record.

Kárahnjúkar's opponents, however, saw no reason to sacrifice Iceland's pristine wilderness just to feed the world's energy gluttony and lower the cost of beer cans. On a per capita basis, Iceland is already one of the world's 10 richest countries. The overall unemployment rate is low, and most of Kárahnjúkar's new jobs have been filled by foreign workers. Kárahnjúkar has soaked up capital that could have been invested in more forward-looking sectors, such as universities, scientific research institutions, or software companies.

The dams have drastically altered the most intact and extensive glacier-to-sea ecosystem in Iceland and flooded 57sq km (22 sq miles) of Europe's largest unspoiled wilderness. The feeding grounds of reindeer and nesting grounds of pink-footed geese and other birds have already disappeared. Sand and clay have washed down from construction sites and devastated local fishing grounds. Soil erosion now sends storms of dust and sand on to farmland. The dams could prove vulnerable to volcanoes and earthquakes. Vatnajökull glacier, the source of the dammed rivers, is melting rapidly and reservoirs could eventually dry up.

Support for Kárahnjúkar among Icelanders has slipped and support for similar, planned projects is waning. In April, 2007, residents of Hafnarfjörður voted to reject a $1.2-billion smelter expansion by the Alcan corporation. Since the bank collapse in 2008 opposition has dwindled, with Icelanders having other things to worry about.

Where to Dine

If driving around Lagarfljót, your best lunch option is the **cafe at Skriðuklaustur ★★** (p. 351), which doesn't require museum admission. A fabulous, homemade, all-you-can-eat lunch buffet is served until 2pm, costing only 2,190kr for adults, 1,100kr for children 6 to 12. A cake buffet from 2pm to museum closing time costs 1,650kr adults, 850kr for children. In **Hallormsstaðaskógur,** the **Fosshótel Hallormsstaður** off Route 931 has a summer-only restaurant, and the **Shell station** has seating space and serves burgers, pizzas, and sandwiches.

SEYÐISFJÖRÐUR

Icelandic villages nestled in fjords are likened to pearls in a shell, and none fit this description better than Seyðisfjörður ★★. The 17km (11-mile) fjord is lined with sheltering, snow-capped mountains and tumbling waterfalls. The dizzying descent into the fjord makes drivers feel like swooping gyrfalcons. The village, enlivened by Norwegian wood kit homes from the 19th and early-20th centuries, is a popular summer retreat for artists and musicians; the ferry from Europe arrives here weekly.

Seyðisfjörður is an ideal port, and became a trading hub in the early-18th century. In the late-19th century it became a boom town, thanks to the herring trade, largely controlled by Norwegian merchants. In 1906, Seyðisfjörður was chosen as the entry point for Iceland's first undersea telegraph link to the outside world. During World War II, Allied forces built a camp on the fjord, and a German air raid sank the *El Grillo* oil tanker, which still lies at the fjord bottom. Seyðisfjörður's economy still relies on fishing, and is prone to the same uncertainties faced by other Eastfjord villages. The fish factory went bankrupt in 2003 but is now back in operation.

Essentials

GETTING THERE

BY CAR Seyðisfjörður is at the end of Route 93, only 26km (16 miles) from Egilsstaðir. From the Ring Road, take Route 92 through central Egilsstaðir, then turn left on Route 93.

Route 93 to Seyðisfjörður is often foggy, which could reduce your breathtakingly-scenic drive to a blind, harrowing crawl. **Viewing conditions** can be checked on three live web-cams run by the Icelandic Road Administration; visit www.nat.is, click "travel guide," navigate to Seyðisfjörður, and click "Web Camera Fjarðarheidi."

About 7km (4⅓ miles) before reaching Seyðisfjörður, a gravel road branches off to the left. This road enabled construction crews to build avalanche barricades, which can be seen from Route 93 further downhill. In 1885, Seyðisfjörður suffered the most deadly avalanche in Icelandic history. Twenty-four people were killed, many more were injured, and several houses were knocked right into the fjord. In 1996 another avalanche leveled a factory, but no one died. A **memorial sculpture** made from the factory's twisted girders stands in the town, at the intersection of Ránargata and Fjarðargata.

BY BUS From June through August, **Ferðaþjónusta Austurlands** (✆ **472-1515;** www.sfk.is/gamli/ferdamal/fas.htm) connects Seyðisfjörður and Egilsstaðir with two **buses** daily on weekdays, with an extra bus on Wednesdays and Thursdays, and one bus a day at weekends. Tickets are 800kr for adults, 600kr for seniors and teens (13–19 years), and 400kr for children (5–12 years).

Seyðisfjörður

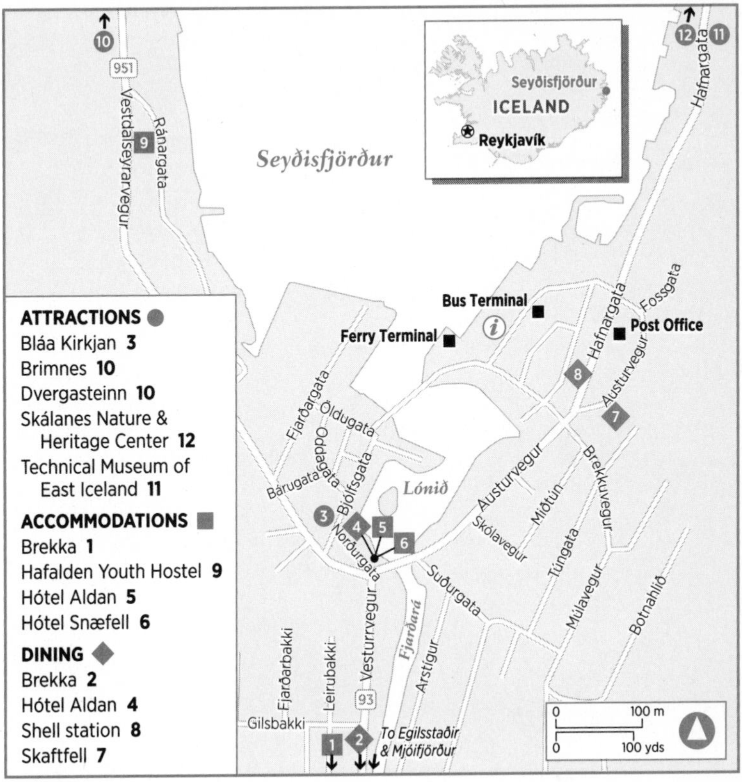

BY FERRY In summer, the **Norröna car and passenger ferry** (p. 41) arrives from Europe on Thursday mornings, departing at noon the same day.

VISITOR INFORMATION

The **tourist office** (✆ **472-1551;** www.sfk.is; May 1 until Sept Mon–Fri 9am–noon and 1–5pm; Jan through April Tues–Wed 9am–noon and 1–5pm) is inside the ferry terminal building. It is closed from October to December but should be open on ferry arrival days and possibly the day before. The staff sells bus passes and can help book places to stay.

What to See & Do

Among Iceland's smaller towns, Seyðisfjörður has perhaps the best concentration of **historic buildings and homes.** Most compelling are the chalet-style houses, inspired by German and Swiss models, clustered along Bjólfsgata and Norðurgata streets. Well-off merchants imported these houses from Norway—assembly required—roughly between 1890 and 1910. The free brochure *Historic Seyðisfjörður,* which can be found all over town, provides an in-depth history and walking tour of the architectural highlights.

Despite Seyðisfjörður's reputation as a magnet for Iceland's artsy community, the population is under 800, and visitors should not expect to find streets bristling with shops and galleries. Things do liven up the nights before and after the ferry arrival, however. It's also a good idea to check with the tourist office for **special events.** The various cultural festivities known as **Á seyði** are concentrated in early June but extend through July. The less-known **LungA festival** (✆ **861-5859;** www.lunga.is), takes place on the third weekend of July and invites young people aged 16 to 25 to join workshops led by artists focusing on everything from visual art to circus performance to fashion design. Non-Icelanders are welcome, and the week culminates with live concerts by prominent Icelandic bands. Classical concerts are presented in **Bláa Kirkjan** (✆ **472-1775**), a blue-painted church in the middle of town, on six consecutive Wednesdays from July 7 to August 11 at 8:30pm. Tickets cost 2,000kr adults; 1,500kr senior and students; free for 16 years and under; and go on sale half an hour before the performance.

The **Skaftfell Bistro and cultural center** (listed below in "Where to Dine") is the main hub for visual artists in the east of Iceland. The bistro is dedicated to the late artist Dieter Roth (known for his book creations and biodegradable works) and furnished in the spirit of his art; some of his book works are on display. Apart from the Skaftfell, Seyðisfjörður has not had consistent art gallery locations. Exhibitions have been held at **Skálinn,** an old service station on Bjólfsgata near the church, but the building's future is unclear.

From mid-May to mid-September, a **crafts market (handverkmarkaður)** is held on Austurvegur 23 from 1 to 5pm every day; call ✆ **866-7859** or contact the tourist office for an update. The tax-free shop **Þrýði,** Norðurgata 8 (✆**472-1535;** Mon–Fri 3–6pm), sells souvenirs, woolens, and local handicrafts.

Technical Museum of East Iceland (Tækniminjasafn Austurlands) ★
Seyðisfjörður was quite the cradle of modern technology, with Iceland's first telegraph station (1906), the first machine shop to run on hydroelectricity (1907), and the first modern electric power station (1913). This museum encompasses the original telegraph station and the machine shop, which has original belt-driven metalworking machines, turbines, a foundry furnace, and a blacksmith's forge. Upstairs from the machine shop is an exhibit recounting Seyðisfjörður's technical triumphs and an old telephone switchboard to play with.

The highlight here is the telegraph station, located 100m (328 ft.) from the machine shop inside a blue-gray house, which was bought from a rich Norwegian merchant in 1905. That same year, a telegraph cable was laid under the ocean to the Faeroe Islands, and then on to Scotland and the rest of Europe. In the summer of 1906, a crew of over 300 Icelanders and Norwegians planted 14,000 telegraph poles in a 614km (382-mile) course from Seyðisfjörður to Reykjavík.

The devoted staff maintains the original telegraph equipment, which must be seen in action to be truly appreciated. Ask them to demonstrate the transmission of Morse code on to hole-punched rolls of paper, using a machine powered by a spring and hand crank. A specially-adapted typewriter then converts the paper to words.

Hafnargata 44. ✆ **472-1596.** www.tekmus.is. Admission 600kr adults; free for seniors and children aged 18 and under. Free admission Fri. June–Sept 15 daily 11am–5pm; Sept 16–May Mon–Fri 1–4pm.

A DAY hike IN SEYÐISFJÖRÐUR ★★

The 5- to 6-hour hiking route from **Stafdalur to Vestdalur ★★** is a spectacular traverse through peaceful upland heath, past the mountain-sided lake Vestdalsvatn, and down into Seyðisfjörður along the cascading Vestdalsá River. Other than the steep downhill stretch at the end, the trail isn't too difficult or strenuous. It's a one-way route, and you'll need to arrange transport at either end. Any clear day from late June to early September is suitable, though late June and early July have the best show of wildflowers. The trail is poorly-staked, so bring a topographical map. Early in the season, ask about snow conditions and bring sunglasses to protect your eyes from glare.

The trail begins from a ski lift along Route 93, about 8km (5 miles) outside of Seyðisfjörður. The turnoff is indicated by a large sign with the Shell Oil logo and the words "VELKOMIN Á SKÍÐASVÆÐIÐ Í STAFDAL" The trail is marked with yellow-tipped stakes and leads north, away from Route 93, with Stafdalsfell mountain on the left and the boggy Stafdalsá River Valley on the right. In the pass between Stafdalsfell and Bjólfur peaks, the trail crosses the Stafdalsá. At this point you are about halfway to Vestdalsvatn Lake. Make sure to round the lake clockwise; another yellow-staked trail takes the near side of the lake and will lead you astray. At the northeast corner of Vestdalsvatn, you can sign the guestbook in the Vatnsklettur shed. From there it's all downhill, due east, along the Vestdalur Valley, with waterfalls and fabulous fjord views the whole way. Upon reaching the Vestdalsá River, the trail divides and proceeds down both banks; the southern (right-hand) trail is a little easier. Both trails end up on the coastal road, 2km (1¼ miles) north of the village.

The reverse route uphill from Seyðisfjörður through Vestdalur to Vestdalsvatn, then back the same way, does not require one-way transport and is almost as rewarding. Allow 5 hours for the round-trip, or 6 if you start from the village.

Tours & Activities

Local sailor **Hlynur Oddsson** (✆ **865-3741;** www.iceland-tour.com) offers individually tailored **fishing, cycling, and kayaking** trips. Fishing trips generally pursue cod, haddock, and coalfish. Mountain-bike rental starts at 2,500kr for a half-day. Guided kayak tours range from 1 hour (2,500kr) to 2-day excursions to Skálanes and back (27,000kr).

For **birdwatching tours** of Skálanes, 19km (12 miles) from Seyðisfjörður, see below.

VENTURING FROM SEYÐISFJÖRÐUR

The lonely, pristine, and beautiful fjords north and south of Seyðisfjörður make for wonderful adventures off-the-beaten-track. The best **topographical hiking map** of this entire region, including Borgarfjörður Eystri to the north, is titled *Víknaslóðir: Trails of the Deserted Inlets.* To buy this map in advance, contact Hafþór Snjólfur Helgason (✆ **863-2320** or helgima@mi.is/hsh2@hi.is).

A road leads along the **north shore** of Seyðisfjörður, reaching halfway to the tip of the peninsula. Close to the water, about 6km (3¾ miles) from the village and a 5-minute walk from the road, is **Dvergasteinn** (Dwarf's Rock), a 3m-high (10 ft.) rock that looks like a petrified cross-section of pock-marked foam. At the end of the road, a 4WD track extends another 5.5km (3½ miles) to **Brimnes,** an abandoned farm with a lighthouse, and a good destination for a coastal walk. Campers should definitely consider the hike overland to **Loðmundarfjörður,** which once had several farms but was abandoned in 1973. Loðmundarfjörður is an 8-hour walk from the village, or 6 hours from further up the coastal road. For more information on Loðmundarfjörður and other deserted inlets to the north, see Borgarfjörður Eystri (p. 359). Another wonderful trek leads from the southern shore of Seyðisfjörður overland to **Mjóifjörður**—yet another incredible find for connoisseurs of obscure fjords. Mjóifjörður is particularly long, steep, and narrow, with a beautiful series of waterfalls at its base, abundant crowberries in August, and about 35 inhabitants. **Brekka** (see "Where to Stay," below) lies right where the trail meets the fjord, and a gravel road (Rte. 953) leads back to Egilsstaðir.

The isolated **Skálanes Nature and Heritage Center ★** (✆ **690-6966** or 861-7008; www.skalanes.com; May 15–Sept 15), 19km (12 miles) from the village on Seyðisfjörður's south shore, is a great day trip or overnight from Seyðisfjörður, especially for birdwatchers. Skálanes provides very basic, shared accommodation, with en-suite bedrooms (each sleeping four), and leads guided tours of the area, including high cliffs and a beach popular with seals. The lack of privacy is compensated for by uninterrupted views of the surrounding landscape and full board of three hearty meals a day—largely fish, lamb, reindeer, and eggs harvested by the staff. Meals are by reservation only, but traditional Icelandic soup is usually on hand for drop-ins. Cars can reach within 6km (3¾ miles) of Skálanes, and 4WD vehicles go all the way. Transportation can be arranged from as far as Seyðisfjörður; other options include biking or kayaking with the help of Hlynur Oddsson (p. 357). The **Hótel Aldan** (below) can also put together a Skálanes package.

Where to Stay in & Around Seyðisfjörður

The ferry from Europe arrives on Thursdays, so it's near impossible to find a room for Wednesday or Thursday nights in summer without booking far in advance. Early June is also difficult, because of the *Á seyði* festival. Many arriving passengers move on to Egilsstaðir, which has more choices and is only 26km (16 miles) away. Check with the tourist information office (p. 355), which can help book places to stay anywhere in the region.

The friendly, offbeat **Hafalden Youth Hostel,** Ránargata 9 (✆ **472-1410** or 891-7010; fax 472-1610; www.simnet.is/hafaldan; 7 units, none w/bathroom; 8,400kr double; 3,200kr sleeping-bag accommodation in four-person room; 1,000kr sheet rental; MC, V; closed Oct 16–Apr 14) has straightforward bunk-bed rooms, Wi-Fi, access to a guest kitchen, Internet terminal, and washer. The common room, with large windows overlooking the fjord, is a perfect spot for writing postcards.

In Mjóifjörður, 30km away on the other side of the peninsula, **Brekka** (✆ **476-0007;** mjoi@simnet.is) offers a few bedrooms with a guest kitchen, plus two cottages with small private kitchens (7,600kr double; 3,000kr sleeping-bag accommodation; 9,000kr cottage). A basic **cafe** (1–6pm daily July 1–Aug 15) serves sandwiches and cakes.

Hótel Aldan ★★ With its deft arrangements of hand-crafted bedspreads, embroidered rugs, and real and fake antiques, this former bank building has the classiest interior decoration of any hotel in east Iceland. The rooms offer no views to choose from, but speak up if you like bathtubs. Iceland's president and his wife stay in one of the top-floor corner triples, where the extra single bed is tucked inside a cute alcove. The summer can get booked-up quickly, especially during events and festivals.

Oddagata 6 (reception in the Hótel Aldan restaurant, at Norðurgata 2). ✆ **472-1277.** Fax 472-1677. www.hotelaldan.com. 9 units. June–Aug. 22,900kr double; 27,900kr triple/suite. Rates around 13% lower May and Sept; around 27% lower Oct–Apr. Rates include breakfast. MC, V. **Amenities:** Laundry/dry cleaning service for stays of 3 nights or more. *In-room:* TV/DVD, minibar, hair dryer, no phone, Wi-Fi.

Hótel Snæfell ★ Snæfell is under the same ownership as Hótel Aldan (above), and is basically a simpler and humbler but no-less homey version. The two cheaper doubles are very small and—unlike most of the regular doubles—have no fjord view.

Austurvegur 3 (reception in the Hótel Aldan restaurant, at Norðurgata 2). ✆ **472-1277.** Fax 472-1677. www.hotelaldan.com. 9 units. June–Aug. 16,900kr–18,900kr double, 20,900kr triple. Rates around 15% lower May–Sept; around 20% lower Oct and Apr. Rates include breakfast. MC, V. Closed mid-Oct to Apr. *In room:* TV/DVD, hair dryer, no phone.

Where to Dine in & Around Seyðlsfjörður

The **Shell station,** Hafnargata 2 (✆ **472-1700;** daily 9am–10pm), serves fish soup or even a main course as well as hot-dogs.

Brekka (see "Where to Stay," above) serves snacks in its simple eatery in Mjóifjörður.

Hótel Aldan ★ ICELANDIC/MEDITERRANEAN The cooking may be a bit orthodox and unsurprising, but the Aldan compensates with super-fresh, organic ingredients and recipes that ease up on the cream and butter without compromising flavor. The herbal-marinated salmon is perfection. Good main courses include the grilled catfish, roasted lamb prime steak, and the beef dish. Ask for a table in the small room overlooking the waterfront.

Norðurgata 2. ✆ **472-1277.** Reservations required. Main courses 3,200kr–4,900kr MC, V. May–Sept 15 daily 7:30–10am, noon–2pm, and 6:30–9pm. Closed Sept 16–Apr.

Skaftfell ★★ CAFE/BISTRO Drawing tables become dinner tables in this cement-floored, art-themed bistro, furnished in the spirit of Dieter Roth. One large table is dedicated to the artistic skills of customers, who add their own doodles to a history of others. The menu offers mid-range lasagna, lamb, fish, and the locally made veggie-burger. Free Wi-Fi, an Internet terminal, perusable art books, and a table with paper and pencils for guest to indulge in their artistic skills complete the scene.

Austurvegur 42. ✆ **472-1633.** Reservations recommended Wed–Thurs in summer. Main courses 2,000kr–3,600kr; pizzas 1,500kr–2,200kr. MC, V. May 1– Sept 30 Mon–Thurs 10am–11pm; Fri–Sun 11am–1am. Oct–April open weekends, or call ahead for group bookings.

BORGARFJÖRÐUR EYSTRI

Borgarfjörður Eystri ★★★ is one of Iceland's supreme hiking areas, but recognition has been slow in coming. Road access is bumpy and limited; some of the best trails are free of snow for only 3 months, from early June to early September; and the scenery lacks immediate, overwhelming visual impact. It's the second-biggest rhyolite area in Iceland, with mountainsides draped in silky swaths of minerals in bright shades, but can't compete with Landmannalaugar. The fjords, inlets, and coastline are lovely but cannot match the majestic grandeur of Seyðisfjörður or the staggering cliffs of Hornstrandir. The flowering plants may be the most beautiful and diverse in all of Iceland, yet the vegetation does not overtake the senses as it does in Þórsmörk. Put all of its assets together, however, and the comparisons fade away. Most hikers here are Icelanders, ahead of the tourist curve.

Borgarfjörður Eystri means "East Borgarfjörður," to distinguish it from Borgarfjörður in the west. The main village in the area, Bakkagerði, is in the fjord Borgarfjörður, and is sometimes itself referred to as Borgarfjörður. Borgarfjörður Eystri can refer to the village, the fjord, the village and the fjord, or the entire municipality, north to Njarðvík and south to Loðmundarfjörður.

Getting the best of Borgarfjörður Eystri requires venturing far from the village of Bakkagerði and ideally spending two or more nights by the abandoned inlets of Breiðavík, Húsavík, and Loðmundarfjörður, which have mountain huts with 4WD access. Trails are well-marked and signposted, and there are excellent arranged tours.

Essentials

GETTING THERE Bakkagerði is 71km (44 miles) from Egilsstaðir. From the Ring Road, take Route 92 through Egilsstaðir, turn left on Route 93, and turn left again 1km (½ mile) later on Route 94, which goes all the way to Bakkagerði. Transportation between Egilsstaðir and Bakkagerði is available in the postal van with **Jakob Sigurðsson** (✆ **472-9805** or 894-8305; hlid@centrum.is). Tickets are 2,000kr adults, 1,500kr seniors, and 1,000kr for children aged 12 and under. Departures are on weekdays only, leaving Bakkagerði at 8am and the Egilsstaðir tourist information office at noon.

VISITOR INFORMATION **Egilsstaðir's tourist information office** (p. 347) covers this area and is a good place to buy a map. In Bakkagerði, limited tourist information is available at **Alfasteinn** and the **Fjarðarborg** tourist office (✆ **472-9920/848-5515;** fjardarborg@simnet.is; Jun–Aug daily 12noon–10pm), both of which should stock maps. The best website is **www.borgarfjordureystri.is**. The essential map ***Víknaslóðir: Trails of the Deserted Inlets,*** with trail descriptions in English, costs 700kr and is widely available in the summer, otherwise contact Hafþór Snjólfur Helgason (✆ **863-2320** or helgima@mi.is/hsh2@hi.is) to buy the map in advance of your trip.

Group & Self-Guided Tours

You can arrange camping or lodging at the three mountain huts independently, but guided tours have definite advantages. Tour companies have 4WD access all the way south to Loðmundarfjörður and can transport baggage and food. Guides are also well-versed in local history, geology, flora, and fauna, and can lead you to that unique milky waterfall, rare wildflower, or elf church off the main trail routes.

Ferðafélag Fljótsdalshéraðs (✆ **863-5813;** www.fljotsdalsherad.is/ferdafelag; ferdafelag@egilsstadir.is) operates the mountain huts at Breiðavík, Húsavík, and Loðmundarfjörður and occasionally leads tours in the area.

Elftours (Ferðaþjónustan Álfheimar), Borgarfjörður Eystri (✆ **861-3677;** www.elftours.is; info@elftours.is), offers tours of Borgarfjörður Eystri under the heading "In the foosteps of elves." Costs are from 139,900kr for 7-day tours, including hotel accommodation in double rooms, transportation from Egilsstaðir, local guide, day tour to Mývatn, and full board using local cusine.

Hafþór Snjólfur Helgason (✆ **863-2320;** helgima@mi.is or hsh2@hi.is), who lives in Bakkagerði, leads trips and knows everything about the area. He can also put together **self-guided tours,** with food and supplies delivered to the huts. 4WD delivery services are also offered by Fjarðarborg and Guesthouse Borg; see "Where to Stay," below. You can drive these routes yourself in a 4WD vehicle.

Exploring the Area

Route 94 traverses Fljótsdalshérað Valley before entering Borgarfjörður Eystri through a dramatic mountain pass. From Fljótsdalshérað, **Mt. Dyrfjöll**—distinctively notched, like the blunt end of a razorblade—is visible on the right. After the mountain pass, the road descends steeply into **Njarðvík,** a tiny settlement northwest of Bakkagerði. Near the bottom of the descent, on the right-hand side of the road, look for a sign for **Innra-Hvannagil ★**, a narrow rhyolite gorge. A 5-minute trail leads from the parking area into the gorge, which has banks of rock shards, a vertical surface of intricately patterned stone, and a stream running over slabs of gleaming yellow rhyolite. Walking further into the gorge is impossible.

After Njarðvík, the road follows a sinuous, knuckle-whitening coastal route along the **Njarðvíkurskriður** (Njarðvík Screes), steep banks of loose rock at the base of the cliffs and mountains. On the ocean side is the **Naddakross,** a wooden cross with the Latin inscription *Effigem Christi qui transit pronus honora. Anno 1306* ("You who pass the sign of Christ, bow your head in reverence. Year 1306"). This marks the legendary spot where, in 1306, a farmer named Jón Árnason killed a half-human, cave-dwelling monster named Naddi by wrestling him into the ocean. Naddi had been gnawing loudly on rocks and striking terror into the hearts of anyone crossing the screes after nightfall. The present cross dates from the 1950s, but is apparently planted on the original site.

BAKKAGERÐI ★ (BORGARFJÖRÐUR)

Njarðvík and Bakkagerði are the only inhabited parts of Borgarfjörður Eystri, with a total population of around 145. Borgarfjörður has a nice seaweedy **beach,** and seals often congregate on the eastern shores. A **submarine mine** from World War II is mounted along the main road. On the south side of the village, the **Álfacafé** store and cafe, Iðngarðar (✆ **472-9900;** May 20–Aug daily 11am–8pm; Sept–May 11am–5pm), sells souvenirs made from rock, including candle holders, clocks, and, of course, trolls. Next to Álfasteinn is a small **fish factory;** you could drop in and ask to look around, if you don't mind some fishy splatter on your clothes.

Borgarfjörður takes its name from **Álfaborg,** the distinct rocky hill behind the village. Álfaborg is home to the elf queen herself—the name translates either to "elf rock" or "elf town." A stroll up the hill is a pleasant way to orient yourself to the valley. At the top is a view disc identifying the surrounding mountains.

Bakkagerðiskirkja ★ is a 1901 church, and aligned facing the fjord, rather than east–west, like every other Icelandic church of its day. According to local legend, the town planned to build the church on top of the Álfaborg, but an elf appeared to a town elder in a dream and requested the current site. Bakkagerðiskirkja hosts the town's most treasured possession: an **altarpiece painting** of Christ on the Mount by Jóhannes S. Kjarval. Christ stands on what looks like a miniature Álfaborg, with the unmistakable outline of Dyrfjöll in the background. The townspeople commissioned the painting in 1914, when Kjarval was 29 and studying in Copenhagen. Iceland's bishop hated the painting and refused to consecrate it. The church is easy to locate by sight, and is generally open all day.

HIDDEN people, ELVES & MODERN ICELAND

In polls, only about 20% of Icelanders rule out the existence of elves. Construction projects can still be thwarted by fears of disturbing elf dwellings. In 1996, as ground was prepared for a graveyard in a Reykjavík suburb, two bulldozers leveling a suspected elf hill mysteriously broke down. Elf arbitrators were called in. "We're going to see whether we can't reach an understanding with the elves," the project supervisor told Iceland's daily newspaper, *Morgunblaðið*.

Many Icelanders are tired of being asked if they really believe in elves, because they can't give a simple yes or no answer. Saying "yes" would not mean they believe, in the most literal sense, that little people emerge from rocks every night and dance around. And saying "no" would not mean they dismiss related supernatural concepts and phenomena.

Icelanders by necessity have always been strongly attuned to their strange and harsh environment. Spend enough time outdoors in Iceland's long twilights—which play strange tricks on the eyes—and Icelanders' unwillingness to rule out hidden people starts to make intuitive sense.

On the main street is **Lindarbakki,** an oft-photographed, turf-roofed house with reindeer horns over the door. If you knock, the friendly summer resident will probably invite you in to sign the Gestabók. Note the now-framed rat skeleton she found in the wall.

Six kilometers (3¾ miles) northeast of the village, next to the fishing boat dock, **Hafnarhólmi** ★ has two excellent platforms for viewing puffins and cliff-nesting birds. The best time to visit is in the morning or late afternoon, when puffins are least likely to be off fishing. The platforms are closed in May for nesting season, and open from 11am to 7pm in June and July. In August the platforms are open 24 hours, though the puffins disappear by mid-month. The fence atop the cliff is to prevent puffins from digging burrows in the territory of eider ducks, whose nest feathers are harvested once the nests have been abandoned for the winter. The lower platform by the picnic table is ideal for observing the gull-like kittiwakes.

The Kjarval Experience (Kjarvalsstofa) is on Bakkagerði's main road at Fjarðarborg community building, on the second floor. Jóhannes Sveinsson Kjarval (1885–1972), Iceland's most highly-regarded painter, grew up in Borgarfjörður. This museum pays tribute to the man more than his art, which is featured at the Kjarvalsstaðir in Reykjavík (p. 129). Even Kjarval's admirers can probably skip the displays of his soiled hat and ties, but the gallery with prints of his portrait drawings of locals is touching. A screening room shows old Super 8 movies and TV news clips of Borgarfjörður Eystri in Icelandic. Children can play in a room with paints.

Two prints of Kjarval's landscape paintings are posted outdoors east of town, the idea is to reflect the painter's inspiration. To find them, take the short trail (marked #18 on the *Víknaslóðir* map) to the Hólar mounds.

Argarður. ✆ **862-6163.** Admission 500kr adults; free for children aged 15 and under. June–Aug daily noon–6pm.

HIKING ROUTES

As mentioned above, *Víknaslóðir: Trails of the Deserted Inlets* is essential for exploring the region. Trails are well-marked from the main road, and a map is posted at each trailhead. The best time for hiking is from early July to early September, though many routes are clear of snow by June. In late August you can eat your fill of *krækiber* (black crowberries)—keep an eye out for the rare albino variety. The weather is rainier in September, but you'll have plenty of solitude.

The best trips in Borgarfjörður Eystri last 2 to 7 days, but if you have just 1 day (and no access to a 4WD vehicle), the two best **day hikes** are to Stórurð and Brúnavík. Both destinations take around 5 to 6 hours for the round-trip.

Stórurð ★★ is a mystical jumble of oddly-shaped boulders around a blue-green stream and pond with grassy banks. Don't come before early July, when the snow lifts. The best trail route (marked #9 on the *Víknaslóðir* map) starts at the 431m (1,414 ft.) Vatnskarð pass on Route 94, west of Njarðvík, and crosses the 634m (2,080 ft.) Geldingafjall peak, before descending into Stórurð. This trail has some ankle-twisting stretches of loose gravel and scree. Somewhat easier trails (#8 and #10) reach Stórurð from different parts of the road, but #9 has the best approach to Stórurð, as well as astounding views of Njarðvík, Fljótsdalshérað Valley, and even Snæfell and Vatnajökull. You could return by one of the easier trails, but would have to walk back to your car along the road.

Brúnavík ★★, the first cove east of Borgarfjörður, has a lovely beach of rhyolite sand and was inhabited by two families until 1944. Two trails lead to Brúnavík from the coastal road on Borgarfjörður's eastern side. For the dramatic descent into Brúnavík, the best circular route is clockwise, heading to Brúnavík through the 345m (1,132- ft.) Brúnavíkurskarð Pass (the trail marked #19 on the map) and returning through the 321m (1,053 ft.) Hofstrandarskarð Pass (trail #20).

The trails and 4WD tracks—and the best **multi-day trips**—extend all the way south to **Loðmundarfjörður,** or perhaps even to Seyðisfjörður. Loðmundarfjordur had 87 residents at the outset of the 20th century, but the last ones left in 1973, after failing to convince authorities to build a road around the coast from Seyðisfjörður. A partially restored 1891 church is still standing but stays locked up. (Húsavík also has a cute church near the ocean; it dates from the late 1930s and always remains open.)

The scenic highlights of Borgarfjörður Eystri are manifold, but **Hvítserkur** should be singled out, as many consider it the most strangely beautiful mountain in Iceland. The main bulk is pale-rose rhyolite, but glacial erosion has exposed dark basaltic ribbons that look like paint splattered by Jackson Pollock. Hvítserkur's best side faces south, and can be seen from Húsavik and the 4WD road leading there.

Where to Stay

The **mountain huts** at Breiðavík *(Breiðuvíkurskáli)* and Húsavík *(Húsavíkurskáli)* are operated by **Ferðafélag Fljótsdalshéraðs** (**✆ 863-5813;** ferdafelag@egilsstadir.is). The Breiðavík hut has a warden in the morning and evening. Both huts sleep 33 in bunks (4,200kr adults; 1,100kr children aged 7–12) and neither has reception for phones.

Camping is allowed at Bakkagerði (next to the Breiðavík), Húsavík, and Loðmundarfjörður mountain huts (1,000kr per night).

The **Ásbyrgi Youth Hostel** (© **472-9962** or 866-3913; fax 472-9961; www.hostel.is; 6 units, none w/bathroom; AE, DC, MC, V) is a cheap place to bed down for the night, and has two double rooms available (7,000kr).

Guesthouse Borg This is spread over three houses around town, all with unexciting but serviceable rooms and guest kitchens. The manager, Skúli, doesn't speak much English, but can transport food and bags to the mountain huts for guests.

Bakkagerði, 720 Borgarfjörður Eystri (off Rte. 946) © **472-9870** or 894-4470. Fax 472-9880. www.borgarfjordureystri.is. 11 units, none w/bathroom. 9,000kr double; 3,500kr per person sleeping-bag accommodation per person. Breakfast available (1,200kr). MC, V. **Amenities:** Guest kitchen. *In room:* No phone, Wi-Fi.

Réttarholt This simple but homey guesthouse is the best option in town. Two rooms are doubles, and one has five beds. Owner Helgi also doubles as a tour guide and is your best possible resource for local travel information. Breakfast is no longer available, so bring your own food.

Bakkagerði, 720 Borgarfjörður Eystri, (off Rte. 946) © **472-9913.** www.borgarfjordureystri.is. 3 units, none w/bathroom. Made-up beds 4,400kr per person; 3,400kr sleeping-bag accommodation per person. No credit cards. **Amenities:** Guest kitchen. *In room:* No phone.

Skólasel Fjarðarborg community center operates this basic guesthouse building, with access to the guest kitchen and laundry at the youth hostel. It has three large rooms with up to six beds in each (you can book a whole room for an extra 1,000kr). Skúli, who runs Fjarðarborg and Guesthouse Borg, speaks limited English but also arranges 4WD transport of food, baggage, and passengers to and from the mountain huts.

Fjarðarborg, Bakkagerði, 720 Borgarfjörður Eystri (off Rte. 947) © **472-9920.** 3 units, none w/bathroom. Made-up beds 4,500kr per person; 3,500kr sleeping-bag accommodation. MC, V. Closed Sept–May. **Amenities:** Restaurant. *In room:* No phone.

Where to Dine

Consider stocking up at Egilsstaðir's **supermarkets** before heading to Borgarfjörður Eystri. Since Bakkagerði has few dining options, all places to stay have guest kitchens, and food must be brought in to mountain huts. From June to August, the community office **Fjarðarborg** (above) offers passable burgers, soup, sandwiches, vegetable pitas, lamb chops, and fried fish from 11.30am to 9pm daily. Main courses are 1,100kr–3,200kr. **Álfacafé** (p. 361) has a limited cafe, serving drinks, snack food, and 1,550kr servings of tasty fish soup with traditional Icelandic brown-rye flatbread.

FLJÓTSDALSHÉRAÐ VALLEY

Fljótsdalshérað is the broad, flat valley that extends from Egilsstaðir northeast to the ocean, providing an outlet for two major rivers, Jökulsá á Brú (aka Jökulsá á Dal) and Lagarfljót. The Jökulsá á Brú has been drastically affected by the new Kárahnjúkar Dam (p. 353), far upstream. The diversion of water and blockage of sediments is disrupting the local ecosystem and could devastate the hundreds of seals that breed in the river delta. Nonetheless, the valley—walled in by mountains, with plenty of pretty farms and bird ponds—is a beautiful place to do some **horseback riding.**

Want to feel totally removed from the world in an adorable rustic farmhouse, cooking your own meals and riding horseback along peaceful ocean beaches, grasslands, and riverbanks in search of birds and seals? If so, **Húsey ★**, (✆ **471-3010** or 847-8229; www.husey.de; 7 units, none w/bathroom. 6,700kr double; sleeping-bag accommodation 3,350kr. Jan 15– Dec 10 AE, DC, MC, V; between Oct–May no credit cards), a picturesque farm at the headwaters of the Jökulsá á Brú, is the place for you. Horse trips are tailored for beginners and experts and range from 2-hour seal-watching jaunts to 2-day excursions to a historic farmstead. Non-riders may be perfectly content walking the trails and reading on the porch all day. Breakfast is available for 1,500kr, but all other food must be brought in and can be prepared in the guest kitchen. For more places to stay, click on the "gisting" link at **www.fljotsdalsherad.is**.

The drive from Egilsstaðir to Húsey is about an hour. Take the Ring Road north for 26km (16 miles), then turn right on Route 925, just before the Jökulsá á Brú bridge (ignore the earlier junction with Rte. 925. At the farm Litlibakki, as Route 925 turns off to the right, go straight on Route 926 and continue to the end. If you need a ride, inquire at Húsey (above). For up to six people, the round-trip price is 13,000kr from Egilsstaðir or you can get a lift to the main road for 8,000kr for bus connections to Akureyri, Egilstaðir, and Höfn. A taxi costs far more.

EGILSSTAÐIR TO MÝVATN

The lonely 167km (104 miles) stretch of the Ring Road between Egilsstaðir and Mývatn can be a blur of barren, gravelly plains—but it also affords beautiful vistas, especially on a clear day when Mt. Herðubreið is visible to the south. Make sure your gas tank is full before setting out.

Almost halfway from Egilsstaðir to Mývatn and 13km (8 miles) south of the Ring Road, **Sænautasel ★** (✆ **892-8956** or 855-5399)—a reconstructed turf farm on a 60km-long (37-mile) heathland called Jökuldalsheiði—is a great detour to break up the trip. Sænautasel was abandoned in 1875 after the Askja eruption fouled the area with ash. In 1992, a descendant of Sænautasel's first settler reconstructed the original farm, which now welcomes visitors daily from June through August 31 (10am–10pm). To reach Sænautasel, exit the Ring Road at its western junction with Route 901, roughly 70km (43 miles) northwest of Egilsstaðir. A few kilometers later, turn left on Route 907 and continue for another 10 minutes. After desolate expanses of nothingness, the road arrives at a vision from another age: two turf-roofed houses next to a pleasant lake surrounded by vegetation. Pancakes and coffee are served inside the Welcome building. Admission to the farmhouse, close to the Welcome building, costs 500kr for adults, and is free for children aged 11 and under. If no warden is there, ask to be shown around.

Buses connecting Egilsstaðir and Mývatn stop at **Möðrudalur,** an isolated sheep farming settlement along Route 901, 8km (5 miles) south of Route 901's western junction with the Ring Road. Möðrudalur dates back to the Saga Age, and at 469m (1,539 ft.) above sea level is Iceland's highest working farm. The **Fjalladýrð Cafe and Guesthouse** (✆ **471-1858** or 894-8181; www.fjalladyrd.is) offers pastries, lamb and vegetable soups, sandwiches, and hot-dogs. The owners also arrange 4WD trips to Vatnajökull, Askja, and Kverkfjöll.

THE INTERIOR

12

Almost a third of Iceland is covered by highland plateaus blanketed with volcanic gravel, and punctuated only by glacial rivers, scattered mountains and lakes, smatterings of vegetation, and perhaps a stray boulder. Amid this pristine desert wasteland, visitors often pose for pictures next to directional signs at road junctions. The signs seem to point nowhere, and, in the photo, the visitor invariably grins at the absurdity—and otherworldly beauty—of the scene. The Apollo astronauts came to Iceland's interior to train, and until tourism reaches the moon, this place may be the closest substitute.

The interior is often described as Europe's last great-untouched wilderness. This is somewhat misleading, as much of the land was vegetated before settlers and their voracious sheep first arrived. In efforts to reseed the desert, Icelandic scientists are experimenting with dropping bombs full of fertilizer from a World War II-era DC-3 plane.

Early settlers often traversed the interior for parliamentary meetings at Þingvellir, but many routes were closed off when temperatures cooled in the 13th century. In popular mythology, the interior became a refuge for outlaws and outcasts, much like the Wild West in the American imagination.

The two main south–north routes through the interior are Kjölur, in the western half of the country, and Sprengisandur, right in the middle. The Kjölur Route is relatively hospitable, and can be crossed easily in a 4WD vehicle. The Sprengisandur Route passes through Iceland's most fantastically bleak territory, with more hazardous road conditions. Further east is the Askja caldera, a dramatic ring of mountains formed largely in the aftermath of a catastrophic 1875 eruption.

South of Askja is Kverkfjöll, where intense geothermal activity and the Vatnajökull glacier surreally converge. Some interior highland destinations find their place elsewhere in this book, notably Landmannalaugar and Þórsmörk in the south (chapter 9), Snæfell in the east (chapter 10), and the Kaldidalur Route in the west (chapter 7).

The travel season is generally restricted to mid-summer. In July the sparse plant life heroically blooms, but August is generally prettier, since more snow has lifted. River crossings are often more difficult in July, because of higher water levels. July can also be buggier.

High winds and severe temperature fluctuations are endemic to the highlands. Volcanic sands are lightweight and swirl easily in the wind, so eye and face protection can be crucial. Driving in the interior presents serious challenges; see "Getting Around," in chapter 3 (p. 41), for details.

KJÖLUR ROUTE

Leaving aside the much shorter Kaldidalur Route in the west, Kjölur—which runs from Geysir and Gullfoss in the southwest to Húnaflói and Skagafjörður in the north—is the most accessible, most trafficked, and least barren route through Iceland's highland interior. The highest point of the road, 600m (1,968 ft.) above sea level, is in the valley between Langjökull and Hofsjökull, Iceland's second- and third-largest glaciers. Strictly speaking, Kjölur refers only to this valley, but the word commonly applies to the entire 165km (103 miles) course of mountain road F35. Kjölur is often called a "shortcut" to Akureyri, but this only makes sense if you're already near Geysir and Gullfoss—*and* you have a 4WD car. In a regular car, Kjölur is usually navigable, and all rivers are bridged, but your insurance will likely be voided.

There were tentative plans for a paved toll road through Kjölur which would have cut a straighter path and remained open all year. Some said it would improve access for all, but Iceland's Travel Industry Association argued that visitors entranced by the interior's unspoiled landscape didn't want trucks echoing across the plains. Either way, the plans were shelved after an environmental assessment in summer 2010.

Essentials

GETTING THERE The Kjölur Route opens in early- to mid-June, and can remain open even into October. If you're **driving,** note that the only **filling station** (Jun–Sept 20) is at Hveravellir, 93km (58 miles) from Gullfoss.

From mid-July through August, the **Sterna** bus company (© **553-3737;** www.sterna.is) connects Reykjavík and Akureyri via Kjölur daily in both directions, leaving Reykjavík at 8pm and Akureyri at 8:30am. **SBA Norðurleið** (© **550-0700;** www.sba.is) covers the same route daily for more of the year (mid-June until early September) with buses leaving at 8am from both Reykjavík and Akureyri. Both companies charge 11,000kr one-way, and stop at Hveragerði, Selfoss, Geysir, Gullfoss, Hvítárnes, Kerlingarfjöll, Hveravellir, Svartábrú, and Varmahlíð, with short sightseeing breaks at Geysir, Gullfoss, and Hveravellir. The SBA bus takes 10 hours in either direction, while the Sterna bus takes 15 hours from Reykjavík to Akureyri, including breaks at Þingvellir and Kerlingarfjöll; this route does travel via Hveragerði or Selfoss. The Akureyri–Reykjavík Sterna trip takes 11 hours, and does not travel through Þingvellir. The Kjölur Route is also included in two of SBA's bus package deals, the **Highlights Passport** (from 37,600kr) and **Highland Circle Passport** (34,200kr)—both offered by **SBA Norðurleið** (© **550-0700;** www.sba.is), an affiliate of Reykjavík Excursions.

VISITOR INFORMATION The best information sources for Kjölur are the people or groups who run accommodations along the route. The hiking group **Ferðafélag Íslands** (© **568-2533;** www.fi.is) operates five mountain huts around Kjölur and has the most regional expertise. The folks at **Ásgarður** (© **894-2132;** www.kerlingarfjoll.is) know the Kerlingarfjöll area. **Hveravallafélag** (© **452-4200** or 894-1293; www.hveravellir.is) supervises Hveravellir and the website has printable maps of all hiking routes from there. Ample information on Kjölur's geology, flora, and fauna is found at

The Interior

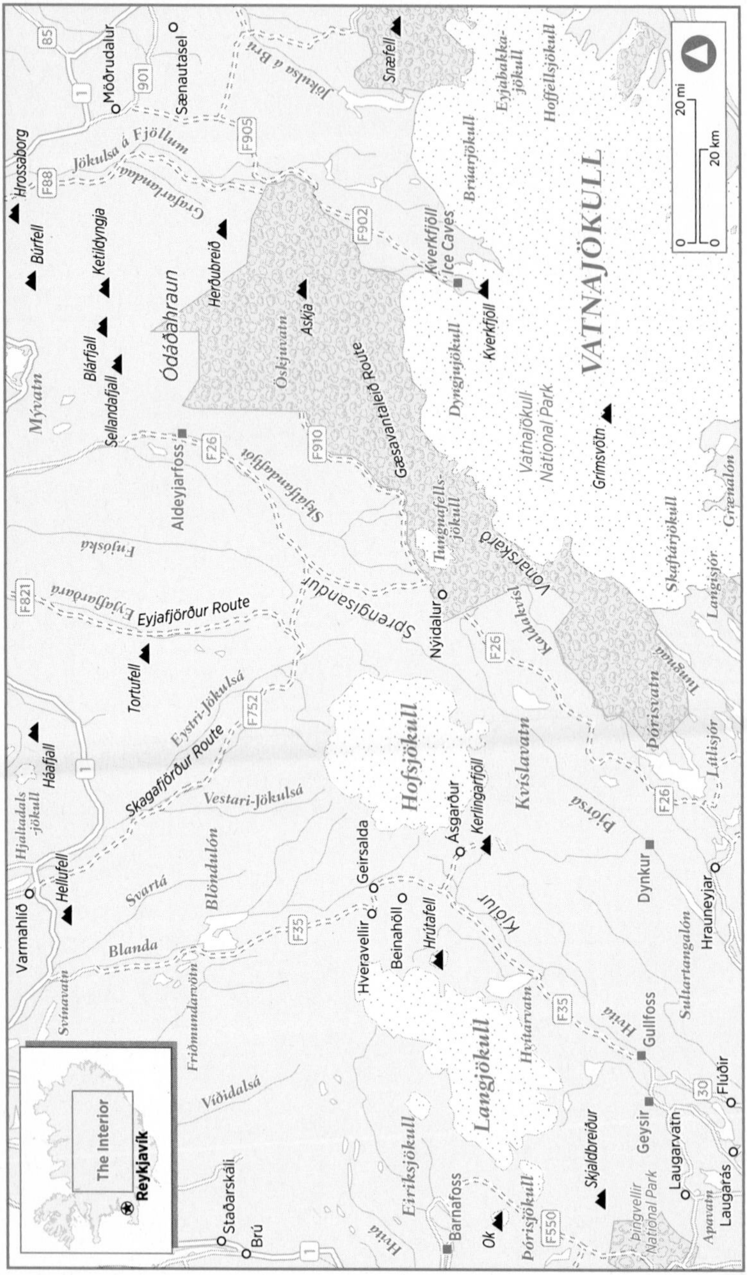

www.ust.is, the website of the **Environment and Food Agency of Iceland** (click "Protected Areas," then "Hveravellir").

Outdoor Activities

HIKING **Ferðafélag Íslands** (✆ **568-2533;** www.fi.is), Iceland's premier hiking group, leads a couple of multi-day trips around Kjölur each summer. **Fannborg ehf** (✆ **664-7000/**664-7878; www.kerlingarfjoll.is) operates a popular women's hiking and yoga tour to Kerlingarfjöll for 35,000kr in June. Prices include facilities, food, and guiding (contact: hhardard@gmail.com).

HORSEBACK RIDING Two of Iceland's most reputable stables run Kjölur tours on horseback. The **Íshestar** (✆ **555-7000;** www.ishestar.is; 297,000kr per person) tour is 9 days, while **Eldhestar** (✆ **480-4800;** www.eldhestar.is) tours are 8; both give you 6 days in the saddle. Food, accommodation, and transportation to and from Keflavík airport are included.

Exploring the Area

The map *Kjölur: Arnarvatnsheiði–Kerlingarfjöll,* available at tourist offices and online at www.nordicstore.net, has good detail on hiking and driving routes.

HVÍTÁRVATN & HVÍTARNES ★

Around 45km (28 miles) northeast of Gullfoss, a turnoff from Route F35 leads 6km (4 miles) to Hvítárnes, a well-vegetated, marshy plain overlooking Hvítárvatn, a broad aquamarine lake, sometimes with floating icebergs calved from Langjökull. The scenery is austere but captivating, and the Hvítárnes mountain hut, built in 1930, is a charming throwback with white gables and turf-insulated side walls. For engaging hikes around Hvítárvatn, ask at the hut or click the "Hiking Tracks" link at www.hveravellir.is.

KERLINGARFJÖLL ★★

This vast volcanic system near the southwest corner of Hofsjökull is one of the most glorious and underappreciated hiking areas in Iceland. The range of highland scenery is astounding, with peaks ranging in height from 800 to 1,477m (2,625–4,846 ft.); rhyolite

THE KJÖLURVEGUR trek

The **Kjölurvegur ★★** (aka Kjalvegur) is a rewarding and very manageable 3-day hike along an old horse trail from Hvítárnes to Hveravellir, with mountain huts spaced at 4- to 6-hour (12–14km/7½–9-mile) intervals. The route skirts Langjökull, with interesting but optional detours from the Þjófadalir hut east through the Kjalhraun lava field or west toward Langjökull. Buses stop at both ends of the Kjölurvegur, though you'll have to walk the 6km (4 miles) from Route F35 to the Hvítárnes hut. (Reserving bus seats in advance is a smart precaution.) Online, **www.fi.is** has a day-by-day breakdown of the route—under the heading "Hveravellir-Hvítárnes (the Old Kjalvegur Hiking Trail)"—but it takes you from north to south. Hiking south to north lets you end the trek with a valedictory dunk in Hveravellir's geothermal hot tub. To reserve space in the huts, see "Where to Stay," below.

mountainsides in spectral shadings of red, yellow, and green; shimmering glaciers; chiseled ravines; and steaming geothermal hotspots, some with swimmable ponds and springs. If Landmannalaugar is not on your itinerary, Kerlingarfjöll is a very worthy alternative, and spending 2 or 3 nights here is an ideal way to break up the Kjölur Route. The website www.kerlingarfjoll.is has downloadable maps of all the hiking trails.

Kerlingarfjöll is reached via Route F347, which branches off from Route F35 about halfway between Hvítárnes and Hveravellir. The places to stay at Ásgarður (see below) are about 10km (6 miles) down the road. If you're coming by bus, note that the SBA bus can drop you at the crossroads, but only the Trex bus goes right to Ásgarður.

HVERAVELLIR ★

About 93km (58 miles) from Gullfoss, Route F735 detours 2km (1¼ miles) from Route F35 to reach Hveravellir (Hot Spring Plains), an intriguing geothermal hot spot and Kjölur's main summer service hub, with restaurant, bar, small market, and sleeping-bag accommodation in mountain huts. There is no filling station here, but they have a supply for emergencies. Hveravellir's weather station is staffed year-round, providing one of Iceland's best jobs for loners. The geothermal field is worth a stop, especially to bathe in the waist-deep pool, or to see Öskurhólshver, a white-crusted conical fumarole hissing eggy steam. Stick to the boardwalks to protect both yourself and the land. Hveravellir is also a terminus for the Kjölurvegur trek; see box, above.

Where to Stay & Dine

The only **restaurants** along the Kjölur Route are at Ásgarður (in Kerlingarfjöll) and Hveravellir, which also has a small **market.** Don't expect fine dining.

For mountain huts in **Hvítárnes** and along the **Kjölurvegur Route** (except for Hveravellir), sleeping-bag space must be reserved online and at least 1 month in advance through **Ferðafélag Íslands** (✆ **568-2533;** www.fi.is; 3,200kr per person per night). All huts have kitchens but no utensils. None have showers, and only Hvítárnes has a warden. All food must be brought in, and all rubbish must be packed out.

At **Kerlingarfjöll,** from mid-June until the end of September, **Ásgarður** (✆ **664-7878**; www.kerlingarfjoll.is) offers a wide range of lodging, from sleeping-bag accommodation in a bunk room for 28 people (4,000kr) to made-up beds in private cottages (10,000kr per person). Facilities include guest kitchens, a restaurant, and a bathhouse with showers and three hot tubs. All cottages have heat and electricity, and the website outlines each rooming option, with photos.

The mountain huts at **Hveravellir** are run by **Hveravallafélag** (✆ **452-4200** or 894-1293; www.hveravellir.is; 5,000kr sleeping-bag accommodation) and are open between June and September (depending on weather conditions and road access). One hut has three bedrooms and sleeps 33, while the other sleeps 20 and is split into three rooms. Both have fully equipped kitchens and hot water. It's possible to book meals in advance, otherwise soup and sandwiches are available.

SPRENGISANDUR ROUTE

Sprengisandur, the desert expanse at Iceland's heart, is a true moonscape—so much so, in fact, that conspiracy theorists believe this is where the U.S. government "faked" the moon landing. Such bleak, lifeless scenery is transporting and sublime to some, depressing and monotonous to others, but on a clear day, no one can fail to be unimpressed by the grand tableau of mountains and glaciers in all directions. If you've ever doubted the world is round, come here and witness the sky arching overhead.

The Sprengisandur Route has no strict beginning or end, but loosely corresponds to Route F26, which spans 196km (122 miles) from the Hrauneyjar highland area to the Aldeyjarfoss waterfall. However desolate the route, it's hardly featureless, and opportunities for exploration abound.

Essentials

GETTING THERE

BY CAR With its rough surfaces and hazardous river fords, Route F26 is only for rugged 4WD vehicles with good clearance. The road's opening date varies, but usually falls at the end of June. The **Public Roads Administration** (✆ **522-1000;** www.vegagerdin.is; weekdays 8am–4pm or the inland service ✆ 1777; May–October 8am–4pm; Nov–April 7:30–10pm) continually monitors road conditions; but for the latest on water levels or other dangers at river crossings, the warden at **Nýidalur** (✆ **854-1194**) is the better source. Traffic on the Sprengisandur Route has increased greatly, so in high season—as long as you stick to Route F26—driving in convoy is not a necessary precaution. ⚠ Fuel is not available on Route F26, and the service stations at Hrauneyjar and Goðafoss are 240km (149 miles) apart. (Unprepared drivers are often seen begging for fuel at Nýidalur.)

From the south, Route F26 is reached via Route 26 or Route 32; for sights en route, see "Þjórsárdalur and Hekla," p. 298.

Three significant interior routes branch off from Route F26. A few kilometers north of Nýidalur, Route F910 links Route F26 to Askja. This road—also known as the **Gæsavantaleið Route**—has incredible scenery but should only be attempted by experienced drivers in convoy; allow 9 hours from Nýidalur to Askja's Drekagil huts. Route F752, also known as the **Skagafjörður Route**, links Route F26 to the town of Varmahlíð and Skagafjörður. Routes F881 and F821, jointly known as the **Eyjafjörður Route,** link Route F26 to Akureyri. At its north end, Route F26 connects with Route 842, which leads 41km (25 miles) through the Bjarðardalur valley to the Ring Road near Goðafoss. The northern end of Route F26 is far more dependable than the Skagafjörður and Eyjafjörður routes, which are sometimes closed to traffic altogether.

BY BUS **Reykjavík Excursions** (✆ **562-1011;** www.re.is) connects Landmannalaugar and Lake Mývatn via the Sprengisandur Route from July 1 to September 3. Departures from Mývatn (Reykjahlíð) are Monday, Wednesday, and Friday at 8:30am, and departures from Landmannalaugar are Sunday, Tuesday, and Thursday, also at 8:30am. The full one-way trip lasts 10 hours and costs 11,600kr, with stops at Hrauneyjar, Nýidalur, and Skútustaðir, plus sightseeing breaks at the Aldeyjarfoss and Goðafoss waterfalls. Passengers taking the bus from Mývatn to Landmannalaugar must wait until the following day for connections to Reykjavík and elsewhere. The duration of stops can differ so be sure to keep informed of the time: you don't want to be left behind in no-man's land. The Sprengisandur Route is included in two multi-trip bus package deals—the **Highlights Passport** and **Highland Circle Passport** (p. 367).

VISITOR INFORMATION

No specific tourist information office is assigned to the Sprengisandur Route, but regional offices in Hveragerði, Varmahlíð, Akureyri, and Mývatn can provide help. The **Hrauneyjar Highland Center** (✆ **487-7782;** www.hrauneyjar.is) is a useful resource, and the warden at **Nýidalur** (✆ **860-3334;** July–Aug)—while not responsible for helping non-guests—is usually happy to answer questions.

Tours

HIKING **Icelandic Mountain Guides** (✆ **587-9999;** www.mountainguide.is) lead epic, unforgettable treks off the beaten path, including Askja to Nýidalur in 6 days (113,100kr) and Nýidalur to Eldgjá in 7 days (180,900kr). Plan on carrying a heavy pack.

HORSEBACK RIDING **Eldhestar** (✆ **480-4800;** www.eldhestar.is) offers an 8-day Sprengisandur traverse with 6 days spent on horseback (280,000kr), while **Íshestar** (✆ **556-7000;** www.ishestar.is), an equally experienced and reputable company, tackles the route in 12 days with 9 in the saddle.

Exploring the Area

At the northern end of Route F26, make sure to stop at the enthralling waterfall Aldeyjarfoss (p. 263).

Hrauneyjar Highland Center, a year-round highland oasis at the southern terminus of the Sprengisandur Route, has two hotels and restaurants (see "Where to Stay & Dine," below), an information desk, and the last service station for the next 240km (149 miles). A trail map of the surrounding area is available at reception.

As a base, Hrauneyjar is best for those with their own 4WD transport. The Highland Center arranges tours only for groups, and the best local destinations—such as the Veiðivötn lakes (below), or the lovely **Dynkur ★**, a waterfall on the Þjórsá river—are inaccessible to regular cars. Hrauneyjar is especially handy for visitors who want to explore Landmannalaugar by day and then retire to a private room with a made-up bed. Landmannalaugar is an hour from Hrauneyjar via Route F208, which opens up in late June. (Regular cars can negotiate the route, but this would void your insurance.)

The Hrauneyjar area has some excellent fishing, and the Highland Center sells licenses and rents rods. Prices are steep, however, with licenses starting around 4,900kr per rod, per day in lakes.

VEIÐIVÖTN ★

Trout fishermen are particularly drawn to this idyllic and peaceful cluster of 50 volcanic crater lakes, located close to Landmannalaugar but accessed through Hrauneyjar on Route F228. Fishing permits (8,000kr) and sleeping-bag accommodation (3,300kr per person) in four bunk-style cottages are handled by **Landmannahellir** (✆ **893-8407;** www.landmannahellir.is). Make sure to book well in advance, accommodation and fishing permits are usually sold out by April.

NÝIDALUR ★

An overnight stay at this remote desert outpost, combined with a day hike east to **Vonarskarð Pass ★★**, makes for a memorable episode along the Sprengisandur Route. Nýidalur is right on Route F26, about 120km (74 miles) from Hrauneyjar and 20km (12 miles) from the northwest corner of Vatnajökull. Vonarskarð forms a dramatic saddle between Vatnajökull and the small glacier Tungnafellsjökull, and the hiking route skirts some restless geothermal fields. Sudden releases of glacial meltwater can make stream crossings difficult, so speak to the warden before setting out. Those just passing through Nýidalur can still take the short easy hike east to a nearby hill with panoramic views.

Where to Stay & Dine

No food is sold anywhere on the 240km (149-mile) stretch between Hrauneyjar and Goðafoss.

Hrauneyjar may be the last outpost at the desert frontier, but for those with 4WD vehicles, it's also a central base for exploring Þjórsárdalur, Hekla, Landmannalaugar, and Veiðivötn. Hrauneyjar's two hotels, run by the same management, are 1.4km (1 mile) apart, and each has its own restaurant (see below).

The **Nýidalur mountain huts** (✆ **860-3334;** 4,200kr sleeping-bag accommodation; MC, V; July–Aug) sleep 120 people and are operated by **Ferðafélag Íslands** (✆ **568-2533;** www.fi.is). Advance bookings can be made online, but walk-ins are usually accommodated. Showers cost an additional 400kr, and the kitchen has pans and utensils. Camping in the area costs 1,000kr per person. All food must be brought in. Come prepared to sleep in a packed room with 30 other visitors, or in bunks that look like singles but are meant for two.

Hótel Highland Walking into this high-end hotel and restaurant is a surreal transition from the wild and remote landscape outside. The Highland was farm accommodation as recently as 2005, and some rooms are still in transition design-wise, but you won't suffer for sheets with an insufficient thread count. The fine **restaurant** ★ is open for dinner only, 7–10pm, with main courses in the 4,500kr to 5,100kr range. The menu has the expected elegant dishes—surf and turf, game platters, and the like—but we recommend the grilled local char or trout with white wine sauce and potatoes.

Rte. 26, Hrauneyjar. ✆ **487-7750.** www.allseasonhotels.is. 24 units. June 15–Sept 33,000kr double; 39,350kr–46,850kr suites for 2–6 people. Rates include breakfast. AE, DC, MC, V. Closed Oct–May 15. **Amenities:** Restaurant; hot tub; sauna. *In room:* TV, hair dryer, Wi-Fi.

Hrauneyjar Highland Center This hotel is adjoined to Hrauneyjar's service station and information desk, and the Reykjavík Excursions bus through Sprengisandur stops here. The rooms are spartan but comfortable, and, if you've just come through the desert interior, the whole place is Shangri-La. Confusingly, 17 of the rooms—which share a guest kitchen—and the four apartments are located next to Hótel Highland but classified with the Highland Center. The restaurant, open from 11:30am to 10pm daily, is limited to basic grilled dishes plus salads, sandwiches, wraps, and a daily special. The burgers are surprisingly delicious. Late at night the staff put leftovers outside for the foxes, and you can watch them cavorting.

Rte. 26, Hrauneyjar. ✆ **487-7782.** www.hrauneyjar.is. 73 units, 20 w/bathroom. June–Aug 22,150kr double w/bathroom; 17,000kr without bathroom; 9,350kr sleeping-bag accommodation. Rates 20% lower Sept–early June. Rates include breakfast (except sleeping-bag accommodation: breakfast 2,000kr). AE, DC, MC, V. **Amenities:** Restaurant, bar. *In room:* No phone, Wi-Fi.

ASKJA, KVERKFJÖLL & EASTERN INTERIOR ROUTES

Among the scenic landmarks of Iceland's desert highlands, the vast stratovolcano **Askja** ★★ is the most visited—and not just for its stark, elemental beauty and grandeur. If the weather cooperates, you can take a warm unforgettable swim in a crater lake with milky-blue, sulfurous water. Trips to Askja often extend to **Kverkfjöll** ★★, a mountain spur protruding from the northern margin of Vatnajökull amid a bleak expanse of rugged hills and gritty lava. The Kverkfjöll region is suffused with geothermal activity, and hot springs sculpt elaborate ice caves as they emerge from the glacier's edge.

These areas can only be accessed in sturdy 4WD vehicles or on group tours. The only places to stay are mountain huts, and all food must be brought in. Clear skies can switch suddenly to rain, and snowstorms can arise even in midsummer. Askja can be reached on day tours from the Mývatn, but seeing Kverkfjöll requires at least 1 night apart from the world. Two nights at Kverkfjöll should be the minimum, since the best hikes take the better part of a day.

Essentials

GETTING THERE The 4WD roads to Askja and Kverkfjöll generally remain open from mid-June through mid-September or later. No mountain roads (designated by an "F" before the route number) in the region have fuel stops. Inexperienced drivers may have trouble negotiating rock shards, potholes, and fords over rivers.

The standard route to **Askja** is Route F88, which branches off from the Ring Road (Route 1) 32km (20 miles) east of Mývatn and stretches 95km (59 miles) to the Drekagil mountain hut at Askja's outskirts. From there, it's a bouncy 8km (5 miles) drive on Route F894 to the Vikraborgir parking area, a 2.5km (1½-mile) walk from Víti crater in central Askja.

Drivers headed from Askja to **Kverkfjöll** backtrack from Drekagil on Route F88 and then take Route F910 southeast to Route F902 (confusingly, another branch of Route F910 heads directly from Drekagil west to Nýidalur in Sprengisandur). Those headed straight from the Ring Road to Kverkfjöll usually start on Route F905 (by the Möðrudalur filling station/cafe, 65km/40 miles east of Mývatn), and then take Route F910 to Route F902. The distance from Möðrudalur to the Sigurðarskáli hut at Kverkfjöll is 108km (67 miles).

For **bus travel** to Askja and Kverkfjöll, see "Tours," below.

VISITOR INFORMATION Offices in Akureyri, Mývatn, and Egilsstaðir can all provide information on the Askja and Kverkfjöll region. For consultation on hikes in the Askja area, contact **Ferðafélag Akureyrar** (p. 247). This group runs the mountain huts at **Þórsteinsskáli,** Route F88, at Herðubreiðarlindir (✆ **822-5191**), and **Drekagil,** Route F88, at Drekagil (✆ **853-2541**), and the hut wardens have current information on road and weather conditions. For hikes in the Kverkfjöll area, the authority is **Ferðafélag Fljótsdalshéraðs** (p. 352), which runs the **Sigurðarskáli hut** (p. 377); again the wardens have the local lowdown. The huts are generally staffed from mid-June to August or mid-September; see "Where to Stay" below.

Tours

Most visitors to Askja and Kverkfjöll come on arranged tours, which makes sense, given the poor roads and other logistical hassles. However, except for the infrequent hiking trips led by Ferðafélag Akureyrar and Ferðafélag Fljótsdalshéraðs, no tours allow extensive time for exploring either destination. For Askja, Mývatn Tours is usually willing to leave you at the Drekagil hut and pick you up a day or two later. The SBA-Norðurleið tour allows 2 nights and a day at Kverkfjöll, but for more time you'll need your own 4WD vehicle.

Mývatn Tours (✆ **464-1920;** www.askjatours.is) leads a popular 11- to 12-hour guided tour of Askja, starting from the Mývatn information kiosk, for 18,000kr adults and 9,000kr for children aged 6 to 12. Departures are daily from June 25 to August 31. Bring lunch, warm clothes, strong shoes, and a bathing suit and towel. **Saga Travel** in Akureyri (✆ **659-8888;** www.sagatravel.is) offers roughly the same tour, but in Super Jeeps instead of a bus. The cost is 33,000kr for adults, half price for children up to 12, with a two-person minimum. Off-road driving is prohibited, however, so the much higher price is hard to justify. Departures are from June 1 until October by advance request.

From early July 5 to August 15, **SBA-Norðurleið** (✆ **550-0700;** www.sba.is) offers a 3-day trip from Akureyri or Mývatn to Askja and Kverkfjöll, with 2 nights at Kverkfjöll's Sigurðarskáli hut. Departures are Mondays only, and the 29,000kr price (half-price for children aged 4–11) includes a guide but no food or accommodation. If you ask, they can at least reserve a bed for you at the hut.

In July, **Ferðafélag Akureyrar** (p. 247), Akureyri's hiking body, leads an adventurous 5-day backpacking trek (65,000kr per person, including accommodation, food, and guide) from Drekagil to Askja and onward to Svartárkot, at the southern terminus of Route 843. The website now has an English translation. A 3-day trip to climb Herðubreið should also be listed. **Ferðafélag Fljótsdalshéraðs** (p. 352) occasionally leads hiking trips in the Askja–Kverkfjöll region (click on the "ferðir" link to glean tour listings, or just call instead, tours can also be arranged with the staff).

For **aerial tours** of Askja and Kverkfjöll from Mývatn, see p. 269.

Exploring the Area

ROUTE F88 TO ASKJA

Starting from the Ring Road, the first 60km (37 miles) of Route F88 follow the western side of the Jökulsá á Fjöllum—the same river that forms the canyon in Jökulsárgljúfur further downstream. Just south of the Ring Road and west of Route F88 is **Hrossaborg,** a 10,000-year-old crater formed when rising magma heated groundwater, prompting a massive explosion of steam and rock. Horses were once grazed well into the winter around the area; the horses would sometimes seek shelter in Hrossaborg during bad weather—thus the name, which means "Horse City." A small road leads from Route F88 right into Hrossaborg's natural amphitheater through a collapsed crater wall.

In roughly 40km (25 miles), Route F88 comes to its first major ford at the **Grafarlandaá river,** known for its pure-tasting water. Twenty kilometers (12 miles) further south is **Herðubreiðarlindir,** a lovely highland oasis of moss, wildflowers, and springs gushing from beneath the lava rock to converge on the Lindaá River. **Herðubreið ★**, a majestic table mountain, looms 6km (3¾ miles) to the west. Herðubreiðarlindir has a mountain hut and summer warden, and is also the launch point for the **Öskjuvegurinn ★**, a memorable 5-day trek through some of Iceland's starkest wastelands. (Most of the route traverses the Ódáðahraun, which translates to "Lava Field of Evil Deeds.") The Öskjuvegurinn skirts Herðubreið, and reaches Askja's Drekagil hut on the second night. For further details on all the huts along the route, contact **Ferðafélag Akureyrar** (p. 247). A 5-minute trail leads from Herðubreiðarlindir to the remains of a tiny underground shelter, where Fjalla-Eyvindur—Iceland's most legendary outlaw—reportedly survived the winter of 1774–75 on a diet of raw horsemeat and angelica roots. The original shelter collapsed and was renovated in 1922. A map available at the hut outlines other short, pleasant hikes in the Herðubreiðarlindir area.

In clear weather, the view of Herðubreið is awe-inspiring. In 2002 a national poll was conducted to determine "Iceland's favorite mountain," and Herðubreið was the overwhelming winner. Its name means "Broad Shoulders," and its flattened top is the result of eruptions beneath the crushing weight of a glacier. With its steep screes and vertical cliff faces, Herðubreið is a very challenging and somewhat dangerous climb. If you do make the attempt, consult the warden at Herðubreiðarlindir first, and allow 12 hours for the round-trip.

ASKJA ★★

In Iceland's recorded history, no cataclysm produced more ash than the 1875 volcanic eruption at Askja, which means "Caldera" in Icelandic. The ash blanketed 10,000sq. km (3,861 sq. miles) of land, killing livestock and forcing hundreds of Icelandic farmers to emigrate to North America. Askja—designated a stratovolcano because of its layers of lava from periodic eruptions—erupted most recently in 1961, but most of the current topography took form in 1875. Askja is also Iceland's most dramatic illustration of a subsidence cauldron, formed when underground passageways of molten rock empty and collapse, leaving an enormous bowl in the middle of the volcanic edifice. Askja's collapsed heart, dominated by **Öskjuvatn Lake,** is 4.5km (3 miles) wide and still sinking. Öskjuvatn is Iceland's deepest lake, at 220m (722 ft.).

The mountain hut closest to Askja is at **Drekagil gorge,** 33km (21 miles) from Herðubreiðarlindir. From Drekagil, Route F894 extends 8km (5 miles) to **Vikraborgir,** a crater row formed during the 1961 eruption. Tour buses park at Vikraborgir for the easy 35-minute walk south to **Víti ★**, a lake-filled crater formed in 1875 and separated from Öskjuvatn by a narrow ridge. (*Víti,* by the way, means "Hell.") The Icelanders are usually the least hesitant to scoot down Víti's steep walls and plunge into the warm, opaque, eggy-smelling water, which reaches a depth of 60m (197 ft.). The water temperature ranges from 72°F to 86°F (22°C–30°C)—a bit tepid at times, but it's warmer if you swim out to the middle. You can also dig your toes into the hot mud on the lake floor, but be careful not to get burned. Trails proceeding from Víti around Öskjuvatn are difficult, dangerous, and often blocked by signs prohibiting access, so check with the warden at Drekagil before setting out.

A longer, more suspenseful approach to Víti starts at the Drekagil hut and proceeds through Dyngjufjöll, bypassing Vikraborgir. Consult the warden on the status of the trail, and allow 3 hours each way. A stroll up the Drekagil gorge is also worthwhile.

KVERKFJÖLL ★★

The Kverkfjöll volcanic system—which reaches 1,929m (6,329 ft.) in height and extends 10km (6 miles) on a south–north axis—is mostly buried beneath Vatnajökull, but its northern rim protrudes from the glacier's edge. With so much geothermal activity churning beneath Europe's largest mass of ice, Kverkfjöll is usually seen as a collision of natural extremes. Yet the most lasting impressions are of its austere and solemn beauty: the hypnotic pattern inside an ice cave, perhaps, or a view over reddish-black wastes with the barest etching of pale gray lichen.

The most common tourist mistakes are to wear jeans, a real encumbrance in the rain, or sneakers, which shred on lava trails and soak through in snow or mud. Also remember to bring a water bottle, as it can be difficult to find drinking water free of silt.

HIKING ROUTES The wardens at Sigurðarskáli, the only mountain hut in the Kverkfjöll vicinity, sell hiking maps and dispense excellent advice.

From Sigurðarskáli, a well-marked, manageable trail leads up **Virkisfell ★** for fabulous views; allow at least 90 minutes for the round-trip. From the mountain, the trail continues past several volcanic fissures to **Hveragil ★**, a river gorge and oasis of vegetation nurtured by hot springs; a wonderful natural bathing pool is fed by a waterfall. Hveragil is 12km (7½ miles) from Sigurðarskáli, and the round-trip hike takes around 7 hours. A rough 4WD track extends to Hveragil from Route F903, but talk to a warden before braving it.

A road extends 4km (2½ miles) from the hut to the edge of the Kverkjökull glacial tongue; a more direct walking trail is only 3km (2 miles). From the end of the road, it's a 10-minute walk west to where a river emerges from a spectacular **ice cave *(íshellir)* ★★** at the edge of the glacier. The play of light on the sculpted hollows and undulating walls is utterly entrancing. Eerie crashing sounds emanate from deep within the cave, and venturing inside is very dangerous. The escaping river is warmer in winter, when hot springs are less diluted by glacial meltoff.

Each day in summer, a Sigurðarskáli warden leads a **day hike ★★** onto Kverkjökull. The maximum group size is 20, and slots often fill up; call the hut and reserve in advance. The price is low—just 5,000kr to 11,500kr, depending how long the hike is—and includes crampons, walking poles, and safety harnesses. In good weather, the hike lasts 8 to 10 hours and extends past the Langafönn slope to **Hveratagl ★**, an expanse of steaming springs, bubbling mud cauldrons, and ice caves along the glacier's margin. The hike may continue further to **Gengissig,** a pretty lagoon next to a small mountain hut. For independent hikers, it's possible to spend the night here and continue to **Skarphéðinstindur,** Kverkfjöll's highest mountain; from the peak, the trail loops more directly back to Sigurðarskáli by a different route. All unguided hikes on the glacier are discouraged, but if you do go, be sure to tell the wardens where you're headed and stick to established trails.

Where to Stay

Mountain huts in the Askja–Kverkfjöll region are generally open from mid-June to mid-September. Expect costs to be between 3,800kr–4,200kr per person per night, with an extra charge for showers (usually around 400kr). The Þórsteinsskáli, Drekagil, and Sigurðarskáli huts all have kitchens with cookware and utensils. No food is sold at the huts, and you must bring your own sleeping bag. As usual, guests are packed into large rooms with minimal privacy. If you bring a tent, expect to pay around 1,000kr per person for use of the facilities. In July and August advance reservations are strongly advised.

All mountain huts in the Askja area, including **Þórsteinsskáli** and **Drekagil,** are owned and operated by **Ferðafélag Akureyrar** Strandgata 23, Akureyri (✆ **462-2720;** www.ffa.is). The wardens at Þórsteinsskáli (✆ **822-5191**) and Drekagil (✆ **822-5190**) can be reached directly, but reservations are made with Ferðafélag Akureyrar by email (ffa@ffa.is).

The **Sigurðarskáli hut,** Route 902, at Kverkfjöll (✆ **863-9236**) sleeps up to 85 people and is booked through **Ferðafélag Fljótsdalshéraðs** (✆ **863-5813;** ferdafelag@egilsstadir.is; www.fljotsdalsherad.is/ferdafelag); e-mail contact is preferred. The remote hut at Gengissig—simply known as **Kverkfjöll hut**—has no electricity or running water and sleeps six (or 12, more intimately). For reservations, contact the **Icelandic Glaciological Society** (✆ **893-0742;** skalar@jorfi.is).

FAST FACTS

13

Area Codes Calls to Iceland from overseas require **country code prefix 354.** See also "Staying Connected" (p. 59).

Business Hours **Banks** are generally open Monday through Friday 9:15am to 4pm. **Shopping hours** vary enormously. Many places are open Monday to Friday from 10am to 6pm, and Saturday from 10am to early afternoon, but many others—including markets—don't open until noon; filling station convenience stores are open longer. Reykjavík and Akureyri have 24-hour supermarkets. Hours for **museums and sights** are highly irregular.

Drinking Laws The legal drinking age in Iceland is 20. Drink-driving laws are extremely strict; just one drink could put you over the blood alcohol limit (0.05).

Driving Rules See "Getting There and Getting Around," p. 39.

Electricity Iceland uses 220 Volts, 50 Hz AC, the European standard, and plugs have two round prongs. Remember to bring a power adapter and perhaps an Ethernet cable and phone cord as well. You may need an "international" power adapter that properly regulates the current to prevent computer damage. Icelandic phone jacks are the same as in North America, so Europeans will need an adapter.

Embassies & Consulates U.S. Embassy, Laufásvegur 21, Reykjavík (✆ **562-9100;** www.usa.is; Mon–Fri 8am–5pm). Canadian Embassy, Túngata 14, Reykjavík (✆ **575-6500;** www.canada.is; Mon–Fri 9am–noon). British Embassy, Laufásvegur 31, Reykjavík (✆ **550-5100;** www.britishembassy.is; Mon–Fri 9am–noon). Republic of Ireland Honorary Consulate, Ásbuð 106, Garðabær, near Reykjavík (✆ **554-2355**). Australia has no embassy or consulate in Iceland. Services for Australian citizens in Iceland are handled through Denmark's Australian Embassy, Dampfaergevej 26, Copenhagen (✆ **7026-3676;** www.denmark.embassy.gov.au). New Zealand does not have an embassy in Iceland either; the nearest is in the Hague in the Netherlands at Carnegielaan 10, 2517 KH (✆ **31/70-346-9324;** nzemb@xs4all.nl). South Africa Honorary Consul, Borgartún 35, Reykjavík (✆ **591-0355**).

Emergencies Phone ✆ **112** for all fire, police, or ambulance emergencies.

Gasoline (Petrol) Gasoline—*bensín*—tends to be more expensive in Iceland than in the U.S. or rest of Europe, but taxes are already included in the printed price. (One U.S. gallon equals 3.8 liters or .85 imperial gallons.)

Holidays Businesses close on the following holidays in Iceland (see also "Calendar of Events" in Chapter 3, p. 32): New Year's Day; Maundy Thursday; Good Friday; Easter Sunday; Easter Monday; First Day of Summer—3rd Thursday in April; Labor Day—1 May; Ascension; Whit Sunday and Monday; National Day—*17 Jun*; Bank holiday weekend—1st Monday in August; Christmas Eve; Christmas Day; Boxing Day; and New Year's Eve.

Insurance For information on travel insurance, trip cancelation insurance, and medical insurance while abroad please visit www.frommers.com/planning.

Internet Access There is widespread free Wi-Fi in Iceland. Aside from libraries, public Internet access terminals are rare. Outside Reykjavík (p. 98) and Akureyri (p.245), cafes with free Wi-Fi are less common. See also "Staying Connected," p. 59.

Language Icelandic is the national language. English is widely understood and spoken in Iceland, though a few older guesthouse owners in country areas speak Danish or German much better than they speak English. See the next chapter for some useful Icelandic words and phrases.

Legal Aid For legal advice, the best first-stop would be the **Intercultural Center** (Ofanleiti 2, Reykjavík; ✆ **530-9300**) which offers all sorts of advice to foreigners in Iceland, mostly targeting immigrants. The friendly staff will point you in the right direction if they can't assist you directly.

Mail At press time, international postage for letters and postcards costs 165kr to Europe, 220kr to elsewhere. Less if not by airmail (*A-póstur*). The postal service is reliable, though mail often takes longer than the postal service's estimated delivery times between Iceland and more distant countries such as Australia and New Zealand. Mail typically takes 3 to 5 business days to reach Europe or the U.S. General post office hours are 9am to 6pm weekdays: www.postur.is; ✆ **580-1200**. Mailboxes are bright red and marked *Pósturinn*. **To receive mail in Iceland,** you can have letters and packages sent "Poste Restante" to any Icelandic post office. Mail should be addressed to the recipient at "Poste Restante/[name of town] Post Office" (check the website for addresses). When collecting the mail, bring your passport for identification. Beware import taxes imposed on new goods being sent to Iceland; you may be asked to pay if gift packages are not clearly marked.

Newspapers & Magazines Many English language newspapers and magazines are readily available in the main bookstores (p. 138).

Passports See www.frommers.com/planning for information on how to obtain a passport. See also p. 37.

Police In an emergency dial ✆ **112**.

Smoking Smoking is prohibited by law in all restaurants, cafes, bars, and places to stay.

Taxes Iceland's 25.5% VAT (sales tax) is included in prices, but tourists can get most of that back on qualified purchases; see p. 137.

Telephones See "Staying Connected" (p. 59) for information on phone calls in Iceland.

Time Iceland is on Greenwich Mean Time—even when Greenwich isn't! It has no daylight saving time. Thus during the winter, Iceland is 5 hours ahead of Eastern Standard Time (E.S.T.) in the U.S. and in the same time zone as the U.K. In summer, Iceland is 4 hours ahead of E.S.T. and 1 hour behind the U.K.

Tipping Icelanders don't tip, not even in restaurants or taxis. Tipping is never expected, but if you do tip, you are unlikely to offend anyone; it would be graciously accepted or politely refused. The practice is becoming a little more common in Reykjavík bars and nightclubs.

Toilets The vast majority of Icelandic public toilets are clean and safe.

Visas Nationals of very few countries need a Visa to enter Iceland for travel purposes. See Iceland's Department of Immigration website www.utl.is for details. See also "Entry Requirements" (p. 37).

Visitor Information Regional visitor information offices are listed under "Visitor Information" in Chapters 6 to 12. See also "The Best of Iceland Online" (p. 11).

Water Enjoy Iceland's water! Iceland has some of the world's best drinking water, and all tap water is safe to drink. Even surface water is generally potable, but avoid drinking from streams that have flowed through areas with livestock or birds. When in doubt, boil water for 10 minutes or use purifying treatments founds at camping stores.

AIRLINE, HOTEL & CAR RENTAL WEBSITES

MAJOR AIRLINES

Icelandair
www.icelandair.com

Iceland Express
www.icelandexpress.com

Scandinavian Airlines
www.flySAS.com

HOTEL CHAINS

Edda Hotels
www.hoteledda.com

Fosshótel
www.fosshotel.is

Hilton Hotels
www.reykjavik.nordica.hilton.com

Icelandair Hotels
www.icelandairhotels.com

KeaHotels
www.keahotels.com

Radisson Hotels & Resorts
www.radissonblu.com

Reykjavík Hotels
www.reykjavikhotels.is

CAR RENTAL AGENCIES

ALP Bílaleiga
www.alp.is

ÁTAK Car Rental
www.atak.is

Avis
www.avis.is

Berg
www.carrental-berg.com

Budget
www.budget.is

Europcar
www.europcar.is

Geysir
www.geysir.is

Hertz
www.hertz.is

National—Bílaleiga Akureyrar
www.nationalcar.is

SS Bílaleiga
www.carrentalss.com

Thrifty
www.thrifty.is

ICELANDIC PRONUNCIATION & USEFUL VOCABULARY

Most Icelanders speak English, often with remarkable fluency—especially among younger and more urban demographics. (In 1999, English replaced Danish as the first foreign language taught in every school.) You can easily get by without learning Icelandic, but it pays to familiarize yourself with the rules of pronunciation. Asking for directions will go far more smoothly, and Icelanders are extremely appreciative when you say their names correctly.

If you do absorb some vocabulary, be aware that Icelandic words are notorious for constantly shifting in form. All nouns are gendered, and adjectives have to match the gender, number, and case of the nouns they modify. Even proper names have multiple forms: a restaurant on a street called Strandgata would give its address as *Strandgötu,* and a guesthouse run by a woman named Anna Sigga is called *Gistiheimili Önnu Siggu.*

PRONUNCIATION GUIDE

Icelandic inflections are difficult, but pronunciation rules are relatively straightforward and consistent. Stress almost always falls on the first syllable of a word. The Icelandic alphabet has 36 letters, with 12 vowels. Two consonants, the *eth* (ð, Ð) and the *thorn* (þ, Þ), are common to Old English. Icelandic letters are often pronounced as in English; the most notable exceptions are listed below. For a free online lesson in Icelandic pronunciation, visit www.travlang.com/languages. But to get a feel for the basics, we recommend just reading aloud the basic vocabulary listed below.

VOWELS

á	*ow* as in *owl*
é	*ye* as in *yet*
í, ý	*ee* as in *seen*
ó	*o* as in *note*
ö	*i* as in *whirl*
ú	*oo* as in *pool*
æ	*i* as in *life*
au	œ as in the French *œil*, or *uh-ee* as in *perky* (without the *p* or *rk*)
g	Wait, that's not a vowel! But if between certain vowels, it sounds like one. Such as *stigi* meaning *stairs*, pronounced *stee-yee*. At other times *g* is usually close to the English *g* as in *goat* or, when before an *s* or *t*, the guttural *ch* as in *Achtung*.

CONSONANTS

ð (Ð)	*th* as in *bathe*
þ (Þ)	*th* as in *bath*
dj	*j* as in *juice*
hv	*kv* as in *kvass*, but softer
j	*y* as in *yes*
ll	*tl* as in *Atlantic*
r	rolled, as in Spanish

ICELANDERS: ON A first-name BASIS

Iceland is the only Scandinavian country to retain the Old Norse system of patronymics (and occasionally metronymics) as opposed to surnames which exist but are rare. If a man named Jón has a son named Páll and a daughter named Ólöf, their names are Páll Jónsson and Ólöf Jónsdóttir. Women do not change names when they marry, so if a married couple has a son and a daughter, every family member has a different last name.

Children are often named after their grandparents, further adding to the confusion, with generation after generation called, for example, Páll Jónsson or Jón Pálsson alternately. The upside is that when you address Icelanders, you always use the first name. Icelanders all call each other by first name, no matter what their social relations. Even the phone book is alphabetized by first name.

One Word to Get Right: kehb-lah-veehk

Some Icelandic consonants have identity crises when followed by certain other consonants—*f* becomes *v* between vowels and *b* before *l* or *n*; *p* becomes *f* before an *s* or *t*, and see *g* listed with vowels above—so here's a tip to avoid the most common mistake made by foreigners: ***Keflavík*** (as in Keflavík International Airport) is pronounced ***Keblavík***. Get this right and you'll earn a few points with Icelanders before you've even passed through customs.

BASIC VOCABULARY & PHRASES

English	Icelandic	Pronunciation
Yes/No	**Já/Nei**	yow/nay
Hello	**Halló** *or* **Góðan daginn**	hah-lo/gohth-an dai-yin
Goodbye	**Bless**	blehss
Excuse me	**Afsakið**	ahf-sahk-ith
Please	**Vinsamlega**	vin-sahm-lehgah
Thank you	**Takk** *or* **Takk fyrir**	tahk/tahk firr-irr
You're welcome	**Þú ert velkominn**	thoo ehrrt vehl-kohm-in
Do you speak English?	**Talar þú ensku?**	tah-larr thoo ehn-sku
I (don't) understand	**Ég skil (ekki)**	yehkh skil (ehk-i)
My name is . . .	**Ég heiti . . .**	yehkh hay-ti
What is your name?	**Hvað heitir þú?**	kvahth hay-tirr thoo
Nice to meet you	**Gaman að kynnast þér**	gah-mahn ahth kihn-nahst th-yerr
Cheers!	**Skál!**	skowl
Where is the . . . ?	**Hvar er . . . ?**	kvahrr ehrr
Tourist information/ services	**Ferðamannaþjónusta**	fehrr-tha-mahn-nah-thyohn-uhs-tah
Toilet	**Snyrting**	snihrr-ting
Bank	**Banki**	bown-khi
ATM	**Hraðbanki**	hrahth-bown-khi
Restaurant	**Veitingahús**	vay-teen-kha-hoos
Bus	**Strætó** (city bus) *or* **Rúta** (longer distance)	strrai-tow/roo-dah
Airport	**Flugvöllur**	fluhk-vertl-urr
Post office	**Pósthús**	pohst-hoos
Police station	**Lögureglustöð**	lerkh-rrehkl-ö-sterhth
Pharmacy	**Apótek**	ah-poh-tehk
Hospital	**Sjúkrahús**	syook-rrah-hoos
Doctor	**Læknir**	laik-nirr

English	Icelandic	Pronunciation
Help	**Hjálp**	hyowlp
Left/Right	**Vinstri/Hægri**	vinst-rri/haihk-rri
North/South	**Norður/Suður**	norr-thr/su-thr
East/West	**Austur/Vestur**	œs-tr/ves-tr
Map	**Kort**	korrt
Passport	**Vegabréf**	vehkh-ah-brryehv
How much is it?	**Hvað kostar þetta?**	kvahth kost-ahrr theh-tah
Do you have . . .	**Áttu . . .**	owh-tu
Could I have ...	**Má ég fá...**	mow yehk fow
Do you have any vacancies?	**Eru herbergi laus?**	ehrr-u hehrr-behrr-khi lœs
Room	**Herbergi**	hehrr-behrr-khi
Reservation	**Bókun**	boh-kuhn
Sleeping bag/sleeping bag accommodation	**Svefnpoki/ svefnpokapláss**	svehbn-po-ki/svehbn-po-ka-plows
Today	**Í dag**	ee dahk
Tomorrow	**Á morgun**	ow morrhk-n
Open/Closed	**Opið/Lokað**	ohp-ihth/lohk-ahth

NUMBERS, DAYS & MONTHS

English	Icelandic
Zero	**Núll**
One	**Einn**
Two	**Tveir**
Three	**Þrír**
Four	**Fjórir**
Five	**Fimm**
Six	**Sex**
Seven	**Sjö**
Eight	**Átta**
Nine	**Níu**
Ten	**Tíu**
One hundred	**Eitt hundrað**
One thousand	**Eitt þúsund**
Monday	**Mánudagur**
Tuesday	**Þriðjudagur**
Wednesday	**Miðvikudagur**
Thursday	**Fimmtudagur**
Friday	**Föstudagur**
Saturday	**Laugardagur**
Sunday	**Sunnudagur**

English	Icelandic
January	**Janúar**
February	**Febrúar**
March	**Mars**
April	**Apríl**
May	**Maí**
June	**Júní**
July	**Júlí**
August	**Ágúst**
September	**September**
October	**Október**
November	**Nóvember**
December	**Desember**

GLOSSARY OF GEOGRAPHICAL TERMS

Icelandic place names are usually pieced together from local geographical features and other landmarks. The village of *Kirkjubæjarklaustur,* for example, means "Church Farm Cloister," while *Jökulsárgljúfur* is "Glacial River Canyon." Farm names are usually inspired by nearby topography; *rauða skriða,* for instance, means "red scree," hence *Rauðaskriða* farm is surrounded by slopes of red scree. Identifying the components of place names provides a key to local environments, both scenically and historically, as you travel through Iceland.

English	Icelandic
á	river
alda	ridge of several hills
bær	farm, small settlement
bakki	riverbank
berg	rock, cliff
bjarg	cliff
brekka	slope, scree
brú	bridge
bruni	lava
dalur	valley
djúp	long coastal inlet
eiði	isthmus
engi	meadow
ey	island (plural *eyjar*)
eyri	spit of land, point
fell	hill, mountain

English	Icelandic
fjall	mountain, (plural *fjöll*)
fjörður	broad inlet or fjord
fljót	wide river
flói	large bay
foss	waterfall
gígur	crater
gil	gorge
gjá	fissure
gljúfur	canyon
gnúpur	steep mountain, promontory
hæð	hill
háls	ridge
heiði	heath, moor
hlíð	mountainside
höfði	promontory, headland
höfn	harbor or port
hóll	knoll (plural *hólar*)
hólmur	small island
holt	hill
hraun	lava flow
hver	hot spring
jökull	glacier
jökulsá	glacial river
kirkja	church
klauster	cloister
klettur	cliff, crag (plural *klettar*)
kot	croft, small farm
laug	hot spring (plural *laugar*)
mörk	periphery
múli	headland
nes	headland, peninsula, point
ós	estuary, mouth of river
reykur	smoke, steam
sandur	sands, beach
sjór	ocean, sea
skagi	peninsula, cape, headland
skarð	mountain pass
sker	rocky islet, reef, skerry
skógur	woodland, scrubland
skriða	scree, rockslide

English	Icelandic
staður	place, stead (plural *staðir*)
stapi	crag
stígur	trail
tangi	spit of land, point
tindur	peak
tjörn	small lake, pond
tunga	spit of land, point
vað	ford
vatn	lake, water (plural *vötn*)
vegur	path, road, way
vellir	plains (singular *völlur*)
vík	small inlet, bay, cove
vogur	inlet, creek, cove

Index

See also Accommodations and Restaurant indexes, below.

General Index

C

G

I

J

K

L

M

Accommodations

Restaurants

NOTES

NOTES

NOTES

NOTES